HIGH YIELD BONDS

Market Structure,
Portfolio Management,
and Credit Risk Modeling

Edited by

THEODORE M. BARNHILL, JR.

WILLIAM F. MAXWELL, and

MARK R. SHENKMAN

McGraw-Hill

New York   San Fransico   Washington, D.C.   Auckland   Bogotá
Caracas   Lisbon   London   Madrid   Mexico City   Milan
Montreal   New Delhi   San Juan   Singapore
Sydney   Tokyo   Toronto

Library of Congress Cataloging-in-Publication Data

High yield bonds : market structure, portfolio management, and credit
  risk modeling / edited by Theodore M. Barnhill, William F. Maxwell,
  and Mark R. Shenkman.
    p.   cm.
  ISBN 0-07-006786-4
   1. Junk bonds.   2. Portfolio management.   3. Credit.
  I. Barnhill, Theodore M.   II. Maxwell, William F.,
  III. Shenkman, Mark R.
  HG4963.H528   1998
  332.63'23—dc21   98-40324
                                             CIP

McGraw-Hill

*A Division of The **McGraw·Hill** Companies*

  2 3 4 5 6 7 8 9 0 DOC/DOC 9 0 3 2 1 0 9

ISBN 0-07-006786-4

The sponsoring editor for this book was *Roger Marsh* and the production
supervisor was *Suzanne W. B. Rapcavage*. It was set in Times Roman by *Electronic
Publishing Services, Inc.*

Printed and bound by R. R. Donnelley & Sons Company.

McGraw-Hill books are available at special quantity discounts to use as premiums
and sales promotions, or for use in corporate training programs. For more information, please write to the Director of Special Sales, McGraw-Hill, 11 West 19th Street,
New York, NY 10011. Or contact your local bookstore.

This book is printed on recycled, acid-free paper containing a minimum of
50% recycled de-inked fiber.

Theodore M. Barnhill, Jr. is Professor of Finance and Director of the Financial Markets Research Institute at The George Washington University in Washington, D.C. Prior to joining the university in 1978, he held managerial and investment analysis positions at the United States Treasury Department and the Prudential Insurance Company. His research and publications cover a range of topics, including financial institution asset/liability modeling, fixed- income arbitrage, and project finance. He is also the developer of ValueCalc, a computer software package that values a range of financial assets and derivative securities and provides market and credit risk management analysis. Dr. Barnhill received a Ph.D. in finance and a M.B.A. and M.S. in chemical engineering from the University of Michigan. He also received a B.S. in chemical engineering from Tennessee Technological University.

William F. Maxwell is a visiting Assistant Professor of Finance at The Georgetown University. He specializes in the areas of fixed income valuation and risk management. Dr. Maxwell has published in academic and professional journals including *Financial Management* and has experience as a research fellow at the Financial Markets Research Institute. His professional background includes work in mergers and acquisitions and security valuation. Dr. Maxwell received a Ph.D. in finance at The George Washington University, a M.B.A. from the University of Colorado, and a B.S. from Indiana University.

Mark R. Shenkman is a pioneer in the field of high yield bonds. He started his investment career in 1969 and has been actively involved in the high yield market since 1977. Mr. Shenkman is the founder and Chief Investment Officer of Shenkman Capital Management, Inc., a New York-based investment management firm that focuses exclusively on the high yield market. He is the former President of First Investors Asset Management Co., was cohead of the high yield department of Lehman Brothers Kuhn Loeb and has held portfolio management and research positions with Fidelity Management and Research Company in Boston. Mr. Shenkman is a member of the Boston Society of Security Analysts, the New York Society of Security Analysts, the Association for Investment Management and Research, the American Statistical Association, and the American Bankruptcy Institute. He is a graduate of the University of Connecticut and received an M.B.A. from The George Washington University.

CONTRIBUTING AUTHOR BIOGRAPHIES

Edward I. Altman, Max L. Heine Professor of Finance, Stern School of Business, New York University. Since 1990, Ed Altman has directed the research effort in Fixed Income and Credit Markets at the NYU Salomon Center and is currently the Vice Director of the center. Dr. Altman's primary areas of research include bankruptcy analysis and prediction, credit and lending policies, and risk management in banking, corporate finance, and capital markets. Professor Altman is one of the founders and an executive editor of the international publication, the *Journal of Banking and Finance* and has published over a dozen books and over 100 articles in scholarly finance, accounting, and economic journals.

Norman B. Antin, Partner, Elias, Matz, Tiernan & Herrick L.L.P. Mr. Antin specializes in public and private offerings, general corporate financings, reorganization transactions, mergers and acquisitions, and general corporate and securities law matters, primarily representing financial institutions, savings associations, savings banks, commercial banks, and thrift and bank holding companies. Mr. Antin, in addition to general corporate and regulatory counseling, is extensively involved in mergers and acquisitions, mutual and stock holding companies, branch acquisitions, conversions, public and private stock and debt offerings (representing both issuers and underwriters), and supervisory issues. Mr. Antin is a graduate of the George Washington University and the University of Connecticut School of Law.

Ned Armstrong, Managing Director, Friedman, Billings, Ramsey, & Co. Mr. Armstrong joined Friedman, Billings, Ramsey, & Co. at its inception in 1989 and has been involved in its research and capital raising efforts since. Over that time, Mr. Armstrong has generated many successful research ideas in both equity and debt securities. In addition, Mr. Armstrong has been involved in the underwriting of several equities and high yield bonds. Prior to joining FBR, Mr. Armstrong did sell side research, recommending the equity and high yield issues of companies in a variety of businesses. He also worked for a buyout boutique analyzing prospective investments and devising financing structures. Mr. Armstrong received his B.S. in Accountancy from Miami University and his M.B.A. from the University of Chicago.

Jonathan Blau, Vice President, High Yield Research Department, Donaldson, Lufkin & Jenrette. Mr. Blau is the quantitative analyst for high yield at Donaldson, Lufkin & Jenrette. Prior to joining DLJ, Mr. Blau was quantitative analyst in High Yield Research at Chase Securities Inc. He also worked in the Fixed Income Trading Technology department at CS First Boston, where he supported both high yield and mortgages. Prior to his six years in the financial community, Mr. Blau was a CPU design engineer at Alliant Computer Systems, Tandem Computers, and Data General.

Lea V. Carty, Vice President and Senior Credit Officer, Moody's Investors Service. Lea Carty manages Moody's research concerning bond and commercial paper defaults as well as trends in corporate credit quality. He has published articles concerning these topics in academic journals, professional journals, and books. Prior to joining Moody's in 1992, Mr. Carty worked at Bear, Stearns, and Company, Inc., New York and Thomson–CGR, Paris. He holds a B.A. in Mathematics and French from Washington University in St. Louis, an M.A. in Mathematics from the University of Colorado, and a Ph.D. in Economics from Columbia University.

Sam DeRosa-Farag, Managing Director, High Yield Research Department, Donaldson, Lufkin & Jenrette. Mr. DeRosa-Farag is the head of Global High Yield Strategy and Portfolio Research at Donaldson, Lufkin & Jenrette. He has 12 years of experience in the high yield industry. Prior to joining DLJ, Mr. DeRosa-Farag acted as Head of High Yield Portfolio and Strategic Research at Chase Securities Inc. He also developed and managed the High Yield Quantitative & Portfolio Strategies Group at CS First Boston where he was employed for nine years. Mr. DeRosa-Farag is a member of Institutional Investors All-American Fixed Income Research Team, ranked for Strategy and Economics in 1993 through 1997.

Allan C. Eberhart, Associate Professor of Finance, Georgetown University, and Associated Consultant with A.T. Kearney. During the 1993–94 school year, Dr. Eberhart was a Visiting Assistant Professor of Finance at the New York University Stern School of Business. He conducts research in valuation, corporate finance, volatility and bankruptcy, and teaches advanced corporate finance to graduate students and advanced financial management to undergraduates. Professor Eberhart is on the editorial board of the *Journal of Banking and Finance* and has published articles in the *Journal of Finance, Financial Management, Journal of Banking and Finance,* and other journals. Besides his work for A.T. Kearney, Professor Eberhart has served as a consultant for many other firms including Standard and Poor's and MCI Communications.

Mark J. Flanagan, C.P.A., C.F.A., Vice President, Director of Credit Research at Shenkman Capital Management, Inc. Shenkman Capital is a New York-based investment management firm that focuses exclusively on the high yield market. Formerly, he was with Hamption Ventures and Arthur Andersen. Mr. Flanagan received his graduate and undergraduate degrees from the State University at Albany.

Martin S. Fridson, CFA, Managing Director, Merrill Lynch & Co. Martin Fridson is Director of Global High Yield Strategy at Merrill Lynch & Co. He was dubbed "the dean of the high yield bond market" in conjunction with being voted to the *Institutional Investor* All-America research team. *The New York Times* called Fridson "one of Wall Street's most thoughtful and perceptive analysts." Fridson received his B.A. cum laude in history from Harvard College and his M.B.A. from Harvard Business School. In January 1990, *Institutional Investor* selected Martin Fridson for its list of "The Next Generation of Financial Leaders." The New York Society of Security Analysts, in July 1994, called Fridson "one of our best known members." In 1997, *Worth Magazine* included Fridson's *Investment Illusions* among the 22 books published since 1841 constituting its investors' core library. Economist Henry Kaufman said of Fridson's *It Was A Very Good Year (1998)*, "There are important lessons in this book for all investors."

Yan Gao is a Ph.D. candidate in Finance at Northwestern University's Kellogg School of Management. Previously he worked for Merrill Lynch & Co. in high yield bond research and Cathay Financial LLC as a convertible bond analyst. Mr. Gao also holds a BS in computational math from Beijing University, a MS in applied math from Michigan State University and a MBA from Baruch College.

M. Christopher Garman, Assistant Vice President, Global High Yield Strategy, Merrill Lynch & Co. Christopher Garman supports research and analysis in the High Yield Strategy group at Merrill Lynch. His responsibilities include modeling high yield credit risk premiums, default rates, and portfolio allocations. Before joining the high yield strategy group in 1995, he was associated with Financial Engineering Associates and the London Traded Options Market. His published works include coauthored contributions to *Bondweek, The Journal of Fixed Income,* and *Financial Analysts Journal.* Mr. Garman holds a Master of International Affairs degree in international political economy from Columbia University and a B.A. with distinction in Diplomacy and World Affairs from Occidental College.

Stuart C. Gilson, Professor of Business Administration, Harvard Business School. Professor Gilson's research focuses on how companies can create value by restructuring their financial claims and contracts. He has written extensively in the area of corporate bankruptcy and high yield debt, and teaches a course called "Creating Value through Corporate Restructuring" in Harvard's M.B.A. and executive programs. He is currently studying techniques for valuing distressed companies, and the market for investing in distressed securities. Professor Gilson's publications have appeared in *The Journal of Finance, The Journal of Financial Economics, The Journal of Applied Corporate Finance,* and *The Financial Analysts Journal.* His research has also been cited in a number of national news and business periodicals, including *The Wall Street Journal, The New York Times, Business Week, The Economist, Institutional Investor,* and *U.S. News and World Report.*

Jeffrey D. Haas , Partner, Elias, Matz, Tiernan & Herrick L.L.P. Mr. Haas specializes in public and private offerings, general corporate financings, reorganization transactions, mergers and acquisitions, and general corporate and securities law matters, primarily representing financial institutions, savings associations, savings banks, commercial banks, and thrift and bank holding companies. Mr. Haas, in addition to general corporate and regulatory counseling, is extensively involved in mergers and acquisitions, mutual and stock holding companies, branch acquisitions, conversions, public and private stock and debt offerings (representing both issuers and underwriters), and supervisory issues. Mr. Haas is a graduate of the University of Connecticut, the George Washington University National Law Center, and the George Washington University, School of Business and Public Management.

Vellore M. Kishore, Research Associate, NYU Salomon Center. Mr. Kishore graduated from the N.Y.U. Stern School of Business and is a research associate at the Salomon Center as well as a financial and real estate consultant.

Robert S. Kricheff, Managing Director, Fixed Income Department, Credit Suisse First Boston. Bob is group head of the High Yield Research Department, which produces market strategy and credit research. Along with his other duties, he oversees the quantitative and portfolio analysis product and covers the media and telecommunications industries, which he has followed for over a decade. He joined the firm in 1987. Prior to this time, Mr. Kricheff worked on the high yield trading desk at Paine Webber. He began his career at S.N. Seidman & Co., which specialized in corporate and bankruptcy valuations and investments. Mr. Kricheff attended New York University where he received degrees in Economics.

Frederick L. Joutz, Associate Professor of Economics, The George Washington University. Frederick L. Joutz has held the position of associate professor of economics at The George Washington University since 1988. His primary research interests are in applied macroeconomic and energy modeling and forecasting. His publications have appeared in professional journals such as *American Economic Review, Energy Economics, International Journal of Forecasting, Journal of Business and Economic Statistics, Journal of Forecasting,* and *Journal of Macroeconomics.* He produces the Benchmark Forecasts of macroeconomic and financial series in the *Survey of Professional Forecasts* conducted by the Federal Reserve Bank of Philadelphia. He has consulted for government agencies and private corporations on modeling and forecasting.

Dana Lieberman was an Associate Analyst in default research at Moody's Investor Services from 1994 to 1997. Prior to working at Moody's she received a Bachelor of Arts majoring in Economics and Business Administration at the Hebrew University of Jerusalem, Israel. She currently works for SG Cowen in the Credit Risk Monitoring division.

Frank X. Reilly, Bernard J. Hank Professor of Business Administration, University of Notre Dame. Dr. Reilly has published over 60 articles in the *Journal of Fixed Income, Journal of Finance, Journal of Financial and Quantitative Analysis, Journal of Accounting Research, Journal of Financial Research, Financial Analysts Journal, Financial Management,* and *Journal of Portfolio Management,* among others. Dr. Reilly (with Edgar Norton) is the author of *Investments* and *Investment Analysis* and *Portfolio Management* (with Keith Brown). His professional experience includes a position with Goldman Sachs & Company, a senior security analyst for Technology Fund, and a consultant for the World Bank and Ryan Lab, Inc. He is on the Board of Directors of Brinson Global Funds (Chairman of the Board), Fort Dearborn Income Securities, Greenwood Trust Co., NIBCO, Inc., the Association for Investment Management and Research, Morgan Stanley Dean Witter Trust FSB, and Battery Park High Yield Funds.

Vesna Strenk, Vice President, Fixed Income Department, Credit Suisse First Boston. Vesna is group head of the High Yield Research Department's quantitative and portfolio analysis product. She joined the firm in 1989. Ms. Strenk received her B.A. in Corporate Finance from CUNY's Baruch College.

Frank X. Whitley, Senior Vice President, Shenkman Capital Management, Inc. Shenkman Capital is a New York-based investment management firm that focuses exclusively on the high yield market. Prior to joining Shenkman Capital in 1988, Mr. Whitley held analyst and managerial positions at Integrated Resources and Collins & Aikman Corp. He is a graduate of Seton Hall University and received an M.B.A. from Fordham University.

David J. Wright, Associate Professor of Finance, University of Wisconsin–Parkside. Dr. Wright is currently an associate professor of finance in the School of Business and Technology at the Unviersity of Wisconsin–Parkside, where he teaches investments, working capital management, and corporate finance. Previously, he worked at the Universtiy of Notre Dame in the College of Business and at the Graduate School of Business, Indiana University, Bloomington. Dr. Wright has done extensive research in the field of bonds, with special emphasis on bond indices and their implications for fixed-income portfolio performance measurement. He has published numerous articles in prestigious publications. Dr. Wright received his B.S., M.B.A., and Ph.D. from the University of Illinois.

Mitchell Weiman, Vice President, High Yield Trading, Friedman, Billings, Ramsey & Co. Inc. Mr. Weiman currently heads the high yield trading department at Friedman, Billings, Ramsey. Mr. Weiman makes markets in over 50 high yield bond and preferred securities, while coordinating the growth of the high yield effort. Mr. Weiman joined FBR in 1992, and has been a high yield analyst and trader since that time. Mr. Weiman graduated from Babson College with a B.S. in Finance.

Sheng Wu, Investment Bond Analyst, Morgan Stanley. Sheng Wu is currently an analyst with Morgan Stanley in Hong Kong. Prior to joining Morgan Stanley, he worked as an analyst with the Merrill Lynch investment bond department in Hong Kong. Before coming to Hong Kong, he worked as a research assistant in Merrill Lynch's High Yield Strategy Research in New York. Sheng Wu received a Bachelor of Art degree in Economics from the University of Chicago in 1997.

The high yield bond market has grown dramatically since the early 1980s to a current size of over $500 billion. This rapid growth has been fueled by domestic U.S. and international institutional investors seeking higher yields, and emerging companies in need of capital to finance growth. In 1997, new issue volume reached $135 billion, as compared to about $45 billion in initial public equity offerings. The high yield market is now truly a global market with 16 percent of new issues in 1997 coming from international firms.

The purpose of this book is to bring together articles by many of the leading finance professionals and academics, working and writing in the high yield area to provide a comprehensive overview of the market. Given the unique investment characteristics of high yield bonds, where both interest rate changes and credit risk are major factors, a comprehensive treatment is necessary to truly understand the risks and rewards of the area. Hence, the book is organized into seven parts dealing with market structure, security risk analysis, security valuation, market valuation models, portfolio management, distressed security investing, and corporate finance considerations.

Part One looks at the growth, structure, and evolution of the high yield market. The role of investment banks in security innovation and market development, the major types of institutional investors, and the array of uses to which high yield financing has been applied are detailed. The evolution of analytical methodologies applied to high yield securities is also examined. Recent developments in the leveraged loan market are identified. Finally, the globalization of the high yield market is discussed.

Part Two examines crucial aspects of high yield bond risk analysis. Topics covered include historical bond default rates, the relationship between real interest rates and default rates, and recovery rates on defaulted bonds. Also, information is provided on historical bond rating transition probabilities as well as new simulation methodologies for modeling changes in credit quality.

Part Three discusses major factors that affect the pricing of high yield securities. The topics examined include the impact of seniority and security on bond pricing and return. Fundamental factors involved in security valuation are detailed, including financial analysis, covenant review, evaluation of senior management, and trading factors. Finally, a Monte Carlo simulation methodology for valuing bonds and options on bonds in an environment having correlated interest rate and credit risk is demonstrated.

To fully understand the pricing of high yield securities, an investor must also have a perspective on what drives overall market yield levels and spreads. Part Four reviews econometric studies that detail the importance of monetary influences, risk-free interest rates, default rates, mutual fund flows, seasonal fluctuations, and other factors.

Part Five surveys high yield portfolio management issues. A historical perspective is provided for the risk and return on high yield securities as well as a comparison to alternative investments. Indices are utilized to measure the performance of security classes as well as to serve as benchmark to compare portfolio managers. An analysis of the indices available to investors is discussed as well as the problems of utilizing the indices. A historical examination of the number of high yield bonds necessary to diversify a portfolio's default risk is also provided. Next, a description is provided by professional fund managers about how they manage and build a portfolio of high yield assets, as well as how they manage the overall risk of the portfolio. Finally, a Monte Carlo simulation methodology for modeling interest rate and credit risk as a correlated random process and providing improved portfolio risk assessments is demonstrated.

Part Six considers the unique issues involved in investing in distressed securities. Historical risk and return information on distressed securities is detailed. Finally, an academic overview of the market as well as a professional investment manager's decision criteria for investing in specific securities is outlined.

Part Seven discusses selected corporate finance topics. An overview of emerging firms' strategic choice between external debt and equity financing is provided. Finally, the advantages and disadvantages of issuing public versus private (Rule-144a) securities are examined. By bringing together a broad spectrum of the best research and writing on high yield bonds, this book will provide a useful reference for both finance professionals and academics.

ACKNOWLEDGMENTS

We would like to thank The George Washington University for creating The Financial Markets Research Institute (FMRI), as well as providing significant funding and facilities to support this and other projects. In addition, we want to recognize Shenkman Capital Management, Sallie Mae, NASD, Friedman Billings Ramsey, Inc., and FinSoft, Inc. for their financial support for FMRI. Without tangible commitments such as these, this project would not have been possible. Marjorie Barnhill provided very helpful detailed editorial comments. Also thanks to our families for allowing us the time required to complete the needed research and writing.

Finally, and most importantly, the contributing authors made this book a reality. They made time in busy schedules to complete their chapters. Thanks to them for a job well done.

Theodore M. Barnhill, Jr.
William F. Maxwell
Mark R. Shenkman

BRIEF CONTENTS

CONTENTS

Chapter 12

Analyzing a High Yield Issue   220

Chapter 13

Valuing Bonds and Options on Bonds Having Correlated Interest Rate and Credit Risk   232

Chapter 16

The January Effect in the Corporate Bond Market: A Systematic Examination   280

PART FIVE

PORTFOLIO MANAGEMENT

Chapter 17

High Yield as an Asset Class   305

Chapter 18

An Analysis of High Yield Bond Indices   336

Chapter 25

Analyzing the Credit Risk of Distressed Securities   473

PART SEVEN

CORPORATE FINANCE

Chapter 26

Strategic Financing Choices for Emerging Firms: Debt versus Equity   489

PART ONE

Market Structure

CHAPTER 1

The High Yield Market

Bob Kricheff

Vesna Strenk

INTRODUCTION

The modern high yield market began in the 1980s. Wall Street firms began to develop new buyers willing to buy corporate bonds that did not have investment grade ratings. Simultaneously, these firms, led by Drexel Burnham Lambert, sought out smaller and mid-sized companies that needed capital to grow their businesses and were willing to add debt to their balance sheets to get it. This gradually led to a liquid market for the issuance and trading of below-investment-grade corporate bonds.

Financings in the early days of the modern high yield market were used by mid-sized companies either to fund growth opportunities, requiring heavy upfront capital spending, or for acquisitions. Initially, only a few billion dollars of bonds were being issued each year; however, by the latter part of the 1980s, new issuance began to boom. The major driver of this expansion was the corresponding acquisition boom of the late 1980s. This period created some of the most innovative financing techniques, and many are still in vogue today.

This era also helped finance numerous growth companies and several industries that could not get financing elsewhere. These companies included MCI Communications, McCaw Cellular (now AT&T Wireless), and Turner Broadcasting. Some of the industries such as cable television and gaming used high yield bonds as the primary source of financing for their tremendous growth during the 1980s. The aggressiveness of many

3

high yield financed buyouts and recapitalizations were much more responsible for the record level of defaults that followed in 1990 and 1991 than the general corporate issuance. For example, some of the last leveraged buyouts of the 1980s were financed with bonds that had almost usurious rates of 16½ and 17½ percent[1], making it very difficult for a company to grow into its capital structure without a booming economy.

The painful adolescence that the high yield market experienced during 1990 and 1991 helped it mature from a club, dominated by one underwriter, into a market. It also helped establish greater discipline in covenants and structures.

During the 1990s, the high yield market has become a source of financing for numerous types of companies funding growth, business expansions, and acquisitions. The market now regularly utilizes many of the structures developed in the late 1980s. These include discounted deferred interest securities, pay-in-kind securities, and holding company securities which are now used to fund acquisitions and also used to finance companies on the forefront of developing new competitive technology. The market remains an institutional market. However, it now attracts a broad array of investors including mutual funds, insurance companies, pension funds, hedge funds, high grade funds that "cross-over," and an increasing number of foreign money managers rather than the small group of mutual funds and insurance companies that were the main investors in the 1980s.

THE EARLY TO MID-1980s

The original investors in high yield bonds primarily had "fallen angels" to choose from. These were issues of bonds that originally had investment grade ratings but had been downgraded to a rating BB+ or Ba1 or below. Such a rating designated it below investment grade and restricted most traditional fixed income investors from buying the issue.

Prior to the mid-eighties, most companies without an investment grade rating that were looking to issue bonds generally had to go to the private placement market. Frequently, the buyers were a specialized division of insurance companies. Buyers insisted on strict features and restrictive covenants and with a limited universe of buyers, they had the negotiating leverage. Additionally, because they were buying private placements there

---

1. Rates on two tranches of the SCI Television securities issued in 1987.

was virtually no meaningful secondary market for these securities so the buyers had to assume that they were being held until maturity or other scheduled retirement.

By the mid-eighties, there were a growing number of issuers that were accessing a market for public registered bonds being issued with an original rating below investment grade. The prime underwriter in this market was the firm Drexel Burnham Lambert.

The buyers consisted primarily of insurance companies, savings and loans associations, and a gradually growing pool of mutual funds that focused on this market. Additionally, there were corporations that had raised excess cash through bond offerings and were investing this cash into other high yield securities as they waited to find acquisition opportunities.

There were several different types of credits that were issuing high yield bonds. One type of issuer was the fallen angel that still needed to raise more money. These issuers were originally heavily weighted in the airline, energy, and steel industries. Then there were issuers that could not generally get financing from banks or other traditional lenders for their expansion projects. These issuers were predominately in the gaming and cable television industries. There also was a mixed bag of growth companies. These companies were typically too small and had too much debt to qualify for an investment-grade rating. Lastly, there were companies that came to market to fund acquisitions—sometimes the funding was for a specific acquisition and sometimes it was for a "blind pool" in which the company was expected to find acquisitions in the future.

THE GROWTH OF ACQUISITION FINANCING

These acquisitions funded with debt were increasingly known as leveraged buyouts (LBOs) because debt was being used to "leverage" up the balance sheet to fund the acquisition. LBOs were the dominant feature of the high yield market during the late 1980s. The escalation of "hostile" LBOs and increasingly aggressive issuers began to raise the risk profile for investors.

In 1985, there were approximately $14.5 billion of below-investment-grade bonds issued.[2] Approximately $3.2 billion were raised for LBO refinancing, $2.1 billion for other acquisitions and blind pools, and $1.4 billion for other acquisition refinancing. So even in the early days of high yield new

---

2. *High Yield Handbook,* First Boston, February 1986, p. 5.

issuance, almost half of the supply was related to merger and acquisition activity. By 1989 the new supply was about $25 billion and about $14 billion, or about 56 percent, were acquisition related; another $8 billion entered the market from "cram-down" paper related to M&A activity, bringing the percentage up to 67 percent.[3] Cram-down paper was a bond issued in exchange for a portion of the outstanding equity of a company in an LBO transaction or in a leveraged recapitalization (recap). Typically, these cram-down securities and a cash component were paid out to shareholders on a pro-rata basis in these transactions. Cram-down paper was typically the most junior piece of debt in the post transaction capital structures.

As hostile takeover offers escalated during the late 1980s, the acquirers were increasingly arranging commitments from financial institutions ahead of time. The entrenched management of these target companies appealed to their shareholders to hold out against adding debt onto the company and to invest for the long term, but were increasingly losing out to the high prices being offered to shareholders by the acquirers. One defense that developed was the use of leverage itself.

In the defense of hostile takeovers, some companies raised debt to counteract an outside bid. Companies would mount a pool of borrowings that would allow for the payment of a special dividend to shareholders. This would give existing shareholders a payment that was large relative to the price of the stock and still allow them to hold onto the stock. This "stub" stock was then part of a levered entity and traded at a significantly lower value than it had prior to the transaction. The lower stock price was due to the high leverage that had been added to the balance sheet. These transactions are generally referred to as leveraged recaps. In some cases, these have been done as a method of maximizing shareholder value even without a hostile bid being present.

SOME STRUCTURAL DEVELOPMENTS

Traditionally high yield issues were cash paying securities with ten- or twelve-year maturities and no call features for the first five years. As prices for takeovers escalated, new structures began to appear. Features were developed to allow a company to cover its cash interest expense with its own cash flow. The most common structure was the use of discounted deferred pay securities, also known as zeros or zero/fix securities. These bonds were

---

3. *High Yield Handbook,* First Boston, January 1990, pp. 36–38.

issued at a discount to their face value[4] and accreted to face value usually over a five-year period. At that time companies were required to begin to pay the interest on the bonds in cash. This structure was put in place to allow the companies that were subject to highly levered transactions a chance to increase their available cash flow and/or sell assets to pay down debt. A comparable security structure was one that gave the company the option to pay the interest on the security for a period of time, typically five years, by issuing additional securities. These pay-in-kind, or PIK, securities were not only issued as bonds but also as preferred stock. These high yield preferred stocks, while structurally equity, differed from traditional perpetual preferred shares. These PIK preferred securities typically had a mandatory redemption date. If the issue was not redeemed on that date, the preferred shareholders could typically block payment of dividends to the public equity and also would get to elect several seats to the board. These preferred shares were also typically exchangeable into debt at the company's option, should it be advantageous on a tax basis.

While these deferred pay securities were usually subordinated in nature, banks and/or other lenders often required these securities to be structurally subordinated as well. For these reasons a holding company was frequently formed to separate the entity where the operating assets and the bank lines resided away from where all or some of the public securities would be issued.

By the end of 1988 it was estimated that 10.3 percent of the high yield universe were zero/fix issues and 4.1 percent were PIKs.[5]

LBO RETURNS

The logical question is why were investors willing to invest in these highly levered transactions? The answer was: returns. When these LBOs were successful, returns for the bond investors were dramatic. The quick streamlining of operations, or the successful pay-down of debt through asset sales resulted in rapid price acceleration of the related high yield securities. In many cases the companies would refinance the capital structure, including

---

4. Typical face value or par value of a bond is $1,000. These bonds would be issued at a discount, say $550. The bond's claim value, or accreted value, increased at a rate equal to the coupon of the bond and would typically reach the face value at the same time that it would begin to pay cash interest. It is important to note that in a bankruptcy the bondholders' claim would be the accreted value not the sale value. A formula for annual accreted value is the following: Beginning Accreted Value $(1+ Coupon/2)^2$.

5. *High Yield Handbook,* First Boston, January 1989.

reequitizing the company through a public stock offering and retiring public debt at a premium.

One good example of this was Union Carbide Corporation. The company undertook a leveraged recap in early 1986 and issued several billion dollars face amount of debt. By year-end, the company retired approximately $2.5 billion face amount of public high yield debt at a 24 percent premium to face value.

Early retirement of bonds at premiums have been a hallmark of the high yield market and have regularly enlarged returns for high yield portfolios. As a company experiences improvements in cash flow and the value of the underlying equity increases, the cost of available borrowing declines. It frequently becomes economically feasible for a company to retire its high coupon bonds at a premium, even if they are not callable, thus leading to returns for investors substantially above the stated coupon on the bonds.

OTHER DEVELOPMENTS OF NOTE

There were some other features of the high yield market worth mentioning during this era. One was a distressed exchange offer and the other was "usable" bonds.

During the 1980s numerous companies got into financial difficulties. These companies often got to the point where they were unable to meet their debt obligations. In order to avoid a bankruptcy these companies attempted to undertake a negotiated exchange offer with bondholders. These *distressed* exchange offers usually offered bondholders some combination of a reduction in the face value of the bonds, a reduction in coupon, or an extended maturity. Bondholders frequently received some form of equity in return. The exchange offers were considered distressed when the terms of the offered security were in any way weaker than the terms of the existing one.

While some exchange offers worked out well, and bondholders benefited from the greater upside in the equity, others did not. Many companies over time needed to undertake more than one exchange offer to stay afloat. In some cases, despite several exchange offers, the company eventually filed for bankruptcy anyway. In these cases, the series of exchange offers frequently reduced the bondholders' claim in bankruptcy substantially from the original bond's claim. Over time bondholders began to work together to protect their own interests and became less willing to give up any of their claims prior to a bankruptcy. Additionally, when necessary, creditors tried to negotiate "prepackaged" bankruptcies so they could force all the securities in an asset class to exchange their securities. Distressed exchange offers, as they existed in the 1980s, have effectively disappeared over time as the use of the bankruptcy code has generally helped investors.

During the 1980s, underwriters looked for ways to attract more investors and enhance returns. One way was to offer more upside with the inclusion of some type of equity component. The equity was usually attached in the form of warrants. Popular in the 1980s were "usable" bonds. In these cases warrants were issued along with the bonds. Investors had the choice of using cash to exercise the warrants or to exchange the existing bonds as currency for the exercise price of the warrants. In this case the bonds would be valued at face value for purposes of the exchange.

These types of securities generally became less popular, as management generally preferred to get cash from the exercise of warrants which they could use at their discretion. However, the use of "equity kickers" has remained popular. During the 1990s, early stage developmental telecommunications companies have frequently attached warrants to a bond offering to help entice investors to buy the securities. These bundled securities are called units and initially trade as one security. The two securities are usually separated after some period of time. Of note, it has been commonplace for companies to issue warrants even if they do not have public stock outstanding; these warrants are usually exercisable at $0.01 and have provisions for various take-outs if an initial public offering of stock is not undertaken.

THE RATING AGENCIES VERSUS THE MARKET

Rating agencies have given significant weighting to a company's book-equity-to-debt ratio, the ratio of earnings to fixed charge obligations, and the size of the company's book capitalization in arriving at its rating conclusions. These types of statistics were generally not strong for high yield companies. This was especially true when the company was growing by acquisitions and/or extensive capital expenditures, and was building assets with economic lives much longer than their balance sheet lives. The high level of depreciation and amortization for these companies led to earnings declines and weakened book values. However, in many cases, the cost of the maintenance capital was significantly less than the depreciation being charged on the income statement. Therefore, underwriters and bond purchasers looked to other measures besides traditional earnings and book values to arrive at the relative creditworthiness of these bond issuers.

First, investors tended to ignore earnings because of the dispropor-
tionate depreciation and amortization in these high growth companies.
Investors looked toward a measure of cash flow, using earnings before
interest, taxes, depreciation and amortization, EBITDA. Investors then utilized an EBITDA/interest expense ratio to explore the ability of a company
to meet its debt obligations. In some cases, to be more conservative,
investors adjusted the numerator in this ratio from EBITDA, to EBITDA
less required maintenance capital expenditures.

To examine leverage, investors would use the ratio of total
debt/EBITDA. Investors could rationalize this ratio relative to cash flow
multiples that were being paid for comparable assets or valuations of comparable public equities. For example, if a company had a 5× debt/EBITDA
ratio, and asset sales of properties comparable to those owed by the company were occurring at 10× EBITDA, it would imply that there were 2×
more asset value than debt, regardless of the book value of the company.
Investors and underwriters also began to use debt to *market value* of equity
rather than debt to book equity. The market value of the equity is calculated
by multiplying the total number of shares by the market price of the stock.

The use of all of these ratios put increased emphasis on cash flow and
on the market value of assets rather than on earnings and traditional book
accounting for equity. These are still some of the same key components of
high yield credit analyses used today.

PEAK DEFAULT AND REDEMPTION

By 1989, the major underwriter in the high yield market was under investigation for insider trading and the economy was slowing. This all occurred
as leverage was increasing in many LBOs. What ensued was several years
of historically high default rates within the high yield market. Default rates
peaked in 1990 and 1991 with rates of 7.9 percent and 9.3 percent.[6]

The average price of securities in the high yield market was also at historic lows. At the end of 1990 the average price was 65.9 percent of face
value and there was very limited liquidity in the market. Many so called
"vulture" funds began to enter the market, buying securities at depressed
prices and frequently willing to take control of the company's underlying
assets in bankruptcy should the bond issuer not maintain adequate liquidity.

---

6. *High Yield Handbook,* First Boston, January 1993, p. 44.

These huge discounts in market prices would not remain and, by the end of 1991, the average price was back into the low 80s.[7] During 1991 the market posted a 44 percent return and then in 1992 it posted a 17 percent return.[8]

These returns were enough to attract numerous investors back to the market. Funds began to flow into mutual funds, and insurance company and pension fund allocators began to look at the high yield market again. However, most pension advisors and insurance company asset allocators waited to see several years of positive annual returns before aggressively addressing the market. New issuance of bonds also returned. After there were only $11 billion of new bonds that came to market during 1990 and 1991 combined, $40 billion came to market in 1992. New issuance has continued to accelerate and grow the market; in 1997 over $135 billion face amount of new bonds came to market.

While the high yield market remains an unlisted market, the increased diversity of issues and credit quality in the market, as well as the increased diversity of market participants and underwriters, implies a much more liquid market. The market can be readily accessed by issuers, and investors have a variety of marketmakers to go to. In the late 1980s, Drexel Burnham Lambert still accounted for about 60 percent of all underwriting. In 1997, this same market share was split among 11 underwriters, with the largest having less than a 12 percent share. Additionally, since 1991, the number of high yield mutual funds tracked by MorningStar has more than doubled, and this does not account for the increase in pension and insurance funds investing in the high yield market.

NEW ISSUING TRENDS IN THE 1990s

Initially, much of the high yield financing that came to market in the early 1990s was used to refinance higher coupon debt that had already been outstanding. Eventually, acquisition financing returned to the market and LBOs did too. However, much of the boom in financing that has been seen during 1995 to 1998 has come in response to deregulation and changes in technology.

Some of the fastest growing sectors of the high yield market in the 1990s have been the media, cable television, and communications industries. Within the media industry, deregulation of ownership rules on the

---

7. Ibid., p. 15.
8. Ibid., Appendix I.

number of broadcast properties a company could own led to massive consolidation. This consolidation required financing that came from the high yield, equity, and bank markets. Several regulatory changes that improved the ability of new competitors to enter the cable television business and to develop these businesses internationally led to a new round of cable television-related financing in the 1990s. However, the most dramatic boom in new high yield paper has come from the communications sector. The domestic and international deregulation of the telecommunications industry, coupled with the rapid growth in the use of the Internet and electronic data and technological innovations, has led to a plethora of developmental telecommunications companies being formed to challenge the incumbents. Many of these insurgent companies have turned to the high yield market for financing because bank financing has not been available. These new companies have been the dominant feature of the market during the 1990s. The communications sector alone accounted for only 4 percent of the market in early 1995 but was up to 15 percent by year-end 1997.

These industries have been largely responsible for the resurgence in the issuance of deferred pay securities. Generally, these developmental credits have utilized zero-fix bonds to fund their period of negative cash flow and heavy capital expenditures. The use of PIK bonds has largely disappeared though PIK preferreds remain a popular financing vehicle. These have been particularly popular among broadcasters whose banks count the preferred shares as equity, freeing up bank availability for acquisitions.

OTHER STRUCTURAL DEVELOPMENTS

Several new structural developments also appeared during the 1990s; two of note were *overfunded* bonds and *equity clawbacks*.

First, developmental credits began to issue overfunded cash-pay bonds to address investors' concerns regarding overexposure to zeros. Despite these companies having the inability to pay cash interest with cash flow, these bonds have cash paying coupons. The bond financing raises extra proceeds beyond what the company needs for capital spending and operating capital. These "extra" proceeds are escrowed in order to pay interest on the bonds, typically for the first three years. The cost to the issuer is (1) the higher level of debt outstanding initially after the transaction and (2) the negative arbitrage between what the company can earn from investing escrowed proceeds in Treasuries and the coupon on the high yield debt. The first of these types of structures appeared in the financing for Mobile Telecommunications Technology.

The levered companies of the high yield market have had increasing access to the equity markets during the 1990s. With the increased potential of raising public equity at attractive levels, companies wanted greater options in being able to refinance their high yield debt. Thus the equity clawback was developed. This initially appeared in an issue for General Nutrition Centers. This feature allows a company to use proceeds from an equity offering to call a set percentage of the bonds outstanding at a premium. Typically, this option is available to the company during the first three years of a bond. (Remember, typically a bond is not callable for five years.) The call price is usually at par plus the coupon and the call is for a maximum of 25–35 percent of the amount outstanding. Bond buyers initially felt they were compensated by the premium call price and the credit improvements inherent from the raising of additional equity. However, the feature clearly limits the upside for original issue buyers. Additionally, when bonds trade to very high premiums in the secondary market, due to declining rates and credit improvements, the clawbacks can represent downside pressure on the bond prices.

NEW ANALYSIS TOOLS

With more bonds being issued by early stage developmental credits, many traditional financial ratios became less useful, because most of the companies had minimal revenue and negative EBITDA. Investors have needed to be more forward looking. Investors have used projections of cash needs and future EBITDA and the comparison of items such as the ratio of invested capital to debt, percentage of the business plan that is fully funded, and the projected EBITDA level at the time when cash interest payments are required. These ratios are considered along with market value for the type of assets that the company is building.

CLOSING COMMENTS

Overall, the risks in the high yield market have changed dramatically. Initially the market had limited diversity and minimal trading liquidity. A single credit default had a meaningful impact on overall market returns.

The growth of the market has allowed portfolio diversification to help insulate the impact of any one credit problem. The growth in the number of money managers and underwriters has helped to improve the trading liquidity.

Additionally, the credit risks have changed. Due to the dominance of LBOs in the late 1980s, the credit risks were frequently structural in nature (i.e., how much debt and in what structure). In the 1990s, issuance has been dominated by media, cable, and communications. These industries have changed the credit risk in the market so that it now comes from business competition and technology and has caused the market to be more dependent on continued deregulation.

One feature that has remained a constant in high yield is that the face value or par value is not the only upside for bondholders. The ability of these high yield companies to post dramatic credit improvements frequently leads to the early retirement of the bonds at a premium. Since 1991, these premium retirements have far outstripped defaults and we expect this trend to continue as original issue high yield bonds rarely reach maturity.

E X H I B I T   1–1

Typical Features of a Cash-Paying High Yield Corporate Bond

Ranking	Senior or senior subordinated
Coupon	Cash paying semiannual
Maturity	10 or 12 years
Sinking Fund	None
Call	Noncall for five years First call at a price equal to par and half the coupon, declining each year to reach par in year nine

E X H I B I T   1–2

Typical Features of a Zero-Fix High Yield Corporate Bond

Ranking	Senior or senior subordinated
Coupon	Bond accretes at the coupon rate compounding semiannually First cash coupon begins accruing in year five, pays semiannually
Maturity	10 or 12 years
Sinking Fund	None
Call	Same as cash pay bonds

E X H I B I T   1–3

Typical Features of a High Yield PIK Preferred Stock

Ranking	Preferred stock
Coupon	Payable at the company's option in cash or in additional shares of preferred valued at par. Payable quarterly or semiannually
Maturity Redemption	10 or 12 years
Exchangeable	At the company's option into a subordinated bond with comparable terms and a maturity equivalent to the redemption date
Sinking Fund	None
Call	Same as cash pay bonds

SUMMARY OF TYPICAL HIGH YIELD BOND COVENANTS

Covenants in high yield securities are almost always based on incurrence rather than the maintenance covenants that are typical of a private placement or a bank agreement. This means that the high yield covenants prevent a company from undertaking certain actions unless these tests are met. Covenants vary widely and this brief only tries to outline a few of the most widely used covenants in very rough terms.

It is important to note that terms may be defined differently in each covenant package. Defined terms usually appear capitalized in the prospectus. The definition for the purpose of the fund appears somewhere in the document. Covenants can typically be changed with an affirmative vote of over 50 percent of the bondholders.

Debt Incurrence   Limits the ability to draw additional borrowings unless certain terms are met. Typically the test includes a Debt/EBITDA test; e.g., "no additional borrowings may be drawn if pro forma the Debt/EBITDA for the latest twelve months reported period is 7x or less." Sometimes the test includes an interest coverage ratio or a test based on invested equity, typically for developmental issues.

Typical exceptions or *carve-outs* include room for use of an existing bank line, receivables financing, vendor financing, or debt used for refinancing of existing debt and working capital lines. Sometimes there is a carve-out for the issuance of debt that is junior to the existing securities.

Restricted Payments   Limit the ability to pay dividends, retire equity or junior debt except if proceeds come from an equity offering and certain terms are met. Typically the test includes a pro forma interest coverage test and requires that the company be able to meet the pro forma debt test outlined above. Payments cannot usually exceed a cumulative "basket" of proceeds, consisting of cumulative net income from the time of the debt offering.

Change of Control   This covenant typically requires the company to make an offer to purchase the bonds at 101 percent of face value should the controlling ownership structure change. The definition of the ownership varies greatly for each bond. Additionally, sometimes the offer to purchase must be undertaken only if a rating downgrade or a decline in net worth occurs.

CHAPTER 2

Changes in the High Yield Market, A Historic Perspective

Sam DeRosa-Farag

Jonathan Blau

INTRODUCTION

As we examine our outlook for the leveraged finance market (both high yield bonds and leveraged loans) we are faced with a large number of changes that have impacted these markets. Key changes include a dramatic growth in the market size on the new issue side (see Exhibit 2–1), an increase in the risk profile of certain sectors such as build-outs and LBOs, a rapid increase in the number of issues and issuers in the high yield market, a dramatic shift in the seniority and credit ratios of new issues, and a significant improvement in the average single B/BB credit statistics over the 1984–1997 period. In 1997, we believe the changes were so dramatic that a whole review of the asset class is in order. On the new issue side changes included a proliferation in the number of non-U.S. issuers, high yield issuers tapping the non-U.S. dollar high yield market in Europe, and a rapid shift in the number of underwriters that incorporated new entrants and the consolidation of existing players. The investor base also has shifted to include a prominent role for structured funds (CBOs/CLOs) in excess of a $55 billion market size in 1997(see Exhibit 2–2). The average money management firm has decided it must have a presence in high yield, and a large number of European and other international investors are now involved in this market.

The intention of this section is to highlight the major changes in the high yield and leveraged loan markets and review the evolution of these markets to maintain perspective.

E X H I B I T   2-1

High Yield Market Size to New Issue Volume

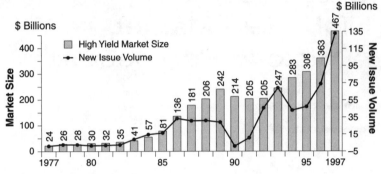

Sources: DLJ; Securities Data Corporation (SDC).

E X H I B I T   2-2

CBO/CLO Volume, 1987–1997

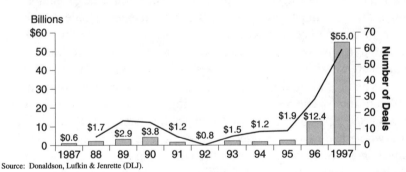

Source: Donaldson, Lufkin & Jenrette (DLJ).

EVOLUTION OF THE MARKET: HIGH YIELD LEVERAGED LOANS, INFANCY, AND PRIVATE PLACEMENT

From 1980 to 1997, the analytical tools utilized within the high yield market changed dramatically in conjunction with the market's development phases. While one of the basic tasks of credit analysis is to understand the drivers affecting a credit's profitability and competitive position, the ability to develop the same driver approach to the overall high yield market is a very recent development. This was a function of a cultural issue in the high yield market that stemmed from the lack of readily available data. Also, when an asset is in its infancy, small numbers do not suggest a law of large number approach. Without the information of a full economic cycle, it was difficult to arrive at any substantial long-term conclusions about the high yield market. For a long time, a large number of practitioners believed there were no measurable drivers. The prevailing belief was that the market was entirely credit driven, and therefore, the aggregate behavior was somewhat random. It was not until recently that the high yield market had enough analytical tools, the results of answering different questions over many years, to successfully locate and quantify drivers. This is enabling us to have hedging methodologies, however imperfect, and helps us anticipate the behavior of the asset.

In addition, one of the most fundamental conclusions is that credit analysis only contributes an estimated 8 percent of overall portfolio returns while market posture, or beta, contributes 80 percent. These conclusions are in line with other findings in financial literature and have substantial repercussions on resource allocation in line with costs/fees in both the money management business and for underwriters attempting to provide value to their clients. We believe that these tools were developed in three distinct phases of the high yield market.

PHASE I

In the beginning of the modern high yield market, 1978–1986, the market focused primarily on the delivery of efficient execution for below-investment-grade companies accessing the capital markets. This placed high yield in somewhat of a competition with bank debt and the fragmented private-placement markets. This was an era of securitization where the mortgage, asset-backed, and high yield markets provided a more cost effective, less complicated, and less time consuming way, due to the standardization of documentation, for issuers to access capital. Therefore, these new developments created more liquid markets than the markets they were intended to replace. In this phase, the benchmark of success was the comparison to bank debt and private placements, and in this comparison, high yield was successful. The U.S. capital markets remain, to this day, one of the few global markets that can efficiently price and deliver capital to non-investment-grade credits. Having said that, we are currently witnessing the evolution of the European high yield market.

PHASE II

In the second phase, market practitioners applied similar analytical tools that had been utilized in other security markets to the high yield market. Investors began to view high yield as they did any other security, not just as a private-placement alternative, and they started to ask security questions about high yield. The market was concerned with issues such as whether or not the pricing of market risk and market efficiency were existent in high yield. In more detail, the questions presented were:

- Are we pricing the market risks (i.e., default and liquidity) appropriately?
- Is the market an attractive alternative investment?
- Other than its main investors such as mutual funds and the insurance companies, should anybody else invest in high yield?

Unfortunately, it took a recession, the disappearance of the largest underwriter from the market, and the intervention of regulators (FIRREA, NAIC, and HLTs) to arrive at the answers. The outcome was a body of analytical work that addressed whether the current spread over Treasuries compensated investors for the modern experience of default loss rates. Also included in this category were studies to show where high yield bonds fell on the efficient frontier—specifically, were we getting compensated for the risks from a historical return perspective? This was made possible by 17 years of data on the high yield market, a substantial number that validates asset allocation models, risk and reward graphs, correlation and autocorrelation studies, and diversification analysis. The outcome of this analysis seems to show that high yield is a very attractive asset. Similar questions currently are being asked about emerging markets and bank debt, and until we have data from a full economic cycle on these assets, we will not be able to comprehensively answer these questions.

PHASE III

The high yield market is currently in what we would classify as the third phase, characterized by enough analytical tools to give market outsiders the understanding of how high yield would affect a multiasset portfolio. High yield currently has a body of analytical work that allows an outsider to determine its attributes, its risks and rewards (see Exhibit 2–3), its relationships with other assets, its relative liquidity, and its role in a diversified portfolio. The availability of work such as tactical asset/sector allocation models for multiasset portfolios and for high yield portfolios, a somewhat robust benchmarking system, and performance attribution methodology (i.e., multifactor models) all help an outsider determine a level of interest to exposure to high yield assets, and the profile of that exposure. The outsider would also have the ability to estimate the net positive impact of adding high yield to an existing multiasset portfolio. In 1997 alone, we have witnessed the shift in the high yield market from a three-factor model to a four-factor model where international risk is an added high yield market driver.

With more than 17 years of historical data, long-term trends can be assessed and quantified. Among the advantages of building a fundamental model are:

- It allows for the construction of a forecasting model for high yield assets, even though the accuracy of any of these models lacks a high level of robustness. This is primarily due to the large number of variables to which the asset responds. A multivariable model is always more difficult to work with than a single variable model. However, the direction and magnitude of measures, given certain drivers, can highlight implicit risks and attractive sectors in the market.

- Sensitivities to certain variables—interest rates, economic and international risks—can be run while addressing the relative value of sectors within the asset or among multiasset portfolios. A basis for a performance attribution model can be built so as to decompose the returns into market components, credit contributions, and other factors.

- The ability to create a portfolio management system, where the results of sensitivity analysis along with a tactical optimization model would result in useful guidelines for sector weightings within a portfolio.

In general, high yield returns can be attributable to four overall components: (1) economic risk; (2) interest rate risk; (3) international risk; and (4) market specific risk, as defined by the equation:

$$R = \alpha + \beta_i(R_i) + \epsilon$$

where: R is the return net the risk free rate
α is the return due to credit selection
β_i is the return attributable to market drivers
R_i are the high yield market drivers
ϵ is the return attributable to random risk

THE MAJOR SHIFTS

Information Overload/Management Challenge

The high yield market has achieved critical mass, with its size currently at $467 billion. Furthermore, the task of following individual issues has become formidable as the market has grown to over 2,300 issues and 1,400 issuers (see Exhibit 2–3). We believe these factors will lead to the rapid adaptation of data/information management tools to maximize an organization's given resources. In addition, a wave of consolidation will hit the underwriters as market knowledge shifts from new issue volume and AMG inflows to a more sophisticated decision-making information framework to deal with the information overload. One of the key market changes in the 1980–1997 period is the migration of the market from "information scarcity" to "information overload." This shift requires a data/information/market driver framework to back the decision-making process.

The Sector Exposure to a Footprint Argument

In the high yield market's infancy, a portfolio manager and maybe one analyst could oversee a 30- to 40-issue portfolio which would provide them with satisfactory diversification. In sharp contrast, a large number of analysts are now required, because the average fund consists of 170–250 different credits. In addition, the ability to get allocations in desired deals is somewhat related to the footprint or size of assets under management.

E X H I B I T   2–3

High Yield Market Evolution,
Number of Issues and Issuers

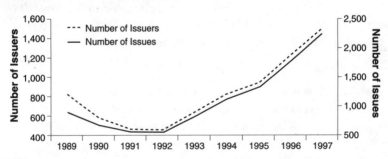

Source: DLJ.

E X H I B I T   2–4

High Yield Mutual Fund Investors

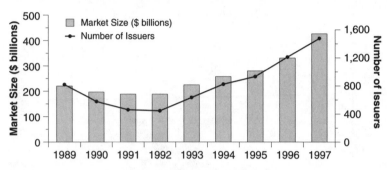

Source: DLJ.

Therefore, the identification of the undervalued issues in the market is challenging given the size of the market and the lack of pricing and data information feeds.

Management Fee Compression

Another shift is the rapid fee compression in managing high yield assets for the institutional market. One of the key challenges is the lack of indexed funds in the high yield market. If an investor would like an exposure to the asset class but is not convinced that a manager provides much incremental return over time, the result is fee compression. In other assets, if a managed/indexed fund choice existed, fee compression would be minimized. Also, the sophistication of the current performance attribution methodologies should help. In conclusion, the driving factor behind the success of high yield managers will be the ability to unbundle risk.

The Inflation/Growth Shift

One of the major trends of 1982 through 1997 has been the credit themes that are perceived to be favorable credit/industry profiles. In the late 1980s, a supermarket was considered to be the ultimate leveraged instrument. A low growth in earnings with an assumed 3 to 4 percent food price inflation resulted in a 25 to 30 percent internal rate of return after leverage. In an environment where inflation is no longer a factor, we have shifted from a stable play with leverage to growth credits. The large number of build-outs has proliferated in response. Overall, the high yield market has shifted from inflation bets to growth bets.

E X H I B I T   2–5

Project Finance Issues in the DLJ High Yield Index (market value)

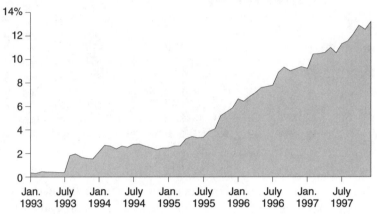

| Jan. | July | Jan. | July | Jan. | July | Jan. | July | Jan. | July |
| 1993 | 1993 | 1994 | 1994 | 1995 | 1995 | 1996 | 1996 | 1997 | 1997 |

Source: DLJ.

E X H I B I T   2–6

New Issue Credit Characteristics

	1982	1983	1984	1985	1986	1987
Total Amount, $Bil	$2.7	$5.8	$14.7	$16.6	$33.2	$30.4
Total Proceeds, $Bil	$2.4	$5.5	$13.4	$13.4	$29.7	$27.6
Number of Issues	49	43	110	148	218	182
Average Size (MM)	$54.7	$135.7	$133.6	$111.8	$152.2	$167.2
Yield at Issuance	16.44%	13.32%	15.47%	13.97%	12.58%	12.82%
Spread at Issuance	400 bp	387 bp	307 bp	385 bp	504 bp	436 bp
Sales Growth	54.8%	23.4%	11.1%	59.2%	18.4%	33.7%
EBITDA Growth	76.8%	23.7%	21.1%	61.9%	40.8%	29.9%
EBITDA Margin	27.6%	26.6%	35.8%	19.3%	24.6%	19.7%
Sales Volatility	34.9%	23.4%	16.2%	34.1%	16.6%	16.2%
EBITDA Volatility	55.0%	30.3%	69.9%	48.4%	31.5%	23.0%
EBITDA/Cash Interest	2.4 x	2.2 x	2.3 x	1.7 x	1.5 x	1.7 x
EBITDA-Capex/Cash Interest	1.7 x	1.8 x	1.4 x	1.4 x	1.0 x	1.4 x
EBITDA/Total Interest	2.4 x	2.2 x	2.2 x	1.6 x	1.5 x	1.6 x
Senior Debt/Cash Interest	4.0 x	4.1 x	4.8 x	3.6 x	4.4 x	5.0 x
Senior Debt/EBITDA	2.7 x	2.0 x	3.4 x	3.5 x	3.5 x	3.5 x
Senior Debt/Total Debt	53.1%	51.8%	57.2%	50.2%	49.5%	53.5%
Debt/EBITDA	4.9 x	4.0 x	6.1 x	6.6 x	6.6 x	5.8 x
Debt/Cap	62.2%	62.5%	71.0%	73.8%	72.3%	83.7%
Debt/Market Cap	NA	57.5%	NA	67.9%	NA	41.6%

Source: DLJ.

E X H I B I T   2-7

Media/Entertainment Issues in the DLJ High Yield index (market value)

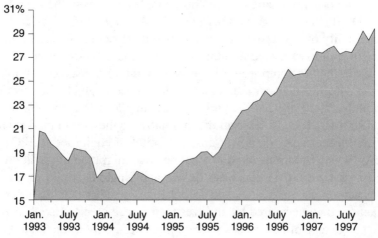

Source: DLJ.

	1988	1989	1990	1991	1992	1993	1994	1995	1996	1997
	$31.9	$28.1	$2.3	$15.2	$47.0	$77.1	$42.7	$45.3	$72.1	$133.0
	$26.9	$24.3	$1.8	$11.5	$42.8	$71.8	$39.0	$41.0	$66.0	$125.4
	158	124	11	58	266	439	244	224	380	704
	$202.2	$226.5	$212.0	$261.4	$176.8	$175.7	$174.8	$202.2	$189.7	$188.9
	13.37%	13.47%	11.34%	10.73%	10.59%	10.18%	11.04%	11.10%	10.56%	10.20%
	459 bp	487 bp	338 bp	362 bp	387 bp	450 bp	434 bp	474 bp	421 bp	392 bp
	24.6%	12.4%	4.2%	16.4%	6.2%	10.2%	17.6%	55.3%	45.0%	53.6%
	23.3%	31.6%	7.5%	22.6%	9.7%	15.4%	25.1%	48.6%	46.2%	43.9%
	31.6%	22.4%	18.0%	22.8%	25.5%	19.7%	19.0%	27.3%	24.4%	27.4%
	19.4%	12.7%	4.3%	15.6%	14.6%	10.2%	15.4%	30.8%	25.4%	29.1%
	28.0%	25.6%	18.0%	25.6%	15.1%	22.5%	28.0%	33.3%	33.9%	42.8%
	1.4 x	1.8 x	2.7 x	2.1 x	1.7 x	2.2 x	2.3 x	2.4 x	2.5 x	2.2 x
	0.7 x	1.2 x	0.9 x	1.3 x	1.1 x	1.4 x	1.6 x	1.7 x	1.7 x	1.7 x
	1.3 x	1.6 x	2.7 x	2.0 x	1.7 x	2.0 x	2.0 x	2.2 x	2.2 x	2.0 x
	3.6 x	6.8 x	4.8 x	5.9 x	5.2 x	6.9 x	6.5 x	6.3 x	6.0 x	5.7 x
	2.9 x	4.2 x	2.1 x	3.2 x	3.6 x	3.9 x	3.9 x	3.5 x	3.8 x	3.6 x
	41.1%	71.6%	48.9%	70.8%	57.0%	71.7%	77.2%	76.2%	81.7%	69.2%
	7.7 x	6.1 x	3.5 x	4.9 x	5.7 x	5.3 x	5.4 x	5.0 x	5.1 x	5.5 x
	85.0%	80.4%	79.7%	82.1%	95.8%	71.2%	69.1%	69.8%	67.0%	69.1%
	72.1%	80.4%	76.4%	78.6%	96.4%	54.4%	54.8%	52.6%	50.0%	48.4%

RAPID INCREASE IN RISK OF THE SECONDARY MARKET IN 1980s RELATIVE TO DECLINE IN RISK IN THE 1990s

One of the primary changes in the high yield market is in the overall risk trend. During the high growth period of 1984–1989 (see Exhibit 2–8), the credit quality of new issues had a significant impact on the credit quality of the overall market (see Exhibit 2–7). The reason was twofold: (1) The new issue market comprised a large percentage of the secondary market and (2) debt was cheaper than equity, which encouraged higher leverage. In contrast, in the 1992–1997 period, as the market size grew, new issues' credit statistics became less significant relative to the overall market credit profile. Furthermore, the lower cost of capital of equity led to IPOs and M&As, which in turn resulted in a net positive migration of credit quality (see Exhibit 2–9). Consequently, the average Single B issue over the last 3–5 years has been upgraded and deleveraged by either tapping the equity markets or being acquired by an investment grade credit. Also, because a large percentage of new issues were refinancings, only a small number of "new" issues came to the market. All else being equal, refinancing in a declining interest rate environment results in an instantaneous improvement in coverage ratios.

E X H I B I T   2–8

High Yield Market Growth, 1987–1997

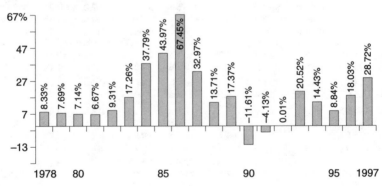

Source: DLJ.

EXHIBIT 2–9

Ratio of Upgrades to Downgrades, 1987–1997

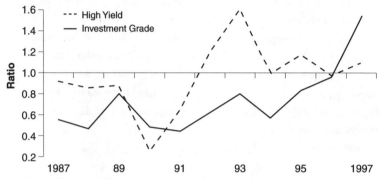

Sources: DLJ; Standard & Poor's (S&P).

EXHIBIT 2–10

Risk and Reward Characteristics of Various Assets, 1980–1997

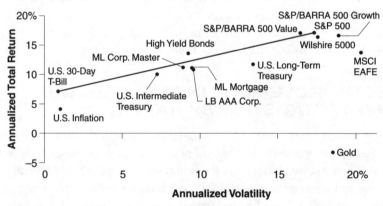

Sources: DLJ; Ibbotson Associates.

The proliferation of high yield portfolio management styles

Default minimization

Yield optimization

Total return maximization

EBITDA growth style

Spread compression play

Value/vulture investing

Consolidation/deleveraging plays and overall positive event risk plays

Insurance companies/risk-based capital institutions

Mutual funds/retail channels

Pension funds/hedge funds

Cyclical rebound and media plays

Investment grade buyers

Distressed investing

THE ROLE OF DERIVATIVES/STRUCTURED PRODUCTS: A RISK REWARD SPECTRUM

The increased understanding of risk and of the drivers in the high yield market has led to increased use of derivatives to manage risk. A classical example would be to modify portfolio duration by buying or selling Treasury derivatives to manage the effective duration of high yield assets. Another is the proliferation of the total return swaps on high yield indices. Also, the impact of an equity market correction can be managed though equity derivatives with S&P 500 or small-cap options, or with forward contracts.

THE IMPROVEMENT IN THE AVERAGE CREDIT STATISTICS BY RATING

One of the arguments made to demonstrate the overall credit risk in the high yield market is the percentage of new issues that are Single B or below versus BB and above. The implicit assumption is that the Single B category is a constant measure of credit quality over time. In effect, the rating agencies continuously release historic default rate studies to prove that their ratings have merit. The higher the rating the lower the default rate, and vice versa. Our study however indicates that Single B rated credits have been improving over time. A comparison of the 1992–1997 and 1985–1991 time periods shows that Single B and BB issues have had increasingly better interest coverage and leverage statistics over time (see Exhibit 2–11).

E X H I B I T   2-11

Average Leverage (Debt/EBITDA) by Rating

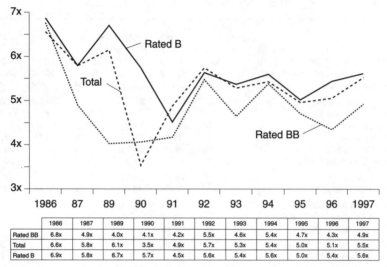

	1986	1987	1989	1990	1991	1992	1993	1994	1995	1996	1997
Rated BB	6.8x	4.9x	4.0x	4.1x	4.2x	5.5x	4.6x	5.4x	4.7x	4.3x	4.9x
Total	6.6x	5.8x	6.1x	3.5x	4.9x	5.7x	5.3x	5.4x	5.0x	5.1x	5.5x
Rated B	6.9x	5.8x	6.7x	5.7x	4.5x	5.6x	5.4x	5.6x	5.0x	5.4x	5.6x

Source: DLJ.

E X H I B I T   2-12

Number of BB and B New Issues

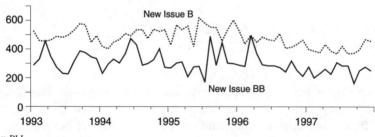

Source: DLJ.

The other argument is that the average new issue has deteriorated in credit quality. In effect, from 1991–1997 the percentage of new issues rated BB and above has increased versus the 1986–1989 time period (see Exhibit 2–12).

E X H I B I T   2–13

Credit Characteristics of New Issues by Industry Type, Cyclical

	1983	1984	1985	1986	1987	1988
Total Amount, ($ billions)	$5.3	$14.3	$16.4	$30.0	$27.7	$27.8
Total Proceeds, ($ billions)	$5.1	$13.0	$13.2	$27.3	$25.0	$23.4
Number of Issues	39	107	144	194	167	135
Average Size (MM)	$136.3	$133.6	$114.0	$154.6	$166.0	$206.2
Yield at Issuance	13.29%	15.47%	14.00%	12.54%	12.85%	13.47%
Spread at Issuance	NA	305 bp	385 bp	498 bp	437 bp	464 bp
Sales Growth	24.2%	9.6%	59.2%	19.2%	16.3%	22.0%
EBITDA Growth	24.5%	19.7%	61.9%	43.7%	28.2%	25.8%
EBITDA Margin	27.8%	36.5%	19.3%	26.5%	19.6%	33.9%
Sales Volatility	23.6%	15.1%	34.1%	17.2%	13.0%	18.3%
EBITDA Volatility	31.8%	71.5%	48.4%	32.4%	22.4%	27.1%
EBITDA/Cash Interest	2.3x	2.4x	1.7x	1.5x	1.9x	1.5x
EBITDA-Capex/Cash Interest	1.6x	1.4x	1.4x	1.0x	1.5x	0.7x
EBITDA/Total Interest	2.2x	2.2x	1.6x	1.5x	1.7x	1.3x
Senior Debt/Cash Interest	4.3x	4.9x	3.6x	4.4x	5.1x	3.7x
Senior Debt/EBITDA	2.1x	3.4x	3.5x	3.5x	3.5x	2.9x
Senior Debt/Total Debt	55.3%	58.5%	50.2%	50.3%	55.0%	41.0%
Debt/EBITDA	4.0x	6.0x	6.6x	6.6x	5.7x	7.6x
Debt/Cap	63.6%	70.6%	73.8%	69.8%	82.4%	83.6%
Debt/Market Cap	57.5%	NA	67.9%	NA	41.6%	68.8%

Source: DLJ.

THE SHIFT IN CAPITALIZING CYCLICAL CREDITS

During the 1989–1990 period, a large number of issues that defaulted were cyclicals in the housing, retail, transportation, and chemicals sectors. Consequently, cyclical issuers' capitilization was measured by normalized cash flow rather than current cash flow. In other words, rather than pricing the debt at peak pricing power, the EBITDA volatility was recognized and the capital structure was priced at mean EBITDA. All else being equal, this should lead to lower default rates.

1989	1990	1991	1992	1993	1994	1995	1996	1997
$19.3	$2.0	$9.0	$23.2	$44.0	$23.6	$15.7	$30.1	$51.6
$18.0	$1.4	$5.3	$20.6	$41.1	$23.1	$15.5	$29.5	$50.0
105	9	31	139	269	141	94	187	341
$184.1	$220.2	$290.8	$167.2	$163.5	$167.3	$167.3	$161.1	$151.4
13.46%	10.77%	10.65%	10.50%	10.18%	10.96%	10.98%	10.57%	10.14%
490 bp	284 bp	437 bp	393 bp	453 bp	431 bp	464 bp	420 bp	386 bp
11.0%	6.7%	18.9%	−2.9%	8.5%	8.0%	29.5%	44.0%	35.1%
34.6%	8.2%	17.6%	1.3%	15.9%	19.9%	65.7%	51.9%	36.8%
21.6%	23.0%	19.4%	22.9%	14.6%	15.7%	21.6%	16.9%	24.5%
11.7%	6.8%	15.2%	15.2%	10.0%	11.6%	21.5%	21.4%	21.5%
27.5%	8.4%	23.8%	13.3%	25.1%	27.5%	37.8%	34.5%	34.6%
1.9x	3.1x	2.1x	1.9x	2.2x	2.2x	2.5x	2.6x	2.3x
1.3x	0.6x	1.3x	1.5x	1.5x	1.6x	1.9x	1.9x	1.9x
1.7x	3.2x	2.1x	1.9x	2.0x	2.0x	2.4x	2.3x	2.1x
6.7x	7.3x	5.2x	4.9x	6.9x	7.2x	6.5x	6.3x	5.6x
4.0x	2.2x	2.8x	3.1x	3.9x	4.3x	3.5x	3.6x	3.2x
71.8%	64.0%	68.1%	66.5%	71.4%	80.3%	82.9%	81.3%	65.9%
5.9x	2.6x	4.7x	4.8x	5.3x	5.7x	4.3x	4.8x	5.3x
76.6%	77.2%	84.3%	97.2%	70.6%	72.0%	72.4%	68.6%	68.9%
76.6%	76.4%	87.5%	98.9%	54.9%	58.7%	53.1%	54.9%	49.2%

EVENT RISK: A SHIFT FROM THE ROLE OF EQUITY ISSUANCE TO M&A TRANSACTIONS

Event risk in the high yield market has been shifting toward the positive during the last few years. The escalation of IPOs and M&A transactions (see Exhibit 2–19) has overshadowed the impact of defaults. In effect, default rates have been running below the 1982–1988 annual rates of 3–4 percent to the current annual average of 1–2.5 percent (see Exhibit 2–15).

The volume of IPOs has been declining and so, too, has their impact on credit quality in the high yield market. The impact of IPOs has been replaced by the higher frequency of M&A transactions, which now affect overall credit quality.

E X H I B I T   2–14

Annual High Yield Defaults

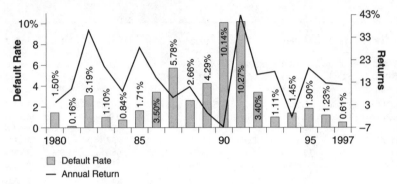

    Default Rate
—— Annual Return

Source: DLJ (1997); Altman Default Study (1971–1996).

E X H I B I T   2–15

Annual High Yield Defaults, 1980–1997

	Par Value Defaults ($ millions)	Default Rate
1980	224	1.50%
1981	27	0.16%
1982	577	3.19%
1983	301	1.10%
1984	344	0.84%
1985	992	1.71%
1986	3,156	3.50%
1987	7,486	5.78%
1988	3,944	2.66%
1989	8,110	4.29%
1990	18,354	10.14%
1991	18,862	10.27%
1992	5,545	3.40%
1993	2,287	1.11%
1994	3,418	1.45%
1995	4,551	1.90%
1996	3,336	1.23%
1997	2,537	0.61%

Sources: DLJ (1997); Altman Default Study.

E X H I B I T   2–16

1997 Default Calendar

Company	Principal Amt ($ MM)	Proceed Amt ($ MM)	Status	Sector
January 1997				
In-Flight Phone	285.8	190.0	Filed Chapter 11	Media/Entertainment
Defaulted Debt:	285.8			
Number of Companies:	1			
February 1997				
RXI Holdings	60.0	60.0	Missed cpn. pymt. (1/15/97)	Manufacturing
Defaulted Debt:	60.0			
Number of Companies:	1			
March 1997				
Flagstar	1,422.4	1,422.4	Filed reorganization plan in anticipation of filing Chapter 11.	Food/Tobacco
Defaulted Debt:	1,422.4			
Number of Companies:	1			
May 1997				
Harvard Industries	299.9	299.9	Filed Chapter 11	Transportation
Barry's Jewelers	50.0	50.0	Filed Chapter 11	Consumer Nondurables
Defaulted Debt:	349.9			
Number of Companies:	2			
July 1997				
Alliance Entertainment Corp.	125.0	125.0	Filed Chapter 11	Retail
First Merchants Acceptance Corp.	66.1	66.1	Filed Chapter 11	Financial
Koll Real Estate Grp	186.0	186.0	Filed prepackaged	Financial
Payless Cashways Inc.	200.0	200.0	Filed Chapter 11	Retail
Rymer Foods	23.5	23.5	Filed voluntary Chap. 11 in Ct.	Food/Tobacco
Defaulted Debt:	600.6			
Number of Companies:	5			
August 1997				
RDM Sports (Roadmaster Industries)	3.0	3.0	Filed Chapter 11	Gaming/Leisure
Reeves Industries	138.4	137.5	Missed int. pymt. (7/15/97)	Manufacturing
Defaulted Debt:	141.4			
Number of Companies:	2			
September 1997				
Consolidated Hydro	202.3	112.1	Filed prepackaged	Utility
Levitz Furniture	191.6	191.6	Filed Chapter 11	Retail
Defaulted Debt:	393.9			
Number of Companies:	2			
November 1997				
Town & Country	53.5	53.5	Filed Chapter 11	Consumer Nondurables
Farm Fresh	201.0	201.0	Missed cpn. pymt. (10/1/97)	Food & Drug
Defaulted Debt:	254.5			
Number of Companies:	2			
Full Year 1997				
Defaulted Debt:	3,508.5			
Number of Companies:	16			
1997 Default Rate	**0.84%**			

E X H I B I T   2–17

High Yield Bond Defaults by Industry, 1997

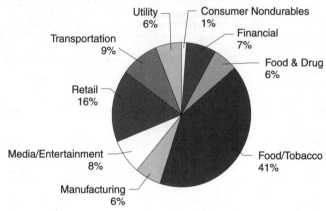

Sources: DLJ; Moody's; Bloomberg & Bond Investors Association.

E X H I B I T   2–18

Public Equity Issuance versus S&P 500 P/E Ratio

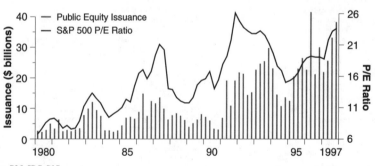

Sources: DLJ; SDC; S&P.

Another shift in issuance has been the decline of calls exercised by issuers. This has occurred as an increasing number of the new issues coming to market now carry a five-year call protection. Consequently, there has been an increase in the number of tendered issues, which, in turn, results in a higher tender price and hence better returns for investors.

E X H I B I T   2-19

M&A Transaction Volume

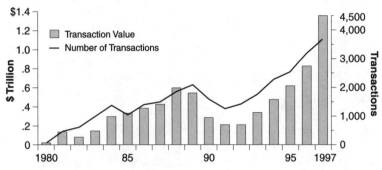

Sources: DLJ; SDC.

E X H I B I T   2-20

Amount of High Yield Debt Redemptions

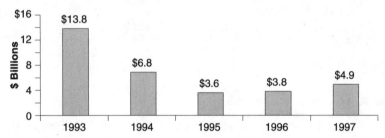

Sources: DLJ; Indepth data.

E X H I B I T   2-21

Amount of High Yield Debt Tendered

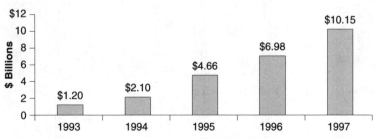

Sources: DLJ; Indepth data.

EXHIBIT 2-22

Issuance by Seniority in the Capital Structure (proceeds)

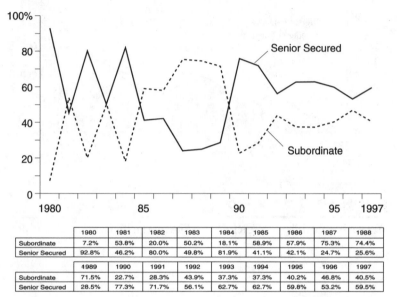

	1980	1981	1982	1983	1984	1985	1986	1987	1988
Subordinate	7.2%	53.8%	20.0%	50.2%	18.1%	58.9%	57.9%	75.3%	74.4%
Senior Secured	92.8%	46.2%	80.0%	49.8%	81.9%	41.1%	42.1%	24.7%	25.6%

	1989	1990	1991	1992	1993	1994	1995	1996	1997
Subordinate	71.5%	22.7%	28.3%	43.9%	37.3%	37.3%	40.2%	46.8%	40.5%
Senior Secured	28.5%	77.3%	71.7%	56.1%	62.7%	62.7%	59.8%	53.2%	59.5%

Sources: DLJ; SDC.

EXHIBIT 2-23

Defaulted Debt Recovery Rate Estimates by Seniority of Claim, 1989-1997

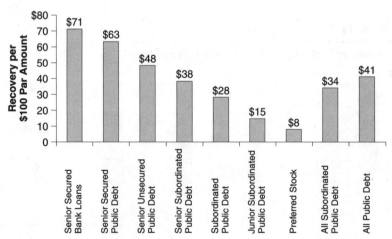

Sources: DLJ; Moody's.

E X H I B I T   2–24

Correlations among Various Assets, 1980 to 1997

Asset	U.S. 30-Day Treas	U.S. Inter Treas	U.S. Long Treas	ML Mortgages	LB AAA Corp.	ML Corp.	DLJ HY Bonds	S&P 500	Wilshire 5000	S&P/BARRA Growth	S&P/BARRA Value	MSCI EAFE	Gold
U.S. Intermediate Treasury	0.17												
U.S. Long-Term Treasury	0.07	0.89											
ML Mortgage	0.13	0.91	0.87										
LB AAA Corp.	0.11	0.93	0.94	0.95									
ML Corp. Master	0.09	0.93	0.94	0.93	0.99								
DLJ HY Bonds	0.01	0.59	0.55	0.63	0.65	0.68							
S&P 500	−0.09	0.30	0.37	0.28	0.35	0.37	0.47						
Wilshire 5000	−0.10	0.27	0.35	0.26	0.33	0.36	0.49	0.99					
S&P/BARRA 500 Growth	−0.08	0.27	0.35	0.25	0.32	0.34	0.42	0.98	0.97				
S&P/BARRA 500 Value	−0.09	0.32	0.38	0.29	0.37	0.39	0.50	0.97	0.96	0.90			
MSCI EAFE	−0.06	0.22	0.24	0.19	0.21	0.23	0.34	0.46	0.46	0.42	0.48		
Gold	−0.12	0.00	−0.03	0.01	0.00	0.01	0.10	0.07	0.10	0.04	0.09	0.20	
U.S. Inflation	0.52	−0.12	−0.21	−0.14	−0.18	−0.18	−0.22	−0.17	−0.17	−0.16	−0.16	−0.20	0.04

Sources: DLJ; Ibbotson Associates.

Dramatic Shift in Seniority

During the 1980–1997 period, one of the most fundamental shifts has been the average seniority in the high yield market (see Exhibit 2–22). One of the drivers behind this shift is the realization of the critical role of seniority. Yet another driver has been the lower leverage ratios, which have allowed high yield issues to be senior/senior secured as leverage (debt/EBITDA) declined and the average equity contribution to the capital structure went to the current 27–30 percent from 7 percent.

One can imply that while the historic default rates might shift due to the improvement in the average credit quality, seniority would be expected to have a profound effect on the recovery rates. Historically, the more senior the issue, the higher the default recovery rates, due to the application of the strict priority rules (see Exhibit 2–23).

THE INCREASED IMPORTANCE OF DIVERSIFICATION IN A GLOBAL LINKED MARKETS ENVIRONMENT

One of the basic risk management tools in finance is diversification across different asset classes in order to minimize volatility. In the 1994–1997 environment, as many global markets moved in tandem, adding assets to a

E X H I B I T   2–25

Who Owns High Yield? December 1997

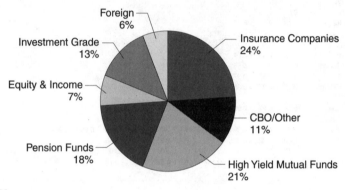

Foreign
6%

Investment Grade
13%

Insurance Companies
24%

Equity & Income
7%

CBO/Other
11%

Pension Funds
18%

High Yield Mutual Funds
21%

Source: DLJ.

E X H I B I T   2–26

Who Owns High Yield?

	1989	1992	1997	89–97% Change	92–97% Change
Insurance Companies	30%	29%	24%	−20%	−17%
CBO/Other	1	18	11	1000	−39
High Yield Mutual Funds	30	18	21	−30	17
Pension Funds	15	13	18	20	38
Equity & Income		9	7	NA	−22
Investment Grade		9	13	NA	44
Foreign	9	3	6	−33	100
RTC		1		NA	−100
Savings & Loans	7			−100	NA
Individuals	5			−100	NA
Corporations	3			−100	NA

Source: DLJ.

portfolio became an even higher priority. In this context, high yield and leveraged loans continue to be excellent diversification tools for both U.S. and global portfolios (see Exhibit 2–24).

Toward a diversification objective, adding an efficient asset that is above the market line is even more desirable. As interest rate volatility increased in the 1994–1997 period, interest rate sensitive instruments shifted below the market line as the market has continuously underpriced interest rate volatility. This inefficiency further enhanced the relative value of high yield assets, particularly leveraged loans, as a floating rate asset.

THE UNITED STATES VERSUS THE GLOBAL BET SHIFT

Historically, the high yield market has been a U.S. backyard industry. Recently, however, non-U.S. issuances in the new issue market have escalated. Chapter 4 provides statistics and a discussion on this important development.

CHAPTER 3

The Leveraged Loan Market

Sam DeRosa-Farag

Jonathan Blau

The use of the word *market* to describe the ancient and arcane world of loan syndications is a recent event. Though banks have syndicated loans for decades as a way to lay off exposure to downstream correspondence institutions, it was not until the LBO market crystallized in the mid-1980s that banks began to create true primary and secondary markets for syndicated loans.

In recent years, syndicated leveraged loans—those of $50 million or more that are (1) priced at a spread over LIBOR of 125 basis points or higher and (2) made to noninvestment-grade and unrated issuers—have attracted a deep and increasingly broad institutional following. During 1997, institutional loan investors supplanted foreign banks to become the largest discrete market for highly leveraged loans (see Exhibits 3–1 and 3–6). This is an event of surpassing importance as the market completes its evolution into a return-driven segment of the capital markets.

In this chapter, we provide a review of the syndicated leveraged loan market, including a primer of the loan product and a review of recent market developments.

BACKGROUND

Leveraged loans are the largest source of high yield paper with new issue volume of $194 billion in 1997, according to Loan Pricing Corporation. Syndicated leveraged loans typically are secured, floating-rate instruments that run between 5 and 10 years and occupy the senior place in an issuer's balance sheet.

E X H I B I T   3–1

Primary Market for Highly Leveraged Loans by Broad Investor Type

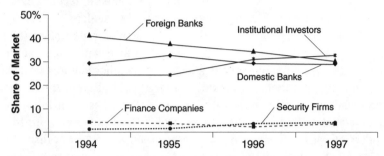

Note: Excludes All Left and Right Agent Commitments (including Administrative, Syndication and Documentation Agent as well as Arranger).

Source: Donaldson, Lufkin & Jenrette (DLJ); Portfolio Management Data (PMD).

Until the credit crunch of the early 1990s, the investor market for leveraged loans was comprised primarily of foreign and domestic banks, with Japanese banks representing far and away the largest segment. This all changed when a confluence of events—most notably, the economic slowdown in 1990—severely depressed asset valuations and fictionalized many ambitious projections on which high yield transactions were based. The result was a shocking increase in default rates during 1991 and 1992 that led to a liquidity crisis in the high yield bond and leveraged loan markets. Liquidity was limited further when many banks sold off leveraged loans in the face of regulatory and shareholder scrutiny and higher capital reserve requirements instituted by the Bank for International Settlements.

E X H I B I T   3–2

Institutional Loan Investors, 1993–1997

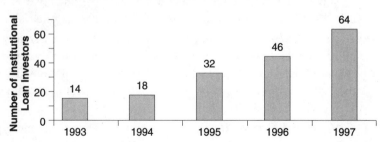

Sources: DLJ; PMD.

Several money center banks seized on the trading opportunity presented by this liquidity crisis, as regional and foreign banks sold off par and distressed leveraged loans in order to boost capital. From these humble beginnings, the secondary loan market has blossomed in recent years and now includes roughly 25 dealers and 3 inter-broker dealers.

The development of an active secondary market put in place the liquidity that was critical to attracting institutional investors to the loan market. In recent years, the market has adopted many other features associated with mature capital markets, including a large field of competitive underwriting institutions, a broad institutional investor base, securitization vehicles, data/analytic tools, credit ratings, professional managers, third-party providers of back-office functions, and portfolio management disciplines. As a result, the institutional loan investor base has grown to 64 mutual funds, hedge funds, insurance companies, securitization vehicles, and derivative structures at year-end 1997, up from just 14 institutions four years ago (see Exhibit 3–2). This is a startling development for a financing segment that just 10 years ago was a closed, price-inefficient, bank-only market virtually without any institutional investor representation.

LEVERAGED LOAN RISK/RETURN PROFILE

The driving factor in bringing new investors into the loan market in recent years has been the compelling risk/return opportunity offered by this asset class. Exhibits 3–3 and 3–4 show that leveraged loans have offered risk-adjusted returns since 1992 that exceed equities, corporate bonds, high yield bonds, and Treasuries. The reason: Loans display extraordinarily low risk when measured by return volatility, the standard CAPM risk benchmark. The low level of variance can be traced to three primary factors:

- *Floating Rate*   Loans are floating rate instruments that are reset normally every three to six months at a margin above LIBOR. Therefore they are virtually without interest rate risk.
- *Prepayable*   Loans are prepayable at any time, in virtually all cases without penalty. Therefore, loans rarely trade over par. Because loans tend to repay far ahead of schedule, particularly if the issuer is improving, their average duration is estimated at just 18 months. This short duration further restricts volatility.
- *Collateral Protection*   Because loans are secured and typically the senior obligations in an issuer's capital structure, they are the last security to experience tremors—and are affected the least—when an issuer's financial condition deteriorates.

E X H I B I T   3–3

Risk/Reward Characteristics
of Various Assets, 1992–1997

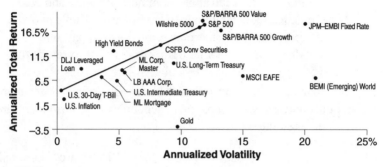

Sources: DLJ; Ibbotson Associates.

E X H I B I T   3–4

Risk/Return Profile, 1992–1997 (annualized)

Asset	*Annualized*		
1992–1997	Return	Volatility	Return/Risk
U.S. Intermediate Treasuries	6.53%	4.81%	1.36
ML Corp. Master	8.65	5.27	1.64
DLJ Leveraged Loan Index	8.96	1.92	4.67
High Yield Bonds	12.68	4.55	2.79
S&P 500	18.05	11.99	1.51
JPM-EMBI Fixed Rate	18.30	20.14	0.91

Sources: DLJ; Ibbotson Associates.

LEVERAGED LOAN PRODUCTS AND MARKET SEGMENTS

Leveraged loans can be divided into two product types and two market segments.

Product Types

There are two principal leveraged loan instruments: unfunded commitments and funded term loans.

- Unfunded commitments are principally revolving credits (RC) but also include acquisition facilities that are drawn down over time and term-out after a certain date and letters of credit (LC) that guarantee trade receivables, commercial paper, and other obligations. RCs are analogous to credit cards. They are open lines of credit that the issuer may draw down, repay, and reborrow during a contractual term. Lenders will often, at the borrower's request, issue letters of credit under RCs.
- Term loans are simple installment lines with defined drawdown amounts and dates and repayment schedules. The term loan can be segmented into:

1. Amortizing term loans ("A" term loans). These are traditional bank installment loans. "A" term loans typically run for five to seven years, are co-terminus with revolving credits, and require progressive repayments throughout the term.
2. Institutional term loans ("B," "C," and "D" term loans) were introduced on a broad scale in 1992 with reverse LBO transactions (IPO-related recapitalizations) like Burlington Northern and CNW. They are carved out specifically for institutional loan investors and feature longer maturities, more back-end loaded repayment schedules, and incrementally higher spreads than revolving credit and "A" term loans. Institutional term loans typically run from six to ten years, or six months to three years longer than revolving credit and "A" term loans of the same issuer. As a result, they are usually priced 25–50 basis points higher than associated revolving credits and "A" term loans.
3. Hybrid term loans are a 1997 innovation. Hybrid (or *Covenant-lite*) term loans incorporate some features of loans with those of bonds and are sold primarily to institutional loan investors and, on a small scale, to traditional high yield investors.

These instruments are like loans in that they are floating rate and prepayable at the borrower's option. They are like bonds in that they lack compliance covenants (hence the Covenant-lite label) and carry modest prepayment fees. The prepayment fees typically start at 2–3 percent in year one and are phased out by year four. Security, which ranges from full pari passu status to junior or second lien, is negotiated and reflected in the pricing of the loans. The following charts show that pari passu hybrids are

E X H I B I T   3-5

Hybrid Loan Volume by the Gap between Hybrid Loan
and Pro Rata Spread of the Same Issuer for 1997

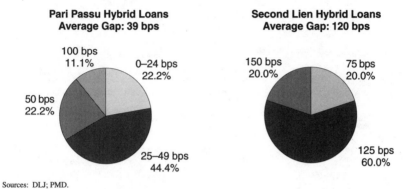

Sources: DLJ; PMD.

priced, on average, 39 bps higher than associated revolving credits and "A"
term loans while, not surprisingly, second lien hybrids are priced at a far
higher premium—120 bps, on average.

Market Segments

Over the past five years, most arrangers have syndicated revolving credits
and "A" term loans (pro rata tranches) separately from institutional term
loans (institutional tranches). Banks are the primary market for pro rata
tranches while nonbanks are the primary buyers of institutional tranches.
Though there is some crossover investment between the pro rata and institutional markets, it is largely at the margin. Some banks will play in the
institutional market, usually to create trading opportunities. Institutional
investors will buy "A" term loans but only when a comparable institutional
loan is not available.

PRICING: SPREADS AND FEES

- ***Spreads***   Leveraged loans are almost always floating rate
  instruments priced at a spread over LIBOR. The rate is reset at
  the issuer's option in one-month to one-year intervals. Most
  loans also have a pure floating rate *prime* option that is tied to
  a spread over a reference bank's prime lending rate. This is a
  more expensive option, from the issuer's perspective, and is used

E X H I B I T   3–6

Primary Market for 1997 Highly Leveraged and All Institutional Term Loans

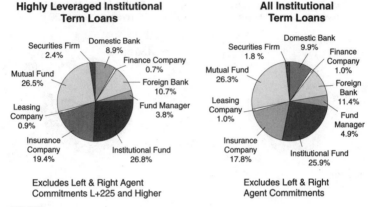

Highly Leveraged Institutional Term Loans

Securities Firm 2.4%
Domestic Bank 8.9%
Finance Company 0.7%
Mutual Fund 26.5%
Foreign Bank 10.7%
Leasing Company 0.9%
Fund Manager 3.8%
Insurance Company 19.4%
Institutional Fund 26.8%

Excludes Left & Right Agent Commitments L+225 and Higher

All Institutional Term Loans

Securities Firm 1.8 %
Domestic Bank 9.9%
Finance Company 1.0%
Mutual Fund 26.3%
Foreign Bank 11.4%
Leasing Company 1.0%
Fund Manager 4.9%
Insurance Company 17.8%
Institutional Fund 25.9%

Excludes Left & Right Agent Commitments

Sources: DLJ; PMD.

primarily for overnight and very short-term borrowing. The spread of most loans is tied to a grid that adjusts pricing to the issuer's financial performance as measured primarily by objective financial ratios and less often by ratings. See Appendix 1 at the end of this chapter for broad parameters of pricing and fees in the leveraged loan market.

• **Fees**   Loans have several types of fees.

1.   Upfront fees are the most common type of fee associated with leveraged loans. These fees are paid at closing to participants based on the amount they commit to the transaction and are the loan market's equivalent of discounts in the bond market. Arrangers typically set several upfront fee tiers tied to participants' commitments with higher commitments receiving higher fees. The fees are paid on the final allocation, though for large complex transactions lenders sometimes will receive flat fees paid on their initial commitment. Because the institutional market has been particularly robust in recent quarters, arrangers typically offer incrementally higher upfront fees for pro rata commitments than for institutional commitments (see Exhibit 3–7).

E X H I B I T   3–7

Average Retail Upfront Fee for Each Million
Dollar Commitment to Acquisition-Related Highly
Leveraged Loans by Pro Rata and Institutional
Tranches, 1992/93–1997

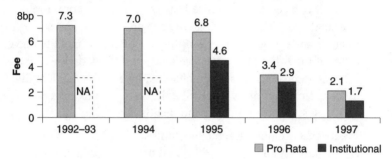

Note: There were too few fee schedules specifically for institutional tranches before 1995 to form a meaningful sample.
Sources: DLJ; PMD.

2. Commitment fees are paid on available and undrawn amounts
   under revolving credit and acquisition facilities and typically
   range from 25–50 bps in the leveraged loan market. These
   fees also are tied to grids described in the spread section
   above. The fees are paid to compensate lenders for keeping
   capital reserved against undrawn amounts. Under the Bank
   for International Settlement's capital adequacy guidelines,
   banks must reserve 4 percent against undrawn amounts under
   commitments, as opposed to 8 percent against drawn amounts
   under loans. Therefore, lenders charge a fee to hold amounts
   in abeyance.

3. Letter of credit fees are typically set equal to the credit spread
   of the revolving credit. The reason for this convention is that
   banks must reserve capital on LCs equal to a fully drawn loan
   even though the commitment is rarely drawn down. Therefore,
   banks charge the full credit spread on LCs even though they are
   unfunded commitments.

STRUCTURE AND COVENANTS

Leveraged loans are highly customized and active agreements which share common features, including:

- **Compliance Covenants**   With the exception of hybrid loans, leveraged loans require issuers to meet two or more sets of financial tests. These tests usually are progressive and set tightly to an issuer's projections. Compliance covenants include one or more of the following: coverage tests, cash flow divided by cash interest, debt service or fixed charges; leverage tests, debt divided by cash flow and/or by total capitalization; capital expenditures; and leases, mostly for retail and health care deals.

- **Baskets**   Credit agreements almost always restrict an issuer's ability to take on additional debt and make acquisitions or investments.

- **Mandatory Prepayments**   The issuer is usually required to prepay credit agreements from: asset sale proceeds that are not reinvested within a stated timeframe, usually six months to a year; debt issuance proceeds; some percentage of equity issuance proceeds; and excess cash flow. Prepayments from equity proceeds and excess cash flow generally range from 50–75 percent and are reduced or waived if the issuer achieves a specified financial objective (e.g., a debt/EBITDA ratio of 3x or less). The percent of leveraged loans with such triggers increased to 50 percent last year from 20 percent in 1995, according to *Portfolio Management Data*.

- **Security**   Leveraged loans usually are secured by all material assets of the issuer, including: receivables, inventory and cash; capital stock of subsidiaries; fixed assets and real property; intangible assets; downstream guarantees from a holding company; and upstream guarantees from subsidiaries. Issuers with the strongest equity and corporate sponsors often are able to negotiate loans backed by only capital stock of operating units. Some agreements are structured with collateral release provisions that oblige lenders to relinquish security if the borrower's financial performance improves. These provisions almost always are triggered if the issuer achieves an investment grade rating and are reserved for the largest near-investment-grade borrowers.

RECENT TRENDS

1997 was a watershed year for the leveraged loan market in which institutional investors surpassed foreign banks to become the largest discrete primary buyers of highly leveraged loans (please refer to Exhibit 3–1), those priced at LIBOR plus 225 basis points or higher. The growth of the institutional loan investor base has been a boon to issuers, resulting in:

- Increased deal capacity to finance new technologies, construction projections and buy-and-build platforms as well as once taboo industries like retail and apparel.
- Spread and fee compression.
- Longer maturities and looser structures.
- More aggressive credit statistics.

These trends have been pervasive in the market since 1995 but accelerated during the first three quarters of 1997. In the fourth quarter, however, a startling increase in loan volume—particularly in the institutional term loan segment where volume reached a record $11 billion, nearly as much as that of the prior two quarters combined—caused the secondary market to back up. Institutional investors, faced with many new transactions became more critical buyers and began to rebalance their portfolios by selling off assets with lower spreads in favor of richer margin loans. This is reflected in the average secondary bid for par institutional term loans which eased to slightly less than par in December 1997 from roughly 100.28 percent in September (see Exhibit 3–8). This backup has also been felt in the primary market, where upfront fees to investors have moved up incrementally.

E X H I B I T   3–8

Average Bid for Par Institutional Term Loans

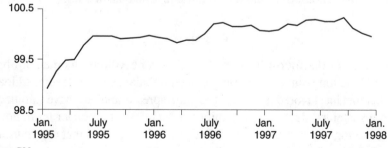

Source: DLJ.

E X H I B I T   3–9

Average Retail Upfront Fee for Each Million
Dollar Commitment to Acquisition-Related Highly
Leveraged Institutional Loans: Rolling Three-Month
Periods through December 1997

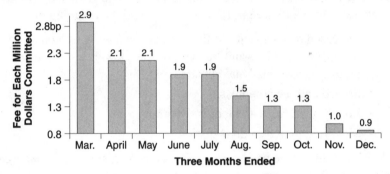

Sources: DLJ; PMD.

The "Asian effect" on the leveraged loan market has not been significant, yet. Japanese banks, which in the 1980s were far and away the largest
market for leveraged loans, withdrew after the 1991 credit crunch and have
never come back in a meaningful way. By the fourth quarter of 1997, these
banks accounted for just 6.6 percent of the primary retail market for leveraged loans (see Exhibit 3–10). Even the Japanese credit banks that have
been consistent players since the late 1980s significantly scaled back
involvement before the 1997 fourth quarter. The strength of the institutional investor base and the lack of Asian bank participation has helped
shield the leveraged loan market. The Asian impact may be damaging,
however, to several industry segments with significant leveraged loan
activity where even marginal players are important, including media,
health care, automotive, and telecommunications businesses.

Pricing

Beginning in the fourth quarter of 1997, strong volume momentum has
arrested the long-standing supply/demand imbalance in the leveraged loan
market that has favored issuers. As a result, spreads and fees have stabilized
after a sustained decline (see Exhibits 3–9 and 3–11). Longer term, however, leveraged loans remain an underinvested asset class that continues to

E X H I B I T   3–10

Asian Banks as a Percent of Retail Primary Commitments to Leveraged and Highly Leveraged Loans, 1995 to Fourth Quarter, 1997

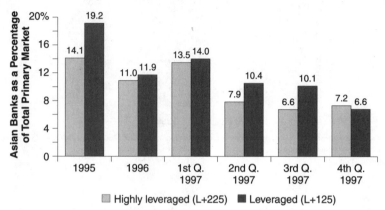

Sources: DLJ; PMD.

E X H I B I T   3–11

Average Pro Rata Spread of Leveraged Loans by Debt/Adjusted EBITDA Ratio, 1993/4–1997

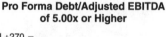

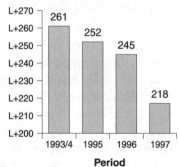

Excludes Media and Retail Issuers

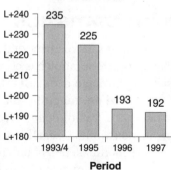

Excludes Media and Retail

Sources: DLJ; PMD.

E X H I B I T   3-12

Percent of Institutional Term Loans
with Pricing Grids, 1995–1997

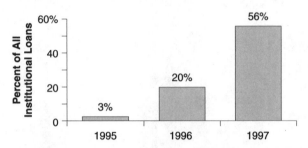

Note: Excludes media loans. The data are compiled by deal, rather than facility; therefore a deal with a TLb, TLc, and TLd, all of
        which were tied to a pricing grid, would count once, not three times, for this chart.

Sources: DLJ; PMD.

attract new investors. This liquidity undoubtedly will mean that spreads
and fees will continue their long-term downward trend, particularly for the
largest, most liquid deals.

In addition to lower spreads and fees, the growing acceptance of grid
pricing by institutional investors is a less subtle form of pricing compression
(see Exhibit 3–12). Pricing grids in the leveraged loan market favor the
issuer because they primarily adjust pricing downward as an issuer's financial condition improves.

CREDIT STATISTICS

Credit structures have deteriorated in the face of increased liquidity,
although this deterioration has been more subtle. Broad credit statistics, as
measured by average debt/EBITDA multiples of highly leveraged loans,
have not moved meaningfully since 1995 (see Exhibit 3–13). This stability is indicative less of stable credit standards and more of increases in
middle market volume. Smaller deals, of course, are often structured with
little or no subordinated debt providing less cushion for bank debt lenders.
It is therefore more meaningful to look at the largest, most liquid segment
of the market—loans of $500 million (see Exhibit 3–14). The average pro
forma debt/EBITDA multiple for the largest, most liquid deals have
increased to 6.2x in 1997 from 5.6x in 1996.

E X H I B I T   3–13

Average Debt Multiple of Highly Leveraged Loans, 1987–1997

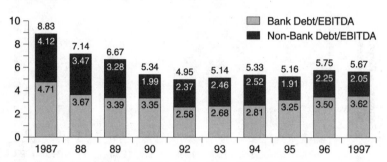

Note: Criteria: Pre-1996: L+250 and Higher; 1996 to Date: L+225 and Higher; Media Loans Excluded.

Sources: DLJ; PMD.

E X H I B I T   3–14

Average Pro Forma Credit Statistics of Highly Leveraged Loans of $500 Million or More (nonadjusted ratios), 1995–1997

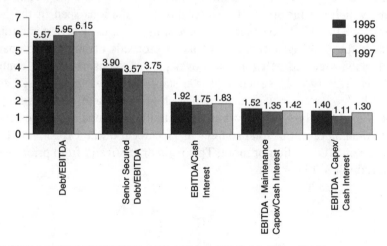

Note: Criteria: Loans Priced at L+225 and Higher (L+250 and Higher in 1995); Excludes Media and Retail Issues.

Sources: DLJ; PMD.

E X H I B I T   3-15

Average Equity Contribution to
Leveraged Buyouts, 1987-1997

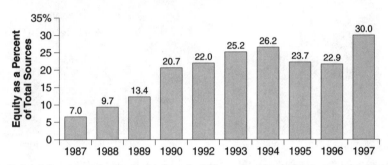

Note: Equity includes common equity and preferred stock as well as holding company debt and seller note proceeds downstreamed to
       the operating company as common equity.

Sources: DLJ; PMD..

At the same time, LBO purchase-price multiples have increased dramatically since 1995 following skyrocketing stock prices and active fund
raising by equity sponsors (see Exhibit 3–16). While this increase in purchase multiples has been paid mostly through increased equity contributions, which are far above the wafer-thin contributions seen in the late
1980s (see Exhibit 3–15), there are some warning signs. The first and foremost is the growing acceptance of using proceeds of holding company
debt, downstreamed as equity, to cover part of sponsors' equity contributions. This type of structure was a staple of late 1980s deals. Until
recently, however, it was anathema to high yield and leveraged loan
investors. In early 1998, downstreamed holding companies represented
more than 5 percent of total sources in 17 percent of the LBOs with total
sources of $100 million or more. This is up dramatically from prior years
(see Exhibit 3–17).

E X H I B I T   3–16

Average Leveraged Buyout Purchase Price as a Multiple of Nonadjusted Pro Forma Trailing EBITDA by Total Sources, 1994/5–1997

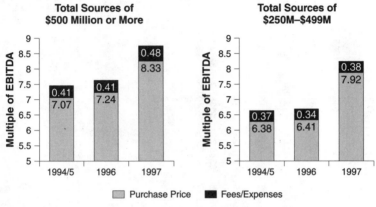

Sources: DLJ; PMD.

E X H I B I T   3–17

Percent of LBOs Where Downstreamed Holding Companies Represent More Than 5% of Total Sources (transactions with total sources of $100 million or more)

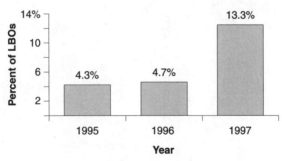

Sources: DLJ; PMD.

E X H I B I T 3–18

Syndicated Loan Volume by Purpose ($ billions), 1987–1997

Purpose	1987	1988	1989	1990	1991	1992	1993	1994	1995	1996	1997
Leverage Debt	66.12	162.74	186.45	57.86	20.87	39.90	28.18	81.10	101.30	134.80	193.96
Repayment	11.48	42.30	44.38	42.58	46.53	58.46	40.69	57.80	227.10	297.80	353.80
Specialty Finance	17.02	8.64	7.05	17.39	16.60	22.96	8.16	15.50	25.30	15.20	12.45
General Corporate	42.49	70.71	95.31	123.43	150.38	254.16	312.29	510.90	463.30	439.80	551.65
Total	**$137.11**	**$284.39**	**$333.19**	**$241.26**	**$234.38**	**$375.48**	**$389.32**	**$665.30**	**$817.00**	**$887.60**	**$1,111.86**
Growth Rate		**107.4%**	**17.2%**	**-27.6%**	**-2.9%**	**60.2%**	**3.7%**	**70.9%**	**22.8%**	**8.6%**	**25.3%**

Sources: DLJ; Loan Pricing Corporation (LPC).

Syndicated Leveraged Loan Characteristics

Leveraged credits typically are divided into tranches, with longer-dated, term loan facilities (institutional term loans) carved out for institutional investors. These "B," "C," or "D" term loans (TL B/C/D) have back-end loaded maturities and are priced incrementally higher than amortizing bank term loans.

- Ranking: Senior, secured instruments that sometimes have pari passu public or private debt.
- Stated Maturity and Average Life (typical):

	Average Life	Final Maturity
Revolving Credit	Bullet Maturity	5–7 years
Amortizing TL	3–5 years	5–7 years
TL B	5–7 years	6–8 years
TL C	6–7.5 years	7–9 years
TL D	7–8.5 years	8–10 years

- Typical Pricing (spread over LIBOR):

Single B/B- (senior unsecured rating)	
Revolving Credit	200–300
Amortizing TL	200–300
TL B	250–350
TL C	300–375
TL D	350–400
BB-/B+ (senior unsecured rating)	150–200*
BB+/BB (senior unsecured rating)	62.5–149*

*Typically, loans to these companies do not have TL B/C/D tranches.

- Pricing Options:

Borrowers tend to use a loan's fixed-rate, LIBOR option, which is reset every 1 to 12 months at the borrower's option. A short-term, prime option also is available. This is almost always a more costly alternative, and is used mainly for overnight or short-term borrowings.

- Covenants: Tight financial compliance is required. Leveraged loans usually have at least one coverage and one leveraged covenant, both set tightly to projections. The borrower's ability to take on more debt, sell assets, pay dividends, or make investments is restricted.
- Voting Rights:

Issue	Typical Consent
Amendments/waivers/consents	51–67%
Material collateral release	67–100%
Interim amortization	67–100%
Final maturity	100%
Rate reduction	100%
Tranche voting	Any changes that affect an individual facility usually require the approval of 51% of the affected lenders.

- Typical Mandatory Prepayments

The borrower must prepay most leveraged loans from proceeds of

Excess cash flow	50–75%
Asset sale proceeds	Typically 100% of nonreinvested proceeds
Net equity proceeds	25–100%
Net debt proceeds	Typically 100%

- Optional Prepayments: The borrower is always allowed to prepay, usually without penalty
- Interest Payments: Quarterly

Secondary Loan Sales and Trading

Loans almost always are sold without accrued interest. The administrative agent usually divides the interest payment at quarter-end between the buyer and seller. Loans can be sold in two ways: assignments and participations.

- Assignments. An assignment is a direct sale of the credit. The assignee generally pays a fee to the administrative agent (typically $2,000–$3,000), becomes a direct party to the credit agreement and, among other things, assumes full voting rights under the agreement.

- Participation. Under a participation, the buyer acquires an interest (a participating interest) in the seller's loan and commitment. The loan is not transferred and the seller continues to receive interest and principal payments, which it passes through to the participant. No assignment fee is paid and consent is rarely required. The participant's voting rights are limited to material issues, usually amortization, rate, term, and collateral.

- Minimum Assignment. Usually, assignments must be sold in minimum amounts of $5 million–$10 million, unless the lender sells its entire commitment.

- Minimum Hold. Some agreements require banks that do not sell their entire position to hold a certain minimum amount. It is typically the same as the assignment minimum, although the amount may be higher for the agent bank. This provision is not common in leveraged loans.

- Assignment Fee. An assignment fee is paid to the administrative agent. The fee is usually $2,000–$3,500 and can range from $1,000–$5,000. In some cases, the fee for assignments to existing lenders is less than those for assignments to new lenders.

- Consent. The consent of the borrower and administrative agent is typically required. This is more common with revolving credits than with term loan tranches. The agreements usually provide that consent may not be unreasonably withheld. Borrower consent is often waived in defaults.

- Default Exclusion. Many assignments waive borrower consent to assignments if the borrower is in default.

- Eligible Assignee. Agreements often list eligible assignee criteria. These tend to limit potential assignees to large commercial banks or other financial institutions, accredited investors (under SEC Rule 144a), and institutional and retail mutual funds that invest primarily in bank loans.
- Confidentiality. Loans typically trade subject to confidentiality agreements, which may affect the ability of the parties to trade public securities. For this reason, institutional investors set up "Chinese walls" around their bank loan trading groups.
- Other. In rare cases, lenders in the bank group have the right of first refusal on sales at distressed levels.

The Globalization of the High Yield Market

Sam DeRosa-Farag

Jonathan Blau

The recent volatility in the emerging markets, particularly in the Far East, and its impact on the U.S. capital markets has highlighted the relationship between the different sectors of the global economy. Historically, this was not an issue in the high yield market. High yield, after all, has been a U.S. cottage industry with little exposure to the global markets except for a second-order effect. This effect primarily has been estimated to be the operational exposure to the international market from U.S.-based corporations (e.g., American Standard's European and Far East operations, Exide's European operations, etc.).

A number of key changes in the high yield market and in the overall capital markets during the 1993–1997 period:

- In 1997, there were 134 new bonds issued outside of the United States, compared to only 57 in 1996 (see Exhibit 4–1).
- By the end of 1997, nearly 6 percent of the market value of the DLJ High Yield Index consisted of emerging markets debt. This proportion was less than 1 percent just four years ago (see Exhibit 4–3).

E X H I B I T   4–1

Non-U.S./Canada New Issues (proceeds)

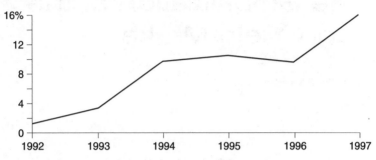

Sources: Donaldson, Lufkin & Jenrette (DLJ); Securities Data Corporation (SDC).

E X H I B I T   4–2

Credit Statistics of New Issues by Region

	Non–U.S./Canada			
	1992	1994	1995	1996
Total Amount, $Bil	$1.2	$4.1	$6.0	$8.3
Total Proceeds, $Bil	$0.9	$3.8	$4.3	$6.7
Number of Issues	4	17	18	37
Average Size (MM)	$301.6	$241.8	$336.0	$223.4
Yield at Issuance	11.09%	11.18%	11.54%	11.59%
Spread at Issuance	464bp	436bp	544bp	519bp
Sales Growth	11.3%	18.9%	123.8%	91.4%
EBITDA Growth	13.2%	16.5%	6.8%	19.6%
EBITDA Margin	27.0%	28.8%	34.9%	28.3%
Sales Volatility	10.7%	20.2%	48.9%	33.8%
EBITDA Volatility	12.3%	29.2%	16.4%	27.4%
EBITDA/Cash Interest	1.4x	2.3x	3.5x	2.1x
EBITDA-Capex/Cash Interest	1.1x	1.2x	0.6x	1.0x
EBITDA/Total Interest	1.4x	1.7x	2.6x	1.7x
Senior Debt/Cash Interest	7.5x	8.2x	9.7x	4.1x
Senior Debt/EBITDA	5.6x	3.4x	3.7x	6.3x
Senior Debt/Total Debt	81.3%	95.5%	100.0%	94.7%
Debt/EBITDA	6.8x	7.3x	3.7x	6.7x
Debt/Cap	99.7%	56.2%	49.7%	63.1%
Debt/Market Cap	99.8%	70.6%	NA	37.8%

Source: DLJ.

- The correlation of the DLJ High Yield Index with the JPM EMBI has grown to about 90 percent in 1997 from about 30 percent in 1993 (see Exhibit 4–4).
- As illustrated in Exhibits 4–6 and 4–7, the expected return and volatility of high yield assets in the United States, Asia, and Latin America are distinctly different. When an asset has a different mean-variance from other assets it is considered to have a separate driver and forms a distinct segment.
- Historically, the G7 have had the highest GDP growth rates versus others in the global economy. This relationship shifted starting in the early 1990s (see Exhibit 4–8). The implementation of the IMF and World Bank guidelines on convertibility,

1997	U.S./Canada				
	1992	1994	1995	1996	1997
$21.6	$32.1	$35.1	$38.8	$63.6	$111.3
$20.6	$30.7	$31.9	$36.3	$59.0	$104.8
104	188	199	202	340	599
$208.0	$170.6	$176.4	$192.1	$186.9	$185.8
10.55%	10.82%	11.03%	11.09%	10.45%	10.14%
427bp	401bp	435bp	470bp	410bp	387bp
77.9%	8.6%	17.9%	51.5%	43.0%	51.4%
85.3%	12.6%	23.7%	48.9%	47.6%	40.5%
44.3%	26.0%	19.0%	27.2%	24.3%	25.8%
36.6%	13.1%	15.5%	29.8%	25.1%	28.5%
54.4%	14.8%	27.8%	33.2%	34.3%	41.8%
2.2x	1.7x	2.3x	2.3x	2.5x	2.2x
2.0x	1.0x	1.6x	1.7x	1.7x	1.7x
2.0x	1.6x	2.0x	2.1x	2.3x	2.1x
5.3x	5.2x	6.7x	6.4x	6.1x	5.8x
3.7x	3.7x	4.1x	3.5x	3.6x	3.6x
74.2%	55.1%	77.2%	75.1%	80.6%	68.6%
5.4x	5.9x	5.4x	5.0x	4.9x	5.5x
65.3%	95.1%	69.4%	71.3%	67.2%	69.6%
44.8%	95.0%	54.9%	52.7%	50.9%	48.5%

E X H I B I T   4–3

Developing Countries in the DLJ
High Yield Index (market value)

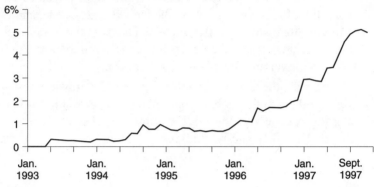

Source: DLJ.

E X H I B I T   4–4

20-Month Rolling Return Correlation of the
JPM EMBI with the DLJ High Yield Index

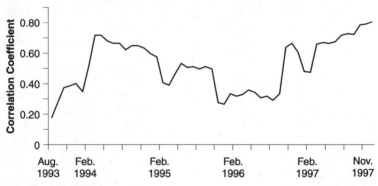

Sources: DLJ; Ibbotson Associates.

economic liberalization and the encouragment of local financial
markets' evolution, and reformation of the banking system have
resulted in the rapid decline in sovereign credit risk over the last
several years. This decline has led to a higher growth rate and
declining inflation for the emerging markets, which have led to

E X H I B I T   4–5

20-Month Rolling Return Correlation of the DLJ High Yield Index with U.S. Treasuries and the S&P 500

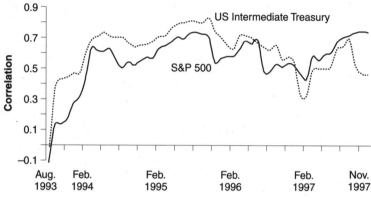

Sources: DLJ; Ibbotson Associates.

E X H I B I T   4–6

Annual Returns

Asset	1992	1993	1994	1995	1996	1997
U.S. Intermediate Treasury	7.19%	11.24%	–5.14%	16.80%	2.10%	8.38%
High Yield Bonds	16.66	18.00	–2.04	19.68	13.03	12.21
U.S./Canada	NA	17.58	–2.09	19.56	12.39	12.75
Non–U.S./Canada	NA	24.16	–4.45	26.07	18.20	7.55
Asia	NA	NA	1.86	17.13	20.56	–6.70
Latin America	NA	6.49	–19.59	37.47	19.65	12.26
EMBI Fixed Rate	10.42	48.99	–25.69	41.85	30.45	21.15
S&P 500	7.67	9.99	1.31	37.43	23.07	33.36

Sources: DLJ; Ibbotson Associates.

the ability of emerging market companies to access the high yield market as emerging market spreads have compressed versus the U.S. high yield market (see Exhibits 4–9 and 4–10).

- With the rapid decline in the U.S. capital market's risk including high yield, higher risk/higher yielding segments such as build outs (project finance) and non-U.S. issuance have grown.

E X H I B I T   4–7

Recent Risk and Reward Characteristics, 1996–1997

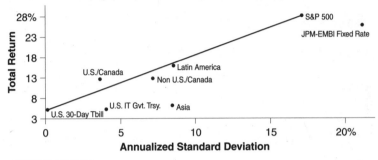

Sources: DLJ; Ibbotson Associates.

E X H I B I T   4–8

| Historic Annual GDP Growth by Region (%) | | | | | | | Projected |
	1992	1993	1994	1995	1996	1997	1998
G7	1.9	1.2	3.2	2.5	2.7	2.8	2.3
Latin America	3.1	3.7	5.0	1.3	3.4	5.2	3.5
Southeast Asia	5.8	6.3	7.6	7.4	6.4	6.2	3.6
Historic Annual Inflation Rate by Region (%)							Projected
	1992	1993	1994	1995	1996	1997	1998
G7	3.2	2.8	2.2	2.3	2.2	2.0	2.1
Latin America	153.2	212.5	213.9	41.7	20.5	13.7	9.4
Southeast Asia	5.9	4.6	5.7	4.6	4.3	3.7	4.7

Source: International Monetary Fund.

Conclusions drawn as a result of these changes:

- *The high yield market in 1997 has shifted from a three-factor
  model to a four-factor model.* Historically, the high yield market
  has been driven by 3 factors: interest rates, the equity markets,
  and intrinsic risk. Intrinsic risk is the overall leverage in the high
  yield market (liquidity, etc.) along with other high yield market-
  specific conditions. The escalating correlation between high yield
  and emerging market debt indicates that a new non-U.S. risk is at
  play. We will refer to this non-U.S. driver as *the global factor.*

E X H I B I T   4–9

Spreads of DLJ High Yield Index versus JP Morgan EMBI Euro Index

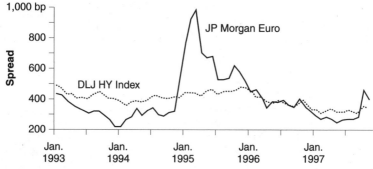

Sources: DLJ; Bloomberg.

E X H I B I T   4–10

Regional STW versus DLJ HY Index

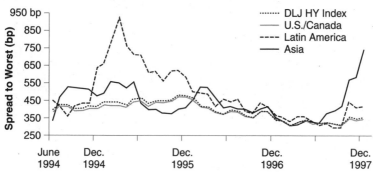

Source: DLJ.

- From a portfolio perspective, *an investor who is bearish on the U.S. economy can be overweighted in the non-U.S./Canada high yield market, and vice versa.* The growth of the global factor is built on other factors such as low cost, which can be detected by higher overall margins compared to U.S. issues. The higher growth rates of non-U.S. companies also combine with higher sales and EBITDA volatility (see Exhibits 4–11 and 4–12).

- *The risk of the high yield market declines as more sectors with different drivers are introduced.* The incremental diversification

E X H I B I T   4–11

20-Month Rolling Return Volatility (annualized) of Various Assets

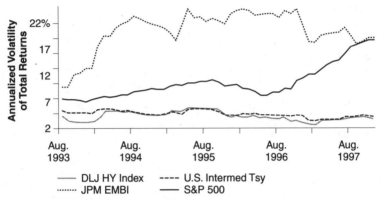

Sources: DLJ; Ibbotson Associates.

E X H I B I T   4–12

20-Month Rolling Return Volatility (annualized) of the DLJ High Yield Index versus the Asian and Latin American Components

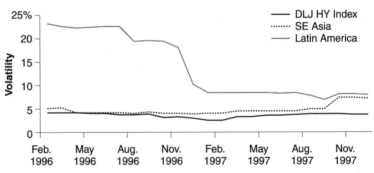

Sources: DLJ; Ibbotson Associates.

E X H I B I T   4–13

U.S./Canada Market Weight by Industry, December 31, 1997

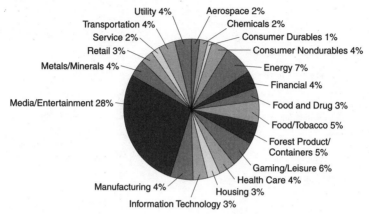

Source: DLJ.

in the high yield market has resulted in a lower volatility. In contrast, the volatility of the Treasury and equity markets has escalated over the past 1–2 years.

- The higher growth rate of the non-U.S./Canada sectors has led to the spread compression observed in non-U.S./Canada issues from 1993–1997. The volatility of these sectors caused by political risk, exchange rate risk, and transfer risk can lead to a rapid spread widening. This is consistent with the events of the last few months of 1997.

- From a tactical asset allocation perspective, a fundamental risk/reward methodology leads to two strategies. One is underweighting the emerging market sector of the high yield market. The other is the mean reversal approach, which dictates that as spreads widen from a fundamental level assets are either richer or cheaper.

Historically, non-U.S. issues have been in infrastructure and other basic industries, versus the high diversification of U.S. companies. Non-U.S. issues also have higher ratings, and an overweighting in DIS and prefunded issues (30 percent versus 14 percent), and project finance (29 percent versus 11 percent) as compared with U.S. issues (see Exhibits 4–13 through 4–19).

E X H I B I T   4–14

Non-U.S./Canada Market Weight by Industry, December 31, 1997

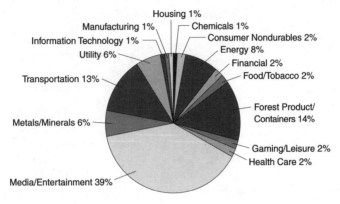

Source: DLJ.

E X H I B I T   4–15

Domestic and Nondomestic Sectors of the DLJ High Yield Index by Security Type, December 31, 1997

	Market Weight	
	Non-U.S./Canada	U.S./Canada
Cash (nonprefunded)	69.6%	85.4%
Prefunded Interest	9.0%	3.1%
Deferred Less Than 2 Years	0.0%	3.5%
Deferred 2 Years and Over	21.3%	7.1%
Default	0.0%	0.9%
Cushion Paper	3.0%	22.4%
Noncushion Paper	97.0%	77.6%
Project Finance	29.1%	11.4%
Nonproject Finance	70.9%	88.6%

Source: DLJ.

E X H I B I T   4—16

U.S./Canada Market Weight by Rating Tier, December 31, 1997

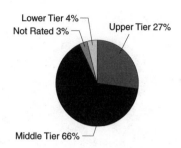

Source: DLJ.

E X H I B I T   4—17

Non-U.S./Canada Market Weight by Rating Tier, December 31, 1997

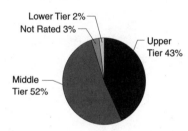

Source: DLJ.

E X H I B I T   4—18

Non-U.S./Canada Market Weight by Region, December 31, 1997

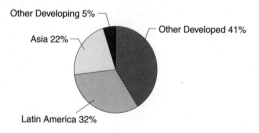

Source: DLJ.

E X H I B I T   4–19

Breakdown of Non-U.S./Canada Components of the DLJ HY Index by Country, 12/31/97

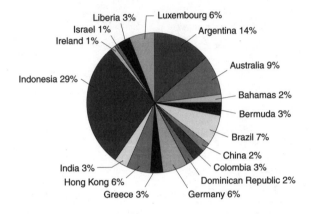

Source: DLJ.

PART TWO

Security Risk Analysis

CHAPTER 5

Historical Default Rates of Corporate Bond Issuers, 1920–1996

Lea V. Carty

Dana Lieberman

INTRODUCTION

As a complement to Moody's ongoing default research, we extended our study of historical corporate bond defaults to cover the 77-year period beginning in 1920. Moody's corporate bond default research began in 1987 as part of an effort to ensure the uniformity of our long-term debt ratings across asset classes. We initiated this upgrade of that research to further

E X H I B I T   5—1

One-Year Default Rates by Rating and Year

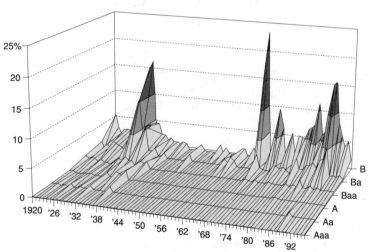

examine the performance of our ratings as indicators of credit quality over a wider variety of economic cycles. We also intend to use these data to study patterns and correlations in the incidence of default and rating changes among industries, domiciles, and rating categories.

In keeping with the spirit of previous Moody's default studies, we limit this report to a general overview of defaults, default rates, and recovery rates. Also, under the rationale that more recent experience is of greater interest to investors, we continue to place special emphasis on the period since 1970. We first present a summary of the 1996 default activity in the following section. In subsequent parts, we explore the entire period from 1920 through 1996.

1996 DEFAULT OVERVIEW

Globally, just 27 issuers defaulted on $5.4 billion of long-term, publicly held corporate debt in 1996. This is the second lowest yearly total of defaulted issuers for the last 10 years and represents a marked decrease in default activity from the 49 issuer defaults in 1995 involving $8.5 billion. The low incidence of defaults dragged Moody's trailing 12-month, issuer-based, and dollar-based speculative-grade default rates to just 1.6 percent each by the end of the year—less than half of their levels as of the end of 1995.

In terms of dollar amounts, manufacturers accounted for the largest portion of last year's defaulted public debt—$1.4 billion (27 percent). Following in second place were media firms that contributed another $894 million (16 percent). The third-place slot was filled by financial firms, which defaulted on another $700 million (13 percent). In terms of the number of defaulting issuers, the recently default-prone textiles and apparel industry shared a joint first place with the leisure, casino, and lodging industry as each experienced four defaults. Exhibit 5–2 gives more detail of the industrial composition of the 1996 defaults.

In response to diminishing credit risk, the spread between Moody's median speculative-grade bond yield and seven-year Treasuries narrowed by 92 basis points over the course of 1996. Tightening spreads helped support gains in the speculative-grade bond market relative to Treasury securities. Moody's speculative-grade total return index outperformed Treasuries by a wide margin last year, returning 12.14 percent to investors versus a negative 0.78 percent total return for long-term Treasuries.

Favorable trends in default risk and bond pricing, and a surging equity market laid the foundation for a surge in new speculative-grade bond issuance, as the 1996 total matched the 1993 record issuance, $67 billion.

E X H I B I T   5–2

Defaulted Debt by Industry, 1996*

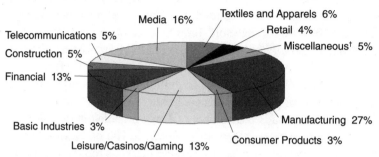

*$5.4 billion = 100%.
†Includes Autos, Energy, Utilities, Computers, and Electronics.

New issuance was skewed towards the riskier end of the credit scale with 71 percent of the new debt carrying a B or lower rating. Additionally, nearly half ($32 billion) of the new speculative-grade debt sold in 1996 was issued under Rule 144a. This debt was of lower average credit quality than public speculative-grade issuance as 78 percent of it was rated B or lower versus 65 percent for public issuance. Despite the trend towards riskier issuance in 1996, after taking into account the effects of upgrades, downgrades, calls and other retirements, the rating composition of speculative-grade issuers remained constant. The percentage of speculative-grade issuers carrying the B or lower ratings at the senior unsecured level remained at the 1995 level, 52 percent. This, however, represents a considerably riskier credit mix than existed before the speculative-grade market meltdown of the early 1990s. At the start of 1989, for example, only 43 percent of speculative-grade issuers carried B or lower ratings at the senior unsecured level. The significant supply of lower-rated debt and the relatively risky mix of junk bond issuers will put upward pressure on speculative-grade default rates in 1997 and beyond.

RATINGS AND DEFAULT DATA

Moody's bases the results of this study on a proprietary database of ratings and defaults for industrial and transportation companies, utilities, financial institutions, and sovereigns that issued long-term debt to the public. Municipal debt issuers, structured finance transactions, and issuers with only short-term debt ratings are excluded. We compiled the ratings data from four main sources: Moody's ratings database, Moody's "dead ratings" files, Moody's manuals (Industrial, Utilities and Transportation), and Moody's investment letters. In total, the data cover the credit experiences of over 14,000 issuers that sold long-term debt publicly at some time between 1919 and 1996. As of January 1, 1997, approximately 3,500 of those issuers held Moody's ratings. These issuers account for the bulk of the outstanding dollar amount of U.S. public long-term corporate debt and a substantial part of public issuance abroad.

Exhibit 5–3 details the number of firms included in our ratings database as of the start of each decade since 1920. The downward trend from 1920 through 1950 reflects the public bond market's retrenchments following the Great Depression and World War II, increasing financial intermediation and consolidation in the railroad and utilities industries. Since 1950, however, the number of rated firms has increased steadily with sharp increases in the 1980s and 1990s. The increase in the 1980s reflects, in part, the development of the junk bond market in the United States which attracted a new set of issuers to the public bond market. The increase in the 1990s, on the other hand, primarily reflects Moody's expansion into non-U.S. markets. It was not until 1994 that Moody's again rated as many corporate issuers as it did in 1920 when, according to the study by W. Braddock Hickman ("Corporate Bond Quality and Investor Experience," NBER, 1958), nearly 98 percent of straight corporate bonds outstanding were rated.

Non-U.S. issuers comprised nearly as large a percentage of the Moody's rated universe in January of 1930 (15 percent) as they did in January of 1990 (18 percent). The portion of rated issuers domiciled outside the United States hit a high in 1930 but trailed off to an all-time low in 1970. Since then, this fraction has grown significantly higher than in the past and stood at 38 percent at the beginning of 1997. Before 1980, the non-U.S. issuers Moody's-rated were predominantly those that tapped the U.S. bond market. In recent years, however, Moody's has extended ratings to many more issuers placing debt in non-U.S. markets. Currently, the two non-U.S. countries contributing the largest number of Moody's-rated companies are Japan and the United Kingdom.

Historically, the industrial cross section of U.S. bond issuers has shifted with broad patterns in the country's capital formation process. Consequently, the industrial composition of firms with Moody's-rated debt has also shifted. Exhibit 5–4 traces the industrial composition of Moody's-rated, corporate issuers from 1920 to the present. In the early part of the

E X H I B I T   5–3

Moody's-Rated Issuers, 1920–1997

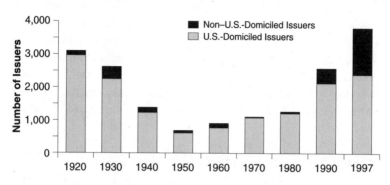

E X H I B I T   5–4

Industrial Composition of Issuers, 1920–1997

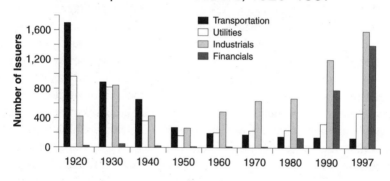

century, railroads absorbed the majority of the country's investment. As of 1920, more than half of the issuers Moody's rated were railroad companies. Following the railroads were the utilities, industrials, and financial companies: these comprised over 31 percent, 14 percent, and 1 percent, respectively, of rated issuers in 1920. Since 1920, railroads have consolidated so that by January 1997, the entire transportation industry comprised only 4 percent of Moody's-rated, corporate public debt issuers. On the other hand, industrials have expanded to represent 44 percent of the total number of rated firms. Since Moody's began rating bank debt in 1971, financial companies have expanded significantly to comprise 39 percent of the Moody's rated universe as of the start of 1997.

We compiled the default histories used in this study from a variety of sources, including our own *Industrial, Railroad,* and *Public Utilities Manuals;* reports of the National Quotation Service; various issues of *The Commercial and Financial Chronicle;* our library of financial reports; press releases; press clippings; internal memoranda; and records of analyst contact with rated issuers. We also examined documents from the Securities and Exchange Commission, The Dun & Bradstreet Corp., the New York Stock Exchange, and the American Stock Exchange. The default database covers nearly 3,000 defaults by issuers both rated and unrated by Moody's.

DEFAULTS AND DEFAULT RATES
Definitions and Methodology

Moody's defines default as any missed or delayed disbursement of interest and/or principal, bankruptcy, receivership, or distressed exchange where (1) The issuer offered bondholders a new security or package of securities that amounted to a diminished financial obligation (such as preferred or common stock, or debt with a lower coupon or par amount), or (2) The exchange had the apparent purpose of helping the borrower avoid default.

To calculate default rates, which are estimates of the default probability component of ratings, we use the issuer as the unit of study rather than individual debt instruments or outstanding dollar amounts of debt. Because Moody's intends its ratings to support credit decisions, which do not vary with either the size or number of bonds that a firm may have outstanding, we believe this methodology produces more meaningful estimates of the probability of default. Because the likelihood of default is essentially the same for all of a firm's public debt issues, irrespective of size, weighting our statistics by the number of bond issues or their par amounts would simply bias our results towards the characteristics of large issuers.

The default rates we calculate are fractions in which the numerator represents the number of issuers that defaulted in a particular time period and the denominator represents the number of issuers that could have defaulted in that time period. In this study, the numerators are the numbers of issuers defaulting on Moody's-rated debt. The denominators are the numbers of issuers that potentially could have defaulted on Moody's-rated debt. Hence, if all of an issuer's ratings are withdrawn, it is subtracted from the denominator. Failing to correct the denominators in this way tends to generate artificially low estimates of the risk of default. It is important to note that Moody's does not withdraw ratings because of a deterioration in credit quality. In such cases, the issuer's bonds are simply downgraded.

Moody's ratings incorporate both the likelihood and the severity of default. So, in order to calculate the default probability component of ratings, we must hold severity considerations constant. We do this by taking the rating on each company's senior unsecured debt or, if there is none, by statistically implying such a rating on the basis of rated subordinated or secured debt. In most cases, this will yield an assessment of risk that is relatively unaffected by special considerations of collateral or of position within the capital structure. We have incorporated some improvements to the algorithm used to imply senior unsecured ratings. In the process, some of the implied rating histories have been revised, thereby generating some changes in previously reported default rates. The resulting figures represent a more accurate estimate of the actual risk of default associated with each Moody's rating.

Defaults Since 1920

Moody's corporate bond default database contains records for nearly 3,000 rated and unrated defaults as of January 1, 1997. The incidence of these defaults is spread unevenly over this century with large numbers of defaults in the 1920s, the Depression of the 1930s, and again in the late 1980s and early 1990s. The number of recorded defaults per year peaked in 1933 at 317.

At 40 percent, industrials account for the largest fraction of the total number of defaults in our database. The remaining defaulters are divided between transportation companies (36 percent), utilities (16 percent), financial companies (5 percent), and another 3 percent miscellaneously affiliated firms. However, closer inspection reveals that the contributions made by industries to the total number of defaults have varied substantially through time.

Exhibit 5–5 portrays the total number of defaults, sorted by industry, in each of five time periods that span the period from 1920 through the present. In the 1920s, transportation companies made up the majority of defaulters, with industrial firms coming in a distant second place. During the depression years of the 1930s, all industries experienced sharp increases in the incidence of defaults. However, the number of industrials defaulting during this period surged past those for other industries to 537. The 35-year period beginning after World War II was characterized by a low incidence of defaults within all industries. Defaults began to build again near the beginning of the 1980s, reaching a peak during the first two years of the 1990s.

Non-U.S. defaults peaked during the 1930–1949 period when they constituted 16 percent of all defaults. By contrast, during the 1990s, non-U.S. defaults have comprised only 10 percent of the number of defaults.

E X H I B I T   5–5

Default Count by Decade and Industry

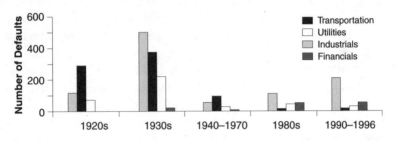

The large fraction of non-U.S. defaults in the 1930s is at least partially attributable to Germany's 1933 payment moratorium. Of the 317 defaulters on record for the year, 62 (20 percent) were German companies restricted from making payments under the German Transfer Moratorium. All of these companies carried speculative-grade ratings at the senior unsecured level at least six months prior to the decree. Half were utility companies, a third were industrials, and the remainder were transportation companies. Subsequent related defaults were registered in Austria and Czechoslovakia. Other countries that have declared payment moratoriums and therefore generated defaults include Rhodesia, Chile, and Uruguay.

Over 2,000 of the more than 14,000 corporate issuers that Moody's has rated since 1920 have defaulted at some point in time. One year prior to default, only 184 of these carried actual or implied senior unsecured ratings at the investment-grade level. However, at various lengths of time before default, more issuers carried investment-grade ratings. To capture the evolution of ratings as default approached, we calculated the median senior or implied senior unsecured rating of issuers between zero and 15 years before default. Exhibit 5–6 displays this information and clearly shows a decline in the median rating as the time of default approaches.

Nine years prior to default, the median rating of defaulting companies is speculative grade, and one year before default it is B. This indicates that over the last 77 years, Moody's has rated at least half of its defaulters B one year prior to default. Exhibit 5–6 also shows an increase in the median credit quality of defaulters from B to Baa between 1 and 15 years prior to default. This pattern is partly generated by construction. That is, for an issuer to service its debt for the 15 years required for it to be considered in the calculation of the median rating 15 years before default, it must have

E X H I B I T   5—6

Median Rating of Years before Default

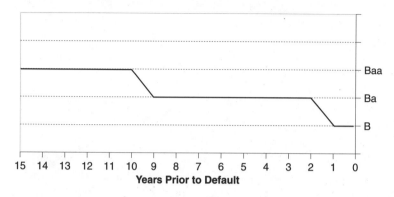

Years Prior to Default

been relatively safe at the time the Baa rating was assigned. Consequently, it is not surprising that the median rating 15 years before default is investment grade.

One-Year Default Rates

Exhibit 5–7 portrays a monthly time series of one-year, corporate default rates (calculated as the number of Moody's-rated issuers that defaulted over the following 12-month period divided by the number of Moody's-rated issuers that could have defaulted over that 12-month period). It provides an overall picture of how quickly, and to what extent, aggregate corporate default risk has ebbed and flowed since 1920.

January 1920 through mid–1929 was a period of cyclical and declining default risk that resembled the 1980s in terms of the average default rate. Interest rates started the 1920s at high levels and drifted lower, supporting booms in corporate debt issuance and the stock market that helped suppress default rates. The next period, from mid–1929 through December 1939, witnessed the heaviest default activity of the period examined in this report. The Great Depression generated a 77-year high, one-year corporate default rate of 9.2 percent in July 1932, indicating that nearly 1 in 10 Moody's-rated corporate issuers defaulted over the following year. The severity of the Depression and its characteristic asset depreciation ensured that the high rates of default did not subside quickly. For the eight-year

EXHIBIT 5-7

One-Year, Corporate Issuer Default Rate
versus Baa–Aaa Yield Spread, 1920–1996

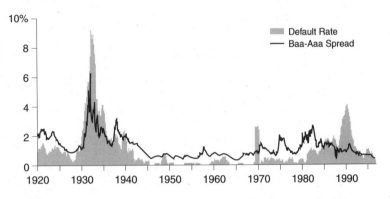

period beginning in January 1930, this default rated averaged 3.7 percent—nearly as high as the recent peak set in July 1991—4.1 percent. The default rate jumped at the beginning of World War II, reflecting the war-related defaults of Italian, German, French, Japanese, Czechoslovakian, and Austrian companies. Following the war, default risk subsided to very low levels that persisted until 1970, when the defaults of Penn Central Railroad and 25 of its affiliates shook fixed income markets. From 1970, default risk has been moderate to low by historical standards until 1982, when the modern period of relatively high default risk began.

Exhibit 5–7 also tracks the spread between Moody's average, long-term Baa- and Aaa-rated bond yields. Month-to-month, the Baa–Aaa spread varies with a variety of market conditions including, and most important, the market's perception of the credit risk differential between Aaa- and Baa-rated debt. This spread generally tracked the corporate default rate from 1920 through the early 1980s. In the early 1980s, however, it began a pronounced downward trend that it has maintained through today despite the highest corporate default rates seen since the Great Depression. This signals a fundamental difference between the episodes of high credit risk investors faced in the 1930s versus those recently experienced during the speculative-grade market meltdown of the early 1990s. During the Depression, the economy experienced the most severe contraction of this century while deflation increased the real value of fixed debt obligations, placing even highly creditworthy borrowers at considerable risk of default. Consequently, defaults in the 1930s reached quite far up the credit scale, even affecting some investment-grade debt. The market reacted to the surge in credit risk for Baa-rated debt over Aaa-rated debt by demanding greater Aaa–Baa spreads. On the other hand, the economic recession that occurred during the early 1990s proved to be the mildest since World War II and was devoid of deflation. Consequently, very little invest-ment-grade debt defaulted in this recent period, even though defaults were numerous within the speculative-grade bond ratings. The falling Baa–Aaa yield spread during this period reflects the bond market's accurate assess-ment that the recent period's credit risk was not due to significant overall and unexpected weakness in the economy, but rather to phenomena specific to the speculative-grade bond market (e.g., the many ill-conceived LBOs of the 1980s).

We define one-year default rates for any rating classification in a manner analogous to that used for calculating overall, one-year corporate default rates. For the B rating, for example, the one-year default rate is the number of Moody's-rated issuers that defaulted over the following one-year period divided by the number of Moody's-rated issuers that could have defaulted over that one-year period. The issuer-weighted average of default rates (defined at the start of each year) represents an estimate of the risk of default within any one-year period. (The underlying one-year default rates for each rating category from 1970 through the present are included in Exhibit 5–17 of the appendix to this chapter.) Exhibit 5–8 pre-sents weighted-average default rates defined over the periods from 1920 and from 1970 to the present.

The weighted-average default rates defined over both time horizons clearly show an increased risk of default associated with lower rating cat-egories. The average, one-year default rates for the Aa through Baa rating categories are higher for the 1920–1996 period than for the 1970–1996 time period. This reflects the influence of the Great Depression during which greater numbers of investment-grade issuers succumbed to the period's severe economic pressures and defaulted. The average default rates for the Ba rating category differed only by 12 basis points when meas-ured over either time period, but those for the B rating category differed by nearly three percentage points. This difference reflects the 25-year period following World War II during which few firms defaulted, generating a long string of near-zero default rates.

The last three rows of Exhibit 5–17 in the appendix give the one-year default rates for investment-grade issuers, speculative-grade issuers, and all corporate issuers since 1970. There is a clear pattern of higher risk of default associated with the speculative-grade rating categories. This pattern persists over the entire period considered in this study. For all but 28 of the past 77 years, the one-year default rate for the investment-grade sector was

One-Year, Weighted-Average Default Rates by Rating

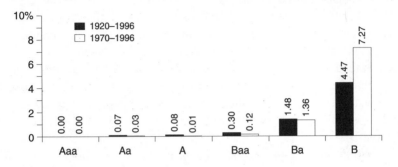

zero. By the methodology outlined above, an average of 3.25 percent of speculative-grade issuers defaulted per year, compared with just 0.16 percent of investment-grade issuers.

Moody's refined its rating scale in April 1982 by adding numerical modifiers. The ratings from Aa to B were expanded to include three numerical modifiers each in order to provide finer gradations of credit risk. Exhibit 5–9 and Exhibit 5–18 in the appendix present one-year and weighted-average one-year default rates for each of these rating categories. These default rates are drawn from the relatively high default risk period extending from 1983 through 1996. The results suggest that the relationship between ratings and the likelihood of default holds for numerically modified rating categories as well as for the nonmodified categories, because average one-year default rates climb from 0.0 percent for Aaa to 13.7 percent for B3. Another interesting aspect of Exhibit 5–9 is the great dispersion within speculative-grade rating categories. The Ba3 rating has a default rate three times as great as that of the Ba1 category, and the B3 default rate is of a similar magnitude greater than the B1 default rate.

Multiyear Default Rates

Although one-year default rates may be the most commonly reported, some investors find default rates for longer time horizons more relevant. A 10-year default rate, for example, estimates the share of a portfolio of bonds expected to default over a 10-year period. To quantify the risk of default over time horizons longer than one year, we formed cohorts of issuers at the start of each year since 1920. A cohort consists of all issuers holding a given senior rating at the start of a given year. These issuers are

E X H I B I T 5—9

One-Year Default Rates by Numerically
Modified Ratings, 1983–1996

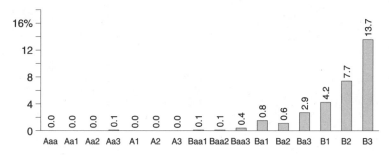

then followed through time, keeping track of when they default or leave the
rated universe, in order to estimate the cumulative risk of default over multiyear horizons. Moody's approach, by forming cohorts of all Moody's-
rated issuers with debt outstanding at January 1 of each year, provides an
indicator of the experience of a portfolio of both seasoned and new-issue
bonds purchased in a given year.

Exhibit 5–21 in the appendix traces, for up to 20 years, the cumulative default rates of cohorts of Moody's-rated issuers formed at the beginning of each year from 1970 to 1996. For example, this table answers the
question, "What was the risk that a B-rated issuer with bonds outstanding
as of January 1, 1983 would default by 1996?" The answer is found in the
last row and last column of the section labeled "Cohort Formed January 1,
1983": 58.5 percent. The cohort methodology has the advantage that year-
by-year comparisons of actual default experiences can be made. In cases
in which an investor feels that the business conditions of the current year
are similar to those of a previous year, she may consult the previous year's
cohort directly to ascertain what default patterns to expect.

To estimate the average risk of default over time horizons longer than
one year, we calculate the risk of default in each year since a cohort was
formed. The issuer-weighted average of each cohort's one-year default rate
forms the average cumulative one-year default rate. The issuer-weighted
average of the second-year default rates, cumulated with that of the first
year, yields the two-year average cumulative default rate. In this manner,
we compute average cumulative default rates for 1 to 20 years for each
rating category. Exhibit 5–10 presents average cumulative default rates for
5-, 10-, 15-, and 20-year time horizons based on all data available since

E X H I B I T   5—10

5-, 10-, 15-, and 20-Year Default Rates, 1920–1996

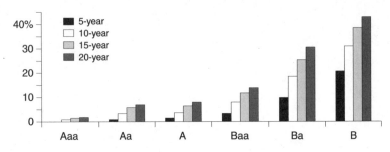

1920. Exhibit 5–19 in the appendix presents these data in detail for the period 1970 to 1996, and Exhibit 5–20 presents average cumulative default rates by numerically modified ratings for up to six years.

Exhibit 5–10 shows that higher default risk for lower rating categories remains evident over investment periods exceeding one year. For example, average default rates for five-year holding periods climb from 0.1 percent for the Aaa rating category to 20.6 percent for the B rating category. Exhibit 5–10 also shows that the pattern recurs for average default rates for 10- and 15-year holding periods.

Comparison with Hickman's (1958) Default Rates

W. Braddock Hickman conducted one of the earliest and most complete studies of credit risk in corporate bond markets ("Corporate Bond Quality and Investor Experience," NBER, 1958). Among the analyses conducted was one that correlated defaults with ratings over four-year periods. For both investment-grade and speculative-grade rating groupings, Hickman calculated cumulative default rates for each nonoverlapping four-year period from 1912 through 1943. Exhibit 5–11 compares his results with analogous results drawn from Moody's default database over the time period covered by both studies. On average, Moody's default analysis generates a higher average investment-grade default rate than Hickman's, 3.4 percent versus 2.2 percent. On the other hand, for the speculative-grade rating categories, Moody's analysis, on average, generates lower default rates than Hickman's, 13.7 percent versus 24.0 percent.

E X H I B I T   5–11

Comparison of Hickman and Moody's
Four-Year Default Rates

	Investment-Grade		Speculative-Grade	
	Moody's	**Hickman**	**Moody's**	**Hickman**
1920–23	1.5%	1.0%	7.9%	18.2%
1924–27	1.9	1.1	11.6	23.5
1928–31	2.0	1.4	13.6	22.6
1932–35	11.3	6.2	33.9	48.9
1936–39	2.8	3.3	9.9	21.7
1940–43	0.6	0.4	5.4	8.9
Average	3.4%	2.2%	13.7%	24.0%

Differences between the methodologies employed by Hickman and Moody's make reconciling discrepancies between the average investment-grade and speculative-grade default rates of Exhibit 5–11 difficult. For example, Moody's results are based upon the experience of its rated universe, which includes both U.S. and non-U.S. issuers. Hickman's results, on the other hand, are based on a sample drawn solely from the U.S. debt markets. (Hickman considered all debt issues with an original issue amount of at least $5 million and selected a sample of issues with an original issue amount of less than $5 million.) Additionally, Hickman focuses attention on the par amount of defaulted debt whereas Moody's uses the debt issuer as the unit of study. However, at least part of the reason that Moody's average investment-grade default rate is higher than Hickman's is because of Moody's stricter definition of default. In contrast to the Hickman methodology, Moody's considers distressed exchanges as defaults. For the once-investment-grade defaults of the period covered by Exhibit 5–11, such exchanges accounted for about 15 percent of the aggregate number of defaults.

Default Rate Volatility

An examination of cohorts of bonds formed in various years reveals that default rates vary from one year to the next for a given rating category. For the B rating category in the period from 1920 through 1996, for instance, the one-year default rate ranged from a low of zero in several years to a high of 23.4 percent in 1970. The sources of this variation are many, but macroeconomic trends are certainly among the most influential factors. To quantify this variability, Moody's calculated the standard deviations of the one-year default rates for each letter rating category. Exhibit 5–12 presents these statistics defined over the periods from 1920 and from 1970 to 1996.

This exhibit highlights a pattern of higher default rate volatility for lower credit ratings for both time periods examined. That is, while the average risk of default is higher for lower rating categories, the chances of the default rate differing significantly from the average in any given year is also higher. Additionally, the greater investment-grade default rate volatilities—except that of the Aaa rating—for the period including the experience of the Great Depression, reflect the uncertainty over invest-ment-grade default rates provoked by the extreme economic circumstances of that time. The volatility of default rates has important implications in bond pricing. The returns investors earn on lower-rated debt must not only compensate them for the higher average risk of default, but also for the increased risk that the default rate could differ substantially from its his-torical average.

RECOVERY RATES

A critical aspect of a corporate bond default is the severity of the loss incurred. Eventually, most bond default resolutions provide bondholders with some amount of recovery, which may take the form of cash, other securities, or even a physical asset. The recovery rate, defined here as the percentage of par value returned to the bondholder, is a function of several variables. These variables include the seniority of the issue within the issuer's capital structure, the quality of collateral (if any), the overall state of the economy, and the market for corporate assets.

What may seem the most straightforward methodology for calculating recovery rates is not particularly practicable. This methodology would track all payments made on a defaulted debt instrument, discount them back to the date of default, and present them as a percentage of the par value of the security. However, this methodology is problematic because it relies on many assumptions. One must make a separate estimate of the discount rate that will apply to each payment generated by the defaulted instrument. Fur-thermore, one must often make assumptions concerning the values of cer-tain payments. The resolution may hand bondholders various equity and

E X H I B I T   5–12

One-Year Default Rate Volatilities

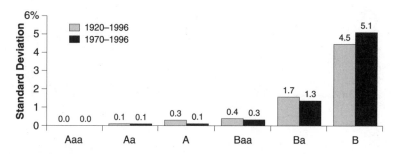

derivative instruments, enhancements to the terms of the surviving debt, or sometimes even a physical asset in place of cash. As there is frequently no market for such payments, there is no definite measure of their value.

For these reasons, we use the trading price of the defaulted instrument as a proxy for the present value of the ultimate recovery. Although it is only an estimate of the actual recovery, it has the advantage of being the definite measure of the recovery realized by those debtholders who liquidate a position soon after default.

We collected, from several sources, prices for many of the bonds that defaulted between January 1, 1920, and December 31, 1996. For each defaulted issue, we considered the seniority, date of default, and the price approximately one month after default. Exhibit 5–13 maps out the yearly average of defaulted bond prices in our database from 1920 to 1996. The average for the 77-year period is $40. The data reveal tremendous volatility in average defaulted bond prices year-over-year as well as correlations with macroeconomic variables and the risk of default. The lows of $21 and $30 in 1932 and 1990 respectively, correspond to peaks in the corporate default rate, suggesting a negative correlation of defaulted bond prices and the risk of default. Additionally, the low values during the late 1970s and early 1980s suggest a negative correlation with interest rates.

W. Braddock Hickman (in "Corporate Bond Quality and Investor Experience," NBER, 1958) also examined defaulted bond prices as indicators of the recovery investors retrieve on default debt. For the period from 1930 through 1943, Hickman's average price for 394 "large" (greater than $5 million) straight defaulted bonds was $34, and his average for 105

E X H I B I T   5–13

Yearly Average Defaulted Bond Prices, 1920–1996

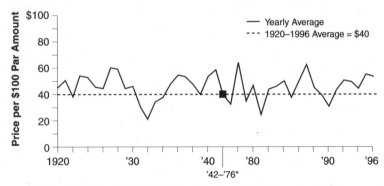

*Because of the dearth of defaults between 1942 and 1976, we have prices for only 68 bonds from this period. We have grouped them
  together in order to make this chart more easily read.

"small" straight defaulted bonds was $35. The average for the 1,106 defaulted bonds from this period for which Moody's has prices is just slightly higher—$36.

We translate defaulted debt prices into recovery rate estimates by presenting them as percentages of par (not percentages of original issue prices or accreted values). Investors are entitled to receive face value at maturity, even though they may have paid somewhat less or more for the bond either at issue or in the secondary market. Expressing recoveries as a fraction of some price other than par could improperly bias recovery rates. Because discount bonds and convertible bonds have unique pricing features, we have removed them from the sample.

Trends in bond market financing make the averaging of recovery rate estimates derived from defaulted bond prices over very long time horizons unreliable. For example, a much higher percentage of the bonds Moody's rated from 1930 through 1943 were secured than were those Moody's rated between 1980 and 1996. The especially dismal circumstances of the Great Depression era combined with the preponderance of secured financing conspired to generate an average 1920–1996 senior secured bond price lower than that for senior unsecured bonds. In order to mitigate this difficulty and to incorporate and facilitate comparison with recent Moody's recovery analysis of senior secured bank loans, we have limited the sample period to 1989 through 1996. Exhibit 5–14 breaks out

E X H I B I T   5–14

Defaulted Debt Recovery Rate Estimates by Seniority of Claim, 1989–1996

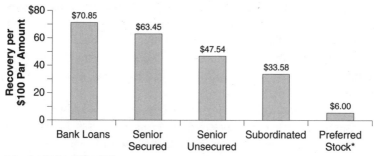

*Estimate based on data from 1980 to 1994.

average recovery estimates by seniority of claim and includes Moody's estimate of the recovery investors can expect to receive on bank loans and preferred stock.[1] The average bank loan recovery estimate is $71. Considering prices for 57 senior secured bonds, our recovery estimate is $63; prices for 156 senior unsecured bonds generate a recovery estimate of $48. The 293 subordinated bonds sold for $34 on average. Preferred stockholders can only expect to retrieve about $6 per $100 par or liquidation value of defaulted preferred stock.

Recoveries, on average, decline as priority of claim declines, lending support to Moody's practice of assigning lower ratings to an issuer's subordinated debt. Generally speaking, a bond default is an issuer-level event that will in time affect all of the issuer's outstanding debt obligations. That is, the probability of an issuer defaulting on a particular debt issue is independent of the seniority of that issue relative to the company's other obligations. However, holding all else constant, severity considerations suggest that although default likelihood is the same across an issuer's debts, Moody's should reflect the greater expected losses for subordinated issues with lower ratings.

---

[1]See the December 1994 *Moody's Special Comment,* "Preferred Stock Dividend and Credit Risk" and the November 1996 *Moody's Special Comment,* "Defaulted Bank Loan Recoveries."

Defaulted Bond Price Volatility

The recovery estimates presented in Exhibit 5–14 are simple averages of defaulted bond prices. They approximate the most likely bond prices to arise from particular defaults, but they do not convey the range of possible outcomes. For example, while the estimated recovery for all subordinated bonds is $34 per $100 par amount, one of the underlying issues had a price of just $1 while another had a price of $107. In addition to the expected defaulted bond price, an important consideration is the volatility of defaulted bond prices.

Exhibit 5–16 of this chapter's appendix provides additional statistics describing the distribution of prices underlying Exhibit 5–14. The standard deviations for the senior secured bank loans, senior secured, senior unsecured, and subordinated defaulted public debt prices are $21, $26, $26, and $23, respectively. The relative sizes of these standard deviations indicate that defaulted subordinated debt prices are more tightly distributed about their sample mean than are either the prices of defaulted senior unsecured or senior secured debt. Although investors can expect defaulted subordinated debt to be worth less than defaulted senior unsecured debt, they can have greater confidence that the value of the subordinated issue will be close to its mean, $34. Senior unsecured debt prices, on the other hand, are more dispersed. Even though investors can expect a senior unsecured issue to be worth more upon bankruptcy than subordinated debt, there is greater uncertainty about the value of senior secured debt after bankruptcy than about the value of subordinated debt.

LOSS RATES

Moody's long-term debt ratings are statements about protection against credit loss. For a given economic environment, the credit loss one can expect to incur is higher for lower ratings. Conceptually, expected credit loss depends upon both the probability of a default occurring and the extent of the loss investors can expect to incur upon default. Previous sections have detailed Moody's estimation of the historical average probability of default associated with each rating category as well as average recovery rates for secured debt and unsecured debt of various seniority levels (the severity of loss is simply one minus the recovery rate). Multiplying Moody's estimates of the risk of default by our estimate of the severity of

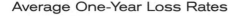

E X H I B I T   5–15

Average One-Year Loss Rates

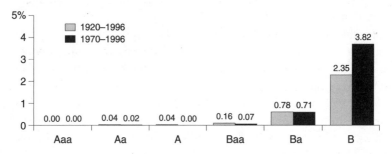

loss for senior unsecured debt yields estimates of the credit losses historically associated with each rating category. Exhibit 5–15 presents these estimates using both the 1920–1996 and 1970–1996 average default rates and
the 1989–1996 average recovery rate estimates for senior unsecured debt.
(The 48 percent recovery rate implies a 52 percent loss rate.)

Exhibit 5–15 indicates that expected credit loss increases dramatically as Moody's credit opinion slips from investment-grade to speculative-
grade. The safest speculative-grade rating category, Ba, has generated more
than four times the credit loss of the riskiest investment-grade rating category, Baa. That the expected credit loss increases as Moody's opinion
of credit quality decreases is an indication that Moody's ratings have
meaningfully differentiated securities on the basis of the credit risks
investors have faced over the last 77 years.

CONCLUSION

This study of corporate bond defaults extends Moody's previous research
to cover the period from 1920 through 1966. Moody's ratings and default
databases cover the credit experiences of over 14,000 U.S. and non-U.S.
corporate debt issuers. The long time horizon we have examined allows us
to correlate our ratings with the incidence and severity of default over many
business, interest rate, and other economic cycles. The results indicate that
over the last 77 years, the average risk of default has been higher for issuers
with lower-rated Moody's debt.

Moody's has also examined prices for defaulted debt as indicators of the recovery investors can expect to retrieve. The results reveal a tremendous intertemporal and cross-sectional volatility in defaulted bond prices that may be partially attributable to correlations with macroeconomic and business conditions as well as the supply of defaulted debt. It is important to note that investors in credit-risky debt must not only be compensated for the likelihood of default, but also for the volatility of default and recovery rates.

Our calculations of both the likelihood and severity of default permit the estimation of the default losses that have historically been associated with each of our ratings. That greater average default losses are associated with the lower rating categories is evidence that for the better part of this century Moody's has consistently differentiated debt on the basis of the credit risks facing investors.

EXHIBIT 5-16

Descriptive Statistics for Defaulted Bond Prices, 1989–1996

Seniority and Security	Number	Average	Standard Deviation
Senior Secured Bank Loans	59	$71.18	$21.09
Senior Secured Public Debt	57	63.45	26.21
Senior Unsecured Public Debt	156	47.54	26.29
Senior Subordinated Public Debt	166	38.28	24.74
Subordinated Public Debt	119	28.29	20.09
Junior Subordinated Public Debt	8	14.66	8.67
All Subordinated Public Debt	293	33.58	23.34
All Public Debt	506	$41.25	$26.55

One-Year Default Rates by Letter Rating Category, 1970–1996

Rating	1970	1971	1972	1973
Aaa	0.00%	0.00%	0.00%	0.00%
Aa	0.00	0.00	0.00	0.00
A	0.00	0.00	0.00	0.00
Baa	0.26	0.00	0.00	0.43
Ba	2.78	0.40	0.00	0.00
B	23.40	0.00	2.99	3.33
Investment-Grade	0.13%	0.00%	0.00%	0.22%
Speculative-Grade	8.46	1.02	1.39	1.15
All Corporates	2.55%	0.27%	0.34%	0.42%

Rating	1980	1981	1982	1983
Aaa	0.00%	0.00%	0.00%	0.00%
Aa	0.00	0.00	0.00	0.00
A	0.00	0.00	0.26	0.00
Baa	0.00	0.00	0.30	0.00
Ba	0.00	0.00	2.73	0.91
B	4.82	4.60	4.49	6.25
Investment-Grade	0.00%	0.00%	0.20%	0.00%
Speculative-Grade	1.60	0.71	3.53	3.81
All Corporates	0.33%	0.16%	1.00%	0.93%

Rating	1990	1991	1992	1993
Aaa	0.00%	0.00%	0.00%	0.00%
Aa	0.00	0.00	0.00	0.00
A	0.00	0.00	0.00	0.00
Baa	0.00	0.27	0.00	0.00
Ba	3.30	5.51	0.30	0.55
B	14.87	15.33	7.90	5.77
Investment-Grade	0.00%	0.06%	0.00%	0.00%
Speculative-Grade	9.18	10.67	4.62	3.49
All Corporates	3.19%	3.26%	1.22%	0.91%

1974	1975	1976	1977	1978	1979
0.00%	0.00%	0.00%	0.00%	0.00%	0.00%
0.00	0.00	0.00	0.00	0.00	0.00
0.00	0.00	0.00	0.00	0.00	0.00
0.00	0.00	0.00	0.27	0.00	0.00
0.00	0.96	0.94	0.50	1.05	0.48
9.38	6.06	0.00	3.28	5.26	0.00
0.00%	0.00%	0.00%	0.10%	0.00%	0.00%
1.22	2.02	0.82	1.28	1.72	0.41
0.26%	0.42%	0.17%	0.33%	0.33%	0.08%

1984	1985	1986	1987	1988	1989
0.00%	0.00%	0.00%	0.00%	0.00%	0.00%
0.00	0.00	0.00	0.00	0.00	0.58
0.00	0.00	0.00	0.00	0.00	0.00
0.36	0.00	1.32	0.00	0.00	0.59
0.83	1.75	1.75	2.47	1.43	2.96
6.67	7.48	11.08	5.42	6.31	9.21
0.09%	0.00%	0.31%	0.00%	0.00%	0.27%
3.31	3.66	5.25	3.77	3.67	5.99
0.89%	0.98%	1.74%	1.31%	1.36%	2.35%

1994	1995	1996
0.00%	0.00%	0.00%
0.00	0.00	0.00
0.00	0.00	0.00
0.00	0.00	0.00
0.24	0.68	0.00
3.83	4.81	1.54
0.00%	0.00%	0.00%
1.82	3.28	1.61
0.51%	0.99%	0.48%

E X H I B I T   5–18

One-Year Default Rates by Year and Numerically Modified Rating Category, 1983–1996

	1983	1984	1985	1986	1987	1988	1989
Aaa	0.00%	0.00%	0.00%	0.00%	0.00%	0.00%	0.00%
Aa1	0.00	0.00	0.00	0.00	0.00	0.00	0.00
Aa2	0.00	0.00	0.00	0.00	0.00	0.00	0.00
Aa3	0.00	0.00	0.00	0.00	0.00	0.00	1.36
A1	0.00	0.00	0.00	0.00	0.00	0.00	0.00
A2	0.00	0.00	0.00	0.00	0.00	0.00	0.00
A3	0.00	0.00	0.00	0.00	0.00	0.00	0.00
Baa1	0.00	0.00	0.00	0.00	0.00	0.00	0.00
Baa2	0.00	0.00	0.00	0.00	0.00	0.00	0.80
Baa3	0.00	1.06	0.00	4.82	0.00	0.00	1.06
Ba1	0.00	1.16	0.00	0.88	3.73	0.00	0.79
Ba2	0.00	1.61	1.63	1.20	0.94	0.00	1.79
Ba3	2.61	0.00	3.77	2.75	2.44	2.97	4.67
B1	0.00	5.67	4.26	6.35	4.86	4.35	6.33
B2	10.00	18.75	3.70	16.67	4.30	7.02	8.22
B3	18.46%	2.99%	14.14%	16.07%	7.35%	10.53%	18.84%

1990	1991	1992	1993	1994	1995	1996
0.00%	0.00%	0.00%	0.00%	0.00%	0.00%	0.00%
0.00	0.00	0.00	0.00	0.00	0.00	0.00
0.00	0.00	0.00	0.00	0.00	0.00	0.00
0.00	0.00	0.00	0.00	0.00	0.00	0.00
0.00	0.00	0.00	0.00	0.00	0.00	0.00
0.00	0.00	0.00	0.00	0.00	0.00	0.00
0.00	0.00	0.00	0.00	0.00	0.00	0.00
0.00	0.75	0.00	0.00	0.00	0.00	0.00
0.00	0.00	0.00	0.00	0.00	0.00	0.00
0.00	0.00	0.00	0.00	0.00	0.00	0.00
2.67	1.05	0.00	0.79	0.00	0.00	0.00
2.74	0.00	0.00	0.00	0.00	0.00	0.00
3.86	10.24	0.74	0.76	0.61	1.76	0.00
8.27	6.20	1.08	3.49	1.97	3.31	1.28
22.36	12.58	1.56	4.80	3.57	7.96	0.00
23.03%	29.59%	20.36%	10.69%	7.79%	4.37%	3.77%

E X H I B I T   5–19

Average Cumulative Default Rates from 1 to 20 Years (based on data from 1970 to 1996)

Rating	1	2	3	4	5	6	7	8	9	10
Aaa	0.00%	0.00%	0.00%	0.04%	0.13%	0.22%	0.33%	0.45%	0.59%	0.74%
Aa	0.03	0.05	0.10	0.25	0.40	0.57	0.73	0.91	1.04	1.13
A	0.01	0.07	0.22	0.39	0.57	0.76	0.96	1.18	1.44	1.73
Baa	0.12	0.39	0.76	1.27	1.71	2.21	2.79	3.36	3.99	4.61
Ba	1.36	3.77	6.29	8.88	11.57	13.87	15.69	17.55	19.23	20.94
B	7.27	13.87	19.94	25.03	29.45	33.26	36.34	39.01	41.45	44.31
Investment-Grade	0.05%	0.16%	0.34%	0.60%	0.84%	1.12%	1.42%	1.74%	2.08%	2.43%
Speculative-Grade	3.93	7.81	8.82	12.22	15.44	18.19	20.34	22.39	24.21	26.09
All Corporates	1.12%	2.22%	2.87%	3.86%	4.75%	5.55%	6.22%	6.87%	7.49%	8.10%

Rating	11	12	13	14	15	16	17	18	19	20
Aaa	0.91%	1.10%	1.31%	1.42%	1.55%	1.69%	1.86%	2.05%	2.05%	2.05%
Aa	1.23	1.35	1.49	1.80	1.90	2.00	2.23	2.37	2.52	2.71
A	2.03	2.35	2.65	2.89	3.22	3.60	3.98	4.37	4.82	5.08
Baa	5.29	6.01	6.70	7.42	8.18	8.99	9.82	10.60	11.25	11.78
Ba	22.84	24.87	26.97	28.68	30.34	32.14	33.59	34.91	36.32	37.81
B	46.07%	47.26%	48.30%	49.15%	50.19%	51.39%	52.85%	52.85%	52.85%	52.85%
Investment-Grade	2.82%	3.22%	3.62%	4.02%	4.45%	4.92%	5.41%	5.88%	6.32%	6.64%
Speculative-Grade	27.92	29.77	31.66	33.19	34.71	36.38	37.79	38.91	40.10	41.36
All Corporates	8.73%	9.38%	10.02%	10.60%	11.20%	11.85%	12.48%	13.05%	13.59%	14.05%

E X H I B I T   5–20

Average Cumulative Default Rates from 1 to 6 Years
(based on data from 1970 to 1996)

	1	2	3	4	5	6
Aaa	0.00%	0.00%	0.00%	0.06%	0.21%	0.29%
Aa1	0.00	0.00	0.00	0.28	0.28	0.49
Aa2	0.00	0.00	0.08	0.26	0.60	0.73
Aa3	0.08	0.13	0.25	0.38	0.55	0.76
A1	0.00	0.04	0.45	0.73	0.93	1.16
A2	0.00 ·	0.03	0.20	0.54	0.82	1.10
A3	0.00	0.18	0.35	0.49	0.57	0.76
Baa1	0.05	0.36	0.73	1.09	1.42	1.69
Baa2	0.05	0.25	0.32	1.00	1.59	2.31
Baa3	0.40	0.96	1.65	2.65	3.42	4.37
Ba1	0.78	2.51	4.39	7.14	9.62	12.55
Ba2	0.65	3.14	6.05	8.97	11.67	13.95
Ba3	2.93	7.84	13.19	18.22	22.84	26.75
B1	4.22	10.76	17.28	23.22	28.79	34.00
B2	7.71	14.51	21.50	27.15	30.91	34.53
B3	13.66%	22.58%	29.30%	34.40%	39.42%	42.80%

CHAPTER 6

Almost Everything You Wanted to Know about Recoveries on Defaulted Bonds*

Edward I. Altman

Vellore M. Kishore

INTRODUCTION

Perhaps the most critical analytical factor determining required yields on risky corporate debt is the expected default probability and the severity of default. Default rate calculations have long been a commonly documented statistic (e.g., Hickman 1958), with the modern era focusing on high yield *junk bond* default rates (Altman and Nammacher 1984). Bond rating agencies focus almost exclusively on the probability of default and the timeliness of payment of interest and principal in their assigned risk categories. There is, however, a fairly standard rule of thumb that lowers a firm's subordinate bond issues by two notches compared to its senior issues, if the senior bond is non-investment grade, and one notch if it is investment grade. This *ad-hoc* adjustment is more than likely based on the expectation that the junior bonds will recover less than the more senior issues. Lately, the rating agencies have explicitly incorporated severity expectations in their private placement and structured finance analytics (e.g., Standard & Poor's 1995).

The severity issue impacts the expected loss from defaults and has been highlighted both in traditional calculations (Altman and Nammacher

---

*Source: Reprinted with permission from *Financial Analysts Journal,* November/December 1996.
Copyright 1996, Association for Investment Management and Research, Charlottesville, VA.
All rights reserved.

1987) and in aging and mortality rate approaches (Altman 1989 and Moody's 1990). In addition to arithmetic and weighted average default losses, analysts have further refined the data to consider the critical element of debt seniority. Indeed, Standard & Poor's (1991), with Altman and Eberhart (1994), examine recovery rates on defaulted debt by seniority, both at the default date and also upon emergence from the distressed corporate restructuring (in most cases, upon emergence from Chapter 11 bankruptcy reorganization). They find that recovery rates and loss rates are a function of the debt's seniority, as expected, but also that realized returns during the bankruptcy reorganization period are more favorable for the senior secured and senior unsecured priorities than is the case for the more junior classes.[1]

The term *recovery* can refer to the price that bonds can be sold for at the time of default or the value at the end of the distressed reorganization period. In this study we examine the experience at the time of default.

Recovery rates for defaulted bonds now often share equal importance with default rate expectations and hence deserve increased scrutiny. This study continues that scrutiny by focusing on the industry affiliation of the defaulted debtor and, where possible, the seniority of the issue within each industry.

The reason why industry affiliation is likely to be important is that the enterprise's business activity will dictate the types of assets and the competitive conditions of the firms found within different industrial sectors. Assuming other factors such as leverage structure equal, the more tangible and liquid the assets, the higher their liquidation value and, hence, the greater the expected price of the debt securities in a distressed situation. In addition, if future earnings of the distressed entity in certain industries are more certain, the higher the enterprise value and its debt component will be. For example, the asset structure and regulatory environment of public utilities bodes for better recovery rates in this industry than in industries with little or no tangible assets that operate in a highly competitive environment. Since these factors need to be assessed in the pricing of debt securities throughout their duration—from original issuance and most definitely in a distressed situation—the actual recovery experience by industry and priority is likely to be useful and welcome information.

---

1. This is perhaps surprising because one would expect that the market would properly discount the junior bonds at default, and the postdefault return experience would be about the same for junior bonds versus those with senior priority—especially because the variance of returns is about the same for each class of bonds.

RECOVERY RATES BY SENIORITY

The ability to sell debt securities at nonsignificant values just after default has always been an attractive attribute of publicly held and traded bonds. Hence, average prices at default have been calculated for decades with the venerable overall conclusion of "40 cents on the dollar." (Hickman 1958). Indeed, this average overall recovery rate still persists today. We find (Altman and Kishore 1996) that the arithmetic average recovery rate on a sample of over 700 defaulting bond issues from 1978 to 1995 is $41.70.[2] The weighted average recovery rate by seniority over this period is shown in Exhibit 6–1. Seniority does play the expected important role with senior secured debt averaging about 58 percent of face value, senior unsecured 48 percent, senior subordinated 34 percent, and junior subordinated about 31 percent. Note that we interchange dollar and percent recoveries, since the average issue price is very close to par ($100).

Perhaps the finding that secured debt recovers only 58 percent of its face value is surprising. It should not be, however, if one considers that the assets providing collateral vary from factories, buildings, and rolling stock to less tangible guarantees. And, distressed firms assets' economic value will typically depreciate as its earning power erodes. In addition, because we observe that secured bonds earn over 20 percent per year during a two-year bankruptcy-reorganization period (Altman and Eberhart 1994), in order for the post-reorganization price to approximate par ($100), which it does, the price at default should be about what we observe. The relatively high returns observed for the reorganization period can perhaps be explained by the uncertainty that surrounds a Chapter 11 bankruptcy's result and its duration.

RECOVERY RATES BY INDUSTRY

We stratified our sample of 696 defaulted bond issues, which we were able to categorize by industrial sector, into three-digit Standard Industrial Classification (SIC) codes.[3] A firm is assigned a SIC code corresponding to the product group that accounts for the greatest value of its sales. The

---

2. Altman and Nammacher (1987) find that the average recovery rate on a much smaller sample covering the period 1974–1985, was essentially identical at $41.60. It should be noted that our defaulted bond sample includes bonds which were issued at both investment grade (25 percent) and noninvestment grade (75 percent).

3. These Standard Industry Codes (SICs) are from Standard & Poor's *Compustat* and Securities Data Company's compilations and may be different from industrial classifications found in other data sources. Indeed, Kahle and Walkling (1996) find nearly 80 percent of the four-digit

E X H I B I T   6–1

Weighted Average Recovery Rates on Defaulted Debt by Seniority per $100 Face Amount, 1978–1995

Default Year	Senior Secured		Senior Unsecured		Senior Subordinated		Subordinated		Discount & Zero Coupon	
	No.	($)	No.	($)	No.	($)	No.	($)	No.	($)
1995	5	$44.64	9	$50.50	17	$39.01	1	$20.00	1	$17.50
1994	5	48.66	8	51.14	5	19.81	3	37.04	1	5.00
1993	2	55.75	7	33.38	10	51.50	9	28.38	4	31.75
1992	15	59.85	8	35.61	17	58.20	22	49.13	5	19.82
1991	4	44.12	69	55.84	37	31.91	38	24.30	9	27.89
1990	12	32.18	31	29.02	38	25.01	24	18.83	11	15.63
1989	9	82.69	16	53.70	21	19.60	30	23.95	—	—
1988	13	67.96	19	41.99	10	30.70	20	35.27	—	—
1987	4	90.68	17	72.02	6	56.24	4	35.25	—	—
1986	8	48.32	11	37.72	7	35.20	30	33.39	—	—
1985	2	74.25	3	34.81	7	36.18	15	41.45	—	—
1984	4	53.42	1	50.50	2	65.88	7	44.68	—	—
1983	1	71.00	3	67.72	—	—	4	41.79	—	—
1982	—	—	16	39.31	—	—	4	32.91	—	—
1981	1	72.00	—	—	—	—	—	—	—	—
1980	—	—	2	26.71	—	—	2	16.63	—	—
1979	—	—	—	—	—	—	1	31.00	—	—
1978	—	—	1	60.00	—	—	—	—	—	—
Total/Average	85	$57.89	221	$47.65	177	$34.38	214	$31.34	31	$21.66
Median		51.04		40.65		27.86		31.96		18.66
Std. Dev.		$22.99		$26.71		$25.08		$22.42		$18.35

Source: Altman and Kishore (1996).

arithmetic and weighted average (by amount outstanding in each industry) and median recovery price at default for this categorization are shown in Exhibit 6–2. Note that while many of the sectors (14) include 20 or more observations, the majority of SIC codes (41) had under 20; several had less than 10 observations. We cannot feel very comfortable about summary

classifications (the most finely separated categories) are different between Compustat and the CRSP stock data files, with about 50 percent differences at the three-digit level and 36 percent at the two-digit level. Other sources of SIC codes are Lexis, *SEC Directory, Million Dollar Directory,* and the *Value Line Investment Survey.* Kahle and Walkling tested the differences between Compustat and CRSP and, in a controlled experiment, concluded that Compustat's SIC codes tend to "outperform" CRSP, despite the fact that Compustat does not provide historical information of industry affiliations of firms.

E X H I B I T   6–2

Recovery Price by Industry:
Defaulted Bonds, 1971–1995

Code	Industry	Number of Observations	Average Price	Weighted Price
492	Gas Utilities	25	$81.75	$90.42
150	Construction Contracting	1	71.00	71.00
616	Mortgage Bankers	4	67.60	49.80
290	Petroleum & Energy Products	23	67.29	84.18
730	Personal Business Services—Computer	3	64.87	70.90
491	Electric Utilities	29	62.57	51.43
560	Apparel & Accessory Stores	1	61.00	61.00
790	Recreation Services	10	59.00	60.70
280	Chemicals & Allied Products	6	58.00	61.63
470	Transportation Services	5	52.73	43.16
350	Machinery except Electric	20	50.54	49.95
300	Rubber & Plastic Products	6	49.96	56.55
500	Wholesale & Retail Trade	7	49.54	52.00
610	Finance Companies	3	49.50	53.91
380	Instruments & Related Products	2	49.38	49.30
770	Casino Hotels	11	48.91	44.22
609	Noncredit Institutions	12	48.75	54.76
520	Retail Trade	2	48.50	47.56
390	Manufacturing, Miscellaneous	6	47.40	51.18
260	Paper & Allied Products	6	46.83	44.37
270	Printing & Publishing	8	46.77	47.76
330	Steel & Metal Products	32	46.07	42.92
360	Electrical & Electronic Equipment	14	46.06	35.90
200	Food & Related— Manufacturing	18	45.28	37.40
208	Beverage Bottler	1	44.50	44.50
496	Steam & Air Conditioning Supply	2	44.00	43.99
420	Trucking	4	43.63	40.59
620	Financial Services	7	42.07	36.46
100	Mining	10	40.69	33.34
410	Bus Transit	1	40.50	40.50
998	Diversified Manufacturing	14	40.11	23.64
450	Air Transportation	39	39.50	41.25
483	Radio & TV Broadcasting	32	38.97	39.81
720	Laundry Service	2	38.50	39.31

(continued)

E X H I B I T   6-2

(concluded)

Code	Industry	Number of Observations	Average Price	Weighted Price
220	Textile & Mill Products	18	37.22	38.52
590	Retail, Miscellaneous	20	36.95	38.37
780	Movie Production	15	35.00	35.41
540	Food Stores	21	34.47	26.68
650	Real Estate	34	34.21	27.93
320	Building Materials	26	32.31	25.25
340	Fabricated Metal Products	10	32.15	24.62
130	Oil & Gas Drilling	33	31.54	31.91
580	Eating & Drinking Places	3	31.50	38.74
630	Insurance	10	31.48	35.17
530	Department Stores	37	30.69	27.99
533	Variety Stores	5	30.33	18.28
370	Transportation Equipment	8	30.28	40.77
602	Commercial Banks	22	29.33	21.60
510	Wholesale Trade-Nondurable Goods	3	28.08	34.15
800	Hospitals & Nursing Facilities	11	26.89	18.47
482	Telegraph & Related Communications	10	26.43	34.85
701	Lodging Places	11	26.09	22.12
230	Apparel & Related Products	13	23.96	26.13
570	Furniture, Furnishings & Equipment Stores	2	23.00	23.20
632	Hospitals & Medical Services	3	22.50	31.41
670	Investment Funds & Trusts	2	20.82	28.21
138	Oil & Gas Field Services	2	19.07	19.08
310	Leather Products	1	13.00	13.00
250	Furniture	3	9.50	11.59
603	Savings Institutions	6	9.25	19.68
240	Wood & Related Products	1	5.00	5.00

averages with so few datapoints, nor is it meaningful to present measures of variance. Still, we present this data for analysts to use, as is, or to combine SIC categories in some meaningful aggregations (as we now do).

We have combined a number of the 3-digit SIC codes to arrive at a reduced number of reasonable aggregations. Exhibit 6–3 shows the recovery price aggregated into 18 categories, most of which have over 20 observations, some with over 50. The highest arithmetic average recoveries came

E X H I B I T   6-3

Recovery Price by Industry: Defaulted Bonds, 1971–1995 (by 3–digit SIC code)

Industry	SIC Codes*	Number of Observations	Average Price	Weighted Price	Standard Deviation	Median Price
Public Utilities	490	56	$70.47	$65.48	$19.46	$79.07
Chemicals, Petroleum, Rubber & Plastic Products	280, 290, 300	35	62.73	80.39	27.10	71.88
Machinery, Instruments & Related Products	350, 360, 380	36	48.74	44.75	20.13	47.50
Services—Business & Personal	470, 720, 730	14	46.23	50.01	25.03	41.50
Food & Kindred Products	200	18	45.28	37.40	21.67	41.50
Wholesale & Retail Trade	500, 510, 520	12	44.00	48.90	22.14	37.32
Diversified Manufacturing	390, 998	20	42.29	29.49	24.98	33.88
Casino Hotel and Recreation	770, 790	21	40.15	39.74	25.66	28.00
Building Materials, Metals, and Fabricated Products	320, 330, 340	68	38.76	29.64	22.86	37.75
Transportation & Transportation Equipment	370, 410, 420, 450	52	38.42	41.12	27.98	37.13
Communication, Broadcasting, Movie Production, Printing & Publishing	270, 480, 780	65	37.08	39.34	20.79	34.50
Financial Institutions	600, 610, 620, 630, 670	66	35.69	35.44	25.72	32.15
Construction & Real Estate	150, 650	35	35.27	28.58	28.69	24.00
General Merchandise Stores	530, 540, 560, 570, 580, 590	89	33.16	29.35	20.47	30.00
Mining & Petroleum Drilling	100, 130	45	33.02	31.83	18.01	32.00
Textile & Apparel Products	220, 230	31	31.66	33.72	15.24	31.13
Wood, Paper and Leather Products	240, 250, 260, 310	11	29.77	24.30	24.38	18.25
Lodging, Hospitals & Nursing Facilities	700 through 800	22	26.49	19.61	22.65	16.00
Total		696	$41.00	$39.11	$25.56	$36.25

*For example, 490 includes 490 through 499; 280 includes 280 through 289; 700 includes 700 through 709.

from public utilities (70 percent) and chemical, petroleum, and related products (63 percent). These two sectors reversed themselves in terms of weighted (by the amount outstanding within each SIC code) average recoveries.[4] The difference in recovery rates of these two industrial aggregations compared to all the rest was quite large. (We will return to test these differences later after the discussion on seniority.) Next came heavy machinery

---

4. The relatively high price and size of Texaco's defaulting issues were primarily responsible for this reversal.

and electrical instruments, services, food, wholesale and retail trade, conglomerates, and casino hotel/recreation industries (all over 40 percent). The remaining industrial sectors, with the exception of lodging, hospital, and nursing facilities (26 percent) had recovery rates in the 30–40 percent range. Weighted average recoveries had similar results with a few exceptions. As noted above, chemicals and related products actually exceed utilities and the lowest category had recoveries of under 20 percent.

While it may appear that the remaining industrial categories listed in Exhibit 6–3 were fairly tightly clustered in the 30–40 percent recovery range, in reality there may be a large difference between recoveries in the high 40 percent range compared to the low 30 percent. Hence machinery, instruments and related products, services, and food product companies have recovered considerably more, for example, than retailers, drilling companies, and textile and apparel firms.[5]

We also list standard deviations of the average recovery rates in Exhibit 6–3 and find that most are in the 20–28 percent range. Interestingly, public utilities, which have the highest recovery rates, are among the lowest in terms of variance. Textile and apparel manufacturers and mining and petroleum drilling have both low average recoveries and relatively low variance. In general, the variability is quite high, relative to the mean, indicating that knowledge of specific issuer characteristics is still very important.

RECOVERY RATES BY SENIORITY WITHIN INDUSTRIES

While data on industry recovery rates are useful, we should be mindful of the seniority factor. Despite the small sample problem that comes from slicing data into ever finer categories, we do think it important to display recovery rates by seniority within industries. Exhibit 6–4 shows our 18-industry categorization for up to five seniority classes.[6] We observe the expected ordinal hierarchy in such industries as mining and petroleum drilling, chemicals, petroleum, rubber and plastics, building materials, metals and fabricated metals, diversified manufacturing, retail trade, and financial institutions.

---

5. We were somewhat surprised that services (personal and business) recovered over 46 percent of face value. This sector's sample size, however, was quite small with a few outliers.
6. While we do include discounted/zero coupon bonds in our compilation, this category is less meaningful since it can encompass several of the seniority classes, for example, senior subordinated or subordinated zero coupon bonds.

E X H I B I T   6–4

Recovery Price by Industry and Seniority
Defaulted Bonds, 1971–1995

Industry	Seniority	Number of Observations	Average Price	Weighted Price
Mining & Petroleum Drilling	Senior Secured	1	$71.00	$71.03
	Senior Unsecured	9	43.60	37.37
	Senior Subordinated	12	37.78	36.51
	Subordinated	21	25.41	27.48
	Discount & Zero Coupon	2	17.75	19.84
Construction & Real Estate	Senior Secured	1	40.00	40.00
	Senior Unsecured	12	41.91	39.16
	Senior Subordinated	10	37.31	24.59
	Subordinated	12	26.52	22.79
Food & Kindred Products	Senior Unsecured	6	54.42	48.27
	Senior Subordinated	6	31.00	36.22
	Subordinated	6	50.42	36.68
Textile & Apparel Products	Senior Unsecured	8	34.47	36.24
	Senior Subordinated	14	31.65	36.56
	Subordinated	6	28.25	24.80
	Discount & Zero Coupon	3	31.00	32.51
Wood, Paper and Leather Products & Publishing	Senior Unsecured	3	47.33	58.54
	Senior Subordinated	8	36.63	27.32
	Subordinated	5	44.33	47.14
	Discount & Zero Coupon	3	15.00	8.27
Chemicals, Petroleum, Rubber & Plastic Products	Senior Secured	6	75.04	89.17
	Senior Unsecured	16	71.91	81.71
	Senior Subordinated	7	63.07	77.81
	Subordinated	6	25.54	31.46
Building Materials, Metals, and Fabricated Products	Senior Secured	7	48.33	47.66
	Senior Unsecured	20	44.23	36.55
	Senior Subordinated	9	44.08	33.02
	Subordinated	28	35.39	31.83
	Discount & Zero Coupon	4	6.31	7.15
Machinery, Instruments & Related Products	Senior Unsecured	11	47.55	51.36
	Senior Subordinated	8	58.41	35.40
	Subordinated	15	44.75	41.60
	Discount & Zero Coupon	2	46.50	50.52
Diversified Manufacturing	Senior Unsecured	3	85.71	82.37
	Senior Subordinated	7	36.73	29.33
	Subordinated	10	33.16	21.58

(continued)

E X H I B I T   6–4

(concluded)

Industry	Seniority	Number of Observations	Average Price	Weighted Price
Transportation & Transportation Equipment	Senior Secured	14	55.72	58.12
	Senior Unsecured	22	30.83	36.28
	Senior Subordinated	8	45.81	48.02
	Subordinated	8	21.60	15.00
Services—Business & Personal	Senior Secured	6	56.61	54.37
	Senior Subordinated	6	35.18	47.96
	Subordinated	2	48.25	43.06
Communications, Broadcasting & Movie Production	Senior Secured	2	36.88	38.64
	Senior Unsecured	12	34.97	53.73
	Senior Subordinated	13	39.77	38.10
	Subordinated	21	33.16	35.56
	Discount & Zero Coupon	9	36.61	38.16
Public Utilities	Senior Secured	21	64.42	59.64
	Senior Unsecured	32	77.74	71.53
	Subordinated	2	44.00	43.99
	Discount & Zero Coupon	1	17.75	17.75
Wholesale & Retail Trade	Senior Unsecured	2	39.00	33.50
	Senior Subordinated	2	76.45	69.18
	Subordinated	7	37.88	47.17
	Discount & Zero Coupon	1	32.00	32.00
General Merchandise Stores	Senior Unsecured	26	44.55	45.59
	Senior Subordinated	27	36.37	30.20
	Subordinated	26	25.95	28.83
	Discount & Zero Coupon	10	13.67	10.18
Financial Institutions	Senior Secured	6	49.20	52.70
	Senior Unsecured	37	38.68	42.70
	Senior Subordinated	12	29.70	30.78
	Subordinated	11	24.81	21.28
Lodging, Hospitals & Nursing Facilities	Senior Unsecured	4	20.50	19.39
	Senior Subordinated	8	26.75	15.49
	Subordinated	9	28.08	18.63
	Discount & Zero Coupon	1	34.00	34.00
Casino Hotel & Recreation	Senior Secured	10	40.78	37.18
	Senior Unsecured	1	100.00	100.00
	Senior Subordinated	5	34.20	44.59
	Subordinated	4	26.13	26.22
	Discount & Zero Coupon	1	60.00	60.00
Total		696	$41.00	$39.11

There are, however, several industries where the expected hierarchy does not manifest itself. This is, no doubt, due to recoveries that are individual firm and issue dependent rather than seniority dependent. We have observed this before (Altman and Eberhart 1994) and when we restrict the sample only to firms that have *both* senior and subordinated issues, the expected hierarchy does indeed result. This again points toward an important conclusion: While industry categorization is a factor in recovery rates, the particular situation of each firm and its idiosyncratic characteristics, that is, earnings outlook, capital structure tranches, and the particular collateral, if any, will also determine recovery rates.

TESTING FOR STATISTICAL SIGNIFICANCE

As noted above, we observed that public utilities and chemicals, petroleum, and plastics manufacturers experienced much higher recoveries than did the rest of the industrial sectors. We also observed, in Exhibits 6–1 and 6–4, that senior bonds recover more than junior bonds. One might therefore try to explain the higher recoveries in certain industries by a greater preponderance of senior secured bonds or senior unsecured bonds in the higher recovery sectors. And, at first glance, it does appear in Exhibit 6–4 that, for example, public utilities had the vast majority of its bonds in the senior classes (53/56 = 95 percent). Chemicals, et al., had a lower senior priority ratio (63 percent) but was still higher than most, but not all, others.

We now test for the difference between average recovery rates of specific industries compared to all other sectors, holding the seniority of debt constant. For example, in Exhibit 6–5 we analyze the average recovery of senior secured public utilities (64.42 percent) versus all other senior secured (55.75 percent) defaults. The latter figure is taken from Exhibit 6–1, modified by removing public utilities from the other industries. We do the same test for the senior unsecured class (77.74 percent) versus all other senior unsecured defaults (42.56 percent).

Our results show the differences among public utilities and all other industries and among chemicals, petroleum, and plastics and all other groups are significantly different, with t-tests significant at the 0.01 or 0.05 levels. That is, the observed differences do not happen by chance and also they are not determined by seniority. We therefore conclude that it is the nature of the firms' assets, the industry's competitive structure, or other variables that explains differential recovery rates.

We have reported on some rather obvious large differences between individual industry/priority results and the combined data for all industries.

E X H I B I T   6–5

Significance Test for Selected Industry versus Aggregate Recovery Rates by Seniority

Industry Group(s)/Seniority	Industry Group(s)			Entire Sample*			
	N	Average Price	Standard Deviation	N	Average Price	Standard Deviation	t-Test
Public Utilities							
Senior Secured	21	$64.42	$14.03	64	$55.75	$25.17	1.98†
Senior Unsecured	32	77.74	18.06	189	42.56	24.89	9.59††
Chemicals, Petroleum, Rubber & Plastics							
Senior Secured	6	75.04	25.83	79	56.59	22.16	1.70†
Senior Unsecured	16	71.91	18.41	205	45.76	26.52	5.27††
Senior Subordinated	7	63.07	25.74	170	33.20	24.45	3.01††

*From Exhibit 6–1, excluding observations from the particular industrial groups(s) being tested.
†Significant at .05 level.
††Significant at .01 level.

The recovery comparison significance tests have been applied to every industry versus the entire sample, and between any two industries, but we do not report each and every comparison.

RECOVERY RATES BY SENIORITY AND ORIGINAL CREDIT RATING

A question that we are sometimes asked is whether an issue's original bond rating plays any role in the recovery rate, should the bond default. One might expect that since a bond issue is almost always noninvestment grade just prior to default,[7] its original rating should play no role in determining recoveries. On the other hand, if firms affiliated with certain industries have a greater preponderance of higher rated, senior secured and senior unsecured original debt, then one might expect higher recoveries. An obvious example of this would be public utilities; we have seen earlier that utilities do recover more than other sectors.

---

7. We observe (Altman and Kishore 1996) that about 6 percent of bonds that default had an investment-grade rating six months prior to default, but it is very rare for the bond to be investment grade just prior to default (perhaps in just two or three cases in the last 25 years).

Exhibit 6–6 shows the average recovery price for highly rated investment-grade original issues versus low rated noninvestment-grade issues. The results show clearly that original rating, at least in terms of the broad investment grade versus junk bond rating categories, has *no effect* on recoveries, once we account for seniority.[8] While this is perhaps consistent with intuition and expected values, it is counter to what we had observed when the original rating was not stratified by seniority.

Finally, we tested for the association between the size of an issue (face value), stratified by seniority, and the default recovery rate. We find absolutely no statistical association between size and recoveries.

CONCLUSION

This report has documented average recovery rates (i.e., prices) on defaulted bonds stratified by industry and also by seniority. When we aggregate by 3-digit SIC codes, we do observe great differences in a few sectors. However, the results show similar recoveries for a large number of industries. The original bond ratings of an issue have virtually no effect on recoveries, once we account for seniority.

We have not calculated default rates by industry which would require assembling new issue and cumulative totals of amounts outstanding stratified by the accepted definitions of industries. We intend to pursue this compilation in a subsequent study.

REFERENCES

Altman, E.I. (1989). "Measuring Corporate Bond Mortality and Performance." *The Journal of Finance*. September, pp. 909–22.

Altman, E.I. and Allan C. Eberhart (1994). "Do Seniority Provisions Protect Bondholders' Investments?" *Journal of Portfolio Management* 20, pp. 67–75.

Altman, E.I. and Scott Nammacher (1984). "The Default Rate Experience of High Yield Corporate Debt." *Financial Analysts Journal*. July/August, pp. 25–41.

Altman, E.I. and Scott Nammacher (1987). *Investing in Junk Bonds*. New York: John Wiley & Sons.

Altman, E.I. and Vellore M. Kishore (1996). "Defaults and Returns on High Yield Bonds: Analysis Through 1995." *NYU Salomon Center Special Report*.

---

8. Altman and Kishore (1996) show that the time it takes for an issue to default from its origination date also has no impact on the recovery rate at default.

E X H I B I T   6–6

Recovery Price by Seniority and Original Bond Rating, 1971–1995

Seniority	Rating	Number of Observations	Average Price	Weighted Price	Standard Deviation	Median Price
Senior Secured	Investment	16	$54.80	$48.58	$15.11	$55.82
Senior Secured	Noninvestment	58	56.42	56.82	24.93	50.50
Senior Unsecured	Investment	49	48.20	41.34	30.63	40.00
Senior Unsecured	Noninvestment	175	48.73	55.61	25.64	42.50
Senior Subordinated	Investment	26	32.74	37.26	20.43	29.75
Senior Subordinated	Noninvestment	136	39.93	35.01	25.67	32.00
Subordinated	Investment	63	31.89	33.97	18.75	30.00
Subordinated	Noninvestment	136	31.67	27.58	21.07	28.40
Discount & Zero Coupon	Investment	7	24.14	23.57	10.79	23.50
Discount & Zero Coupon	Noninvestment	30	24.42	17.21	19.14	19.90
Total		696	$41.00	$39.11	$25.56	$36.25

Hickman, W. Braddock (1958). *Corporate Bond Quality and Investor Experience.* Princeton University Press, Princeton, N.J.

Kahle, Kathleen and Ralph Walkling (1996). "The Impact of Industry Classification on Financial Research." Working Paper, Ohio State University, College of Business, February.

Moody's Special Reports (1990–1995). "Corporate Bond Defaults and Default Rates." *Moody's,* New York.

Standard & Poor's (1991). "Corporate Bond Defaults Study." *Credit Week.* September 16, pp. 1–5 and December 21, 1992.

Standard & Poor's (1995). *Structured Finance Ratings: Asset Backed Securities.* New York.

Moody's Rating Migration and Credit Quality Correlation, 1920–1996

Lea V. Carty

INTRODUCTION

Practitioners and academics alike have made great strides in the measurement and management of many financial risks including those attributable to interest rates, exchange rates, and market fluctuations. Noticeably absent from this list of financial risks is credit risk. The tremendous informational requirements and complexity of issuer-specific credit analysis combined with the difficulty of directly observing the price of credit risk has conspired to hinder progress in the theory and practice of credit risk management. Yet there is a real need to more precisely quantify credit exposures, particularly within a portfolio context, and investors are increasingly adapting variants of the theories and methodologies previously used to address other financial risks to credit risk. The new approaches are typically differentiated from previous credit risk management methodologies in that they require more detailed knowledge of the statistical characteristics of credit quality. One specific need is for a better understanding of the evolution, through time, of firm credit quality. This report begins to address this need by examining historical patterns in the movements and co-movements of Moody's ratings.

Changes in credit quality are of interest to investors for a variety of reasons. The accurate pricing of total return and default swaps, as well as of other credit derivatives, depends critically upon the distribution of the reference asset's future credit quality. The ability of a structured transaction to meet contractual payments may be dependent on the credit quality of an underlying pool of corporate debt issues. Loan indentures may offer a rated entity the option to repay a loan before maturity in the event of an upgrade. Finally, for a "total return"-oriented fixed-income investor, the movements and comovements of credit qualities are of critical importance in understanding the credit risk characteristics of his or her portfolio and the effects of prospective purchases or sales.

A factor critical to understanding the future distribution of the value of a credit-sensitive investment is the likelihood that a change in credit quality will occur. The rating transition matrices presented in this report describe various aspects of the probability of rating changes and defaults for corporate debt issuers for some or all of the last 77 years. A factor critical to understanding the future distribution of the value of a *portfolio* of credit-sensitive investments is the likelihood that changes in the credit quality of several issuers will occur jointly. We therefore present additional statistics—summarized in joint rating transition matrices—that describe the likelihood of various joint rating changes and defaults.

The first section of this report describes the database and methodology that underlie this research, as well as Moody's corporate bond default research. The second section gives an overview of the broad patterns rating changes have displayed over the past 77 years. The third section addresses the volatility and correlation of rating changes, while the final section summarizes broadly the report's findings and their implications for investors.

DATA AND METHODOLOGY

Moody's bases the results of its study on a proprietary database of ratings and defaults for industrial and transportation companies, utilities, financial institutions, and sovereigns that issued long-term debt to the public. Municipal debt issuers, structured finance transactions, and issuers with only short-term debt ratings are excluded. In total, the data cover the credit experiences of over 14,000 issuers that sold long-term debt publicly between 1919 and 1996. As of January 1, 1997, approximately 3,500 of those issuers held Moody's ratings. These issuers account for the bulk of the outstanding dollar amount of U.S. public long-term corporate debt and a substantial part of public issuance abroad.

As with Moody's special reports on long-term public debt defaults, the unit of study is the long-term, public corporate debt issuer, as opposed to either the par amount of debt or the number of debt issues. The rationale for this methodology is that Moody's intends its ratings to support credit decisions. Separately tabulating multiple issues or the par amounts of a single issuer would bias the results toward the default characteristics of issuers with multiple issues or large amounts of outstanding debt and would therefore be of less utility to an investor contemplating credits without these features. We have also omitted firms whose rated debt consists solely of issues backed by entities that are not members of the issuer's corporate family, since the ratings of such debt would reflect that support and not the credit quality of the issuing firm.

In order to count each legal entity separately, we track each issuer's actual, or implied, senior unsecured long-term debt rating. If the issuer has rated senior unsecured debt, we use that rating as the measure of the issuer's credit quality for as long as such obligations' ratings are outstanding. In cases where an issuer does not have senior unsecured debt, we estimate what this debt would likely be rated if it did exist. We derive the estimated senior unsecured rating from actual ratings assigned to an issuer's other rated debt by a simple notching algorithm intended to reflect observed ratings relationships. While correct on average, in any particular case the estimated senior unsecured ratings may differ from what Moody's would have actually rated a particular senior unsecured obligation. The estimated senior unsecured ratings have not been examined by Moody's analysts and benefit only indirectly from the full scope of analysis that underlies Moody's bond ratings.

We compiled the default histories used in this study from a variety of sources: our own Industrial, Railroad, and Public Utilities Manuals; reports of the National Quotation Service; various issues of *The Commercial and Financial Chronicle;* our library of financial reports; press releases; press clippings; internal memoranda; and records of analyst contact with rated issuers. We also examined documents from the Securities and Exchange Commission, The Dun & Bradstreet Corporation, the New York Stock Exchange, and the American Stock Exchange. The default database covers approximately 3,000 defaults by issuers both rated and unrated by Moody's.

Exhibit 7–1 details the number of firms included in our ratings database as of the start of each decade since 1920. The downward trend from 1920 through 1950 reflects the public bond market's retrenchment following the Great Depression and World War II, increasing financial intermediation, and consolidation in the railroad and utilities industries. Since 1950, however, the number of rated firms has increased steadily, with sharp increases over the 1980s and 1990s. The increase of the 1980s reflects, in part, the development of the junk bond market in the United States, which attracted a new set of issuers to the public bond market. The increase of the

E X H I B I T   7–1

Moody's-Rated Corporate Bond Issuers, 1920–1997

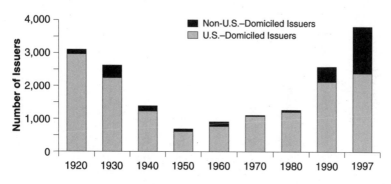

1990s, on the other hand, primarily reflects the growth of, and Moody's continued expansion into, non-U.S. markets. It was not until 1994 that Moody's again rated as many corporate issuers as it did in 1920.

Non-U.S. issuers comprised nearly as large a percentage of the Moody's rated universe in January of 1930 (15 percent) as they did in January of 1990 (18 percent). The portion of rated issuers domiciled outside of the United States hit a high in 1930 but trailed off to an all-time low in 1970. Since then, this fraction has grown significantly to higher than it has ever been in the past and stood at more than 35 percent as of the beginning of 1997. Before 1980, the non-U.S. issuers Moody's rated were predominantly those that tapped the U.S. bond market. In recent years, however, Moody's has extended ratings to many more issuers placing debt in non-U.S. markets.

Historically, the industrial cross section of U.S. bond issuers has shifted with broad patterns in the country's capital formation process. Consequently, the industrial composition of firms with Moody's-rated debt has also shifted. Exhibit 7–2 traces the industrial composition of Moody's-rated, corporate issuers from 1920 to the present. In the early part of the century, railroads absorbed the majority of the country's investment. As of 1920, more than half of the issuers Moody's rated were railroad companies. Since 1920, railroads have consolidated, so that by January 1997, the entire transportation industry comprised only 4 percent of Moody's-rated, corporate public debt issuers. On the other hand, industrials have expanded to represent 44 percent of the total number of rated firms from 14 percent in 1920. Since Moody's began rating bank debt in 1971, financial companies have expanded significantly to comprise more than 35 percent of the Moody's-rated universe at the start of 1997.

E X H I B I T   7–2

Industrial Composition of Issuers, 1920–1997

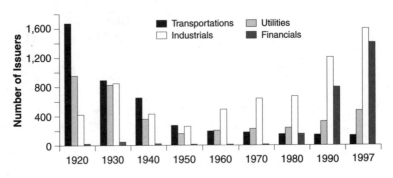

RATING MIGRATION

Trends in Corporate Credit Quality from 1920 through 1996

In order to measure general trends in the credit quality of the Moody's-rated corporate universe through time, we consider annual rating drift. To calculate annual rating drift we subtract from the total number of upward rating changes (weighted by the number of ratings changed per upgrade) per year, the total number of downward rating changes (similarly weighted) per year, and divide this difference by the number of nondefaulted issuers at risk of a rating change during the course of the year.[1] Rating drift summarizes the overall increase or decrease in the credit quality of the rated universe as a percentage of one rating grade per issuer.

We measure annual rating activity in this report by computing the sum of all upward and downward letter rating changes (again, weighted by the number of ratings changed) and dividing by the number of nondefaulted issuers at risk of a rating change during the course of the year. This measurement captures both the effects of multiple rating changes for a single issuer within a given year and the relative sizes of rating changes. In effect, it shows the pace at which ratings change, based on units of ratings changed per issuer.

---

1. The number of issuers at risk of a rating change during the course of the year is the number of nondefaulted issuers holding ratings at the start of the year less one-half of the number of issuers whose ratings were withdrawn during the course of the year. The adjustment for the issuers whose ratings were withdrawn reflects the assumption that, on average, such issuers were at risk of a rating revision for only one-half of one year.

Exhibit 7–3 details annual rating drift and activity from 1920 through 1996 and is based upon letter rating changes as opposed to changes of alphanumeric ratings. Moody's altered its long-term rating scale in April 1982. The traditional nine-tiered letter rating scale (Aaa, Aa, A, Baa, Ba, B, Caa, Ca, C) was expanded by attaching three numerical modifiers (1, 2, or 3, in order of increasing credit risk) to each of the ratings from Aa through B. The new alphanumeric rating system is comprised of 19 grades (Aaa, Aa1, Aa2, Aa3, A1, ...etc.). Because the alphanumeric ratings did not exist before April 1982, none of the statistics reported for these rating categories are based on pre-April 1982 ratings data. Statistics reported for the original letter rating scale are extended through the post-April 1982 period by collapsing the alphanumeric ratings into the original letter rating categories. For example, the Baa1, Baa2, and Baa3 ratings all would be considered Baa.

Since 1920, annual rating drift has averaged a negative 6 percent while annual rating activity has averaged 15 percent. The rating drift time series illustrates prolonged deteriorations (represented by negative values) in overall corporate credit quality during the depression of the 1930s and the 16-year period beginning in 1980. Annual rating drift averaged −24 percent during the 1930s and −0.9 percent during the eighties and the first half of the nineties, versus an average of just −0.1 percent for the period from 1940 to 1979. Annual rating drift was nonnegative in 1996 for the first time since 1975.

The negative average annual drift for the 1930s reflects the most severe economic contraction of this century, coupled with severe asset deflation. This combination put even highly creditworthy borrowers at considerable risk of default. The increased risk of default was reflected by an increase in the incidence and size of downgrades relative to upgrades.

The significant credit deterioration beginning in 1980 was the result of a slew of special events and an overall trend towards increased corporate leverage. The recession of 1982 proved to be the most severe of the post-World War II era. Sharply lower oil prices in the mid-1980s prompted large numbers of industrial and financial company downgrades. Concerns about problem loans in the banking system led to numerous downgrades in 1989, just one year before the onset of another recession.

Rating Change Magnitude

We define the magnitude of a rating change as the number of rating categories that a rating change spans. For example, an upgrade from Ba to Baa covers one letter rating category while a downgrade from Ba to Caa

E X H I B I T   7–3

Long-Term Rating Activity and Drift, 1920–1996*

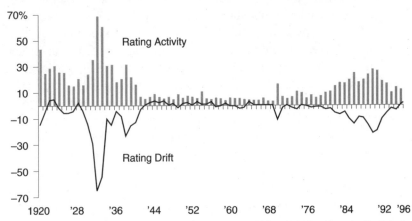

*Figures for 1982 are straight-line interpolations between 1981 and 1983. We use this interpolation because our algorithm for imply-
ing senior ratings artificially inflated the numbers of upgrades and downgrades during our 1982 adoption of numerically
modified ratings. For example, an issuer with subordinated debt rated Ba prior to 1982 has a senior implied rating of Baa.
If, upon adoption of the modified rating system, this issue comes in at the lower end of the Ba scale, say Ba3, then its senior
implied rating is now Ba1. This corresponds to the letter rating Ba. Hence our algorithm has artificially created a downgrade
from Baa to Ba even though there has been no rating revision. The actual numbers occurred in nearly the same ratio as those
presented here.

covers two categories. This same concept applies analogously to our
alphanumeric ratings. Exhibits 7–4 and 7–5 display the frequency of rating revisions by reflecting the magnitude of change for the entire period
spanned by our database.

Changes of smaller magnitude are relatively more frequent than are
large rating revisions. Rating changes of three ratings or more have
occurred historically only about 2 percent of the time. For the alphanumeric ratings, changes of four or more rating notches have also occurred
historically only about 2 percent of the time.

Rating Change Magnitude and Direction— Rating Transition Matrices

Unlike the charts on the next page, an average transition matrix is a concise representation not only of the size, but also the direction of typical rating changes. Exhibit 7–6 depicts an average rating transition matrix
defined for a one-year time horizon. Each row indicates the rating at the
beginning of a one-year time period. Each column corresponds to a rating,

E X H I B I T   7–4

Frequency of Letter Rating Changes of Various
Magnitudes, January 1920–March 1997

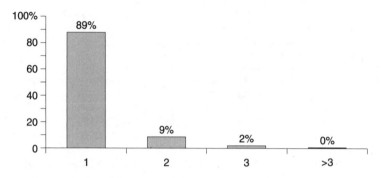

E X H I B I T   7–5

Frequency of Alphanumeric Rating Changes
of Various Magnitudes, April 1982–March 1997

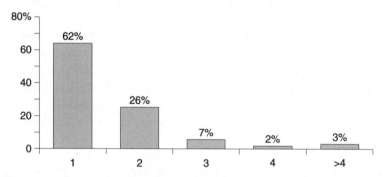

default, or withdrawn rating (WR) at the end of the one-year period. Each
cell entry, excluding the "Default" and "WR" columns, is the average fraction of issuers who held the row rating at the beginning of the time period
and the column rating or status at the end of the time period.

The upper left-hand corner, for example, indicates that on average
over the period from 1920 to the present, 88.32 percent of Aaa's have
remained at that level over the course of one year. The next percentage to
the right indicates that 6.15 percent of Aaa's have, on average, suffered a

E X H I B I T   7–6

Average One-Year Rating Transition Matrix, 1920–1996

				Rating To:					
		Aaa	**Aa**	**A**	**Baa**	**Ba**	**B**	**Caa–C**	**Default**	**WR**
Aaa	88.32%	6.15%	0.99%	0.23%	0.02%	0.00%	0.00%	0.00%	4.29%
Aa	1.21	86.76	5.76	0.66	0.16	0.02	0.00	0.06	5.36
A	0.07	2.30	86.09	4.67	0.63	0.10	0.02	0.12	5.99
Baa	0.03	0.24	3.87	82.52	4.68	0.61	0.06	0.28	7.71
Ba	0.01	0.08	0.39	4.61	79.03	4.96	0.41	1.11	9.39
B	0.00	0.04	0.13	0.60	5.79	76.33	3.08	3.49	10.53
Caa–C	0.00	0.02	0.04	0.34	1.26	5.29	71.87	12.41	8.78

(Rows labeled "Rating From:")

downgrade to Aa. Also, by way of example, the chart indicates that 2.30 percent of all A-rated companies enjoyed a net improvement of one letter rating (to Aa) by the end of any one-year period.[2]

The largest values in the transition matrix are along the diagonal, indicating that the most likely rating for an issuer at the end of a one-year time horizon is the rating with which the issuer started the period. Moving off of the diagonal, the values fall off very quickly as very large changes in credit quality over a one-year period are infrequent.

The patterns in the alphanumeric rating transition matrix in Exhibit 7–7 are roughly similar to those of the average one-year letter rating transition matrix. However, note that the estimated likelihood that an Aaa rating is maintained over the course of one year is just 84.64 percent versus an estimated 88.34 percent in Exhibit 7–6. Part of the reason for this difference is that the alphanumeric transition matrices are estimated on data available since April 1982, when Moody's adopted the current alphanumeric rating scale. From 1982 until just recently, there has been an overall trend towards decreasing credit quality as documented by Moody's rating drift statistics in Exhibit 7–3. Hence, while the average letter rating transition matrices incorporate the entire post-WW II to 1979 period of very low credit risk and volatility, the average alphanumeric rating transition matrices are estimated over a period characterized by historically high credit risk.

---

2. The increase in credit quality is net since a rating transition matrix is a snapshot of the evolution of the rating profile at a specific point in time. Therefore, it does not address the dynamics of how the hypothetical A-rated issuer arrived at the Aa rating one year later. It may well have been upgraded to Aaa and then downgraded to Aa between the beginning and end of the one-year period.

Additionally, the diagonal elements of Exhibit 7–7 are smaller than those of Exhibit 7–6. This is because the alphanumeric ratings represent a finer gradation of credit risk than the letter rating scale. Consequently, finer movements in credit quality that would not have been substantial enough to warrant an entire letter rating change can be registered by rating changes of one or two notches. Because finer changes in credit quality are being measured, more rating changes are registered and the average rating transition rates estimated in Exhibit 7–7 reflect the greater rating change volatility of the alphanumeric ratings.

Withdrawn Ratings

The withdrawn rating category (column heading "WR") in Exhibit 7–6 corresponds to cases where Moody's has withdrawn all of an issuer's ratings. The likelihood of a rating withdrawal generally increases as credit quality decreases. Exhibit 7–6 indicates that over a one-year time period, Aaa-rated issuers have an average 4.29 percent risk of rating withdrawal while B-rated issuers have more than double the risk, 10.53 percent. At least part of the reason for this pattern is that private debt markets are relatively more attractive for many of the smaller borrowers that generally carry lower ratings. Consequently, such issuers have been more likely to replace rated public bonds with unrated private debt.

The rationale for the withdrawal of all of a company's debt ratings could be important in the overall understanding of the credit dynamics implied by the rating transition matrices given above. For example, Moody's might withdraw a debt rating because the underlying issue has been retired. In this case, the withdrawn ratings simply reflect the issuer's exit from the public bond market and have no negative credit implications. On the other hand, in some cases, Moody's withdraws ratings because the information necessary to accurately rate the company's debt is not available. In such cases, it is conceivable that the withdrawn rating may correlate with increased credit risk.

In order to better understand the reasons why ratings are withdrawn, we examined Moody's corporate bond ratings database. Of the over 35,000 withdrawn long-term individual debt ratings considered, 92 percent were withdrawn because either an issue had matured or had been called. In the remaining 8 percent of cases, the reason for the withdrawn rating was not specified, or the rating withdrawal was associated with any of a variety of situations including conversions, mergers, defeasances, bankruptcies, or

E X H I B I T   7-7

Average, One-Year Alphanumeric Rating Transition Matrix, 1983–1996

	Rating To:								
	Aaa	**Aa1**	**Aa2**	**Aa3**	**A1**	**A2**	**A3**	**Baa1**	**Baa2**
Aaa	84.64%	5.53%	3.13%	0.67%	0.77%	0.36%	0.14%	0.00%	0.00%
Aa1	2.53	74.04	8.63	7.87	2.61	0.23	0.00	0.24	0.00
Aa2	0.61	2.54	76.97	9.15	4.30	1.15	0.73	0.21	0.00
Aa3	0.10	0.43	2.90	76.85	10.25	3.83	0.85	0.10	0.25
A1	0.04	0.10	0.65	4.45	78.75	7.25	2.93	0.70	0.22
A2	0.03	0.04	0.20	0.63	5.46	77.32	7.23	3.04	0.76
A3	0.03	0.11	0.00	0.20	1.53	8.56	71.59	6.47	3.68
Baa1	0.06	0.00	0.09	0.11	0.15	3.11	8.49	69.73	7.61
Baa2	0.00	0.12	0.16	0.15	0.14	0.93	3.58	7.49	69.65
Baa3	0.04	0.00	0.00	0.06	0.24	0.57	0.44	4.09	9.89
Ba1	0.11	0.00	0.00	0.00	0.16	0.10	0.62	0.84	2.77
Ba2	0.00	0.00	0.00	0.00	0.00	0.17	0.12	0.30	0.47
Ba3	0.00	0.03	0.03	0.00	0.00	0.21	0.13	0.13	0.20
B1	0.03	0.00	0.03	0.00	0.06	0.05	0.18	0.08	0.31
B2	0.00	0.00	0.08	0.00	0.15	0.00	0.06	0.15	0.11
B3	0.00	0.00	0.06	0.00	0.00	0.00	0.00	0.10	0.16
Caa–C	0.00%	0.00%	0.00%	0.00%	0.00%	0.00%	0.00%	0.00%	0.60%

Rating From: (row axis label)

the lack of sufficient information to accurately rate the debt. Of the 8 percent of all rating withdrawals that were not related to debt maturities, calls, or defaults[3], one-half were withdrawn for unspecified reasons and an additional 1 percent of the total number of withdrawals occurred for reasons that could be connected with negative credit developments (e.g., insufficient information to maintain the rating or an indenture amendment). In total, 95 percent of the rating withdrawals were not associated with any deterioration in credit quality. An additional 4 percent occurred for unspecified reasons and so may have been associated with a credit deterioration. However, this category also included cases in which the par amount of the obligation outstanding had fallen to such a low level that there was little or no trading or investor interest in the maintenance of the rating. In only 1 percent of the cases was a deterioration in credit quality likely.

The ratings examined in this report are not Moody's published individual debt ratings, but instead senior unsecured, or estimated senior unsecured, ratings for firms. The circumstances that led Moody's to withdraw

---

3. We do not consider withdrawals associated with a default in this analysis under the rationale that a default has already occurred in such cases, and the question of whether the withdrawn rating carries information about the future creditworthiness of the issuer is moot.

Baa3	Ba1	Ba2	Ba3	B1	B2	B3	Caa–C	Default	WR
0.00%	0.05%	0.00%	0.00%	0.00%	0.00%	0.00%	0.00%	0.00%	4.71%
0.00	0.12	0.00	0.00	0.00	0.00	0.00	0.00	0.00	3.74
0.00	0.00	0.00	0.07	0.07	0.00	0.00	0.00	0.00	4.20
0.22	0.00	0.05	0.12	0.00	0.00	0.00	0.00	0.00	4.06
0.18	0.37	0.37	0.07	0.17	0.00	0.00	0.00	0.00	3.76
0.28	0.20	0.13	0.13	0.03	0.07	0.00	0.03	0.00	4.42
1.43	0.45	0.18	0.26	0.41	0.04	0.00	0.00	0.00	5.06
3.03	0.95	0.38	0.45	0.62	0.12	0.00	0.00	0.06	5.05
7.41	1.89	0.40	0.68	0.40	0.47	0.29	0.00	0.06	6.20
64.87	6.53	2.94	1.90	0.89	0.31	0.07	0.13	0.52	6.52
6.12	68.60	4.49	3.75	0.76	1.27	0.91	0.11	0.81	8.59
2.22	7.23	66.67	5.59	1.25	3.85	1.60	0.24	0.68	9.62
0.77	2.31	4.59	69.25	2.45	5.69	2.41	0.49	2.69	8.62
0.39	0.33	2.42	5.88	70.45	1.48	4.88	0.90	4.04	8.48
0.00	0.23	1.95	3.42	5.35	62.02	7.30	2.53	8.67	7.99
0.18	0.21	0.29	1.37	4.52	2.28	64.57	3.84	13.36	9.05
0.60%	0.79%	0.00%	2.17%	2.14%	1.34%	2.54%	51.08%	28.33%	10.41%

ratings on all of a company's debts may be different from those that would lead Moody's to withdraw a rating on any particular debt. To explore this possibility, we looked at each withdrawn rating in Moody's database of senior unsecured, and estimated senior unsecured, rating histories. In 87 percent of the cases in which Moody's had withdrawn all of a company's debt ratings, the withdrawal was the result of debt maturity, call, conversion or other means consistent with the debts' indentures. Therefore, in only 13 percent of all cases were ratings withdrawn under circumstances that could be correlated with an increase in credit risk. In 9 percent of the cases, the reason for the rating withdrawal was unspecified. In the remaining 4 percent of the cases, ratings were withdrawn because of a lack of sufficient information. The increases in the percentages of rating withdrawals associated with either unspecified, and therefore possibly risky developments, or developments likely associated with a credit deterioration, indicates that the reasons that lead Moody's to withdraw a bond's rating are not necessarily the same as those that lead Moody's to withdraw all ratings on debt that a company may have outstanding.

An important use of rating transition data is in the modeling of the prices of credit sensitive securities. In many cases, an investor enters into a long-term agreement and would like to summarize the likely credit position of a counterparty at the end of the transaction. Because the withdrawn rating is most commonly associated with exit from the debt markets, such investors are interested in rating transition matrices that are estimated for rating histories that do not include rating withdrawals.

Because rating withdrawals are not directly related to credit risk, a transition matrix can be created that excludes such withdrawals without generating significant distortion. Such a matrix can be created by distributing the probability mass associated with rating withdrawals across the remaining categories on a probability weighted basis. Another approach, demonstrated in Exhibit 7–8, is to estimate rating transition matrices that are conditioned upon the issuer's rating remaining outstanding over the entire period spanned by the matrix. The two methodologies bear similar results.

Multiyear Rating Transition Matrices

We can define average rating transition matrices over a variety of time horizons. Exhibit 7–17 in this chapter's appendix includes average letter rating transition matrices similar to those previously shown, but defined over 2- through 10-year, and 15-year time horizons. Exhibit 7–18 of this chapter's appendix presents alphanumeric average rating transition matrices for 2- through 10-year time horizons. These transition matrices include rating withdrawal as a possible transition state. For those readers interested in estimating a transition matrix that does not include rating withdrawal as a state, a simple approximation can be obtained by distributing the probability associated with the rating withdrawal across the remaining ratings on a probability weighted basis. As mentioned in the previous section, because rating withdrawal is not directly related to credit deterioration, the error introduced by this technique is generally small.

Higher ratings are more likely to be maintained than are lower ratings over the 2- to 15-year time horizon presented in these matrices. The higher likelihood of ratings remaining unchanged for higher credit ratings indicates that the higher rating categories are not only associated with lower default risk (as indicated by the default transition rates posted in the "Default" column) but are also more stable.

Considering the matrices listed in Exhibit 7–17 of this chapter's appendix, one sees that for the Aa and A ratings, the frequency of net downgrades generally exceeds that of net upgrades. For any of the given time horizons, it is more likely for an issuer starting with one of these ratings to have a lower rating than a higher rating at the end of the period. For

E X H I B I T   7–8

Average One-Year Rating Transition Matrix, 1920–1996, (conditional upon no rating withdrawal)

	Aaa	Aa	A	Baa	Ba	B	Caa–C	Default
				Rating To:				
Aaa	92.18%	6.51%	1.04%	0.25%	0.02%	0.00%	0.00%	0.00%
Aa	1.29	91.62	6.11	0.70	0.18	0.03	0.00	0.07
A	0.08	2.50	91.36	5.11	0.69	0.11	0.02	0.14
Baa	0.04	0.27	4.22	89.16	5.25	0.68	0.07	0.31
Ba	0.02	0.09	0.44	5.11	87.08	5.57	0.46	1.25
B	0.00	0.04	0.14	0.69	6.52	85.20	3.54	3.87
Caa–C	0.00	0.02	0.04	0.37	1.45	6.00	78.30	13.81

(Rating From: rows, Rating To: columns)

issuers rated Baa that have not defaulted, however, this pattern is not as pronounced. Within a one-year horizon, Baa-rated issuers are only slightly more likely to be rated below Baa as above. As the time horizon covered by the transition matrix expands, Baa-rated issuers that have not defaulted are more likely to have a higher rating than lower until, after ten years, there is nearly two times as great a chance of having a single-A rating (11.71 percent) as there is of having a Ba rating (6.36 percent). Continuing down the credit spectrum, there is a relatively greater chance of a non-defaulted B-rated issuer enjoying a net upgrade than there is for a Ba-rated issuer. Caa- and-lower-rated issuers, however, tend to be too weak to make the uphill climb and tend to fall into default.

RATING TRANSITION RATE VOLATILITY AND CREDIT QUALITY CORRELATION

Rating Transition Rate Volatility

The rating transition matrices above summarize the average risk of changes in credit quality over a specified time period. However, the risk of a change of credit quality varies from year to year as unexpected changes in macro-economic variables and the business environment in general alter firms' credit outlooks. Consequently, there is volatility in rating transition rates from year to year. The average rating transition matrices reported above are calculated over as many as 77 years; they smooth over variations in the year-to-year rating transition rates caused by fluctuating macroeconomic and business conditions. To investigate rating transition rate volatility, we have, by way of example, expanded the average, one-year, A to Baa transition rate into its 77 constituent observations—one for each year since 1920 as shown in Exhibit 7–9. The gray bars indicate years for which the annual growth rate of real U.S. gross domestic product was negative, hinting at downgrade risk countercyclicality—that is, economic contractions seem to be associated with greater downgrade risk.

As presented in the A row, Baa column of Exhibit 7–8, the average fraction of issuers downgraded from A to Baa over the course of one year is 5.11 percent. However, in three different years during the long period of very low default risk, extending from WW II to the 1970s (1942, 1944, and 1956), no issuer (with an A, or estimated A, senior unsecured debt rating) experienced this downgrade. At the height of the Great Depression in 1932, 32 percent of A-rated issuers were downgraded to Baa.

Statistically, the median value of 3.68 percent is a more insightful measure of the center of the distribution of A to Baa transitions (shown in Exhibit 7–10), than is the mean. Exhibit 7–10 reveals that the annual risk of downgrade from A to Baa is concentrated in the 0% to 10% range, but that substantially larger fractions have not been uncommon historically. The frequency distribution of this rating transition rate is truncated on the left at zero and has a long right-hand tail. Consequently, reliance on the mean and standard deviation statistics to describe the distribution's center and dispersion is questionable.

The standard deviation of the transition rates pictured on page 133, 5.33 percent, coupled with the assumption that rating transition rates are normally distributed generates negative transition rates at the 90 percent level of confidence. Specifically, a 90 percent confidence interval for the average transition rate, 5.11 percent, is (−1.73 percent, 11.94 percent). Considering the data directly, approximately 90 percent of the observations (69 of the 77) lie between 0.56 percent on the low side and 16.44 percent on the high side. This indicates that not only are A to Baa transition rates below 0.56 percent relatively rare, but that transition rates greater than 11.94 percent are not rare. This highlights the limitations of the mean and standard deviation in describing the distribution of transition rates.

The asymmetry of the A to Baa transition rate is not unique. Exhibit 7–19 of this chapter's appendix provides selected summary statistics describing the distributions of all of the one-year transition rates. The medians listed in that table can be compared with the average values presented in Exhibit 7–8. The averages presented there may be used in conjunction with the standard deviation and the 5 percent and 95 percentiles to gain a better understanding of the asymmetry of each one-year transition rate's distribution.

E X H I B I T   7–9

Yearly Fraction of Issuers Downgraded from A to Baa

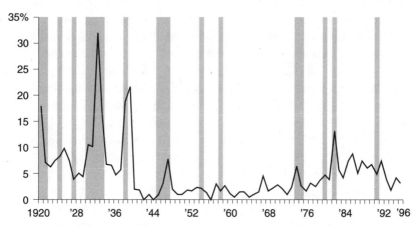

Note: Gray bars indicate years of negative growth in real U.S. GDP.

E X H I B I T   7–10

Histogram of Yearly A to Baa Rating Transition Rates, 1920–1996

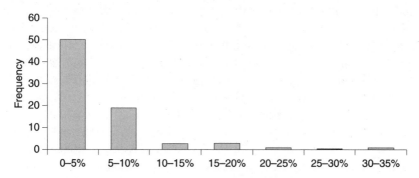

Credit Quality Correlation

Differences in the outlooks for firms' credit risks arise as conditions in firms' factor and output markets, and macroeconomic and regulatory environments adjust. For example, Exhibit 7–9 highlights the sensitivity to economic growth of the risk of downgrade for A-rated issuers. Because operating conditions adjust dynamically and movement in any one macroeconomic variable may affect several issuers, the credit ratings of different obligors are likely to be linked and therefore to move together. In this section, we examine some of the evidence ratings provide on the existence of credit quality correlation and also provide some indication of their economic importance to the understanding of the portfolio characteristics of credit risk.

To examine the question of whether credit quality is correlated across firms, we first examine the patterns in the co-movements of ratings that we would expect to see if credit quality were not correlated. We then examine actual rating co-movements in our database of rating histories. Finally, we compare the two results to answer the question of whether the credit qualities of different firms are likely to be correlated or not.

Consider, for example, two issuers with Baa-rated senior unsecured debt. Historically, over the course of one year, Baa-rated issuers have maintained the same rating, moved to another rating category, or defaulted with the probabilities reported in the Baa row of the one-year transition matrix in Exhibit 7–8. Because there are eight possible transitions (seven different rating groupings + default) for each of the two issuers, there are a total of 64 (8×8) possible credit quality combinations for the two issuers at the end of one year. If we impose the assumption that the credit qualities of these issuers are uncorrelated, the likelihoods of each possible credit quality combination for the two issuers at the end of one year are easily calculated. They are simply the products of the likelihoods of each issuer making the specified transitions. For example, the probability of the first Baa-rated issuer moving to the A rating over a one-year time horizon is estimated to be 4.22 percent (the Baa–A entry of Exhibit 7–8). The probability of the second Baa-rated issuer moving to the Ba rating over a one-year time horizon is estimated to be 5.25 percent (the Baa–Ba entry of Exhibit 7–8). Assuming no credit quality correlation, the likelihood of the first issuer's rating changing to A *and* the second issuer's rating changing to Ba over the course of one year is simply the product of these two likelihoods, 0.22 percent. If we perform this calculation for each of the 64 possible rating combinations, we obtain a matrix describing the joint probability distribution of rating migrations for the portfolio of two issuers at the end of one year. These are detailed in Exhibit 7–11.

Each cell entry of Exhibit 7–11 is an estimate of the likelihood that the first Baa-rated issuer will move to the corresponding row rating *and* the second issuer will move to the corresponding column rating. The first row of numbers represents the sum of each column of probabilities and sums to our likelihood estimate that a Baa-rated issuer will move to the corresponding column rating over the course of one year (the Baa row of the

E X H I B I T   7–11

Joint Rating Transition Matrix Assuming No Credit Quality Correlation

		Second Issuer's End-of-Period Rating							
		Aaa	Aa	A	Baa	Ba	B	Caa–C	Default
		0.04%	0.27%	4.22%	89.16%	5.25%	0.68%	0.07%	0.31%
	Aaa	0.04%	0.00%	0.00%	0.00%	0.03%	0.00%	0.00%	0.00%	0.00%
	Aa	0.27	0.00	0.00	0.01	0.24	0.01	0.00	0.00	0.00
First Issuer's End-of-Period Rating	A	4.22	0.00	0.01	0.18	3.76	0.22	0.03	0.00	0.01
	Baa	89.16	0.03	0.24	3.76	79.49	4.68	0.61	0.06	0.28
	Ba	5.25	0.00	0.01	0.22	4.68	0.28	0.04	0.00	0.02
	B	0.68	0.00	0.00	0.03	0.61	0.04	0.00	0.00	0.00
	Caa–C	0.07	0.00	0.00	0.00	0.06	0.00	0.00	0.00	0.00
	Default	0.31%	0.00%	0.00%	0.01%	0.28%	0.02%	0.00%	0.00%	0.00%

Note: Two initially Baa-rated issuers. Based on data available since 1920.

one-year rating transition matrix of Exhibit 7–8).[4] Similarly, the first column of numbers represents the sum of each row of probabilities and also sums to our likelihood estimate that a Baa-rated issuer will move to the corresponding row rating over the course of one year. The 64 interior cells of the joint rating transition matrix in Exhibit 7–11 sum to 100 percent. They completely describe the probabilities associated with the range of possible joint rating outcomes at the end of one year for the two Baa-rated issuers under the assumption that their credit qualities are not correlated. The most likely outcome for the two initially Baa-rated issuers at the end of one year is that they both remain at the Baa rating. The likelihood of this outcome is estimated at 79.49 percent (the entry in the Baa row and the Baa column of Exhibit 7–11). The next most likely outcome is for one issuer to be downgraded to Ba while the other remains at Baa, 4.68 percent. This can happen in either of two ways: The first issuer could be the one downgraded, while the second maintains its Baa rating (this likelihood is given in the Ba row, Ba column cell of Exhibit 7–11) or vice versa (the Baa row, Ba column cell). There is an estimated 0.00 percent risk that both issuers default by the end of one year.

---

4. The columns of this matrix, as reported here, do not all sum exactly to the corresponding entry of the first row because of the roundoff error associated with reporting only four decimal points of accuracy.

We derived Exhibit 7–11 under the assumption of no credit quality correlation. We obtain evidence about the true nature of credit quality correlation by comparing these results with those we obtain directly from our database of rating histories.

In Exhibit 7–12 we directly estimate an empirical joint rating transition matrix without imposing the assumption of no correlation. To do this, we formed a dataset of all possible pairs of Baa-rated issuers as of the start of each year since 1920 and then examined the ratings combinations of those pairs at the end of each one-year period. The relative frequency of the actual historically observed ratings co-movements for each pair of issuers are estimates of the joint migration probabilities. These are presented in Exhibit 7–12.

The first row and the first column of numbers in Exhibit 7–12 are the same as those of Exhibit 7–11 and give the "stand-alone" likelihood of each issuer moving to each rating category. Each cell entry gives an estimate of the probability that, of a pair of Baa-rated issuers, the first will move to the row rating while the second will move to the column rating. For example, the entry in the Aa row and Baa column is 0.21 percent, indicating that there is an estimated 0.21 percent chance that the first issuer will move to Aa and that the second will remain at Baa.

A comparison of Exhibit 7–11 with Exhibit 7–12 provides evidence that the credit qualities of these two Baa-rated issuers are positively correlated. Positive credit quality correlation between the two Baa-rated issuers would imply that if one issuer improves in credit quality over the course of one year, the other issuer would be more likely also to improve in credit quality. Similarly, if one issuer deteriorates in credit quality, the other issuer would be more likely also to deteriorate in credit quality. The shaded cells in the upper left hand quadrants of Exhibits 7–11 and 7–12 correspond to the probabilities that both issuers will experience an improvement in their credit ratings. The shaded cells in the lower right hand quadrants correspond to the probabilities that both issuers will experience a deterioration in their credit ratings. If the credit quality of the Baa-rated obligors is positively correlated, then the total likelihood that both obligors' ratings improve (the sum of the shaded cells in the upper left-hand corner) or deteriorate (the sum of the shaded cells in the lower right-hand corner) should be larger than those calculated under the assumption of no correlation. The total likelihood of an upgrade for both issuers under the assumption of no correlation is 0.21 percent, versus the 0.42 percent actually observed. The total likelihood of downgrades or default for both issuers under the assumption of no correlation is 0.40 percent, versus the 0.97 percent actually observed

E X H I B I T   7–12

Empirical Joint Rating Transition Matrix

		Second Issuer's End-of-Period Rating							
		Aaa	Aa	A	Baa	Ba	B	Caa–C	Default
		0.04%	0.27%	4.22%	89.16%	5.25%	0.68%	0.07%	0.31%
First Issuer's End-of-Period Rating	Aaa 0.04%	0.00%	0.00%	0.00%	0.03%	0.00%	0.00%	0.00%	0.00%
	Aa 0.27	0.00	0.00	0.03	0.21	0.03	0.00	0.00	0.00
	A 4.22	0.00	0.03	0.36	3.46	0.31	0.04	0.00	0.02
	Baa 89.16	0.03	0.21	3.46	80.50	4.14	0.52	0.05	0.25
	Ba 5.25	0.00	0.03	0.31	4.14	0.63	0.10	0.01	0.04
	B 0.68	0.00	0.00	0.04	0.52	0.10	0.02	0.00	0.01
	Caa–C 0.07	0.00	0.00	0.00	0.05	0.01	0.00	0.00	0.00
	Default 0.31%	0.00%	0.00%	0.02%	0.25%	0.04%	0.01%	0.00%	0.00%

Note: Two initially Baa-rated issuers. Based on data available since 1920.

The joint rating transition matrix derived under the assumption of no credit quality correlation and the empirical joint rating transition matrix, together with the issuer counts used to generate them, can be combined in a more rigorous statistical test of the assumption of no credit quality correlation.[5] Under this test, we can reject the hypothesis of no credit quality correlation at the 1 percent level of confidence.

The discussion above reveals evidence of credit quality correlation for Baa-rated issuers over the better part of this century. It does not, however, address variations in this outcome across different combinations of rating categories, industries, geographies, or time periods, nor does it provide an indication of the economic impact of such correlation. In the following sections, we provide some indicative calculations that more directly quantify the effects of the credit quality correlation explored above and provide an example of how correlations may vary across rating categories, industries, geographies, and the period considered.

The Impact of Credit Quality Correlation

The correlation of credit quality movements has implications for the credit risk characteristics of portfolios of credit exposures. In general, the higher the correlation, the greater the volatility of a portfolio's value that is attributable to credit risk. Exhibits 7–11 and 7–12 yield evidence of positive

---

5. We used Pearson's Chi-square statistic to test the hypothesis of no credit quality correlation.

credit quality correlation for Baa-rated obligors. It is of interest to determine how meaningful this correlation is. Towards that end, we consider one measure of the volatility of a portfolio's value—the standard deviation.[6] We also consider a hypothetical portfolio consisting of two similar obligations: Baa-rated, 7.5 percent bonds with 20 years remaining to maturity.[7] We estimate the values of these securities at the end of a one-year time horizon under each possible change in credit quality.[8] Exhibit 7–13 presents these valuations. If a 7.5 percent bond were upgraded to A, for example, we estimate that the note's value would climb to $102.06 (the figure on the row corresponding to the Baa-rated note, under the A column).

A portfolio consisting of two of these bonds can then be easily valued under each possible joint credit outcome. For example, if one bond experienced an upgrade to Aa, we estimate its value would climb to $104.26. If the other bond were downgraded to Ba, we estimate its value would be $81.18. The portfolio's value would then be $185.44 ($104.26 + $81.18).

Under the assumption of no credit quality correlation, the expected value and standard deviation of the portfolio's value may be calculated using the probabilities given in the joint rating transition matrix estimated under the assumption of no credit quality correlation (see Exhibit 7–11). However, we need not impose the assumption of no credit quality correlation between these bonds. We can reestimate the expected value and standard deviation of the portfolio's value without imposing any assumptions about how credit quality moves by instead using the probabilities reported in the empirical joint rating transition matrix instead (see Exhibit 7–12). Exhibit 7–14 presents the results of these calculations.

The positive credit quality correlation manifests itself as an increase in the standard deviation (risk) of the portfolio's future value from $8.12 under the assumption of no credit quality correlation to $8.43, a 3.8 percent increase. The greater standard deviation implies more variability, or risk, in the distribution of the portfolio's future value.

---

6. The standard deviation is only one of many possible measures of portfolio risk (volatility). We examine it here not because we feel that it is the most appropriate measure but because its wide usage promotes easy understanding.
7. We consider debt of similar characteristics here in order to focus attention on the effects of credit quality correlation.
8. We estimate these values by discounting the bonds' remaining promised cash flows along a forward, zero coupon spot yield curve for that bond's rating. The valuation calculation is not central to this discussion and so we do not comment on it in detail here.

E X H I B I T   7–13

Estimated Bond Values at the End of One Year

Rating at Start of Year	Debt Description	Rating/Status at End of Year							
		Aaa	Aa	A	Baa	Ba	B	Caa–C	Default
Baa	7.5%, 20-Year Bond	$104.96	$104.26	$102.06	$100.31	$81.18	$75.47	$58.59	$44.00

E X H I B I T   7–14

Mean and Standard Deviation of Portfolio Value

	Expected Value	Standard Deviation
Without Correlation	$198.04	$8.12
With Correlation	198.04	8.43

The difference between the standard deviation calculated using historical credit quality correlations and that calculated under the assumption of no credit quality correlation increases with the number of exposures. In the example in Exhibit 7–14, if we were to include another similar bond, the difference between the standard deviation as calculated with and without correlation climbs to 7.5 percent. After adding 40 exposures, the standard deviation as calculated with correlation is double that calculated without correlation.

Industrial and Geographic Considerations for Credit Quality Correlations

The ambient business environment, including capital market conditions, regulatory considerations, and economic growth are likely to contribute to the credit quality correlation highlighted by the empirical joint rating transition matrix in Exhibit 7–12. However, prevailing business conditions vary across countries, industries, and time. For these reasons, the correlation of credit qualities can be expected to also vary across industries, geographies, and time. Rather than explore the gamut of possible rating and joint rating transition matrices presented by industrial, geographic, and temporal segmentations, we present a sample calculation that suggests that these factors are, in fact, important determinants of the rating and joint rating migrations.

To explore industry- and geography-specific credit quality correlation further, we have appealed to patterns in ratings movements between debt issuers of different industries and geographies. Proceeding as in the previous sections, we have estimated a joint rating transition matrix for two issuers, except this time we chose one A-rated European financial company and one A-rated U.S. industrial company (see Exhibit 7–15). These results have been obtained from ratings data available since January 1990.

As in the discussion of the previous section, the first row of numbers in Exhibit 7–15 represents the sum of each column and hence, the stand alone likelihood of a U.S. industrial issuer's (estimated) senior unsecured rating migrating to each other rating category or to default. We estimate that an A-rated U.S. industrial will maintain that rating over the course of one year with about 94.33 percent probability. The first column of numbers represents the sum of each row and so presents the stand alone likelihood of an A-rated European financial issuer's (estimated) senior unsecured rating migrating to each other rating category or to default. Note that these values differ from those of the A-rated U.S. industrial.

At first glance, the evidence in favor of a credit quality correlation between A-rated U.S. industrials and A-rated European financials does not appear to be as strong as the evidence considered earlier for all Baa-rated issuers. Based on the assumption that the credit qualities of these firms are uncorrelated, the total probability of joint upgrade comes to four basis points, while the total risk of joint downgrade amounts to 23 basis points. Exhibit 7–15 reveals that the historically observed probability of joint rating upgrade also amounts to four basis points, while that observed for joint downgrade climbs slightly to 27 basis points.

To quantify the effects of any possible correlation in these data, consider a portfolio of two A-rated bonds—one issued by a U.S. industrial firm and one issued by a European financial firm. For the sake of simplicity, assume that the terms of these bonds are the same as those of the previous section. We can then reconstruct the calculations of that section using the same bond and portfolio valuations, but replacing the Baa–Baa one-year, joint rating transition matrix with the joint rating transition matrix presented in Exhibit 7–15. The results are presented in Exhibit 7–16.

E X H I B I T   7–15

Empirical Joint Rating Transition Matrix

A-rated U.S. Industrial Issuer

		Aaa	Aa	A	Baa	Ba	B	Caa–C	Default
		0.07%	1.46%	94.33%	3.89%	0.25%	0.00%	0.00%	0.00%
	Aaa	0.00%	0.00%	0.00%	0.00%	0.00%	0.00%	0.00%	0.00%	0.00%
A-rated Euro. Financial Issuer	Aa	2.29	0.00	0.04	2.15	0.09	0.01	0.00	0.00	0.00
	A	92.13	0.06	1.34	86.96	3.54	0.23	0.00	0.00	0.00
	Baa	5.57	0.00	0.08	5.22	0.26	0.01	0.00	0.00	0.00
	Ba	0.00	0.00	0.00	0.00	0.00	0.00	0.00	0.00	0.00
	B	0.00	0.00	0.00	0.00	0.00	0.00	0.00	0.00	0.00
	Caa–C	0.00	0.00	0.00	0.00	0.00	0.00	0.00	0.00	0.00
	Default	0.00%	0.00%	0.00%	0.00%	0.00%	0.00%	0.00%	0.00%	0.00%

Note: One A-rated European financial issuer and one A-rated U.S. industrial issuer used.

E X H I B I T   7–16

Mean and Standard Deviation of Portfolio Value

	Expected Value	Standard Deviation
Without Correlation	$203.99	$1.56
With Correlation	203.99	1.55

Note: One A-rated U.S. industrial and one A-rated European financial used.

Using the rating and joint rating migration patterns documented in Exhibit 7–15, the expected value of this portfolio climbs to $203.99. This is as expected since we have effectively upgraded both bonds in the previous example from Baa to A. The standard deviation in both cases falls considerably. This is due, in part, to the increase in ratings from Baa to A. However, it is also because we have estimated these joint rating transition matrices over the period from 1990 to the present, during which there have been few situations in which either a U.S. industrial or a European financial with an A rating has suffered a large downgrade.

The relative difference in the portfolios' risk, as measured by the standard deviation, is very small in absolute value and suggests a slight negative correlation (thereby reducing the portfolio standard deviation in the case with correlation). This small degree of correlation between these two very different companies hints at the importance of industrial and geographic considerations when estimating the effects of credit quality correlations.

CONCLUSION

This study of corporate rating drift, defaults, and correlations expands the scope of Moody's previous research in this area and extends it to cover the period from 1920 through the present. Moody's ratings and default data-bases now cover the credit experiences of over 14,000 U.S. and non-U.S. corporate debt issuers. The long time horizon examined allows us to study rating migration patterns over a variety of business, interest rate, and other economic cycles.

The results indicate that not only are Moody's higher ratings associated with a lower incidence of default, but they are also more stable in the sense that they are generally less likely than are lower rating categories to be revised over any time period from 1 to 15 years.

Moody's has also examined the variability of rating transition rates. The distribution of rating transition rates is necessarily asymmetric, and there is evidence suggesting that the distribution is affected by macroeconomic factors. That macroeconomic variables may affect the credit quality of many borrowers, in turn suggests that different issuers' credit qualities may be linked. A statistical test rejected the hypothesis that the credit qualities of Baa-rated issuers is not correlated at the 99 percent level of confidence, providing additional evidence of credit quality correlation.

The impact of credit quality correlation was explored by examining the increase in risk, as measured by the standard deviation of a portfolio's distribution of future values, between the case of no credit quality correlation and the case where it is correlated to the extent suggested by Moody's database of historical rating changes and defaults. The results suggest that such correlation is an important feature for those wishing to understand the credit risk characteristics of credit portfolios. Finally, we performed simple indicative calculations suggesting that credit quality correlations are, in part, determined by factors specific to both the issuer's industry and geographic domain.

APPENDIX TO CHAPTER 7

Exhibit 7-17

Average Letter Rating Transition Matrices for 2 through 10- and 15-Year Time Horizons

Two-Year Average Rating Transition Matrix, 1920–1995

		Aaa	Aa	A	Baa	Ba	B	Caa–C	Default	WR
					Rating To:					
Rating From:	**Aaa**	79.70%	9.51%	2.01%	0.45%	0.15%	0.01%	0.00%	0.00%	8.16%
	Aa	2.00	76.26	9.50	1.43	0.42	0.03	0.02	0.16	10.18
	A	0.10	3.77	75.79	7.17	1.28	0.22	0.04	0.28	11.34
	Baa	0.05	0.42	6.42	69.73	6.71	1.29	0.12	0.73	14.53
	Ba	0.03	0.14	0.74	7.50	63.73	7.06	0.81	2.37	17.62
	B	0.00	0.05	0.23	1.18	8.63	60.42	3.95	6.32	19.22
	Caa–C	0.00%	0.02%	0.03%	0.77%	2.07%	6.97%	56.11%	18.11%	15.92%

Three-Year Average Rating Transition Matrix, 1920–1994

		Aaa	Aa	A	Baa	Ba	B	Caa–C	Default	WR
					Rating To:					
Rating From:	**Aaa**	72.27%	12.33%	2.89%	0.66%	0.32%	0.02%	0.00%	0.03%	11.48%
	Aa	2.65	67.47	12.47	2.17	0.65	0.08	0.02	0.25	14.25
	A	0.15	4.88	67.66	8.63	1.84	0.38	0.06	0.53	15.87
	Baa	0.06	0.61	8.19	60.24	7.63	1.69	0.21	1.23	20.14
	Ba	0.04	0.19	1.22	9.16	52.22	7.99	1.09	3.56	24.52
	B	0.01	0.07	0.32	1.66	10.04	48.37	4.11	8.84	26.58
	Caa–C	0.00%	0.00%	0.02%	0.82%	3.06%	7.97%	44.74%	22.17%	21.23%

Four-Year Average Rating Transition Matrix, 1920–1993

		Aaa	Aa	A	Baa	Ba	B	Caa–C	Default	WR
					Rating To:					
Rating From:	**Aaa**	66.18%	13.91%	3.68%	0.79%	0.46%	0.07%	0.00%	0.08%	14.82%
	Aa	3.07	60.24	14.52	2.85	0.94	0.14	0.02	0.40	17.81
	A	0.18	5.54	61.07	9.65	2.28	0.49	0.07	0.82	19.91
	Baa	0.07	0.76	9.30	52.93	7.95	1.95	0.28	1.79	24.95
	Ba	0.04	0.24	1.63	9.95	43.41	8.26	1.19	4.81	30.47
	B	0.01	0.09	0.39	2.15	10.45	39.06	3.89	11.12	32.84
	Caa–C	0.00%	0.00%	0.02%	1.31%	3.40%	8.04%	36.26%	25.54%	25.44%

E x h i b i t 7–17

(continued)

Five-Year Average Rating Transition Matrix, 1920–1992

				Rating To:					
Rating From:		Aaa	Aa	A	Baa	Ba	B	Caa–C	Default	WR
	Aaa	60.78%	15.21%	4.33%	0.96%	0.49%	0.09%	0.03%	0.14%	17.96%
	Aa	3.43	54.14	15.93	3.42	1.16	0.20	0.02	0.58	21.12
	A	0.20	5.85	55.74	10.34	2.58	0.69	0.08	1.08	23.43
	Baa	0.09	0.92	10.01	47.06	8.03	2.00	0.32	2.28	29.28
	Ba	0.04	0.26	1.92	10.40	36.48	8.09	1.29	5.90	35.62
	B	0.02	0.09	0.48	2.41	10.25	32.12	3.53	12.91	38.19
	Caa–C	0.00%	0.00%	0.02%	1.57%	4.03%	7.77%	29.60%	27.98%	29.04%

Six-Year Average Rating Transition Matrix, 1920–1991

				Rating To:					
Rating From:		Aaa	Aa	A	Baa	Ba	B	Caa–C	Default	WR
	Aaa	56.03%	16.24%	4.97%	1.12%	0.58%	0.09%	0.03%	0.21%	20.72%
	Aa	3.74	48.82	17.00	3.93	1.40	0.24	0.03	0.78	24.06
	A	0.21	6.05	51.35	10.67	2.88	0.84	0.10	1.31	26.59
	Baa	0.10	1.04	10.52	42.42	7.79	2.09	0.32	2.75	32.98
	Ba	0.05	0.26	2.13	10.64	31.00	7.73	1.32	6.89	39.98
	B	0.02	0.07	0.64	2.42	9.81	26.73	3.15	14.43	42.73
	Caa–C	0.00%	0.00%	0.00%	2.01%	3.72%	7.44%	24.82%	30.17%	31.84%

Seven-Year Average Rating Transition Matrix, 1920–1990

				Rating To:					
Rating From:		Aaa	Aa	A	Baa	Ba	B	Caa–C	Default	WR
	Aaa	51.82%	17.14%	5.30%	1.44%	0.61%	0.13%	0.01%	0.27%	23.28%
	Aa	4.01	44.24	17.82	4.28	1.62	0.30	0.03	0.97	26.72
	A	0.23	6.13	47.55	10.77	3.08	0.94	0.13	1.54	29.63
	Baa	0.07	1.14	10.88	38.74	7.36	2.12	0.32	3.20	36.17
	Ba	0.06	0.26	2.36	10.55	26.66	7.35	1.34	7.69	43.74
	B	0.03	0.06	0.73	2.34	9.28	22.47	2.77	15.81	46.50
	Caa–C	0.00%	0.00%	0.00%	2.50%	2.89%	7.05%	21.13%	31.97%	34.46%

Eight-Year Average Rating Transition Matrix, 1920–1989

				Rating To:					
Rating From:		Aaa	Aa	A	Baa	Ba	B	Caa–C	Default	WR
	Aaa	48.19%	17.90%	5.60%	1.62%	0.71%	0.14%	0.01%	0.38%	25.45%
	Aa	4.22	40.36	18.64	4.43	1.80	0.40	0.05	1.16	28.94
	A	0.25	6.28	44.28	10.92	3.17	1.00	0.16	1.76	32.17
	Baa	0.06	1.23	11.22	35.58	6.95	2.08	0.32	3.64	38.92
	Ba	0.07	0.25	2.62	10.51	23.12	6.98	1.29	8.50	46.66
	B	0.03	0.07	0.86	2.40	8.82	19.03	2.52	16.89	49.39
	Caa–C	0.00%	0.02%	0.00%	2.54%	2.52%	6.53%	18.53%	33.87%	36.00%

E x h i b i t   7–17

(concluded)

Nine-Year Average Rating Transition Matrix, 1920–1988

				Rating To:					
	Aaa	**Aa**	**A**	**Baa**	**Ba**	**B**	**Caa–C**	**Default**	**WR**
Aaa	44.96%	18.39%	5.95%	1.84%	0.70%	0.15%	0.01%	0.50%	27.50%
Aa	4.35	36.93	19.27	4.64	1.98	0.50	0.08	1.30	30.96
A	0.27	6.44	41.43	11.03	3.20	1.06	0.18	1.99	34.41
Baa	0.07	1.27	11.56	32.79	6.62	2.08	0.31	4.04	41.26
Ba	0.07	0.29	2.81	10.38	20.05	6.58	1.28	9.16	49.37
B	0.03	0.08	0.85	2.60	8.27	16.28	2.36	17.71	51.82
Caa–C	0.00%	0.02%	0.00%	2.33%	2.94%	5.39%	16.10%	35.63%	37.60%

Rating From: (left axis label)

10-Year Average Rating Transition Matrix, 1920–1987

				Rating To:					
	Aaa	**Aa**	**A**	**Baa**	**Ba**	**B**	**Caa–C**	**Default**	**WR**
Aaa	41.57%	19.00%	6.09%	2.11%	0.77%	0.19%	0.02%	0.64%	29.62%
Aa	4.48	33.35	19.84	4.88	2.21	0.59	0.13	1.45	33.08
A	0.30	6.52	38.62	11.07	3.28	1.10	0.20	2.24	36.65
Baa	0.08	1.33	11.71	30.00	6.36	2.05	0.30	4.41	43.76
Ba	0.07	0.32	3.00	10.13	17.06	6.08	1.26	9.91	52.18
B	0.02	0.06	0.81	2.74	7.78	13.75	2.10	18.62	54.11
Caa–C	0.00%	0.02%	0.00%	2.12%	3.21%	5.06%	13.50%	36.92%	39.17%

Rating From: (left axis label)

15-Year Rating Transition Matrix, 1920–1996

				Rating To:					
	Aaa	**Aa**	**A**	**Baa**	**Ba**	**B**	**Caa–C**	**Default**	**WR**
Aaa	32.12%	20.88%	8.10%	2.70%	1.23%	0.31%	0.00%	1.11%	33.55%
Aa	4.39	24.10	20.38	6.18	3.07	0.84	0.28	2.13	38.64
A	0.36	6.69	31.07	11.15	3.37	1.05	0.22	3.23	42.86
Baa	0.09	1.34	12.43	22.71	5.26	1.79	0.31	5.69	50.39
Ba	0.04	0.38	3.71	8.97	10.62	4.49	0.97	12.27	58.56
B	0.03	0.05	0.65	4.00	4.99	7.88	1.56	20.98	59.87
Caa–C	0.00%	0.02%	1.17%	1.02%	3.46%	4.03%	7.11%	41.11%	42.09%

Rating From: (left axis label)

EXHIBIT 7–18

Average Alphanumeric Rating Transition Matrices for 2- through 10-Year Time Horizons

2-Year Average Rating Transition Matrix, 1983–1995

Rating From:	Rating To: Aaa	Aa1	Aa2	Aa3	A1	A2	A3	Baa1	Baa2
Aaa	72.7%	8.1%	5.2%	2.3%	0.9%	1.0%	0.2%	0.0%	0.0%
Aa1	3.8	53.7	13.5	11.9	5.7	1.7	0.4	0.3	0.0
Aa2	1.2	4.6	58.4	13.8	6.7	4.0	1.6	0.9	0.2
Aa3	0.2	0.9	4.0	58.6	16.6	6.7	2.4	0.8	0.4
A1	0.1	0.2	1.6	7.6	62.4	11.1	4.6	1.7	0.8
A2	0.1	0.1	0.2	1.5	8.3	59.9	11.6	4.5	2.0
A3	0.1	0.1	0.1	0.5	3.3	13.2	51.6	9.7	5.7
Baa1	0.1	0.0	0.3	0.3	0.9	6.1	11.5	49.0	10.6
Baa2	0.1	0.3	0.2	0.3	0.7	2.2	6.5	9.9	50.0
Baa3	0.0	0.0	0.1	0.1	0.4	0.9	2.0	7.4	13.3
Ba1	0.2	0.0	0.0	0.0	0.2	0.5	1.1	1.3	5.1
Ba2	0.0	0.0	0.1	0.0	0.0	0.3	0.3	0.9	1.5
Ba3	0.0	0.1	0.0	0.1	0.0	0.2	0.2	0.5	0.4
B1	0.0	0.0	0.1	0.0	0.1	0.2	0.2	0.2	0.5
B2	0.0	0.0	0.1	0.0	0.3	0.1	0.1	0.2	0.2
B3	0.0	0.0	0.0	0.0	0.0	0.0	0.0	0.1	0.2
Caa–C	0.0%	0.0%	0.0%	0.0%	0.0%	0.0%	0.0%	0.8%	0.0%

3-Year Average Rating Transition Matrix, 1983–1994

Rating From:	Rating To: Aaa	Aa1	Aa2	Aa3	A1	A2	A3	Baa1	Baa2
Aaa	62.9%	9.5%	6.8%	3.4%	0.8%	1.5%	0.4%	0.0%	0.0%
Aa1	4.5	40.2	14.8	12.5	9.6	2.6	0.8	1.1	0.1
Aa2	1.6	5.4	44.8	16.1	9.0	5.9	2.6	1.6	0.6
Aa3	0.5	1.2	4.5	45.7	18.4	9.3	3.6	1.5	0.7
A1	0.3	0.3	2.0	9.2	51.0	12.3	5.6	2.4	1.7
A2	0.0	0.1	0.2	1.9	10.0	47.3	13.9	5.1	3.3
A3	0.1	0.1	0.1	1.1	4.1	15.5	39.3	11.0	6.2
Baa1	0.1	0.0	0.5	0.3	1.5	7.0	14.7	37.3	11.0
Baa2	0.1	0.4	0.2	0.5	1.3	3.3	6.6	10.1	39.3
Baa3	0.1	0.0	0.1	0.1	0.5	1.7	2.7	9.1	14.8
Ba1	0.2	0.0	0.0	0.0	0.2	1.2	1.5	1.9	6.8
Ba2	0.0	0.0	0.1	0.0	0.1	0.4	0.8	1.1	1.6
Ba3	0.0	0.1	0.0	0.1	0.0	0.3	0.4	0.7	0.9
B1	0.1	0.0	0.2	0.0	0.1	0.1	0.2	0.6	0.7
B2	0.0	0.0	0.1	0.1	0.1	0.1	0.1	0.2	0.2
B3	0.0	0.0	0.0	0.0	0.0	0.0	0.3	0.3	0.4
Caa–C	0.0%	0.0%	0.0%	0.0%	0.0%	0.0%	0.0%	0.0%	0.7%

Baa3	Ba1	Ba2	Ba3	B1	B2	B3	Caa–C	Default	WR
0.0%	0.3%	0.0%	0.0%	0.0%	0.0%	0.1%	0.0%	0.0%	9.2%
0.3	0.7	0.0	0.0	0.0	0.0	0.0	0.0	0.0	8.1
0.0	0.0	0.0	0.1	0.1	0.0	0.0	0.1	0.0	8.4
0.4	0.2	0.2	0.4	0.1	0.0	0.0	0.0	0.0	8.3
0.4	0.3	0.4	0.4	0.5	0.0	0.0	0.0	0.0	7.7
0.8	0.7	0.3	0.4	0.3	0.2	0.0	0.1	0.0	9.1
2.7	0.9	0.3	0.8	0.3	0.1	0.1	0.0	0.2	10.3
4.8	1.9	0.7	1.3	0.8	0.5	0.1	0.2	0.3	10.5
9.2	3.8	0.9	1.2	0.8	0.8	0.6	0.1	0.2	12.4
44.4	7.6	3.7	1.9	2.5	0.9	0.3	0.4	1.1	12.9
8.6	46.0	6.3	5.2	1.2	2.1	1.5	0.5	2.3	17.8
3.0	10.2	43.7	7.6	2.1	5.7	2.5	0.7	3.0	18.4
1.0	3.9	6.0	47.4	3.9	7.6	3.9	0.8	6.7	17.2
0.8	1.2	3.7	6.4	50.1	2.4	6.8	1.2	9.7	16.2
0.4	0.8	2.3	6.6	6.6	40.1	9.5	3.0	15.1	14.5
0.2	0.9	0.6	2.6	6.8	2.9	41.9	4.1	21.5	18.5
2.4%	0.2%	0.0%	1.9%	2.8%	2.2%	2.8%	32.0%	33.9%	21.0%

Baa3	Ba1	Ba2	Ba3	B1	B2	B3	Caa–C	Default	WR
0.0%	0.6%	0.0%	0.0%	0.0%	0.0%	0.1%	0.0%	0.0%	13.8%
0.6	0.7	0.0	0.0	0.0	0.0	0.0	0.0	0.0	12.5
0.0	0.0	0.0	0.2	0.1	0.0	0.0	0.1	0.1	12.0
0.6	0.4	0.2	0.5	0.2	0.0	0.0	0.0	0.1	12.6
1.0	0.2	0.5	0.4	0.7	0.1	0.2	0.2	0.4	11.7
1.4	0.9	0.6	0.6	0.3	0.2	0.0	0.1	0.2	13.9
3.1	1.4	0.7	1.3	0.4	0.4	0.0	0.0	0.4	14.8
5.4	2.1	0.7	1.6	1.0	0.7	0.3	0.3	0.7	15.0
9.9	3.8	1.1	1.8	1.0	1.0	0.8	0.3	0.3	18.2
32.3	7.6	3.7	2.7	2.7	0.4	0.6	0.5	1.8	18.7
9.4	31.7	6.3	5.8	1.8	2.7	1.5	0.6	3.7	24.7
4.2	10.2	29.6	8.6	2.2	5.6	2.7	1.2	5.4	26.2
0.8	4.6	6.8	32.5	4.6	7.6	4.3	0.8	10.4	25.2
1.0	1.8	3.5	6.0	36.7	3.4	7.1	0.9	14.1	23.6
1.1	1.4	2.8	5.4	7.7	26.3	8.9	3.1	21.1	21.4
0.5	0.5	1.1	2.9	7.4	2.4	28.0	3.9	26.2	26.2
0.9%	0.0%	0.3%	3.4%	4.2%	1.5%	2.8%	22.1%	36.3%	27.6%

E X H I B I T   7–18

(continued)

4-Year Average Rating Transition Matrix, 1983–1994

	Rating To :								
	Aaa	**Aa1**	**Aa2**	**Aa3**	**A1**	**A2**	**A3**	**Baa1**	**Baa2**
Aaa	54.9%	10.3%	7.5%	3.8%	2.2%	1.5%	0.5%	0.0%	0.0%
Aa1	4.7	32.4	13.3	13.1	11.7	3.4	1.3	1.5	0.7
Aa2	1.6	5.2	36.6	16.3	9.6	7.0	3.6	2.5	0.7
Aa3	0.7	1.1	4.7	38.9	17.5	10.7	3.9	2.4	0.9
A1	0.3	0.4	2.1	9.6	43.5	12.8	6.4	3.0	1.6
A2	0.0	0.2	0.1	2.2	10.3	40.0	14.6	5.8	3.8
A3	0.1	0.1	0.1	1.7	4.1	16.6	32.3	10.0	6.7
Baa1	0.0	0.0	0.5	0.3	2.5	7.0	14.9	30.8	10.5
Baa2	0.1	0.4	0.3	0.6	1.4	4.0	6.4	10.6	34.2
Baa3	0.2	0.0	0.1	0.1	0.5	2.0	4.0	8.6	14.6
Ba1	0.2	0.0	0.1	0.1	0.2	1.3	1.5	2.5	7.4
Ba2	0.0	0.1	0.0	0.0	0.2	0.7	0.8	1.3	2.2
Ba3	0.0	0.1	0.0	0.1	0.1	0.4	0.3	0.4	1.0
B1	0.1	0.1	0.2	0.0	0.2	0.1	0.4	0.4	1.1
B2	0.0	0.0	0.0	0.2	0.1	0.1	0.2	0.3	0.2
B3	0.1	0.0	0.0	0.0	0.0	0.0	0.5	0.5	0.4
Caa–C	0.0%	0.0%	0.0%	0.0%	0.0%	0.0%	0.0%	1.4%	0.0%

(Rating From: shown along the left margin)

5-Year Average Rating Transition Matrix, 1983–1992

	Rating To :								
	Aaa	**Aa1**	**Aa2**	**Aa3**	**A1**	**A2**	**A3**	**Baa1**	**Baa2**
Aaa	48.8%	9.9%	8.0%	4.0%	3.3%	1.4%	0.8%	0.3%	0.0%
Aa1	4.7	28.3	11.8	14.1	9.6	3.5	2.6	3.0	1.2
Aa2	1.4	4.5	31.4	16.7	9.8	7.6	3.9	2.7	1.0
Aa3	0.7	1.1	5.1	33.6	17.6	11.1	4.5	2.8	0.9
A1	0.4	0.3	2.0	9.5	39.5	13.7	6.2	3.3	1.8
A2	0.0	0.2	0.1	2.1	10.1	35.9	14.5	6.3	4.0
A3	0.1	0.1	0.2	1.7	4.7	16.2	28.7	9.3	6.8
Baa1	0.0	0.0	0.5	0.3	2.8	6.9	14.7	27.1	10.1
Baa2	0.2	0.4	0.3	0.8	1.2	3.9	6.7	10.8	30.7
Baa3	0.3	0.0	0.1	0.1	0.8	2.2	4.0	8.4	14.6
Ba1	0.1	0.0	0.1	0.1	0.3	1.2	1.5	3.0	7.6
Ba2	0.0	0.1	0.2	0.0	0.4	0.7	0.9	1.2	2.4
Ba3	0.0	0.1	0.0	0.1	0.1	0.3	0.2	0.5	0.7
B1	0.1	0.1	0.3	0.0	0.2	0.2	0.8	0.1	0.7
B2	0.1	0.0	0.0	0.2	0.0	0.2	0.3	0.2	0.2
B3	0.1	0.0	0.0	0.0	0.0	0.1	0.7	0.7	0.4
Caa–C	0.0%	0.0%	0.0%	0.0%	0.0%	0.0%	0.0%	1.4%	0.0%

(Rating From: shown along the left margin)

Baa3	Ba1	Ba2	Ba3	B1	B2	B3	Caa–C	Default	WR
0.0%	0.4%	0.0%	0.1%	0.1%	0.0%	0.1%	0.0%	0.1%	18.4%
0.2	0.3	0.0	0.0	0.2	0.0	0.0	0.2	0.4	16.6
0.5	0.0	0.1	0.2	0.2	0.1	0.0	0.1	0.2	15.6
0.7	0.4	0.2	0.7	0.3	0.0	0.0	0.0	0.2	16.7
1.4	0.5	0.5	0.5	0.6	0.2	0.2	0.2	0.7	15.5
1.7	1.1	0.6	0.6	0.4	0.2	0.0	0.1	0.4	17.9
3.8	1.6	1.0	1.5	0.7	0.5	0.0	0.0	0.5	18.7
5.9	2.0	1.2	1.4	1.1	0.8	0.4	0.3	1.1	19.2
9.0	3.1	1.4	1.8	1.0	1.0	0.8	0.4	0.7	22.6
26.4	6.8	3.7	3.2	2.5	0.6	0.5	0.7	2.4	23.2
8.9	24.4	5.5	5.6	2.1	3.1	1.3	0.4	5.3	30.4
4.1	9.6	21.3	7.8	2.4	5.5	2.5	1.1	7.5	33.0
1.1	4.4	6.5	23.9	4.5	6.9	4.4	0.6	13.3	32.0
0.9	1.7	3.8	5.4	27.2	3.4	7.2	0.7	17.5	29.7
0.8	1.2	2.8	4.7	8.4	19.2	7.7	3.9	24.0	26.5
0.7	0.3	1.0	3.1	6.7	2.0	19.4	3.9	29.0	32.3
0.2%	0.0%	0.7%	3.1%	5.4%	0.8%	3.1%	15.4%	38.2%	31.6%

Baa3	Ba1	Ba2	Ba3	B1	B2	B3	Caa–C	Default	WR
0.0%	0.0%	0.1%	0.1%	0.2%	0.0%	0.1%	0.2%	0.3%	22.7%
0.1	0.2	0.5	0.2	0.0	0.0	0.0	0.0	0.4	19.7
0.7	0.3	0.3	0.3	0.1	0.0	0.0	0.0	0.5	18.9
0.7	0.4	0.3	0.3	0.5	0.0	0.0	0.1	0.4	20.0
1.4	0.8	0.1	0.5	0.6	0.3	0.2	0.2	0.9	18.4
1.8	1.1	0.7	0.7	0.4	0.2	0.0	0.1	0.6	21.3
3.6	1.8	1.1	1.8	0.8	0.3	0.1	0.1	0.5	22.1
5.7	1.8	1.2	1.6	0.9	0.7	0.2	0.2	1.4	23.6
9.0	2.5	1.6	1.5	1.0	0.7	0.4	0.6	1.1	26.6
22.7	6.3	3.9	3.4	1.9	0.9	0.6	0.3	2.9	26.6
8.1	19.6	4.9	5.5	2.2	3.1	1.2	0.5	6.3	34.8
4.0	8.8	16.8	6.4	2.7	5.0	2.6	0.7	9.0	38.2
1.2	4.1	5.9	19.0	4.7	6.1	4.1	0.5	15.4	37.0
0.9	2.0	3.6	4.9	20.8	3.1	6.2	0.7	20.1	35.2
0.6	1.4	2.6	3.1	9.0	16.1	6.3	3.6	25.6	30.4
0.5	0.4	1.0	2.4	6.2	2.1	14.7	3.5	31.0	36.2
0.2%	0.0%	1.3%	2.8%	4.7%	0.5%	3.1%	12.3%	39.5%	34.3%

E X H I B I T   7–18

(continued)

6-Year Average Rating Transition Matrix, 1983–1991

	Aaa	**Aa1**	**Aa2**	**Aa3**	**A1**	**A2**	**A3**	**Baa1**	**Baa2**
Aaa	43.9%	9.7%	8.0%	4.7%	3.8%	2.1%	1.0%	0.4%	0.1%
Aa1	4.6	26.1	11.3	13.2	8.6	2.3	3.0	4.6	1.6
Aa2	1.3	4.2	28.2	16.0	10.2	7.5	4.3	2.4	1.5
Aa3	0.7	0.8	5.5	30.1	17.1	10.9	5.5	3.0	1.1
A1	0.4	0.2	1.8	8.9	36.3	15.0	6.5	3.0	1.9
A2	0.0	0.2	0.1	2.2	9.6	33.4	14.1	6.5	4.0
A3	0.1	0.1	0.2	1.6	5.0	15.4	26.9	9.0	6.5
Baa1	0.0	0.0	0.3	0.3	3.3	7.1	13.8	25.1	9.6
Baa2	0.1	0.4	0.3	0.6	1.3	3.6	6.4	11.2	28.7
Baa3	0.3	0.0	0.2	0.3	0.8	2.3	4.3	8.0	14.0
Ba1	0.1	0.1	0.1	0.1	0.2	1.5	1.5	3.4	7.9
Ba2	0.1	0.1	0.3	0.0	0.5	0.7	1.0	1.2	2.6
Ba3	0.0	0.0	0.1	0.0	0.2	0.2	0.3	0.3	0.9
B1	0.1	0.1	0.3	0.0	0.2	0.5	0.8	0.2	0.5
B2	0.2	0.0	0.0	0.1	0.0	0.3	0.2	0.2	0.1
B3	0.1	0.0	0.0	0.0	0.0	0.1	0.7	0.9	0.2
Caa–C	0.0%	0.0%	0.0%	0.0%	0.0%	0.0%	0.0%	1.4%	0.0%

Rating From: (left margin label) — Rating To: (top label)

7-Year Average Rating Transition Matrix, 1983–1990

	Aaa	**Aa1**	**Aa2**	**Aa3**	**A1**	**A2**	**A3**	**Baa1**	**Baa2**
Aaa	40.3%	9.3%	7.3%	5.9%	4.1%	2.2%	1.2%	0.3%	0.3%
Aa1	4.6	24.7	11.1	12.6	7.0	2.7	3.0	4.9	1.8
Aa2	1.1	3.6	26.0	15.7	10.8	7.2	4.5	2.7	1.6
Aa3	0.7	0.7	5.4	27.5	16.5	10.5	6.6	2.9	1.0
A1	0.4	0.1	2.1	8.3	33.9	15.7	6.7	3.1	1.9
A2	0.0	0.2	0.1	2.2	9.4	31.3	14.2	6.5	4.1
A3	0.1	0.1	0.0	1.7	5.0	14.9	25.4	8.7	6.0
Baa1	0.0	0.0	0.1	0.3	3.7	7.3	13.2	23.4	9.3
Baa2	0.0	0.4	0.3	0.3	1.7	3.2	5.8	11.8	26.9
Baa3	0.3	0.0	0.2	0.5	0.6	2.5	4.3	8.1	14.1
Ba1	0.0	0.1	0.0	0.1	0.2	1.4	1.5	3.9	8.1
Ba2	0.3	0.1	0.1	0.0	0.6	0.7	0.9	1.3	2.6
Ba3	0.0	0.0	0.1	0.0	0.2	0.2	0.3	0.4	0.7
B1	0.1	0.1	0.3	0.0	0.1	0.5	0.8	0.3	0.5
B2	0.3	0.0	0.0	0.0	0.0	0.4	0.3	0.1	0.3
B3	0.1	0.0	0.0	0.0	0.0	0.1	0.7	0.7	0.2
Caa–C	0.0%	0.0%	0.0%	0.0%	0.0%	0.0%	0.0%	0.0%	1.4%

Rating From: (left margin label) — Rating To: (top label)

Baa3	Ba1	Ba2	Ba3	B1	B2	B3	Caa–C	Default	WR
0.0%	0.0%	0.1%	0.1%	0.1%	0.0%	0.1%	0.1%	0.3%	25.6%
0.5	0.0	0.5	0.4	0.0	0.1	0.0	0.0	0.6	22.7
0.9	0.4	0.4	0.2	0.3	0.1	0.0	0.0	0.5	21.6
0.6	0.4	0.2	0.1	0.3	0.0	0.0	0.1	0.6	23.0
1.8	0.6	0.1	0.4	0.3	0.4	0.2	0.1	1.1	21.1
1.9	1.0	0.9	0.8	0.4	0.1	0.0	0.1	0.8	23.8
3.8	1.5	1.0	2.1	0.6	0.4	0.1	0.1	0.6	25.1
5.4	1.5	1.4	1.3	0.5	0.8	0.2	0.2	1.6	27.4
8.1	2.7	1.9	1.7	0.8	0.6	0.3	0.4	1.4	29.3
20.9	6.1	3.7	3.1	1.9	1.1	0.4	0.3	3.4	28.9
7.3	16.2	4.6	5.0	2.4	2.9	1.0	0.4	7.3	38.0
4.1	8.0	13.8	5.5	3.0	4.6	2.4	0.4	9.8	42.0
1.3	4.2	5.4	15.8	5.0	5.3	3.5	0.4	17.2	40.0
1.0	1.8	3.4	4.6	16.1	2.9	5.6	0.6	22.5	39.0
0.6	2.3	2.6	2.9	8.5	13.1	5.6	3.2	27.4	32.8
0.3	0.4	1.3	2.5	5.6	1.9	11.2	3.5	32.0	39.4
0.2%	0.0%	2.0%	1.5%	4.7%	1.1%	2.8%	9.7%	40.2%	36.5%

Baa3	Ba1	Ba2	Ba3	B1	B2	B3	Caa–C	Default	WR
0.0%	0.1%	0.1%	0.0%	0.2%	0.0%	0.0%	0.1%	0.4%	28.4%
1.1	0.0	0.6	0.5	0.0	0.0	0.1	0.0	0.6	24.8
0.9	0.3	0.4	0.2	0.2	0.0	0.0	0.1	0.6	24.1
0.5	0.4	0.1	0.0	0.3	0.0	0.0	0.1	0.6	26.1
1.2	0.7	0.1	0.5	0.2	0.4	0.1	0.0	1.1	23.5
2.1	0.7	1.1	0.7	0.5	0.0	0.1	0.2	0.9	25.8
3.4	1.6	0.9	2.3	0.8	0.4	0.0	0.1	0.8	27.8
5.4	1.6	1.3	0.9	0.2	0.9	0.2	0.3	1.9	30.1
7.6	2.7	2.4	1.4	1.0	0.7	0.3	0.2	1.6	31.7
19.5	5.1	3.1	2.8	1.7	1.4	0.5	0.4	3.9	31.0
6.7	14.2	4.9	4.4	2.7	2.9	0.5	0.3	7.9	40.1
4.5	7.6	12.0	5.3	3.2	3.8	1.8	0.5	10.6	44.3
1.4	4.0	5.2	13.1	4.8	5.0	3.0	0.5	18.7	42.3
0.9	1.6	3.2	4.5	12.7	2.6	5.2	0.6	24.3	41.7
0.9	1.7	2.8	3.9	7.5	11.7	5.1	2.4	28.3	34.3
0.0	0.4	1.0	3.1	5.2	1.8	9.4	3.5	32.7	41.2
0.2%	0.0%	2.0%	0.8%	4.7%	1.7%	2.8%	6.8%	40.5%	39.1%

EXHIBIT 7–18

(continued)

8-Year Average Rating Transition Matrix, 1983–1989

Rating From:	Rating To: Aaa	Aa1	Aa2	Aa3	A1	A2	A3	Baa1	Baa2
Aaa	37.1%	8.3%	7.4%	6.6%	4.3%	2.1%	1.5%	0.4%	0.3%
Aa1	4.0	24.2	11.0	12.5	6.8	2.3	3.3	4.4	1.9
Aa2	1.1	3.1	24.6	15.0	10.9	7.4	4.8	2.7	1.6
Aa3	0.7	0.5	5.4	26.1	15.9	10.8	6.8	2.9	0.9
A1	0.3	0.1	2.2	8.2	31.7	16.3	6.6	2.6	2.1
A2	0.0	0.2	0.1	2.2	9.3	29.8	14.3	6.5	3.9
A3	0.1	0.1	0.0	1.5	5.0	14.8	24.3	8.1	6.1
Baa1	0.0	0.0	0.1	0.3	3.6	7.2	12.7	22.4	8.8
Baa2	0.0	0.4	0.2	0.4	1.8	3.1	5.5	11.9	25.6
Baa3	0.2	0.0	0.1	0.6	0.6	2.7	4.3	8.3	13.5
Ba1	0.0	0.1	0.0	0.1	0.2	1.4	1.4	4.2	8.1
Ba2	0.3	0.1	0.0	0.0	0.7	0.6	0.6	1.3	2.7
Ba3	0.0	0.0	0.1	0.0	0.3	0.3	0.3	0.4	0.7
B1	0.1	0.1	0.3	0.0	0.1	0.5	0.8	0.4	0.5
B2	0.4	0.0	0.0	0.0	0.0	0.5	0.3	0.0	0.5
B3	0.1	0.0	0.0	0.0	0.0	0.1	0.7	0.8	0.2
Caa–C	0.0%	0.0%	0.0%	0.0%	0.0%	0.0%	0.0%	0.0%	0.0%

9-Year Average Rating Transition Matrix, 1983–1988

Rating From:	Rating To: Aaa	Aa1	Aa2	Aa3	A1	A2	A3	Baa1	Baa2
Aaa	34.7%	7.5%	7.6%	6.8%	4.2%	2.1%	1.8%	0.4%	0.3%
Aa1	3.7	23.8	10.5	12.6	6.9	3.2	3.7	3.1	2.1
Aa2	1.0	2.9	23.6	14.3	11.0	7.7	4.5	3.1	1.3
Aa3	0.7	0.5	5.1	24.8	15.8	10.8	6.8	3.1	0.9
A1	0.3	0.1	2.4	8.0	30.3	15.5	6.6	2.6	2.5
A2	0.0	0.3	0.1	1.9	9.3	29.2	14.2	6.3	3.8
A3	0.1	0.1	0.1	1.3	5.1	14.5	23.3	8.0	6.5
Baa1	0.0	0.0	0.1	0.4	3.4	7.0	12.7	21.2	8.6
Baa2	0.0	0.3	0.2	0.3	1.7	3.5	5.6	12.0	24.2
Baa3	0.1	0.0	0.0	0.7	0.7	2.8	4.8	8.0	13.4
Ba1	0.0	0.1	0.0	0.1	0.3	1.4	1.2	4.7	7.9
Ba2	0.3	0.1	0.0	0.0	0.5	0.5	0.4	1.5	2.8
Ba3	0.0	0.0	0.1	0.0	0.3	0.3	0.2	0.5	0.6
B1	0.1	0.1	0.4	0.0	0.1	0.5	0.8	0.5	0.6
B2	0.4	0.0	0.0	0.0	0.0	0.5	0.3	0.0	0.8
B3	0.1	0.0	0.0	0.0	0.0	0.1	0.7	0.9	0.2
Caa–C	0.0%	0.0%	0.0%	0.0%	0.0%	0.0%	0.0%	0.0%	0.0%

Baa3	Ba1	Ba2	Ba3	B1	B2	B3	Caa–C	Default	WR
0.1%	0.1%	0.1%	0.0%	0.0%	0.0%	0.0%	0.0%	0.5%	31.1%
1.4	0.0	0.0	0.6	0.0	0.0	0.0	0.0	0.6	26.9
0.9	0.3	0.2	0.2	0.2	0.0	0.0	0.2	0.7	26.2
0.3	0.4	0.2	0.0	0.2	0.1	0.0	0.1	0.6	28.0
1.2	0.6	0.1	0.5	0.3	0.2	0.0	0.0	1.2	25.7
2.2	0.6	1.0	0.6	0.5	0.1	0.0	0.2	1.1	27.4
3.3	1.7	1.1	1.6	1.0	0.3	0.1	0.2	0.8	29.9
5.8	1.7	0.9	0.7	0.2	0.7	0.2	0.2	2.4	32.0
7.2	2.8	2.0	1.4	1.1	0.9	0.2	0.1	1.8	33.7
19.0	4.6	3.0	2.6	1.4	1.4	0.5	0.4	4.2	32.7
6.5	13.0	5.1	4.3	3.0	2.3	0.5	0.3	8.4	41.2
4.7	7.1	11.0	5.2	3.0	3.5	1.5	0.5	11.0	46.1
1.3	3.9	5.2	11.4	4.6	4.9	2.4	0.5	20.0	43.8
0.8	1.6	3.3	4.1	10.8	2.5	4.4	0.7	25.4	43.6
0.9	1.6	2.9	3.9	6.4	10.3	4.9	2.5	28.7	36.2
0.0	0.3	0.8	2.6	4.7	1.6	8.4	3.3	33.9	42.5
1.6%	0.0%	2.0%	0.1%	4.0%	2.4%	2.8%	6.7%	40.5%	39.9%

Baa3	Ba1	Ba2	Ba3	B1	B2	B3	Caa–C	Default	WR
0.1%	0.2%	0.1%	0.0%	0.0%	0.0%	0.0%	0.0%	0.5%	33.8%
1.3	0.0	0.0	0.0	0.0	0.0	0.0	0.0	0.6	28.4
1.1	0.3	0.1	0.0	0.1	0.0	0.0	0.2	0.7	28.0
0.4	0.6	0.1	0.0	0.1	0.1	0.0	0.0	0.6	29.5
1.0	0.5	0.2	0.5	0.2	0.2	0.0	0.0	1.2	27.8
2.1	0.7	1.1	0.4	0.4	0.1	0.0	0.1	1.2	28.7
3.4	1.7	1.0	0.9	1.3	0.2	0.2	0.2	0.9	31.4
5.9	1.6	0.9	0.6	0.2	0.7	0.2	0.2	2.7	33.8
6.7	2.9	2.1	1.1	1.1	1.1	0.2	0.1	1.9	35.1
18.5	4.1	2.6	2.7	1.3	1.2	0.5	0.3	4.6	33.6
6.5	11.9	5.5	4.0	2.9	2.2	0.6	0.2	8.6	42.1
4.2	7.5	10.3	5.0	2.9	3.6	1.3	0.5	11.2	47.3
1.4	3.9	5.0	9.8	4.7	4.9	1.8	0.6	21.0	45.1
0.7	1.5	3.4	4.1	9.8	2.4	3.6	0.6	26.1	44.8
1.1	1.4	1.8	3.9	5.2	8.8	5.1	2.9	29.0	38.7
0.0	0.2	1.1	1.5	4.6	1.8	8.0	3.1	34.8	42.9
0.2%	0.7%	2.0%	0.8%	3.3%	2.4%	2.8%	6.7%	40.5%	40.5%

E X H I B I T   7–18

(concluded)

10-Year Average Rating Transition Matrix, 1983–1987

					Rating To :				
	Aaa	Aa1	Aa2	Aa3	A1	A2	A3	Baa1	Baa2
Aaa	29.2%	6.8	7.9	7.3	4.6	2.3	1.9	0.4	0.0
Aa1	3.4	20.3	10.9	12.6	7.0	4.2	4.2	2.5	2.2
Aa2	1.1	2.4	19.4	13.8	12.0	8.1	4.3	3.8	0.9
Aa3	0.6	0.4	5.0	21.8	15.0	10.9	7.4	3.5	1.0
A1	0.2	0.1	2.7	7.2	27.8	15.3	6.5	2.9	2.7
A2	0.0	0.3	0.1	2.0	8.9	27.0	13.9	6.6	4.0
A3	0.1	0.1	0.1	0.9	4.8	14.0	21.5	7.4	6.6
Baa1	0.0	0.0	0.1	0.4	3.5	6.1	11.7	18.5	9.1
Baa2	0.0	0.2	0.2	0.3	1.7	3.9	5.6	11.7	20.7
Baa3	0.1	0.0	0.0	0.7	0.9	2.5	5.4	8.0	13.0
Ba1	0.0	0.1	0.0	0.0	0.3	1.5	1.2	4.9	7.7
Ba2	0.3	0.1	0.0	0.0	0.5	0.4	0.3	1.2	2.9
Ba3	0.1	0.0	0.1	0.0	0.3	0.4	0.2	0.3	0.7
B1	0.0	0.0	0.4	0.0	0.1	0.4	0.7	0.7	0.5
B2	0.4	0.0	0.0	0.0	0.0	0.5	0.4	0.3	0.9
B3	0.1	0.0	0.0	0.0	0.0	0.1	0.5	1.1	0.1
Caa–C	0.0%	0.0%	0.0%	0.0%	0.0%	0.0%	0.0%	0.0%	0.0%

Rating From: (row label axis)

E X H I B I T   7–19

Rating Transition Rate Distribution Summary, (%)

	Aaa	Aa	A	Baa
Aaa	(78.2,94.1,8.3,100.0)	(5.6,5.6,6.5,6.5)	(0.0,0.0,2.7,2.7)	(0.0,0.0,0.8,0.8)
Aa	(0.0,1.2,1.2,3.4)	(92.2,92.2,7.1,7.1)	(4.8,4.8,5.7,5.7)	(0.0,0.0,1.3,1.3)
A	(0.0,0.0,0.2,0.4)	(1.9,1.9,2.6,2.6)	(94.8,94.8,8.4,8.4)	(3.7,3.7,5.3,5.3)
Baa	(0.0,0.0,0.1,0.3)	(0.0,0.0,0.5,0.5)	(2.7,2.7,4.4,4.4)	(91.2,91.2,10.2,10.2)
Ba	(0.0,0.0,0.1,0.0)	(0.0,0.0,0.2,0.2)	(0.2,0.2,0.6,0.6)	(3.9,3.9,3.9,3.9)
B	(0.0,0.0,0.0,0.0)	(0.0,0.0,0.2,0.2)	(0.0,0.0,0.3,0.3)	(0.0,0.0,1.1,1.1)
Caa–C	(0.0,0.0,0.0,0.0)	(0.0,0.0,0.2,0.2)	(0.0,0.0,0.2,0.2)	(0.0,0.0,2.1,2.1)

Note: Each table entry is comprised of the following (5th percentile, Median, Standard Deviation, 95th percentile). All numbers in percents.

Baa3	Ba1	Ba2	Ba3	B1	B2	B3	Caa–C	Default	WR
0.4%	0.3%	0.0%	0.0%	0.0%	0.0%	0.0%	0.0%	0.6%	38.3%
0.5	0.0	0.0	0.0	0.0	0.0	0.0	0.0	0.6	31.6
1.1	0.2	0.0	0.0	0.1	0.1	0.0	0.1	0.9	31.7
0.5	0.7	0.2	0.1	0.1	0.1	0.0	0.0	0.6	32.3
0.8	0.5	0.1	0.5	0.3	0.2	0.0	0.0	1.3	30.8
2.2	0.8	0.9	0.4	0.4	0.2	0.0	0.1	1.3	31.1
3.5	1.8	1.3	0.8	1.3	0.0	0.2	0.2	1.1	34.4
5.7	1.7	1.1	0.5	0.5	0.6	0.2	0.2	2.9	37.3
6.5	2.9	2.1	0.7	1.1	1.2	0.4	0.1	2.2	38.6
16.1	3.1	2.9	2.9	1.2	1.1	0.5	0.2	4.8	36.6
6.0	9.5	5.1	3.5	2.8	2.3	0.8	0.2	9.4	44.8
4.0	7.0	8.4	4.0	2.8	3.5	1.2	0.6	12.2	50.8
1.4	3.7	3.7	7.9	4.5	4.4	1.5	0.7	22.8	47.5
0.6	1.4	2.8	3.6	7.8	2.3	3.0	0.5	28.0	47.1
0.9	2.8	1.3	2.7	3.8	8.5	3.9	3.3	30.7	39.6
0.0	0.2	1.2	0.9	4.5	1.5	6.1	2.5	36.8	44.3
0.0%	0.0%	3.0%	0.1%	3.6%	2.4%	2.6%	4.9%	42.0%	41.4%

Ba	B	Caa–C	Default
(0.0,0.0,0.1,0.1)	(0.0,0.0,0.0,0.0)	(0.0,0.0,0.0,0.0)	(0.0,0.0,0.0,0.0)
(0.0,0.0,0.5,0.5)	(0.0,0.0,0.1,0.1)	(0.0,0.0,0.0,0.0)	(0.0,0.0,0.2,0.2)
(0.0,0.0,1.3,1.3)	(0.0,0.0,0.3,0.3)	(0.0,0.0,0.1,0.1)	(0.0,0.0,0.4,0.4)
(3.2,3.2,6.1,6.1)	(0.2,0.2,1.2,1.2)	(0.0,0.0,0.2,0.2)	(0.0,0.0,0.5,0.5)
(90.4,90.4,9.9,9.9)	(3.4,3.4,6.4,6.4)	(0.2,0.2,0.8,0.8)	(0.6,0.6,2.0,2.0)
(4.7,4.7,5.6,5.6)	(86.7,86.7,10.5,10.5)	(2.3,2.3,4.7,4.7)	(2.4,2.4,4.7,4.7)
(0.0,0.0,3.4,3.4)	(4.5,4.5,6.0,6.0)	(82.5,82.5,20.1,20.1)	(8.3,8.3,18.1,18.1)

Modeling Bond Rating Changes for Credit Risk Estimation

Theodore M. Barnhill, Jr.

William F. Maxwell

INTRODUCTION

Credit risk analysis requires a methodology for estimating the change in credit quality of the individual assets in a portfolio. Some methodologies rely on average historical rating transition probabilities. However, this type of analysis does not address the correlated nature of credit rating changes and defaults. Contingent claims models (e.g., CreditMetrics™ and Value-Calc™) are being developed to model the correlated nature of such credit events. This chapter reviews the methodology used in ValueCalc and the type of output it produces.

Credit risk analysis assesses the effect of stochastic changes in credit quality (including default) on the value of a fixed income security or a portfolio of fixed income securities. The output of such credit risk analysis is utilized by banks, insurance companies, and mutual funds to set acceptable risk levels and capital requirements over a preset time horizon.

Credit risk methodologies initially estimate the probability of financial assets migrating to different risk categories (i.e., bond ratings) over a preset horizon. The values of the financial assets are then typically estimated for each possible future risk category using forward rates from the term structure appropriate for each risk class. There are currently a number of different packages available to assess credit risk including CreditMetrics™, Credit Risk +, Credit View, Loan Analysis System (LAS), and ValueCalc™.

This chapter discusses and demonstrates the Monte Carlo simulation methodology developed by Barnhill and incorporated in the ValueCalc™ (1998) financial software to model credit rating change probabilities. The statistical calibration of the model required to complete this analysis was drawn from Barnhill and Maxwell (1998). The focus of this chapter is to demonstrate how an appropriately calibrated simulation model can produce bond rating change probabilities that are very similar to the historical ones reported by major rating services for a one-year time step. This type of analysis is necessary to correctly assess the credit risk of owning high yield assets.

HISTORICAL TRANSITION MATRICES

The historical probabilities of credit transition by rating category are compiled by a number of different organizations with the two most prevalent being Moody's Investors Service and Standard & Poor's. For example, Moody's one year transition matrix for senior unsecured debt adjusted to eliminate the rating withdrawn category is found in Exhibit 8–1. (See Chapter 7 for a full discussion of historical transition probabilities.) The diagonal in this table gives the probability of remaining at the initial rating. It is striking to note that for every category, over 95 percent of the time the bond's rating one year in the future is within one rating category of its initial rating.

There are clearly problems utilizing a historical transition matrix calculated over a number of years in assessing the credit risk of bonds at any particular time. For example, in Chapter 9 Fridson, Garman, and Wu identify a relation between macroeconomic conditions and default probabilities. Thus one-year transition probabilities will likely differ considerably during an economic recession and during an economic expansion. Further, the rating transition probabilities are usually not the same for all firms in a particular rating category that operate in different industries, face a wide variety of risk, and have much different capital structures. It is also important to model correlated credit changes in a portfolio of financial instruments. Thus, a flexible methodology for estimating credit transition probabilities based on current economic and firm-specific conditions is needed.

CREDIT RATING SIMULATION

The bond rating simulation methodology utilized in this study is based on a contingent claims framework. It is assumed that for a given firm a deterministic relationship exists between the firm's debt ratio [Total liabilities/(Total liabilities + Market value of equity)] and its bond rating. For example, a debt ratio below 0.1 implies an Aaa bond rating, and a debt ratio over 0.9 implies a defaulted bond.

Moody's Transition Matrices Adjusted
for Withdrawn Ratings (1920–1996)

Initial Rating	**Probability of Rating after One Year**							
	Aaa	Aa	A	Baa	Ba	B	Caa–C	Default
Aaa	92.28%	6.43%	1.03%	0.24%	0.02%	0.00%	0.00%	0.00%
Aa	1.28	91.68	6.09	0.70	0.17	0.02	0.00	0.06
A	0.07	2.45	91.59	4.97	0.67	0.11	0.02	0.13
Baa	0.03	0.26	4.19	89.41	5.07	0.66	0.07	0.30
Ba	0.01	0.09	0.43	5.09	87.23	5.47	0.45	1.23
B	0.00	0.04	0.15	0.67	6.47	85.32	3.44	3.90
Caa–C	0.00	0.02	0.04	0.37	1.38	5.80	78.78	13.60

A summary of the contingent claims approach used in this study to simulate the evolution of credit ratings on a bond is as follows. The first step is to simulate the return on an equity market index (e.g., S&P 500). Second, a one-factor model is used to estimate the return on a firm's equity as a function of the return on the equity index plus a firm-specific random change. Third, the firm's simulated return on equity is used to calculate the future market value of its equity and its debt ratio. Finally, as the firm's debt ratio increases (decreases) its assigned credit rating decreases (increases).

SIMULATING EQUITY RETURNS AND DEBT TO VALUE RATIOS

The simulation of the market value of a firm's equity starts by simulating a return on an equity market index (S&P 500, manufacturing, etc.) using a standard lognormal stochastic process where the volatility of return is a function of the square root of time. For the present analysis, which focuses on simulating bond ratings for a broad cross section of manufacturing firms, the S&P 500 index was simulated with an assumed expected return of 12 percent (0.12). The historical volatility (1926–1996) for large capitalization firms of 20.3 percent (Ibbotson 1997) is used as the estimate for market return volatility.

Once the return on the S&P 500 is simulated the return on equity for the individual firm is simulated using a modified version of the following one-factor model:

$$K_i = R_F + \text{Beta}_i \, (R_m - R_F) + \sigma_i \Delta z$$

where

K_i = The return on equity for firm$_i$
R_F = The risk-free interest rate
Beta$_i$ = The systematic risk of firm$_i$
R_m = The simulated return on the S&P 500
σ_i = The firm specific volatility in return on equity
Δz = A Wiener process with Δ_z being related Δt by the function $\Delta z = \epsilon \sqrt{\Delta t}$

The first step in calculating the expected return on equity for a typical firm in a particular bond rating is to understand how beta coefficients change with bond ratings. To do this, a cross-sectional time series analysis was undertaken on data drawn from Compustat to calculate the average manufacturing firm's beta by bond rating. This analysis found as expected that as bond ratings decline, the firm's systematic risk increases. As shown in Exhibit 8–2, the average beta is 0.90 for A-rated bonds and 1.26 for B-rated bonds.

To simulate a firm's return on equity its unsystematic risk must also be determined. As with the measurement of systematic risk, unsystematic risk also increases as bond rating declines. As shown in Exhibit 8–3, the mean firm-specific equity return volatility for companies with A-rated bonds, is 0.062, compared to an average of 0.148 for companies with B-rated bonds.

E X H I B I T   8–2

Mean Beta for Manufacturing Firms with Various Bond Ratings Relative to the S&P 500 over the Period 1993–1996

Bond Rating	Mean Beta
Aaa	0.859
Aa	0.842
A	0.902
Baa	1.024
Ba	1.095
B	1.258
Caa	1.501
D	NA

E X H I B I T   8–3

Mean Firm-Specific Equity Return
Volatility for Manufacturing Companies
by Bond Rating (1993–1996)

Bond Rating	Mean Firm-Specific Volatility
Aaa	.044
Aa	.055
A	.062
Baa	.079
Ba	.110
B	.148
Caa	.246
D	NA

Once the firm's simulated return on equity is determined, its end-of-period market value of equity is calculated along with its debt ratio based on a target level of total liabilities.

MAPPING DEBT RATIOS INTO BOND RATING CATEGORIES

For the current analysis, the ranges of debt ratios corresponding to bond ratings were estimated using linear regressions of bond ratings versus mean debt ratios by rating class for all manufacturing firms during the 1992 to 1996 time period. The data utilized in this analysis was again obtained from Compustat. The corresponding relation between bond rating and debt ratios is found in Exhibit 8–4.

Credit Transition Matrices

Utilizing the parameters described in Exhibits 8–2 and 8–4, the credit transition probabilities for bonds with debt ratios starting at the middle of the various ranges identified can be simulated. The simulated credit transition matrix for a one-year time horizon is found in Exhibit 8–5. The results are demonstrative for a typical firm within each rating category. It is important to keep in mind that the simulated credit transition probabilities can change

E X H I B I T   8–4

Implied Break Points for Bond Rating Categories

Bond Rating	Debt Ratio Break Point
AAA	Less than 0.1875
AA	Less than 0.3125
A	Less than 0.4375
BBB	Less than 0.5625
BB	Less than 0.6875
B	Less than 0.8125
CCC	Less than 0.9375
Default	Greater than or equal to 0.9375

dramatically for bonds within a particular category based upon the assumed volatility of market equity returns, the systematic and unsystematic risk characteristics of the firm, and the assumed ranges of debt ratios that correspond to various bond ratings.

COMPARISON OF HISTORICAL AND SIMULATED TRANSITION MATRICES

A comparison of Moody's historical and simulated credit rating transition matrices indicate many similarities and one important difference. First, the percent of the time that the rating stays in the initial category is similar for all ratings. For example, Exhibit 8–5 shows that 94.25 percent of the time the simulated rating for an initially Aaa-rated bond retained that rating one year later. This compares to the somewhat lower 92.28 percent given in the historical data in Exhibit 8–1. Alternatively, for B-rated bonds, the simulation model produced a B rating 77.35 percent of the time versus 85.32 percent for the historical data. A second similarity is that for both approaches a very high percentage of all observations fall within one rating category on either side of the initial rating. A significant difference between the historical and simulated rating transition probabilities is that the historical rating transitions show a larger probability of multicategory rating changes including defaults. In Chapter 13, this will be shown to be an important factor that must be dealt with when valuing bonds with credit risk.

E X H I B I T   8–5

Simulated Implied Transition Matrices

	Aaa	Aa	A	Baa	Ba	B	Caa–C	Default
Aaa	94.25%	5.75%	0.00%	0.00%	0.00%	0.00%	0.00%	0.00%
Aa	2.30	93.30	4.40	0.00	0.00	0.00	0.00	0.00
A	0.00	6.95	85.15	7.90	0.00	0.00	0.00	0.00
Baa	0.00	0.00	11.05	77.95	11.00	0.00	0.00	0.00
Ba	0.00	0.00	0.10	14.85	72.00	13.05	0.00	0.00
B	0.00	0.00	0.00	0.20	13.40	77.35	9.05	0.00
Caa–C	0.00%	0.00%	0.00%	0.00%	0.20%	14.10%	74.05%	11.65%

SIMULATING CORRELATED CHANGES IN THE CREDIT RATING FOR A PORTFOLIO OF BONDS

In portfolio valuation and risk analysis it is important to be able to model the correlated changes in value for individual securities. From a credit risk modeling perspective this can be accomplished by modeling the correlated returns on a set of equity indices (auto industry, entertainment, manufacturing, etc.) as a multinominal stochastic process. Subsequently, the return on each firm's equity is modeled as a function of the return on an appropriate index or indices, plus a firm-specific random term. Using the methodology described above, correlated credit rating changes for each firm can then be calculated. This methodology is implemented in Chapter 22.

CONCLUSION

The value of a bond fluctuates based upon changes in market interest rates as well as changes in its credit quality. Thus, to assess the risk of owning high yield bonds, an investor must understand the probability of the asset migrating up or down in credit quality. Historical transition probabilities are useful in understanding the long-run probabilities of changes, but the historical approach does not factor in the present macroeconomic and market conditions, nor does it take into account firm-specific information. As a result of the shortcomings of relying on historical data, methodologies have been developed to simulate credit rating migrations utilizing a contingent claims framework (CreditMetrics™, KMV[1], and ValueCalc™). This chapter provides a basic conceptual framework about how one of these methodologies simulates credit migration probabilities. For the current study, the simulation model was calibrated with parameters estimated from data on a broad cross section of manufacturing firms. Under these conditions, the simulated rating transition probabilities were very similar to historical data reported by major bond rating agencies.

REFERENCES

Barnhill, T. and W. Maxwell (1998). "Valuing Options with Interest Rate and Credit Risk." Working paper, The George Washington University.

Fridson, M.; C. Garman; and S. Wu (1997). "Real Interest Rates and the Default Rates on High-Yield Bonds." *Journal of Fixed Income,* September, pp. 27–34.

Gupton, Greg M.; Christopher C. Finger; and Mickey Bhatia (1997). *CreditMetrics™– Technical Document.* 1st Edition. New York: J. P. Morgan & Co.

Ibbotson (1997). *Stock, Bonds, Bills, and Inflation (1997 Yearbook).* Chicago: Ibbotson Associates.

---

1. An example of KMV's transition probabilities is found in Credit Metrics–Technical Document, p. 70.

CHAPTER 9

Real Interest Rates and the Default Rate on High Yield Bonds*

Martin S. Fridson

M. Christopher Garman

Sheng Wu

MOTIVATION FOR RESEARCH ON DEFAULT RATES

Determinants of the aggregate default rate on high yield bonds have attracted increased research interest in recent years. In 1990–1991, the proportion of defaulting issues reached essentially its highest level since the Great Depression of the 1930s.[1] Consequences included negative rates of return on high yield bonds during 1990, substantial outflows of capital from the sector, and concerns about potential strains on other segments of the financial markets. By the mid-1990s, the high yield market had recovered fully. A new record volume of primary issuance was recorded in 1993. Analysts understandably began to wonder whether another wave of financial failures would inevitably follow.

---

1. The 11.388 percent (principal-amount basis) reported by Altman and Nammacher (1987) for 1970 may be viewed as anomalous. It reflects that year's bankruptcy of a single large issuer, Penn Central Transportation Company (including its numerous affiliates). Thanks to dramatic growth of new issuance of noninvestment-grade bonds beginning in 1977, no similar degree of concentration of principal amount by issuer has distorted the default statistics in a comparable fashion in the intervening years.

High yield bond investors, mutual fund organizations, and regulators all had clear stakes in these matters. Likewise taking a keen interest in projections of the aggregate default rate were the growing numbers of money managers specializing in distressed securities. As these "vulture capitalists" raised investment pools from institutions and wealthy individuals, they wondered whether the supply of investable paper would be sufficient.

LITERATURE OVERVIEW

Research studies spawned by the 1990–1991 default surge have linked the high yield default rate to both the market's quality mix and measures of macroeconomic performance. Multiple regression models based on these factors explain as much as 81 percent of the annual variance in default rates reported by Moody's Investors Service.

Vanderhoof, Albert, Tenenbein and Verni (1990) and Fons (1991) develop the premise that the greater the concentration of outstanding issues in the lowest (riskiest) bond rating categories, the higher the default rate, all else being equal. Helwege and Kleiman (1996), Jónsson and Fridson (1996), and Jónsson, Fridson and Zhong (1996) refine the actuarial, ratings-mix approach to account for the variability of default probability over the life of an average noninvestment-grade bond. As a function of this "aging" effect, a surge of bottom-quality-tier issuance alters the high yield universe's quality mix immediately but raises the default rate with a delay.

Macroeconomic variables that display explanatory power in established models include:

- Growth in Gross National Product
- Corporate profits as a percentage of Gross National Product
- Current liabilities of business failures

Helwege and Kleiman (1996) model growth in Gross Domestic Product (GDP) as a dummy variable. They assign it a value of "1" when growth exceeds 1.5 percent per annum and "0" when it falls below that level. The authors surmise that a shift from growth or to expansion has a material impact on the default rate, but that acceleration from high to very high growth does not. Helwege and Kleiman achieve good results with their dummy variable, which is not highly sensitive to the somewhat arbitrarily selected 1.5 percent cutoff. They derive additional explanatory value by combining the dummy GDP variable with a proxy for the aging effect, described above, to create an "interaction" variable.

THE CURIOUS ABSENCE
OF INTEREST RATES

Surprisingly, perhaps, previous empirical investigations have not identified interest rates as an important determinant of default rates on high yield bonds. Indeed, in a study dealing primarily with risk premiums, Fridson and Kenney (1994) find that contemporaneous U.S. Treasury yields explain little of the variance in annual default rates reported by Edward I. Altman of New York University.

Interest rates, in economic theory, represent the price of hired capital. At the margin, a rise in interest rates should price some borrowers out of the market. The ranks of companies priced out in this manner are likely to include financially strained enterprises that cannot satisfy their current obligations without obtaining new credit or additional capital. A second impact of rising interest rates, at the margin, is that for some companies, the cost of capital will begin to exceed the rate of return on capital employed. By definition, the result is negative equity value, that is, bankruptcy. In these instances, a default on debt may be delayed until accumulated cash reserves have been exhausted, but no longer. In light of the twofold influence that theory predicts for interest rates, their lack of inclusion in default rate models is curious, at least to theoreticians.

Perhaps, however, the inconsequential explanatory power of interest rates reported by Fridson and Kenney (1994) reflects those authors' focus on *nominal,* as opposed to *real,* rates. Nominal rates include no adjustment for changes in purchasing power. Real rates, in direct contrast, are defined as the stated interest rate minus the expected rate of inflation.

Escalating nominal rates will not necessarily drive borrowers, at the margin, into insolvency. Imagine, for example, that a company is paying interest at a 10 percent rate, while increasing its prices to customers at a 4 percent annual pace, in line with the general inflation rate. Its real cost of debt is $10\% - 4\% = 6\%$. Now suppose that inflation rises by four percentage points to 8 percent, while the nominal rate of interest climbs only to 13 percent. If the company continues to raise prices in line with inflation, it may actually improve its interest coverage ratio, implying a decrease in default risk. (The outcome also depends on such factors as the sensitivity of sales to price increases and the impact of inflation on operating expenses.)

On the face of it, default risk would appear more likely to increase in response to a rise in real rates, the result (among other possibilities) of a rise in nominal rates that is less than fully offset by a rise in the inflation rate. Such reasoning led us to test empirically whether historical real rates were in fact correlated with the default rate.

MEASURING CORRELATIONS

We began by compiling quarterly series of the following data for the period 1971–1995:

Default Rate
Trailing-12-months default rate on high yield bonds, percentage-of-issuers basis. (Source: Moody's Investors Service)

Nominal Interest Rates
Yield on 10-year U.S. Treasuries. (Source: Federal Reserve Board)

Inflation
Year-over-year percentage change in the Consumer Price Index. (Source: Bureau of Labor Statistics)

For purposes of this study, we defined the real interest rate as simply the nominal interest rate minus the inflation rate for the same period. In effect, we treated the present inflation rate as a proxy for the expected inflation rate demanded by a formal definition of the real rate.[2]

Our first test (see Exhibit 9–1) found a correlation (R) of just 17.6 percent between the default rate and nominal interest rates. The negligible percentage-of-variance-explained (R^2) of 3.1 percent confirmed the Fridson and Kenney (1994) finding, which was based on a different proxy for default rates. A negative t-statistic on the correlation coefficient implied, contrary to intuition, that high nominal interest rates were associated with *low* default rates. At -1.77, however, the t-statistic's absolute value was too low to justify strong confidence in any conclusion.

When we plotted default rates against real interest rates (see Exhibit 9–2), a very different picture emerged. This time, we found a 33.1 percent correlation, resulting in a nontrivial 11.0 percent percentage-of-variance-explained. Consistent with our hypothesis, the regression statistics showed that high real interest rates were associated with high default rates. The t-statistic of 8.13 indicated significance at a confidence level greater than 99.99 percent.

---

2. As a function of the trailing-12-months basis of Moody's default rates, the 1971 statistics include impact from the Penn Central Transportation Company, the distorting effects of which are described in Footnote 1. For the same reason, the impact of the huge default surge of 1990–1991 obliged us to include 1992 in our outlier group. While we do not suggest that the extraordinarily high default rates recorded in 1970 and 1990–1991 could never be seen again, we also think it is worth considering how real interest rates act on the system in more ordinary years.

E X H I B I T   9–1

Nominal Interest Rates versus Default Rates (quarterly), 1971–1995

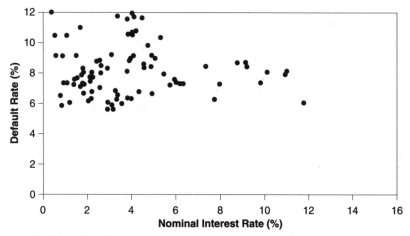

Sources: Federal Reserve Board; Moody's Investors Service.

E X H I B I T   9–2

Real Interest Rates versus Default Rates (quarterly), 1971–1995

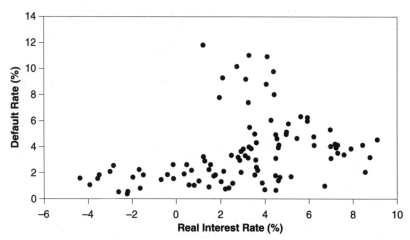

Sources: Bureau of Labor Statistics; Federal Reserve Board; Moody's Investors Service.

Real rates explained a still higher 35.0 percent of the quarterly variance in default rates when we excluded as outliers the years 1971 and 1990–1992.[3] The confidence level for significance remained high, at 99.99 percent, as indicated by a t-statistic of 6.64. Eliminating outliers achieved no comparable result with nominal rates. Excluding 1971 and 1990–1992, nominal rates explained a mere 1.0 percent of the variance in default rates, that is, less than the R^2 we calculated for all years, including outliers.

As another means of potentially squeezing additional explanatory value out of real interest rates, we tested them as a leading, rather than contemporaneous, influence on default rates. We have already suggested one rationale for such a model. That is, a rise in the cost of capital will not immediately render companies insolvent if they have substantial liquidity on their balance sheets. Instead, the surge in corporate failures will come only after a delay corresponding to the period required for debtors to exhaust whatever cash they have on hand or can raise quickly. Another reason to test for lags is that the contraction in economic activity resulting from a rise in real interest rates may occur only gradually. For example, much of the economy's manufacturing output is sold in advance of production. When real interest rates rise, causing new orders to slow down, a manufacturer can continue shipping products (from both finished goods inventories and new production) until its backlog has been erased. Only then will revenue (and the associated cash flow) decelerate, potentially putting the manufacturer in financial jeopardy.

As it turned out, a two-year lag produced the maximum correlation between real interest rates and default rates. Including all 25 years between 1971 and 1995 in the sample, we found a correlation (R) of 50.5 percent, resulting in a percentage-of-variance-explained (R^2) of 25.46 percent. A still higher correlation (69.1 percent) and R^2 (47.70 percent) resulted from plotting two-year lagged real interest rates against default rates of the 21 nonoutlier years (see Exhibit 9–3).

---

3. In comparing the impact of nominal and real rates, we considered the possibility that the two were not statistically very different, as a practical matter. This might be the case if inflation were highly stable or consistently represented a small percentage of the nominal rate. As it turned out, though, the quarterly correlation between nominal and real rates for the period 1971–1995 was only 33.1 percent. This was not a high enough correlation to render it redundant to analyze the two series separately. (Note that by sheer coincidence, the real rate/nominal rate correlation was identical to the real rate/default rate correlation.)

E X H I B I T   9–3

Real Interest Rates (lagged two years) versus
Default Rates (quarterly), Nonoutlier Years Only

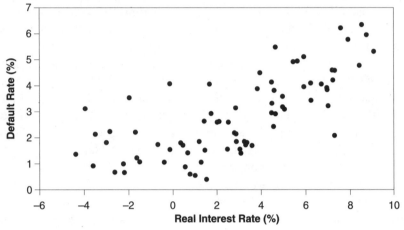

Sources: Bureau of Labor Statistics; Federal Reserve Board; Moody's Investors Service.

MODELING DEFAULT RATES WITH A REAL INTEREST RATE VARIABLE

The power of lagged real interest rates to explain default rates is immensely valuable from a forecasting standpoint. Without having to forecast either nominal interest rates or the inflation rate, chancy propositions at best, we can infer a great deal about the likely range of default rates as far out as two years.

Better still, we can combine the already known real interest rates with in-hand information about the aging effect discussed above. As an empirically validated proxy for the quality mix of past issuance, Jónsson and Fridson (1996) and Helwege and Kleiman (1996) employ the percentage of issuers rated B-minus or lower by Standard & Poor's, lagged by three years. A regression analysis utilizing real interest rates and the B-minus or lower percentage explains 74.7 percent of the annual variance in default rates in the period 1980–1995[4] (see Exhibit 9–4). Put another way, the figures indicate that on average, three-quarters of the current year's default rate is "locked in" by economic and financial forces of two to three years ago.

---

4. Prior to 1980, there was little issuance in the rating categories of B-minus or lower. The aging
    variable makes no meaningful contribution to explaining default rates prior to that date, yet is
    a critically important factor in the "modern era." Accordingly, Helwege and Kleiman (1996)
    and Jónsson, Fridson and Zhong (1996) begin their test periods in 1980.

E X H I B I T   9–4

Multiple Regression Analysis of Default Rate "Locked-in" Variables Only

$R^2 = 0.747$
Adjusted $R^2 = 0.708$
Observations $= 16$

	Coefficient	t-Statistic	P-Value
Intercept	0.0169	2.71	0.0176
Bottom-Tier Issuance (lagged)	0.086	5.51	0.0001
Real Interest Rates	0.001988	1.627	0.127

To be sure, more recent events will make some difference. We therefore propose a more complete model of default rates consisting of the variables listed in Exhibit 9–5. This model simply adds real interest rates to the model described in Jónsson, Fridson and Zhong (1996), which explained 76.7 percent of the annual variance in default rates.

Adding the new variable produces a percentage-of-variance-explained (R^2) of 93.9 percent (see Exhibit 9–6). All four variables are significant at confidence levels of 95 percent or higher. Exhibit 9–7 illustrates the historically tight fit between actual annual default rates and the values estimated by our proposed new model. From 1980 on, the standard error of estimate has been 0.61 percent.

A "jackknife test" of the data confirms that the model's high explanatory value is not intolerably period-dependent. Dividing the observation period in half, we calculate coefficients for the four explanatory variables, based only on the first half. We then test those coefficients on the second-half data. The percentage-of-variance-explained is approximately the same in the first (89.6 percent) and the second (99.2 percent) halves.[5]

Notwithstanding its generally close fit with actual default rates, our proposed new model characterizes the 1996 trailing twelve-months' rate (2.06 percent through October) as surprisingly low. The model shares this overestimation with other empirical attempts to explain aggregate default

---

5. Although the model derived solely from the first-half data achieved a high R^2, it greatly overestimated the default experience of 1990–1991. Considering that those years essentially represented the post-Depression peak in defaults, overestimation was a less blameworthy error than underestimation. In any event, the division of data into subperiods is an exercise undertaken solely to test the full-period model's robustness. With 15 years of data now under its belt, the full-period model should perform well, even under extreme conditions such as those witnessed in 1990–1991.

E X H I B I T   9–5

Explanatory Variables of Proposed New Model

Variable	Source
Unseasoned Bottom-Tier Issuance Percentage of Principal Amount of High Yield Issuance Rated B-Minus or Lower by Standard & Poor's (annually, lagged by three years)	Securities Data Company
Stock Market Relative Value (3 x Standard & Poor's Price/Earnings Ratio) minus (Nasdaq Index Price/Earnings Ratio)*	Standard & Poor's, National Association of Securities Dealers
Interaction Variable Unseasoned Bottom-Tier Issuance × Growth in Gross Domestic Product (Dummy variable: 1 if greater than 1.5% per annum, 0 if less than or equal to 1.5%)	Bureau of Labor Statistics
Real Interest Rates Nominal Interest Rate on Ten-Year U.S. Treasuries (quarterly average) minus Same-Period Year-over- Year Percentage Change in Consumer Price Index	Bureau of Labor Statistics, Federal Reserve Board

*Multiplication of the S&P 500's multiple by 3 is a transformation demanded by the outcome of the regression analysis.

E X H I B I T   9–6

Regression Output of Final Default Rate Model

$R^2 = 0.939$
Adjusted $R^2 = 0.916$
Observations = 16

	Coefficient	t-Statistic	P-Value
Intercept	0.004	0.727	0.483
Bottom-Tier Issuance	0.027	2.203	0.050
(3 × S&P) − (NASD)	0.001	2.739	0.019
Interaction	0.617	4.780	0.001
Real Interest Rates	0.003	3.633	0.004

E X H I B I T   9–7

Actual versus Estimated Default
Rate (yearly), 1980–1996*

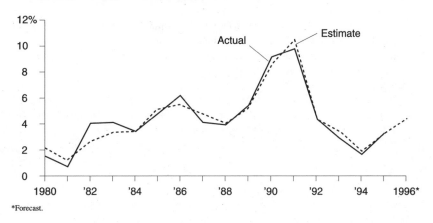

*Forecast.

rates. Unusually favorable monetary conditions may be responsible, but no research to date has satisfactorily explained the disappointing (to analysts and vulture capitalists) shortfall of defaults during 1996.

CONCLUSION

Previous research on the determinants of aggregate default rates on high yield bonds has strangely neglected the role of real interest rates. From a macroeconomic perspective, real rates would loom as the first explanatory variable worth testing.

Our new empirical work finds that real interest rates, lagged by two years, significantly enhance the explanatory power of previously established models of aggregate default rates. The lag is significant in that it helps investors to identify a likely range of future default rates, without having to forecast the future state of the economy or financial markets.

REFERENCES

Altman, Edward I. and Scott A. Nammacher (1987). *Investing in Junk Bonds: Inside the High Yield Debt Market.* New York: John Wiley & Sons.

Fons, Jerome S. (1991). *An Approach to Forecasting Default Rates.* New York: Moody's Investors Service, August.

Fridson, Martin S. and James F. Kenney (1994). "How Do Changes in Yield Affect Quality Spreads?" *Extra Credit,* July/August, pp. 4–13.

Helwege, Jean and Paul Kleiman (1996). "Understanding Aggregate Default Rates on High Yield Bonds." *Current Issues in Economics and Finance.* Federal Reserve Bank of New York, May.

Jónsson, Jón G. and Martin S. Fridson (1996). "Forecasting Default Rates on High-Yield Bonds." *The Journal of Fixed Income,* June, pp. 69–77.

Jónsson, Jón G.; Martin S. Fridson; and Hong (Harry) Zhong (1996). "Advances in Default Rate Forecasting." *Extra Credit,* May/June, pp. 4–9.

Vanderhoof, Irwin T.; Faye S. Albert; Aaron Tenenbein; and Ralph F. Verni (1990). "The Risk of Asset Default: Report of the Society of Actuaries C-1 Risk Task Force of the Committee on Valuation and Related Areas." *Transactions 1989,* pp. 547–91. St. Joseph, Michigan: Imperial Printing Company.

PART THREE

Security Valuation

Valuing Like-Rated Senior and Subordinated Debt[*]

Martin S. Fridson

M. Christopher Garman

INTRODUCTION

A little-remarked-upon feature of Moody's and Standard & Poor's bond rating systems is the fact that a given rating can apply to issues with quite different estimated probabilities of default. For instance, S&P uses its B+ rating not only for senior issues of companies with default probabilities in the high Single-B range, but also for subordinated issues of companies with default probabilities in the mid-Double–B range.[1]

Recognizing that difficulties may arise when ratings do double duty, Moody's compiles its default rate statistics on a senior-equivalent basis, rather than grouping issues according to their actual ratings. With few other exceptions, however, research on credit experience and on the relationship between ratings and yields lumps senior B1 issues with subordinated B1 issues, senior BB– issues with subordinated BB– issues and so forth.

As we shall demonstrate, the failure to distinguish between like-rated bonds of different priorities in the capital structure can foster misperceptions about the relationship between agency ratings and bond pricing. In particular, our informal surveying of practitioners discloses a widespread belief that a senior bond ought to yield less than a like-rated subordinated bond, yet we show the opposite to be true, in both theory and practice. We also find that the relative premium on senior debt should and does increase as ratings decrease. Finally, we offer a possible explanation for the paradox of how the market seems to arrive, by an incorrect line of reasoning, at the correct relative valuation of like-rated senior and subordinated bonds.

---

*Reprinted by permission. Copyright © 1998 Merrill Lynch, Pierce, Fenner & Smith Incorporated.
1. See Exhibit 10–1 for a comparison of the Moody's and Standard & Poor's rating scales.

E X H I B I T   10–1

Comparison of Moody's and
Standard & Poor's Rating Scales

Moody's	Standard & Poor's
Aaa	AAA
Aa1	AA+
Aa2	AA
Aa3	AA–
A1	A+
A2	A
A3	A–
Baa1	BBB+
Baa2	BBB
Baa3	BBB–
Ba1	BB+
Ba2	BB
Ba3	BB–
B1	B+
B2	B
B3	B–
Caa1	CCC+
Caa2	CCC
Caa3	CCC–
Ca	CC
C	C
—	D

THE TRADE-OFF BETWEEN DEFAULT
PROBABILITY AND EXPECTED RECOVERY

To analyze the relationship between equivalently rated senior and subordinated bonds, we shall first consider two of the most important dimensions
of bond valuation, namely, probability of default and severity of default.[2]
Note that Moody's attempts, just as Standard & Poor's does, to reflect both
of these aspects of risk on a single letter-grade scale. For example, a Ba3
rating on a subordinated bond indicates not only a measurable probability
that default will occur, but also the fact that the subordinated holder has a
lesser standing in the event of bankruptcy than a senior holder.

2. The ratings of Moody's and S&P focus largely on probability of default, with severity of default
    addressed to a more limited extent through the gradation between senior and subordinated
    issues. Bond covenants likewise have some rating impact, but there are few if any examples
    of two pari passu issues of a single company being rated differently because of nonequivalent
    covenant packages. Several other dimensions of valuation are explicitly excluded from the

Let us imagine, for a moment, a world in which companies issue only senior bonds. In this world, the holders of all of a company's issues have equivalent standing in a liquidation or reorganization. Accordingly, there is no analytical need to differentiate bonds according to their expected recoveries in bankrupctcy. Under such conditions, a rating system is satisfactory as long as it accurately classifies companies (which, given the assumptions, is tantamount to classifying issues) according to their default probabilities. The customary means of pursuing this objective is to group companies on the basis of identifiable risk factors (e.g., cash flow coverage of interest charges, ratio of debt to cash flow).

A close analogy to a bond-rating scheme based solely on default risk is an actuarial system designed for life insurance underwriters. By way of illustration, actuaries regard 30-year-olds, as a group, as better risks than 60-year-olds. This judgment is valid if the former group proves to have lower observed mortality over a reasonable, stated period. Similarly, the rating agencies' criteria for assigning companies to risk buckets (Triple-A, Double-A, etc.) are vindicated if each bucket's observed incidence of default is greater than that of the bucket rated one step higher. (In the case of the highest rating category, Triple-A, the default rate should exceed that of "risk-free" government bonds.)

Exhibit 10–2 confirms that over a one-year horizon, the default rate rises with each step down the Moody's senior-equivalent rating scale. Similar graphs for longer horizons (over which even Triple-A companies have a nonzero default rate) likewise reveal an inverse relationship between rating and default rate. In our imaginary world of senior issuance only, rational investors would simply demand a larger risk premium (that is, more yield) on a Single-B bond than they would demand on a Double-B bond, adjusting for any differences in duration, covenants, secondary market liquidity, and so forth.[3]

---

rating process (e.g., duration, vulnerability to premature redemption, issue size—which affects liquidity in the secondary market—and transient supply/demand factors). The frequently voiced criticism that ratings correspond imperfectly to secondary market yields is rather unjust. It is reasonable to chastise an organization for not achieving its stated objective, but not for "failing" to accomplish a mission that others have falsely ascribed to it. The agencies make no representation that their ratings are in and of themselves sufficient for the determination of appropriate yields.

3. Even in our imaginary world, an investor might perceive a particular company to be misclassified by the agencies, even while acknowledging the accuracy of ratings, in aggregate. The investor might then be rational, in light of her belief, to demand a higher yield on a Double-B than on a Single-B. Alleged misratings are a murky topic, however. Rating errors cannot be demonstrated on the basis of purely objective, quantitative measures, given that the agencies emphasize the role of certain subjective factors in their analysis. Neither can after-the-fact experience establish whether a credit was previously misrated. The fact that a Single-B

E X H I B I T   10–2

One-Year Default Probabiliity, 1970–1994

Note: Based on 1970–1994 data.
Source: Moody's Investors Service.

The world becomes much more complicated when we add subordinated debt issuance to the picture. Now we must take into account the
severity, as well as probability, of default.

Generally speaking, when a company becomes unable to meet its
obligations, it defaults on both its senior and its subordinated bonds.
Accordingly, the two classes of debt have equivalent probability of default.
Under the absolute priority rule, however, the bankruptcy settlement must
satisfy the senior holders' claims in full before any asset value is conveyed
to the subordinated holders.[4] Bankruptcy usually implies that asset value
is insufficient to satisfy all claims in their entirety. Subordinated holders,
standing further back in line than senior holders, ordinarily wind up with
less than full recovery. Therefore, although subordinated debt is no more
likely to default than senior debt, its expected *severity* of default is greater.

In this more complicated world of subordinated as well as senior
issuance, a difficulty arises from the use of a single rating scale to characterize both probability and severity of default risk. Specifically, a rational
investor will value a bond according to its *total default risk,* defined as
probability of default times severity of default. Unfortunately, there is no

---

borrower escaped default all the way until maturity does not prove that it was underrated;
the published default rate for such credits is less than 100 percent. Returning to the actuarial
analogy, if some of the 30-year-olds die in airplane accidents or natural disasters within the
next five years, it surely will not indicate that they were misclassified. An individual's
experience may diverge widely from the average experience of the population.

4. For a discussion of how the absolute priority rule works in practice, see Chapter 23. On the whole,
seniority in the capital structure is indeed associated with superior recoveries in bankruptcies,
even if the principle of absolute priority is not always honored to the letter.

assurance that the total default risk of an average senior B+ bond will be equivalent to the total default risk of an average subordinated B+ bond. That is, it would be pure serendipity if the product of B+ default probability and senior default severity happened to equate to the product of BB– (senior-equivalent) default probability and subordinated default severity. Consequently, two bonds, both rated B+, may have quite dissimilar total default risks. In this light, it often makes eminent sense for two identically rated bonds to carry different yields, even though the market concurs with the agencies' default risk assessments in both cases.[5] (Small wonder, then, that many noninvestment-grade analysts perceive little connection between ratings and yields.)

Thanks to statistical analysis conducted by the rating agencies, as well as studies such as Altman and Eberhart (1994), expected default losses by rating and capital structure priority are not matters of conjecture. Exhibit 10–3 provides direct comparisons for all ratings in the range of Double-B to Single-B, using Moody's notation. At each level, the table shows the one-year expected default rate[6] on a senior unsecured issue of the indicated rating, along with the comparable figure for a like-rated senior subordinated issue. In no instance, as it turns out, does a rating connote the same degree of risk on a senior bond as it does on a senior subordinated bond.

By way of illustration, let us consider the B1 rating, for which the S&P equivalent is B+. Exhibit 10–3 indicates that a senior bond rated B1 has a 5.7 percent probability of defaulting within the next year, according to Moody's historical data. Also according to Moody's, the average price of a senior unsecured bond shortly after default is 44.62 percent of par. The *annual default loss rate* for a B1 senior unsecured bond, which takes into account both probability and severity, is $5.7\% \times (1 - 0.4462) = 3.16\%$.[7]

---

5. Strictly speaking, default premiums should vary with maturity, cf. Fons (1994). In this discussion, readers should take "identically rated" to mean "carrying the same rating and all other valuation factors, excluding priority in the capital structure."

6. It is feasible, using Moody's data, to construct similar tables based on cumulative probability of default over multiyear periods. The general conclusions drawn from such analysis would be similar to those derived from Exhibit 10–3, given that the incidence of default rises monotonically with each descent down the rating scale, over multiyear periods, as well as over one year.

7. This analysis is a bit simplistic in the sense that the full implied 55.38 percent loss (from par) will not necessarily occur within the year of default. In many cases, the market anticipates defaults far in advance, with the result that the imperiled bonds are valued at substantial discounts more than one year before the obligor fails on its obligations. (This is not even to consider discounts that may occur for noncredit reasons, i.e., increases in interest rates subsequent to issuance.) All of these facts apply to both senior and subordinated debt, however. The comparative risk relationship between the two classes is fairly depicted by the table, even though the analysis is not a perfect simulation of expected performance in the period immediately preceding default.

E X H I B I T   10–3

Rating-for-Rating Comparison of Expected Default Loss by Capital Structure Priority

	Senior Unsecured			Senior Subordinated			
				Annual Default Rate			
Bond Rating	Annual Default Rate (%)	Adjustments for Recoveries	Annual Default Loss Rate (%)	Implied Senior Rating	(%)	Adjustment for Recoveries	Annual Default Loss Rate (%)
Ba1	1.0	× (1−.4462) =	0.55	Baa3	0.3	× (1−.3604) =	0.19
Ba2	1.0	× (1−.4462) =	0.55	Baa3*	0.3	× (1−.3604) =	0.19
Ba3	2.8	× (1−.4462) =	1.55	Ba1	1.0	× (1−.3604) =	0.64
B1	5.7	× (1−.4462) =	3.16	Ba2	1.0	× (1−.3604) =	0.64
B2	10.7	× (1−.4462) =	5.93	Ba3	2.8	× (1−.3604) =	1.79
B3	14.5	× (1−.4462) =	8.03	B1	5.7	× (1−.3604) =	3.64

Note: Based on 1983-1994 data.

*As a consequence of the general rule for "notching" of subordinated debt (one level down if the senior rating is investment grade, two levels down if the senior rating is noninvestment grade), some ambiguity arises at the borderline between Triple-B and Double-B. Companies with bonds rated Ba2 (BB) at the subordinated level may have senior-equivalent ratings of either Baa3 (BBB–) or Ba1 (BB+). In the latter case, the annual default loss rate would be 0.64 percent, nominally higher than the 0.55 percent indicated for Ba2 senior issues. As a practical matter, there are very few nonconvertible subordinated bonds rated Ba2 or BB. The majority of those that we can currently identify are rated investment grade (Baa3 or BBB–) at the senior level.

Source: Moody's Investors Service.

Moving across to the senior subordinated side of the table, the comparable annual default loss number is derived from the default probability of the senior-equivalent rating (Ba2), which is 1.0 percent. Factoring in as well the average postdefault price of 36.04 percent of par for senior subordinated issues, we calculate an annual default loss rate of 0.64 percent.

For every rating from Ba1 down to B3, the senior unsecured issue has a higher annual default loss rate than the equivalently rated senior subordinated issue. Note as well that the default loss differential increases as ratings decrease. At the Ba1 level, annual default losses on senior unsecured bonds exceed annual default losses of senior unsubordinated bonds by 0.55% − 0.19% = 0.36%. Down at the B3 category, the difference is a much greater 8.03% − 3.64% = 4.39%.

If the market is pricing risk correctly, then yields should be higher on senior bonds than on equivalently rated subordinated bonds, a proposition that practitioners generally find counterintuitive. In addition, the default loss comparisons suggest that the yield spread between like-rated senior and subordinated debt should be wider at lower rating levels.

EVIDENCE FROM THE PRIMARY MARKET

To determine whether the market is correctly pricing the effects of seniority and subordination, we first studied risk premiums on new issues. This approach offered comparatively few observations, but highly accurate data, to wit:

Using primary market data largely overcomes the difficulty of obtaining reliable historical pricing of high yield bonds, which trade primarily in a noncentralized, over-the-counter secondary market. On the pricing date, a high yield issue has a recorded, bona fide clearing price. It is established through the auctionlike process of "building a book." The underwriter determines the amount of demand at various yields and then sets the price with the objective of getting the bonds fully distributed and well placed. To be sure, minor deviations from pure clearing prices may arise, as when underwriters "leave a little on the table" to ensure good performance in the aftermarket. Occasionally, too, a deal that has met a frosty reception from investors during the marketing period may be priced richer than the level at which all bonds have been spoken for. In such a case, the underwriter runs the risk of being stuck with unsold securities, but hopes for a rally that will make the issue's fixed price a fair value as other bonds move higher. Notwithstanding such nuances, high yield new issue prices represent a marked improvement in reliability over secondary prices.

We focused our new issue analysis on the B+ rating category. From a comprehensive list of noninvestment-grade bonds floated during the period 1989 through the first half of 1995, we created a matched sample. Each senior bond (secured or unsecured) was paired with a subordinated bond (designated either as senior subordinated or just subordinated) that was priced no more than 30 days earlier or later. We purged our preliminary sample of the one pair that included a bond labeled "senior" but which our analysis determined to be, in reality, structurally subordinated, as explained in Appendix B of this chapter. To minimize distortions arising from other pricing factors, we excluded from our sample all bonds with maturities of less than 5 years or more than 15 years. When more than one potential match was available within our designated pricing period and maturity band, we selected the subordinated issue that most closely resembled the senior issue according to these two criteria. We did not set specific constraints on call protection, which was fairly uniform within the sample. Of the 70 individual issues, 55 had exactly five years of call protection, none had fewer than three years, and just three were noncallable for more than eight years. As a final means of ensuring comparability between the matched bonds, we limited our sample to conventional fixed-coupon issues (i.e., we excluded floating rate, variable rate, zero coupon, and payment-in-kind obligations). Our final sample (see Exhibit 10–4 on pages 186–189) consisted of 35 matched pairs of senior and subordinated issues. This is generally considered a sufficient number to establish statistical significance at the 95 percent confidence level.

To isolate the risk premium specifically related to priority in the capital structure, we subtracted from each bond's yield to maturity, as of its pricing date, the yield to maturity of the Merrill Lynch Single-B Corporate Index on the same date. The differences were generally negative numbers, consistent with the sample's B+ (connoting less than average risk within the Single-B universe) quality.

Note that a more common practice in research of this type is to measure risk premiums against risk-free U.S. Treasury obligations. Such an analysis, however, may introduce distortion related to changes over time in the yield spread between Treasuries and bonds rated in the broad Single-B category. That is, a senior bond may misleadingly appear to be priced richer than a subordinated bond was priced a week earlier, simply because the entire Single-B sector has widened against Treasuries in the interim. Comparing yields to a rating-specific benchmark captures a purer premium for seniority or subordination. One disadvantage of this striving for purity is that our observation period could not begin earlier than the late-1988 inception date of the Merrill Lynch Single-B Corporate Index.

For each matched pair, we subtracted the subordinated issue's spread over the Single-B index from the senior issue's comparable spread. A positive difference indicated that the senior issue had a larger risk premium, controlling for changes in the market during the brief interval between pricing of the two matched bonds. To test whether the market had priced seniority and subordination correctly, at least in a directional sense, we calculated the mean of the differences in spreads for each matched pair. If, on average, the differences were positive, then we could infer that the market correctly viewed senior bonds as riskier than comparably rated subordinated issues, notwithstanding the practitioners' diametrically opposed intuition.

Exhibit 10–5 summarizes the findings of our new issue analysis. On average, the risk premiums on senior B+ issues were 75.74 basis points greater than the risk premiums on subordinated B+ issues. We can reject the null hypothesis that the 75.74–basis-point gap was statistically indistinguishable from zero. Given our sample size of 35 matched pairs, there is a 95 percent probability that the true mean was within a range of 75.74

E X H I B I T   10–5

Comparison of Risk Premiums on Senior and
Subordinated Issues, Primary Market Data

	Basis Points
Mean of Difference of Spread	75.74
Standard Deviation	130.94
Confidence Interval*	43.38

*At 95 percent confidence level, based on sample size of 35 matched pairs.

plus-or-minus 43.38, or 32.36 to 119.12 basis points. As a precaution against being misled by outliers, we reran the test excluding two extreme values shown in Exhibit 10–4 (398 basis points for a June 1993 pair and 389 basis points for a June 1995 pair). Even in this case, we were able to reject the null hypothesis at the 95 percent confidence level. In short, we can be quite confident that B+ senior new issues are priced at larger risk premiums than B+ subordinated issues, notwithstanding practitioners' impressions to the contrary.

EVIDENCE FROM THE SECONDARY MARKET

For corroboration of our findings in the primary market, as well as to examine the impact of seniority and subordination at different rating levels, we next turned to secondary market data. In doing so, we sacrificed a certain degree of price accuracy (see the above discussion of new issue pricing) for the benefit of larger sample sizes and elimination of possible distortion related to changes over time. Specifically, we drew our test sample from a universe (approximating 600 noninvestment-grade issues) tracked in a Merrill Lynch research periodical, *Yield-to-Worst Rankings*. All issues in the sample were priced on the same date, July 20, 1995, a procedure that eliminated timing differences as a potential pitfall in our analysis. The loss of pricing accuracy, vis-á-vis the primary market, was mitigated by the fact that the approximately 600 bonds in the *Rankings* generally represented the most regularly quoted issues within a larger universe of more than 2,000 nondefaulted, noninvestment-grade bonds identified by Merrill Lynch.

E X H I B I T   10–4

Comparison of Risk Premiums on
Senior and Subordinated New Issues

Issuer	Offer Date	Type of Security	Offer Yield (%)
Memorex Telex	7/26/89	Gtd Sr Notes	13.250
Hyster-Yale Materials	7/27/89	Sr Sub Debs	12.375
American Medical Int'l	10/19/91	Senior Notes	11.000
Safeway	11/13/91	Sr Sub Notes	10.000
Coltec Industries	3/24/92	Senior Notes	9.750
Safeway	3/17/92	Sr Sub Notes	9.350
Plastic Containers	4/02/92	Sr Secured Nts	10.750
Owens-Illinois	4/01/92	Sr Sub Notes	10.250
Cinemark USA	6/03/92	Senior Notes	12.000
Continental Cablevision	6/15/92	Sr Sub Notes	10.625
K&F Industries	6/03/92	Sr Secured Nts	11.875
Continental Cablevision	6/15/92	Sr Sub Debs	11.000
Del Webb	4/09/92	Senior Notes	11.000
Embassy Suites	4/08/92	Gtd Sr Sub Nts	10.875
Riverwood International	6/17/92	Senior Notes	10.750
Owens-Illinois	6/15/92	Sr Sub Notes	10.500
Rexnord	7/01/92	Senior Notes	10.750
Riverwood International	6/17/92	Sr Sub Notes	11.250
Grand Union	7/15/92	Senior Notes	11.250
Owens-Illinois	7/28/92	Sr Sub Notes	10.000
AMC Entertainment	8/05/92	Gtd Sr Notes	12.000
Bradlees	7/29/92	Sr Sub Notes	11.000
ComputerVision	8/14/92	Senior Notes	10.875
Continental Medical Sys.	8/06/92	Sr Sub Notes	11.000
Century Communications	8/14/92	Senior Notes	9.625
Owens-Illinois	8/14/92	Sr Sub Notes	9.750
Coltec Industries	10/16/92	Senior Notes	9.750
IDEX	9/16/92	Sr Sub Notes	9.750
Farm Fresh	10/02/92	Senior Notes	12.250
Owens-Illinois	10/01/92	Sr Sub Notes	9.95
Foamex L.P.	10/02/92	Senior Notes	11.250
American Reinsurance	9/21/92	Sr Sub Debs	10.875
Western Co. of North Amer.	11/12/92	Senior Notes	13.330
California Hotel Finance	11/20/92	Sr Sub Notes	11.000

B Index Market-Weighted Yield (%)	Spread Differential to B Index (%)	Difference of Spreads (%)	Maturity	Offer Price	Call Protection (years)
13.796	−0.546		8/01/96	100.000	5.0
13.790	−1.415	0.869	8/01/99	100.000	5.0
13.570	−2.570		10/15/00	100.000	4.9
13.041	−3.041	0.471	12/01/01	100.000	10.0
11.775	−2.025		4/01/00	100.000	8.0
11.518	−2.168	0.143	3/15/99	100.000	7.0
11.844	−1.094		4/01/01	100.000	5.0
11.844	−1.594	0.500	4/01/99	100.000	5.0
11.725	0.275		6/15/02	100.000	5.0
11.636	−1.011	1.286	6/15/02	100.000	5.0
11.725	0.150		12/01/03	100.000	5.0
11.636	−0.636	0.786	6/01/07	100.000	7.0
11.861	−0.861		3/31/00	99.336	5.0
11.868	−0.993	0.132	4/15/02	100.000	5.0
11.627	−0.877		6/15/00	100.000	5.0
11.636	−1.136	0.259	6/15/02	100.000	5.0
11.585	−0.835		7/01/02	100.000	5.0
11.627	−0.377	−0.458	6/15/02	100.000	5.0
11.525	−0.275		7/15/00	100.000	5.0
11.451	−1.451	1.176	8/01/02	100.000	5.0
11.331	0.669		8/01/00	99.36	5.0
11.424	−0.424	1.093	8/01/02	100.000	5.0
11.850	−0.975		8/15/97	100.000	3.0
11.312	−0.312	−0.663	8/15/02	99.250	5.0
11.850	−2.225		8/15/00	99.310	8.0
11.850	−2.100	−0.125	8/15/04	100.000	5.0
11.671	−1.921		11/01/99	100.000	7.0
11.201	−1.451	−0.470	9/15/02	100.000	5.0
11.197	1.053		10/01/00	100.000	5.0
11.256	−1.306	2.359	10/15/04	100.000	5.0
11.197	0.053		10/01/02	100.000	5.0
11.195	−0.320	0.373	9/15/04	100.000	5.0
11.675	1.655		12/01/02	97.501	5.0
11.536	−0.536	2.191	12/01/02	100.000	5.0

(continued)

E X H I B I T   10–4

(concluded)

Issuer	Offer Date	Type of Security	Offer Yield (%)
Geneva Steel	3/08/93	Senior Notes	11.125
Toll Corporation	3/10/93	Sr Sub Notes	9.625
Pacific Lumber	3/12/93	Senior Notes	10.500
Mark IV Industries	3/19/93	Sr Sub Notes	8.750
Coast Savings Financial	4/01/93	Senior Notes	10.000
Petroleum Heat and Power	3/30/93	Sub Notes	10.125
Container Corp. of America	4/07/93	Senior Notes	9.750
Payless Cashways	4/13/93	Sr Sub Notes	9.125
Essex Group	4/30/93	Senior Notes	10.000
Sealy	4/30/93	Sr Sub Notes	9.500
Bell & Howell	6/11/93	Senior Notes	9.250
Musicland Group	6/10/93	Sr Sub Notes	9.000
Stone Container	6/24/93	Senior Notes	12.625
AnnTaylor Stores	6/14/93	Sub Notes	8.750
USAir	6/30/93	Senior Notes	10.000
Blount	6/30/93	Sr Sub Notes	9.000
Jordan Industries	7/16/93	Senior Notes	10.375
AES Corporation	6/09/93	Sr Sub Notes	9.750
Carbide/Graphite Group	8/19/93	Senior Notes	11.500
General Chemical	8/12/93	Sr Sub Notes	9.250
Cole National	9/24/93	Senior Notes	11.500
Best Buy	10/04/93	Sr Sub Notes	8.625
Stone-Consolidated	12/07/93	Sr Secured Nts	10.250
Sinclair Broadcast Group	12/02/93	Sr Sub Notes	10.000
Geneva Steel	1/24/94	Senior Notes	9.500
Gulf Canada Resources	1/20/94	Sr Sub Debs	9.350
USAir	1/26/94	Sr Unsec Nts	9.625
Petroleum Heat and Power	1/27/94	Sub Debs	9.375
Container Corp. of America	5/04/94	Senior Notes	11.250
Garden State Newspapers	5/13/94	Sr Sub Notes	12.000
MVE	2/10/95	Sr Secured Nts	12.500
Petroleum Heat and Power	2/02/95	Sub Debs	12.250
Westinghouse Air Brake	6/19/95	Senior Notes	9.375
Berkeley Federal	6/07/95	Sub Debs	12.000
Kelley Oil & Gas	6/14/95	Senior Notes	13.625
Gulf Canada Resources	6/28/95	Sr Sub Notes	9.749

B Index Market-Weighted Yield (%)	Spread Differential to B Index (%)	Difference of Spreads (%)	Maturity	Offer Price	Call Protection (years)
10.977	0.148		3/15/01	100.000	5.0
10.926	−1.301	1.449	3/15/03	99.207	5.0
10.936	−0.436		3/01/03	100.000	5.0
10.927	−2.177	1.741	4/01/03	100.000	5.0
10.909	−0.909		3/01/00	100.000	5.0
10.903	−0.778	−0.131	4/01/03	100.000	5.0
11.002	−1.252		4/01/03	100.000	10.0
10.896	−1.771	0.519	4/15/03	100.000	5.0
10.891	−0.891		5/01/03	100.000	5.0
10.891	−1.391	0.500	5/01/03	100.000	15.0
10.502	−1.252		7/15/00	100.000	4.0
10.502	−1.502	0.250	6/15/03	100.000	5.0
10.380	2.245		7/15/98	100.000	5.0
10.485	−1.735	3.980	6/15/00	100.000	5.0
10.198	−0.198		7/01/03	100.000	5.0
10.198	−1.198	1.000	6/15/03	100.000	5.0
10.227	0.148		8/01/03	100.000	5.0
10.544	−0.794	0.942	6/15/00	100.000	4.0
10.324	1.176		9/01/03	100.000	5.0
10.322	−1.072	2.248	8/15/03	100.000	5.0
10.464	1.036		10/01/01	98.714	5.0
10.468	−1.843	2.879	10/01/00	100.000	5.0
10.157	0.093		12/15/00	100.000	5.0
10.215	−0.215	0.308	12/15/03	100.000	5.0
9.745	−0.245		1/15/04	100.000	5.0
9.749	−0.399	0.154	1/15/04	99.367	5.0
9.746	−0.121		2/01/01	100.000	7.0
9.682	−0.307	0.186	2/01/06	100.000	5.0
11.008	0.242		5/01/04	100.000	8.0
10.906	1.094	−0.852	7/01/04	100.000	5.0
11.763	0.737		2/15/02	100.000	5.0
11.849	0.401	0.336	2/01/05	100.000	5.0
10.967	−1.592		6/15/05	100.000	5.0
10.782	1.218	−2.810	6/15/05	100.000	5.0
10.895	2.730		6/15/99	99.629	4.0
10.907	−1.158	3.888	7/01/05	99.216	5.0

As in our primary market analysis, we strove for homogeneity in our secondary test sample by selecting only issues with 5 to 15 years of remaining maturity. The *Yield-to-Worst* universe from which we drew our test sample excludes floating rate, payment-in-kind, and multicoupon bonds. We further refined the selection criteria to eliminate zero coupon issues. Once again, we divided our sample into senior (including both secured and unsecured) and subordinated (including any degree of subordination) issues. We did not go to great lengths to control for structural subordination in our large test sample, having found it to be an almost negligible consideration in the primary sample. Our final sample consisted of 298 issues, distributed as follows:

Rating	Senior	Subordinated	Total
B+	46	41	87
B	50	75	125
B–	32	54	86
Total	128	170	298

From a statistical standpoint, the comparative sizes of all six subsamples promised robust results.

Exhibit 10–6 details the first portion of our secondary market data analysis. Note that we simplified this analysis by expressing all quantities in yield-to-worst.[8] There was no need to convert the figures to spreads, given that all yields were measured on the same day and that the risk premiums would be calculated by subtracting the same quantity (the yield on the Single-B index) in every case. Under these conditions, analyzing yields would reduce to the same procedure as analyzing spreads.

On July 20, 1995, our sample of actively quoted B+ senior issues had a mean yield of 11.34 percent. The comparable figure for B+ subordinated issues was 10.18 percent. Because the confidence intervals of the two means do not overlap, we can infer, at the 85 percent confidence level, that the B+ senior issues truly had greater risk premiums than the B+ subordinated issues. Similarly, B senior issues had a higher average yield (11.92 percent) than B subordinated issues (10.58 percent), a difference that was significant at a higher 95 percent confidence level. Finally, the average yield of B– senior issues (14.03 percent) exceeded the average yield of B– subordinated yields (11.45 percent) by a margin that again was significant at the 95 percent confidence level.

---

8. "Yield-to-worst" is a term of art, defined as a bond's lowest possible realized yield, considering all redemption scenarios, i.e., retirement at maturity plus redemption on all possible call dates at the specified call prices, but not default or exchange.

E X H I B I T   10–6

Comparison of Risk Premiums on Senior and Subordinated Issues, Secondary Market Data

Rating	Priority	Sample Size	Mean Yield-to-Worst (%)	Standard Deviation of Yield	Confidence Interval (%) Low	Confidence Interval (%) High	Significant at Confidence Level (%)
B+	Senior	46	11.34	3.60	10.58	12.11	85
	Subordinated	41	10.18	1.20	9.91	10.45	
			Difference: 1.16				
B	Senior	50	11.92	2.22	11.30	12.53	95
	Subordinated	75	10.58	1.44	10.26	10.91	
			Difference: 1.34				
B–	Senior	32	14.03	3.48	12.83	15.24	95
	Subordinated	54	11.45	1.24	11.12	11.78	
			Difference: 2.58				

Secondary comparisons, in short, reinforce the conclusion derived from the new issue evidence: The market correctly perceives senior issues as *more* risky, not less risky, than like-rated subordinated issues.

Observe as well that the B+ seniors outyielded the B+ subordinated issues by 11.34% – 10.18% = 1.16%. That was less than the gap between B senior and subordinated yields of 11.92% – 10.58% = 1.34%, which in turn was less than the B- differential of 14.03% – 11.45% = 2.58%. The monotonic increase in the senior/subordinated yield spread (from 1.16% to 1.34% to 2.58%) as we move down the rating scale suggests that the market is getting the senior/subordinated relationship right with respect to magnitude, as well as direction. That is, the greater yield differential between like-rated senior and subordinated bonds at lower rating levels is consistent with the evidence (see Exhibit 10–3) that the differential in annual default losses increases as ratings decline.

HOW DOES THE MARKET GET IT RIGHT?

Our results indicate that the high yield market is rational in pricing the differences in default probability and severity between like-rated senior and subordinated bonds. This finding is reassuring from the standpoint of efficient allocation of capital within the economy, yet at the same time presents a riddle. When we ask practitioners how a senior bond ought to trade in comparison to a like-rated subordinated bond, they almost invariably respond that the senior issue should yield less than the subordinated issue. How can investors in aggregate price the issues correctly if, individually, they analyze the question incorrectly?

The best answer to this riddle, we believe, is that, in practice, high yield investors and marketmakers do not discover prices from ratings and capital structure priority. Doing so is not a realistic option, because as they readily observe, issues within a single noninvestment-grade rating category concurrently trade at widely varying yields. (For documentation, see Exhibit 10–6.) Practitioners typically begin the valuation process by assigning a bond to one of many general risk categories that are determined fairly independently of ratings. A common procedure is to classify companies according to their cash flow coverage of interest expense, then to adjust the indicated risk premium upward or downward according to the relative favor with which the company's industry is currently being viewed.[9]

As an illustration of how this line of thought could lead to the same relative valuation as we have justified on the grounds of default loss rates, consider the following two bonds of similar coupon and maturity, issued by fictitious companies in the same industry:

Bond	A	B
Issuer	Adam Corp.	Betty Inc.
Priority	Subordinated	Senior
Issuer's Coverage Ratio	2.0x	1.3x

To determine an appropriate spread for a proposed swap between the two bonds, a practitioner may begin by considering the yields on comparable issues. Perfectly substitutable bonds are not generally available in the high yield market, but let us suppose that there are other issuers in the same industry with coverage ratios in the neighborhood of 2.0x. We shall further assume that the bonds of such companies are currently trading in a range around 11 percent, with variances related to the structures and the secondary market liquidity of individual issues.

Having examined these facts, practitioners can conclude that a starting point for valuing Bond A is 11.00 percent. Then, to adjust for the

---

9. Investors' industry preferences vary over time as a function of the business cycle. In addition, high yield funds generally have industry concentration limits, established by charter or by policy, to ensure adequate portfolio diversification. If a particular industry happens to be subject to a large volume of financing during a period in which most funds are already near their maximum allowed concentration in that industry, the new supply will be absorbed only at levels cheaper than the ratings or financial ratios would otherwise justify. For these and other reasons, yields and ratings correlate imperfectly, not because the ratings are "wrong" or the yields are "right," but because many factors other than ratings legitimately influence yields.

issue's subordination, they add on 50 additional basis points. Note that the magnitude of this rule-of-thumb adjustment varies with the market conditions and the credit quality of the senior bond. In short order, without ever having considered Moody's or Standard & Poor's ratings, practitioners have assigned an 11.50 percent yield to Bond A. (Later on, though, a trader or portfolio manager may attempt to negotiate a better price on the basis of the issue's rating, while in the next breath dismissing ratings as irrelevant because they do not happen to favor his cause in another trade.)

Proceeding to Bond B, the practitioners use as a benchmark the 12.50 percent level around which various issuers in the industry with approximately 1.3 times coverage are trading. This time, there is no need to adjust for subordination, so it is 12.50 percent. The indicated spread between Bond A and Bond B is 12.50% − 11.50% = 1.00%, with senior Bond B carrying the higher yield.

If the practitioners took note of the ratings, they might find them to be identical. Fixed charge coverage is by no means the sole determinant of ratings, but at the ratios indicated, Adam Corp. and Betty Inc. might very well be rated BB− and B+, respectively, at the senior-equivalent level. Bond A's subordination would likely put its rating at B+. Under these far from implausible circumstances, practitioners' deductions from financial ratios produce exactly the same result as our analysis of default losses: A senior bond should yield more than a like-rated subordinated bond.

By considering the valuation process actually employed by investors and dealers, we can resolve the paradox of the market pricing the senior/subordinated relationship correctly, even though most market participants analyze the problem incorrectly. The truth is that unless prodded by mischievous research types, traders and portfolio managers never analyze this particular problem. They derive satisfactory valuations (as evidenced by their survival in a highly competitive environment) by a reasoning process that bypasses both ratings and the magnitude of risk represented by a subordinated position in the capital structure.

CONCLUSION

We have shown that in the noninvestment-grade market, senior bonds should and do yield more than like-rated subordinated bonds. The premium yield on seniors increases as ratings decrease. All of this happens despite the opinion of most practitioners that the subordinated issues should carry higher yields.

Armed with new insight into the value of seniority and subordination, investors may from time to time spot exploitable pricing disparities. If another market participant acts on the mistaken belief that a senior bond should yield less than a like-rated subordinated bond, the two issues involved may temporarily deviate from their appropriate relative values. It may even pay to search systematically for examples of such mispricing in the secondary market.

From a research standpoint, our findings may facilitate additional useful discoveries regarding valuation. As an example, the relative default loss statistics that we report represent averages over many years. Most risk factors in the high yield market are priced variably over time. For example, liquidity premiums respond to market fluctuations and the term structure of interest rates changes from one period to the next. It is therefore reasonable to suppose that subordination is valued differently, on a rating-for-rating basis, in some periods than in others. Detailed empirical analysis may be able to explain such variance in the senior/subordinated spread, enabling investors to capitalize on short-run deviations of the spread from fundamentally supportable levels.

Notching Policies for Senior and Subordinated Ratings

To capture both probability and severity of default on a single rating scale, a rating agency must devise rules for "notching," that is, specifying the number of gradations between an issuer's senior and subordinated debt. Further complications arise when the capital structure includes both senior secured and senior unsecured debt, for which recoveries are likely to differ in the event of bankruptcy.

A number of interesting issues arise in connection with rating policies on subordinated issues. For example, the agencies may rate a subordinated (most likely convertible) issue of a company with a Triple-A senior rating no lower than the senior debt. The reasoning is that the extremely low probability of default renders a distinction based on severity irrelevant. There may likewise be little point in notching for fine gradations within the subordinated portion of the debt structure. In practice, bankruptcy judges try to aggregate creditors into as few classes as possible. Subordinated creditors may wind up being recognized separately from senior unsecured creditors, but junior subordinated holders may be lumped with senior subordinated holders. In that case, the two groups of subordinated bondholders will receive equivalent settlements for their claims, so that with hindsight, differentiating them on the basis of severity will prove invalid.

For the majority of high yield issuers, rated debt is limited to, at most, senior unsecured and one class of subordinated debt. Notching for such companies has tended to follow a rule of thumb. The subordinated debt has typically been rated two notches lower than the senior debt, for example, senior Ba1, subordinated Ba3; senior BB–, subordinated B, etc. By a similar rule of thumb, a one-notch differential usually has prevailed when the senior debt has carried an investment grade rating (Baa3 or higher by Moody's or BBB– or higher by Standard & Poor's). The rating agencies, however, have consistently emphasized (Moody's perhaps a bit more emphatically) that this practice is not a hard-and-fast rule. Recently, S&P has more explicitly added flexibility to its notching (Sprinzen and Samson 1995). Under the revised policy, though, it remains the case that "subordinated debt is almost always notched to the fullest extent," which is generally two notches down from the company's highest rating.

    Whatever notching policy the rating agencies may adopt, properly reflecting both probability and severity of default in a single scale remains a challenge. Perhaps it would help to set a specific objective of notching in such a way that bonds of a given rating have roughly equivalent default losses. Examining the data in Exhibit 10–3, we find that the seemingly arbitrary rule of "two notches down if the senior debt is noninvestment grade" performs reasonably well, at least based on the one-year default statistics. Rearranging the figures a bit, as shown below, we find similar default loss rates for senior ratings and subordinated ratings two notches lower, at levels within Moody's Ba and B tiers for which statistics are available.

Senior/Subordinated Rating	*Annual Default Loss Rate (%)*	
	Senior Unsecured	**Senior Subordinated**
Ba1/Ba3	0.55	0.64
Ba2/B1	0.55	0.64
Ba3/B2	1.55	1.79
B1/B3	3.16	3.64

Structural Subordination

An investor may hold a bond labeled "senior" yet still be a residual receiver of earnings. Probably the most familiar case of such "structural subordination" involves a senior bond of a pure holding company. A pure holding company is defined as a parent corporation that owns the stock of one or more operating companies but does not directly own any operating assets. In this case, debt service is completely dependent on dividends from the operating subsidiaries, which are junior to any senior claims at those entities. If the operating subsidiaries are bond issuers, the senior bond-holder is effectively subordinated to the subsidiaries' bondholders.

The phrase structural subordination appeared in many of the prospectuses we used in our primary market analysis, but the term was applied rather broadly. Upon close examination, we found that in some cases, the operating subsidiaries guaranteed the holding company debt, eliminating the effect of structural subordination. In other instances, the subsidiaries had no debt of their own and were precluded from issuing any, again negating the structural subordination. We checked cases that were not clear-cut against Standard & Poor's ratings tables to verify that issues labeled senior by Securities Data Company indeed carried the agency's senior ratings. (S&P acknowledges genuine structural subordination by notching down the senior debt.) In the end, we were obliged to eliminate only one senior issue from our sample on grounds of structural subordination.

REFERENCES

Altman, Edward I. and Allan C. Eberhart (1994). "Do Seniority Provisions Protect Bond-holders' Investments?" *The Journal of Portfolio Management.* Summer, pp. 67–75.

Carty, Lea; Dana Lieberman; and Jerome S. Fons (1995). *Corporate Bond Defaults and Default Rates 1970–1994.* New York: Moody's Investors Service, January.

Fons, Jerome S (1994). "Using Default Rates to Model the Term Structure of Credit Risk." *Financial Analysts Journal.* September/October, pp. 25–32.

Fridson, Martin S. and Rock Gao (1995). *Yield-to-Worst Rankings.* New York: Merrill Lynch & Co., July.

Sprinzen, Scott and Solomon Samson (1995). "Notching Criteria Refined for U.S. Corpo-rates." *High Yield Directions.* New York: Standard & Poor's, June, pp. A13–A17.

CHAPTER 11

Determinants of Spreads on New High Yield Bond Offerings*

Martin S. Fridson

M. Christopher Garman

Sheng Wu

INTRODUCTION

Most portfolio managers who specialize in the high yield bond sector rely heavily on the new issue market. As a result of the limited liquidity of many seasoned issues, it can be difficult to deploy large sums quickly and cost-effectively through the secondary market alone. By implication, the performance of high yield managers is highly sensitive to their valuation skills in the primary market.

In this light, it is curious that almost nothing appears to have been published on the subject of pricing high yield new issues. High yield handbooks such as Altman (1990), Altman and Nammacher (1987), Fabozzi and Cheung (1990), Fridson (1989), Howe (1988), Lederman and Sullivan (1993), Reilly (1990), and Yago (1991) discuss credit analysis but do not explicitly link the resulting risk assessments to valuation.

Perhaps researchers have shied away from the subject of high yield pricing because of its popular reputation as a black art. During the 1980s, market participants commonly portrayed high yield securities as "story bonds," for which value was not a direct function of quantifiable financial

---

*Reprinted by permission. Copyright © 1998 Merrill Lynch, Pierce, Fenner & Smith Incorporated.

ratios. Before going bankrupt in 1990, leading high yield bond underwriter Drexel Burnham Lambert actively represented the intangibles of management vision and drive as offsets to risky-looking balance sheets. Even during the 1990s, it has frequently been possible to observe wide discrepancies between underwriters' "preliminary price talk" and a bond's pricing at issue. This suggests that at least for certain issues, objective pricing criteria are difficult to identify.[1]

We undertook to fill the research gap on high yield primary pricing by analyzing the variance in a sample of prices as a function of quantitative factors. In this way, we hoped to measure the extent to which the new issue market reflects objective considerations, as opposed to "stories." We also expected our analysis to shed light on the value added by underwriters in high yield financing transactions. To the extent that institutional investors cannot derive completely objective prices for a newly floated noninvestment-grade bond, the quality of the issuer's execution will depend at least partly on the underwriter's effectiveness in presenting the deal to analysts and portfolio managers.

METHODOLOGY

We chose 1995–1996 as our observation period. This two-year span offered reasonable variation in market conditions, ensuring that our results would not be skewed by prolonged, atypical risk premiums or extreme supply/demand conditions. The spread between Merrill Lynch's High Yield Master Index and 10-year Treasuries ranged from 291 to 414 basis points.[2] Quarterly high yield new issue volume[3] varied between $21.8 billion and $5.4 billion, while monthly high yield bond mutual fund flows were as low as $280 million and as high as $2.2 billion.[4]

---

1. An underwriter might deliberately overstate the value of an underwriting client's bonds at an early stage of the marketing process. The firm risks a loss of credibility, however, if it goes public with a valuation that diverges radically from the eventual clearing price. The typical procedure is for the underwriter to remain mum about probable pricing until the deal has been exposed sufficiently to get a notion of where investment interest will materialize.
2. To put these numbers into perspective, the mean spread in the period subsequent to the 1989–1991 high yield market upheavals has been 382 basis points, with a standard deviation of 63 basis points. Our observation period is not distributed exactly evenly between bull and bear markets, but captures a substantial portion of the variation in conditions that occurs over longer periods.
3. Source: Securities Data Company.
4. Source: Investment Company Institute.

From Securities Data Company we collected an initial sample of 521 high yield bonds floated during our observation period. After eliminating issues that were nonrated, were rated less than B3 by Moody's, or had floating-rate coupons, we obtained a final sample of 428 issues. The sample included both conventionally underwritten public bonds and bonds distributed under Securities and Exchange Commission Rule 144a.[5]

In seeking to explain variance in new issue pricing, we specifically sought to exclude variance related to the general rise and fall of default-free bond yields. To filter out those fluctuations, we expressed each noninvestment-grade issue's initial offering yield as a spread over the same-day yield on a Treasury security of similar maturity. We then set out to identify the factors that caused this spread to vary from issue to issue. (In more technical terms, the new issue spread became the dependent variable in our multiple regression analysis.)[6]

To identify sources of variance in the spread, we tested a variety of factors that market participants commonly regard as material. Our list included both company-specific and environmental factors. Detailed descriptions of the test variables appear in Exhibit 11–1.

COMPANY-SPECIFIC VARIABLES
Rating

As measures of credit risk, agency ratings by Moody's and Standard & Poor's or other organizations may be expected to correlate with risk premiums on newly offered bonds. In general, the lower the rating (that is, the higher the indicated probability of default), the wider should be the spread (see Exhibit 11–2).

To obtain pure default risk measures, we express all ratings in senior-equivalent terms. As explained by Fridson and Garman (November 1995),

---

5. The convention in the high yield market is for 144a deals to be done with registration rights attached. Once registered, the obligations become effectively indistinguishable from conventionally underwritten issues.

6. As noted above, the spread between Treasuries and the high yield market as a whole was not completely stable during the period. In testing our variables, we investigated whether the issue-to-issue variance in spread was partly a function of changes in the overall level of risk premiums, as indicated by the spread versus Treasuries. As our discussion of empirical findings indicates, the coincident high yield spread versus Treasuries had a modestly positive, but statistically insignificant, correlation with the individual issue spread. Accordingly, we conclude that our results were not compromised by the hidden influence of fluctuations in the general level of spreads.

E X H I B I T   11–1

Descriptions of Test Variables

Short Title	Description	Source
Company-Specific		
Rating	Moody's Senior-Equivalent Rating	Moody's Investor Service
Seniority	Dummy Variable: 0–Senior,	
	1–Subordinated	Securities Data Company
Term	Maturity (Years)	Securities Data Company
Callability	Dummy Variable: 0–Noncallable,	
	1–Callable	Securities Data Company
Zero Coupon Status	Dummy Variable: 0–No, 1–Yes	Securities Data Company
Float	Principal Amount at Issue ($ millions)	Securities Data Company
144a Status	Dummy Variable: 0-Public, 1–144a	Securities Data Company
First-Time Issuer	Dummy Variable: 0–No, 1–Yes	Securities Data Company
Underwriter Type	Dummy Variable: 0–Investment Bank,	
	1-Commercial Bank	Securities Data Company
Environmental		
Spread versus	Yield Differential: Merrill Lynch High	
Treasuries	Yield Master Index minus Ten-Year	
	Treasuries (basis points)	Merrill Lynch
BB/B Spread	Yield Differential: Merrill Lynch Single-B	
	Index minus Double-B Index (basis points)	Merrill Lynch
Yield Curve	Yield Differential: Ten-Year Treasuries minus	
	Three-Month Treasuries (basis points)	Merrill Lynch
Default Rate	Moody's Trailing-12-Month Issuer-Based	
	Default Rate	Moody's Investor Service
IPO Volume	Monthly Initial Public Offerings (dollars)	Securities Data Company
Forward Calendar	Volume of Announced but Uncompleted	
	High Yield Offerings (dollars)	Merrill Lynch
Mutual Fund Flows	Monthly Net Inflows to High Yield	
	Mutual Funds, Including Dividend	
	Reinvestments (dollars)	Investment Company Institute
Mutual Fund	Liquid Assets as a Percent of Total Assets	
Cash Position	of High Yield Mutual Funds	Investment Company Institute
Interest Rate Change	Month-over-Month change in Yield on	
	Ten-Year Treasuries (basis points)	Merrill Lynch
High Yield Return	Total Return on Merrill Lynch High Yield	
	Master Index (percent)	Merrill Lynch

the correlation between ratings and spreads is constrained by the fact that ratings measure both *probability* and *severity* of default.[7] The consequent problem is that like-rated bonds do not always have equivalent implied *total*

---

7. "Severity" refers to the percentage of principal amount of claim that investors can expect to lose in the event of default. Severity is in large measure a function of priority within the corporate structure. That is, expected recoveries are higher for senior than for subordinated creditors, all other things being equal.

E X H I B I T   11–2

Comparison of Moody's and Standard & Poor's Rating Scales*

	Moody's	Standard & Poor's
Lowest Risk	Aaa	AAA
	Aa1	AA+
	Aa2	AA
	Aa3	AA–
	A1	A+
	A2	A
	A3	A–
	Baa1	BBB+
	Baa2	BBB
	Baa3	BBB–
	Ba1	BB+
	Ba2	BB
	Ba3	BB–
	B1	B+
	B2	B
	B3	B–
	—	CCC+
	Caa	CCC
	—	CCC–
	Ca	CC
Highest Risk	C	C
	—	D

*June 16, 1997 Moody's announced that it would subdivide its Caa category into Caa1, Caa2 and Caa3 subcategories. It will take at least a few quarters for sufficient data to accumulate in order to determine whether the explanatory power of ratings is enhanced by this change.

risk (probability times severity). For example, a B+ bond may be either a senior issue of a company with B+ default probability or a subordinated issue of a company with (considerably lower) BB default probability. Fridson and Garman demonstrate that the senior bond's lesser severity does not fully offset the disadvantage of its greater default probability. Furthermore, Fridson and Garman show empirically that market yields correctly reflect the nonequivalent total risks of the senior B+ and subordinated B+ issues. They find that when bonds are classified according to their senior-equivalent ratings (see Exhibit 11–3), rather than their actual ratings, the percentage of variance in yield explained by ratings nearly doubles.

E X H I B I T   11–3

Conversion Key for Senior Equivalency, Moody's Scale, Noninvestment-Grade Range

Subordinated Rating	Senior-Equivalent Rating
Ba1	Baa3
Ba2	Baa3
Ba3	Ba1
B1	Ba2
B2	Ba3

The general rule applied here is that if the senior equivalent is Baa3 or higher, the subordinated rating is one "notch" lower, while if the senior-equivalent rating is Ba1 or lower, the subordinated rating is two "notches" lower. (Subordinated Ba2 issues fall through the cracks.) This rule-of-thumb approach is not an absolutely rigid rule, but as a practical matter, generally produces the correct senior-equivalent rating. See Chapter 10.

Seniority

Given two bonds of equivalent default probability, a rational investor will demand a larger risk premium for the one that has greater default severity. Accordingly, we should observe a correlation between the initial offering yield and ranking within the capital structure. As a practical matter, ranking boils down to whether the issue is senior or subordinated, with the latter implying greater default severity and hence a higher yield. Following Fridson and Garman (November 1995), we use a dummy variable to indicate subordination. We do not model gradations within the broad rankings (senior secured versus senior unsecured, senior subordinated versus junior subordinated, etc.). Our sample contains no cases of multiple issues of a single issuer that would necessitate such distinctions.

Term

In examining term as a possible pricing influence, we are not dealing with the familiar "term structure of interest rates."[8] That effect is captured in the prevailing yield curve of pure interest rates (i.e., rates on default-free

---

8. Elementary discussions of the debt markets (see, for example, Fabozzi, 1993, pp. 187–188) point out that at a point in time, pure (default free) interest rates vary by term. The yield curve, a plot of interest rates on the vertical axis against bond maturity on the horizontal axis, is positively sloped in some periods, negatively sloped in others, and "humped" (peaking in the middle maturities) in still others.

Treasuries). Instead, we quantify the correlation between a noninvestment-grade bond's term and its spread over Treasuries. We use final maturity as a measure of term, although alternatives such as average life and duration are available at the cost of considerable additional data-gathering effort.

Kim, Ramaswamy, and Sundaresan (1993) present a theoretical model for yield spread as a function of maturity. In the case of callable bonds (the type that accounts for 78.3 percent of our sample), they predict a general pattern of spreads being smallest in very short maturities, peaking in intermediate maturities, and declining with maturity in the long end. Fons (1994), on the other hand, predicts and empirically observes a pattern of the spread increasing with maturity for investment-grade bonds, but decreasing with maturity for noninvestment-grade bonds. Longstaff and Schwartz (1995) derive a more complex relationship in which spread increases between the first five to ten years of maturity, then declines. We hypothesize that our own data on noninvestment-grade issues will corroborate Fons's results.

Callability

From the issuer's standpoint, an option to retire a bond prior to its final maturity has considerable value (see Kalotay 1997). If the general level of interest rates declines between issuance and the scheduled maturity, the issuer can refinance at a lower rate. It may also become attractive for the issuer to call the bond if its credit quality improves, enabling the company to obtain a lower default risk premium on new borrowings. This second type of trigger for the call option is especially pertinent for noninvestment-grade issues. They typically trade hundreds of basis points above the default-risk-free Treasury rate, meaning that reduced-rate refinancing can represent sizable cost savings for issuers.

While an early redemption realizes a benefit for the issuer, it represents a cost to the investor, who is forced to reinvest at a reduced interest rate. The rational investor will demand compensation for incurring this risk, so we hypothesize that callable bonds carry wider spreads than noncallable bonds. We model callability as a simple Yes/No proposition, even though the value of the call option varies according to particulars of the call provision. (These include the length of the call protection period and the required premiums to be paid to investors.) As a practical matter, there is a fair amount of standardization in high yield call features, with five years being the typical call protection on a ten-year deal.

Zero Coupon Status

Zero coupon (or "deferred-interest") bonds display greater volatility of returns than conventional cash-pay issues. Over the period 1987–1996, which includes all full-year periods for which returns on the Merrill Lynch High Yield Deferred-Interest Bond Index are available, the mean monthly return of 1.02 percent had a standard deviation of 3.20 percent. The cash-pay only Merrill Lynch High Yield Master Index's 0.88 percent mean return, by contrast, displayed a standard deviation of just 1.58 percent. In terms of this conventional measure, zeros were considerably riskier than cash-pays. Accordingly, we hypothesize that primary buyers will demand wider spreads on zeros than on cash-pays.[9]

Float

Marketability is a valuable benefit. It enhances the ability of a security's holders to shift their portfolio mixes in response to changes in personal circumstances, market conditions, or the security's expected return or risk. Fisher (1959) uses as a proxy for marketability the market value of all of a firm's publicly traded bonds, arguing:

> Other things being equal, the smaller the amount of bonds a firm has outstanding, the less frequently we should expect its bonds to change hands. The less often its bonds change hands, the thinner the market; and the thinner the market, the more uncertain is the market price. Hence, the larger the market value of publicly traded bonds a firm has outstanding, the smaller is the expected risk premium on those bonds.

Fridson and Bersh (1996) demonstrate a correlation between the amount outstanding of an *individual bond* and the risk premium assigned it in the primary market. We follow this practice, hypothesizing that the larger the issue size, the smaller is the risk premium.

---

9. The comparatively high volatility of zeros derives at least in part from their comparatively long duration. At the end of 1996, for example, the Merrill Lynch High Yield Deferred-Interest Bond Index's duration was 6.40, versus 5.52 for the cash-pay-only Merrill Lynch High Yield Master Index. The disparity in volatility is accentuated by the tendency of dealers to sell zeros short when they perceive a need to hedge against a marketwide decline. (Shorting cash-pays is considerably more expensive, in light of the short seller's obligation to pay out cash interest, while remaining short, to the buyer.) As a result of this practice, zeros not only fall precipitously when a perceived market downside increases, but rise sharply if the danger passes, causing dealers to scramble to cover their shorts.

144a Status

Securities and Exchange Commission Rule 144a is an effort to combine certain advantages of the private and public markets. A company that uses the mechanism can move swiftly to capitalize on favorable financing conditions because it is not obliged to go through the registration process first. At the same time, a 144a issue can be traded in the secondary market more readily than a conventional private placement, which enhances its attractiveness to investors.

In the noninvestment-grade market, 144a offerings are invariably done with registration rights attached. Except in the rare instance of an underwriter's failure to get an issue registered, a 144a high yield bond eventually becomes undifferentiated from conventionally underwritten public issues.

The distribution process (including road shows) for public and 144a deals is essentially the same, except that in the latter case, registration follows distribution. Nevertheless, many institutions continue to classify 144a bonds as "illiquid securities" until they are registered. Institutions typically limit (by charter or by internal policy) the proportion of their portfolios that illiquid securities may represent. If a large volume of 144a offerings comes to market within a short span, those limits may be reached.

As the issues get registered, they leave the illiquid category, restoring the institutions' ability to buy additional 144a paper. In the interim, however, an issuer that desires the swift market access of the 144a mechanism must sell to a reduced universe of investors. This implies that the borrower may have to pay a yield premium. Accordingly, we hypothesize that 144a issuance (modeled as a yes/no dummy variable) is associated with a larger spread than public issuance.

First-Time Issuer

Remarks "heard on the street" suggest that portfolio managers demand an incremental risk premium on bonds of companies that have not been in the public markets previously. One possible rationale is that in such cases, there is no basis for judging management credibility. For seasoned issuers, in contrast, investors can match a record of management's stated plans and performance projections against actual outcomes.

We classify a company as a first-time issuer if it has not floated public debt during the ten years preceding our observation period.[10] To the

---

10. An alternative classification scheme would also differentiate between companies on the basis of whether they have public stock outstanding. Publicly held companies are likely to have a traceable record of planned versus actual corporate strategy and performance.

fullest extent possible, we check for name changes that may identify an observation-period issuer as a preobservation-period issuer under a different guise. We hypothesize that companies identified by a dummy variable as first-time issuers have larger spreads than other issuers.

Underwriter Type

Portfolio managers report that they need an extra yield inducement to participate in a high yield offering by an underwriter that lacks a strong reputation for supporting its deals in the aftermarket. Furnishing a supporting bid in a volatile market requires capital commitment. This is a hidden cost that novice underwriters may not consider when projecting the profitability of their entry into the high yield bond sector.

As a class, commercial banks are comparative newcomers to corporate bond underwriting. The Glass–Steagall Act of 1933 imposed restrictions on such activity that have eroded only gradually. Anecdotal evidence suggests that, fairly or otherwise, some portfolio managers regard commercial banks as less reliable than investment banks in terms of supporting their deals. Recognizing that the question is highly sensitive from a competitive standpoint, we allow the empirical results to speak for themselves. In line with portfolio managers' comments, we hypothesize that issues underwritten by commercial banks (represented by a dummy variable) have larger spreads than issues underwritten by investment banks.

ENVIRONMENTAL VARIABLES
Spread versus Treasuries

It would be surprising if an individual high yield new issue's risk premium were insensitive to changes in the marketwide risk premium. According to the law of one price, its valuation must be affected by the returns available on substitutable assets. Seasoned high yield bonds are substantially (albeit not completely) substitutable for new issues. Accordingly, an increase or decrease in the yield spread on an index of seasoned issues should be accompanied by a roughly parallel move in new issue spreads. Our hypothesis, by this logic, is that the wider the high yield sector's spread versus Treasuries at the time of issue, the wider will be the new issue's spread.

BB/B Spread

New issue spreads may be sensitive not only to changes in risk premiums on high yield bonds as a group, but also to changes in intramarket spreads. (By this we mean yield differentials among various quality tiers within the noninvestment-grade category.) As Exhibit 11–4 shows, the marketwide spread versus Treasuries and the spread between BB and B corporates move somewhat independently over time. Therefore, it is reasonable to surmise that the BB/B spread may have explanatory power distinct from that of the marketwide spread versus Treasuries.

In particular, our past studies of the BB/B spread have led us to believe that it captures fluctuations in the supply/demand dynamics of the high yield market. Over the intermediate term, its range appears to be determined by the level of spreads generally. In the short run, however, the BB/B spread tightens when high yield mutual fund inflows temporarily outpace the generation of new issues. Once the primary market catches up, the BB/B spread widens again.

We hypothesize that a wide BB/B spread is associated with wide new issue spreads.

Yield Curve

The risk premium on high yield bonds may be affected by general money market conditions, as well as conditions within the noninvestment-grade arena. One key gauge of the broader interest rate environment is the slope of the Treasury yield curve. When short-term interest rates are high relative to long-term bond yields (indicated by a flat or negatively sloped yield curve), the usual interpretation is that the Federal Reserve is keeping credit tight. Tight money, in turn, may lead to a recession, which implies increased default risk. Accordingly, we hypothesize that the Treasury yield curve (long-term yield minus short-term yield) is negatively correlated with the spread versus Treasuries.

Default Rate

It seems reasonable to suppose that the risk premium on high yield new issues increases when perceived credit risk increases in the market as a whole. Perceptions of credit risk, in turn, are likely to be influenced by fluctuations in the default rate on high yield bonds. We hypothesize that high default rates coincide with wide spreads.

IPO Volume

Investors may accept comparatively modest risk premiums on high yield bonds when the stock market is ebullient. For one thing, high equity valuations connote general optimism about the economic outlook. Additionally,

E X H I B I T   11–4

High Yield Spread versus Treasuries and
Intramarket Spread, Monthly, 1992–1996

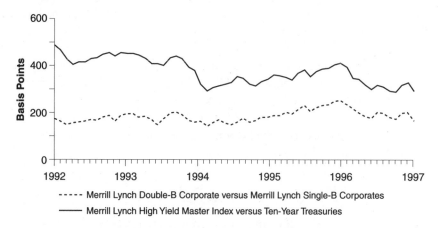

----- Merrill Lynch Double-B Corporate versus Merrill Lynch Single-B Corporates
——— Merrill Lynch High Yield Master Index versus Ten-Year Treasuries

a bull market in stocks can enable noninvestment-grade companies to strengthen their balance sheets by raising new equity. As a proxy for the tone of the stock market, we use the volume of initial public offerings (IPOs). Large IPO volume, we hypothesize, is associated with narrow high yield new issue spreads.

Forward Calendar

Among environmental factors, investors may consider not only indications of credit risk (listed above), but also supply/demand conditions. One potentially useful gauge of supply is the volume of announced, but not yet completed, high yield offerings. Based on elementary economic principles, we would expect a large forward calendar to be associated with a wide spread over Treasuries.

Mutual Fund Flows

The demand side of the supply/demand equation may be captured reasonably well by the flow of capital into or out of high yield bond mutual funds. Mutual funds, to be sure, are not the sole buyers of high yield bonds. Their flows have the merit of being reported on a weekly basis, however, and may be representative of total flows across all categories of investors. Based again on elementary economics, we would expect large inflows to the high yield funds to be associated with narrow spreads over Treasuries.

Mutual Funds Cash Position

Fridson and Jónsson (1996) find a positive correlation between the high yield secondary market's spread versus Treasuries and the percentage of assets held in cash by high yield mutual funds. The most likely explanation is that when portfolio managers are uneasy about the market outlook, they increase their cash positions rather than take on additional price-vulnerable assets. Under such circumstances they may also accumulate cash in anticipation of increased shareholder redemptions. Either way, investors reduce market liquidity when they stay on the sidelines. We hypothesize that new issues must carry large risk premiums when liquidity is low, implying a positive correlation between the primary market spread and the cash percentage in the funds.

Interest Rate Change

Fridson and Kenney (1994) find a negative correlation between changes in the yield on ten-year Treasuries and changes in the spread versus Treasuries. Yields on corporates do not immediately respond basis point for basis point to changes in government bond yields. In the short run, the spread between the two asset classes compresses when Treasury rates rise and expands when rates fall. We therefore hypothesize a negative correlation between the spread versus Treasuries and the monthly yield change in Treasuries.

High Yield Return

Investors may tend to evaluate the future by looking in the rear-view mirror. Putting it another way, they may accept comparatively low risk premiums on an asset class that has provided strong returns recently.

CORRELATION RESULTS

Exhibit 11–5 ranks the proposed independent variables in order of their absolute correlation (R) with the spread versus Treasuries over the period 1995–1996. Signs of the correlations are indicated in a separate column. For convenience, the table also lists each variable's percentage-of-variance-explained (R^2), which is considered in assessing its fitness as a variable in the final model.

E X H I B I T   11–5

Proposed Variables Affecting New Issue Spreads,
by Absolute Correlation, 1995–1996

Short Description	Absolute Correlation (%)	Sign	R^2(%)
Rating	68.81	+	47.35
Callability	39.94	+	15.95
144a Status	27.24	+	7.42
Zero Coupon Status	21.08	+	4.44
First-Time Issuer	19.58	+	3.84
Underwriter Type	16.54	+	2.73
Seniority	10.30	+	1.06
Term	9.54	–	0.91
Float	9.45	–	0.89
Default Rate	8.00	–	0.64
Yield Curve	7.93	–	0.63
Spread versus Treasuries	5.79	+	0.34
Mutual Fund Flows	5.70	+	0.33
IPO Volume	5.47	–	0.30
Forward Calendar	5.16	–	0.27
BB/B Spread	4.38	+	0.19
High Yield Return	2.47	+	0.06
Interest Rate Change	0.34	–	0.00
Mutual Fund Cash Position	0.02	+	0.00

Most of the correlation signs are consistent with our hypotheses. For all three exceptions (Default Rate, Maturity, and High Yield Return), the absolute correlations were weak, that is, below 0.10. We therefore tend to regard the variables in question as immaterial to new issue spreads, rather than indicators of irrational behavior by investors.

Ratings, contrary to the self-serving claims of rating-agency bashers, have by far the highest correlation with new issue spreads of any variable. It is simply an error to assert, as recently did an investor who refused to be quoted by name, "I don't think rating agencies' ratings in and of themselves have much of a bearing on pricing."[11] In fairness, the connection is more apparent when ratings are analyzed on a senior equivalent basis, as we have done here, than when they are viewed in the more usual (nonsenior-equivalent) format.

---

11. Monroe (1997), p. 34.

The strength of the correlations with new issue spreads drop off rather sharply after Ratings (0.69). Perusing the other variables that appear to have a material influence on primary market pricing, we find support for the proposition that all other things being equal, a high yield offering will carry a larger risk premium if it is a 144a transaction, a new name in the market or a bond underwritten by a commercial bank.

CREATING A MULTIPLE REGRESSION MODEL

Individual variables that displayed high correlations (R) with new issue spreads became candidates for our final regression model. We sought to maximize the model's explanatory power (R^2), subject to avoiding statistical distortions that might arise from effects such as multicollinearity. Stepwise regression was among the tools, but not the sole technique that we employed in identifying the optimal combination of variables.

Various combinations of the proposed independent variables explained respectable percentages of the variance in new issue spreads. No matter how many combinations we tried, however, we could not break through an "R^2 ceiling" of approximately 55 percent.

Exhibit 11–6 represents the best obtainable model, in our judgment. The percentage-of-variance-explained is 56 percent (adjusted $R^2 = 55$ percent). All nine explanatory variables are significant at the 97 percent confidence level or higher and have P-values (indicating the probability of the indicated correlation sign being wrong) of 3 percent or less.

The explanatory variables that "make the cut," ranked by absolute value of t-statistic, are:

1. Rating
2. Zero coupon status
3. BB/B spread
4. Seniority
5. Callability
6. Term
7. First-time issuer
8. Underwriter type
9. Interest rate change

Worth noting is the fact that 144a Status does not make the cut, despite its comparatively high correlation with new issue spread, as shown in Exhibit 11–5. Additional testing of the model indicates that the explanation appears

E X H I B I T   1 1 – 6

Multiple Regression Model of High
Yield New Issue Spread, 1995–1996

R^2	0.56
Adjusted R^2	0.55
Observation	428

	Coefficient	*t*-Statistic	*P*-Value	Confidence Level (%)
Intercept	−213.67	−3.39	0.00	99
Rating	66.19	16.02	0.00	99
Zero Coupon Status	136.54	4.16	0.00	99
BB/B Spread	95.31	3.84	0.00	99
Seniority	41.46	3.47	0.00	99
Callability	51.65	3.35	0.00	99
Term	−8.51	−3.14	0.00	99
First-Time Issuer	25.23	2.30	0.02	98
Underwriter Type	28.13	2.22	0.03	97
Interest Rate Change	40.44	2.12	0.03	97

to be the high correlation of 144a Status with Rating. Evidently, the periodic filling up of 144a baskets per se does not create statistically significant price discrimination. Rather, 144a deals carry comparatively high yields because they tend to be lower-rated issues. As was reported by Fridson and Garman (1997), only 20.6 percent of 144a high yield volume during 1992–1996 was rated in the Double-B category or split-rated (in the Triple-B category by Standard & Poor's, but below the Baa category by Moody's). The comparable figure for conventional public underwritings was 43.4 percent. If 144a Status does not genuinely result in wider spreads, all other things being equal, it may be that when investors cite 144a constraints as an objection, they are using an excuse to reject a deal on credit grounds.

Surprising too, is the absence of Float from the final model. The inconsequentiality of issue size persists in additional testing, in which we model principal amount as a dummy variable (assigning a value of zero for $100 million or greater and one for less than $100 million). Fridson and Bersh (1996), in contrast, find a strong issue-size effect in pricing. This result is generally consistent with Fisher (1959), the seminal article on corporate bond risk premiums. The low (9.45 percent) absolute correlation that we find for Float raises a caution about possible time dependency in our observation period. That is, investors may have been compensated unusually meagerly during 1995–1996 for the relative illiquidity of small issues. Perhaps an analysis of a longer period would show Float to have meaningful explanatory power, making possible a multiple regression model with a higher R^2 than we have achieved in the present study.

TESTING FOR PERIOD DEPENDENCE

One hazard in multiple regression analysis is that a model may explain variance extremely well within the test period, yet prove a very poor model subsequently. To test for this potential weakness (period dependence), we divided our test period into two subperiods, 1995 and 1996. (See Exhibits 11–7 and 11–8.) Encouragingly, adjusted R^2 was similar in the two subperiods at 57 percent and 54 percent, respectively. Additionally, Rating stood out with a very high t-statistic in both subperiods, as it did in the full observation period.

Somewhat less reassuring, while yet not damning, is the fact that four other explanatory variables display a greatly reduced statistical significance (t-statistic) and have very high probabilities of wrong correlation signs (P-value) during 1996. The four that appear to fall by the wayside are: BB/B Spread, First-Time Issuer, Underwriter Type, and Interest Rate Change. Perhaps their reduced significance reflects reduced discrimination by the market, as evidenced by an average secondary market spread between high yield bonds and ten-year Treasuries of just 328 basis points during 1996. During 1996, the spread averaged 371, only slightly less than the 1992–1996 average of 382. (The high yield sector's yield is measured by the Merrill Lynch High Yield Master Index.) It is also possible, although only time will tell, that one or more of the variables of reduced importance in 1996 are genuinely losing explanatory power over time. (For example, commercial banks may be gaining credibility as underwriters and therefore ceasing to have a spread-widening impact.)

POSSIBLE SOURCES OF UNEXPLAINED VARIANCE

The 55 percent R^2 ceiling that we encountered suggests that high yield new issue pricing is highly dependent on factors that do not lend themselves to the sort of modeling used in this study. Based on testimony of market participants, we suspect that the following exert considerable influence.

E X H I B I T   11–7

Multiple Regression Model of High Yield New Issue Spread, Subperiod–1995

R^2	0.60			
Adjusted R^2	0.57			
Observation	168			

	Coefficient	t-Statistic	P-Value	Confidence Level (%)
Intercept	−191.64	−1.43	0.16	84
Rating	66.71	8.16	0.00	99
Zero Coupon Status	115.93	1.98	0.05	95
BB/B Spread	113.83	2.29	0.02	98
Seniority	46.28	1.94	0.05	95
Callability	73.29	2.49	0.01	99
Term	−17.77	−3.00	0.00	99
First-Time Issuer	47.25	2.29	0.02	98
Underwriter Type	53.29	2.15	0.03	97
Interest Rate Change	77.83	1.82	0.07	93

E X H I B I T   11–8

Multiple Regression Model of High Yield New Issue Spread, Subperiod–1996

R^2	0.56			
Adjusted R^2	0.54			
Observations	260			

	Coefficient	t-Statistic	P-Value	Confidence Level (%)
Intercept	−3.94	−0.04	0.97	3
Rating	62.75	14.06	0.00	99
Zero Coupon Status	162.12	4.26	0.00	99
BB/B Spread	−2.22	−0.06	0.95	5
Seniority	35.48	2.76	0.01	99
Callability	32.43	1.87	0.06	94
Term	−5.14	−1.87	0.06	94
First-Time Issuer	8.53	0.68	0.50	50
Underwriter Type	10.09	0.73	0.47	53
Interest Rate Change	13.63	0.66	0.51	49

Issuer's Industry Category

The issuer's industry classification could affect pricing in at least two different ways. For one thing, it is possible that the market exacts a larger risk premium when a company is at the bottom of its profit cycle than when it is at the top.[12] Additionally, the relative scarcity of an industry's paper within the high yield universe may cause its new issues to be priced at variance with the levels indicated by our model. In general, high yield bond funds (and to an even greater extent, collateralized bond obligations) must diversify their holdings by industry. As a result of this constraint, a large volume of financing within a single industry during a brief time span, can create a glut. It may prove impossible to resolve this somewhat artificial oversupply through a smooth price adjustment.

It would not be difficult to classify the new issues in our sample by industry. Incorporating the classifications into our model, however, would be difficult, for at least two reasons:

1. Some industries would inevitably wind up with extremely small sample sizes. Even some of the most heavily represented industries would fall below the generally accepted cutoff of 30 observations required to validate statistical significance, given the overall sample size of 857 and the 40 industry classifications currently in use in the Merrill Lynch High Yield Index system.

2. The implications of a given industry classification would likely vary over the course of a two-year observation period. For example, an industry might progress from a high point to a low point in its operating cycle. Similarly, an industry with scarcity value in the early months might issue heavily and become a drag on the market in later months.

Notwithstanding these obstacles, future research might devise a workable approach and increase the 56 percent R^2 of our present model.

---

12. Ratings, in principle, should not vary in response to ordinary fluctuations in cash flow over the course of the cycle. In practice, though, it is sometimes difficult for the rating agencies to distinguish between cyclical and secular changes in profitability.

Quality of Management Presentation

Investors commonly report that their evaluation of a proposed new issue is influenced by the presentation skills that the company's management displays at the "road show." (This term refers to a series of group presentations and one-on-one meetings that a high yield company's management ordinarily makes to institutional investors over a period of several days preceding pricing. Road shows are nearly mandatory for both public and 144a transactions.)[13]

In the worst construction, the impact of the road show might suggest a triumph of style over substance. More positively, a good road show may be one in which bona fide investment merits are communicated effectively. The effective communication may simply involve such techniques as following a logical plan, speaking in clear and unconvoluted sentences, employing easily understandable graphics, and so forth.

CONCLUSION

Pricing of newly issued high yield bonds is sensitive to quantifiable characteristics of the issue and the prevailing market environment. In the issue-characteristics category, a noninvestment-grade bond's yield spread will be greater, all other things being equal, the lower its senior-equivalent rating, the lower its seniority in the capital structure, and the longer its maturity and also, if it is callable prior to maturity, a zero coupon security, the bond of a first-time issuer, or if it is underwritten by a commercial bank. As for the market environment, the yield will be higher, all other things being equal, the wider the secondary market spread between Double-B and Single-B corporates and if Treasury yields rise in the month preceding issuance.

The statistically demonstrable feasibility of modeling primary prices refutes the notion sometimes advanced that high yield issues are "story bonds," for which no objective evaluation standards apply. On the other hand, we find that no more than 56 percent of the variance in pricing of high yield new issues can be explained by objective factors.

---

13. For anecdotal evidence of the impact of road shows on high yield new issue pricing, see Celarier (1997). "Bonds are sold; they are not bought," comments one banker. "If they were bought, you could just put them on a screen, and investors would dial in and buy them."

This is encouraging news for underwriters in the sense that they have considerable potential for adding value to the underwriting process. In particular, by orchestrating an effective road show, a lead manager may obtain a narrower spread for an issuer than for another issuer that ought to be priced identically, based on numbers alone. To the extent that high yield debt is inherently a product with high value added by underwriters, it may remain a noncommoditized, high profit margin line of business for financial intermediaries.

REFERENCES

Altman, Edward I. (1990). *The High-Yield Debt Market: Investment Performance and Economic Impact.* Homewood, Illinois: Dow Jones-Irwin.

Altman, Edward I. and Scott A. Nammacher (1987). *Investing in Junk Bonds: Inside the High Yield Debt Market.* New York: John Wiley & Sons.

Celarier, Michelle (1997). "Borrowers: It's the Roadshow, Stupid!" *Euromoney,* June, pp. 60–62.

Fabozzi, Frank J. (1993). *Bond Markets, Analysis and Strategies,* 2nd ed. Englewood Cliffs, NJ: Prentice Hall.

Fabozzi, Frank J. and Rayner Cheung, eds (1990). *The New High-Yield Debt Market: A Handbook for Portfolio Managers and Analysts.* New York: HarperBusiness.

Fisher, Lawrence (1959). "Determinants of Risk Premiums on Corporate Bonds." *Journal of Political Economy.* June, pp. 217–37.

Fons, Jerome S (1994). "Using Default Rates to Model the Term Structure of Credit Risk." *Financial Analysts Journal.* September/October, pp. 25–32.

Fridson, Martin S. (1989). *High Yield Bonds: Identifying Value and Assessing Risk of Speculative Grade Securities.* Chicago: Probus Publishing Company.

Fridson, Martin S. and Jeffrey A. Bersh (1996). "Measuring Liquidity Premiums in the High-Yield Bond Market." In *The Yearbook of Fixed Income Investing 1995.* Edited by John D. Finnerty and Martin S. Fridson, pp. 84–116. Chicago: Irwin Professional Publishing.

Fridson, Martin S. and M. Christopher Garman (1995). "How Well Do Ratings Explain Yields?" *This Week in High Yield.* November, pp. 1, pp. 3–5.

_____ (1995). "Valuing Like-Rated Senior and Subordinated Debt." *Extra Credit,* July/August, pp. 4–17.

_____ (1997). "This Year in High Yield—1996." *Extra Credit.* January/February, pp. 4–33.

Fridson, Martin S. and Jón G. Jónsson (1996). "Spread versus Treasuries and the Riskiness of High Yield Bonds." *Financial Analysts Journal.* May/June, pp. 79–88.

Fridson, Martin S. and James F. Kenney (1994). "How Do Changes in Yield Affect Quality Spreads?" *Extra Credit.* July/August, pp. 4–13.

Howe, Jane Tripp (1988). *Junk Bonds: Analysis & Portfolio Strategies.* Chicago: Probus Publishing Company.

Kalotay, Andrew J. (1997). "Optimum High Yield Bond Calling." *Extra Credit.* January/February, pp. 34–39.

Kim, Joon; Krishna Ramaswamy; and Suresh Sundaresan (1993). "Does Default Risk in Coupons Affect the Valuation of Corporate Bonds?: A Contingent Claims Model." *Financial Management.* Autumn, pp. 117–31.

Klein, April (1996). "Can Investors Use the Prospectus to Price Initial Public Offerings?" *The Journal of Financial Statement Analysis.* Fall, pp. 23–38.

Lederman, Jess and Michael P. Sullivan (1993). *High Yield Bond Market: Investment Opportunities, Strategies and Analysis.* Chicago: Probus Publishing Company.

Longstaff, Francis A. and Eduardo S. Schwartz (1995). "A Simple Approach to Valuing Risky Fixed and Floating Rate Debt." *The Journal of Finance.* July, pp. 789–819.

Monroe, Ann (1997). "Do Bond Ratings Matter to High-Yield Buyers?" *Investment Dealers' Digest.* April 14, p. 34.

Reilly, Frank K (1990). *High-Yield Bonds: Analysis and Risk Assessment.* Charlottesville, VA: Association for Investment Research and Management.

Yago, Glenn (1991). *Junk Bonds: How High Yield Securities Restructured Corporate America.* New York: Oxford University Press.

CHAPTER 12

Analyzing a High Yield Issue

MARK R. SHENKMAN

INTRODUCTION

High yield bonds primarily trade on the basis of corporate developments. If the fundamental story is favorable and the company is exhibiting improving credit statistics, the bonds should show upward price movement. Conversely, if the credit fundamentals are showing erosion, the price of the bonds is likely to deteriorate. Therefore, credit analysis must be the driving force in high yield bond selection and portfolio management.

There are many methodologies that can be employed to dissect a company's financial and operating results. Analysts must determine a company's strengths and weaknesses and evaluate a company's financial prospects over a 12–24 month period. Forecasts beyond two years tend to be somewhat suspect given the rapidly changing global, economic, and financial markets. Whatever methodology is utilized, it should be a disciplined approach to ensure consistency in the selection process. Experience has shown that a more disciplined credit selection and analysis process should lead to lower volatility, and hence, higher risk adjusted returns. Consistent returns are of paramount importance for most investors in high yield securities.

This chapter explores the five key components of assessing the creditworthiness of a noninvestment-grade rated bond. Specifically, these five key components are industry analysis, financial analysis, covenant review, . senior management, and trading factors.

INDUSTRY ANALYSIS

High yield companies tend to be more vulnerable to the changing forces within their industry. Because noninvestment-grade rated companies have a higher level of debt in their capital structure, the competitive environment plays a vital role in a high yield issuer's ability to thrive or survive. Industry characteristics such as the cyclicality, seasonality, pricing flexibility, size, growth rates, technology, capital requirements, labor situation, consolidation trends, and foreign competition are all elements that may impact the creditworthiness of a borrower.

Some industries are more conducive to leverage because their operating margins and high growth rates enable a company to service a higher degree of indebtedness. However, for other industries that have low operating margins and growth rates, a heavy debt burden may weaken a company's ability to service its debt in an economic downturn or a prolonged period of sluggish product demand.

Barriers to entry in a specific industry are a crucial determinant of the amount of debt a high yield issuer should assume. Industries with low barriers to entry represent a more intensive competitive environment; therefore, the burden of debt should be lower in order to survive an economic downturn. Companies that operate in industries with high barriers to entry or in an oligopolistic environment can be saddled with greater indebtedness because competitive conditions allow companies' price flexibility to withstand adversity without impacting revenue generation and profitability.

Market share position is another vital indicator of a company's financial survivability. All companies, regardless of credit rating, that have dominant or market leadership positions should have the staying power to prosper against weaker competitors. However, high yield issuers that have niche market positions or one or more unique characteristics (such as a given franchise territory, patented technology, application process, or distribution network) may be better able to thrive despite more creditworthy competitors.

Pricing flexibility represents a key variable in a company's ability to utilize more financial leverage. Companies with constant margin pressures may not be able to maintain or increase their cash flows when margins are squeezed due to higher raw material or labor costs or their general inability to raise prices. Companies with the most price elasticity should have greater revenue stability and therefore should be able to assume more financial leverage in their capital structure. When competition is keen, or demand is sluggish, the inability to generate top-line revenue growth can impair cash flows needed to service debt.

Industry comparables must be incorporated in the analysis to show the relative financial condition of companies within the same industry sector. All relevant companies within the same industry should be examined. The financially weaker issuers should have a higher yield, reflecting their ranking within the industry. Many times the market may not differentiate the credit quality between one or more companies within the same industry. Any discrepancies identified in the comparative analysis may offer an opportunity for investors to exploit these market inefficiencies.

FINANCIAL ANALYSIS

The depth of financial analysis can range from comprehensive to cursory. Numerous financial textbooks offer detailed techniques of analysis. However, from a high yield credit analyst's perspective, there are eight key elements to the financial analysis of a high yield company.

Within the scope of the high yield investment process, the following factors should be carefully examined. There are many financial statistics that can be calculated and compared, but the eight key ratios for high yield analysis are as follows:

1. Analysis of Cash Flow Generation

Cash flow stability and predictability are of paramount importance in high yield analysis. Quite simply, cash flow services debt. Without sufficient cash to service debt, an issuer's bonds become impaired. Reviewing the companies' historical records, quarter-by-quarter, for a five-year period is essential in determining the stability of cash flow. Borrowers with erratic or declining cash flow are inherently riskier credits.

2. The Ability to Deleverage

Once a company has borrowed funds, and its cash flow trends have been ascertained, the next question should be: "How is that company going to repay its principal at maturity?" Bond investors generally prefer companies that generate excess free cash flow (i.e., the amount of cash available after payment of capital expenditures and interest) and use their excess free cash flow to pay down existing bank debt or purchase their high yield bonds in the open market. Investors need to be aware of companies that draw down additional debt for capital expenditures, borrow to pay interest on existing borrowings, or declare large dividends to shareholders. These practices should serve as warning signals that financial difficulties may occur in the future.

3. Amortization Schedules

Companies with aggressive debt repayment schedules to either banks or bondholders (i.e., sinking fund payments) run a higher risk that there will be a short fall in their cash positions, which could imperil their ability to remain financially sound. Many companies need to "grow into" their cash flow projections and amortization schedules, potentially representing a dangerous situation. Bondholders typically prefer that companies have a cushion of several years before their debt begins to amortize, thereby allowing needed flexibility to build cash and generate higher returns on new capital expenditure projects. The combination of erratic cash flow and early debt payment schedules must be carefully monitored and evaluated.

4. Quality and Salability of Assets

One frequently employed strategy to meet a pending debt amortization payment is the sale of assets. Hence, analysts should examine the various corporate assets that can be divested on a quick timetable in order to generate cash for required debt prepayments. Many high yield companies with inherently weak operating results and leveraged balance sheets have avoided defaulting on their bonds by selling or liquidating some strategic and/or noncore assets.

5. Priority of Debt in the Capital Structure

Credit ranking is another essential ingredient in the analysis process. Is the debt senior secured, senior, or subordinated? Are the subordinated debentures pari passu with trade creditors? Is there a negative pledge on senior notes? These are important questions, particularly for weaker high yield issuers. The price of the security should reflect the creditor's position in the event of a default. Other critical questions to ask are: How complex is the company's capital structure? Are the bonds being issued by a holding company or an operating company? and, What is the market capitalization of the public equity compared to the total debt of the issuer?

6. Capital Expenditure Requirements and Company's Life Cycle

Examining the company's capital expenditure requirements over the next several years is critically important to determine the potential drain on the firm's cash flow. Although the company may be investing the money in new projects, it may take several years before these projects generate sufficient returns to service indebtedness.

Companies that have significant capital requirements due to ambitious business plans need to develop a model that takes into account the timing of debt and/or equity offerings and near-term capital expenditures. For example, if the high yield company is a startup company or otherwise engaged in a relatively new business, and presently does not have sufficient cash flow to pay cash interest on its debt, then zero coupon or pay-in-kind bonds may be the preferable method to borrow funds to build a new enterprise. A company's ability to access the capital markets depends on market conditions as well as the company's historic record to meet cash flow projections. The latter criteria helps to develop credibility with Wall Street analysts and portfolio managers.

7. Event Risk

Certain unforeseen events can interfere with a company's obligation to pay interest and repay principal. Analysts should consider the regulatory environment and other governmental laws and regulations that can materialize to determine the probability of risks of such events causing a significant deterioration in cash flow. Other event risks may include litigation, technological obsolescence, or structural changes within the industry. Companies with financial cushions may survive such event risks. Analysts should weigh the probability of such event risks occurring prior to the maturity of the debt.

8. Liquidity

Cash is king! In analyzing a credit, the amount of cash on the balance sheet combined with the company's lines of credit with banks, or bank availability, serves as a cushion to meet capital expenditure requirements, seasonal needs, or unexpected cash payments. The liquidity of a high yield company is a paramount consideration in the serviceability of a company's debt obligations in the event of unforeseen business reversals.

COVENANT REVIEW

Contained within the indenture of virtually all high-yield bond offerings are certain covenants (or agreements) between the issuing company and bondholders. These covenants are primarily designed to protect the bondholders from having the company remove capital from the business or incur additional debt. Four key covenants are discussed below:

Limitation on Indebtedness

One of the covenants typically contained in the indenture is the additional indebtedness test, or "debt test", which is written in one of two ways: minimum interest coverage ratio or maximum leverage ratio. Neither test allows the company to incur supplementary debt unless the test is satisfied after taking the new debt into account. These two credits statistics are important factors in determining credit quality because the "debt incurrence test" protects the bondholders from a deterioration in credit quality resulting from the new debt. It is very important to compare these ratios with the company's pretest ratios. For example, if a company's leverage test for additional indebtedness is 6.5x (Total debt/EBITDA) and the company's prevailing or present ratio is 5.5x, then this would imply that the company can add additional debt (perhaps ahead of the existing bondholders) under its covenants and possibly impair existing bondholders. Similarly, with the interest coverage ratio, if the covenant test is 2.5x (EBITDA/Interest expense) and the company's ratio is 3x, then the company can take on additional debt, thereby increasing its interest expense and lowering the ratio. Such action may also impair the credit quality of the borrower. Additional indebtedness covenants may also be structured to enable the company to incur new debt under certain specified circumstances called "carve-outs," that do not have to meet the above-mentioned tests. The type of circumstances will vary depending upon the industry in which the company competes. For example, if a company's business strategy includes making acquisitions, it will usually have the ability under its bank line of credit to incur debt regardless of its debt test. It is very important to review the issuer's carve-outs in tandem with the debt test ratios.

Restricted Payments

It is important to analyze the company's ability to take capital out of the entity that has issued bonds. Bond indentures typically contain restrictions on payments of this kind, which are referred to as restricted payments. The ability of business owners to take money out of their company as either dividends or payments to other corporate entities can, like additional debt, impair the position of a bondholder. In most cases, the company will be allowed to make payments limited to a formula, generically defined as 50 percent of net income, plus other miscellaneous additions. Also, a company's ability to make restricted payments will be tied to its ability to incur further debt—meaning the company can make restricted payments if it "can incur $1.00 of additional debt." Under this scenario, as long as the company has the flexibility under its debt tests, it can make restricted payments. Similar to having additional indebtedness covenants, the company may have the ability to make restricted payments under various circumstances. These events will be determined by several factors, including the industry and the company's current capital structure (i.e., if the company is owned by a holding company that has tax and interest obligations, the covenants may allow the borrower to make payments to the holding company in order to satisfy these obligations).

Change of Control

High yield bond indentures also typically include a "change of control" provision at a price per bond which would represent a small premium, usually 101 percent of the principal amount, to the price paid by the bondholder. For example, the change of control provision may be triggered if the majority owner of the company ceases to maintain a majority ownership. This covenant protects the bondholder from a company's change of ownership that might deteriorate its credit quality. The bondholder's ability to force the company to buy back the bonds protects it from potential principal impairment.

Asset Sales

High yield bond indentures may also limit asset sales by the company and the manner in which proceeds of such sales may be applied. It is important to carefully ascertain how asset sale proceeds will be utilized. When a company sells assets, the assets usually generate earnings and cash flow for debt service. Because this cash flow will no longer be available after the assets are sold, the indenture may contain a covenant that obligates the company to either reinvest the proceeds in cash-flow-generating assets or repay its existing debt in order to maintain its ability to service debt.

In reviewing asset sale covenants in the indenture, analysts should keep in mind several factors. First, if the company has an existing senior secured credit facility with a group of banks, the bank agreement will typically require that 100 percent of asset sale proceeds be used to repay bank borrowings under that agreement. This requirement may be addressed in the bond covenants, where the company will have a specific period of time in which it will be required to repay senior debt or other indebtedness. Second, the company will usually have the right to reinvest asset sale proceeds in related business assets or other assets that will allow it to operate in the industry or business in which the company already operates. Third, and most important, if the above scenarios are not consummated within a specified time period (i.e., 270 days), the company may be required to offer to repurchase the bonds under the "optional redemption" covenant in the indenture.

SENIOR MANAGEMENT

In many cases, high yield companies are controlled by entrepreneurs. Identifying management capabilities is a crucial variable in analysis of the issuer. Evaluation of management should consider the following.

Track Record and Reputation of Management

CEOs of many high yield companies are effective promoters, salesmen, and financial backers, but can they operate a company with a leveraged balance sheet? The experience of management running a company with a high degree of leverage becomes an extremely important factor.

Equity Ownership

High yield bondholders prefer investing in companies where operating management owns a significant amount of equity. These managements have an incentive to succeed because their equity ranks below that of the bondholders.

LBO Sponsors

Approximately 20 percent of high yield issues are the result of leveraged buyout transactions. Accordingly, the track record of the LBO sponsor should be evaluated. The LBO sponsor's default history and acquisition record in paying down debt quickly should be taken into consideration. Another consideration is the potential relationship between the LBO sponsor and bondholders. Some LBO sponsors consider bondholders to be important in their long-term financial plans, while other LBO sponsors take a cavalier or arrogant view toward their debtholders.

Corporate Goals and Vision

It is important to talk with management about their strategic five-year goals. Given a leveraged balance sheet, analysts must know whether a company's primary goal is internal growth, deleveraging, or external growth through acquisitions. Each of these objectives can influence bond valuation and credit rating.

Style of Management

Many high yield companies have a strong visionary as CEO, but may have a weak team surrounding its aggressive CEO. It is imperative to determine if the company has a deep and solid senior management team or whether the CEO is an authoritarian leader or, at the other end of management style, a hands-off delegator.

Direct contact with management (e.g., road show, one-on-one, or conference call) is the best way to understand and evaluate management. This type of contact can provide greater insight into the risk and return parameters for a specific high yield issuer. In some cases, which are "true story bonds," the strength and quality of management can actually override the company fundamentals. Weak management in a leveraged company or a highly cyclical industry is an invitation to financial disaster. On the other hand, embryonic companies in new industries led by experienced management teams are oftentimes able to overcome a weak balance sheet. Investors can capitalize on start-up companies with low credit ratings if they can get comfortable with the management and its corporate vision.

TRADING FACTORS

While investment grade securities and U.S. Treasury bonds correlate with the direction of interest rates, high yield bonds trade on both fundamental and technical considerations and are more highly correlated to equity markets. Analysts must not only discern the industry and company fundamentals, but must incorporate various trading aspects of a bond into their analysis. The following variables should be factored into the investment decision process.

Size of Issue

The size of the issue affects the issue's liquidity, and, in turn, may affect the issue's availability and price. Smaller deals (i.e., under $100 million in size) typically have less liquidity. Consequently, the ability to buy or sell based upon the investor's analysis may not be achieved. On the other hand, larger deals (i.e., in the $150–200 million range) have greater demand and increased liquidity. Under favorable market conditions the more liquid issues tend to trade higher due to their availability to investors.

Number of Market Makers and Wall Street Sponsorship

The vast majority of high yield bonds trade in the dealer-to-dealer market; therefore, a greater number of broker/dealers trading a particular bond facilitates easier and quicker execution. The more market makers, the more trading volume, and hopefully a more efficient market. Wall Street sponsorship is critical for research coverage and the flow of information, which may create demand for the high yield bonds. Again, the most active issues in the high yield marketplace tend to have several broker/dealers trading their bonds. The more credit research available to investors generally enhances the "comfort level" of investing in a particular security.

Duration

Duration is the calculation of the relationship of time value and a bond's interest and principal payments. Duration takes into account interest payments as well as the final principal payment at maturity. The longer the duration, the more sensitive the price will be to interest rate fluctuations. Overall, bonds with high yields will have shorter durations than lower yielding issues.

Analysts must calculate a bond's duration, and factor in the duration based on the investment strategy of the portfolio.

Relative Yield Spreads

As a benchmark, high yield bonds trade off of 10-year U.S. Treasury bonds. Financial analysts should include spread relationships to determine if the market risk is commensurate with the credit risk. For example, a B-rated issue yielding only 225 basis points over riskless Treasuries may exhibit greater market risk compared to another B-rated issue with a spread of 500 basis points. However, the credit risks may be similar.

Credit analysis should not be performed in a price vacuum. One way to identify both credit risk and market risk is to construct a risk/return matrix such as that shown in Exhibit 12–1.

The inverse relationship displayed in Exhibit 12–1 is logical. For example, credits in Quadrant I have strong credit statistics and moderate leverage and their bonds have a correspondingly low yield. Typical characteristics of a Quadrant I credit include companies with predictable and improving cash flows; industries that are consolidating; deleveraging companies; and companies that have substantial assets. Conversely, credits in Quadrant III have thin cash flow, are generally start-up in nature, utilize zero coupon securities, and have large capital requirements, *or* have deteriorating statistics due to increasing competitive pressures. In order to compensate bondholders for these risks, their bonds have a higher yield. Credits in Quadrant II fall in the middle and can appreciate or depreciate depending upon their ability to execute their business plan and deliver their balance sheet. Quadrant IV credits are troubled, stressed, or distressed and may be in actual or technical violation of debt or bank covenants.[1]

---

1. For more information on quadrant analysis, please refer to Chapter 20.

E X H I B I T   12–1

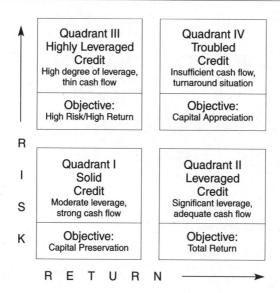

The market risk matrix is an important tool that credit analysts and portfolio managers can use to visualize risk/reward criterion based on fundamental credit statistics.

CONCLUSION

Financial analysis is a continuous process. Quarterly, annual, and last 12-month results must be re-examined to determine if creditworthiness has strengthened or deteriorated. The financial condition of a company is never static given the dynamics of the economy. Holding a bond to maturity in today's economic and financial climate may be an invitation to disappointment for noninvestment-grade bondholders. Frequent reviews should ensure investors that the company that issued the high yield bond purchased three years ago has the financial capacity to meet its obligations over the next three years.

CHAPTER 13

Valuing Bonds and Options on Bonds Having Correlated Interest Rate and Credit Risk

Theodore M. Barnhill, Jr.

William F. Maxwell

INTRODUCTION

This chapter provides a demonstration of a Monte Carlo simulation methodology for valuing bonds and options on bonds in an environment having correlated interest rate and credit risk.[1] The approach taken is to simulate a future financial environment consisting of eight correlated interest rate terms structures (i.e., risk-free, Aaa, . . . , Caa) and an equity index (for example, S&P 500). Using a one-factor model and the methodology described in Chapter 8 ("Modeling Bond Rating Changes for Credit Risk Estimation"), the firm's return on equity, market value of equity, debt-to-value ratio, and credit rating are simulated as a function of the return on the equity index and other firm-specific information. With a simulated credit rating, default recovery rate, and term structures, the value of the bond can be calculated at a selected target date. Given an assumed strike price, the payoff on a European call option on the bond can also be calculated at the target date. Using risk neutral valuation techniques, the current value of the bond and bond option can be calculated. It is demonstrated that the correlation between interest rate changes and equity returns affects the value of such bond options.

---

1. See Longstaff and Schwartz (1995), Das and Tufano (1996), Duffie and Singleton (1997), and Madan and Ural (1998) for alternative approaches to valuation and risk assessment of fixed income securities with interest rate and credit risk.

CREDIT EVENT

Credit risk is commonly thought of as the probability of default. However, this definition of credit risk views a bond in only two states, defaulted or not defaulted, and is only appropriate when valuing bonds held to maturity. However, in the more complex setting necessary to price bonds that may be sold before maturity, credit risk is a continuum with multiple states, with each state representing an associated probability of default. Hence, temporal credit risk is a function of the probability of a change in the value of the bond, associated with a transition in the probability of default over time.

A positive credit change decreases the likelihood of a bond defaulting and is commonly related to an increase in the bond's rating—an upgrade. An upgrade lowers the required yield on the bond, driving up the bond's price. Given the prevalence of embedded call options in bonds, care must be used in assessing the upside potential of a bond. The embedded call options effectively limit the upside. This is true even when the bond has call protection for a period of time.

A negative credit event is either a default or a downgrade, which can result in a significant loss in the value of the bond. However, even in the event of default, bonds do not become worthless. Thus a careful treatment of default recovery rates is required.

A credit event is normally associated with a change in the bond's rating. Rating categories serves as a means of grouping bonds into discrete categories with similar credit qualities and are commonly used as an indicator of risk level for a fixed income security. While there may be a lag between the market's perception of a change in credit quality and a change in the firm's actual credit rating, overall credit ratings provide a useful assessment of the firm's credit quality. Third parties and financial regulators place importance on credit ratings for assessing the risk of financial institutions, mutual funds, and pension funds.

STOCHASTIC CREDIT RISK

Changes in bond ratings reflect changes in the perceived ability of the firm to meet its financial obligations. Such credit quality changes may result either from changes in macroeconomic or firm-specific factors. The effect of macroeconomic changes on credit quality implies a correlation of credit risk across firms in various industries. Credit quality changes may also result from changes in the unique financial conditions of the firm.

An increase in credit quality lowers the credit risk of owning the security and increases the value of the security. A decrease in credit quality will decrease the value of the security.

Exhibit 13–1 demonstrates the effect on the value of a bond if the bond rating shifts up or down one major rating category. The example utilizes the noncallable term structures estimated for December 31, 1996. The results demonstrate the significance of a credit event on the value of a bond. This is especially true as credit rating declines. A credit migration from Aaa to Aa for a five-year bond decreases the value of the bond by 0.6 percent, while a credit migration from Ba to B decreases the value of the bond by 14.95 percent. An examination of the effect of credit migration between the five- and ten-year bonds, as well as the discrepancy of the change in the price based upon an upgrade versus a downgrade, demonstrates the influence of duration and convexity on credit migration.

RECOVERY RATES IN THE EVENT OF DEFAULT.

To value bonds with credit risk, the distribution of the amount recovered in the event of default must also be modeled. Historical recovery rates have been studied by Carty and Lieberman (1996) and Altman and Kishore (1996). The results of Carty and Lieberman's study are found in Exhibit 13–2.

A number of conclusions can be drawn from this study. First, average recovery rates increase with the seniority and security of the bonds. Second, within a seniority class there is a wide distribution of realized recoveries. Additionally, Altman and Kishore (1996) found some indication that recovery rates may be a function of industry.

UTILIZING TRANSITION MATRICES AND RECOVERY RATES TO VALUE BONDS BEFORE MATURITY

The recovery rate can be modeled as either a deterministic or stochastic process. If the recovery rate is assumed to be deterministic, the value of the bond at any time step, $t = j$ can be easily calculated by multiplying the probability of ending up at each possible state in nature—the term structure—by the value of the bond if it ends up at that term structure. The calculation of the expected value of a bond with credit risk at time $t = j$ is found in equation 13–1.

E X H I B I T   13–1

Changes in the Value of a Bond
Due to Rating Changes

Rating Category	Aaa	Aa	A	Baa	Ba	B	Caa
5-Year Bond Yield	6.51	6.53	6.65	6.88	7.93	8.85	13.12
Downgrade to Next Category	99.94	99.50	99.06	95.77	96.40	85.05	38.52
% Change Downgrade	−0.06%	−0.50%	−0.94%	−4.23%	−3.60%	−14.95%	−61.48%
Upgrade to Next Category	NA	100.06	100.50	100.94	104.35	103.69	116.65
% Change of Upgrade		0.06%	0.50%	0.94%	4.35%	3.69%	16.65%
10-Year Bond Yield	6.77	6.86	7.00	7.22	8.01	10.06	14.33
Downgrade to Next Category	99.36	99.02	98.47	94.70	87.41	78.04	38.52
% Change Downgrade	−0.64%	−0.98%	−1.53%	−5.30%	−12.59%	−21.96%	−61.48%
Upgrade to Next Category	NA	100.64	100.99	101.55	105.49	113.78	126.13
% Change Upgrade		0.64%	0.99%	1.55%	5.49%	13.78%	26.13%

Note: The five- and ten-year bond yields by rating category are as of 12/31/96. The change in the value of the bond is calculated by changing the yield to the adjacent yield requirement category. The initial bond value is 100.00. For example, a five-year Ba bond priced at 100 would be priced at 96.40 if downgraded to B, or it would be priced at 104.35 if upgraded to Baa.

E X H I B I T   13–2

Recovery Rates and Seniority

	Average (%)	Std. Deviation
Senior Secured	53.80	28.86
Senior Subordinated	51.13	25.45
Senior Unsuborinated	38.52	23.81
Subordinated	32.74	20.18
Junior Subordinated	17.09	10.90

$$E(V_j) = \sum_{i=1}^{n} P_{i,j} V_{i,j} \qquad (13\text{–}1)$$

$E(Vj)$ is the expected value of the fixed income instrument at time j, $P_{i,j}$ is the probability of being in state i at time j, and $V_{i,j}$ is the value of the instrument at time j in state i expressed as:

$$V_{i,j} = \sum_{t=0}^{m} C_{i,t}\, e^{R_{i,t}} \qquad (13\text{–}2)$$

$C_{i,t}$ is equal to the cash flow in state i at time t and $R_{i,t}$ is the continuously compounded spot interest rate to time t $(t \geq j)$.

The variance and standard deviation of $V_{i,j}$ is equal to:

$$\sigma_{V_j}^2 = \sum_{i=1}^{n} P_{i,j} (V_{i,j} - E(V_j))^2 \qquad (13\text{–}3)$$

$$\sigma_{V_j} = \sqrt{\sigma_{V_j}^2} \qquad (13\text{–}4)$$

The cash flows from the bond after the first year are equal to the known coupon payments plus the face value of bond at maturity. These payments are known with certainty unless the bond defaults. Nevertheless, if the bond's credit quality has changed, it must be revalued using the appropriate new term structure.

Exhibit 13–3 shows an example of a standard credit risk analysis for a five-year Ba bond trading with an initial PAR value of 100. The value of the cash flow from the bond is then revalued at the end of the first year utilizing the implied forward rates as of December 31, 1996. Since the yield curve is upward sloping in this example, the value of the bond at the end of the first year is worth less than its original value even if the bond stays in the same rating category. The distribution of possible returns multiplied by the probability of arriving at that credit quality is the mean expected value of the bond at the end of one year, $105.62 in this example. The standard deviation of the bond's value at the end of one year can then be easily calculated. The distribution of the value at the end of one year is nonparametric but the 99 percent and 95 percent confidence levels can be easily calculated given that there are known probabilities.

Two obvious limitations of the above analysis are that it does not take into account correlated interest rate risk or stochastic default rates. The importance of modeling the stochastic nature of recovery rates increases as the bond's rating decreases, because there is a higher likelihood of being in default. In the following analysis, recovery rate is modeled stochastically as a truncated normal distribution.[2] The distribution is truncated to ensure that the minimum recovery rate is 0 percent and the maximum is 100 percent with a mean recovery rate of 34 percent and a standard deviation of 25 percent (Altman and Kishore 1996).

---

2. If detailed data on recovery rate distributions is available, other modeling approaches may be more appropriate. For example, CreditMetrics suggests that recovery rate be modeled as a Beta distribution.

E X H I B I T   13–3

Credit Risk Analysis for a Five-Year Ba-Rated Bond

	Probability Transition	Coupon	Bond Value	Bond & Coupon	Probability Weighted	Change from Mean
Aaa	0.01%	$8.09	$104.33	$112.43	0.01	$6.81
Aa	0.09	8.09	104.30	112.39	0.10	6.77
A	0.43	8.09	103.80	111.89	0.48	6.27
Baa	5.09	8.09	102.88	110.97	5.65	5.35
Ba	87.23	8.09	98.41	106.50	92.90	0.89
B	5.47	8.09	95.10	103.19	5.64	(2.43)
Caa	0.45	8.09	82.93	91.03	0.41	(14.59)
Default	1.23	—	—	34.00	0.42	(71.62)
				Average	$105.62	
				Standard Deviation	8.17	

Note: The forward yields were estimated from 12/31/96 yield curves. The coupon is paid annually.

TERM STRUCTURE ESTIMATION BY RATING CATEGORY

As demonstrated from the transition matrices, corporate bonds have a probability of migrating to different rating categories over time. Hence, to value the bond and the option on the bond at any time before maturity, the various term structures to which the bond may migrate must be modeled.

The first step in modeling the different term structures is to determine the appropriate initial yield curves. Hence, the noncallable term structures, by rating category, are calculated as of 12/31/96. Exhibit 13–4 shows the noncallable term structures for Treasury Securities, and corporate bonds rated A, Ba, B, and Caa.

MODELING MULTIPLE STOCHASTIC TERM STRUCTURES

After estimating the initial term structures, a methodology for modeling correlated changes in multiple term structures and an equity index is required. There are numerous methodologies [for examples see Vasicek (1977); Cox, Ingersoll, and Ross (1985); Heath, Jarrow, and Morton (1992);

E X H I B I T   13–4

The Term Structure of Credit Risk
as of December 31, 1996

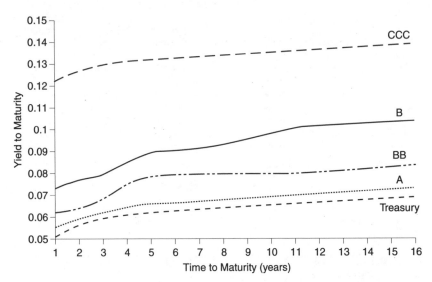

Hull and White (1990a, 1990b, 1993, 1994); and Jamshidian (1989)]. For
this study the Hull and White (1994) extended Vasicek model is utilized to
model the term structures.

The Hull and White (1994) model for r is:

$$\Delta r = a(\frac{\Theta(t)}{a} - r)\Delta t + \sigma \Delta z$$

Δr = The risk-neutral process by which r changes.

a = The rate at which r reverts to its long-term mean.

r = The instantaneous short-term interest rate.

$\Theta(t)$ = Theta is an unknown function of time that is chosen so that
          the model is consistent with the initial term structure.

Δt = A small increment to time.

σ = Sigma is the instantaneous standard deviation of r, which is
          assumed to be constant.

Δz = A Wiener process driving term structure movements with
          Δz, related to Δt by the function $\Delta z = \epsilon \sqrt{\Delta t}$.

ϵ = A random draw from a unit normal distribution.

The Hull and White (1994) model incorporates both a time-dependent mean reversion rate and a volatility measurement. The mean reversion and volatility rates can be estimated from a time series of historical data on spot interest rates or from the market prices of interest rate options. Using implied volatilities calculated from the observed market price of options has the advantage of calibrating the model to the current market environment. In this chapter, the model is calibrated from LIBOR cap price quotes as of December 31, 1996.

After estimating the required parameters, the risk-free instantaneous spot rate can then be simulated over the selected time step. The spot rates for the other term structures, as well as for the equity index, are simulated as a correlated multivariate normal distribution (see Hull 1997, p. 362). To ensure that the simulated spot rates for lower credit ratings would never be lower than those for higher credit ratings, all spot rates were modeled with the same volatility and mean reversion rate and a high correlation (i.e. .99) between the rates was assumed. This methodology produces essentially constant simulated credit spreads, which are approximately equal to the forward rate spreads calculated from the initial term structures.

MODELING THE VALUE OF THE UNDERLYING BOND

The next step is to simulate the evolution of the value of the underlying bond. In order to integrate interest rate and credit risk in a coherent valuation framework, it is necessary to simulate the correlated evolution of the credit quality of the financial instruments, as well as the future financial environment in which this instrument will be valued. The future financial environments are simulated to include eight arbitrage-free term structures (GOV, Aaa, . . . ,Caa) and an equity index (for example, the S&P 500).

The importance of this correlated evolution of interest rates and equity values is demonstrated by the correlation structure between the change in interest rates and return on the S&P 500 Index (Exhibit 13–5). Changes in interest rates are negatively correlated with returns on the S&P 500 Index. For example, the change in the short Aa and Caa bond rates are negatively correlated to the S&P 500 at –0.44 and –0.33 respectively. To the extent that equity returns are related to a firm's creditworthiness, this implies that the valuation of interest rate instruments having credit risk requires the joint modeling of equity returns and interest rates.

E X H I B I T   13-5

Correlation of the Change in Interest Rates by
Rating Category and Return on the S&P 500

	ΔAaa	ΔAa	ΔA	ΔBaa	ΔBa	ΔB	ΔCaa	SP500
ΔAaa	1	0.92	0.90	0.81	0.26	0.06	0.00	−0.33
ΔAa		1	0.93	0.85	0.27	0.04	0.05	−0.44
ΔA			1	0.90	0.28	0.06	0.05	−0.43
ΔBaa				1	0.32	0.09	0.01	−0.34
ΔBa					1	0.34	0.31	−0.29
ΔB						1	0.51	−0.16
ΔCaa							1	−0.33
SP500								1

CREDIT RATING SIMULATION

A complete discussion of the methodology utilized to estimate the credit migration probabilities for use in risk analysis is found in Chapter 8. However, a brief overview of the contingent claims framework utilized is as follows. First, the return on an equity market index is simulated with a set of spot interest rates for different credit ratings as a correlated random process. Second, a one-factor model is used to estimate the return on a firm's equity which is used to calculate the future market value of its equity and debt-to-value ratio. As a firm's debt-to-value ratio increases (decreases) its assigned credit rating decreases (increases).

There is one significant difference in the credit risk modeling methodology when the object is to value an instrument (bond or option) in a risk-neutral framework. In such a risk-neutral valuation the appropriate mean simulated return on the firm's equity is the risk-free rate. Thus in the valuation analysis in this chapter, the return on the firm's equity is modeled directly without going through the capital asset pricing model.

CALIBRATING THE MODEL (ARBITRAGE TESTS OF SIMULATIONS)

To test the validity of the results, comparisons are made between the known values of Ba- and B-rated coupon bonds and the simulated values for these bonds. Coupon bonds, with a maturity of six years for each term structure, are priced from the known yield curves for the rating classes. The values of the coupon bonds are then simulated out one year ($t = 1$) and discounted

E X H I B I T   13–6

Test of Arbitrage Opportunities Implied in the Model for Six-Year Bond Paying an Annual Coupon at $t = 1$

	Analytical Value ($t = 0$)	Mean	Simulated Output Standard Dev.	Error
		Test of Arbitrage (one year)		
Ba	100.00	100.85	7.19	0.85%
B	100.00	100.74	11.45	0.74%

Note: The value at $t = 0$ represents the analytical valuation of a six-year coupon bond (as a percentage of par) from the known term structure. The simulation output contains the mean value ($V_0 = V_1 e^{-rt}$), the maximum and minimum simulated values, and the standard deviation of the simulated values. The estimated error represents the over- or undervaluation of the simulated mean compared to the analytical solution.

back at the average simulated spot risk-free rate. For the model to be arbitrage free, the known value at $t = 0$ should equal the mean of the simulated value at $t = 1$, discounted back at the average simulated risk-free rate.

The estimated error represents the over- or undervaluation of the simulated value compared to the analytical solutions (Exhibit 13–6). The simulation valuation errors of approximately one percent reflect the underestimations of the number of defaults in the Ba and B categories produced by the credit rating simulation. Such pricing errors can be reduced by calibrating the equity volatility and the other parameters used in the simulation model.

THE EFFECT OF THE CORRELATION STRUCTURE ON THE RESULTS

The simulation results produced by this methodology are significantly affected by the assumed correlations between the returns on the equity indices and interest rates. Other methodologies do not account for these correlations. We have found that this omission leads to a substantial misestimation of the risk associated with owning corporate bonds.

Correlation analyses between the changes in short-term interest rates for the various rating categories compared to S&P 500 returns are found in Exhibit 13–5. However, this is an incomplete picture. Industries' and companies' returns are correlated to changes in interest rates differently. The correlation between industry equity indexes and interest rates vary dramatically, ranging from slightly greater than 0.0, to –0.5.

To examine the effect of correlation assumptions, valuation results are presented for a range of assumed correlations (i.e. –0.75, –0.50, –0.325, –0.25, 0.00, 0.25) structures between the equity index and interest rates. In addition, the results are reported assuming no credit risk, which is comparable to a traditional interest rate value at risk analysis.

THE SIMULATED CREDIT RISK OF Ba- AND B-RATED BONDS

The methodology discussed above can be utilized to undertake an integrated risk analysis, combining both interest rate and credit risk. On a bond or portfolio of bonds. For comparison purposes, results from value-at-risk analyses, which assume only interest rate risk and no credit risk, are also reported. The results of integrated risk analyses utilizing the methodology described above for Ba- and B-rated bonds are reported in Exhibits 13–7 and 13–9. The increase in the standard deviation of the bond's value, as compared to an interest rate risk analysis, is also provided. The risk confidence levels simulated for these bonds are reported in Exhibits 13–8 and 13–10. The risk confidence level information can be utilized for capital adequacy and risk measurement purposes.

By examining the standard deviations and confidence levels found in Exhibits 13–7 through 13–10, the traditional value-at-risk analysis, which assesses only interest rate risk, is demonstrated to dramatically underestimate the potential change in the valuation of a high yield bond. As credit quality decreases, the risk associated with credit quality change increases, as reflected in the higher standard deviation and lower confidence level for the B-rated bonds compared to Ba-rated bonds. Finally, the assumed correlation structure between equity returns and interest rates and thus on credit quality changes, is demonstrated to be significant. As the negative correlation increases so does the risk of owning the high yield bond. These findings are even more significant when the time until the maturity of the bond and the risk analysis time horizon increases.

VALUING OPTIONS WITH CREDIT RISK

The risk-neutral valuation variant of the methodology developed above can also be utilized to assess the effect of credit risk on the valuation of European call options on bonds. Since 90 percent of noninvestment-grade bonds have call options, this is of significant concern to investors. As shown previously, credit risk increases volatility. This increased price volatility

E X H I B I T   13–7

Integrated Risk Analyses of a Ba-Rated Bond Assuming Different Correlation between Equity Returns and Interest Rates

Correlation between Equity Index and Interest Rates	Bond Valuation % of PAR	Std. Dev.	Maximum	Minimum	% Δ Std. Dev. Compared to Interest Rate Risk
Interest Rate Risk Only	106.63	5.85	127.71	89.24	—
0.25	106.71	5.99	133.50	85.64	2.39%
0.00	106.75	6.40	131.10	87.09	9.40
−0.25	106.75	6.64	136.40	83.93	13.50
−0.325	106.78	6.91	134.07	85.27	18.12
−0.50	106.78	6.96	135.72	84.31	18.97
−0.75	106.84	7.64	131.57	86.76	30.60

Note: The underlying asset was a six-year Ba-rated bond paying annual coupons valued at the end of the first year.

E X H I B I T   13–8

Risk Valuation Confidence Levels for a Ba-Rated Bond Assuming Different Correlation Structures between Equity Returns and Interest Rates

Confidence Level	Only Interest Rate Risk	Correlations between Equity Returns and Interest Rates					
		0.25	0.00	−0.25	−0.33	−0.50	−0.75
99.0%	93.58%	93.71%	92.92%	92.14%	91.40%	91.72%	90.07%
97.5	95.45	95.68	95.06	94.19	94.00	94.00	92.27
95.0	97.27	97.28	96.80	96.18	95.91	95.63	93.99
90.0	99.35	99.19	98.66	98.37	98.07	98.11	97.36

Note: The underlying asset was a six-year Ba-rated bond paying annual coupons valued at the end of the first year.

would be expected to increase the value of a call option on a bond. Methodologies for valuing the Bermudan style options found in most corporate bonds are still under development.

To demonstrate the effect of credit risk on the valuation of a call option owned by the issuing firm, the value of the European call option on Ba- and B-rated bonds is first valued utilizing the Hull and White extended Vasicek model that assesses only interest rate risk. The options on the

E X H I B I T   13–9

Integrated Risk Analyses of a B-Rated Bond Assuming Different Correlation between Equity Returns and Interest Rates

Correlation between Equity Index and Interest Rates	Bond Valuation % of PAR	Std. Dev.	Maximum	Minimum	% Δ Std. Dev. Compared to Interest Rate Risk
Interest Rate Risk Only	107.61	5.66	128.48	90.41	—
0.25	106.69	7.01	130.57	81.70	23.85%
0.00	106.84	7.47	133.62	78.89	31.98
−0.25	106.69	8.09	128.85	81.51	42.93
−0.325	106.89	8.38	136.17	79.32	48.06
−0.50	106.92	8.42	129.80	80.97	48.76
−0.75	106.91	8.91	137.41	78.90	57.42

Note: The underlying asset was a six-year B-rated bond paying annual coupons valued at the end of the first year.

E X H I B I T   13–10

Risk Valuation Confidence Levels for a B-Rated Bond Assuming Different Correlation Structures between Equity Returns and Interest Rates

Confidence Level	Only Interest Rate Risk	Correlations between Equity Returns and Interest Rates					
		0.25	0.00	−0.25	−0.33	−0.50	−0.75
99.0%	95.04%	88.53%	87.09%	85.20%	84.65%	84.34%	83.03%
97.5	96.95	91.55	89.52	87.31	87.67	86.86	85.12
95.0	98.64	93.74	93.33	90.16	90.69	88.91	87.30
90.0	100.51	97.33	97.72	95.72	95.43	95.78	95.42

Note: The underlying asset was a six-year B-rated bond paying annual coupons valued at the end of the first year.

bonds are then revalued assuming correlated interest rate and credit risk. As before, the values are simulated with a number of different correlation structures to demonstrate the importance of this assumption.

The value of call options with no credit risk is a function of the strike price, option maturity, the current term structure, the mean reversion, and volatility rates. The value of call options with credit risk is a function of the

E X H I B I T   13–11

Valuation of European Call Options as a Percentage of the Face Value on a Ba-Rated Corporate Bond

Correlation between Equity Returns and Interest Rates	Simulation Output				Comparison to IRR Only % Increase
	Mean	Std. Dev.	Maximum	Minimum	
Interest Rate Risk Only	1.45	2.90	22.12	0	—
0.25	1.54	3.02	28.69	0	6.21%
0.00	1.77	3.39	25.99	0	22.07
−0.25	1.89	3.50	25.36	0	30.34
−0.33	2.03	3.80	28.76	0	40.00
−0.50	2.19	4.05	29.67	0	51.03
−0.75	2.37	4.38	29.32	0	63.45

Note: The yield on the bond was set so the bond was trading at 100. The call price was 100. The option maturity was two years and the bond's maturity was four years.

factors listed above plus the probability of transition to a different term structure. Since the value of the call option increases as the required yield decreases, the call becomes more valuable if the bond is upgraded.

The results of this analysis are found in Exhibits 13–11 and 13–12. The increase in the value of the option, as compared to the valuation with no credit risk, is also provided under the different correlation scenarios. As expected, the effect of credit risk is more pronounced on the more volatile B-rated bonds. The results clearly demonstrate that as the correlation between market equity returns and interest rates decreases, the volatility of the underlying asset value increases and, correspondingly, the value of the bond option increases.

CONCLUSION

This chapter described a methodology to value high yield bonds that integrates both interest rate and credit risk. Most valuation methodologies assume that interest rates and equity returns are independent. However, this assumption is clearly erroneous and dramatically underestimates the level of risk of owning a high yield security. An analysis that integrates both interest rate and credit risk is clearly needed to correctly determine risk confidence levels and capital adequacy requirements for institutions holding

E X H I B I T   13–12

Valuation of European Call Options as a Percentage of the Face Value on a B-Rated Corporate Bond

Correlation between Equity Returns and Interest Rates	Simulation Output				Comparison to IRR Only % Increase
	Mean	Std. Dev.	Maximum	Minimum	
Interest Rate					
Risk	1.37	2.83	24.26	0	—
0.25	1.40	2.88	26.95	0	2.19%
0.00	1.66	3.29	29.10	0	21.17
−0.25	1.78	3.51	29.11	0	29.93
−0.33	1.88	3.56	28.53	0	37.23
−0.50	1.96	3.68	33.10	0	43.07
−0.75	2.22	4.21	33.26	0	72.99

Note: The yield on the bond was set so the bond was trading at 100. The call price was 100. The option maturity was two years and the bond's maturity was four years.

risky bonds. The methodology outlined in this chapter also provides a framework to understand the effect of credit risk on the valuation of call options on bonds.

REFERENCES

Altman, E. and V. Kishore (1996). "Almost Everything You Wanted to Know about Recoveries on Defaulted Bonds." *Financial Analysts Journal,* 52, 6, pp. 57–64.

Barnhill, T. (1998). Portfolio Risk Analysis Utilizing Correlated Interest Rate and Credit Risk Simulations, working paper, The George Washington University.

Carty, L. and D. Lieberman (1996). Corporate Bond Defaults and Default Rates 1938–1995, *Moody's Investors Service - Special Report,* January.

Cox, J. C.; J. E. Ingersoll; and S. A. Ross (1985). "A Theory of the Term Structure of Interest Rates." *Econometrica,* 53. March, pp. 385–407.

Das, S. and P. Tufano (1996). "Pricing Credit-Sensitive Debt When Interest Rates, Credit Ratings and Credit Spreads are Stochastic." *Journal of Financial Engineering* vol. 5, no. 2, pp. 166–98.

Duffie, D. and K. Singleton (1997). "An Econometric Model of the Term Structure of Interest-Rate Swap Yields." *Journal of Finance.* September, pp. 1287–1321.

Gupton, Greg M.; Christopher C. Finger; and Mickey Bhatia (1997). *CreditMetrics™– Technical Document.* 1st Edition. (New York: J. P. Morgan & Co.)

Heath, D.; R. Jarrow; and A. Morton (1992). "Bond Pricing and the Term Structure of Interest Rates: A New Methodology for Contingent Claims Valuation." *Econometrica*, 60. pp. 77–105.

Hull, J. (1997). *Options, Futures, and Other Derivative Securities*. Prentice Hall.

Hull, J. and A. White (1994). "Numerical Procedures for Implementing Term Structure Models I: Single-Factor Models." *The Journal of Derivatives*. Fall, pp. 7–16.

Hull, J. and A. White (1993). "One-Factor Interest-Rate Models and the Valuation of Interest-Rate Derivative Securities." *Journal of Financial and Quantitative Analysis*. 28, 2, pp. 235–54.

Hull, J. and A. White (1990a). "Pricing Interest-Rate Derivative Securities." *The Review of Financial Studies*, 3, pp. 573–92.

Hull, J. and A. White (1990b). "Valuing Derivative Securities Using the Explicit Finite Difference Method." *Journal of Financial and Quantitative Analysis*, 25. pp. 87–100.

Jamshidian, F. (1989). "An Exact Bond Option Formula." *Journal of Finance*, 44, pp. 205–9.

Longstaff, F. and E. Schwartz (1995). "A Simple Approach to Valuing Risky Fixed and Floating Rate Debt." *Journal of Finance*. July, pp. 789–819.

Madan, D. and H. Unal (1998). "A Two-Factor Hazard-Rate Model for Pricing Risky Debt in a Complex Capital Structure." working paper, University of Maryland.

Vasicek, O. (1977). "An Equilibrium Characterization of the Term Structure." *Journal of Financial Economics*, 5, pp. 177–88.

PART FOUR

Market Valuation Models

CHAPTER 14

Monetary Influences on the High Yield Spread versus Treasuries[*]

M. Christopher Garman

Martin S. Fridson

INTRODUCTION

Growing participation by asset allocators has stimulated interest in estimating the high yield bond market's relative value at a point in time. Analysts have focused on the sector's risk premium, defined as the interest rate differential between lower-rated corporate bonds and default-free governments. Until 1996, the variance over time in this yield spread was predicted fairly accurately by a model that incorporated measures of credit risk and market liquidity. To explain the recent narrowness of the risk premium, it is necessary to consider monetary conditions as well.

A notable innovation of the mid-1990s is the involvement of dynamic asset allocators in the high yield bond market. To a far greater extent than in previous years, professional money managers actively vary their percentage exposure to the noninvestment grade sector, depending on its near-term relative return potential vis-á-vis other asset classes. The increased use of this strategy for enhancing total return reflects a longer-run change in the mix of high yield market participants.

In earlier periods, the ownership of high yield bonds was dominated by pure high yield portfolios, including dedicated mutual funds.[1] To managers of noninvestment-grade-only portfolios, the relative attractiveness of the high yield sector at a point in time was moot. It was up to the ultimate investor (such as the mutual fund shareholder) to decide whether to be in the asset class, leaving the manager discretion only over the selection of specific securities within the class.[2]

Between 1990 and 1995, however, the number of multisector bond funds in the Morningstar Inc. mutual fund universe increased from 15 to 63. Ratner (1996) describes these portfolios as follows:

> Multisector bond funds seek income at moderate volatility by primarily allocating their assets among three types of bonds. Such funds customarily invest in U.S. government bonds including Treasuries and mortgages; both sovereign- and corporate-foreign debt; and domestic high yield bonds. Allocations among the three markets vary, with most funds keeping a benchmark allocation of one-third of assets in each.

Unlike the managers of dedicated high yield funds, multisector fund managers try to enhance their returns by altering their concentration in the high yield sector according to market conditions.

Some money managers carry the multisector concept a step further. They customize their clients' long-run average distributions among various asset classes, based on their specific investment needs and risk preferences. One client's core high yield position might be 5 percent of assets, while

---

1. Clearly, many institutional investors other than dedicated high yield bond funds were involved in the high yield market prior to the mid-90s. Along with the heavily publicized participation of savings and loan associations, there was substantial investment by life insurance companies, pension plans, and corporate treasury departments. Additionally, investment grade mutual funds often devoted a portion of their assets to issues rated less than Triple-B, in order to beef up their yields. It would not be accurate, however, to portray these investors as actively rotating into and out of the high yield sector on the basis of short-run value judgments.

2. High yield mutual fund charters generally authorize portfolio managers to invest temporarily in cash or other types of securities if they perceive no acceptable investment opportunities within the noninvestment-grade bond category. As a practical matter, though, managers exercise this discretion sparingly. For one thing, they are under intense pressure to generate high dividend yields, a goal that is undercut by keeping large amounts of assets in low yielding cash instruments. Furthermore, noninvestment-grade managers will likely face severe censure if the high yield market rallies, producing high returns at rival funds, while they are in the defensive posture of carrying large cash balances. Finally, shifting assets to an alternative asset class, such as investment grade bonds, creates the potential for criticism if the alternative class underperforms the high yield sector for a time. In that event, disgruntled shareholders will probably complain that their own, astute asset allocation decision was negated by the manager's decision to go "outside the box," i.e., into a different asset class.

another's might be 15 percent or 0 percent, but each client's allocation varies with changing economic conditions and fluctuating risk premiums. Certain pension plan sponsors follow a similar strategy, perennially maintaining some level of exposure to noninvestment-grade bonds, but periodically trimming or augmenting their positions.[3]

In seeking to profit from market-timing the high yield sector, these institutional investors have had to invent new valuation methods. Historically, the bulk of research on high yield valuation has focused on whether the sector represents good long-run value, given its risks.[4] Notwithstanding the importance of this question to investment policymakers, its resolution offers little guidance to dynamic asset allocators. To fill the gap, recent research has turned to variations, over time, in the high yield sector's relative value.

The next section of this study reviews previous approaches to high yield market-timing. We then explore potential refinements of existing methods. Finally, we present a revised model of the high yield spread versus Treasuries that improves materially on the explanatory power of the Fridson-Jónsson model.

HISTORICAL AVERAGE SPREAD

The simplest and perhaps most widely used technique of high yield market valuation is to compare the prevailing spread over Treasuries to its historical average. Suppose, for example, that an index of the high yield market has yielded an average of 400 basis points more than Treasuries over the past ten years. If the present spread is 500 basis points, the noninvestment-grade sector is deemed cheap and therefore worthy of overweighting. Underlying the historical average spread method is a presumption that the spread is mean reverting.

Unfortunately, the intuitively appealing historical-average approach fails as a short-run market-timing method. Fridson and Bersh (1994) demonstrate that over the period of 1985–1992 there was no statistically verifiable difference between high yield bond returns in quarters that began

---

3. One additional group of investors that actively manage their degree of exposure to the high yield sector consists of market-timers. The group includes both a number of specialized money managers and publishers of certain market newsletters. Neither group appears to have been especially active in the high yield market before 1992, although some less specialized market-letters astutely recommended purchase of high yield mutual funds late in 1990. Market-timers express some interest in short-run fundamental valuation models of the high yield market, but they generally rely primarily on technical methods, including momentum models.

4. For an overview of the research on this subject, see Fridson (1994).

with wider-than-average spreads over Treasuries, and those that began with narrower-than-average spreads. Fridson and Bersh acknowledge that the historical average spread method might succeed over longer time horizons, but add, "Investors who would pursue such a strategy, however, must be prepared to sustain highly unfavorable total returns (or significant opportunity costs) while they patiently await the return of 'normal' spreads."

Altman and Bencivenga (1995) propose a model that is a variant of the historical average spread method. The authors derive a "breakeven yield," which does not vary over time. In essence, Altman and Bencivenga subtract a constant quantity from a fluctuating spread and infer that when the resulting remainder exceeds its average, the high yield market represents good value. Altman and Bencivenga corroborate Fridson and Bersh's finding that such methods do not aid market-timing over a three-month horizon. They then assert that an observed correlation between total returns and lagged spreads implies an effective model for predicting returns over 6- and 12-month horizons. (With just six observations in their 12-month sample, these authors are necessarily cautious in their conclusions.)

FRIDSON-JÓNSSON MODEL (1995)

Fridson and Jónsson (1995) argue that the historical average spread approach is conceptually unsound. Its logic implies that the average spread is always the "correct" spread, toward which a momentarily discombobulated market must always return. As Fridson and Jónsson point out, however, the spread over Treasuries is a risk premium. Given that risk is not constant over time, the risk premium should also vary over time. Only when the risk premium is out of line with the prevailing risk, say Fridson and Jónsson, can the market truly be deemed misvalued.

Proceeding empirically, Fridson and Jónsson seek to quantify the high yield market's fluctuating riskiness. Using regression analysis, they model the high yield spread versus Treasuries as a function of five risk variables, which can be grouped into two broad categories:

Credit Risk

Moody's Trailing Twelve-Month Default Rate (percentage-of-issuers basis)

Index of Lagging Economic Indicators

Illiquidity Risk

Mutual Fund Flows as a Percentage of Fund Assets

Cash as a Percentage of High Yield Mutual Fund Assets

Three-Month Moving Average Price of the Merrill Lynch High Yield Master Index

Over the test period of December 1984 to December 1993, the Fridson–Jónsson model generated a percentage-of-variance-explained (R^2) of 0.72. All five variables are statistically significant at the 95 percent confidence level, as indicated by t-statistics greater than 1.96. Exhibit 14–1 shows a fairly tight fit during the test period between actual high yield versus Treasuries spreads and the values estimated in each period by the Fridson–Jónsson model.

MOTIVATIONS FOR FURTHER ANALYSIS

Throughout most of the postobservation period (January 1994, onward), the Fridson–Jónsson model's estimate has remained reasonably close to the actual spread (see Exhibit 14–2). During the first half of 1996, however, the disparity between actual and estimated values became unusually pronounced. At the extreme, on May 31, 1996, the differential stood at 135 basis points. This gap implied that the high yield market's risk premium was more inadequate than it had been at any point since January 1985.

The mere existence of an extreme implied overvaluation does not demonstrate faulty analysis. Indeed, the only other month in which the actual spread fell short of the model-estimated spread by as much as in May 1996 was in May 1987, when the gap was 131 basis points. Over the succeeding two months, the Merrill Lynch High Yield Master Index affirmed the model's verdict that it was overvalued by underperforming intermediate (7 to 9.99 years)[5] Treasuries by 78 basis points (nonannualized). Conversely, the high yield market's greatest implied *undervaluation* occurred in January 1991, when the Fridson–Jónsson model estimated a correct risk premium that was 263 basis points lower than the prevailing spread. That month began the Merrill Lynch High Yield Master Index's best year ever, with a total return of 34.58 percent. If anything, it appears the extreme readings have represented the most valuable output of the Fridson–Jónsson model.

---

5. Fridson and Jónsson (1995), p. 81.

E X H I B I T   14–1

Actual versus Estimated Spread, Fridson–Jónsson Model, 1985 to 1993, Monthly

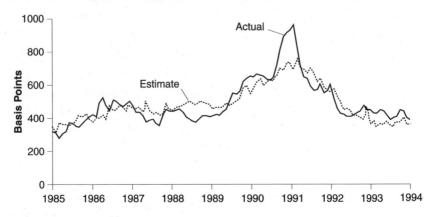

E X H I B I T   14–2

Estimation Error of Fridson-Jónsson Model, January 1985 to July 1996, Monthly

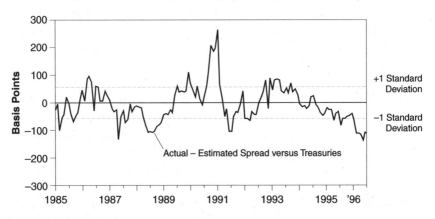

While an extreme valuation does not demonstrate that an analysis is flawed, portfolio managers understandably wish to be quite sure about the conclusion. If they underweight high yield bonds in favor of Treasuries, they must sacrifice 300-plus basis points of yield on an ongoing basis until their judgment is vindicated by a widening of the spread between the two sectors. Time is working against them. Before managers will stake money on the proposition that the high yield market is rich, they will want to assure themselves that they are relying on a robust model.

A number of plausible refinements to the Fridson–Jónsson model have been suggested by academics, as well as by practitioners who employ it as a market-timing tool. In developing a refined model of the spread versus Treasuries, we have focused on three lines of inquiry:

1. Indicators of monetary conditions.
2. Instability of the high yield index's composition.
3. General level of interest rates.

Additionally, we have attempted to improve upon the Fridson–Jónsson model by avoiding reliance on the Three-Month Moving Average Price of the Merrrill Lynch High Yield Master Index. This effort is purely a pragmatic response to investors' preferences, for we believe the variable is conceptually sound.

Observation of the high yield market confirms that a declining price trend ordinarily makes investors cautious. As a consequence, customary intermediaries encounter greatly reduced market depth. To avoid taking on excessive inventory positions, dealers must widen their bid/asked spreads. Secondary market liquidity dries up, increasing the risk of holding bonds. Naturally, the risk premium increases, that is, the spread over Treasuries expands. By an analogous chain of cause and effect, rising prices lead to reduced spreads.

This story makes logical sense to us and is empirically supported. We find that as a practical matter, however, investors perceive the price-change/spread connection to be tautological. Accordingly, a model that is not dependent on the Three-Month Moving Average Price variable is likely to gain better market acceptance.

MONETARY INDICATORS AND THE BABSON MODEL

Fridson and Jónsson (1995) do not overlook indicators of monetary conditions as possible determinants of the high yield spread versus Treasuries. The authors list several variables that they have tested, but reject for lack of explanatory power. Among them is one indicator of monetary conditions, the Broker Loan Rate. Additionally, Fridson and Jónsson note, one variable that "makes the cut" is the Index of Lagging Indicators, among the components of which are Average Prime Rate and Change in Consumer Price Index for Services, Smoothed. Notwithstanding Fridson and Jónsson's search for links between monetary conditions and the high yield risk premium, however, it appears that additional ore can be mined from this vein.

Arce Ruiz, Gunalp, Plotkin, Sezer, and Vasandani (1996) test several variables not incorporated in the Fridson–Jónsson model. (See Exhibit 14–3 for list.) This study, conducted by a group of Babson College students working under the direction of Professors Joel Shulman and Roberto Bonifaz, suggests that monetary conditions may explain a significant portion of the high yield spread versus Treasuries.

The Babson authors take a direction somewhat different from our main interest. In their modeling, they seek to predict the spread versus Treasuries 6 or 12 months ahead, based on the *current* values of their explanatory variables. By contrast, our objective is first to *explain* today's spread on the basis of the *current* values of the variables, then to *forecast* the future spread on the basis of *forecasts of the future values* of the variables.

At the same time, the Babson study underscores the importance of monetary conditions in explaining the spread over Treasuries. Indeed, our own adaptation of the Babson model (see Exhibit 14–4), which does not use the preceding month's spread as an explanatory variable, explains 80 percent of the monthly variance in spread over the period of January 1985 to May 1996. Exhibit 14–5 illustrates the close fit of this modified Babson model and actual spreads.

IMPACT OF THE RATINGS MIX

Aside from incorporating monetary indicators, the other most plausible refinement to the Fridson–Jónsson model suggested by practitioners is to adjust for the changeable ratings mix of the Merrill Lynch High Yield Master Index. The idea springs from the fact that at any given point, Double-Bs yield less than Single-Bs, which in turn yield less than bonds rated Triple-C or lower. Let us suppose (for sake of argument) that the percentage of the Index's market value represented by Double-Bs increases while the Single-B percentage declines by the same amount. Seemingly, the Index's yield should also decline, all other things being equal. This reduction in yield would not be explained by the types of variables represented in the Fridson–Jónsson and Babson models, that is, *systematic* default risk, market liquidity, and monetary indicators. Adjusting the dependent variable (the spread over Treasuries) for this unexplained variance ought to make the existing models more robust.

Exhibit 14–6 lends support to the hypothesis that spreads are affected by the ratings mix. In brief, the exercise shows that on June 30, 1996, the High Yield Master Index was more heavily concentrated in the low-yielding

E X H I B I T   14–3

New Variables Tested by Babson Team

> Assets of High Yield Mutual Funds
> Consumer Price Index
> Housing Completions
> Housing Starts
> Industrial Production
> Manufacturing Production
> Money Supply: M1, M2, M3
> New Manufacturing Orders
> Prime Rate
> Real Personal Income
> Volatile Periods (1989–1991) Dummy Variables

Note: The Babson Team also tested the Index of Leading Economic Indicators, which Fridson and Jónsson rejected.

Source: Arce Ruiz, Gunalp, Plotkin, Sezer, and Vasandani (1996).

E X H I B I T   14–4

Modified Babson Model Regression Statistics

$R^2 = 0.80$
Adjusted $R^2 = 0.78$

Explanatory Variable	Regression Coefficient	t-Statistic	P Value*
Default Risk Indicators			
Moody's Trailing-Twelve-Months Default Rate (percentage-of-issuers basis)	0.33	10.87	0.0000
Index of Lagging Economic Indicators	0.07	1.84	0.0687†
Index of Leading Economic Indicators	−0.17	−3.18	0.0018
Illiquidity Risk Indicators			
Cash as a Percentage of High Yield Mutual Fund Assets	0.27	4.33	0.0000
Three-Month Moving Average Price of the Merrill Lynch High Yield Master Index	0.04	2.18	0.0313†
Monetary Conditions Indicators			
Consumer Price Index	0.00	3.13	0.0022
Money Supply (M1)	0.00	4.88	0.0000

*Significant at 90 percent confidence level, unless noted otherwise.

†Significant at 95 percent confidence level.

E X H I B I T   14–5

Modified Babson Model, Actual
versus Estimated Spread

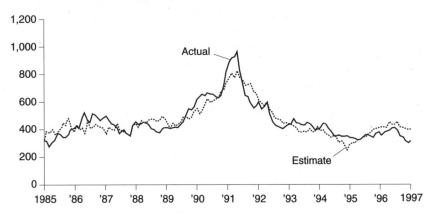

E X H I B I T   14–6

Sensitivity of Spread versus Treasuries to Ratings Mix

Rating Group	Yield to Maturity, June 30, 1996	Percent of Market Weighting*		
		June 30, 1996	Average 1988–1995	Difference
Double-B	8.709%	49.58%	40.0%	9.33%
Single-B	10.739	46.35	51.1	(4.65)
Triple-C/Double-C/Single-C	14.437	4.07	8.8	(4.64)
Weighted Average Yield to Maturity		9.88%†	10.24%	(0.36%)

Note: Columns may not sum to 100 percent due to rounding.

*Based on rated debt only.

†Varies slightly from 9.92 percent yield of Merrill Lynch High Yield Master Index of June 30, 1996. The Master Index contains Canadian and Yankee issues, which although rated, are not included in the rating group subindexes. Accordingly, the three rating subindexes in aggregate represent only 92.6 percent of the Master, by market weighting.

Double-B sector (49.6 percent of market value) than it was on average during the period 1988–1995 (40.0 percent).[6] By the logic outlined in the preceding paragraph, the June 30, 1996 yield (and, by extension, the spread versus Treasuries) of the Master Index was 36 basis points lower than it

---

6. The ratings distribution of the Merrill Lynch High Yield Master Index is not available prior to 1988.

would have been if the market had been at its historical average ratings distribution. Carrying this reasoning to its conclusion, a significant portion of the 107 basis point richness of the high yield market at the end of June 1996, as calculated by the Fridson–Jónsson model, appears to be variance that can be explained by changes over time in the ratings mix.

Notwithstanding this evidence, it remains to be proven that the spread versus Treasuries is genuinely sensitive to the quality distribution of the high yield universe. Hidden in the argument for considering the ratings mix is the assumption that the rating-to-rating yield differentials are insensitive to the proportions of the high yield universe that each rating subcategory represents.

By way of illlustration, let us suppose that on a given date, Single-Bs represent 40 percent of the universe and yield, on average, 11 percent. At the same time, 50 percent of the universe represents Double-Bs, which yield 9 percent, with the balance rated Triple-C or lower. Now let us assume that with nothing else changing in the system, Single-Bs' share increases to 60 percent. According to the proratings-mix argument, the Single-B yield will remain at 11 percent, despite the change in the market's quality distribution. Such an outcome is possible, it seems to us, but only if investors are truly indifferent between holding Double-Bs and Single-Bs, given a spread of 200 basis points (11 percent minus 9 percent). If, on the other hand, some investors are risk-averse, the Single-B yield may have to rise, relative to the Double-B yield, to induce these investors to shift capital to riskier assets. How investors behave, in reality, is an empirical question.

Fortunately, there is a means of testing the proposition. Exhibit 14–7 plots the spread versus Treasuries against a summary measure of the High Yield Master Index's ratings mix.[7] In a one-variable regression, this proxy for the ratings mix explains 27 percent of the monthly variance in spread, with a t-statistic (-6.56) that strongly indicates statistical significance.

When we attempt to incorporate the ratings mix proxy into a multivariate model, however, the possible combinations of results invariably produce unsatisfactory results. In some combinations, the ratings mix proxy contributes no meaningful explanatory power, implying that its effect is captured by other variables in the model. In other combinations of variables, the ratings mix emerges with a positive sign, implying that a higher

---

7. "Par-Weighted Quality," a figure available on The Bloomberg terminals, converts ratings to numerical scores (600 for high Double-B, 576 for medium Double-B, 552 for low Double-B, etc.). This summary statistic is available as far back as January 1986, even though no detailed, rating-by-rating breakdown is available prior to 1988.

E X H I B I T   14–7

Ratings Mix Compared to Spread versus
Treasuries, January 1986–May 1996

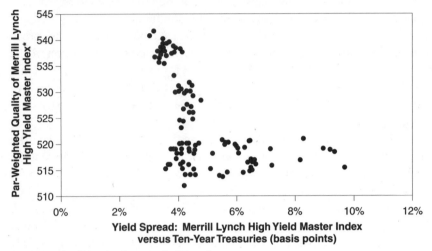

Yield Spread: Merrill Lynch High Yield Master Index
versus Ten-Year Treasuries (basis points)

*Quantitative scale, with largest number representing highest rating.

quality mix is associated with a *larger* risk premium. Not only is the latter
result contrary to our hypothesis, but we cannot think of any reasonable
"story" by which the supposed statistical relationship would make sense.

For the time being, at least, we are obliged to reject the universe's ratings mix as an explanatory variable. The possibility remains that a better
proxy for the ratings mix, with greater explanatory power, will become
available in the future.

INFLUENCE OF THE GENERAL
LEVEL OF INTEREST RATES

Another suggestion frequently made by practitioners is that we attempt to
correlate high yield spreads with the general level of Treasury rates. Fridson and Jónsson (1995) do not pursue this approach, based on earlier
empirical research:

> Many practitioners claim that the high yield spread over Treasuries is
> proportional to the level of Treasury yields, but Fridson and Kenney
> (1994) find no such statistical correlation. (That study does, however,
> find a negative correlation between *changes* in Treasury yields and
> *changes* in high yield spreads versus Treasuries.)

Further testing corroborates Fridson and Kenney's conclusion that, contrary to a stubbornly held belief among practitioners, there is no statistical tendency for the high yield spread to be wider when nominal Treasury rates are higher.[8] This lack of correlation in a one-variable setting, however, may represent the flip side of the ratings mix's seemingly strong correlation with spreads, as discussed above. Just as the ratings mix lacks explanatory power in a multivariate regression model, the Treasury yield may prove helpful in explaining yields when tested in conjunction with other variables. This is, in fact, the result obtained in testing.

A NEW SYNTHESIS: THE GARMAN MODEL

Based on extensive testing, we propose a new model of the high yield spread versus Treasuries consisting of the following variables:[9]

Default Risk

Moody's Trailing Twelve-Months Default Rate (percentage-of-issuers basis)
Capacity Utilization

Illiquidity Risk

Mutual Fund Flows as a Percentage of Fund Assets
Cash as a Percentage of High Yield Mutual Fund Assets

Monetary Conditions

Consumer Price Index (year-over-year change)
Money Supply (M2 minus M1, year-over-year change)
Treasury Yield Curve (ten-year minus three-month)

In general, we have chosen between close proxies on the basis of best fit. For example, our specific Money Supply measure is one of several variants that we tested. The greatest explanatory value emerged from the

---

8. Readers who are reluctant to give up the ghost on this idea can pursue the topic in Fridson (1992).
9. Sources for the variables are as follows: *Moody's Trailing-Twelve-Months Default Rate* (Moody's Investors Service); *Capacity Utilization* (Bureau of Labor Statistics); *Mutual Fund Flows as a Percentage of Mutual Fund Assets* (Investment Company Institute); *Cash as a Percentage of Mutual Fund Assets* (Investment Company Institute); *Consumer Price Index* (Federal Reserve Board); *Money Supply* (Federal Reserve Board).

aggregate M2, stripped of its component, narrower aggregate, M1.[10] Our test period was from January 1985 to May 1996.

Exhibit 14–8 shows that the percentage of variance explained by this new model (R^2 = 0.89) substantially exceeds that of the Fridson–Jónsson model (R^2 = 0.72). On this measure, the Garman model also improves upon the results achieved by the Babson model, absent the preceding month's spread.

On the whole, the signs in Exhibit 14–8 are intuitively satisfying. The risk premium (spread versus Treasuries) decreases, as indicated by a negative sign, when capacity utilization rises or when the yield curve steepens. Both trends imply a strengthening economy and, by implication, reduced risk of business failures. Additionally, the spread narrows when the money supply expands, indicating easier credit conditions, or when cash flows into high yield mutual funds accelerate, enhancing the market's liquidity. The positive sign for the default rate is likewise consistent with a straightforward relationship between risk and the risk premium. Consistent with Fridson and Jónsson (1995), the cash percentage of high yield mutual fund portfolios is positively correlated with the spread. Evidently, fund managers tend to maintain large liquidity balances when market risk is high. Less easy to explain is the positive correlation between the spread and the year-over-year change in the Consumer Price Index. The popular wisdom is that inflation benefits debtors (that is, reduces default risk) by reducing the real cost of liabilities. On the other hand, the predicted response of the Federal Reserve to a surge in the inflation rate is to rein in the money supply. As we have already seen from the sign of our money supply variable, a monetary contraction is associated with an increase in the risk premium. From the conflicting forces generated by escalating inflation, it appears the net impact on the spread versus Treasuries is widening.

Although Exhibit 14–8 shows the correlation coefficients obtained by utilizing the largest possible series of observations, we have also employed the standard "jackknife" procedure of creating a holdout sample. Using the variables listed above, we calculated an R^2 of 0.87 for the period January

---

10. Components of the two aggregates are as follows: M1: Currency; travelers checks of nonbank issuers; demand deposits; other checkable deposits at all depository institutions. M2: All components of M1; money market mutual fund shares (general-purpose and broker/dealer, taxable and nontaxable); savings deposits at all depository institutions; money market deposit accounts at all depository institutions; small-denomination time deposits at all depository institutions. (Source: Board of Governors of the Federal Reserve System, *Federal Reserve Bulletin,* 82:8, (August 1996), pp. AY.)

E X H I B I T   14–8

Garman Model Regression Statistics

$R^2 = 0.89$
Adjusted $R^2 = 0.88$

Explanatory Variable	Regression Coefficient	*t*-Statistic*	*P*-Value
Default Risk Indicators			
Moody's Trailing-Twelve- Months Default Rate (percentage-of-issuers basis)	0.257	9.10	0.000
Capacity Utilization	−0.250	−6.05	0.000
Illiquidity Risk Indicators			
Mutual Fund Flows as a Percentage of Fund Assets	−0.093	−3.98	0.000
Cash as a Percentage of High Yield Mutual Fund Assets	0.258	6.56	0.000
Monetary Conditions Indicators			
Consumer Price Index (year-over-year change)	0.206	3.37	0.001
Money Supply (M2 minus M1) (year-over-year change)	−0.120	−8.94	0.000
Treasury Yield Curve (ten-year minus three-month)	−0.450	−8.68	0.000

*All variables are significant at the 99 percent confidence level.

1985–August 1990 only (one-half of the monthly periods available). Then, with the correlation coefficients derived from that exercise, we estimated values for all of the months from September 1990 forward. Regressing the estimated values against the actual values, we obtained an R^2 of 0.85 in our holdout sample (see Exhibit 14–9). The results of this exercise allayed possible concerns about dependence of our model on period-specific factors.

GARMAN MODEL'S VERDICT ON HIGH YIELD MARKET'S VALUATION

The close fit between actual spreads and the spreads estimated by this model is illustrated in Exhibit 14–10. Monthly differences between actual and estimated spreads are graphed in Exhibit 14–11. For comparison, a graph of the Fridson–Jónsson model's monthly differences appears in Exhibit 14–2.

E X H I B I T   14–9

Jackknife Test of Garman Model
In-Sample Period: January 1985 to August 1990
Holdout Sample Period: September 1990 to May 1996

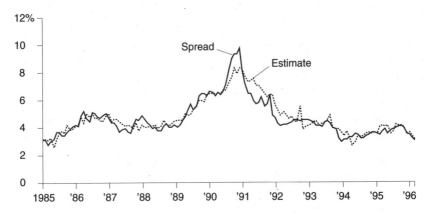

E X H I B I T   14–10

Actual versus Estimated Spread
Garman Model, January 1985 to May 1996, Monthly

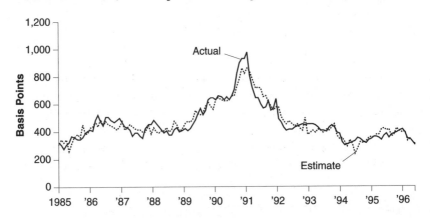

The most conspicuous divergence between the Garman and the Fridson–Jónsson models occurs from the second half of 1995 onward. Estimated and actual spreads converge during the period according to the Garman model which supplements indicators of default and liquidity risk with

E X H I B I T   14–11

Actual Minus Estimated Spread
Garman Model, January 1985 to May 1996, Monthly

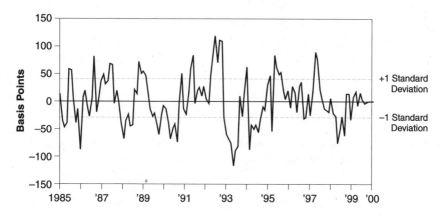

variables representing monetary conditions. By contrast, Fridson and Jónsson's model, which explains the earlier years' spread reasonably well with a more parsimonious model indicates that the risk premium in early 1996 is much too small.

We can hypothesize, based on the divergence between the graphs in Exhibits 14–10 and 14–11, that monetary conditions had an unusually strong influence during 1995 and early 1996. This supposition is corroborated by evidence that the majority of monetary indicators favored narrow spreads during the period. Looking at the underlying data, we find that the mean year-over-year increase in the Consumer Price Index was 3.65 percent between January 1995 and May 1996. The mean for the full observation period was 4.62 percent, representing a difference with high statistical significance. For our money supply indicator, the mean year-over-year increases were 4.95 percent (January 1995 to May 1996) and 3.67 percent (January 1985 to May 1996), a meaningful although not highly significant difference. (Our third monetary conditions variable, the yield curve, was also out of line from historical experience during the 1995–1996 period, but in a direction that implied a wider-than-average spread.)

In summary, between January 1995 and May 1996 two out of three key indicators of monetary conditions call for a narrower-than-average spread versus Treasuries. The Fridson–Jónsson model, which is largely insensitive to monetary factors, signals that a smaller-than-average risk premium cannot be justified. Once monetary conditions are considered, the high yield market ceases to appear overvalued.[11]

By virtue of capturing monetary influences that have substantial, independent explanatory value in selected periods, Garman's highly robust model represents an improvement over previous methods of evaluating the high yield market's risk premium. It is a potentially valuable new tool for investors who hope to beat benchmark returns by varying their high yield concentrations across time.

REFERENCES

Altman, Edward I. and Joseph C. Bencivenga (1995). "A Yield Premium for the High Yield Debt Market." *Financial Analysts Journal.* September/October, pp. 49–56.

Arce Ruiz, Luis; Emre Gunalp; Erik Plotkin; Selim Sezer; and Vinod Vasandani (1996). "High Yield Spread Forecasting Model." Report of project conducted under the supervision of Professors Joel Shulman and Roberto Bonifaz at Babson College, Wellesley, Massachusetts.

Fridson, Martin S. (1994). "Fraine's Neglected Findings: Was Hickman Wrong?" *Financial Analysts Journal.* September/October, pp. 43–53.

——— (1992). "The Proportional Yield Spread Hypothesis." *Extra Credit.* November/December, pp. 13–19.

——— and Jeffrey A. Bersh (1994). "Spread versus Treasuries as a Market-Timing Tool for High Yield Investors." *Journal of Fixed Income.* June, pp. 63–69.

——— and Jón G. Jónsson (1995). "Spread versus Treasuries and the Riskiness of High Yield Bonds." *Journal of Fixed Income.* December, pp. 79–88.

——— and James F. Kenney (1994). "How Do Changes in Yield Affect Quality Spreads?" *Extra Credit.* July/August, pp. 4–13.

Ratner, Hal (1996). "Multisector Bond Overview." *Morningstar Mutual Funds.* May, p. 1,041.

---

11. Another potential contributor to the improvement in accuracy of the Garman model over the Fridson–Jónsson model is the replacement of Lagging Economic Indicators with Capacity Utilization. The latter variable averaged 83.5 percent between January 1985 and May 1996, significantly above the full-period average of 81.78 percent, indicating that a below-average spread versus Treasuries was justified.

CHAPTER 15

Modeling the Yields on Noninvestment-Grade Bonds

Theodore M. Barnhill, Jr.

Frederick L. Joutz

William F. Maxwell

INTRODUCTION

In this chapter we present econometric analyses of the relation between the yields on high yield bond indices and various factors. Long-run relations between noninvestment-grade indices, Treasury yields, and default rates, and several significant short-term dynamic factors including mutual fund flows and equity market levels are identified. We also show that the significance of various factors varies depending on the segment of the high yield considered (for example, BB or B).

The models build upon the yield premium and yield spread models currently being utilized to determine the relative attractiveness of the spreads on high yield instruments. The model formulated in this chapter integrates the long-run relationship implied in the yield premium model and the short-run dynamic factors found in the yield spread models.

Yield premium models (Fons 1987 and Altman and Bencivenga 1995) analyze the market yield premium for holding risky debt (the average yield spread between risky debt securities and the risk-free security). This break-even type analysis calculates whether there is a net return (yield premium minus default rate) for holding risky bonds over a long period. Hence, the yield premium models are long-run models, which focus upon the default risk of holding a noninvestment-grade security versus the additional spread for holding the noninvestment-grade security. The results from these and other studies show that investors earn positive risk-adjusted returns over the long run. However, these models are of limited usefulness to investors trying to determine the relative attractiveness of the current noninvestment grade market.

Fridson and Jónsson (1995) and Garman and Fridson (1996) extend this type of analysis by focusing upon the short-run dynamics of the market by including liquidity risk measures in the analysis and more broadly defining default risk. The authors formulate yield spread models (yield on the risky debt minus the risk-free rate as the dependent variable) that include both default risk and liquidity risk measures.

Our model combines the long-run relationship found in the yield premium models with the short-run dynamic factors found in the yield spread models. CS First Boston provided monthly data on the yields of their aggregate noninvestment-grade index, the BB index, and the B index from January 1987 through July 1996 to estimate the models. Exhibit 15–1 contains information about the general composition of the indices used in the study.

To assess the appropriate Treasury yield to use in this study, a correlation analysis was done on five-, seven-, and ten-year notes (see Exhibit 15–2). The results indicate that the yield on ten-year Treasuries has the highest correlation to the noninvestment-grade bond indices, and hence the ten-year Treasury yield is used for the analysis contained in this chapter.

A LONG-RUN MEAN REVERTING RELATIONSHIP BETWEEN NONINVESTMENT-GRADE YIELDS, TREASURY YIELDS, AND DEFAULT RATES

How are Treasury yields and default rates related to corporate bond yields? A correlation analysis demonstrates that as corporate bond quality goes down, so does the relationship with Treasury yields. However, when examining the correlation between default rates and yields, this relationship is reversed and the lower the credit quality, the higher the correlation. These results are not surprising (see Exhibit 15–3), but instead reinforce the concept of a long-run relationship between Treasury yields and default rates and the yields on noninvestment-grade bonds.

To understand the long-run relation between noninvestment-grade yields, Treasury yields, and default rates, the variables are modeled using econometric techniques (cointegration analysis and error correction modeling). Given the nonstationarity of noninvestment-grade yields, Treasury yields, and default rates, the traditional approach is to model a process with differences to induce stationarity. While this is common practice, it results

E X H I B I T   15–1

Composition by Rating Category of CS
First Boston's High Yield Indices

% Weighting of Index[1995]	BB Index	B Index	CSFB Index
Split BBB	—	—	5.5
BB	100.0	—	22.3
Split BB	—	—	18.1
B	—	100.0	43.2
Split B	—	—	5.0
CCC & Lower	—	—	5.9

E X H I B I T   15–2

Correlation Analysis of the Δ in
Noninvestment-Grade and Treasury Yields

	Δ BB Index	Δ B Index	Δ CSFB Index
Δ 10-Year Treasury Note	0.472	0.395	0.417
Δ 7-Year Treasury Note	0.464	0.394	0.417
Δ 5-Year Treasury Note	0.446	0.362	0.398

in a potential loss of information on the long-run interaction of variables. So instead of moving directly to a model utilizing differences, an analysis was performed to determine if there were a cointegrating vector. The implication of a cointegrating vector is that while the variables may be individually nonstationary a linear combination of variables is stationary. The existence of a cointegrating vector indicates a long-run relationship between the variables and a tendency to revert back to the long-run relationship over time.

We use the Johansen most likely procedure for finite-order vector autoregressions (VARs) to test if there are any cointegrating vectors. The results indicate there is a long-run relation. The long-run relations are found in equations (1), (2), and (3) below.

$$\text{BB index yield} = .9954 \text{ T-bond yield} \qquad (15\text{–}1)$$
$$+ .1150 \text{ Moody's default rate}$$
$$(\alpha \text{ coefficient} = -.2016)$$

E X H I B I T   15–3

Descriptive Analysis of Corporate
Bonds and Treasury Bonds

Bond Index	Mean Yield	Std. Deviation	Correlation with Treasury Bonds	Correlation with Moody's Default Rate
T-Bonds	7.55	1.11	1.00	.301
Aaa	8.52	.96	.973	.302
Aa	8.75	.98	.968	.320
A	8.96	1.04	.966	.327
Baa	9.41	1.13	.959	.329
Split BBB	9.59	1.33	.903	.387
BB	10.54	1.40	.862	.559
Split BB	11.70	1.91	.810	.635
B	12.67	2.17	.745	.677
Split CCC and CCC	18.65	6.90	.151	.712

Note: Bond index information for Treasury bond and investment grade indices was collected from Citibase, which utilizes Moody's
bond ratings. Noninvestment-grade indices were provided by CS First Boston. All index information is monthly from
1987(1) to 1996(7).

$$\text{B index yield} = .7936 \text{ T-bond yield} \qquad (15\text{--}2)$$
$$+ .2914 \text{ Moody's default rate}$$
$$(\alpha \text{ coefficient} = -.0594)$$

$$\text{CSFB index yield} = .8316 \text{ T-bond yield} \qquad (15\text{--}3)$$
$$+ .3458 \text{ Moody's default rate}$$
$$(\alpha \text{ coefficient} = -.0627)$$

The noninvestment-grade indices long-run equilibrium is essentially
the risk-free rate plus a premium to reflect the increased rate of default. The
relationship of the default rate to the different indices is as expected
because as the bond credit quality decreases, signified by the bond rating,
default rate has a larger effect on yield.

The α coefficients found under equations 15–1, 15–2, and 15–3 represent the speed of adjustment to disequilibrium comparable to a mean-
reversion rate. The α coefficients ranged from –0.2016 to –0.0594. The
signs are as expected (a negative sign indicating that as the variables move
away from equilibrium, there is an increasing tendency to move back
towards the equilibrium relationship). The alphas suggest a slow adjustment to disequilibrium in the more volatile B and CSFB indices.

ERROR CORRECTION MODELS AND SHORT-RUN DYNAMICS

After testing for a cointegrating vector in a system of equations, the models are then estimated as a single-equation error correction model (ECM). Error correction models combine the information from the long-run relationship found in the cointegration analysis with short-run dynamics factors.

Short-Run Dynamic Factors Tested

We use Moody's default rate and economic indicators to indicate the relative risk of investing in the noninvestment-grade market. The economic indicators tested are monthly indexes of leading, coincidental, and lagging economic indicators. A note should be made about the default rate measure utilized. The market will anticipate default well in advance of the actual default (Altman 1989), and hence a lag will occur between the market reaction and the default rate. However, default rates are still found to be useful in a market model. This is partly due to the serial correlation of default rates. An increasing default rate can lead to an expectation of future defaults occurring.

A number of authors have demonstrated the correlation of returns on high-yield bonds to equity indices (Bookstaber and Jacob 1986, Ramaswami 1991, and Shane 1994). Such a relationship is consistent with a contingent claims analysis (CCA). Unfortunately, an equity index is not available for firms that have noninvestment-grade debt outstanding. Instead, we performed a correlation analysis on a number of stock indices to determine the best index to utilize in the current study (see Exhibit 15–4). The Russell 2000 Index had the highest correlation across the noninvestment-grade indices and was used. In addition, we also utilized the earnings/price ratio as a proxy for the cost of equity minus the growth rate. Finally, a dummy variable (d.v.) was added to reflect the October 1987 market crash to determine its effect on the yield requirement of high-yield bonds.

Fridson (1995) found that senior debt yields more than like-rated subordinated debt. Fridson's finding at first seems anomalous, but rating agencies factor into account a bond's potential recovery rate, which is a function of seniority, when assigning a rating. Fridson suggests that bondholders, as compared to the rating agencies, place more emphasis on the potential of default, compared to the potential recovery in the case of default. Hence, we examine the effect of a change in the percentage of securities in an index, which are subordinated.

E X H I B I T   15–4

Correlation Analysis of Monthly Δ Bond
Indices Yield and Δ Stock Indices

	Δ Baa Index	Δ BB Index	Δ B Index	Δ CSFB Index
Δ S&P 500	−0.3446	−0.2875	−0.4320	−0.4254
Δ S&P Mid Cap Index	−0.3380	−0.3385	−0.4535	−0.4394
Δ NASDAQ Composite	−0.3337	−0.3756	−0.4628	−0.4596
Δ Russell 1000	−0.3489	−0.3032	−0.4350	−0.4328
Δ Russell 2000	−0.3197	−0.4026	−0.4770	−0.4999
Δ Russell 3000	−0.3498	−0.3156	−0.4428	−0.4430

Note: The change or first difference of a variable is indicated by a Δ before the variable. The stock index information was collected
from COMPUSTAT and the analysis covers the time period of June 1987 to July 1996.

Within each major rating category, there are three more refined categories (+ or − for S&P and 1, 2, or 3 for Moody's). If these minor rating classifications are significant, a change in the percentage of the major rating category that is made up of the lowest credit quality (BB− and B−) should have an effect on the index's yield. We test the effect of the percentage of bonds that are in the lowest minor rating category.

When Iraq invaded Kuwait in August of 1990, the effect on the world's oil supply and thus on the financial markets was unknown. To reflect a possible structural break caused by the Iraq invasion, a dummy variable was included for August of 1990, and lagged one period to encompass the effect in September 1990. An additional dummy variable was included to study the effect the liberation of Kuwait had on the high yield market.

In addition to the long-run relationship found in the cointegration analysis, we also included the change in the Treasury yield to examine how short-run changes affect the yield on noninvestment-grade bonds.

The effect of mutual fund investment flow on stock and bond returns is well understood on Wall Street and in academic work. The Investment Company Institute (ICI) tracks mutual funds by investment category, including one labeled high yield. On a monthly basis, the ICI reports data on the asset value and percentage of assets held in liquid investments. Since mutual funds make up a large segment of the market[1], the change in mutual fund flow and the liquidity position of mutual funds could have a significant effect on market yield.

---

1. Chase Securities Inc. estimates high yield mutual funds comprised 22 percent of the market in 1995 (DeRosa–Farag, 1996).

There is a well-documented January effect in bond returns. A dummy variable was included for December and January to examine if there is any seasonality in noninvestment-grade index yields.

ESTIMATING ERROR CORRECTION MODELS FOR THE NONINVESTMENT-GRADE BOND INDICES

We estimated general error correction models that include both the long-run solution and the variables theorized as possibly affecting the short-run dynamics of the indices. The general models were then reduced to more parsimonious models. The decision criteria used to determine the final specific model was twofold. First, all variables that were statistically significant at the 90 percent confidence level were included. Second, F-tests were performed on the models to determine the significance of the loss of information from removing a variable.

The following is the formulation of the parsimonious error correction models:

$$\Delta \text{BB}_t = -.26[(\text{BB} - .99(\text{T-bond}) - .12(\text{Default rate})]_{t-1} \qquad (15\text{--}4)$$
$$+ .32(\Delta \text{T-Bond})_t + .13(\Delta \text{ Default rate})_{t-1}$$
$$+ .05(\Delta\% \text{ Subordinated}) + .05(\Delta\% \text{ BB}-)_t$$
$$+ .55(\text{Drexel})_{t-2} - .05(\% \text{ Mutual fund flow})_t$$
$$+ .02(\% \text{ Mutual fund flow})_{t-2}$$

$$\Delta \text{B}_t = -.15[\text{B} - .79 \text{ (T-bond)} - .29 \text{ (Default rate)}]_{t-1} \qquad (15\text{--}5)$$
$$+ .15(\Delta \text{T-Bond})_t$$
$$+ .17(\Delta \text{Default rate})_t - .06(\Delta \text{P/E ratio})_t$$
$$+ 1.24(\text{Iraq invasion})_{t-1} - .08(\% \text{ Mutual fund flow})_t$$
$$- .14(\text{January})_t$$

$$\Delta \text{CSFB}_t = -.11[\text{CSFB} - .83 \text{ (T-bond)} - .35(\text{Default rate})]_{t-1} \qquad (15\text{--}6)$$
$$+ .31(\Delta \text{ T-bond})_t + .14(\Delta \text{ Default rate})_{t-1}$$
$$+ .98(\text{Iraq invasion})_{t-1} - .58(\text{Kuwait liberation})_t$$
$$- .09(\% \text{ Mutual fund flows})_t + .01(\% \text{ Mutual fund flows})_{t-2}$$

The error correction models are then converted back into levels to examine the R^2 on the yields. The R^2 is .9736 for the BB index, .9926 for the B index, and .9900 for the CS Aggregate Noninvestment-Grade index. Exhibits 15–5, 15–6, and 15–7 show that there is a very tight fit between the actual versus predicted index yields.

E X H I B I T   15–5

Actual versus Predicted Yields for CS First Boston's Aggregate Noninvestment-Grade Index

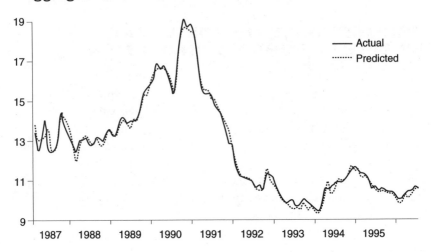

E X H I B I T   15–6

Actual versus Predicted Value for the CS First Boston's BB Index

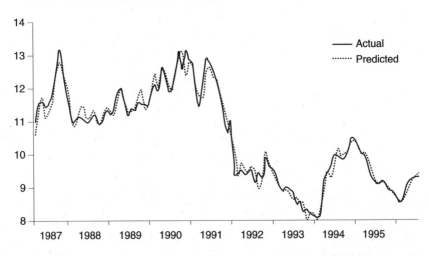

E X H I B I T   15–7

Actual versus Predicted Yields for
CS First Boston's B Index

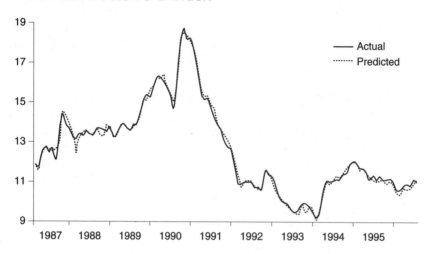

EMPIRICAL FINDINGS

The error correction component representing the long-run relationship was statistically significant in all the models. These results, in conjunction with the cointegration analysis, clearly indicate the significance of the long-run relationship between noninvestment-grade yields, Treasury yields, and default rates. The coefficient was highest for the BB index and lowest for the CSFB index.

Of concern is the stability of this long-run relationship. Is the long-run relationship stable or fluctuating over time? One way to find the answer is to analyze the consistency of the ECM coefficient estimate over time using recursive estimation. The results indicate a stable and consistent long-run relationship for each of the indices.

Mutual Fund Flow had a statistically significant negative effect on all the indices. The results also suggest the lower quality indices, B and CSFB, are more susceptible to price fluctuations as a result of fund flow. The results are consistent with a January effect for all the indices.

Moody's Default Rate was included in the long-run equilibrium models; in addition the Change in Moody's Default Rate was also entered into the error correction models. This clearly indicates the impact of both long- and short-run changes in the default rate on noninvestment-grade yields.

The Russell 2000 stock market index had no statistical effect on the general or specific models when mutual fund flow was included as an explanatory variable. The Standard & Poor's price/earnings ratio had a statistically significant negative impact on the yield of the B index.

The percentage of the index which was rated in the lowest minor rating category had a statistically significant positive effect on the yield; and the percentage of subordinated debt had a statistically significant positive effect on the BB index.

We found that a number of other one-time events had statistically significant effects on the different models separate from any impact of the stock index. The Iraq invasion of Kuwait and the subsequent liberation of Kuwait both had an impact on yield. As expected, these exogenous shocks had a greater impact on the lower quality B and CSFB indices. Economic indicators were not found to have a statistically significant effect on noninvestment grade yields.

SEGMENTATION OF THE HIGH YIELD MARKET

The results clearly indicate the dangers in viewing the noninvestment-grade market as a homogeneous market. Different factors affect the yields of the BB and B indices, and shared explanatory variables have different relationships across the indices. As expected, the lower credit quality B index is more sensitive to the default rate and less so to the Treasury yield in the long and short runs. In general, the B index was also more sensitive to changes in stock prices and mutual fund flows.

CONCLUSION

The yield premium and yield spread models provide frameworks for analyzing factors that affect the risk of holding risky debt instruments. However, since both models utilize spreads, there is assumed to be an instantaneous adjustment between Treasury yields and corporate bond yields. This is not the case, and by not factoring this into account, interest rate risk may be underestimated. We demonstrate by using a correlation and cointegration analysis that interest rate risk is not constant or instantaneous as implied by both models. Instead a broader model that allows interest rate risk (both in the long-run relation and in the short-run dynamic component) and default risk to fluctuate over time provides a better analytical framework to understand the long-term relationship between default rates, Treasury yields, and the yields on noninvestment-grade indices.

The system and single-equation models found varying adjustments to disequilibrium. Thus, even though there is a long-term equilibrium, short-term dynamics can significantly affect yield levels. Lower rated indices exhibit slower reversion toward equilibrium and larger short-run dynamic changes in yield.

In addition to a long-run equilibrium, short-run dynamic factors also affected the monthly yields. The dynamics of the high yield market were explained by changes in the Default Risk Measures including the Moody's Trailing Twelve-Month Default Rates, the Russell 2000 stock index, Percentage of Outstanding Debt in the Lowest Minor Rating Category, and the Percentage of Subordinated Debt Outstanding.

The changes in Liquidity-Risk Measures, including Mutual Fund Flow and Seasonal Variables, had a significant effect on yield levels. The strongest explanatory variable across all models was the Change in Mutual Fund Flow. The results also indicate that the lower credit quality indices are more sensitive to mutual fund flow. We also found a seasonal component in the yields consistent with a January effect.

Finally, the study demonstrated the segmentation of the high-yield market and the dangers in viewing the market as being homogeneous. Explanatory variables affect the indices differently both in the long and short terms.

REFERENCES

Altman, E. (1989). "Measuring Corporate Bond Mortality." *Journal of Finance* 44, pp. 909–22.

Altman, E. and J. Bencivenga (1995). "A Yield Premium Model for the High-Yield Debt Market," *Financial Analysts Journal* 51, pp. 49–56.

Bookstaber, R. and D. Jacob (1986). "The Composite Hedge: Controlling the Credit Risk of High Yield Bonds." *Financial Analysts Journal* 42, pp. 25–35.

Fons, J. (1987). "The Default Premium and Corporate Bond Experience." *Journal of Finance* 42, pp. 81–97.

Fridson, M. (1995). "Seniors Yield More than Like Rated Subs!" *Extra Credit.* July–August, pp. 4–17.

Fridson, M. and J. Jonsson (1995). "Spread versus Treasuries and the Riskiness of High-Yield Bonds." *Journal of Fixed Income* 5, pp. 79–88.

Garman, C. and M. Fridson (1996). "Monetary Influences on the High Yield Spread versus Treasuries." *Extra Credit.* July/August, pp. 13–26.

Ramaswami, M. (1991). "Hedging the Equity Risk of High-Yield Bonds." *Financial Analysts Journal* 47, pp. 41–50.

Shane, H. (1994). "Comovements of Low-Grade Debt and Equity Returns of Highly Leveraged Firms." *Journal of Fixed Income* 3, pp. 79–89.

CHAPTER 16

The January Effect in the Corporate Bond Market: A Systematic Examination*

William F. Maxwell

INTRODUCTION

The January or turn-of-the-year effect is defined in the literature as a positive risk-adjusted premium for holding a security in January. It is a pervasive, well-documented anomaly in financial markets. The anomaly has been established in stock returns using both a CAPM framework (Keim 1983; Reinganum 1983; Roll 1983; and De Bondt and Thaler 1987) and an APT framework (Cho and Taylor 1987, and Gultekin and Gultekin 1987).

A January effect has also been ascertained in corporate bond returns and yields (Chang and Pinegar 1986; Chang and Huang 1990; Fama and French 1993; and Barnhill, Joutz, and Maxwell 1997) and municipal bond returns (Kihn 1996). The prevalence and scope of the January effect is apparent in the findings that international stock markets have similar seasonal variations (Gultekin and Gultekin 1983).

The purpose of this chapter is to examine the January effect in the corporate bond market, systematically examining first its strength, and then its possible causes. The study extends the previous research by examining a larger sample of bonds, testing previously proposed causes using new data and methodologies, and proposing and testing new theories.

The paper is organized as follows. In the first section, I examine previous research on the January effect in the corporate bond market. The second

---

*This chapter is reprinted with permission from William F. Maxwell, "The January Effect in the Corporate Bond Market: A Systematic Examination," *Financial Management,* Vol. 27, no. 2 (Summer 1998), pp. 18–30. Financial Management Association International, University of South Florida, College of Business Administration, Tampa, FL 33620. (813) 974-3318.

section investigates the strength of the anomaly. In the third section, I examine the relationship between the January effect in the bond market and firm size. Section four discusses different supply and demand theories that have been suggested as causes of the January effect. Section five presents conclusions about the causes of the January effect in the corporate bond market.

SEASONAL VARIATION IN CORPORATE BOND RETURNS AND YIELDS

In this section, I review previous work regarding the January effect in the corporate bond markets, examine possible theories for the anomaly, and explore the relation between bond credit quality and the January effect.

The January Effect in the Corporate Bond Market

The January effect in the corporate bond market is well documented. Chang and Pinegar (1986) analyze the monthly holding returns of Treasuries, Aaa, Aa, A, Baa, Ba, and B bonds and find an excess return in January for the noninvestment-grade segments. Specifically, Chang and Pinegar find a positive excess return at the 92 percent confidence level for a sample of Ba-rated bonds and at the 99 percent confidence level for a sample of B-rated bonds in January, but they find no statistically significant excess returns for Treasury or investment-grade bonds.

Chang and Huang (1990) use a different methodology but find similar results. The lower the quality level of the bonds the more pronounced the January effect. In contrast to Chang and Pinegar, Chang and Huang find a statistically significant excess return for the lowest level of investment-grade bonds (Baa).

Fama and French (1993) analyze common risk factors in stock and bond returns. Their study finds a statistically significant excess return in January for portfolios of A, Baa, and noninvestment-grade bonds. The excess return increases monotonically as bond rating decreases.

Barnhill, Joutz, and Maxwell (1997) use cointegration techniques and error correction models to examine factors that affect the yields on noninvestment-grade securities. The authors find statistically significant negative changes in yield on CS First Boston's BB, B, and aggregate noninvestment-grade indices in January. The lowest credit quality B index had a larger January coefficient and statistical significance than the BB index.

Theories that Explain the January Effect

There have been numerous attempts to explain the January effect in the financial markets. One of the most frequently suggested reasons is tax-loss selling. However, numerous studies challenge the validity of this hypothesis (Brown, Keim, Kleindon, and Marsh 1983; Gultekin and Gultekin 1983; Jones, Pearce, and Wilson 1987; Tinic, Barone-Adesi, and West 1987). At best, the previous research suggests that tax-related selling only partly explains the January effect.

DeRosa-Farag (1996) suggests that the January effect in the corporate bond market is the result of supply and demand considerations. Bond coupon payments are not evenly distributed throughout the year, but instead reach their highest level in December and their lowest level in January. DeRosa-Farag therefore suggests that the January price increase is due to fund flow increases in December and decreases in January. However, Fridson and Garman (1995) and Barnhill, Maxwell, and Joutz (1997) find no supporting evidence for a coupon-based payment flow theory.

Several other explanatory hypotheses that apply to the stock market can be ruled out, because they do not apply to the corporate bond market. For example, Bhardwaj and Brooks (1992) find the January effect is closely related to low share price; however, there are no systematic pricing differences across bonds or categories of bonds. Seyhun (1988) finds support for the theory that insider trading by small-firm management is a cause for both the January and small-firm anomalies. However, since management rarely own a company's bonds, this theory cannot be utilized to explain the seasonality of returns in the bond market.

The January Effect and Bond Ratings

As noted, previous research demonstrates that there is an anomaly in the corporate bond market, and the January effect is more pronounced in the lowest quality bonds (low-quality investment-grade and noninvestment-grade bonds). This provides the focus for this paper. First, I examine the seasonality of the lowest-quality investment-grade categories (Split[1] BBB and BBB) and noninvestment-grade bonds. Second, the discrepancy between the strength of the January effect for investment- and noninvestment-grade

---

1. A split rating occurs when Moody's and Standard and Poor differ on the major bond rating
   category.

bonds suggests a systematic difference between the two types. A systematic difference could explain the reason for the anomaly in the corporate bond market.

I note the dangers of viewing the corporate bond market as a homogeneous market. In fact, the market is highly segmented. Describing the causes of the segmentation could clarify the reasons why the January effect is more prevalent in the lowest-quality bonds.

The segmentation between investment- and noninvestment-grade bonds starts with the market participants. Investment- and noninvestment-grade bond investors are different: Noninvestment-grade bonds are held almost exclusively by institutional investors (see Exhibit 16–1).

Another difference is the unique nature of noninvestment-grade bonds. Noninvestment-grade bonds are considered part debt and part equity instruments. This view is consistent with contingent claims theory (Black and Scholes 1973; and Merton 1974). The contingent claims theory implies that as the default probability of the bond increases (and bond rating decreases), the bond becomes less sensitive to changes in interest rates but more sensitive to changes in stock returns. The observed comovements of noninvestment-grade bonds to both debt and equity instruments is thus consistent with the contingent claims theory (Shane 1994; and Fridson 1994).

Portfolio management strategies also differ between investment- and noninvestment-grade bonds. Given the large yield spread between Treasuries and noninvestment-grade bonds, high yield portfolio managers stay close to being fully invested at all times. High yield portfolio managers time the market by shifting a portfolio's weighting across credit qualities, but they rarely shift the portfolio's assets out of the noninvestment-grade market.

The liquidity of investment- and noninvestment-grade bonds can also vary significantly. As credit quality decreases so does the liquidity of the bonds. This is a function of two phenomena. The average size of bond issues decreases with the credit rating, as does the number of bond issues per company. This effectively limits both the secondary market and the number of marketmakers. Also, institutional investors can be restricted from owning over a set percentage of their portfolio in noninvestment-grade bonds. Even noninvestment-grade pension and mutual funds are limited in the percentage of the portfolio held in the lowest rated categories [B, CCC, and NR(not rated)]. Smaller issue size and restrictions on ownership effectively limit the demand for and liquidity of noninvestment-grade bonds.

E X H I B I T   16—1

High Yield Bond Ownership, 1996

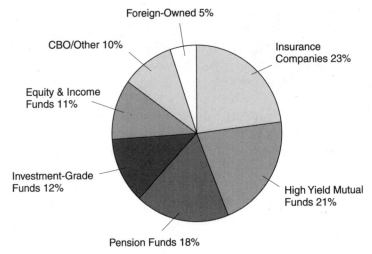

Source: Chase Securities, Inc.

STRENGTH OF THE JANUARY EFFECT

Given that the majority of bonds are not traded on exchanges, reliable yield and return data must be obtained from one of the investment banks that is an active marketmaker. Therefore, to analyze the strength of the anomaly, I collected monthly market return data for noninvestment-grade bonds and the lowest investment-grade category (Split BBB) from CS First Boston from January 1986 to April 1997. CS First Boston calculates return data, based on accrued interest and change in the bond's price, for all bonds in its indices. Because there are new issues and redemptions, the number of bonds tracked in the indices changes monthly, but the indices currently include over 1,200 bonds. Exhibit 16–2 shows the mean and standard deviation of monthly returns by rating category. As expected, the mean and standard deviation of returns increase as credit quality declines.

Exhibit 16–3 shows the monthly return patterns. Previous research finds that the 1987 stock market crash, the Iraq invasion of Kuwait, and the subsequent liberation of Kuwait all had one-month impacts on noninvestment-grade bonds (Barnhill, Joutz, and Maxwell 1997). To account for these exogenous shocks to the market and to reduce "noise" in the model, I

E X H I B I T   16–2

CS First Boston's Noninvestment-Grade Indices Monthly Percent Returns

	Mean Monthly Return	Standard Deviation	% High Yield Market[1995]
Split BBB	0.892	1.109	5.5
BB	0.973	1.101	22.3
Split BB	1.076	1.732	18.1
B	1.174	2.142	43.2
Split B	1.018	2.855	5.0
Split CCC/CCC	1.195	4.379	5.9

Note: This table provides descriptive statistics for the high yield market if the Split BBB category is included. CS First Boston provided monthly returns by rating category from January 1986 to April 1997, except for the Split B index which was only available from January 1990 to April 1997.

E X H I B I T   16–3

Noninvestment-Grade Bond Monthly Percent Returns, January 1986 to April 1997

	Constant	January	December	1987 Market Crash	Iraq Invasion	Kuwait Liberation
Split BBB	0.923	0.170	0.269	−1.603	−1.723	3.157
	(7.78)*	(0.45)	(0.68)	(−1.28)	(−1.38)	(2.53)†
BB	0.974	0.757	.277	−1.464	−3.154	3.866
	(8.22)*	(2.00)†	(0.71)	(−1.17)	(−2.53)†	(3.10)*
Split BB	1.009	0.627	0.300	−3.580	−5.070	9.140
	(7.76)*	(1.51)	(.70)	(−2.61)†	(−3.70)*	(6.66)*
B	1.020	1.014	0.221	−5.120	−10.030	7.510
	(6.36)*	(1.98)†	(0.42)	(−3.03)*	(−5.93)*	(4.44)*
Split CCC/ CCC	0.848	2.477	−1.347	−5.458	−15.918	10.212
	(2.58)*	(2.36)†	(−1.24)	(−1.58)	(−4.60)*	(2.95)*

* Significant at the 0.01 level.

† Significant at the 0.05 level.

Note: This table analyzes several dummy variables to assess their affect on the mean monthly yield by bond rating category. The constant represents the mean monthly yield. The other variables represent the dummy variables. Hence, the January coefficient for the B index represents an average additional and statistically significant return of 1.014 percent in the months of January examined in this study. The results are generated using OLS. The t-statistic appears underneath each coefficient in parentheses. For example, the t-statistic for the January coefficient tests the null hypothesis that the January coefficient is significantly different from zero.

included one-month dummy variables representing these events.[2] Thus, the constant represents the average monthly returns for February through November and excludes January and December. The January and December coefficients represent any additional return above or below the average return. I included the December variables to examine any fluctuations in returns, since several of the theories examined later have implications on return patterns in December. The coefficients for the exogenous shocks represent any change in the average return over the one-month time period the shock took place. The *t*-statistics test the significance of the coefficients.

The January coefficient is positive for all the indices and statistically significant at over the 95 percent confidence level in three of the five indices. While the coefficient is positive for the lowest investment-grade category, it is not statistically significant. The January coefficient ranges from a premium over the average monthly return of 17 basis points for the Split BBB index to 248 basis points for the Split CCC/CCC category. I find no support for a statistically significant negative return in December consistent with year-end selling theories, which are examined in more detail in section V of this chapter.

The strength of the January effect is readily apparent if the excess January return is compared to the average monthly return. The January premium expressed as a percentage of the average monthly return is a 17 percent premium (Split BBB), a 78 percent premium (BB), a 67 percent premium (Split BB), a 99 percent premium (B), and a 292 percent premium (Split CCC/CCC). Overall, the results clearly indicate the strength of the anomaly and the increase in the January premium as the bond rating decreases. These result are consistent with previous findings.

THE JANUARY EFFECT IN THE CORPORATE BOND MARKET AND FIRM SIZE

A number of researchers find the turn-of-the-year effect in stock returns is related to a small-firm effect (Keim 1983; Reinganum 1983; Roll 1983; Cho and Taylor 1987). In the corporate bond market, Chang and Pinegar (1986) conclude that seasonal returns are consistent with the small-firm effect.

---

2. To ensure the robustness of the findings, I also estimated the models without the exogenous variables. The results were similar but the models that excluded the shocks had larger standard errors.

To empirically examine the relation between the small-firm effect and the January anomaly in the corporate bond market, I use Compustat data to compare firm market value to minor bond rating categories (see Exhibit 16–4). On average, as minor bond ratings decrease, there is a monotonic decrease in firm value, except for the change between the AA+ and AA category and the AA- and A+ category.

Because of the small sample size in some rating classes and heterogeneous variances, I use the Wilcoxon rank sum test, a nonparametric test, to compare the significance of the differences between adjacent minor rating categories. Higher rating categories show statistically significant larger market values in 9 of the 15 categories. Though not included, I also compared market value and major rating categories, again using the Wilcoxon rank sum test. All higher major rating categories have statistically significant larger (at the 99 percent confidence level) market values.

Given the relation between firm size, as measured by market value, and bond rating, the results suggest that the January effect in the bond market is indeed related to the small-firm effect found in the stock market.

SEASONAL BUYING AND SELLING PATTERNS

One explanation of financial markets seasonality is the tendency for investors to overreact to information around the end of the year. For example, DeBondt and Thaler (1985, 1987) and Dyl and Maberly (1992) find evidence to suggest that the seasonal returns found in stock prices are related to investor psychology and subsequent seasonal buying and selling patterns. In the same context, Lakonishok, Shleifer, Thaler, and Vishny (1991) find evidence that equity pension fund managers tend to sell "losers" at the end of quarters, especially at the end of the fourth quarter. In the corporate bond market, Cooper and Shulman (1994) find a similar practice of selling "winners" and "losers" at year-end.

While there is support for year-end selling, it does not adequately explain the January effect. Investors may sell their holdings at year-end, but if they reinvest the proceeds the net impact on the market should be neutral unless there is a shifting of investments across categories (see the next section). Therefore, for year-end selling to adequately explain the January effect, there should be a delay between the selling and subsequent reinvestment around the turn of the year. But if there is a delay in reinvestment, the delay would provide the shift in the demand necessary to explain the January effect.

E X H I B I T   16–4

Firm Market Value and Bond Rating

Minor Rating	Observations	Mean Market Value ($ millions)	Wilcoxon Rank Sum Score (z statistic)
AAA	25	42,949.5	2.95*
AA+	13	12,219.6	−0.83
AA	38	20,764.7	1.98†
AA−	56	8,587.8	1.15
A+	7	9,291.0	2.55†
A	153	6,008.3	1.98†
A−	114	4,141.4	1.86
BBB+	115	3,383.5	2.41†
BBB	124	2,425.6	2.11†
BBB−	110	1,719.7	0.79
BB+	76	1,674.6	1.70
BB	91	1,012.7	3.97*
BB−	111	673.2	2.31†
B+	118	440.0	2.26†
B	54	314.7	0.92
B−	20	270.6	NA

* Significant at the 0.01 level.

† Significant at the 0.05 level.

Note: This table compares firm market value between the higher rating category and the next lower rating category. A positive
         Wilcoxon rank sum score indicates the higher rating category has a larger market value. For example, the Wilcoxon rank
         sum score for the AAA category tests if there is a significant difference between the AAA category and the AA+ category.
         Information was derived from Compustat for the 1995 year-end. The Wilcoxon rank sum test is a nonparametric test that
         ranks the observations in two samples from highest to lowest value. The relative proportions of the rankings are then tested.

To examine this theory, I collected data from the Investment Company Institute. Mutual funds report month-end information on the percentage of their portfolios held in liquid assets to the Investment Company Institute. A shift in demand from December to January, as assets are sold but not reinvested until January, suggests the percentage of liquid assets held by mutual funds will increase at the end of December. Moreover, to adequately explain the discrepancy in the strength of the January effect in investment-grade, as compared to noninvestment-grade bonds, there should be an increase in the liquidity position of noninvestment-grade bonds—but not in the investment-grade bond mutual funds.

To examine this theory, I performed a seasonal analysis on the liquidity position of investment- and noninvestment grade bond funds on

E X H I B I T 16–5

Change in Monthly Percent Holdings of Liquid Assets by Bond Mutual Funds, January 1986 to March 1997

Variable	Noninvestment-Grade Funds	Investment-Grade Bond Funds
Constant	−0.074	−0.041
	(0.97)	(−0.50)
January	0.706	0.290
	(2.82)†	(1.09)
December	−0.028	−0.014
	(−0.11)	(−0.05)
1987 Market Crash	2.703	2.426
	(3.40)*	(2.88)*
Iraq Invasion	0.883	0.572
	(1.11)	(0.68)
Kuwait Liberation	−1.364	1.604
	(0.793)	(1.90)

* Significant at the 0.01 level.

† Significant at the 0.05 level.

Note: This table examines the change in the liquid asset holdings of bond mutual funds during January and December, controlling for the other dummy variables listed. The monthly percent holding of liquid assets by bond mutual funds is a nonstationary variable. To induce stationarity, I used the first difference of the monthly holding. The variables are represented as percentages. The results are generated using OLS. The t-statistic appears underneath each coefficient in parentheses.

month-end data from January 1986 to March 1997. The results appear in Exhibit 16–5. The December coefficients represent changes in the liquidity position of the funds. Both the investment- and noninvestment-grade funds have negative, though not statistically significant, coefficients. Clearly, these results indicate that mutual funds do not actively sell assets in December and retain liquid assets until January. A puzzling result is the statistically significant increase in the liquidity position of noninvestment-grade bond funds in January. I suggest an explanation for this in section VI.

In conclusion, even though previous studies have demonstrated the tendency for investors to sell winners and losers around the turn of the year, I can find no evidence that this would lead to the shift in demand necessary to explain the January effect. Nor can I find support for a downward pressure on prices in December which was suggested by year-end selling theories. Lastly, none of the year-end selling theories give a rationale for the strength and prevalence of the January effect for noninvestment-grade bonds but not for investment-grade bonds.

NONINVESTMENT-GRADE BOND SUPPLY

A commonly heard hypothesis on Wall Street for the January effect is an undersupply of noninvestment-grade bonds in January. It has been suggested that there is seasonal variation in new issues of noninvestment-grade bonds or, more specifically, a lack of new issues in January, which drives up the prices of existing bonds. A decrease in the new-issue bond supply of noninvestment-grade bonds in January would certainly provide a good explanation of the January effect in the corporate bond market and a reason for the discrepancy between investment- and noninvestment-grade bonds.

To examine this theory, I obtain monthly supply information for noninvestment-grade bonds from CS First Boston, which collects monthly information on the total supply of noninvestment-grade bonds. Their calculation of the total supply of noninvestment-grade bonds includes new issues (public and 144a), debt retirements, and net rating downgrades and upgrades. New-issue supply is the dominant factor in the change in the total supply of high yield bonds; but, to account for other concurrent changes, I use the total market supply.[3] Unfortunately, the data was only available on a monthly basis starting in January 1992, which clearly limits the conclusions that can be drawn.

While the sample period is limited, the general indication from Exhibit 16–6 is that there is no systematic reduction in the total supply of noninvestment-grade bonds in January. In fact, over the limited sample period, there was an average increase in the net new-issue supply in January. This clearly calls into questions the validity of the theory that the anomaly results from a lack of supply in January.

INDIVIDUAL INVESTOR
SEASONAL DEMAND

The impact of investment flow into mutual funds on market returns is clearly demonstrated in the stock and bond markets (Warther 1995) and on the yield of noninvestment-grade bonds (Fridson and Jónsson 1995). These results suggest that the January effect could be a function of a seasonal shift in demand by individual investors for high yield bonds which would be consistent with DeBondt and Thaler (1985, 1987) and Dyl and Maberly (1992).

---

3. The results are insensitive to the use of new-issue supply or total market supply.

E X H I B I T   16–6

Change in Monthly Supply of High Yield Bonds, January 1992 to April 1997

Variable	Coefficient	Standard Error	t-Value	t-Probability
Constant	−60.46	308.85	−0.196	0.845
January	1,601.50	1,096.30	1.461	0.149

Note: This table presents the results of a regression on the average change in the monthly supply of high yield bonds. The January
coefficient shows an additional change that can be ascribed to that particular month. The monthly supply of high yield bonds
is nonstationary, so the process is modeled using the stationary first difference.

To examine this hypothesis, I modeled the monthly percent change in the total assets invested in high yield mutual funds using Investment Company Institute data (see Exhibit 16–7). Because total assets under management have increased over time, the constant is positive for both the investment- and noninvestment-grade funds. To account for an autoregressive process, I included a single lag of the dependent variable as well as the exogenous shocks discussed in section II. The January and December coefficients reflect any positive or negative change above or below the constant.

The results in Exhibit 16–7 show that the amount of noninvestment-grade mutual fund assets has increased 0.63 percent per month historically. In January, noninvestment-grade mutual fund assets increase an additional, statistically significant, 1.89 percent. This finding of a systematic increase in investment flow in January into the noninvestment-grade market would put upward pressure on prices, which is consistent with the January effect.

For a seasonal increase in demand to be a convincing theory, it must offer a justification for the limited January effect in the investment-grade bond market and explain why the anomaly is stronger for the lower-rated bonds. To examine why there is a limited January effect for investment-grade bonds, I obtained the percent monthly change in total assets for investment-grade bond mutual funds from the Investment Company Institute and examined any seasonal shifts in demand. Exhibit 16–7 reports the results. Unlike the noninvestment-grade mutual funds, there is no statistically significant increase in supply in January for the investment-grade bond funds. This result helps answer the question of why there is little or no corresponding January effect found in the investment-grade bond market.

E X H I B I T   16–7

Percent Monthly Change in Mutual Fund Assets
Held by Investment- and Noninvestment-Grade
Bond Funds, January 1986 to March 1997

Variable	Noninvestment-Grade	Investment-Grade
Constant	0.625	1.26
	(1.93)	(3.33)*
% Mutual Fund Flow$_{t-1}$	0.454	0.07
	(6.14)*	(0.87)
January	1.887	1.03
	(1.98)†	(0.38)
December	−0.515	0.66
	(−0.52)	(0.57)
1987 Market Crash	−6.859	−3.01
	(−2.16)†	(−0.81)
Iraq Invasion	−6.577	−1.09
	(−2.03)†	(−0.77)
Kuwait Liberation	7.670	2.93
	(2.44)†	(0.43)

* Significant at the 0.01 level.

† Significant at the 0.05 level.

Note: This table examines the monthly changes in the amount of funds invested in investment- and noninvestment-grade mutual
funds by individual investors. The constant represents the average increase in mutual fund flow into the fund category. The
% Mutual Fund Flow$_{t-1}$ accounts for any autocorrelation. The other variables represent changes from the average increase.
The Investment Company Institute reports the total assets under management by mutual funds, segmented by investment
criteria. Because both the investment- and noninvestment-grade bond funds have experienced significant growth in the total
assets under management, I calculated the percent change in total assets to induce stationarity. Under each coefficient, the
t-statistic appears in parentheses.

An increase in mutual fund flow into high yield funds could also provide an answer for why the January effect increases as credit quality
decreases. While high yield mutual funds make up 21 percent (see Exhibit
16–1) of the total high yield market, they are believed to be the dominant
holder of B-rated bonds which represent 43 percent of the market.[4] This could
explain why there is a stronger January effect in the lowest bond ratings

A significant increase in investor demand for noninvestment-grade
bonds in January also provides a possible explanation of the anomalous
finding in section V. The increase in the percentage of liquid assets held by
noninvestment-grade bond funds at the end of January that I found in Section V is consistent with increased fund flow into noninvestment-grade
funds in January.

---

4. I reached this conclusion after conversations with market participants. However, I can find no data
   to document this implied market segmentation.

Finally, note the effect of the exogenous shocks on the demand for investment- and noninvestment-grade bonds (see Exhibit 16–7). While the signs of the changes are consistent for both the investment- and noninvestment-grade mutual funds during all of the shocks, the magnitude and statistical significance are very different.

WINDOW DRESSING

Window dressing offers another possible explanation for the anomaly. Window dressing is the year-end practice used by financial institutions and investors to clean up their financial reports. The term can refer to a number of different practices. For example, Lakonishok, Shleifer, Thaler, and Vishny (1991) and Cooper and Shulman (1994) describe the practice as selling "losers" at year-end. Fridson (1994) describes window dressing as the year-end practice of adjusting portfolio weighting to meet compliance restrictions on industry weighting and bond credit quality. In practice, window dressing often results in bond portfolio managers, insurance companies, and pension funds selling lower-quality issues at year-end to raise the average quality level of their portfolios. This practice is then reversed at the beginning of the year as funds are reinvested in the lower credit quality issues. This shift in demand from lower to higher credit quality and then back to lower credit quality could explain the difference in the strength of the anomaly as bond ratings decrease.

The shifting of funds out of the lower credit qualities by funds is not done in a vacuum. If there are significant supply and demand pressures in the market that will impact the BB- and B-rated bonds, these same forces should also apply in the opposite direction to an offsetting asset class.

One possible alternative asset class is liquid investments, discussed in the previous section. Another alternative asset class is Split BBB bonds. The Split BBB category is an attractive alternative asset class to investors who shift funds around the turn of the year. Split BBB bonds are rated investment grade by one of the two major rating categories and noninvestment grade by the other, and regulatory agencies use the highest bond rating in classifying an institution's portfolio. Hence, the Split BBB provides not only an attractive yield but also allows institutional investors to report a higher percentage of investment-grade bonds in their portfolio at the fiscal year-end. To examine the theory that the anomaly is in part a shifting of assets to different classes due to window dressing, I have modeled the seasonal component of the yield on the CS First Boston Split BBB index. For comparison purposes, I have also modeled the two adjacent rating indices, the BBB and BB.

Modeling the Seasonal Component of the BBB, Split BBB, and BB Indices

To accurately examine the impact of seasonal fluctuation on yields and to reduce "noise" in the model, I have controlled for other factors that may affect the yields or relative yields. Barnhill, Joutz, and Maxwell (1997) analyzed factors that affect the yield on noninvestment grade securities. They found that the market drivers for the noninvestment-grade bond market include a long-run mean reverting relationship between the yield on noninvestment-grade securities and Treasury bond yields and default rates. Using error correction models (ECMs), these authors found exogenous shocks impact the short-run dynamics of the different noninvestment-grade indices. Thus, to analyze the January effect, I developed error correction models for the Split BBB index and, for comparison, the BBB and BB indices.

Cointegration Analysis

I have tested corporate bond yields, Treasury yields, and default rates[5] for stationarity utilizing the augmented Dickey–Fuller test statistic. I found that all the variables are nonstationary, but the first differences are stationary. To avoid a potentially spurious regression, the traditional approach in modeling nonstationary variables is to differentiate the variables to induce stationarity.[6] However, this can lead to a loss of information on the long-run relationship among variables. Therefore, I tested to determine if there are any cointegrating vectors. The implication of a cointegrating vector is that, although the individual variables may be nonstationary, a linear combination of the variables is stationary (Enders 1995). Thus, a cointegrating vector implies a long-run stationary relation among the variables.

Two methodologies are available to test for a cointegrating vector. The Engle–Granger methodology (Engle and Granger 1987) is appropriate for a bivariate analysis. However, the Johansen maximum likelihood

---

5. Citibase is used to determine the investment grade and Treasury yield information. Citibase provides Moody's yield information and, for simplicity's sake, the Citibase Baa category is labeled BBB to coincide with the rating method used by CS First Boston, which provided the yield information for the Split BBB, BB, and B indices utilized in this study. Moody's Investors Service furnished the default information.
6. To examine the robustness of the results, I also estimated the models using the traditional approach of differencing the variables to induce stationarity. The results from the differenced models were consistent with the cointegration models. However, the overall fits of the differenced models were at least 20 percent worse based on a comparison of R^2.

procedure for finite-order vector autoregressions (Johansen 1988, 1991) is more appropriate for a multivariate analysis. Given the multivariate nature of the present study, the Johansen methodology is used.

The first step in testing for a cointegrating vector is to determine the appropriate lag structure in the vector autoregression (VAR) which is done by testing the residuals as the lag structure is reduced. The null hypothesis is that there is no significant difference in the residuals as the model lag structure is reduced. The log-likelihood, Schwartz criterion, Hannan–Quinn, and the F-statistics are then used to test the significance of the change in the model's residuals. All the test statistics suggested that a lag structure of two periods is appropriate.

Exhibit 16–8 reports the results of the test of a long-term relation among Treasury yields, default rates, and the yields on the different indices. The maximal and trace eigenvalue statistics test the stationarity of the cointegrating vector and can be considered a multivariate Dickey–Fuller test. For example, the null hypothesis of r(rank) = 0, is that there is no stationary cointegrating vector. The Johansen maximal and trace eigenvalues are the test statistics. All the maximal and trace eigenvalue statistics reject (at the 99 percent confidence level) the null hypothesis that there are no cointegrating vectors for both the Split BBB and BB indices.

The implication is that there is at least one cointegrating (stationary) vector or long-run solution for these indices. The null hypothesis of $r \leq 1$ is that there is one or more cointegrating vector. All the maximal and trace eigenvalue statistics suggest little evidence of more than one cointegrating vector, and I conclude there is a single cointegrating vector for both the Split BBB and BB indices.

By restricting the beta coefficients of the Treasury bond yield and the default rate and then reestimating the cointegrating vectors, the significance of the variables in the cointegrating vectors can be tested by using chi-square statistics. The chi-square [χ^2(degrees of freedom)] statistics suggest that both the Treasury bond yield and the default rate individually add explanatory power to the long-run solution for both the Split BBB and BB indices.

No statistically significant conclusion can be drawn about a cointegrating vector for the BBB index. However, given the cointegration results and the chi-square statistics, the yield on the BBB index seems to be insensitive to the default rate or at least to small changes in the default rate.

The standardized ß/ eigenvectors in Exhibit 16–8 are the estimated cointegrating vectors for the indices long-term market equilibrium or the

E X H I B I T   16–8

Cointegration Analysis of Indices, Treasury Bond Yields, and Default Rate

Index	BBB Index	Split BBB Index	BB Index
Cointegration Statistics			
Eigenvalue	0.112	0.209	0.196
Null Hypothesis	$r = 0$	$r = 0$	$r = 0$
λ_{max}	14.10	27.90*	26.00*
$\lambda^{\alpha}{}_{max}$	13.39	26.49*	24.69*
95% Critical Value	21.0	21.0	21.0
λ_{trace}	21.00	39.16*	35.96*
$\lambda^{\alpha}{}_{trace}$	19.94	37.18*	34.14*
95% Critical Value	29.7	29.7	29.7
Standardized Eigenvectors β/			
T-Bond Yield	−1.183	−0.980	−0.843
Moody's Default Rate	0.003	−0.065	−0.149
Standardized Adjustment,			
Coefficient α	0.078	−0.134	−0.169
Test Statistics for the Significance of the Variable in Cointegrating Vectors			
Variable	$\chi^2(1)$	$\chi^2(1)$	$\chi^2(1)$
T-Bond Yield	7.45*	14.26*	10.95*
Moody's Default Rate	0.01	5.46†	15.08*

* Significant at the 0.01 level.

† Significant at the 0.05 level.

Note: This table shows the cointegration results from the Johansen VAR cointegration analyses. The eigenvalues test the null hypothesis that there are no cointegrating vectors. The λ_{max} and $\lambda^{\alpha}{}_{max}$ are Johansen's maximal eigenvalue statistics, and λ_{trace} and $\lambda^{\alpha}{}_{trace}$ are Johansen's trace eigenvalue statistics. An α signifies the statistics are adjusted for degrees of freedom. The critical values provide the cutoffs for rejection of the null hypothesis that there are no cointegrating vectors. The standardized eigenvector represents the stationary linear combination of the variables. The standardized adjustment coefficients, α, represent the speed of adjustment to disequilibrium which is similar to mean reversion rates in single equation models. The lower the α the faster the reversion toward the equilibrium value represented by the standardized eigenvector. The test statistics for the variables, included in the standardized eigenvector, test the significance of an individual variable by excluding the other variables in the eigenvectors.

long-run solution. The cointegrating vectors for the Split BBB and BB indices are written as follows:

$$\epsilon = \text{Split BBB yield} - 0.980 \text{ T-bond yield} \qquad (16\text{–}1)$$
$$- 0.065 \text{ Moody's default rate}$$

$$\epsilon = \text{BB yield} - 0.843 \text{ T-bond yield} \qquad (16\text{–}2)$$
$$- 0.149 \text{ Moody's default rate}$$

or algebraically manipulated with ε having an expectation of zero as:

$$\text{Split BBB yield} = 0.980 \text{ T-bond yield} \qquad (16\text{--}3)$$
$$+ 0.065 \text{ Moody's default rate}$$
$$(\alpha \text{ coefficient} = -0.134)$$

$$\text{BB yield} = 0.843 \text{ T-bond yield} + 0.149 \text{ Moody's default rate} \qquad (16\text{--}4)$$
$$(\alpha \text{ coefficient} = -0.169)$$

The standardized eigenvector found in equations 16–3 and 16–4 indicates that in the long run, the Split BBB and BB indices' yields are essentially the risk-free rate plus a premium that reflects default-rate risk. As expected, the default premium increases as the bond rating declines. The α coefficients in Exhibit 16–8 (also found under equations 16–3 and 16–4), represent the speed of adjustment to disequilibrium comparable to a mean reversion rate. The sign of the α coefficients are as expected: A negative sign indicates that as the variables move away from equilibrium, there is an adjustment back toward the equilibrium relation. The lower the α coefficient, the quicker the adjustment. Thus, given the smaller α coefficient, the BB index reverts faster to the long-run relation.

Estimating an Error Correction Model for the Indices

After finding a cointegrating vector in a system of equations, I have estimated the indices as single-equation error correction models (ECM). (For further discussion of ECMs, see Enders 1995 and Hendry, 1995.) An error correction model is simply a reparameterized single-equation autoregressive distributed lag (ADL) model. For ease of comparison, I also used an ECM to estimate the yield on the BBB index even though no statistically significant cointegrating vector was found.[7] The resulting ECMs combine a short run dynamic analysis with the long-run relation found in the cointegration analysis. For example, equation 16–5 represents a two-period ADL model of the Split BBB index algebraically manipulated into a one-period ECM that directly incorporates the long run solution:

---

7. The BBB index is also estimated using a differenced model. The results of the differenced model are similar to the results reported in the ECM.

$$\Delta \text{Split BBB}_t = a_0 + b_1 \Delta \text{ Split BBB}_{t-1} + \sum_{i=0}^{1} b_{2i} \Delta \text{ T-bond}_{t-i} \qquad (16\text{--}5)$$
$$+ \sum_{i=0}^{1} b_{3i} \Delta \text{ Default rate}_{t-i} + c_1(\text{Split BBB}$$
$$+ \epsilon \text{ T-bond} + \delta \text{ Default Rate})_{t-1}$$
$$+ a_4 1987 \text{ Crash}_t + a_5 \text{ Iraq invasion}_t$$
$$+ a_6 \text{ Kuwait liberation}_t + a_7 \text{ January}_t$$
$$+ a_8 \text{ December}_t$$

I use the reparameterized general ECM formulations as models to discuss the single equation results. c_1 is the feedback coefficient that reflects a long-run adjustment to disequilibrium, and is comparable to the α coefficients from the cointegration analysis found in Exhibit 16–8. Therefore, the error correction variable (Split BBB + ϵ T- bond + δ Default rate)$_{t-1}$ can be represented from the cointegration results found in equation 16–1 as:

$$\text{ECM}_{\text{SplitBBB}} = [\text{Split BBB} - 0.98(\text{T-bond}) \qquad (16\text{--}6)$$
$$- 0.07(\text{Default rate})]_{t-1}$$

Exhibit 16–9 contains the results of the estimated ECMs on the yield on the different indices. Based upon global F tests, all the models were statistically significant. The ECMs decrease in accuracy, based on R^2 and standard deviation, as the credit quality declines.

In comparing the January effect, the BBB index had little variation in return associated with January or December, and the BB index had a statistically significant decrease in yield in January. The decrease in the BB yield in January is consistent with previous studies and the January effect.

The important result in Exhibit 16–9 is the finding that there is a statistically significant (at the 95 percent confidence level) increase in yield on the Split BBB index in January, and that, though not statistically significant, the coefficient for December is negative. The sign of the January and December coefficients for the Split BBB index is the opposite of what is considered to be the January effect. Overall, a contra January effect on the yield of the Split BBB index supports the theory that part of the January anomaly is the result of window dressing by portfolio managers, because there is a substitution between the lower quality noninvestment-grade bonds and the lowest investment-grade bonds.

CONCLUSIONS

I find a statistically significant January effect in the return data for non-investment-grade bond indexes. While I also find a positive excess return in January in the lowest investment-grade category, the results are not

E X H I B I T   16–9

Error Correction Model of the Yield on the Corporate Bond Indices (January 1987 to March 1997)

Variable	BBB Index	Split BBB Index	BB Index
Long-Run Solution			
ECM$_{Split-BBB}$	−0.070	−0.229	−0.213
	(−2.77)*	(−4.63)*	(−3.93)*
Interest Rate Risk			
Δ T-Bond Yield	0.696	0.620	0.634
	(24.62)*	(6.37)*	(2.29)*
Default Rate Risk			
Δ Moody Default Rate	−0.009	0.209	0.132
	(−0.61)	(3.91)*	(2.32)†
1987 Market Crash	0.249	0.626	0.817
	(3.12)*	(2.27)†	(2.84)*
Iraq Invasion	−0.015	0.047	0.160
	(−0.19)	(0.17)	(0.55)
Kuwait Liberation	−0.156	−0.683	−0.644
	(−1.88)	(−2.39)†	(−2.17)†
Seasonal Factors			
December	0.008	−0.120	−0.026
	(0.31)	(−1.32)	(−0.27)
January	−0.006	0.183	−0.243
	(−0.24)	(2.00)†	(−2.56)†
Model Test Statistics			
R^2	0.854	0.440	0.418
F degrees of freedom (8, 111)	81.26*	10.89*	9.98*
σ	0.079	0.273	0.285

* Significant at the 0.01 level.

† Significant at the 0.05 level.

Note: This table provides the results of the estimated error correction models. The ECMs are estimated from the standardized eigenvectors found in Exhibit 16–8. The other variables are included to reduce the "noise" in the model. The January coefficient
for the Split BBB Index represents the statistically significant increase in the yield of the index in the months of January
studied. The values are in percents, so the January coefficient for the Split BBB Index represents 18.3 basis points.
The t-statistics are under each coefficient in parentheses.

statistically significant. Similar to previous studies, I find that excess returns in January increase as credit quality decreases. Given the demonstrated relation between a firm's market value and bond rating, these results are consistent with the small-firm effect in stocks.

My results reject two hypotheses about the cause of the January anomaly in the bond markets. First, no support is found for a systematic decrease in January of the supply of noninvestment-grade bonds. Second,

I find no seasonal anomaly in the selling and buying patterns of high yield and investment-grade bond mutual funds around the turn of the year.

However, I do find support for the January anomaly in the bond market as being due in part to a seasonal increase in demand by individual investors for high yield bonds in January but not for investment-grade bonds. This discrepancy between the shift in demand for investment- and noninvestment-grade bonds is consistent with previous findings of a January effect in noninvestment-grade but not in investment-grade bonds. Also, the result supports the theories that suggest the January effect is related to individual investor psychology.

I also find evidence that the January effect in the corporate bond market is a function of window dressing. I find a statistically significant increase in yield in the lowest investment-grade bond category (Split BBB) in January. This increase is the opposite of both the normally defined January effect and the results found in this and previous studies that indicate a decrease in the yield on noninvestment-grade bonds in January. Thus an increase in the Split BBB yield, an alternative asset class, is consistent with a window dressing explanation for the January effect as portfolio managers shift their portfolio weighting around the turn of the year. Overall, the results demonstrate that the January effect in the corporate bond market is not a function of a single causal factor, but is in fact a function of several factors coinciding around the turn of the year.

REFERENCES

Barnhill, T.; F. Joutz; and W. Maxwell (1997). "Factors Affecting the Yield of Noninvestment Grade Bond Indices." George Washington University. Working Paper 97–46, August.

Bhardwaj, R. and L. Brooks (1992). "The January Anomaly: Effects of Low Share Price, Transaction Costs, and Bid-Ask Bias." *Journal of Finance.* June, pp. 553–75.

Black, F. and M. Scholes (1973). "The Pricing of Options and Corporate Liabilities." *Journal of Political Economy* 81. pp. 637–54.

Brown, P.; D. Keim; A. Kleidon; and T. Marsh (1983). "Stock Return Seasonality and the Tax-Loss Selling Hypothesis: Analysis of the Arguments and Australian Evidence." *Journal of Financial Economics.* June, pp. 105–28.

Chang, E. and M. Pinegar (1986). "Return Seasonality and Tax-Loss Selling in the Market for Long-Term Government and Corporate Bonds." *Journal of Financial Economics.* December, pp. 391–415.

Chang, E. and R. Huang (1990). "Time-Varying Return and Risk in the Corporate Bond Market." *Journal of Financial and Quantitative Analysis.* September, pp. 323–40.

Cho, C. and W. Taylor (1987). "The Seasonal Stability of the Factor Structure of Stock Returns." *Journal of Finance.* December, pp. 1195–211.

Cooper, R. and J. Shulman (1994). "The Year-End Effect in Junk Bond Prices." *Financial Analysts Journal.* September/October, pp. 61–65.

DeBondt, W. and R. Thaler (1985). "Does the Stock Market Overreact?" *Journal of Finance.* July, pp. 793–805.

DeBondt, W. and R. Thaler (1987). "Further Evidence on Investor Overreaction and Stock Market Seasonality." *Journal of Finance.* July, pp. 557–81.

DeRosa-Farag, S. (1996). *1995 High Yield Market Review.* New York, Chase Securities, Inc.

Dyl, E and E. Maberly (1992). "Odd-Lot Transactions around the Turn of the Year and the January Effect." *Journal of Financial and Quantitative Analysis.* December, pp. 591–604.

Enders, W. (1995). *Applied Econometric Time Series,* New York, John Wiley & Sons, Inc.

Engle, R. and C. Granger (1987). "Cointegration and Error-Correction: Representation, Estimation, and Testing." *Econometrica.* March, pp. 251–76.

Fama, F. and K. French (1993). "Common Risk Factors in the Returns on Stocks and Bonds." *Journal of Financial Economics.* February, pp. 3–56.

Fridson, Martin (1994). "Do High-Yield Bonds Have an Equity Component?" *Financial Management.* Summer, pp. 82–84.

Fridson, M. and C. Garman (1995). "January Effect: Probably Not a Function of Coupon Flows." *This Week in High Yield.* December, pp. 1–3.

Fridson, M. and C. Garman (1995). "January Effect: The Longer-Term Evidence." *This Week in High Yield.* December, pp. 4–6.

Fridson, M. and J. Jónsson (1995). "Spread versus Treasuries and the Riskiness of High-Yield Bonds." *Journal of Fixed Income.* December, pp. 79–88.

Gultekin, M. and B. Gultekin (1983). "Stock Market Seasonality: International Evidence." *Journal of Financial Economics.* December, pp. 469–81.

Gultekin, M. and B. Gultekin (1987). "Stock Return Anomalies and Tests of the APT." *Journal of Finance.* December, pp. 1213–24.

Hendry, D. (1995). *Dynamic Econometrics.* Oxford, England, Oxford University Press.

Johansen, S. (1988). "Statistical Analysis of Cointegration Vectors." *Journal of Economic Dynamics and Control.* June/September, pp. 231–54.

Johansen, S. (1991). "Estimation and Hypothesis Testing of Cointegrating Vectors in Gaussian Vector Autoregressive Models." *Econometrica.* November, pp. 1551–80.

Jones, C.; D. Pearce; and J. Wilson (1987). "Can Tax-Loss Selling Explain the January Effect?" *Journal of Finance.* June, pp. 453–61.

Keim, D. (1983). "Size Related Anomalies and Stock Return Seasonality: Further Empirical Evidence." *Journal of Financial Economics.* June, pp. 13–32.

Kihn, J. (1996). "The Financial Performance of Low-Grade Municipal Bond Funds." *Financial Management.* Summer, pp. 52–73.

Lakonishok, J.; A. Shleifer; R. Thaler; and R. Vishny (1991). "Window Dressing by Pension Fund Managers." *American Economic Review.* May, pp. 227–31.

Merton, R. (1974). "On the Pricing of Corporate Debt: The Risk Structure of Interest Rates." *Journal of Finance.* May, pp. 449–70.

Reinganum, M. (1983). "The Anomalous Stock Market Behavior of Small Firms in January: Empirical Tests for Tax-Loss Selling Effects." *Journal of Financial Economics.* December, pp. 89–104.

Roll, R. (1983). "Vas Ist Das? The Turn-of-the-Year Effect and the Return Premia of Small Firms." *Journal of Portfolio Management.* Winter, pp. 18–28.

Seyhun, N. (1988). "The January Effect and Aggregate Insider Trading." *Journal of Finance.* March, pp. 129–41.

Shane, H. (1994). "Co-movements of Low-Grade Debt and Equity Returns of Highly Leveraged Firms." *Journal of Fixed Income.* March, pp. 79–89.

Tinic, S.; G. Barone-Adesi; and R. West (1987). "Seasonality in Canadian Stock Prices: A Test of the 'Tax-Loss-Selling' Hypothesis." *Journal of Financial and Quantitative Analysis.* March, pp. 51–63.

Warther, V. (1995). "Aggregate Mutual Fund Flow and Security Returns." *Journal of Financial Economics.* October/November, pp. 209–35.

PART FIVE

Portfolio Management

CHAPTER 17

High Yield as an Asset Class

Sam DeRosa-Farag

Jonathan Blau

RISK/REWARD AND ITS ROLE IN STATIC AND TACTICAL ASSET ALLOCATION

Over the last few years, a number of key questions have been asked concerning the high yield market. One of the fundamental issues has been whether high yield should be considered as a separate asset class. Another is its role in asset allocation. We believe that these questions are somewhat related.

A market is considered an asset class if it has a mean/variance (expected return and volatility) that cannot be replicated by a combination of other existing assets. In the case of high yield, there is no mix of equities and Treasuries (both existing and established asset classes) that can produce and replicate high yield returns. Both the equity and the Treasury markets can replicate 60 to 70 percent of the high yield market behavior. The balance is high yield intrinsic risk and international risk.

The argument behind the consideration of the high yield market as a separate asset class also stems from its low correlation with other classes. One of the largest challenges in risk management since 1994 is the evolution of highly interrelated capital markets based on the free movement of capital and coupled yield curves that result in international diversification becoming less effective over time. In addition, the evolution of the European Union is resulting in the convergence of these historically divergent markets. In this context, diversification becomes even more important. As a European interest in high yield develops and the globalization of the high yield market in general continues, the market's diversification virtues are one of the key drivers behind its increasingly important role in global asset allocation.

E X H I B I T   17–1

Risk/Reward Characteristics of Various Assets, 1980–1997

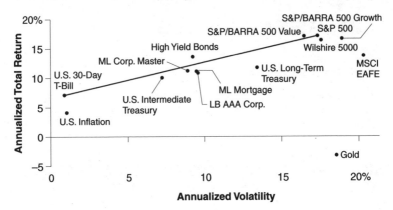

Sources: Donaldson, Lufkin & Jenrette (DLJ); Ibbotson Associates.

E X H I B I T   17–2

Summary Statistics of Various Assets, 1980–1997

Asset 1980–1997	Geometric Mean Annual Return	Arithmetic Mean Annual Return	Annual Volatility*
U.S. 30-Day T-Bill	7.13%	7.17%	0.91%
U.S. Intermediate Treasury	10.16	10.41	7.19
U.S. Long-Term Treasury	11.76	12.53	13.36
ML Mortgage	11.04	11.42	9.44
LB AAA Corp.	10.94	11.39	9.52
ML Corp. Master	11.31	11.69	8.88
High Yield Bonds	13.71	14.35	9.19
S&P 500	17.13	17.89	17.24
Wilshire 5000	16.42	17.24	17.45
MSCI EAFE	13.84	15.80	20.19
Gold	−3.12	−1.90	18.44
U.S. Inflation	4.21	4.24	1.08

*Monthly returns.

Sources: DLJ; Ibbotson Associates.

It is important to view an asset from a fundamental approach to develop a framework from which key questions may be addressed in light of the overall global capital markets:

- What is the relative risk profile of the asset?
- What is the relative expected return (i.e., reward) profile of the asset?
- What is the relative relationship of the asset versus fundamental drivers (the correlation relationships)?
- What is the nature of the asset's behavior: random or trend-oriented?
- How liquid is the asset?

These questions form the framework for addressing an asset's relative value, the role of an asset in a portfolio, and the basis behind expectations of an asset's behavior and role in different market conditions.

This framework also can serve as a form of discipline, useful on a daily basis, to address uncertainties about interest rates, earnings growth, direction of volatility, and other issues. These issues have implications for

First-Order Auto Correlation*	Highest Annual Return	Lowest Annual Return	Annual Median Return	Number of Positive Return Periods	Number of Negative Return Periods
93.68%	14.71%	2.90%	6.26%	18	0
23.66	29.10	−5.14	9.59	17	1
8.86	40.36	−7.77	12.57	14	4
17.88	40.15	−1.56	9.42	17	1
21.07	39.30	−3.63	9.65	16	2
21.67	35.53	−3.34	10.07	17	1
30.34	43.75	−6.38	12.62	16	2
−2.24	37.43	−4.91	19.94	16	2
3.96	36.48	−6.18	18.32	15	3
1.11	69.94	−23.19	11.17	14	4
2.67	23.84	−32.15	−2.50	7	11
63.91	12.40	1.13	3.78	18	0

E X H I B I T   17–3

Correlations among Various Assets, 1980–1997

Asset	U.S. 30-Day Treasury	U.S. Inter Treasury	U.S. Long Treasury	ML Mort	LB AAA Corp.
U.S. Intermediate Treasury	0.17				
U.S. Long-Term Treasury	0.07	0.89			
ML Mortgage	0.13	0.91	0.87		
LB AAA Corp.	0.11	0.93	0.94	0.95	
ML Corp. Master	0.09	0.93	0.94	0.93	0.99
High Yield Bonds	0.01	0.59	0.55	0.63	0.65
S&P 500	−0.09	0.30	0.37	0.28	0.35
Wilshire 5000	−0.10	0.27	0.35	0.26	0.33
S&P/BARRA 500 Growth	−0.08	0.27	0.35	0.25	0.32
S&P/BARRA 500 Value	−0.09	0.32	0.38	0.29	0.37
MSCI EAFE	−0.06	0.22	0.24	0.19	0.21
Gold	−0.12	0.00	−0.03	0.01	0.00
U.S. Inflation	0.52	−0.12	−0.21	−0.14	−0.18

Sources: DLJ; Ibbotson Associates.

E X H I B I T   17–4

Correlations among Various Assets, 1992–1997

Asset	U.S. 30-Day Treasury	U.S. Inter Treasury	U.S. Long Treasury	ML Mort	LB AAA Corp.	ML Corp.	High Yield Bonds	S&P 500
U.S. Intermediate Treasury	0.13							
U.S. Long-Term Treasury	0.14	0.92						
ML Mortgage	0.22	0.90	0.85					
LB AAA Corp.	0.16	0.95	0.98	0.91				
ML Corp. Master	0.16	0.96	0.98	0.90	0.99			
High Yield Bonds	0.11	0.51	0.46	0.56	0.53	0.55		
S&P 500	0.25	0.48	0.51	0.54	0.55	0.54	0.46	
Wilshire 5000	0.23	0.42	0.43	0.47	0.48	0.47	0.48	0.97
S&P/BARRA 500 Growth	0.28	0.40	0.43	0.47	0.47	0.46	0.38	0.96
S&P/BARRA 500 Value	0.19	0.54	0.54	0.56	0.59	0.59	0.53	0.95
CSFB Conv Securities	0.09	0.39	0.32	0.41	0.39	0.41	0.58	0.75
MSCI EAFE	−0.10	0.24	0.19	0.22	0.21	0.24	0.30	0.42
BEMI (Emerging) World	−0.18	0.01	0.00	0.04	0.03	0.06	0.31	0.43
JPM-EMBI Fixed Rate	0.16	0.49	0.52	0.52	0.55	0.55	0.52	0.57
Gold	−0.18	−0.11	−0.11	−0.07	−0.10	−0.08	0.11	−0.10
U.S. Inflation	−0.13	−0.03	−0.11	−0.07	−0.06	−0.03	−0.01	−0.12
DLJ Leveraged Loan	−0.11	0.08	0.07	0.12	0.08	0.09	0.23	0.10

Sources: DLJ; Ibbotson Associates.

ML Corp.	High Yield Bonds	S&P 500	Wilshire 5000	S&P/ BARRA Growth	S&P/ BARRA Value	MSCI EAFE	Gold
0.68							
0.37	0.47						
0.36	0.49	0.99					
0.34	0.42	0.98	0.97				
0.39	0.50	0.97	0.96	0.90			
0.23	0.34	0.46	0.46	0.42	0.48		
0.01	0.10	0.07	0.10	0.04	0.09	0.20	
−0.18	−0.22	−0.17	−0.17	−0.16	−0.16	−0.20	0.04

Wilshire 5000	S&P/ BARRA Growth	S&P/ BARRA Value	CSFB Conv Sec	MSCI EAFE	BEMI (Emerging) World	EMBI Fixed	Gold	U.S. Inflation
0.93								
0.93	0.82							
0.85	0.66	0.79						
0.43	0.32	0.48	0.45					
0.46	0.40	0.42	0.48	0.45				
0.54	0.50	0.60	0.48	0.34	0.58			
−0.07	−0.12	−0.07	0.07	0.16	0.18	0.16		
−0.14	−0.10	−0.14	−0.03	−0.15	−0.06	−0.13	0.00	
0.09	0.07	0.13	0.10	−0.01	0.27	0.05	0.12	0.01

the current stage of the economic cycle and how an investor should be positioned. This discipline also provides a solid foundation for understanding relative value, both among assets and among sectors within these assets. In this discussion, we also address the recent trends among different parts of the capital structure, including bank debt, high yield, and the equity of high yield issuers.

KEY CONCLUSIONS

- The high yield market has an attractive risk/reward profile (an above-average return per unit of risk) due to its multisector composition by tier (lower tier to upper tier), its liquidity, and its high current yield.
- Due to its low correlation to other major assets (equities and Treasuries), the role of high yield assets in portfolio diversification is significant.
- In view of the current demographic trend of aging baby boomers, pension asset managers attempting to match their liabilities (15 years and less) are encouraged to reduce asset exposure to equities, which have durations of 20-plus years, while continuing to pursue above-average returns to meet hurdle rates. It is important to add assets; diversification will lower the overall volatility of a portfolio. The role of high yield assets in this equation explains its relative attractiveness and explains our expectation of continued growth over the next 10–15 years.
- An analysis of the relative performance of high yield in a tactical asset allocation model under various economic scenarios results in an above-average high yield allocation in all scenarios except a recessionary environment.
- Recent trends indicate that bank debt's low volatility and correlations with other assets, due in part to its floater structure and seniority, results in a favorable role in an asset allocation model.
- In the 1990s, as declining inflation leads to global spread compression, an increase in the volatility of interest rates is linked to a shift from taking interest rate risk to taking credit risk. Taking a well-diversified approach to credit risk to minimize that volatility is of great benefit.

E X H I B I T   17–5

Risk/Reward Characteristics of Various Assets, 1992–1997

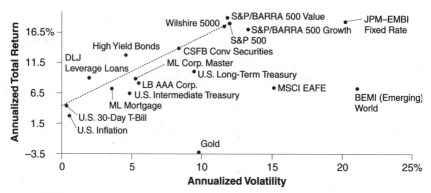

Sources: DLJ; Ibbotson Associates.

E X H I B I T   17–6

Twenty-Month Rolling Volatility (annualized) of Various Assets

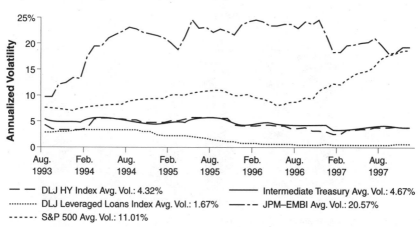

— — DLJ HY Index Avg. Vol.: 4.32%   ——— Intermediate Treasury Avg. Vol.: 4.67%
············ DLJ Leveraged Loans Index Avg. Vol.: 1.67%   — - — JPM–EMBI Avg. Vol.: 20.57%
- - - - - S&P 500 Avg. Vol.: 11.01%

Sources: DLJ; Bloomberg.

E X H I B I T   17–7

Yields of Various Assets

	As of 12/30/94		As of 12/31/97		
	Yield	Yield less YTW for High Yield	Yield	Yield less YTW for High Yield	Difference 94–97 Yield
YTW for High Yield	11.98%	—	9.28%	—	−270bp
A*	8.51	347bp	6.39	289bp	−212
BBB*	8.68	330	6.57	271	−211
BB	10.57	141	8.26	102	−231
CCC/Split CCC	18.98	−700	16.16	−688	−282
S&P 500 (Div Yld)	2.87	911	1.64	764	−123
U.S. Ten Year Tsy	7.82	416	5.74	354	−208
Emerging Markets†	18.99	−701	17.70	−842	−129

*A & BBB are of 10-year maturity.
†JP Morgan EMBI+.
Sources: DLJ; Bloomberg.

E X H I B I T   17–8

Corporate Bond Issuance

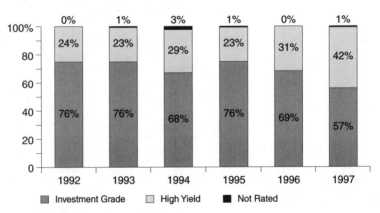

Sources: DLJ; Standard & Poor's.

RISK AND RETURN

From a long-term perspective, high yield bonds continue to provide one of the best risk and return profiles for investors. Over a 15-year period, high yield bonds had an average annual return of 13.21 percent and a return volatility of 7.83 percent (annual returns are a concatenation of monthly returns, and volatility is the annualized standard deviation of monthly returns). This compares favorably with equity (as measured by the S&P 500), which had higher returns (17.52 percent) over the same period with approximately twice as much risk (16.73 percent). High yield's ratio of return at 1.69 per unit of risk is superior to most other asset classes, including many equity indices, corporate bonds, and Treasuries. This is due in part to high yield bonds being a hybrid asset: The high coupon dampens volatility while driving returns in concert with the equity component.

E X H I B I T   17–9

Long-Term Risk and Return of Various Assets

Asset	Geometric Mean Annual Returns				15-Year Volatility	15-Year Return/Risk	Sharpe* Ratio
	1997	5 Year	10 Year	15 Year			
U.S. 30-Day T-Bill	5.26%	4.57%	5.44%	6.15%	0.59%	10.42	NA
Fixed Income							
U.S. Intermediate Treasury	8.38%	6.40%	8.33%	9.47%	5.35%	1.77	0.62
U.S. Long-Term Treasury	15.85	10.51	11.32	11.88	11.29	1.05	0.51
ML Mortgage	9.32	7.32	9.39	10.67	5.91	1.81	0.76
LB AAA Corp.	10.88	8.19	9.56	10.77	6.55	1.64	0.71
ML Corp. Master	10.39	8.56	10.09	11.23	6.39	1.76	0.79
High Yield Bonds	12.21	11.90	11.91	13.21	7.83	1.69	0.90
Equity							
S&P 500	33.36%	20.24%	18.05%	17.52%	16.73%	1.05	0.68
Wilshire 5000	31.29	19.29	17.58	16.68	16.63	1.00	0.63
S&P/BARRA 500 Growth	36.52	19.64	18.48	17.00	18.15	0.94	0.60
S&P/BARRA 500 Value	29.98	20.68	17.36	17.72	16.04	1.10	0.72
CSFB Conv Securities	16.94	13.22	12.97	12.88	11.53	1.12	0.58
International/Emerging Mkts							
MSCI EAFE	2.06%	11.71%	6.56%	15.28%	20.44%	0.75	0.45
BEMI (Emerging) World	−7.87	9.40	NA	NA	NA	NA	NA
JPM-EMBI Fixed Rate	21.15	19.94	NA	NA	NA	NA	NA
Other							
Gold	−21.68%	−2.78%	−5.02%	−3.00%	13.41%	−0.22	−0.68
U.S. Inflation	1.92	2.64	3.43	3.42	0.72	4.75	−3.79
DLJ Leveraged Loan	8.49	9.39	NA	NA	NA	NA	NA

*Returns minus risk-free (30-day T-bill) rate divided by standard deviation of return.

Sources: DLJ; Ibbotson Associates.

E X H I B I T   17–10

Risk and Return of Various Assets, 1995–1997

	1995		1996		1997	
Asset	Return	Volatility	Return	Volatility	Return	Volatility
U.S. 30-Day T-Bill	5.60%	0.13%	5.21%	0.09%	5.26%	0.13%
Fixed Income						
U.S. Intermediate Treasury	16.80%	3.94%	2.10%	3.89%	8.38%	4.10%
U.S. Long-Term Treasury	31.67	9.70	−0.93	9.33	15.85	10.44
ML Mortgage	16.99	3.63	5.42	3.48	9.32	2.93
LB AAA Corp.	21.41	5.07	2.56	5.89	10.88	5.77
ML Corp. Master	21.23	4.98	3.66	5.55	10.39	5.33
DLJ High Yield Index	19.68	4.03	13.03	2.95	12.21	4.48
Equity						
S&P 500	37.43%	6.95%	23.07%	13.29%	33.36%	21.08%
Wilshire 5000	36.48	7.11	21.21	13.01	31.29	19.41
S&P/BARRA 500 Growth	38.13	7.04	23.96	14.65	36.52	24.25
S&P/BARRA 500 Value	36.99	8.58	21.99	12.63	29.98	18.57
CSFB Conv Securities	23.71	8.37	13.85	9.20	16.94	10.85
International/Emerging Mkts						
MSCI EAFE	11.55%	14.28%	6.36%	7.68%	2.06%	16.70%
BEMI (Emerging) World	−5.05	18.90	10.34	14.29	−7.87	22.99
JPM–EMBI Fixed Rate	41.85	25.27	30.45	21.18	21.15	21.83
Other						
Gold	0.98%	5.58%	−4.59%	6.34%	−21.68%	8.97%
U.S. Inflation	2.54	0.60	3.32	0.61	1.92	0.45
DLJ Leveraged Loan	9.31	0.62	7.92	0.48	8.49	0.63

Sources: DLJ; Ibbotson Associates.

PRICE VERSUS RETURN VOLATILITY

When observing volatility on a daily basis, a common view is to look at price volatility. A more meaningful measure, however, may be the volatility of returns, since an investor is concerned ultimately with the realized total returns.

In observing the historical volatility of the DLJ High Yield Index, the S&P 500 and 10-year Treasury, it is apparent that in general, the volatility of returns is significantly less than the volatility of prices, because the coupon/dividend component of total return mitigates the volatility of price alone. The numbers in Exhibit 17–11 fit with our expectations of risk because equities exhibit the highest price volatility and Treasuries (the "risk-free" assets) the lowest, with high yield (a hybrid of equity and fixed-income) in between.

From January 1994 to December 1997, high yield bonds exhibited the lowest volatility of returns of all of these asset classes. This is a historical anomaly, as shown in the long-term table, and may be the result of increasing high yield credit quality coupled with greater-than-expected interest rate volatility, which penalizes Treasuries. For this reason, we see the ratio of return volatility to price volatility being lower for high yield than for Treasuries. While some investors view this as a permanent change, this would imply that the change in cost of capital that occurred in 1992 would also be permanent.

It is interesting to note how different the volatilities are for the various assets within a capital structure. Bank loans, the most senior layer of the capital structure, exhibit the lowest volatility at 1.92 percent. This low volatility is attributable to their senior status, lack of interest rate risk, and the relatively low liquidity of the bank loan market. High yield equity (the equity of high yield issuers) has the highest volatility, reflecting the riskiest segment of the capital structure. High yield equity is more volatile than the S&P 500 due to the generally thin capitalization of high yield issuers. High yield debt, which falls between equity and bank debt, exhibits a volatility level (4.55 percent) between those of these two assets.

SECTOR VOLATILITY

In the second part of this volatility study, we examine the volatilities of various subsectors of the DLJ High Yield Index and compare them to the volatility of the overall index. The subsectors include BB-, B-, and CCC-rated securities and cash paying and deferred interest securities.

The industry volatility and mean returns (Exhibit 17–14) indicate that high yield as an asset experiences a sector effect. This is in sharp contrast to the Investment Grade Corporate Market. However, the overall index returns are lower than most sector returns due to low correlation among the sectors. Having said that, the mean variance graph does indicate that there are certain industries that experience negative credit drift and others that experience positive credit drift. Sectors such as Retail, Food & Drug have been experiencing negative trends since 1993. In effect, that is counter to the mean reversal principle where investors believe that the lowest performer in one year would be the highest in the subsequent one.

Finally, we look at the volatility (measured by the standard deviation) of total returns of these subsectors of the DLJ High Yield Index and compare them to that of the overall DLJ High Yield Index. As expected, the more risky sectors demonstrate higher volatility of returns compared with the less risky sectors and the DLJ High Yield Index.

E X H I B I T   17–11

Annualized Summary Characteristics of Various Assets, 1980–1997

Asset 1980–1997	Geometric Mean Annual Return	Arithmetic Mean Annual Return	Annual Volatility*
U.S. 30-Day T-Bill	7.13%	7.17%	0.91%
U.S. Intermediate Treasury	10.16	10.41	7.19
U.S. Long-Term Treasury	11.76	12.53	13.36
ML Mortgage	11.04	11.42	9.44
LB AAA Corp.	10.94	11.39	9.52
ML Corp. Master	11.31	11.69	8.88
High Yield Bonds	13.71	14.35	9.19
S&P 500	17.13	17.89	17.24
Wilshire 5000	16.42	17.24	17.45
MSCI EAFE	13.84	15.80	20.19
Gold	−3.12	−1.90	18.44
U.S. Inflation	4.21	4.24	1.08

*Monthly returns.

Sources: DLJ; Ibbotson Associates.

E X H I B I T   17–12

Annualized Summary Characteristics of Various Assets, 1992–1997

Asset 1992–1997	Geometric Mean Annual Return	Arithmetic Mean Annual Return	Annual Volatility*
U.S. 30-Day T-Bill	4.39%	4.39%	0.32%
U.S. Intermediate Treasury	6.53	6.76	4.81
U.S. Long-Term Treasury	10.10	10.85	9.46
ML Mortgage	7.32	7.46	3.55
LB AAA Corp.	8.16	8.44	5.46
ML Corp. Master	8.65	8.91	5.27
High Yield Bonds	12.68	12.92	4.55
DLJ Leveraged Loan	8.96	8.97	1.92
S&P 500	18.05	18.81	11.99
Wilshire 5000	17.50	18.19	11.60
MSCI EAFE	7.39	8.19	15.11
Gold	−3.17	−2.48	9.78
U.S. Inflation	2.65	2.65	0.54

*Monthly returns.

Sources: DLJ; Ibbotson Associates.

First-Order Auto Correlation*	Highest Annual Return	Lowest Annual Return	Annual Median Return	Number of Positive Return Periods	Number of Negative Return Periods
93.68%	14.71%	2.90%	6.26%	18	0
23.66	29.10	−5.14	9.59	17	1
8.86	40.36	−7.77	12.57	14	4
17.88	40.15	−1.56	9.42	17	1
21.07	39.30	−3.63	9.65	16	2
21.67	35.53	−3.34	10.07	17	1
30.34	43.75	−6.38	12.62	16	2
−2.24	37.43	−4.91	19.94	16	2
3.96	36.48	−6.18	18.32	15	3
1.11	69.94	−23.19	11.17	14	4
2.67	23.84	−32.15	−2.50	7	11
63.91	12.40	1.13	3.78	18	0

First-Order Auto Correlation*	Highest Annual Return	Lowest Annual Return	Annual Median Return	Number of Positive Return Periods	Number of Negative Return Periods
88.05%	5.60%	2.90%	4.56%	6	0
25.74	16.80	−5.14	7.79	5	1
15.68	31.67	−7.77	11.95	4	2
23.94	16.99	−1.56	7.31	5	1
19.24	21.41	−3.63	9.44	5	1
20.27	21.23	−3.34	9.75	5	1
25.34	19.68	−2.04	14.85	5	1
10.85	11.66	6.84	8.90	6	0
−25.69	37.43	1.31	16.53	6	0
−15.99	36.48	−0.06	16.25	5	1
−8.52	32.94	−11.85	7.21	5	1
−9.93	17.68	−21.68	−3.38	2	4
18.28	3.32	1.70	2.71	6	0

E X H I B I T   17–13

Annualized Summary Characteristics of Various
Sectors of the High Yield Index, 1993–1997

DLJ High Yield Index Sector	Leverage Dec. 31, 97	Coverage Dec. 31, 97	Annualized Volatility (%)	Geometric Annual Return (%)	Correlations Return Corr. w/ S&P 500	Return Corr. w/ 10-yr. Treasury
BB	4.9	2.7	4.45	11.65	0.57	0.74
B	5.6	1.6	4.47	12.44	0.56	0.57
CCC	7.7	1.1	9.13	8.86	0.15	0.22
DIS	8.0	1.9	7.74	11.00	0.62	0.69
Cash-Pay	5.4	1.7	4.22	12.14	0.57	0.54

Source: DLJ.

E X H I B I T   17–14

Comparison of Volatility and Return
by Industry, Annualized, 1993–1997

	Annualized Geometric Mean Return	Annualized Return Volatility
Aeropspace	13.77%	6.22%
Chemicals	12.41	4.64
Consumer Durables	9.98	5.78
Consumer Nondurables	11.11	5.68
Energy	12.82	4.82
Financial	12.07	4.71
Food and Drug	9.06	5.20
Food/Tobacco	9.75	4.70
Forest Products/Containers	10.49	4.56
Gaming/Leisure	12.16	5.51
Health Care	13.31	4.24
Housing	12.09	5.19
Information Technology	11.34	5.17
Manufacturing	13.98	4.20
Media/Entertainment	12.10	6.12
Metals & Minerals	13.22	4.88
Retail	8.64	4.55
Service	11.21	4.56
Transportation	10.69	4.61
Utility	13.28	6.37

Source: DLJ.

E X H I B I T   17–15

Risk/Reward Characteristics by Industry, Annualized, 1993–1997

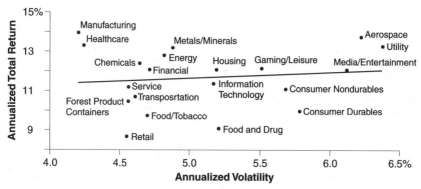

Source: DLJ.

CORRELATION/AUTOCORRELATION

High yield's correlation characteristics make it a favorable asset from a portfolio management perspective. Exhibits 17–3 and 17–4 demonstrate that high yield is not particularly highly correlated with either equities or Treasuries, providing an opportunity for portfolio diversification. From 1980 to 1997, high yield's correlation with the S&P 500 was 47 percent, whereas its correlations with the intermediate-term and long-term Treasuries were 59 percent and 55 percent, respectively.

The implication of the low correlation of high yield with other assets in the preceding charts shows that the overall addition of high yield to equities, corporates, and leveraged loans enhances the efficiency of a portfolio. In the case of investment-grade corporate debt, the argument is very compelling as the total return increases while the overall risk declines. However, in the case of equities, while volatility declines dramatically up to a 55 percent mix, the overall return would be expected to be lower. Portfolio efficiency is becoming an important focus for risk management and institutional investors.

The first-order autocorrelation of an asset demonstrates how much a prior period's return for a particular asset explains the following period's return. A low first-order autocorrelation reflects a random pattern of returns, meaning that a prior period's return does not explain the return of the subsequent period. Equity and other high volatility instruments fall into this category. The S&P, Wilshire 5000, and MSCI EAFE have low autocorrelations of −2.44 percent, 3.96 percent and 1.11 percent, respectively.

E X H I B I T   17–16

Risk/Return Trade-Off, Investment Grade Bonds versus High Yield Bonds, 1992–1997

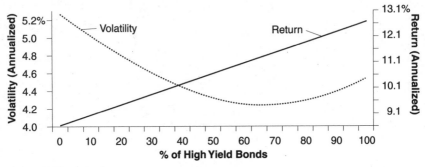

Sources: DLJ; Ibbotson Associates.

E X H I B I T   17–17

Risk/Return Trade-Off, Leverage Loans versus High Yield Bonds, 1992–1997

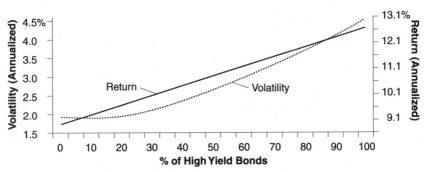

Sources: DLJ; Ibbotson Associates.

Assets that exhibit trends, like interest-rate dependent assets, tend to have higher first-order autocorrelations, because interest rates tend to reflect the long-term economic outlook and only reverse direction when there is a dramatic shift in the outlook for the economy. This explains the mid-20 percent autocorrelation of investment-grade corporate bond funds and intermediate-term Treasuries. In addition to assets that exhibit trends, assets that have lower levels of liquidity (which prevent prices from changing too

E X H I B I T   17-18

Risk/Return Trade-Off, S&P 500 versus
High Yield Bonds, 1992–1997

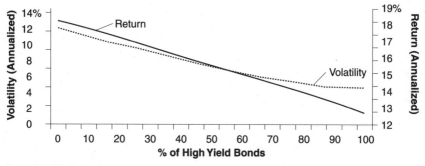

Sources: DLJ; Ibbotson Associates.

drastically) usually have higher autocorrelations. These two factors explain why high yield has one of the highest first-order autocorrelations outside of cash equivalents.

As a result of acquiring sophisticated analytical capabilities over the last 20 years, we can now break down and quantify the market component of high yield returns. In this section, we focus on the drivers of this market component. The market component was derived by using a multifactor approach and is made up of four factors: (1) equity, (2) interest rates, (3) international risk, and (4) high yield market-specific risk. Over an extended period of time, the equity driver explained approximately 30 percent of high yield returns, interest rates 25 percent, international risk 10 percent, volatility 20 percent, and credit and random events explained 15 percent.

At any given point in time, one of these fundamental market drivers can dominate high yield's performance. Throughout 1994 to 1997, a period of extreme interest rate volatility, the Treasury market explained a majority of high yield's returns as well as the market's rapid changes in spread. During this period, duration and its management surfaced as a primary concern for high yield investors. From mid-1985 to the end of 1993, as credit statistics deteriorated from both leverage and coverage perspectives, high yield performed more in line with equity. There are many technologies already available within the high yield market that can help investors manage their exposure to interest rates, volatility, and equity throughout a complete economic cycle.

E X H I B I T   17–19

Twenty-Month Rolling Return Correlation of the
JPM EMBI with the DLJ High Yield Index

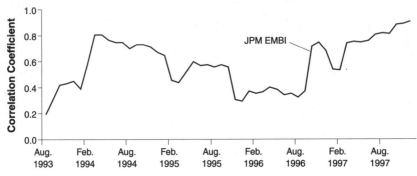

Sources: DLJ; Ibbostson Associates.

E X H I B I T   17–20

Annual Returns for the DLJ High Yield
Index by Region and Other Assets

Asset	1992	1993	1994	1995	1996	1997
U.S. Intermediate Treasury	7.19%	11.24%	−5.14%	16.80%	2.10%	8.38%
High Yield Bonds	16.66	18.00	−2.04	19.68	13.03	12.21
US/Canada	NA	17.58	−2.09	19.56	12.39	12.75
Non-US/Canada	NA	24.16	−4.45	26.07	18.20	7.55
Asia	NA	NA	1.86	17.13	20.56	−6.70
Latin America	NA	6.49	−19.59	37.47	19.65	12.26
EMBI Fixed Rate	10.42	48.99	−25.69	41.85	30.45	21.15
S&P 500	7.67%	9.99%	1.31%	37.43%	23.07%	33.36%

Sources: DLJ; Ibbotson Associates.

INHERENT MARKET VOLATILITY

The Role of Volatility as a
Portfolio Management Tool

As stated above, the high yield market is influenced by four basic sources
of systematic risk: equity, interest rates, international, and market-specific.
Investors have some means of first quantifying and then diversifying or
minimizing each type of risk:

E X H I B I T   17–21

Annual Changes in Spreads for the
DLJ High Yield Index by Region

	1993*	1994	1995	1996	1997
United States	81 bp	(12 bp)	(60 bp)	127 bp	2 bp
Canada	63 bp	30 bp	(118 bp)	150 bp	(81 bp)
US/Canada	79 bp	(10 bp)	(62 bp)	128 bp	(2 bp)
Western Europe	(3 bp)	(54 bp)	(63 bp)	201 bp	(26 bp)
Non-European Developed	157 bp	111 bp	(90 bp)	(52 bp)	(57 bp)
Other Developed	45 bp	(19 bp)	(79 bp)	172 bp	(44 bp)
Latin America	NA	(272 bp)	58 bp	223 bp	(53 bp)
Asia	NA	NA	68 bp	54 bp	(394 bp)
Other Developing	NA	NA	(70 bp)	137 bp	(170 bp)
Developing	(372 bp)	(146 bp)	(3 bp)	174 bp	(196 bp)
Non-US/Canada	62 bp	(51 bp)	(54 bp)	179 bp	(124 bp)
DLJ HY Index	86 bp	(15 bp)	(57 bp)	135 bp	(17 bp)

*January 1993 versus December 1993.
Source: DLJ.

- *Duration* has been somewhat effective as both an interest-rate risk measurement and management tool. To further complicate the issue, spreads would tend to move in the opposite direction of rates, and would move in different magnitudes depending on the imbedded assumptions for every sector.

- A *cyclical* and *defensive* classification (based on correlation with the equity markets) has been useful in identifying economically sensitive sectors and other sectors that are more resilient to this risk. Hence, this classification can be used as a tool to minimize or capitalize on cyclical risk.

- There are a number of classical tools used for measurement and positioning with respect to *credit risk.* From a portfolio perspective, seniority and rating have been effective credit risk adjustment tools.

- *Market volatility,* also referred to as timing, has been used to measure the risk associated with liquidity, default risk, and supply and demand technicals.

E X H I B I T   17–22

Sector Spreads in the High Yield Market, 1992–1997

	1992	1993	1994	1995	1996	1997
BB	417 bp	317 bp	279 bp	308 bp	215 bp	256 bp
Split BB	463 bp	358 bp	342 bp	397 bp	281 bp	291 bp
B	547 bp	470 bp	452 bp	565 bp	388 bp	376 bp
Split B	905 bp	641 bp	754 bp	778 bp	572 bp	513 bp
CCC/Split CCC	1018 bp	606 bp	1116 bp	1000 bp	1123 bp	1047 bp
B vs. BB spread	130 bp	153 bp	173 bp	257 bp	173 bp	120 bp
CCC vs. B spread	471 bp	136 bp	664 bp	435 bp	736 bp	670 bp
Project Finance	NM	NM	739 bp	623 bp	528 bp	484 bp
Latin America	NM	NM	644 bp	586 bp	363 bp	416 bp
Asia	NM	NM	476 bp	408 bp	355 bp	749 bp
10-Year Treasury	6.35%	5.79%	7.82%	5.57%	6.42%	5.74%
High Yield Bonds	490 bp	405 bp	420 bp	477 bp	342 bp	359 bp
DIS vs. Cash spread	−45 bp	115 bp	254 bp	184 bp	181 bp	182 bp
Cyclical vs. Defensive spread	69 bp	103 bp	36 bp	45 bp	−10 bp	11 bp
Small vs. Large Issue spread	26 bp	41 bp	−6 bp	68 bp	41 bp	17 bp

Sources: DLJ; Bloomberg.

   While each of these risks can in time be the dominant source of risk, in other periods we have witnessed these factors acting in tandem or counter to each other. During the 1989–90 period, volatility and cyclical risk worked in concert. In 1994, however, interest rate risk escalated while the cyclical recovery was in full swing (i.e., a decline in cyclical risk).

   We have developed historically a number of tools to measure and help quantify each of these risks. These indicators, or measurement tools, can play a crucial role in our ability to detect each risk and to enhance returns by being appropriately positioned for each one.

Twenty-Month Rolling Volatility

Volatility, measured by the rolling 20-month volatility of returns, is an important tool used to detect risk. Default rates are captured in the volatility measures, but default rates have been a lagging indicator with little contribution to our ability to be positioned in anticipation of that risk. Instead, we try to explain why spreads would widen or tighten as default rates are expected to rise or decline. Volatility is a leading indicator for default rates, supply and demand, and liquidity risks.

E X H I B I T   17–23

Change in the High Yield Market Sector Spreads

	1993*	1994	1995	1996	1997
BB	100 bp	38 bp	(29 bp)	93 bp	(42 bp)
Split BB	104 bp	16 bp	(55 bp)	116 bp	(10 bp)
B	76 bp	18 bp	(113 bp)	177 bp	11 bp
Split B	263 bp	(112 bp)	(24 bp)	206 bp	58 bp
CCC/Split CCC	411 bp	(510 bp)	116 bp	(124 bp)	77 bp
B vs. BB spread	(23 bp)	(20 bp)	(84 bp)	84 bp	53 bp
CCC vs. B spread	335 bp	(528 bp)	229 bp	(301 bp)	65 bp
Project Finance	NA	NA	117 bp	95 bp	44 bp
Latin America	NA	NA	58 bp	223 bp	(53 bp)
Asia	NA	NA	68 bp	54 bp	(395 bp)
10-Year Treasury	56 bp	(203 bp)	225 bp	(85 bp)	68 bp
DLJ High Yield Index	*86 bp*	*(15 bp)*	*(57 bp)*	*135 bp*	*(17 bp)*
DIS vs. Cash spread	(160 bp)	(139 bp)	70 bp	3 bp	(1 bp)
Cyclical vs. Defensive spread	(34 bp)	67 bp	(9 bp)	56 bp	(21 bp)
Small vs. Large Issue spread	(16 bp)	47 bp	(74 bp)	27 bp	23 bp

*January 1993 versus December 1993.
Sources: DLJ; Bloomberg.

The Beta of the High Yield Market

Volatility is the high yield market's equivalent to beta, the equity market's measurement of risk. The well-documented (and in hindsight logical) posture—to have a high beta in anticipation of a bull market and a low beta in anticipation of a bear market—has been a valuable performance-enhancement tool. We would argue that the high yield equivalent is also true. This tends to be a basic market paradigm of the relationship between risk and reward in general. Changes in volatility lead to the outperformance of riskier assets in declining risk environments, and vice versa.

We have examined the relationship between volatility and returns in actively managed funds (our sample is approximately 45 high yield mutual funds) in both declining and increasing risk environments. Funds with high volatility in the 1991–92 period outperformed lower volatility funds by approximately 13 percent. The reverse was true in the 1994–95 period as funds with lower volatility outperformed higher volatility funds by approximately 6 percent. That reversed further in the 1996–1997 period, where investors long volatility were rewarded and higher risk funds outperformed lower risk funds by 2–3 percent.

E X H I B I T   17–24

DLJ High Yield Index, 8-Month Price Volatility versus Spread to Worst

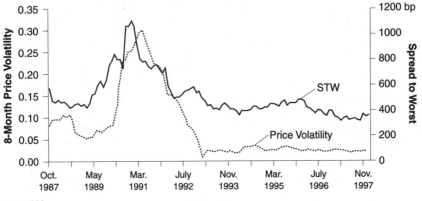

Source: DLJ.

E X H I B I T   17–25

Risk and Reward for Selected High Yield Mutual Funds, 1991–1992

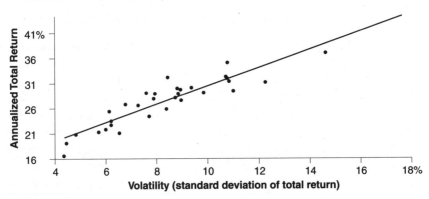

Sources: DLJ; Morningstar.

E X H I B I T   17–26

Risk and Reward for Selected High
Yield Mutual Funds, 1994–1995

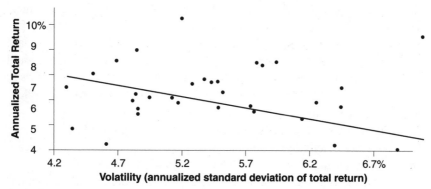

Sources: DLJ; Morningstar.

E X H I B I T   17–27

Risk and Reward for Selected High
Yield Mutual Funds, 1996–1997

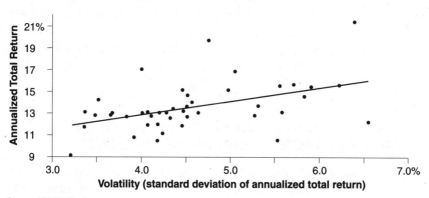

Sources: DLJ; Morningstar.

Yield Dispersion and
Eight-Month Price Volatility

Another measurement of risk, or volatility, is demonstrated through the dispersion of yields in the high yield market. In Exhibit 17–27, the mean yield of the issues in the DLJ High Yield Index is plotted over time. The yield dispersion is measured by plotting the mean plus/minus one standard deviation. This chart attempts to determine what yield differential would be demanded by investors for a credit if this credit were considered risky rather than safe. All else being equal, as in the period from March to September 1994 when credit risk did not increase materially, the yield we demand for the same security in a riskier environment would be higher. We have witnessed yield dispersion widen in 1994–95, in line with the increase of another measure of volatility, the eight-month price volatility.

Eight-month price volatility is more of a coincident indicator and has better resolution than 20-month return volatility. Eight-month price volatility is not affected by the diversification reflected in overall return volatility.

We have indicated that the relationship between risk and reward exists. This analysis is useful if we have a view on the outlook for risk. We believe that risk is on the rise because we have passed the economic peak. Defaults should rise, even though we have been experiencing a decline in default rates and have had the lowest default rate in over 10 years in 1997. In a lower GDP growth environment, even though recession is not imminent, risk would be expected to be higher. Our conclusion is that it would be advantageous in this environment to reduce our risk posture over time in order to outperform other investors.

INTEREST RATE EFFECT: DURATION SIGNIFICANCE IN HIGH YIELD PORTFOLIOS

Prior to 1994, interest rate volatility was not considered a major risk in the high yield market. High yield investors instead focused on credit events such as defaults and ratings changes, and on macroeconomic issues such as the 1991 recession. High yield investors did not seriously consider duration, one of the primary gauges of interest rate sensitivity, when making investment decisions. For the past two years, however, duration has been a fairly important factor contributing to high yield performance. In 1994, as interest rates climbed 203 basis points, securities with long (seven to ten years) durations performed poorly, returning −11.9 percent for the year. Those with short (three to four years) durations outperformed the others with a return of 0.74 percent over the same time period. In 1995, the reverse

E X H I B I T   17–28

Dispersion of Yield for the DLJ High Yield Market

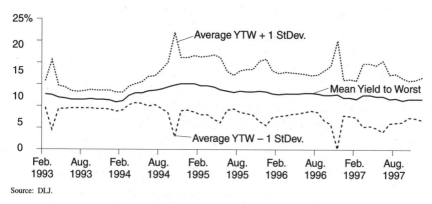

Source: DLJ.

E X H I B I T   17–29

Short versus Long Duration Cumulative Returns, 1993–1997

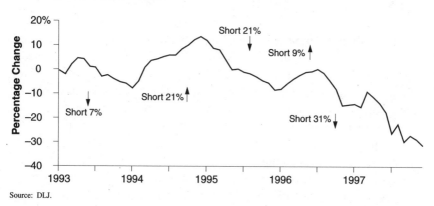

Source: DLJ.

occurred with long-duration securities (seven to ten years) outperforming the others with a 32.2 percent return as interest rates fell approximately 225 basis points. Short-duration securities (less than two years) lagged in 1995, returning 10.0 percent.

Duration alone fails to explain returns in volatile interest rate environments because spreads move directionally opposite the direction of interest rates. Specifically, different ratings would tend to experience very different changes in spread. The fact that spread and rates move in opposite directions leads to the lower volatility of high yield in comparison to other asset classes.

EQUITY/CYCLE COMPONENT

High Yield Correlation with Equity and Treasury Markets

High yield bonds traditionally have been viewed as hybrid securities, exhibiting characteristics of both equity and fixed income securities. One would then expect a strong relationship between returns on high yield corporate bonds and both equity securities (S&P 500 and U.S. small stocks) and Treasury securities (intermediate-term Treasuries). While these relationships are confirmed by empirical evidence, the relative importance of these two factors changes over time, suggesting important investment implications.

Exhibit 17–30 demonstrates, on a 20-month rolling basis, the correlations of high yield bonds with intermediate Treasuries, the S&P 500, and U.S. small stocks. Interestingly, three distinct subperiods emerge: from 1980 to mid-1985, high yield returns demonstrated a stronger correlation with Treasury returns versus equity returns; this reversed for the time period from mid-1985 through 1993; while finally, from 1994 onwards, the correlation with Treasuries regained its dominance.

In Exhibit 17–31, we have performed stepwise multiple regression analysis, which attempts to explain high yield returns (dependent variables) with Treasury and equity returns (independent variables). The relative contribution of Treasuries and small stocks to the R^2 (explanatory power) of the regression equation explains the shift in high yield returns during the three time periods, confirming the changing relative strength of the two relationships.

The observation of these three subperiods is not surprising. For the period of the mid-1980s until the end of the recession, high yield returns and risks were more equity-driven. In times of robust economic activity, default risk/spread widening risk is not of primary concern. With stable spreads, high yield will react more to Treasury returns, which occurred during the periods of 1980–85 and 1994–95. For the overall period from January 1980 to the present, we find that returns in the high yield market can be best explained by Treasuries.

Our outlook for the high yield market reflects these themes. The current environment in which the relationship between high yield and Treasuries is stronger than that with equity is expected to continue through the anticipated economic soft-landing period. This suggests the importance of

E X H I B I T   17–30

Twenty-Month Rolling Return Correlations of Various Assets with the DLJ High Yield Index

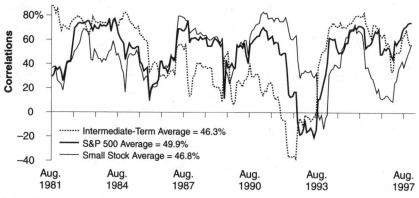

Sources: DLJ; Ibbotson Associates.

E X H I B I T   17–31

Stepwise Multiple Regression Analysis of High Yield Bond Returns

From	To	No. of Observations	R^2 of Linear Regression (HY vs. Tsy.) as a % of R^2 of Multiple Regression	Incremental Explanatory Power of Small Stocks Small Stocks % of R^2 of Multiple Regression	Overall R^2 of Multiple Regression (HY vs. Tsy. & Small Stocks)
Jan-80	Dec-97	216	76%	24%	0.47
Jan-80	Jun-85	66	89	11	0.71
Jul-85	Dec-93	102	23	77	0.25
Jan-94	Dec-97	48	82	18	0.61

Sources: DLJ; Ibbotson Associates.

a continuing focus on duration/spread widening and tightening along with interest rate sensitivity in the short term. Looking forward 12 to 24 months, however, beyond the soft landing, if perceived asset values were to decline and volatility were to increase, equity returns would be a better predictor of these risks.

Cycle Rotation

There are numerous tools to measure and manage the equity component of high yield returns. Cyclical, defensive, and energy sector breakdowns, as well as more specific industry breakdowns, provide an excellent understanding of one's equity exposure. The drastic changes in the spread between cyclical and defensive high yield securities through various stages of the economic cycle provide an opportunity for investors to maximize returns by reallocating their portfolios in anticipation of changes in the economic cycle. By rotating into defensive securities in the late cycle and recession and into cyclical issues in the early recovery, investors can enhance returns by minimizing spread widening risk in a recession and taking full advantage of spread tightening in a recovery.

In addition, as demonstrated in Exhibit 17–32, default rates move in line with the economic cycle, rising to their highest levels during the height of a recession. This default pattern allows high yield managers to adopt a more defensive and conservative position ahead of this trend in order to minimize equity exposure in a high default rate environment.

The basic trend is that risky assets overperform in a declining volatility environment and underperform in an increasing risk environment. Since the major portion of the overall economic cycle exhibits an average to below-average volatility pattern, risky assets are attractive in the overall cycle.

For the overall economic cycle, optimized allocations for a portfolio of Treasuries, corporates, high yield, and equity indicate that high yield assets would have a 19.9 percent allocation for a medium risk profile. Furthermore, the allocation would be approximately 23.2 percent if the objective is to maximize return per unit of risk. There are a number of constraints put on the optimization of this tactical asset allocation model so that assets are not completely ignored or allowed to comprise more than 70 percent of the portfolio at any one time as this would allow for 100 percent certainty and no risk in the outlook.

CONCLUSION

A solid understanding of a market's drivers and how they change over time is a crucial element to successful portfolio management. Numerous management tools already exist that can provide investors with the opportunity to better understand and manage portfolio risks. Duration management

E X H I B I T   17–32

Annual High Yield Default Rates versus Annual High Yield Returns

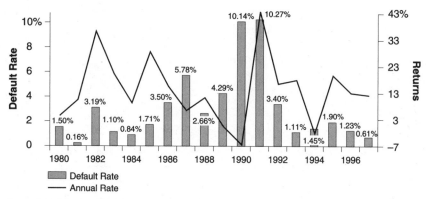

Sources: DLJ, 1997; Altman Default Study, 1971–1996; Ibbotson Associates.

E X H I B I T   17–33

Spread-to-Worst by Rating

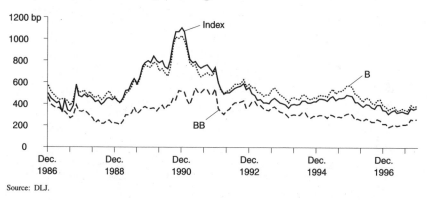

Source: DLJ.

tools can help investors manage interest rate volatility, while various market volatility measurements and cyclical versus defensive studies can help manage exposure to inherent volatility and to the equity markets. By utilizing the existing wealth of information, high yield portfolio managers can make more informed "bets" and enhance portfolio performance.

E X H I B I T   17–34

Difference in Yield-to-Worst of Deferred Interest versus Cash-Pay Securities

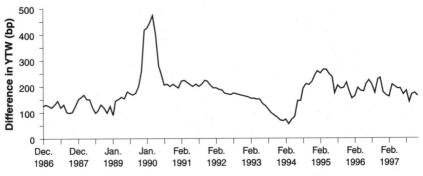

Source: DLJ.

E X H I B I T   17–35

Historical Spread of Cyclical versus Defensive Sectors, 1986–1997

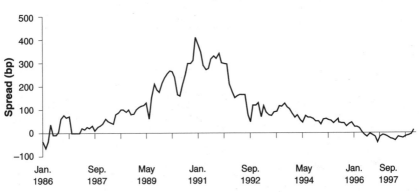

Source: DLJ.

E X H I B I T   17–36

Asset Class Returns by Stage of Economic Cycle (annualized)

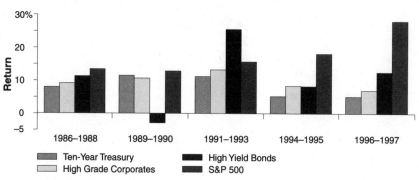

Sources: DLJ; Ibbotson Associates.

E X H I B I T   17–37

Twenty-Month Rolling Return Volatility versus Average Returns

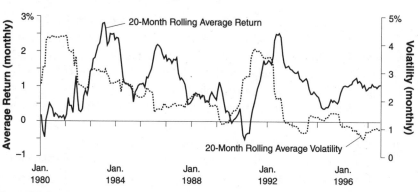

Source: DLJ.

CHAPTER 18

An Analysis of High Yield Bond Indices*

Frank K. Reilly

David J. Wright

INTRODUCTION

The high yield (HY) bond market, which is composed of all bonds below investment grade, has experienced substantial growth during the past 15 years. Although the "modern" HY bond market was born in 1977, its significant growth began in 1983. This market grew because of the increased supply of HY bonds prompted by the capital needs of numerous large and small firms, (Perry and Taggart 1988; Sobel 1989; Yago 1991) and the heavy demand from various institutions that felt HY bonds provided attractive risk-adjusted returns (Altman 1989a, 1990a, 1992; Blume and Keim 1987, 1991a, 1991b; Blume, Keim and Patel 1991; Cheung, Bencivenga and Fabozzi 1992; Cornell and Green 1991; Fridson 1989a). The HY bond market currently contains bonds worth about $494 billion (First Boston 1998). This value estimate has been reduced by defaults, buy-backs, refunds taking advantage of lower interest rates, maturing bonds, and upgrades of bonds to investment grade, while the outstanding value has been increased

*The authors acknowledge the data provided by the following firms: First Boston, Lehman Brothers, Lipper Analytical Services, Merrill Lynch, Ryan Labs, Salomon Brothers, and Professors Marshall Blume and Donald Keim. This chapter is modified and updated from the following article with permission: Frank K. Reilly and David J. Wright, "An Analysis of High Yield Bond Benchmarks," *Journal of Fixed Income*, Vol. 3, no. 4 (March 1994), pp. 6–25.

by new issues and the inclusion of investment grade issues downgraded to the HY bond sector (i.e., fallen angels). After very low rates of return in 1990, subsequent returns on HY bonds have been relatively high since 1991, and the issuance of HY bonds has increased substantially since 1992 (First Boston 1997; Fridson and Garman 1997; Lehman Brothers 1997). Therefore, while nobody is promising an eternal rose garden, most knowledgeable observers anticipate that the HY bond market will become an important component of the aggregate U.S. bond market, although its makeup and performance will differ from its "childhood" prior to 1989 (Altman 1992; Fabozzi 1990; Fridson 1994a; Lederman and Sullivan 1993; Marmer 1989; Mitchell 1992; Rosenberg 1989).

Because of the growth in size and importance of the HY bond market, investors, analysts, and portfolio managers need to measure its risk and return performance over time. To help in this task, several HY bond indexes have been developed that tell different stories (Mitchell 1990). This chapter describes the available HY bond market indexes, highlights their differences in makeup, examines their risk–return performance over time, and compares their performance to that of investment grade bonds, the aggregate equity market, and small cap stocks. Given the additional problems of constructing a composite HY bond market index compared to making an index for the investment grade bond market, we examine the correlation among the HY bond composite indexes and measure how they track each other. In addition, we examine the performance of the alternative benchmarks for the BB, B, and CCC sectors of the HY bond market.

Importance of the Benchmarks

An analysis and comparison of the alternative HY bond indexes is important because the risk-return performance results implied by these indexes are used in academic studies and by money managers when making asset allocation decisions. These indexes are also used by clients and money managers interested in developing an index fund that will track this component of the bond market. Finally, these indexes are used as benchmarks by those evaluating portfolio performance in this market.

Because the HY bond market is relatively new and was fairly small prior to 1983, observers then tended to consider all bonds rated below investment grade (BB, B, and CCC) as part of a composite HY bond market, similar to the investment grade bond market where such an assumption is appropriate (see Reilly, Kao and Wright 1992). Evidence of this tendency is found in several studies of the HY bond market that examined the composite risk–return performance and default record for this total market (Altman 1989a, 1989b, 1990, 1992; Asquith, Mullins and Wolfe 1989; Blume and Keim 1987, 1991a, 1991b; Cornell and Green 1991). Recently, it has been suggested that bonds in the high yield universe might exhibit different characteristics depending upon the bond ratings assigned them (Douglas and Lucas 1989; Fridson and Cherry 1990b; Reilly and Wright 1994). Given the possibility of differences between the bonds in the various rating categories, it is important to examine the risk–return performance of the alternative indexes that represent these rating categories and to analyze the relationship between these sector indexes. Finally, it is important to determine if there have been any changes in the relative makeup of the total HY bond market in terms of rating categories and the duration of this market.

Organization of the Chapter

The first section contains a discussion of the difficulties of constructing a "typical" bond index, and the added problems encountered when creating and maintaining a HY bond index. In section two, we describe the diverse construction of the several HY bond indexes; this diversity is in contrast to the strong similarity in construction of the various investment grade bond indexes. In section three, we analyze the risk-return performance of the various composite HY bond indexes compared to investment grade bonds, aggregate common stocks, and small cap stocks. Section four includes a similar analysis for performance of the HY bonds in the alternative HY rating categories.

In section five, we examine two sets of correlations: (1) among the composite HY bond series, and (2) among HY bonds with different ratings. In section six, we analyze the tracking deviations between indexes as a further test of the relationship between alternative indexes. Section seven contains an analysis of the time series properties of the alternative indexes. In section eight we examine changes in some characteristics of the HY bond market. In section nine we summarize the results of our analyses and consider the implication of these results for those who use these alternative indexes to make asset allocation decisions, to construct HY bond index funds, and as benchmarks to evaluate the portfolio performance of HY bond managers.

CONSTRUCTING A HIGH YIELD BOND INDEX

As noted in Reilly, Kao, and Wright (1992), the following are the difficulties involved in creating and maintaining a bond index, compared to maintaining a stock index.

1. The universe of bonds is much broader than that of stocks. The bond universe ranges from risk-free Treasury bonds to bonds in default. It also varies by sector, coupon, and maturity.

2. The universe of bonds is changing constantly. The numerous bond issues outstanding at a point in time are subject to call provisions, sinking fund redemptions, and redemptions at maturity.

3. The volatility characteristics of alternative bond issues vary substantially and these characteristics change over time because of constant changes in the duration and convexity of the bonds.

4. Significant problems can arise in the pricing of individual bond issues in an index because the major secondary market for most bonds is an OTC market with no reporting requirements and many bonds are subject to infrequent trading.

In addition to these difficulties, constructing a HY bond index introduces additional problems. [For an extensive list of ideal attributes for an index see Fridson 1992.]

1. The range of quality is larger among HY bonds than investment grade bonds.

2. The universe of HY bonds experiences more changes than that of investment grade bonds because HY bonds are affected not only by call provisions, sinking funds, and redemptions at maturity, but also by defaults, upgrades, and downgrades into and out of the HY bond segment.

3. The risk characteristics of HY bonds experience greater and more rapid changes than those of investment grade bonds because HY bonds are affected not only by changes in duration and convexity, but can also experience dramatic changes in credit risk.

4. The illiquidity and pricing problems within the HY bond market are a quantum leap above those encountered in the government

and investment grade bond market (Fridson and Bersh 1993, Mitchell 1990).

The point is, there are clear difficulties in creating and maintaining a HY bond index.

DESCRIPTION OF HIGH YIELD BOND SERIES

There are six creators of HY bond series: Four are investment firms (First Boston, Lehman Brothers, Merrill Lynch, and Salomon Brothers), one is an investment service (Lipper Analytical), and one is an academic source (Professors Blume and Keim from the University of Pennsylvania). In addition, the four investment firms have created indexes for rating categories within the HY bond universe.

Important Index Characteristics

Several characteristics are critical in judging and comparing bond indexes. First, the *sample of securities* must be defined. Users want to know the number of bonds in an index, the maturity and size requirements for the sample bonds, what issues are excluded, and what happens when a sample bond issue defaults. Second, the *weighting of the returns* for individual issues—that is, are the returns market value weighted or equal weighted? Third, the *quality of the price data* used. Specifically, are the prices based on actual transactions, are they provided by bond traders, or are they based upon matrix pricing? Finally, the *reinvestment assumption* for the interim cash flows. Do the creators assume the reinvestment of the interest cash flows during a month, and if so, into what are the flows invested?

The summary of characteristics in Exhibit 18–1 (on pages 342–343) indicates that there are substantial differences among the HY bond indexes. This contrasts with minor differences in the characteristics of investment grade bond indexes (Reilly, Kao, and Wright 1992).

Index Sample

The number of issues in the alternative HY bond indexes vary from 86 HY bond funds in the Lipper series to 735 bonds in the Merrill Lynch High Yield Master (ML) series. Some differences in sample size are due to the maturity size constraints of the particular index. The large number of bonds in the ML series can be partially explained by its maturity guideline. This series includes all HY bonds with a maturity over one year (compared to a seven-year requirement for Salomon Brothers and a ten-year maturity requirement for Blume–Keim (B-K). The minimum issue size also varies; ML has a minimum issue size requirement of $10 million compared to $25 million (B-K), $50 million (SB), $75 million (FBOST), and $100 million (LB). Finally, the alternative indexes handle defaulted issues differently. The treatment varies from dropping issues the day they default (ML), to retaining them for an unlimited period subject to a size constraint (FB).

Return Weights

Only one index differs in how the returns are weighted. The four indexes by investment firms have always been market value-weighted (FBOST, LB, ML, and SB). The B-K index was originally equal weighted, but it currently uses the market value-weighted SB long-term index. The Lipper series computes an equal-weighted mean and median rate of return for its sample of HY bond funds. This is the traditional technique used by investment services.

Bond Pricing

All the bonds in the traditional indexes are trader priced except for ML, which uses matrix pricing for a few of its illiquid issues. The difficulty with trader pricing is that when bond issues do not trade, the price provided by the trader is his or her best estimate of what the price "should be"—which means that it is possible to get significantly different prices from alternative traders. Lipper uses the reported market prices for the funds included in its index. Notably, although the mutual funds have the same pricing problems as the indexes when valuing their portfolios, the funds have significant incentives to get good prices because these prices determine their net asset values (NAV) and the funds must be willing to buy and sell fund shares at these values. As pointed out by Cornell and Green (1991), the returns on the bond indexes are gross, while the returns on mutual funds are net of management fees and trading costs. Also, because bond funds hold cash reserves, it reduces their returns when the yields on HY bonds exceed those on money market securities.

All of the indexes except LB assume the reinvestment of interim cash flows, but at different rates—that is, the individual bond rate, the average portfolio rate, or a T-bill rate. Finally, the average maturity and duration for

E X H I B I T   18–1

Characteristics of Major High Yield Bond Indexes

	Blume–Keim (1)	First Boston
Number of Issues*	233	423
Maturity	Over 10 yrs.	All Bonds
Size of Issues Included	Over $25 million	Over $75 million
Excluded Issues	Convertible Bonds	Convertible Bonds
Treatment of Defaulted Issues	(2)	(3)
Weighting	Equal	Market Value
Pricing	Trader Priced	Trader Priced
Reinvestment Assumption	Yes	Yes
Average Maturity	12.5 (est.)	9.14
Average Duration	6.0 (est.)	3.87

*Approximate number. NA—not available.

1. These characteristics are for the original Blume-Keim index for the period 1982–1989. The results in 1989 are based on the Drexel Burnham long-term index and the results in 1990–1996 are the Salomon Brothers long-term index.

2. Currently the same as the Salomon Brothers Composite.

3. Interest payment not included for month of default. The bond issue is removed from the index if its market value falls below $20 million for six months. While in the index it trades flat and is priced accordingly.

the indexes are consistent with the index constraints—FB, LB, and ML have 1-year minimums and low durations, while SB with a 7-year minimum and B-K with a 10-year minimum have durations that are clearly higher.

In summary, there are significant differences in the characteristics of the alternative HY bond indexes in terms of the samples and pricing. One should expect these differences to have a significant impact on the risk-return performance, the correlations, and the tracking deviations between individual indexes.

Bond and Stock Market Indexes Analyzed

Our analysis considers all of the major indexes from the HY bond universe and some representative investment-grade bond indexes. In addition, we examine the behavior of these bond indexes relative to two equity indexes, the Standard and Poor's 500 Index and the Ibbotson Small Capitalization

Lehman Brothers	Lipper Analytical	Merrill Lynch	Salomon Brothers Composite
624	86 funds	735	411
Over 1 yr. outstanding	NA	Over 1 yr.	Over 7 yrs.
Over $100 million	NA	Over $10 million	Over $50 million
PIKs, Eurobonds, Conv. Bds.	None	Floating Rate, Equip. Trusts, IOs, PIKs	Convertible Bonds or Fltg. Rate Conv. Bds.
(4)	NA	(5)	(6)
Market Value	Equal	Market Value	Market Value
Trader Priced	Market Prices	Trader Priced	Trader Priced
No	No	Yes	Yes
9.29	NA	10.0	12.6
4.53	NA	5.2	5.43

4. The coupon payment during the month of default is included. The bond remains in the index as long as it meets the prevailing requirements, but it is traded flat and is priced accordingly.

5. Monthly return is based on cumulative daily returns. Defaulted bond is dropped out of index on the day they receive information on default. If information is received during day t, it is removed at close of day $t - 1$. No adjustment for prior daily accrued interest.

6. Interest payment not included for month of default. Bond issue kept in the Composite index for a 30-day grade period and then removed from composite index at prevailing price and put into the SB Extended HY Market Index.

Stock Index. All of the indexes except small cap stocks report monthly total returns. The indexes included and the notation for each are as follows:

High Yield Bond Indexes:

BK   Blume–Keim Low Grade Bond Index

FBOST   First Boston High Yield Index

LBCOM   Lehman Brothers Composite High Yield Index

LPAVE   Lipper Analytical Services Corp. Average Return of HY Bond Funds

LPMED   Lipper Analytical Services Corp. Median Return of HY Bond Funds

MLHYM Merrill Lynch High Yield Master

SBLNG   Salomon Brothers Long Term High Yield Index

SBCOM   Salomon Brothers Composite High Yield Index

First Boston High Yield Bond
Indexes by Rating Category:

FB BB   First Boston BB-Rated High Yield Index

FB B   First Boston B-Rated High Yield Index

FB CCC   First Boston CCC-Rated High Yield Index

Lehman Brothers High Yield Bond
Indexes by Rating Category:

LB BB   Lehman Brothers BB-Rated High Yield Index

LB B   Lehman Brothers B-Rated High Yield Index

LB CCC   Lehman Brothers CCC-Rated High Yield Index

Merrill Lynch High Yield Bond
Indexes by Rating Category:

ML BB   Merrill Lynch BB-Rated High Yield Index

ML B   Merrill Lynch B-Rated High Yield Index

ML CCC   Merrill Lynch CCC-Rated High Yield Index

Salomon Brothers High Yield Bond
Indexes by Rating Category:

SB BB   Salomon Brothers BB-Rated High Yield Index

SB B+   Salomon Brothers B+-Rated High Yield Index

SB B   Salomon Brothers B-Rated High Yield Index

SB B−   Salomon Brothers B−-Rated High Yield Index

SB CCC   Salomon Brothers CCC-Rated High Yield Index

Investment Grade Bond Indexes:

LBGC   Lehman Brothers Government/Corporate Bond Index

LBA   Lehman Brothers Aggregate Bond Index

Ryan Treasury Auction Issue
Bond Indexes by Maturity:

RYAN   Ryan Composite Treasury Index

TSY01   Treasury 12-Month Bill Index

TSY03   Treasury 3-Year Index

TSY05   Treasury 5-Year Index

TSY10   Treasury 10-Year Index

TSY30   Treasury 30-Year Index

Stock Market Indexes:

SP500   Standard and Poor's 500 Total Return (with dividends) Index

IBSC   Ibbotson Associates Small Capitalization Stock Index

RISK-RETURN PERFORMANCE: COMPOSITE HIGH YIELD INDEXES

Exhibit 18–2 contains the annual rates of return for the composite HY bond indexes, two representative investment grade bond indexes, and the two stock indexes for the periods available. These annual and cumulative results indicate the diversity of the HY bond series available over the period 1980–1996. The two oldest series are the SB Long HY series which has been available since 1980, and the BK series which has been available for the total period in several different forms. Alternatively, the FB and LB composite indexes were initiated in 1986. Because our goal is to provide a broad examination of the HY bond market, we will concentrate on the period 1986–1996 so we can consider the FB and LB indexes.

The results in Exhibit 18–2 indicate a very wide range of cumulative annualized returns for the period 1986–1996. Specifically, the results for composite indexes ranged from 9.59 for the Lipper funds to 12.07 for the SB Long HY index. If we concentrate on the pure composite HY bond indexes and exclude the fund index, the range is tighter—from 11.44 to 12.07. The investment-grade bond returns were lower than all the composite HY bond indexes. Both the S&P 500 stock results (15.57) and the small cap stock results (13.08) were above all bond results. The range of risk (standard deviations) for HY bonds was larger, going from 5.35 (ML) to 7.77 (BK). The risks for the two investment grade bond indexes were lower (4.95 and 4.67), while the stock index risk measures were about twice as large as the bond index measures with small cap stocks at the peak.

Exhibit 18–3 (on page 348) contains the cumulative wealth ratios for the LB composite HY index, the LB aggregate investment-grade bond index, and the two stock indexes. These results demonstrate the compounding effect of the alternative geometric mean rates of return. The only inconsistent result is that the small cap stocks lagged the S&P 500 during this relatively short test period.

E X H I B I T   18—2

Annual Rates of Return for High Yield Bond,
Investment-Grade Bond, and Stock Indexes:
Annualized Cumulative Rates of Return and Annualized
Standard Deviations of Monthly Returns, 1980–1996

	Blume-Keim	First Boston	Lehman Brothers	Merrill Lynch	Lipper Analytical Services Corp.	
	Low Grade	High Yield	High Yield Composite	High Yield Master	High Yield Bond Funds Mean	Median
Annual Returns (%)						
1980	1.13	—	—	—	—	—
1981	8.02	—	—	—	—	—
1982	32.63	—	—	—	—	—
1983	19.79	—	—	—	—	—
1984	9.68	—	9.70	—	—	—
1985	22.79	—	25.64	—	21.78	21.74
1986	13.63	15.64	17.45	16.35	11.95	13.75
1987	2.08	6.52	4.99	4.66	1.78	2.36
1988	17.89	13.65	12.53	13.47	12.49	12.90
1989	−2.19	0.39	0.83	4.23	−1.25	−0.90
1990	−8.59	−6.38	−9.59	−4.34	−11.21	−10.19
1991	43.29	43.76	46.18	34.58	36.18	35.77
1992	19.18	16.65	15.75	18.16	17.64	17.17
1993	19.95	18.91	17.12	17.18	18.95	18.52
1994	−3.80	−0.98	−1.03	−1.16	−3.73	−3.21
1995	29.34	17.38	19.17	19.91	16.76	17.02
1996	7.86	12.42	11.35	11.07	13.79	13.38
Cumulative Annualized Returns (%)						
1986–1996	11.65	11.85	11.44	11.71	9.59	9.93
Annualized Standard Deviations of Monthly Returns (%)						
1986–1996	7.77	6.80	7.18	5.35	6.13	6.04

Exhibit 18–4 (on page 349) contains a scatter plot of the annual
returns and the standard deviations for the alternative series. The line drawn
is the risk-return regression line for the following six Treasury issues: 1, 2,
3, 5, 10, and 30 years. The two investment grade bond indexes and all of
the HY indexes are above the line. The S&P 500 and the small cap stock
indexes are also above the line, although the S&P 500 experienced a higher
return and less risk than the IBSC index. On a risk-adjusted basis it appears

Salomon Brothers		Lehman Brothers Investment Grade		Stock Indexes	
High Yield Bond Composite	Long	Govt./ Corp.	Aggregate	S&P500	IBSC
—	0.54	3.06	2.71	32.42	39.88
—	4.02	7.26	6.25	−4.91	13.88
—	34.25	31.10	32.62	21.41	28.03
—	22.60	7.99	8.36	22.51	39.67
—	9.47	15.02	15.15	6.27	−6.67
26.06	22.66	21.30	22.10	32.16	24.66
16.49	16.11	15.62	15.26	18.47	6.85
4.57	4.58	2.29	2.76	5.23	−9.30
15.24	16.11	7.58	7.89	16.81	22.87
1.98	−1.10	14.24	14.53	31.49	10.18
−8.45	−8.59	8.28	8.96	−3.17	−21.56
43.23	43.28	16.13	16.00	30.55	44.63
18.28	19.17	7.58	7.40	7.67	23.35
18.33	19.95	11.06	9.75	9.99	20.98
−2.52	−3.80	−3.51	−2.92	1.31	10.05
22.40	29.34	19.25	18.48	37.43	34.46
11.24	7.86	2.89	3.61	23.07	17.61
12.03	12.07	9.02	9.07	15.57	13.08
6.83	7.69	4.95	4.67	14.65	17.14

that the ML index had the best results. In contrast, the Lipper mutual fund series experienced the worst risk-adjusted results because they had risk that was comparable to the other HY bond series, but had lower average returns. As noted previously, these results can be partially explained by the inclusion of fund fees, transactions costs, and the holding of some cash reserves rather than being fully invested in the HY bond market.

E X H I B I T   18–3

Wealth Ratios for Stock and Bond Indexes,
December 1985–December 1996

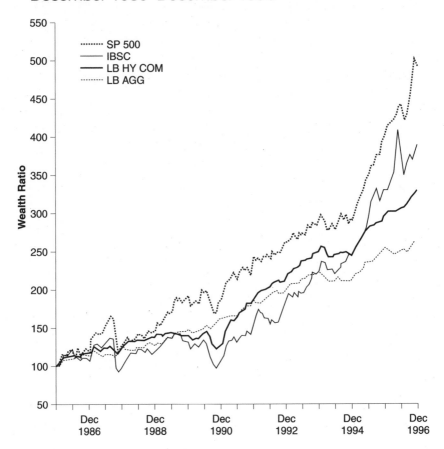

RISK-RETURN PERFORMANCE:
HIGH YIELD RATING CATEGORIES

The annual risk-return results in Exhibit 18–5 (on page 350) for the HY indexes by rating category reveal two important points. First, the indexes that subdivide the HY market by credit risk exhibit *substantial differences in the risk-return performances among the three rating categories*. The range of annualized cumulative total returns over the 11-year period was from 4.05 (SB CCC bonds) to 14.45 (SB B+ bonds). The differences in risk between the HY rating categories were greater than those for returns, but

E X H I B I T   18–4

Annualized Cumulative Return versus the Annualized
Standard Deviation of Monthly Returns:
Stock, Investment Grade Bond, and Composite
High Yield Bond Indexes, 1986–1996

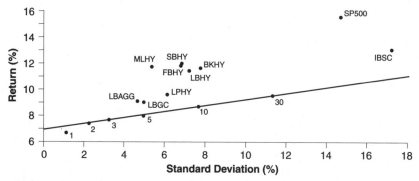

Note: The line represents the linear regression line among the six Treasury indexes, where: Index i (i = 1, 2, 3, 5, 10, 30 years),
Return (i) = 6.65 + .262 Std. Dev. (i) + Error (i), T-Statistics = (49.2) (11.9), R^2 = .973

the differences were always consistent with the ratings (BB, lowest and
CCC, highest). The annualized standard deviation of monthly returns
ranged from 4.59 (FB BB) to 13.93 (FB CCC).

Exhibit 18–6 (on page 352) shows the time series of annual rates of
return for the First Boston HY series by rating categories. The results for
the BB and B series are reasonably consistent, while the CCC series
exhibits substantial volatility including some very good years, but also several very poor ones.

The cumulative effect of the differences in return by rating categories
is demonstrated in Exhibit 18–7 on page 353. An investment of $100 at the
beginning of 1986 in either BB- or B-rated bonds grew to about $400 in
1996. In contrast, $100 invested in very volatile CCC bonds grew to only
about $290 during this period. Notably, these rates of return results are
completely opposite to what one would think on the basis of expected and
actual risk during this period.

Beyond the differences among rating classes, the results in Exhibit
18–5 display a *wide dispersion of risk-return performance within each of
the three rating categories* depending upon which investment firm index is
used. This dispersion is greatest in the CCC category. Depending on which
firm's index is examined, the 1986–1996 annualized returns performance
for CCC bonds was either 4.05 (SB), 9.39 (LB), or 9.90 (FB). Moreover,
for some years, the annual return for the alternative CCC benchmarks

E X H I B I T   18-5

Annual Rates of Return for High Yield
Bond Sector Indexes:
Annualized Cumulative Rates of Return and Annualized
Standard Deviations of Monthly Returns, 1985–1996

	First Boston			*Lehman Brothers*		
	BB	**B**	**CCC**	**BB**	**B**	**CCC**
Annual Returns (%)						
1985	—	—	—	27.06	22.94	17.19
1986	25.56	21.91	21.62	23.33	16.80	9.37
1987	10.51	6.44	6.85	6.12	4.85	3.95
1988	12.70	14.77	6.58	13.77	12.92	9.26
1989	13.33	1.61	−18.35	7.81	0.86	−14.26
1990	4.42	−3.27	−34.01	0.07	−8.62	−22.64
1991	26.84	45.06	100.15	25.02	43.27	83.16
1992	13.86	18.73	40.42	12.08	15.90	22.87
1993	16.09	18.32	38.85	15.86	16.91	20.02
1994	−0.66	0.63	−15.44	−0.39	0.16	−11.93
1995	18.40	16.78	17.13	21.84	16.57	21.82
1996	10.18	15.10	−2.09	8.92	13.58	12.36
Cumulative Annualized						
Returns (%)						
1986–1996	13.48	13.52	9.90	11.91	11.41	9.39
Annualized Standard Deviations						
of Monthly Returns (%)						
1986–1996	4.59	7.15	13.55	5.01	7.07	12.06

varied by as much as 30 to 40 percent in total returns. For example, in 1986 the FB CCC index *increased* by 21.62 percent, while the SB index *decreased* by 14.01 percent. Large return differences were also evident in 1991 when the FB CCC index increased 100.15 percent, while the ML CCC index increased by *only* 61.18 percent.

Exhibit 18–8 on page 354 illustrates the disparity between the three alternative CCC indexes by plotting their wealth ratios from $100 at the beginning of 1986. By the end of 1996, values ranged from only $150 (SB CCC), to about $265 (LB CCC) and about $280 (FB CCC). These differences may be attributed to the unique behavior of the individual CCC bond issues and to the small and varying sample sizes used to track the CCC bond market. For example, there were 55 issues used in the LB CCC index

Merrill Lynch			Salomon Brothers				
BB	B	CCC	BB	B+	B	B-	CCC
—	—	—	37.31	23.18	25.8	27.9	4.99
—	—	—	19.37	19.01	17.31	15.75	−14.01
—	—	—	6.41	6.04	1.94	3.01	19.05
—	—	—	14.39	15.84	14.29	18.36	10.03
12.24	0.79	−13.53	12.10	7.76	3.22	0.57	−25.63
2.20	−6.04	−15.93	5.85	−2.26	−6.80	−16.97	−36.48
22.38	38.43	61.18	23.18	50.86	30.45	53.04	72.35
14.58	19.17	25.07	14.78	21.64	19.73	17.98	16.14
15.83	17.36	22.93	15.88	18.41	17.37	19.25	29.92
−2.16	−0.19	1.87	−1.34	−0.28	0.36	0.94	−11.85
22.50	18.17	9.90	22.62	16.30	17.86	15.43	16.35
7.98	13.68	10.29	8.99	13.77	13.76	15.06	8.99
—	—	—	12.70	14.45	11.29	11.77	4.05
—	—	—	4.79	7.34	6.79	7.70	13.93

in January 1987. Notably, between 1987 and 1996, the number of issues varied from 19 (October 1989) to 86 (June 1989).

The benchmark return differences within the BB and B sectors were not as dramatic as those in the CCC sector, but there was still more return dispersion than among investment-grade bond indexes. The annualized cumulative returns in Exhibit 18–5 for the BB bonds during the 1986–1996 period ranged from 11.91 (LB) to 13.48 (FB) percent, and from 11.29 (SB) to 13.52 (FB) percent among the B indexes. The divergent performance results are because of the problems of constructing a HY bond benchmark described in section one, but those problems particularly plague the CCC sector where the sample of securities is relatively limited and varies over time. In addition, the results for individual CCC bond issues are more volatile.

E X H I B I T   18–6

Annual Returns for First Boston HY
Bonds by Rating Category, 1986–1996

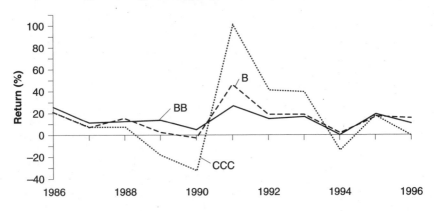

Exhibit 18–9 on page 355 contains a scatter plot of returns and standard deviations for the alternative rating category benchmarks. All of the
indexes except the CCC series were above the Treasury regression line, and
the BB series generally experienced the best risk-adjusted performance.
The LB and FB CCC series were just below the line, while the SB CCC
series had an average annual return of only 4 percent and the highest risk
of any bond series. Although there were observable differences in the rates
of return across benchmarks within a sector, interestingly, there was relative agreement among benchmarks on risk.

CORRELATIONS AMONG
ALTERNATIVE INDEXES

Composite High Yield Bond Indexes

Exhibit 18–10 on page 355 contains the correlations among the composite
HY bond series. These correlations ranging from .885 to .968 are large and
statistically significant. Although there are some long-term differences in
the HY composite indexes' cumulative returns and risk, the high correlations imply similarity in their short-term movements.

E X H I B I T   18–7

Wealth Ratios for Boston HY Bonds by Rating
Category, December 1985–December 1996

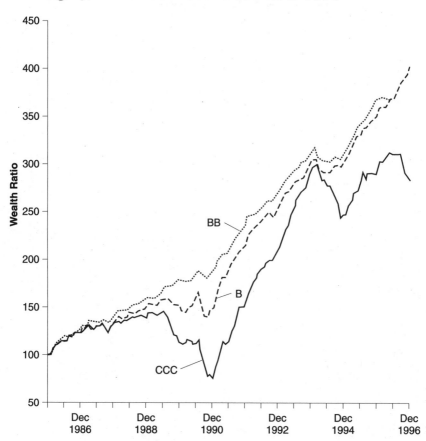

High Yield Rating Category Indexes

Exhibit 18–11 (on pages 356–357) contains the correlations among the HY indexes by rating category. The correlations among indexes with the same rating were significant, but not as high as the correlations among the composite HY bond indexes. Specifically, the correlations among the four BB indexes ranged from .777 to .938 and averaged .861. The correlations

E X H I B I T   18–8

Wealth Ratios for CCC Indexes of First Boston,
Lehman Brothers, and Salomon Brothers,
December 1985–December 1996

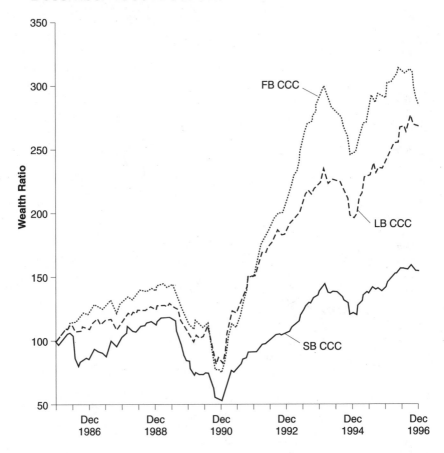

among B-rated bond indexes ranged from .889 to .958 and averaged .926.
Finally, the correlations among the CCC indexes ranged from .729 to .872
and averaged .824.

As expected, the correlations between indexes in different rating categories were lower. Between BB- and B-rated bonds, the average correlation was .802, while between BB and CCC the average correlation was
.666. The average correlation between B and CCC was .803.

E X H I B I T   18–9

Annualized Cumulative Return versus the Annualized
Standard Deviation of Monthly Returns:
High Yield Sector Indexes of First Boston (F), Lehman
Brothers (L), and Salomon Brothers (S), 1986–1996

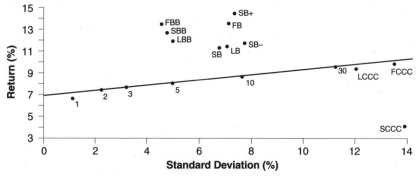

Note: The line represents the linear regression line among the six Treasury indexes, where: Index i (i = 1, 2, 3, 5, 10, 30 years),
Return (i) = 6.65 + .262 Std. Dev. (i) + Error (i), T-Statistics = (49.2) (11.9), R^2 = .973.

E X H I B I T   18–10

Correlation Coefficients among
Monthly Rates of Return:
High Yield Bond Indexes, 1986–1996

	BK	FBOST	LBCOM	LPAVE	MLHYM
BK	—				
FBOST	0.885	—			
LBCOM	0.919	0.962	—		
LPAVE	0.887	0.952		—	
MLHYM	0.925	0.954	0.960	0.966	—
SBCOM	0.960	0.947	0.967	0.943	0.968

Note: All of the correlation coefficients are significant at the 1 percent level.

In summary, the average correlation within a rating category ranged
from .84 to .92, between rating categories the average was .80 if the categories were adjacent, and .67 when categories were not adjacent.

E X H I B I T   18–11

Correlation Coefficients among Monthly Rates
of Return for First Boston, Lehman Brothers,
Merrill Lynch, and Salomon Brothers:
High Yield Indexes by Rating Categories, 1986–1996
(except for ML Indexes, Sept. 1988–Dec. 1996)

	BB Indexes				B Indexes	
	FB BB	LB BB	ML BB	SB BB	FB B	LB B
BB Indexes						
FB BB	—					
LB BB	0.827	—				
ML BB	0.777	0.889	—			
SB BB	0.843	0.893	0.938	—		
B Indexes						
FB B	0.781	0.820	0.663	0.773	—	
LB B	0.777	0.860	0.710	0.799	0.958	—
ML B	0.800	0.798	0.701	0.786	0.938	0.957
SB B+	0.757	0.810	0.648	0.792	0.889	0.915
SB B	0.779	0.865	0.699	0.812	0.925	0.937
SB B-	0.715	0.814	0.686	0.750	0.917	0.959
CCC Indexes						
FB CCC	0.560	0.629	0.535	0.518	0.785	0.789
LB CCC	0.599	0.705	0.609	0.630	0.799	0.861
ML CCC	0.575	0.655	0.548	0.572	0.822	0.849
SB CCC	0.485	0.569	0.573	0.523	0.649	0.709

Note: All of the correlation coefficients are significant at the 1 percent level.

INDEX TRACKING DEVIATION RESULTS

Recently there has been increasing use of bond indexes for portfolio performance measurement. Because there are numerous bond indexes available for measuring the various segments of the bond market, investors and
portfolio managers need to know which indexes provide the most accurate
benchmark for judging portfolio performance. Furthermore, the behavior
of a bond index is critical to those managing bond index funds or enhanced
index funds. The bond portfolio manager's performance is based upon how
accurately the portfolio tracks the client's target index as determined by a
monthly *tracking error,* which is the difference between the total return of
an index fund portfolio and the total return for the selected target index.
Therefore, index fund managers attempt to minimize tracking errors.

B Indexes				CCC Indexes			
ML B	SB B+	SB B	SB B-	FB CCC	LB CCC	ML CCC	SB CCC
—							
0.900	—						
0.900	0.889	—					
0.938	0.886	0.908	—				
0.759	0.706	0.725	0.791	—			
0.855	0.808	0.780	0.864	0.829	—		
0.852	0.735	0.766	0.857	0.847	0.872	—	
0.791	0.647	0.641	0.740	0.729	0.806	0.863	—

Investment-Grade Index Tracking Deviations

The Reilly–Kao–Wright (1992) study examined investment-grade bond indexes and defined the *monthly tracking deviation* as the difference in total monthly returns between two competing bond indexes. Their results for 1976–1990 are similar to the results in Exhibit 18–12 for the recent period, 1986–1996. Specifically, the average performances of the investment-grade indexes converge in the long run, although there are substantial deviations for individual months. These results suggest two key points. First, *the size of the tracking deviations vary based on the type of bond index.* The tracking deviations between alternative corporate bond indexes are about twice as large as the tracking deviations between other bond types. Consequently, the selection of a particular index is a significant decision for those tracking

E X H I B I T   18–12

Monthly Tracking Deviations between the Alternative Investment-Grade Bond Indexes, 1986–1996

	Mean Absolute Deviation (in basis points)	Statistics of Tracking Deviations with Sign (in basis points)				Autocorrelations of Tracking Deviations with Sign		
		Mean	Std. Dev.	Low	High	Lag 1	Lag 2	Lag 3
A. Government Indexes								
LBG–MLG	4.97	−0.08	7.12	−23.20	34.30	−0.44*	−0.06	−0.02
LBG–SBG	7.12	0.17	11.57	−54.10	61.00	−0.37*	−0.05	−0.03
MLG–SBG	6.71	0.25	10.28	−35.60	61.00	−0.33*	0.04	−0.12
B. Corporate Indexes								
LBC–MLC	18.38	−0.06	23.51	−76.00	56.50	−0.28*	−0.17	0.12
LBC–SBC	12.98	0.54	17.16	−42.30	67.20	−0.26*	−0.16	0.09
MLC–SBC	17.49	0.59	23.05	−78.90	65.00	−0.29*	−0.08	0.02
C. Mortgage Indexes								
LBM–MLM	9.27	0.01	14.72	−60.50	64.00	−0.24*	−0.13	0.11
LBM–SBM	8.54	0.06	12.52	−48.80	62.00	−0.27*	−0.01	−0.04
MLM–SBM	8.88	0.05	14.06	−67.60	65.00	−0.30*	0.07	0.01
D. Aggregate Indexes								
LBGC–MLGC	6.57	0.05	8.68	−27.00	29.30	−0.31*	−0.16	0.04
LBA–MLD	5.64	0.04	7.50	−20.00	22.70	−0.22*	−0.24*	0.12
LBA–SBB	5.92	−0.42	8.42	−29.20	32.90	−0.46*	−0.01	−0.05
MLD–SBB	5.85	−0.46	7.88	−33.80	21.00	−0.35*	−0.09	0.04

*Autocorrelation coefficients are significant at the 5 percent level.

a corporate bond series compared to the index decision by those involved with indexing against a government or an aggregate bond market series.

Second, *the first order autocorrelations of the monthly tracking deviations in Exhibit 18–12 were significantly negative,* which suggests that the tracking deviations tended to alternate around the overall mean. These negative autocorrelations were probably caused by the difficulties of pricing the bonds in the index, which would affect the monthly returns for competing indexes. Because these short-term (monthly) price discrepancies tend to reverse themselves as indicated by the negative autocorrelations, the long-term return estimates were similar. In other words, while the firms that maintain the indexes may over- or underestimate bond market values during individual months, these pricing errors tend to correct themselves, so that in the long run, there is approximate agreement on investment-grade bond values.

High Yield Index Tracking Deviations

The previous findings raise several questions with respect to the HY bond indexes. First, because the investment-grade index deviations were probably caused by pricing uncertainties and market illiquidity, how much larger will the tracking deviations be on HY indexes with the substantial illiquidity and pricing problems for HY bonds? It is suggested by Cornell (1992) that the pricing problems will be significant. Second, what is the time series behavior of the tracking deviations for HY bond indexes? Specifically, will the tracking deviations exhibit negative autocorrelation like the investment-grade bond indexes?

The average tracking deviations without a sign (i.e., the mean absolute deviations, MAD) are particularly important for investors attempting to define an "acceptable" portfolio tracking deviation. Although bond indexing has grown substantially, there are no industry standards for acceptable levels of tracking deviations. Therefore, an analysis of tracking deviations between competing HY bond indexes provides important information for establishing standards. Unlike the returns on actual bond portfolios, the returns on indexes are unencumbered by liquidity problems, transaction costs, rebalancing problems, and limitations on the number of securities included. Consequently, the MADs between alternative bond indexes should provide a *lower limit* for acceptable tracking deviations.

The monthly MADs between the HY indexes for the 1986–1996 time period in Exhibit 18–13 vary substantially from those for investment-grade bonds. Specifically, the MADs for the investment-grade bonds ranged from 5 to 18 basis points, while the HY bond results indicate MADs ranging from 40 to 80 basis points per month. These numbers confirm the cumulative return results in Exhibit 18–2, which show that the investment-grade bond indexes exhibit very similar long-run results, while the HY bond indexes show significant differences. The effect of these large tracking deviations between HY bond indexes is that two HY bond funds with identical performance results could have materially different tracking records depending upon the target market index selected.

E X H I B I T   18–13

Monthly Tracking Deviations between the Alternative Composite High Yield Bond Indexes, 1986–1996

	Mean Absolute Deviation (in basis points)	Statistics of Tracking Deviations with Sign (in basis points)				Autocorrelations of Tracking Deviations with Sign		
		Mean	Std. Dev.	Low	High	Lag 1	Lag 2	Lag 3
Composite High Bond Indexes								
BK–FBOST	80.24	−0.94	104.58	−319.50	261.70	−0.07	0.02	0.13
BK–LBCOM	67.42	1.95	88.22	−333.00	222.00	−0.01	0.13	0.16
BK–LPAVE	78.97	16.58	105.82	−256.10	393.00	0.10	0.05	0.16
BK–MLHYM	70.90	0.91	100.32	−411.60	382.50	0.10	0.05	0.11
BK–SBCOM	46.96	−2.24	65.23	−291.10	235.70	−0.05	0.03	0.11
FBOST–LBCOM	40.50	2.89	56.46	−230.71	273.60	−0.19*	0.08	0.03
FBOST–LPAVE	44.06	17.52	60.82	−241.40	206.90	0.22*	−0.15	0.06
FBOST–MLHYM	47.43	1.85	67.11	−327.70	189.60	0.16	−0.15	0.03
FBOST–SBCOM	49.27	−1.30	63.77	−171.40	181.10	−0.07	−0.06	0.10
LBCOM–LPAVE	47.90	14.63	69.86	−208.90	362.01	0.22*	0.02	0.05
LBCOM–MLHYM	46.38	−1.05	73.09	−295.20	351.51	0.18	0.00	0.00
LBCOM–SBCOM	40.46	−4.20	53.20	−188.40	155.30	0.00	−0.05	0.20*
LPAVE–MLHYM	38.51	−15.67	48.42	−195.50	83.00	0.31*	0.22*	0.21*
LPAVE–SBCOM	50.79	−18.82	66.19	−253.50	162.30	0.22*	0.03	0.08
MLHYM–SBCOM	42.91	−3.15	61.20	−243.00	171.50	0.19*	0.02	0.06

*Autocorrelation coefficients are significant at the 5 percent level.

In addition, the tracking deviations of the HY bond indexes are substantially more volatile. The standard deviation and the minimum/maximum values in Exhibit 18–12 and 18–13 indicate that the variability of the HY tracking deviations was *three to five times larger* than that for investment-grade tracking deviations.

High Yield Rating Category Tracking Deviations

The problem with tracking deviations is magnified when we examine the relationship of HY indexes by rating categories, and as we go down in quality. The tracking deviations among the rating category indexes in Exhibit 18–14 show that the MAD statistics between the BB and B indexes were fairly consistent with the composite HY index results in Exhibit 18–13. In contrast, the MAD results for the CCC indexes were three or four times

E X H I B I T   18-14

Monthly Tracking Deviations with Sign
between Alternative High Yield Bond
Indexes by Rating Category, 1986–1996

	Mean Absolute Deviation (in basis points)	Statistics of Tracking Deviations with Sign (in basis points)				Autocorrelations of Tracking Deviations with Sign		
		Mean	Std. Dev.	Low	High	Lag 1	Lag 2	Lag 3
BB Indexes								
FB BB–LB BB	61.24	10.88	82.38	−188.00	388.00	0.01	0.02	−0.12
FB BB–SB BB	56.38	5.94	76.03	−152.00	354.50	−0.02	0.01	−0.03
LB BB–SB BB	47.64	−4.94	65.80	−271.10	212.90	0.12	0.05	−0.02
B Indexes								
FB B–LB B	43.65	15.34	59.50	−181.29	280.00	−0.15	−0.08	0.03
FB B–SB B	56.07	16.91	78.63	−160.60	281.30	0.05	−0.07	0.24*
LB B–SB B	48.22	1.57	71.59	−209.60	396.19	0.17	−0.09	0.02
CCC Indexes								
FB CCC–LB CCC	156.04	8.55	220.06	−776.00	743.00	−0.13	0.08	0.31*
FB CCC–SB CCC	197.40	45.24	292.12	−790.40	1663.00	0.20*	−0.05	0.08
LB CCC–SB CCC	152.02	36.69	239.18	−872.40	1267.00	0.14	−0.03	0.07

*Autocorrelation coefficients are significant at the 5 percent level.

larger than for the other rating categories. The same is true for the mean and standard deviation of tracking deviations with sign. These tracking deviations indicate major differences between the alternative CCC indexes.

Autocorrelations of Tracking Deviations

Finally, the results in Exhibits 18–13 and 18–14 indicate that the returns on HY bond indexes differ in the short run and in the long run, which is inconsistent with the findings for investment-grade bond indexes. Recall that the investment-grade bond indexes had different short-run results but converged in the long run because of the *negative* first order autocorrelations of monthly tracking deviations.

In contrast, the tracking deviations in Exhibits 18–13 and 18–14 between the various HY bond indexes are either not significantly autocorrelated or are *positively* correlated. These results imply that the absolute tracking deviations get progressively worse over longer holding periods— that is, the performances of the HY bond indexes tend to diverge.

TIME SERIES RESULTS

Numerous prior studies have examined the time series properties of equity returns and found no significant dependence in monthly stock index returns. An obvious question is whether there is any dependence in monthly bond index returns. The results in Exhibit 18–15 confirm the insignificant autocorrelation results for large cap stocks. The significant positive autocorrelation for small cap stocks at lag one is probably due to the infrequent trading phenomenon suggested by Fisher (1966). The insignificant autocorrelations for investment-grade bonds are similar to those for large cap stocks. In contrast, *all* of the HY bond indexes exhibit significant positive autocorrelation coefficients at lag one. While not significantly different, the average size of the autocorrelations tend to increase as the credit quality declines.

CHANGES IN THE CHARACTERISTICS OF THE HIGH YIELD BOND MARKET
Makeup of the HY Bond Market

Because of the differences in the risk-return results for the alternative rating categories (especially CCC), it is important to look for any changes in the makeup of the HY bond market. Specifically, what is the proportion of BB, B, and CCC bonds outstanding over time? If these proportions fluctuate, it means that the characteristics of the HY bond market will be constantly changing, which affects how the HY bond market benchmark series can and should be used.

Exhibit 18–16 contains the time series of percent breakdowns for the three rating categories as measured by Lehman Brothers for the period January 1987–December 1996. As shown, there have been dramatic changes over time in the makeup of this market especially in the BB and CCC categories. Specifically, the BB category started at about 18 percent in January 1987, declined to about 12 percent in April 1990, then experienced a dramatic increase during 1993 to about 45 percent, and ended in December 1996 at about 47 percent. Alternatively, the CCC category started at about 15 percent, declined to about 4 percent in late 1989, rebounded to about 20 percent in August 1991, and finished the period at about 5 percent. Finally,

E X H I B I T   18—15

Autocorrelations for the Monthly Index Total Return Series, 1986–1996

	Autocorrelations at Different Lags		
	Lag 1	Lag 2	Lag 3
Stock Indexes			
SP500	−0.02	−0.05	−0.08
IBSC	0.25*	−0.04	−0.11
Investment Grade Bond Indexes			
LBGC	0.17	−0.07	−0.09
LBA	0.18	−0.09	−0.09
High Yield Bond Indexes			
BK	0.41*	0.13	0.00
FBOST	0.45*	0.04	−0.03
LBCOM	0.44*	0.09	−0.04
LPAVE	0.48*	0.18	0.02
MLHYM	0.46*	0.16	−0.02
SBCOM	0.47*	0.12	−0.03
BB Indexes			
FB BB	0.30*	0.06	−0.08
LB BB	0.42*	0.09	−0.12
ML BB	0.49*	0.18	0.02
SB BB	0.36*	0.00	−0.14
B Indexes			
FB B	0.40*	−0.03	−0.03
LB B	0.43*	0.04	−0.05
ML B	0.45*	0.19*	0.05
SB B+	0.43*	0.05	0.01
SB B	0.37*	−0.02	−0.10
SB B-	0.51*	0.15	0.01
CCC Indexes			
FB CCC	0.51*	0.28*	0.15
LB CCC	0.34*	0.20*	0.07
ML CCC	0.51*	0.27*	0.12
SB CCC	0.51*	0.22*	0.05

*Autocorrelation coefficients are significant at the 5 percent level.

E X H I B I T   18–16

Percent Breakdowns of the HY Bond Market by
Rating Categories, January 1987–December 1996

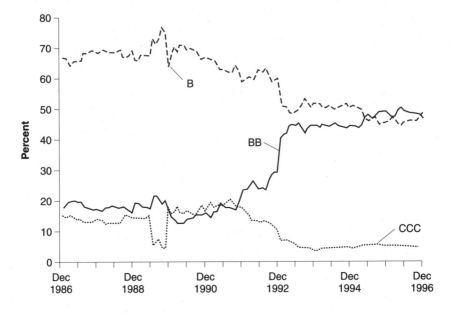

the B-rated bonds started at about 68 percent, reached a peak of over 75 percent, followed by a steady decline to an ending percent very similar to that
of the BB class—about 48 percent.

Changing Duration of the HY Bond Market

Duration is another important characteristic of this market because of how
it impacts bond price volatility. Exhibit 18–17 contains the time series of
average durations for the LB composite HY index and the LB investment-
grade aggregate index for the period 1989–1996. Notably, the durations for
the investment-grade index fluctuated between about 6.0 and 6.4 years. In
sharp contrast, the durations for the HY index experienced fluctuations that
went from over 6 years to about 4.20 years, and ended at about 6 years.
These significant changes in durations over time could be caused by the
changing makeup of the HY bond market as noted, or due to an overall
shift caused by refundings, and so forth.

E X H I B I T   18–17

Modified Durations of the Lehman Brothers High Yield Composite Index and the Aggregate Bond Index

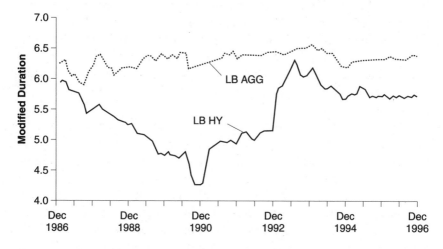

SUMMARY AND IMPLICATIONS
Summary

Because of the growing importance of the HY bond market, several firms have created indexes that can be used to: (1) track the performance of this market; (2) act as benchmarks for index funds; and (3) evaluate portfolio performance. The purpose of this chapter has been to describe and analyze these alternative HY bond indexes. All of the difficulties involved in constructing an investment-grade bond index are generally compounded in the HY bond market. As a result, there are more structural differences among the composite HY bond indexes than among the investment-grade bond indexes.

The composite HY bond indexes experienced a substantial range of return and risk performance during the 1986–1996 period that was much greater than that experienced by investment-grade bonds. An even greater dispersion of returns occurred among indexes within the same rating categories, particularly those for CCC bonds. Finally, there are substantial differences in both risk and return among indexes for bonds in different rating categories (BB, B, CCC).

The correlation results indicated that the HY bond indexes generally move together over time, but these indexes do not exhibit the very high degree of correlations found among the investment-grade bond indexes. Investment-grade bond returns are almost completely determined by fluctuations in interest rates, rather than by unsystematic risk factors. In contrast, the unique credit risk and liquidity factors become very important for HY bonds—more important than the systematic factors. The greater structural differences among HY bonds are especially evident when one considers the lower correlations among bonds within the same rating category—for example, CCC bonds.

The temporal differences among the HY bond indexes were particularly apparent when we examined the absolute tracking deviations that were significantly larger and more volatile than the tracking deviations among investment-grade bonds. Notably, the largest tracking deviations by a multiple of two or more were between alternative CCC indexes. The tracking deviations between HY bond indexes were *positively* autocorrelated, which implies that the absolute tracking deviations get progressively worse over time causing a divergence of performance among the HY bond indexes. In addition, the HY bond indexes exhibited substantially higher return autocorrelation than the investment-grade bonds.

An analysis of changes in the makeup of the HY market indicated substantial changes over time in the proportion of BB and CCC bonds. We also found substantial changes in the average duration for the HY index portfolio.

Implications

The results that show different structural characteristics, risk-return results, and considerable tracking deviations for the alternative composite HY bond indexes, indicate that it makes a difference which HY index is selected as the target series for an index fund or which is used as a benchmark when evaluating a portfolio manager. The selection is especially important when evaluating risk-adjusted performance, because there were large differences in the return measures.

The results for the HY indexes by rating category suggest several implications. First, the choice of a benchmark from each of the three rating categories is very important for performance measurement because of the large annual return differences. Second, the major differences in risk and return between the different rating categories imply that the sector weightings of a particular composite index are critical to its behavior and should be part of the benchmark decision. Specifically, it is absolutely essential to determine the type of HY bond index desired *including the rating category breakdown.* Alternatively, clients must identify the goals and objectives of their HY bond portfolio manager before selecting a HY bond index to use as a benchmark or prior to creating a customized benchmark for evaluating portfolio performance.

The significant difference in results by rating category imply that the HY bond market is not one cohesive unit, and that performance will differ over time. The changes in the makeup of the HY market by rating categories and duration mean that when specifying an index fund, you need to recognize that there are significant changes in the market's makeup over time. Therefore, you can either accept these changes in makeup and the inherent differences in the return-risk performance that they imply, or you should specify what mix of rating categories you want in your portfolio (e.g., 30 percent BB, 60 percent B, 10 percent CCC). When selecting a benchmark for evaluating portfolio performance, you should either select an existing index that has your desired portfolio makeup, or construct a customized benchmark that is consistent with your goals and objectives.

REFERENCES

Altman, Edward I. (1989). "Default Risk, Mortality Rates and the Performance of Corporate Bonds: 1970–1988." Charlottesville, Virginia: The Research Foundation of the Institute of Chartered Financial Analysts.

Altman, Edward I. (1989). "Measuring Corporate Bond Mortality and Performance." *Journal of Finance* 44, no. 4. September, pp. 909–22.

Altman, Edward I. (1990). "Setting the Record Straight on Junk Bonds: A Review of the Research on Default Rates and Returns." *Journal of Applied Corporate Finance* 3, no. 2. Summer, pp. 82–95.

Altman, Edward I. (1992). "Revisiting the High-Yield Bond Market." *Financial Management* 21, no. 2. Summer, pp. 78–92.

Altman, Edward I. ed., (1990). *The High Yield Debt Market.* Homewood, IL: Dow Jones-Irwin.

Asquith, P.; D. W. Mullins, Jr.; and E. D. Wolff (1989). "Original Issue High Yield Bonds: Aging Analyses of Defaults, Exchanges, and Calls." *Journal of Finance* 44, no. 4. September, pp. 923–52.

Blume, Marshall E. and Donald B. Keim (1987). "Lower-Grade Bonds: Their Risks and Returns." *Financial Analysts Journal* 43, no. 4. July–August, pp. 26–33.

Blume, Marshall E. and Donald B. Keim (1991). "Realized Returns and Defaults on Low-Grade Bonds: The Cohort of 1977 and 1978." *Financial Analysts Journal* 47, no. 2. March–April, pp. 63–72.

Blume, Marshall E. and Donald B. Keim (1991). "The Risk and Return of Low-Grade Bonds: An Update." *Financial Analysts Journal* 47, no. 5. September–October, pp. 85–89.

Blume, M. E.; D. B. Keim; and S. A. Patel (1991). "Returns and Volatility of Low-Grade Bonds 1977–1988." *Journal of Finance* 46, no. 1. March, pp. 49–74.

Bookstaber, R. and D. P. Jacob (1986). "The Composite Hedge: Controlling the Credit Risk of High- Yield Bonds." *Financial Analysts Journal* 42, no. 2. March–April, pp. 25–36.

Cheung, Rayner; Joseph C. Bencivenga; and Frank J. Fabozzi (1992). "Original Issue High Yield Bonds: Historical Return and Default Experiences 1977–1989." *The Journal of Fixed Income* 2, no. 2. September, pp. 58–76.

Christensen, D. G. and H. J. Faria (1994). "A Note on the Shareholder Wealth Effects of High-Yield Bonds." *Financial Management* 10, no. 1. Spring.

Cornell, Bradford (1992). "Liquidity and the Pricing of Low-Grade Bonds." *Financial Analysts Journal* 48, no. 1. January–February, pp. 63–67.

Cornell, Bradford and Kevin Green (1991). "The Investment Performance of Low-Grade Bond Funds." *Journal of Finance* 46, no. 1. March, pp. 29–48.

Douglas, S. and D. J. Lucas (1989). "Historical Default Rates of Corporate Bond Issuers 1970–1988." *Moody's Special Report.* July.

Errunza, Vihang and Etienne Losq (1985). "International Asset Pricing under Mild Segmentation: Theory and Test." *Journal of Finance* 40, no. 1. March, pp. 105–24.

Fabozzi, Frank J., ed. (1990). *The New High Yield Debt Market.* New York: Harper Business.

Fabozzi, Frank J.; Mark Pitts; and Ravi Dattatreya (1997). "Price Volatility Characteristics of Fixed Income Securities." in Frank J. Fabozzi, ed. *The Handbook of Fixed Income Securities.* 5th ed. Chicago, IL: Irwin Professional Publishing.

Fama, Eugene F. and Kenneth R. French (1993). "Common Risk Factors in the Returns on Stocks and Bonds." *Journal of Financial Economics* 33, no. 1. February, pp. 3–56.

First Boston. High Yield Handbook. New York: First Boston Corp., Annual.

Fisher, Lawrence (1966 supplement). "Some New Stock Market Indexes." *Journal of Business* 39, no. 1. January.

Fridson, Martin (1989). *High Yield Bonds: Assessing Risk and Identifying Value in Speculative Grade Securities.* Chicago: Probus Publishing Co.

Fridson, Martin S. (1989). "Performance Measurement in High Yield Bonds." *High Performance.* July. Morgan Stanley & Co., Inc.

Fridson, Martin S. (1992). "High Yield Indexes and Benchmark Portfolios." *Journal of Portfolio Management* 18, no. 2. Winter, pp. 77–83.

Fridson, Martin S. (1994). "The State of the High Yield Bond Market: Overshooting or Return to Normalcy?" *Journal of Applied Corporate Finance* 7, no. 1. Spring, pp. 85–97.

Fridson, Martin S. (1994). "Do High-Yield Bonds Have an Equity Component?" *Financial Management* 23, no. 2. Summer, pp. 82–84.

Fridson, Martin S. and Jeffrey A. Bersh (1993). "Measuring Liquidity Premiums in the High Yield Bond Market." *Extra Credit.* May/June, Merrill Lynch Capital Markets.

Fridson, Martin S. and Michael A. Cherry (1990). "Initial Pricing as a Predictor of Subsequent Performance." *Extra Credit.* January, Merrill Lynch Capital Markets.

Fridson, Martin S. and Michael A. Cherry (1990). "Dispersion of Corporate Bond Returns Within Quality Classes." *Extra Credit.* November, Merrill Lynch Capital Markets.

Fridson, Martin S. and M. Christopher Garman (1997). "This Year in High Yield." *Extra Credit*, January/February, Merrill Lynch Capital Markets.

Hessol, Gail I. (1993). "A Study of Corporate Bond Defaults." *The New High Yield Bond Market.* Lederman and Sullivan, eds. Chicago: Probus Publishing.

Howe, Jane Tripp (1988). *Junk Bonds: Analysis and Portfolio Strategies.* Chicago: Probus Publishing Co.

Jorion, Philippe and Eduardo Schwartz (1986). "Integration vs. Segmentation in the Canadian Stock Market." *Journal of Finance* 41, no. 3. July, pp. 603–16.

Kihn, John (1994). "Unravelling the Low-Grade Bond Risk/Reward Puzzle." *Financial Analysts Journal* 50, no. 4. July/August, pp. 32–42.

Lederman, Jess and Michael P. Sullivan, eds. (1993). *The New High Yield Bond Market* Chicago: Probus Publishing Co.

Lehman Brothers (1993). "The Year of the Vanishing Yield." New York: Lehman Brothers, February.

Lehman Brothers (1997). "Global Family of Indices." New York: Lehman Brothers.

Leibowitz, Martin L. (1986). "Total Portfolio Duration: A New Perspective on Asset Allocation." *Financial Analysts Journal* 42, no. 5. September/October, pp. 18–29, 77.

Marmer, Harry S. (1989). "Junk Bonds: When Fact and Opinion Collide." *Risk.* September, pp. 66–67, 84.

Mitchell, Constance (1990). "Junk Bond Indexes Tell a Confusing Story." *The Wall Street Journal.* June, pp. c1, c17.

Monaghan, Kenneth J. and Paul H. Ross (1989). *High Yield Bonds as Loan Substitutes.* New York: Salomon Brothers, September.

Perry, Kevin J. and Robert A. Taggart, Jr. (1988). "The Growing Role of Junk Bonds in Corporate Finance." *Journal of Applied Corporate Finance* 1, no. 1. Spring, pp. 37–45.

Ramaswami, M. (1991). "Hedging the Equity Risk of High-Yield Bonds." *Financial Analysts Journal* 47, no. 5. September–October, pp. 41–50.

Reilly, Frank K., ed. (1990). *High Yield Bonds: Analysis and Risk Assessment.* Charlottesville, VA: The Institute of Chartered Financial Analysts.

Reilly, Frank K. and Keith C. Brown (1997). *Investment Analysis and Portfolio Management.* 5th ed. Fort Worth, TX: The Dryden Press.

Reilly, Frank K.; G. Wenchi Kao; and David J. Wright (1992). "Alternative Bond Market Indexes." *Financial Analysts Journal* 48, no. 3. May–June, pp. 44–58.

Reilly, Frank K. and David J. Wright (1994). "An Analysis of High-Yield Bond Benchmarks." *Journal of Fixed Income* 3, no. 4. March, pp. 6–25.

Reilly, Frank K. and David J. Wright (1997). "Bond Market Indexes." *Handbook of Fixed Income Securities.* 5th ed. Frank J. Fabozzi, ed. Chicago: Irwin Professional Publishing.

Rosenberg, Hilary (1989). "The Unsinkable Junk Bond." *Institutional Investor* 23, no. 1. January, pp. 43–48.

Ross, Paul H.; Vorkhi P. Chaho; Vincent Palermo; and Peter Workich (1989). *High Yield Corporate Bonds: An Asset Class for the Allocation Decision.* New York: Salomon Brothers, February.

Shane, H. (1994). "Comovements of Low-Grade Debt and Equity Returns of Highly Leveraged Firms." *Journal of Fixed Income* 3, no. 4. March, pp. 79–89.

Sobel, Robert (1989). "The Use of High Yield Securities in Corporate Creation." Presented at the Drexel Burnham Lambert 11th Annual Institutional Research Conference, Beverly Hills, CA., April.

Weinstein, Mark I. (1987). "A Curmudgeon's View of Junk Bonds." *Journal of Portfolio Management* 13, no. 3. Spring, pp. 76–80.

Wigmore, Barrie A. (1990). "The Decline in Credit Quality of New-Issue Junk Bonds." *Financial Analysts Journal* 46, no. 5. September–October, pp. 53–62.

Yago, Glenn (1991). *Junk Bonds.* New York: Oxford University Press.

CHAPTER 19

How Many High Yield Bonds Make a Diversified Portfolio?*

Martin S. Fridson

Yan Gao

INTRODUCTION

At some point in the process of launching a high yield bond investment program, most institutions pose the classic question, "How many different issues do we need to own in order to achieve satisfactory diversification?" Typically, they have a vague impression that some magic number of bonds does the trick. They are often encouraged in this belief by promoters of the market, who regard the query as simply one more obstacle to be disposed of before they can begin filling up the account with merchandise.

More serious reflection discloses that a truthful answer is possible only if the investor clearly defines *satisfactory diversification.* Unfortunately, there is no objective basis for deriving a completely acceptable definition of the term. Still, the cause is not hopeless. The institution can begin by establishing a desired level of credit performance, using whatever reasoning process is consistent with its overall investment approach. Then, based on abundant data available concerning historical credit experience, the institution can determine the number of issues required to establish high probabilites of achieving the targeted results.

Clearly, this empirical approach takes more time than it would for a dealer to dispose of the question, "How many issues are required?" by saying, "Thirty. Now let's see what I have in inventory." The more carefully considered response, however, is likely to lead to a better understanding of the investment performance that is genuinely achievable in the high yield sector.

TOTAL RETURN OR DEFAULT EXPERIENCE?

If we are to make any headway on the diversification question, we must first determine whether our goal is defined by total return or by credit performance. Many investors appear to confuse the two, based on dim recollections of past research and sales hype.

In the equity market, financial scholars generally define risk as the volatility of a portfolio's return over time. The relevant theory presumes a high level of market efficiency, implying that no subset of the total universe offers more return per unit of volatility than the total universe (or "market portfolio"). Under these assumptions, a money manager logically should strive to create a portfolio that eliminates essentially all volatility related to individual stock performance, as opposed to overall market fluctuations. Each issue added to a portfolio increases the probability of hitting the index's performance on the nose, but at some point the marginal advantage gained is negligible.

Evans and Archer (1968) used historical prices to simulate the performance of randomly selected stock portfolios. They concluded that it was questionable whether boosting a portfolio's size beyond ten or so issues was economically justified. Elton and Gruber (1977) determined that increasing a portfolio from one to ten stocks eliminated 51 percent of the portfolio's standard deviation. Expanding to 20 issues eliminated another 5 percent of the standard deviation, while only another 2 percent was eliminated by going to 30 issues, suggesting that the benefits of further diversification would be inconsequential. Nevertheless, Statman (1987) concluded that "a well-diversified stock portfolio must include, at the very least, 30 stocks," calculating that the cost-benefit trade-off could be favorable even for additions of securities beyond that point.

Notwithstanding certain differences in methodology, the various analyses of diversification in equities share the framework of a trade-off between return and standard deviation. One result of this work is a vague impression among investors that the number of *securities* needed to achieve satisfactory diversification is something like 30. Applying this idea directly to *high yield bonds* is rather too large a leap. To do so is to transfer a result derived from returns (and of stocks, at that) to a field in which risk is often equated with default risk. Confusion is sure to result.

Thanks to the exertions of high yield bond promoters, investors have fixed in their minds an overly simplistic notion of "putting their eggs into many different baskets." The notion begins with the fact that on average, about 4 percent of outstanding high yield bonds default in any given year. On those bonds, losses come to far less than 100 percent of principal. (Typically, the asset value of a bankrupt company is less than the value of its liabilities, but still greater than zero.) Therefore, by holding a well-diversified portfolio and collecting a promised yield to maturity of four percentage points or more above the default risk-free Treasury yield, an investor *must*—it is alleged—come out ahead on the proposition of taking credit risk.

The shortcomings of this simple-minded analysis are almost too many to enumerate. For one thing, annual default rates fluctuate widely around the 4 percent annual average, so that a spread over Treasuries of 400 basis points may not offset credit losses in a given year. Besides, the bulk of the loss on a defaulting bond is often felt prior to the year in which it defaults. As a result, the spread at the time of default may have little bearing on the defaulting bond's holding-period return. Additionally, promised yield to maturity often has only a passing resemblance in the short run to the return actually realized, owing to fluctuations in the general level of interest rates, redemptions of bonds prior to maturity, and various other factors.

Unsatisfactory though it may be as a basis for gauging the performance of a high yield bond portfolio, the "many different baskets" notion continues to shape the thinking of practitioners. To their way of thinking, satisfactory diversification consists of owning a large enough number of bonds to ensure default experience approximately equivalent to the marketwide historical rate. Based on second-hand, dim memories of textbook discussions of Elton and Gruber's findings, investors conclude that they should buy approximately 30 different issues. It would be pure serendipity, however, if the correct answer turned out to equal the number derived from analysis of total returns and standard deviations of common stocks.

IMPLEMENTING A DEFAULT-BASED APPROACH

During the 1980s, if not necessarily nowadays, the preachers of division of default risk tended to overlook the declining quality of the mix of outstanding high yield bonds. As the universe became more heavily concentrated in highly default-prone issues, the default rate was bound to rise to a level higher than that observed in earlier cycles. This inevitability was realized in 1990–1991 (see Exhibit 19–1). Clearly, one subtlety that must be considered in addressing the question of adequate diversification is the specific risk level of the issues (i.e., Double-B, Single-B or Triple-C), as opposed to simply noninvestment-grade.

E X H I B I T   19-1

Default Rate on Noninvestment-Grade
Corporate Bonds by Number of Issuers,
Trailing-Twelve-Months, 1971-1994

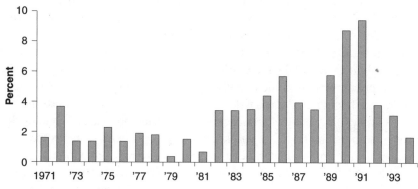

Source: Moody's Investors Service.

In light of the need to make the diversification of default risk rating-specific, it is fortunate that both Moody's and Standard & Poor's publish statistics on corporate failures by rating category. The agencies have tabulated defaults over periods of many years and have demonstrated that their ratings are reasonably consistent measures of credit risk over time. For the present analysis, we shall concentrate on the Moody's figures, which are reported in senior-equivalent terms.[1]

According to Carty, Lieberman and Fons (1995), a company currently rated Single-B at the senior level by Moody's has a 26.5 percent probability of defaulting within the next five years. Put another way, an institution that puts all of its eggs in one basket, that is, which holds just one senior Single-B name, faces more than a one-in-four chance of having its entire portfolio go into default between 1996 and the year 2001. Most institutional investors, we suspect, would consider that risk excessive, even if the potential return were fairly astronomical.

Fortunately, it is a simple matter to reduce substantially the risk of a 100 percent default rate. By adding a second bond to its portfolio, an institution

---

1. Analyzing default rates on a senior-equivalent basis provides a clearer picture, in our experience, than lumping like-rated senior and subordinated issues into a single class. As shown in Chapter 10, market yields correctly reflect the difference in default risk between a senior obligation and a subordinated security of the same rating.

can lower the probability of a total wipeout (before post-default recoveries) to 26.5% × 26.5% = 7.0%.

Note an important assumption, however. This multiplication is valid only if the default probability of Bond A is independent of the default probability of Bond B. The two issuers are not likely to satisfy the independence condition if, for example, they are both oil wildcatters operating primarily in the Gulf of Mexico. To be sure, either might go belly-up without the other following suit. For example, one company's demise could result from an excessive incursion of debt not imitated by its competitor. A sudden drop in energy prices, though, could quickly bankrupt both companies. More effective diversification of default risk would result from creating a portfolio of, for example, one chemical producer and one casino operator. Even then, the two-bond portfolio might experience a 100 percent default rate as the consequence of a single event, that is, a severe economic contraction or credit crunch that left almost no industry untouched. As a practical matter, though, investors must concede the infeasibility of identifying perfectly independent default risks and settle for maximizing the number of industries represented in the portfolio.

By the time investors work their way up to five senior Single-B bonds, they have reduced the probability of a 100 percent default rate within five years to one in a thousand. If we were to accept this particular definition of satisfactory diversification, we would answer the question, "How many bonds do I need?" with the number five. Such a definition would be arbitrary, however. Holders of a five-bond senior Single-B portfolio have a probability of 10.05 percent of suffering a 60 percent default rate (three out of five issues) within five years.[2] For the many investors who still consider the risk too great, a different definition of a well-diversified portfolio must be found.

---

2. The general formula for calculating the probability of a given default rate is:

$$\binom{n}{m} p^m q^{n-m}$$

where:

$$\binom{n}{m} = \frac{n!}{m!(n-m)!}$$

n = Number of issues in portfolio
m = Number of defaulting issues
p = Probability of default within stated period
$q = 1 - p$

In the present example,

$$\frac{5 \times 4 \times 3}{3 \times 2 \times 1} \times 0.265^3 \times 0.735^2 = .1005$$

Ultimately, any such definition will be subjective. An investor must try on various assumptions for size, namely, "Will I be content with x percent probability of y percent default rate cumulatively over z years?" Some investors will be able to reduce the subjectivity of the targeted probability, default rate, and investment horizon by considering the problem in light of a known, corresponding liability schedule. For the rest, the solution must be somewhat arbitrary. By the same token, going through the exercise can valuably increase investors' knowledge about the results they are likely to achieve.

To illustrate, let us for the moment continue our focus on bonds of Single-B senior-equivalent quality. Given the five-year, single-issue default probability of 26.5 percent, the expected average annual default rate is 26.5% / 5 = 5.3%[3]. Many investors would find this level of risk acceptable, in the context of prevailing yield spreads. Under the admittedly simplistic analysis described above, a spread of 500 basis points over Treasuries would more than cover annual defaults of 5.3 percent, net of recoveries (immediately following default) of 40 percent of principal (i.e., average annual credit losses of 530 basis points $\times$ (1 − 0.4) = 318 basis points).[4]

Realistically, though, there is a strong chance that a specific portfolio's default probability will differ from that of the senior-equivalent Single-B universe. Moreover, the senior-equivalent Single-B universe's default rate over any five-year period may vary from its long-run average. Moody's reports that among issuers rated Single B at the senior level as of January 1, 1976, only 9.4 percent defaulted in the ensuing five years. At the other extreme, 34.3 percent of the issuers rated Single B at the senior level as of January 1, 1989 defaulted within five years. Factors potentially influencing this variance include economic conditions, credit availability, and shifts in the distribution within the Single-B category among the B1, B2, and B3 subcategories.[5]

Given the inherent uncertainties regarding expected default experience, the best that an investor can do is state a tolerance. For example, an

---

3. Note that this rate is not equivalent to the one-year default rate reported by Moody's for Single-B senior-equivalent bonds, which is 7.9 percent. Moody's statistics indicate that the probability of default is not level over a bond's life. For example, the two-year cumulative probability of default in this instance is not 7.9% $\times$ 2 = 15.8%, but rather 14.2 percent.

4. These assumptions are all reasonable in view of historical experience. During 1992–1994, a period of comparative stability in credit experience, the Merrill Lynch Single-B Corporate Index (a mixture of senior Single-Bs and subordinated issues of companies with Double-B senior-equivalent quality), yielded on average 454 basis points more than ten-year U.S. Treasuries. The comparable figure for Merrill Lynch's Double-B Corporate Index was 280 basis points. Trading prices immediately after default for nonconvertible bonds of all seniority levels, according to Altman and Eberhart (1994), averaged 41.16 percent of par.

5. It is not feasible to test the impact of changes in subcategory distribution over the full 1970–1994 period reported by Moody's, given that the finer gradations were not introduced until 1983.

institution might *hope* to match the five-year, 26.5 percent default rate recorded over the long run on the full universe of senior-equivalent Single-B bonds, yet be able to *withstand* a default rate 50 percent higher (i.e., 40 percent). Observe that the higher cumulative rate translates into an average annual rate of 40% / 5 = 8%. Under the same simplistic assumptions applied above, 500 basis points is adequate (although by no means generous) compensation for expected default losses: 800 basis points × (1 − 0.4) = 480 basis points.

Having defined a default rate tolerance level, the institution can now calculate the number of issues required to ensure a very high probability that its own default rate will not exceed that level. The general formula is as follows:[6]

$$n = p(1 - p) \left(\frac{z}{pt - p} \right)^2$$

where:

n = Number of bonds required to achieve satisfactory diversification, as defined.

p = Probability of default within five years.

z = Value found in Standard Normal Distribution Table, based on the chosen confidence level.

p_t = Tolerance level default rate of portfolio.

Exhibit 19–2 shows the number of issues required to ensure a maximum cumulative default rate of 40.0 percent, given various confidence levels. With just 29 senior-equivalent Single-B issues, thoroughly diversified by industry, the institution achieves a 95 percent probability of doing no worse than the level it deems tolerable. A few more issues might be advisable as a cushion, given the infeasibility of attaining perfect industry diversification, but there is little incremental benefit in spreading default risk among dozens of additional names.

Indeed, at some point, further diversification becomes counterproductive, as the number of issuers in the portfolio exceeds the institution's credit-monitoring capabilities. While we have discussed credit risk entirely

---

6. Assumes each high yield bond from the same rating category has a default probability of p within the stated period. A random sample of n bonds is chosen to form a portfolio. By the central limit theorem, the default rate of the portfolio approximately follows a normal distribution with mean equal to p and variance equal to $p(1 - p)/n$. Given a tolerance level of default rate p_t and a z value from a refined confidence level, we have $p_t = p + z \sqrt{\dfrac{p(1 - p)}{n}}$. Solve the equation for n.

E X H I B I T   19–2

Minimum Number of Bonds Required for Moody's
Senior-Equivalent Rating, B

Objective: Maximum Default Rate = 150% of Historical Experience
Historical Experience: 26.5% over Five Years

Confidence Level	Number Required
95%	29
90	18
85	12
80	8
75	5

E X H I B I T   19–3

Minimum Number of Bonds Required for Moody's
Senior-Equivalent Rating, Ba

Objective: Maximum Default Rate = 150% of Historical Experience
Historical Experience: 11.1% over Five Years

Confidence Level	Number Required
95%	91
90	55
85	37
80	24
75	15

in probabilistic terms, no rational investment manager will ignore obvious
signals of credit deterioration (huge, unanticipated losses, drastic increases
in financial leverage, etc.) that may enable alert investors to sell out before
a Chapter 11 filing is announced.[7]

---

7. Moody's and Standard & Poor's have developed default-based approaches to diversification for
   the specific purpose of rating collateralized bond obligations. These methods ingeniously
   enable the creator of the financings to trade off the key risk factors (i.e., ratings mix, number
   of issues, and industry distribution) to develop optimal structures. See Lucas et al. (1990).

CREDIT QUALITY'S IMPACT ON THE NUMBER OF ISSUES REQUIRED

One counterintuitive implication of the methodology we have outlined is that the number of issues required to obtain satisfactory diversification *increases* as credit quality improves. The natural assumption is that higher default risk necessitates wider diversification, hence more names in the portfolio. Nevertheless, for a buyer of Double-B (Ba in Moody's parlance) senior-equivalent paper who approaches the tolerance level in the same manner as the investor in our Single-B example, the conclusion is exactly the opposite.

By Moody's reckoning, the five-year cumulative default probability of a company rated Ba at the senior level is 11.1 percent, or 2.2 percent per annum. Let us once again set the tolerance level at 150 percent of historical experience, that is, 16.5 percent over five years, or 3.3 percent annually. The previous spread analysis used indicates that a yield premium of 250 basis points suffices to compensate for the higher expected default loss, that is, 330 basis points x (1 − 0.4) = 198 basis points. Following through with the calculations (Exhibit 19–3), we find that 91 senior-equivalent Ba issues are required to achieve the same 95 percent confidence level obtained with only 29 senior-equivalent Single-B issues.

This mathematical paradox ultimately arises from the simple fact that a 50 percent increase from a default rate of 26.5 percent (13.25 percent) is much greater than a 50 percent increase from a default rate of 11.1 percent (5.55 percent). A less counterintuitive finding might emerge from an alternative approach to setting the tolerance level. Note, however, that the approach we have outlined is not altogether arbitrary. It is supported by the risk premiums commonly available on bonds of Single-B and Double-B senior-equivalent quality.

CONCLUSION

Realized return, adjusted for portfolio volatility, is a key test of investment performance, whether the asset class under consideration is common stocks, noninvestment-grade bonds, or what have you. A high yield manager might achieve a zero default rate, yet post mediocre total returns, by selling at a loss every time a credit took a material turn for the worse.

Notwithstanding these observations, investors will almost certainly persist in equating risk primarily with default risk, rather than variance of return. Over the long run, successfully dodging credit losses is one of the most likely ways to outperform a peer group of high yield managers. The odds are against any manager gaining an edge through superior interest rate forecasting, particularly since the noninvestment-grade sector sometimes diverges from the general trend of the bond market.

As a consequence of their emphasis on default risk, high yield investors tend not to think of diversification in the same terms as equity investors. In any case, the sketchiness of historical prices makes it diffficult for high yield analysts to conduct simulations of the sort that have been used to determine the minimum size of an adequately diversified equity portfolio.

The methodology we have outlined accommodates the desire of high yield investors to consider diversification in terms that directly bear on their performance. It does not generate a single correct answer, as equity-based methods strive to, but instead enables each investor to define a customized objective. Like the approach used by stock investors, though, our technique relies on well-documented data, namely, historical default rates calculated by senior-equivalent rating category.

REFERENCES

Altman, Edward I. and Allan C. Eberhart (1994). "Do Seniority Provisions Protect Bondholders' Investments?" *Journal of Portfolio Management*. Summer, pp. 67–75.

Carty, Lea; Dana Lieberman; and Jerome S. Fons (1995). *Corporate Bond Defaults and Default Rates 1970–1994*. New York: Moody's Investors Service, January.

Elton, Edwin J. and Martin J. Gruber (1977). "Risk Reduction and Portfolio Size: An Analytical Solution." *Journal of Business*. October, pp. 415–37.

Evans, John L. and Stephen H. Archer (1968). "Diversification and the Reduction of Dispersion: An Empirical Analysis." *Journal of Finance*. December, pp. 761–67.

Fridson, Martin S. and M. Christopher Garman (1995). "Valuing Like-Rated Senior and Subordinated Debt." *Extra Credit*. July/August, pp. 4–15.

Lucas, Douglas J.; Noel E. D. Kirnon; Roger M. Stein; and Linda K. Moses (1990). *Rating Cash Flow Transactions Backed by Corporate Debt*. New York: Moody's Investors Service, October.

Statman, Meir (1987). "How Many Stocks Make a Diversified Portfolio?" *Journal of Financial and Quantitative Analysis*. September, pp. 353–63.

CHAPTER 20

Managing a High Yield Portfolio

Mark R. Shenkman

INTRODUCTION

In constructing a high yield bond portfolio, money managers should consider the following elements: investment objectives; investment guidelines and restrictions; diversification; investment philosophy; technical factors; degree of risk needed to achieve investment objectives; volatility considerations; liquidity requirements; yield management; and portfolio turnover. This chapter separately discusses each of these portfolio elements.

INVESTMENT OBJECTIVES

Portfolio managers typically establish certain stated investment goals and objectives at the outset of constructing a portfolio. These investment goals and objectives provide a framework for the overall portfolio and have a domino effect on the other elements. One portfolio manager's objective might be preservation of capital; another's might be total return or high current income. Many portfolio managers seek all three simultaneously but are usually disappointed because each of these three primary objectives has varying and conflicting degrees of risk. Therefore, most portfolio managers have one primary objective and a secondary goal—for example, preservation of capital as the primary objective and high current income as a secondary goal. The more clearly defined the objectives, the more likely the strategy will be effective and successful. Moreover, managers can use comparative performance measurements to determine if the objectives are actually being attained. For example, total return objectives may be measured against various indices (i.e., Credit Suisse First Boston Index or Merrill Lynch High Yield Index). Some pension plan sponsors target their portfolio's objectives in terms of outperforming a benchmark index. A pension plan sponsor may target a 1 percent to 3 percent total return above the Credit Suisse First Boston Index or the Merrill Lynch High Yield Index (or an average of the two indices), in order to obtain a more accurate barometer of market performances. In most situations, bond selection, portfolio strategy, and portfolio construction are tied directly to capital preservation, total return, or current income objectives. Given the fact that different investment vehicles and institutions have varying objectives, a portfolio manager needs to understand the distinction between the various investment goals for a particular portfolio.

GUIDELINES AND RESTRICTIONS

Once the investment objectives are delineated, a portfolio manager needs to establish guidelines and restrictions for the portfolio. Typical guidelines and restrictions might include the following.

1. Diversification. No investment should represent more than 5 percent of the portfolio's total assets and no more than 15 percent of the portfolio's total assets should be invested in any specific industry. (In each case, these limitations should be measured at the time of investment.)

2. Restrictions on the percentage of the portfolio's total assets invested in securities that are not registered under applicable securities laws (i.e., Rule 144a).

3. Restrictions on the types of securities that can be purchased in the portfolio. For example, no investments in distressed securities, convertibles, and non-U.S. dollar denominated securities.

Even with these restrictions, however, a "carve-out" may be provided that allows the portfolio manager to invest a certain percentage of the portfolio's assets in different asset classes within the high yield sector. For example, a portfolio manager may specify that no more than a specific percentage of the portfolio's total assets can be invested in zero coupon bonds or pay-in-kind or preferred securities.

Other guidelines may stipulate the percentage of cash that can be held in the portfolio. Other prohibitions can also include no emerging market securities, no common stock, or the percentage of assets invested in securities with specific credit ratings. For example, the portfolio manager may be prohibited from investing in any security that is rated CCC or below by Moody's Investors Services and Standard and Poor's, or any non-rated security. Furthermore, it may be specified that a security with an investment grade rating above BBB/Baa cannot be held, because the portfolio may take on the characteristics of a high grade bond portfolio, and therefore be subject to increased interest rate sensitivity.

The more restrictions imposed on portfolio managers by a client, the greater the probability that the account will underperform its benchmark index. Certain guidelines and restrictions may be required under Department of Labor regulations for ERISA plans. However, unfettering the manager's ability to capitalize on market opportunities can achieve the highest rates of return.

DIVERSIFICATION

After identifying suitable investment objectives and establishing the investment guidelines and restrictions for the portfolio, the most important consideration in credit selection is diversification. The most effective method to reduce both credit and market risk is through broad diversification by issue, industry, type of security, and percentage of aggregate debt held in a specific credit. The time-tested concept of diversification, simple to implement and understand, has proven a real nemesis for certain portfolio managers over various market cycles.

Discipline is critical to achieve diversification. No matter how strong the financial momentum of a company and its future outlook, or how favorable the industry fundamentals appear to be, a portfolio manager must never become overly enthusiastic about a specific company or industry. Weighting industries based on their structural dynamics and outlook is essential in portfolio construction. Overconcentration increases the volatility and credit exposure of a portfolio; hence, the risk profile of the portfolio can be impacted by a lack of diversification.

On the other hand, if a portfolio has too much diversification, it can take on the characteristics of an index fund. In order to achieve proper diversification, approximately 3 to 5 percent of the portfolio's total assets should be invested in each issue expected to achieve the portfolio's primary objective. Industry concentration (if not mandated by investment guidelines and restrictions) should be held to 15 percent for those industries with the strongest technical and fundamental characteristics.

Typically, the portfolio's 10 largest positions should not exceed 35 percent of the portfolio's total assets, and the 5 largest industry weightings should represent less than 50 percent of the total assets. In addition to decreasing the portfolio's volatility, these weightings should help mitigate the effect of unexpected announcements by the issuer or events that affect an industry in general.

There is a tendency by portfolio managers to overweight positions when the portfolio is underperforming in order to make up for their past poor credit selection or flawed investment strategy. This reaction can compound the problem and result in worse performance. Lack of discipline is the primary factor for disappointing performance.

INVESTMENT PHILOSOPHY

Most portfolio managers have developed a certain investment style or philosophy, which is predicated on their own risk taking instincts and past experience. The three most common methodologies employed by portfolio managers are:

Bottom Up

Under a bottom-up philosophy, the portfolio manager constructs a portfolio based on individual credit decisions. The fundamentals of each credit decision stand on their own merits. While economic scenarios, interest rate forecasts, and current market conditions are factored into the investment decision, these variables are of secondary importance. The creditworthiness of the issuer is the primary focus of the investment process. In other words, the decision to purchase, sell, avoid, or hold is based upon the current and expected financial condition of a specific company.

Top Down

Under this methodology, the portfolio manager is primarily influenced by macroeconomics, monetary policy by the Federal Reserve Board, and technical forces in the market (i.e., mutual fund inflows, new issue supply, historical yield spread, historical default rates, and investor sentiment). The top-down approach is not credit specific. Rather, the portfolio manager has an opinion on the direction of the high yield market over the next few months and invests the portfolio accordingly. Specific credit information on a given issuer is still reviewed and analyzed, however the portfolio manager is making more of an asset allocation decision than a credit decision.

Sector Weightings

Under a sector weighting philosophy, the portfolio manager develops an underweighting or balanced strategy within sectors such as: distressed, zero coupon, global high yield, discounted versus premium price issues, new issues versus secondary issues, low coupon versus high coupon, split-rated, staggering maturities, BB-rated versus B-rated issues, and non-U.S. companies. Each one of ten strategies sectors is assigned a specific emphasis or de-emphasis in the portfolio based upon other variables such as volatility, liquidity, and degree of risk, in order to achieve the portfolio's objectives. While all of these variables may be part of the investment selection and decision-making process, under this methodology these sectors have a greater influence in the selection of specific credits than under the macroeconomic approach.

Although most portfolio managers should examine all the above-mentioned sectors in a bottom-up and/or top-down methodology, portfolio managers with the best long-term and consistent records have cultivated a well-defined methodology. They possess the discipline to adhere to one system under all market conditions. Portfolio managers who bounce from one methodology to another under the guise of being opportunistic tend to have mixed performance records and may subject their portfolios to higher risk and volatility, particularly in down or uncertain markets.

TECHNICAL FACTORS

Portfolios should not be created in a vacuum, or predicated only on credit fundamentals. Since performance is derived from analyzing both credit and market risks, compiling and reviewing the technical aspects of the market must be an integral part of portfolio construction.

Portfolio managers typically utilize technical data that has served them well in the past. In the high yield market, the most commonly compiled and reviewed variables are as follows:

New Issue Supply (Forward Calendar)

The new issue calendar can have a potent impact on the direction of the overall high yield market. Too much supply can increase or cause a back-up in yields. On the other hand, a dearth of new issues can result in a decline in yields because mutual funds need to satisfy their current income requirements by investing in a steady stream of new issues in order to maintain their dividends.

Mutual Fund Inflows/Outflows

Wall Street traders are mesmerized by the weekly net inflows into the approximately 300 U.S. high yield mutual funds. Each week AMG Data Services reports mutual fund subscriptions and redemptions, which are more closely followed by Wall Street traders than by high yield money managers. If the AMG data is weak or negative, it provides a rationale for traders to lower their bids on the most liquid and visible issues in the secondary market. (In the new issue market, AMG data appears to have minimal impact on the pricing of new issues.) On the other hand, strong AMG numbers serve as justification to raise offering prices, particularly in credits in which the trader has built an inventory position.

Yield Spreads

Depending on current yield spreads compared to historical averages, the market may appear "rich" or "cheap." Each month, yield spreads over 10-year U.S. Treasuries are calculated and tracked for the various high yield indices. (The 10-year Treasury is utilized as a benchmark to calculate yield because the vast majority of high yield issues have a 10-year final maturity.) Over the past 10 years, the high yield market has exhibited approximately a 400-basis-point yield differential over 10-year U.S. Treasuries. Hence, if current yield spreads show a 350-basis-point yield spread a portfolio manager may based on a historical perspective, deem the market as rich, or overvalued. Conversely, depending on the stage of the economic cycle and the rate of issuer defaults, a 600-basis-point yield spread may be considered cheap, or undervalued.

Default Rates

The yield spread is a function of the probability of default. If default losses are low (i.e., 1.5 percent on a historical basis), a portfolio manager may not require as high a risk premium for an expectation of increased defaults. Likewise, if default rates jump to 5 percent, a portfolio manager may require a yield spread in excess of 700 basis points in order to compensate for the probability of higher default rates.

As a result, portfolio managers are very cognizant of current default percentages of the total high yield debt outstanding, as well as forecasts of what default rates might be 12 months into the future. In this way, portfolio managers have a benchmark on which to evaluate both current holdings as well as to use as a gauge for the optimum price for new issues.

DEGREE OF RISK: PLACEMENT
ON THE CREDIT SPECTRUM

In building a high yield portfolio, money managers need to be aware of the amount of credit risk within the portfolio. Based on the credit rating systems of nationally recognized credit rating services (in particular, Moody's Investors Services and Standard & Poor's), a portfolio may exhibit a BB overall weighting, B, CCC, or somewhere in the middle of these rating categories. However, of paramount importance to the portfolio manager is the weighting of the aggregate of the issues in the portfolio. Some portfolio managers utilize the terminology upper tier for BB-rated issues; middle tier for B-rated issues; and lower tier for CCC-rated issues.

Other portfolio managers have developed their own internal terminology. For example, Shenkman Capital Management, Inc., a New York-based high yield asset manager, has developed its own proprietary ranking system called Quadrant Analysis. Under this proprietary model, the high yield universe is segmented into four distinct quadrants, as follows:

I.   *Solid Credit.* Moderate leverage with strong cash flow.

II.   *Leveraged Credit.* Significant leverage with adequate cash flow.

III. *Highly Leveraged Credit.* High degree of leverage and thin cash flow.

IV.   *Troubled Credit.* Insufficient cash flow; potential turnaround situation.

Exhibit 20–1 illustrates the Quadrant Analysis. Each quadrant has a different risk-return profile. Quadrant I (QI) has credit characteristics similar to BB issues so that credit risk may be relatively low while the returns offer limited upside potential. Since the yields on QI issues exhibit a higher degree of creditworthiness, they tend to trade primarily off of the U.S. Treasury yield curve; hence, QI issues tend to be more market or interest rate sensitive.

Quadrant II (QII) credits exhibit more of the credit characteristics of a middle tier or B-rated security. QII credits are typically appropriate for portfolios with an investment objective of total return. The vast majority of high yield credits fall into this quadrant.

Quadrant III (QIII) represents most of the discounted, pay-in-kind, and zero coupon securities. QIII issues are speculative securities and often are start-up situations with a brief financial history. QIII credits are categorized as lower tier issues or CCC-rated paper. This quadrant should generate substantial returns but also show a higher degree of risk.

E X H I B I T   20–1

Shenkman's Quadrant Analysis

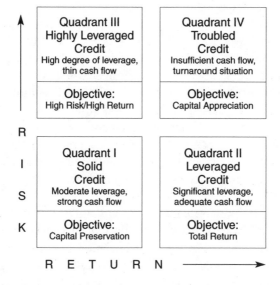

Quadrant IV (QIV) issues are comprised of troubled, distressed, or stressed securities in which the company's ability to service its debts remains questionable. QIV issues are usually designated as D-rated paper and may be in actual or technical violation of its subordinated debt or bank covenants. Distressed securities can be extremely volatile and illiquid with legal considerations sometimes driving prices more than the forecast of financial results. See Chapter 25 for a discussion on Distressed Securities.

In structuring a high yield bond portfolio, money managers should allocate a certain percentage of the portfolio's assets to a given quadrant based upon the investment objectives and degree of risk of the designated portfolio. For example, a portfolio seeking moderate risk may allocate 20 percent to Quadrant I, 70 percent to Quadrant II, 10 percent to Quadrant III and 0 percent to Quadrant IV. In contrast, an aggressive portfolio may allocate 0 percent to Quadrant I, 25 percent to Quadrant II, 50 percent to Quadrant III and 25 percent to Quadrant IV. These allocation weightings should be reviewed quarterly and readjusted based on market conditions, current investment strategy, and actual performance. (While a small percentage change in the quadrant reallocations may not impact performance, a major change in quadrant concentrations could significantly result in under- or overperformance against benchmark indices over a particular holding period.)

VOLATILITY CONSIDERATIONS

Volatility is a multifaceted phenomenon, primarily derived from the following influences: degree of credit quality of the portfolio, percentage of deferred interest securities (e.g., zero coupon, pay-in-kind, step-up coupons), spread over 10-year U.S. Treasuries, size of the issue outstanding, number of dealers making a market in the issue, maturity, priority in the capital structure (i.e., senior vs. subordinated debentures), and expected or perceived changes in interest rates. Volatility can be mitigated by shortening the duration, moving up the capital structure to senior debt, purchasing larger issues with multiple marketmakers, and investing in so-called cushion bonds (securities with high coupons relative to the current interest rates and spreads) trading at or near their call price. Cushion bonds have a certain scarcity value since these bonds tend to be well placed and traded infrequently.

While most portfolio managers are only interested in absolute returns, the more sophisticated portfolio managers look at risk-adjusted returns where the monthly standard deviation is consistently low. The Sharpe Ratio is the primary measurement tool used to determine a portfolio's risk-adjusted returns. The Sharpe Ratio can be used to measure the additional return an investor is compensated for taking on risk. It is calculated as follows:

$$\frac{E\,(rp) - rf}{Op} = \frac{(\text{Portfolio's expected return}) - \text{Risk-free return}}{\text{Portfolio's standard deviation}}$$

Portfolio managers seek a higher Sharpe Ratio because they receive a higher return per unit of risk.

LIQUIDITY REQUIREMENTS

Liquidity is an important driver of performance. Some portfolio managers believe their ability to buy and sell a given high yield security at any time is an important component in their investment strategy. Other portfolio managers believe that credit decisions should be made irrespective of liquidity considerations.

If the ability to liquidate a portfolio or change strategies due to market uncertainties or a client's withdrawal requests are desirable goals, then maximizing liquidity should be the foremost element in the portfolio structure.

A conservative portfolio should have approximately half its assets in highly liquid securities and the other half should be in semiliquid issues. During strong markets, the highly liquid issues tend to demonstrate superior performance. In weaker market environments, the illiquid and/or semi-illiquid situations tend to show better relative price action. This phenomenon is the result of the fact that when portfolio managers need to liquidate positions under adverse market conditions, they are better able to "hit" the dealer bids in order to raise needed cash.

YIELD MANAGEMENT

High yield bond investing requires all portfolio managers to pay close attention to yield considerations. Regardless of a portfolio's investment objectives, the portfolio should generate a certain stream of annual interest income. Hence, yield considerations become of primary significance in the selection of the high yield issues in the portfolio, and the need to maintain that level of interest income throughout the year may dictate which credits get bought and sold. Portfolio managers who become "income hogs" and demonstrate a certain disregard for credit fundamentals, tend to have a higher level of credit default losses and therefore inconsistent performances over time. Current yield considerations should be one of many factors in the credit selection process, and without broad diversification, negative implications may be built into the portfolio. High current yields are generally indicative of higher credit risk although some yields may be artificially high due to the lack of a credit rating, limited Wall Street sponsorship, poor communication by the issuer, or obviously, an issuer's erratic financial record.

PORTFOLIO TURNOVER

Portfolio managers generally have trading styles that minimize or maximize portfolio turnover. Some portfolio managers sell securities at the slightest news event or often act on a broker's recommendation to trade out of one issue and into another under the belief that they are obtaining a better credit as well as a greater yield. These so-called "swaps" can exacerbate portfolio turnover. The well-disciplined manager predicates investment decisions upon a combination of fundamentals and technical factors with a greater emphasis on fundamentals-driven factors.

A company's financial condition must be continuously monitored because it may shift over time due to several factors, including management's capabilities, industry dynamics, and the operating trends of a specific issuer. Some portfolio managers place the predominance of their decision making upon these fundamental factors, while such technical aspects as yield spreads, the size of the new issue calendar, or "swap" opportunities play a minimal role in their decision-making process. In any case, the annual percentage turnover is a vital element in the style of portfolio management.

CONCLUSION

The 10 elements identified in this chapter for constructing a high yield portfolio represent the core concepts of managing high yield assets. However, these 10 elements are not the only ones that are considered by high yield portfolio managers. What is clearly essential is that a well-defined, disciplined, consistent methodology must be utilized to achieve above-average performance results. There are no scientific formulas to constructing a high yield bond portfolio. Rather, these concepts have served professional and experienced portfolio managers well under the vicissitudes of ever-changing and uncertain markets.

CHAPTER 21

Monitoring a High Yield Portfolio

Frank X. Whitley

Mark J. Flanagan

INTRODUCTION

The overall success of a portfolio manager is judged not only on how well a portfolio is initially constructed, but also how well it is monitored. While Chapter 20 discusses the key elements in constructing a high yield portfolio, this chapter outlines the critical elements necessary to adequately monitor a high yield portfolio. Proper monitoring ensures that an optimal portfolio is maintained over the passage of time.

Monitoring a high yield portfolio is a two-step process that must be accomplished at both the overall portfolio level and the individual security level. Moreover, this process must be consistently applied, systematic, and well constructed in order to be as efficient as possible.

MONITORING EXISTING HOLDINGS

In contrast to the performance of investment-grade corporate bonds, which are tied more to changes in the overall level of interest rates, the performance of high yield bonds is more dependent on company-specific developments. Therefore, it is essential that each issue in a high yield portfolio be closely monitored to discern any developing credit trends, both positive and negative.

The data inputs necessary to facilitate this monitoring process may come from several different sources, and the frequency of updating this data may also vary (i.e., daily, weekly, monthly, quarterly). For example, the monitoring of daily price changes may allow early detection of significant price movements, which often are the first manifestation of changing credit fundamentals.

The most important data inputs are derived from a review of the issuer's quarterly financial statements. The most efficient method to gather this data is to develop a standardized form that captures all the relevant data directly from the 10-Q or 10-K. An example of such a form is shown in Exhibit 21–1. This standardized form allows an analyst to compile and analyze relevant data in an efficient manner. One part of the form is for recording specific financial data, such as revenues, cash flow, and capital expenditures. The other part of the form allows the data to be presented in a manner that facilitates quarter-by-quarter comparisons and on a latest twelve-month basis. The form also calls for qualitative comments and a summary of items gleaned from the management discussion and analysis section of the 10-Q or 10-K.

Pertinent items such as revenues, gross profit, selling, general and administrative expenses, and interest expense should be recorded. It may also be important to track balance sheet items such as cash, receivables, inventory, and total debt. Finally, specific items from the cash flow statement should be recorded, such as capital expenditures, changes in working capital, and dividends and taxes paid.

Another analytical tool that is particularly helpful in monitoring an existing high yield portfolio is a one-page historical financial summary of each credit in the portfolio. This historical financial perspective (HFP) provides a clear and concise snapshot of the credit fundamentals for each credit in the portfolio. Exhibit 21–2 shows an example of an HFP. As shown in this figure, this format gives a one-page summary covering a host of credit specific items such as:

Item	Description
A	Quarterly trend in cash flow
B	Credit ratios
C	Historical credit rating
D	Bond data (pricing, yield, spreads, ratings, etc.)
E	Capitalization
F	Debt amortization requirements

As part of the monitoring process, a scoring system should be developed so that easy credit can be scored on a regular basis based on a prescribed qualitative and quantitative criterion. In this way, overall credit improvement or credit deterioration can accurately be monitored.

E X H I B I T   21–1

Shenkman Capital Management, Inc.

Credit Profile Summary Sheet

Company: _____	Credit Rating	
Date of Financials _____	Industry	
	Date Prepared	

	Quarter Ending			____ Months Ending		LTM Ending
		% Chg.			% Chg.	
Sales						
Gross Profit %						
Operating Income						
Deprec. & Amort						
EBITDA						
Capex						
Free Cash Flow						
Cash Interest Expense						
Other Cash Items (Divs, Taxes, etc)						
Net Change in W/C (if applicable)						
Cash Available for Debt Repayment						
Total Interest						
Total Debt						
EBITDA / CIE						
EBITDA-Capex / CIE						
EBITDA / TIE						
EBITDA-Capex / TIE						
Total Debt / EBITDA						
Cash						
Availability						

Amortization 199___		Trend	
Amortization 200___		Event Risk	
Amortization 200___		Covenent Protection	
Amortization 200___		Management	
Amortization 200___		Cyclicality	

EXHIBIT 21-2

Company Contact: _____

(in $ millions)

Historical Performance

		FYE			Quarter Ending	
					Q4	Q4
	12/31/96	12/31/97	12/31/98	12/28/97	12/30/98
Total Revenues	$189.4	$231.3	$220.9	$56.0	$55.9
Gross Profit	28.7	39.3	47.9	14.6	14.6
SG&A	14.4	16.3	15.6	4.4	4.4
EBIT	14.3	23.0	32.3	10.2	10.2
D&A	10.0	11.1	10.0	2.3	2.3
Total EBITDA	24.3	34.1	42.3	12.5	12.5
Capex	11.5	8.4	3.6	0.9	0.9
Free Cash Flow	12.8	25.7	38.7	11.6	11.6
Cash Interest Expense PF	24.0	24.0	24.0	4.5	4.5
CADR	−11.2	1.7	14.7	7.1	7.1
Total Interest Expense	24.0	24.0	24.0	4.5	4.5
Total Debt PF	121.0	121.0	121.0		121.0
Margin Analysis					
Gross Margin	84.8%	83.0%	78.3%	26.1%	26.1%
EBITDA Margin	12.8%	14.7%	19.1%	22.3%	22.4%
SG&A / Revenues	7.6%	7.0%	7.1%	7.9%	7.9%
Percent Change					
Revenue		22.1%	−4.5%		−0.2%
EBITDA		40.3%	24.0%		0.0%
Ratio Analysis					
TD/EBITDA	5.0	3.5	2.9		
EBITDA/CIE	1.0	1.4	1.8	2.8	2.8
FCF/CIE	0.5	1.1	1.6	2.6	2.6

Revenue Detail
Credit Rating OPCO
Credit Rating Holding Co.

| **F** |
| Debt Amortization |
| Requirements |

Capital Structure	**30-Sep-98**		**Amortization**	
			1997	$0.0
Revolver ($50)	$0.0		1998	$0.0
10.5% Sr Notes	$110.0		1999	$0.0
12.5% Sr Debentures	$46.0		2000	$0.0
			2001	$0.0
Total Debt	$156.0		**Liquidity**	
Common Shares Outstanding	n/a		Cash	$7.9
Market Price	n/a		Availability	$65.0
Market Capitalization	n/a			
Total Enterprise Value	n/a		**E**	
			Capitalization	

Date Updated: _____

A
Quarterly Trend in Cash Flow

		Quarter Ending				LTM
Q1 **03/30/97**	**Q1** **03/30/98**	**Q2** **06/30/97**	**Q2** **06/30/98**	**Q3** **09/30/97**	**Q3** **09/30/98**	**09/30/98**
$60.2	$62.2	$56.1	$61.1	$48.7	$57.0	$236.2
12.3	13.6	11.1	14.0	9.9	13.2	55.4
3.9	3.9	3.9	3.9	3.4	4.1	16.3
8.4	9.7	7.2	10.1	6.5	9.1	39.1
3.0	2.7	2.8	2.0	1.9	2.2	9.2
11.4	12.4	10.0	12.1	8.4	11.3	48.3
1.1	1.7	0.9	1.8	0.7	2.4	6.8
10.3	10.7	9.1	10.3	7.7	8.9	41.5
4.5	4.5	4.5	4.5	4.5	4.5	18.0
5.8	6.2	4.6	5.8	3.2	4.4	23.5
4.5	4.5	4.5	4.5	4.5	4.5	18.0
	121.0		121.0		156.0	156.0
20.4%	21.9%	19.8%	22.9%	20.3%	23.2%	23.5%
18.9%	19.9%	17.8%	19.8%	17.2%	19.8%	20.4%
6.5%	6.3%	7.0%	6.4%	7.0%	7.2%	6.9%
	3.3%		8.9%		17.0%	**B** **Credit Ratios**
	8.8%		21.0%		34.5%	
						3.2
2.5	2.8	2.2	2.7	1.9	2.5	2.7
2.3	2.4	2.0	2.3	1.7	2.0	2.3
			90.00		*90.00*	
D **Bond Data**			*83.00*		*84.00*	

High Yield Issue			**High Yield Issue**	
Coupon	10.500%	**C** **Historical Credit Rating**	Coupon	12.500%
Maturity	15-Apr-06		Maturity	15-Jul-07
Size	$110.0		Size	$46.0
Type	Sr Notes		Type	Sr Debs
Ratings	B2/B		Ratings	NR/NR
Price	$109.00		Price	$108.00
Current Yield	9.63%		Current Yield	11.57%
YTW	7.56%		YTW	10.86%
STW	176		STW	504
YTW Term	3.57		YTW Term	5.83
YTM	8.84%		YTM	11.05%
Issue Spread	399		Issue Spread	n/a

Primary Analyst: _____

While in-depth analysis of a company's financial data is crucial, it is important not to rely solely on number crunching in making a final investment decision. Talking to or meeting with a company's management on a regular basis should be an essential part of the investment process. A company's lack of financial ratios can preclude it from being considered an appropriate investment. However, just because a company's financial statistics meet some minimal threshold should not guarantee it a spot in your portfolio. Before making the initial investment, an analyst should discuss with management how the company accomplished its historical results, as well as its prospects for the future. There are clearly some basic questions that should be asked of management in order to get a full picture of the company.

MONITORING ALTERNATIVE INVESTMENTS

In addition to continually monitoring existing holdings within a high yield portfolio, it is important to develop a systematic methodology to allow for the examination of alternative investments that, on a relative basis, may be more attractive than certain existing holdings.

One effective way to monitor alternative investments is to develop an internally maintained database. Exhibit 21–3 provides a sample of the relevant data that a model database should contain. The data contained in the database should be standardized so that the analyst can make the appropriate comparisons between two or more companies. In addition, having a standardized database should enable each analyst within the organization to add every credit that has been reviewed during the course of the year. In this way, the database will be continually updated and can be screened periodically for relative value among virtually every high yield credit reviewed by the firm's analytical staff. Exhibit 21–4 provides a sample screen of several high yield gaming companies—ranked by interest coverage, leverage ratio, and spread premium to an appropriate U.S.Treasury equivalent.

MONITORING THE OVERALL PORTFOLIO

In addition to monitoring each particular security in a portfolio (for default risk), it is equally as important to monitor the overall portfolio's concentration in a particular industry, type of security, or issuer. If a portfolio is too heavily weighted in one of these areas, it may be exposed to unintended risk or volatility. Portfolio managers that adhere to a bottom-up, security-by-security approach to constructing a portfolio may be susceptible to unintended portfolio concentration.

EXHIBIT 21–3

Issuer	New Co.	
Coupon	10.250%	
Maturity	15-May-2003	
Size	$150.0	
Type	Sr Nts	Bond Data
Rating–Moody	B1	
Rating–S&P	B	
Price	**$108.50**	
Primary Analyst	MF	
Secondary Analyst	SS	
YTM	8.20%	
YTW	**7.83%**	
YTW Spread	**224**	Yield and Spreads
YTW Term	4.17	
YTW Treas Equiv.	5.59%	
Current Yield	9.45%	
Industry	Oil & Gas	
Quadrant	1	
LTM Stats.		
	31-Dec-97	
Revenues	$263.6	
EBITDA	$106.7	
Capex	$84.5	
Free Cash Flow (FCF)	**$22.2**	
Cash Interest	$21.2	Financial Data
Cash Avail. for		
Debt Repay (CADR)	**$1.0**	
Total Debt	$203.8	
Total Interest Exp.	$21.2	
Amortization		
1998	$0.0	
1999	$0.0	
2000	$0.0	
2001	$0.0	
2002	$0.0	
Ratios		
TD / EBITDA	**1.9**	
Net Debt / EBITDA	1.6	
EBITDA / CIE	**5.0**	Financial Data
FCF / CIE	**1.0**	
EBITDA / TIE	5.0	
FCF / TIE	1.0	
Liquidity		
Cash	$28.1	
Availability	$35.0	Corporate Liquidity
Latest Period Trend		
Revenue	$74.2	
% Change	59.0%	
EBITDA	$31.8	Operating Trend
% Change	**171.8%**	
Latest 10Q/K on file	**31-Dec-97**	

Source: Reprinted with the permission of Shenkman Capital Management, Inc.

E X H I B I T   21–4

High Yield Comparables–Gaming

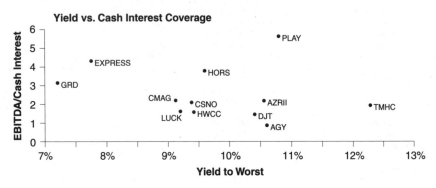

Yield vs. Cash Interest Coverage

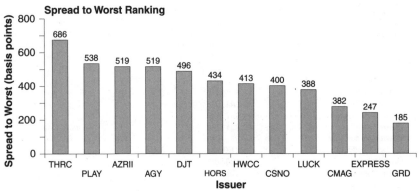

Spread to Worst Ranking

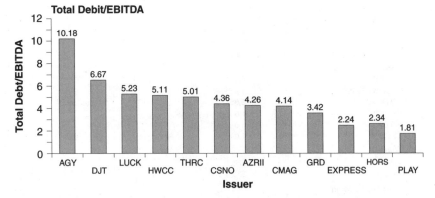

Total Debt/EBITDA

Issuer or Company Concentration

It is only natural for portfolio managers to weight more heavily those investments in which they have the most confidence. However, despite strong convictions, it is prudent and necessary to impose certain restrictions in an attempt to limit the volatility and maintain the integrity of a portfolio. The rationale for these restrictions is simple: the decline of one or two investments would not materially affect the overall performance of the entire portfolio. Specific policies should be established about what an average and maximum portfolio position size should be. In addition, minimum position sizes should be established in order to prevent the portfolio from being overdiversified, in which case a portfolio's performance might simply mimic an index return.

Industry Concentration

A high yield portfolio should be monitored on a regular basis to make sure that it is adequately diversified among various industries. For example, one parameter can be that the portfolio's maximum exposure to any industry cannot exceed 40 percent of the portfolio's total holdings. The actual target weightings may vary, but it is crucial that industry concentration be monitored on a regular basis and that any exceptions be promptly addressed.

When setting the portfolio's industry concentration, portfolio managers should consider the particular industry's historical volatility. For example, in 1997 approximately one-third of all new high yield issues were in the telecommunications and media sector. This sector had most of the highest yielding bonds in the high yield universe and was one of the most volatile industries. Thus, if a portfolio manager maintained the same percentage limitation in each industry, it may have significantly increased the riskiness or volatility of the portfolio even if it was diversified by issuers.

Concentration by Security Type

In response to the investment objectives and constraints of a particular portfolio, portfolio managers may preset maximum target allocations for specific types of securities such as zero coupon issues, preferred stocks, privately-placed securities, and securities with specific ratings. To the extent such limits are set, security type concentrations should be monitored on a regular basis.

Cyclical versus Noncyclical Exposure

Even if a portfolio is diversified by industry, issuer, and security type, there can be significant concentration risk with respect to companies that have a strong operating relationship to the overall levels of GDP growth (i.e., cyclical credits). It is therefore important to monitor a portfolio's exposure to cyclical and noncyclical industries. While cyclical credits can exhibit strong operating performance during a strong economy, they tend to underperform when there is concern over a slowing economy. In addition, cyclical credits have a higher risk of default in a recessionary economic environment. Consequently, the mix of cyclical versus noncyclical credits in a portfolio is an important component in determining its potential volatility and credit risk.

The mix between cyclical and noncyclical credits should be monitored on a regular basis and then integrated with an overall view of the U.S. economy.

MONITORING INVESTOR OBJECTIVES AND CONSTRAINTS

As part of setting up an initial investment program, it is imperative that careful consideration be given to the investment objectives and constraints. Equally as important is the need to consistently monitor each portfolio to ensure that such objectives and constraints are being adhered to. This monitoring process should be systematic and consistently applied to each portfolio. Perhaps the best way to accomplish this is to develop a matrix summarizing each investor's objectives and constraints and then systematically reviewing each portfolio on a monthly basis, confirming that all of the portfolio's objectives and constraints are being satisfied. Examples of such constraints would include maximum industry exposures, maximum security type holdings (i.e., zero coupons, preferreds, Rule 144a's), and maximum credit exposures. Investment objectives are generally goal specific and defined in terms of return requirements and risk tolerance. Although these objectives are subjective in nature, they should be monitored to ensure that the level of risk incurred is commensurate with the investor's tolerance for risk. For example, an endowment fund may be more focused on current income and preservation of capital. As such, a portfolio for this type of investor should avoid zero coupon type securities and gravitate towards higher quality credits (i.e., Ba/BB rated).

SUMMARY

The successful portfolio management of a high yield portfolio requires a systematic and continuous monitoring process. This process should include monitoring of the overall portfolio, each security in the portfolio, and the portfolio's objectives and constraints. The ultimate success of a high yield portfolio is not predicated solely on its initial construction. In fact, the success or failure of a particular portfolio is usually much more a function of the manager's ability to appropriately monitor and adjust the portfolio as conditions change.

CHAPTER 22

Modeling High Yield Bond Portfolios with Correlated Interest Rate and Credit Risk

Theodore M. Barnhill, Jr.

William F. Maxwell

INTRODUCTION

The principal focus of portfolio management is assessing and managing return and risk. Chapter 17 ("High Yield as an Asset Class") provides a historical perspective on the risk and reward of owning a high yield portfolio. Chapter 20 ("Managing a High Yield Portfolio") discusses the construction of a high yield portfolio. This chapter focuses on modeling the return and risk characteristics of a high yield portfolio.

The traditional measurement of risk, standard deviation, underestimates the risk of owning a high yield portfolio (see Duffie and Pan 1995). Market risk models (e.g., interest rate, exchange rate, equity price, and commodity price risk) and credit risk models have been developed to provide improved risk measurement information regarding the frequency with which portfolio values fall below certain levels. However, to date, market and credit risk have been handled as two separate analyses (for example, reference RiskMetrics™ and CreditMetrics™). To fully reflect the risk of owning a high yield portfolio, a methodology to integrate the market and credit risk into one overall risk assessment is needed. This chapter discusses and reports the results of a Monte Carlo simulation methodology where interest rate and credit risk are modeled as correlated random processes allowing the construction of a more complete risk profile of possible future high yield portfolio values.

We will analyze a number of different sample portfolios. Standard risk measures are reported for the different risk assessment approaches (i.e., market risk, credit risk, and integrated market and credit risk). Standard deviation is reported, but since returns are negatively skewed, it will serve only as a general benchmark. Commonly utilized risk measures reported include the portfolio value at 95 percent and 99 percent confidence levels. The analysis provides insights into the number of bonds necessary to diversify a high yield portfolio and the benefits of diversification across industries. We also discuss the information gains from modeling market and credit risk as a correlated process.

SIMULATION METHODOLOGY

The methodology utilized for jointly modeling interest rate and credit risk is the one developed by Barnhill (1998) and incorporated in the Value-Calc™ financial software and is described more fully in Chapters 8 and 13 of this book. In summary, the methodology is as follows.

1. The future financial environment is modeled as a set of correlated interest rate term structures and equity indices. For the current study, eight term structures and up to twenty-four equity indices are simulated. The term structures are modeled using the Hull and White (1994) extended Vasicek model where the stochastic variable is the instantaneous spot interest rate for each term structure.

2. The return on equity for each firm included in the portfolio is estimated using the simulated return on an appropriate equity index, the risk-free interest rate, an assumed beta coefficient for the firm relative to the equity index, and a firm-specific random error term.

3. The firm's market value of equity is calculated using its simulated return on equity and an assumption regarding its initial market value of equity.

4. The firm's simulated debt ratio (i.e., Total liabilities / Total liabilities + Market value of equity) is calculated using its simulated market value of equity and assumed target level of total liabilities.

5. Simulated debt-to-value ratios are mapped into credit ratings. This approach is similar in some regards to that used in Credit-

Metrics™ where simulated asset values for a firm are mapped into credit ratings.

6. Each bond in the portfolio is revalued relative to the appropriate simulated term structure given its simulated credit rating.

7. In the case of default, the recovery rate on the bond is simulated as a truncated normal distribution with a mean of 34 percent, standard deviation of 25 percent, maximum value of 100 percent, and minimum value of zero (Altman and Kishore 1996).[1]

8. The simulation is run ten thousand times and the distribution of simulated portfolio values is analyzed.

STUDY ASSUMPTIONS AND LIMITATIONS

We utilized the following simplifying assumptions in the study.

1. The correlations between all spot interest rates were assumed to be 0.99.

2. The initial term structures were estimated as of December 31, 1996.

3. The stochastic spot interest rate for all term structures were assumed to have the same volatility (1.4 percent) and mean reversion rate (0.004). The mean reversion rate and volatility utilized in this study were those implied by known LIBOR cap prices on December 31, 1996. Assumptions 1 and 3 were made to ensure that the simulated spot interest rates for lower-rated bonds were always higher than the spot interest rates for higher-rated bonds. These assumptions also had the effect of constraining the simulated spreads between the various interest rates to the approximate levels implied by the forward rates calculated from the initial term structures. Using approximately constant interest rate spreads implies that the volatility of high yield bond prices resulting from interest rate spread changes will not be captured in the current analysis.

---

1. If detailed data on recovery rate distributions is available, other modeling approaches may be more appropriate. For example, credit metrics suggests that recovery rates be modeled as a Beta distribution.

4. The expected return and dividend yield on all equity indices were assumed to be 12 percent and 3 percent respectively. The 12 percent expected return is consistent with a medium term risk-free interest rate of 6.2 percent and a historical average equity risk premium of 5.8 percent. The 3 percent dividend yield is approximately equal to the long-term value for the S&P 500.

5. The correlations between all spot interest rates and all equity indices were assumed to be −0.33. This value was chosen as being representative of the correlations between changes in the various spot interest rates and the S&P 500 index, which as shown in Chapter 13 ("Valuing Bonds and Options on Bonds Having Correlated Interest Rate and Credit Risk"), was between −0.18 to −0.44. This is consistent with the assumption that all spot interest rates are perfectly correlated. However, the correlations between the changes in the eight spot interest rates and the return on the twenty-four equity indices actually vary between approximately 0 and −0.50.

6. The correlations between the returns on all equity indices were assumed to be 0.30. This is a commonly used average correlation; however, historical correlations between the twenty-four equity indices range from about −0.09 to 0.77.

7. All bonds included in the test portfolios were assumed to have a ten year maturity, be noncallable, have an annual coupon rate of 10.32 percent, and initially have a 0.75 debt ratio and a B rating.

8. The methodology used to assign bond ratings based on simulated debt ratios is given in Exhibit 22–1. This relationship was estimated from data on manufacturing firms over the 1992 to 1996 period. The 0.85 debt ratio, at which a bond was assumed to default, was chosen so that the simulated default probabilities for a B-rated bond closely match the historical default rates. A more refined approach would be to adjust the relationship between simulated debt ratios and assumed bond ratings to reflect firm- and industry-specific information.

9. The impact of diversification on portfolio risk levels was studied by first varying the assumed number of bonds in the portfolio to between 1 and 24. Then for each of these portfolios, it was either assumed that all of the bonds came from different firms in the same industry or from different firms in different industries.

E X H I B I T 22-1

Relationship Used to Map Simulated Debt Ratios into Bond Ratings

Simulated Debt Ratio	Assigned Bond Rating
Less 0.1875	Aaa
.1875 to .3125	Aa
.3125 to .4375	A
.4375 to .5625	Baa
.5625 to .6875	Ba
.6875 to .8125	B
.8125 to .85	Caa
Over .85	Default

E X H I B I T 22-2

Simulated One-Year Time Step Distribution of Values of a Portfolio of Ten-Year Noncallable B-Rated Bonds Assuming No Credit Risk (per $100,000 of initial value)

Mean	Standard Dev.	Maximum	Minimum	99% Confidence Level	95% Confidence Level
$107,772	$7,865	$139,448	$84,611	$91,150	$95,547

INTEREST RATE RISK SIMULATION RESULTS

Exhibit 22–2 gives the distribution of simulated values for a portfolio of ten-year maturity B-rated bonds at a one-year time step. In this interest rate risk analysis all bonds are assumed to always retain a B-rating, but the level of interest rates is modeled stochastically using the Hull and White (1994) extended Vasicek model.

The assumed annual coupon payment ($10,320) was set so the bond initially traded at par (i.e., $100,000). The mean simulated portfolio value ($107,772) is lower than the par value of the bond plus the coupon payment. This indicates that the simulated interest rate term structures on average rose over the one year simulation period, producing a decline in the market value of the bond. This result is consistent with the initial upward sloping term structure of interest rates (and forward rates) on December 31, 1996. The standard deviation of the portfolio value of $7,865 is consistent with the assumed spot interest rate volatility of 0.014. The maximum and minimum simulated values of the portfolio were $139,448 and $84,611 respectively. For value-at-risk analysis, the simulated portfolio value fell below $91,150 one percent of the time and below $95,547 five percent of the time.

BOND RATING TRANSITION PROBABILITIES

To perform a credit risk analysis it is necessary to assess the probability of a bond migrating between various credit rating categories. The methodologies for assessing rating change probabilities either rely on historical transitions compiled by third party rating agencies (e.g., see Chapter 7—Moody's historical numbers), internally generated historical rating transition probabilities, or simulated transition probabilities. This chapter utilizes the methodology found in ValueCalc™ and discussed in Chapter 8 ("Modeling Bond Rating Changes for Credit Risk Estimation") to simulate credit migration for individual bonds in the portfolio. As a basis for comparison, we also provide Moody's one-year historical probabilities adjusted for withdrawn ratings.

Exhibit 22–3 compares Moody's one-year historical transition probabilities for a B-rated bond to results utilizing the methodology described under two different sets of equity volatility assumptions. The simulated rating transition probabilities given in the third column are based on estimates over the 1992 to 1996 period for the S&P 500 return volatility of 14 percent, mean beta for B-rated firms relative to the S&P 500 of 1.26, and mean firm-specific volatility of equity return of 15 percent for B-rated firms. This will be referred to as the average volatility case. The simulated rating transition probabilities given in the fourth column are based on a long-term estimate for the S&P 500 return volatility of 20 percent, an upper quartile estimate of the beta for B-rated firms relative to the S&P 500 of 1.5, and an upper quartile estimate for firm-specific volatility of equity return of 17 percent for B-rated firms. This will be referred to as the high volatility case.

Comparison of the data in Exhibit 22–3 suggests that the simulation model calibrated for the average volatility case does a very good job of modeling credit migration probabilities except that it significantly underestimates historical average bond defaults. On the other hand, the simulation model calibrated for the high volatility case does a much better job of

E X H I B I T   22-3

Comparison of Simulated Transition Probabilities
and Moody's One-Year Historical Transition
Probabilities for B-Rated Bonds

Bond Rating In One Year	Moody's Historical Transition Probabilities	Simulated Transition Probabilities Assuming: S&P 500 Vol. = .14 Firm Beta = 1.26 Firm Specific Vol. = .15	Simulated Transition Probabilities Assuming: S&P 500 Vol. = .2 Firm Beta = 1.5 Firm Specific Vol. = .17
Aaa	0.0	0.0	0.0
Aa	0.0	0.0	0.0
A	0.2	0.0	0.0
Baa	0.7	0.0	0.6
Ba	6.5	9.0	17.9
B	85.3	85.6	67.1
Caa	3.4	5.2	10.0
Default	3.9	0.2	4.4

matching historical default probabilities. Otherwise, it produces a somewhat broader dispersion of bond ratings than have been observed historically. Since a principal purpose of this chapter is to study the risk characteristics of high yield bond portfolios including default risk, the high volatility case will be the focus of attention in the subsequent analysis. However, the risk characteristics of well-diversified portfolios simulated under both the high and average volatility cases will also be analyzed.

CORRELATED INTEREST RATE AND CREDIT RISK SIMULATION WITH INDUSTRY CONCENTRATION AND HIGH EQUITY VOLATILITY

Exhibit 22–4 gives data on the distribution of simulated portfolio values under conditions of correlated interest rate and credit risk at a one-year time step for portfolios containing various numbers of bonds. Portfolios are assumed to be ten-year maturity, noncallable, B-rated bonds from firms that operate in the same industry (i.e., their simulated return on equity is systematically related to the same equity index). High equity volatility assumptions are used in all portfolios .

As would be expected, the mean portfolio values in Exhibit 22–4 are not affected by the number of bonds in the portfolio. These mean values, reflecting correlated interest rate and credit risk, are approximately $2,000 less than that reported in Exhibit 22–2 reflecting only interest rate risk. This difference reflects average default losses. However, the standard deviation of the portfolio value declines as the number of bonds increases. Between ten and fifteen bonds the standard deviation levels off at under $16,000. This standard deviation is approximately twice that reported in Exhibit 22–2, which reflected interest rate risk only. The results also suggest the downside risk on portfolios of high yield securities concentrated in one industry is very large. Occasionally the entire portfolio value is lost when the portfolio consists of only one or a few securities. Even with fifteen securities in a portfolio, 1 percent of the time 50 percent of the portfolio value is lost. This implies a high correlation in defaults among the securities in the portfolio.

CORRELATED INTEREST RATE AND CREDIT RISK SIMULATION WITH INDUSTRY DIVERSIFICATION AND HIGH EQUITY VOLATILITY

Data on the distribution of simulated portfolio values under conditions of correlated interest rate and credit risk at a one-year time step for portfolios containing various numbers of bonds is reported in Exhibit 22–5. The high equity volatility assumptions are utilized in all portfolios. We also assume all of the bonds are from firms that operate in different industries (i.e., their simulated return on equity is systematically related to different equity indices).

Again, as would be expected, the mean portfolio values in Exhibit 22–5 are not affected by the number of bonds in the portfolio. These mean values, reflecting correlated interest rate and credit risk, are approximately $2,000 less than those reported in Exhibit 22–2 for the bonds without credit risk and are essentially identical to those for the one-industry portfolios reported in Exhibit 22–4. Again, the standard deviation of the portfolio value declines as the number of bonds increases. Between ten and fifteen bonds the standard deviation levels off at under $13,000. This standard deviation is approximately $3,000 less than that for the one-industry portfolios but still about $5,000 greater than that reported in Exhibit 22–2, which reflects interest rate risk only. We attribute this greater volatility to

E X H I B I T   22–4

Simulated Portfolio Values with Correlated Interest Rate and Credit Risk, High Equity Volatility, and Industry Concentration (per $100,000 of initial value)

Number of Bonds in Portfolio	Mean	Standard Deviation	Maximum	Minimum	99% Confidence Level	95% Confidence Level
1	$105,754	$20,864	$167,820	$ 0	$13,921	$78,606
2	105,686	18,940	156,952	0	33,984	66,820
5	106,053	16,196	166,433	16,320	46,643	76,076
7	105,886	16,109	164,182	20,379	48,546	76,205
10	105,867	15,695	159,652	21,685	50,710	76,851
12	105,820	15,904	161,309	21,659	48,036	74,943
15	106,135	15,750	166,284	24,588	52,024	88,480

E X H I B I T   22–5

Simulated Portfolio Values with Correlated Interest Rate and Credit Risk, High Equity Volatility, and Industry Diversification (per $100,000 of initial value)

Number of Bonds in Portfolio	Mean	Standard Deviation	Maximum	Minimum	99% Confidence Level	95% Confidence Level
1	$105,934	$20,600	$163,908	$ 0	$14,094	$80,303
2	106,078	15,702	155,297	0	52,456	72,920
5	106,109	13,312	159,587	39,076	68,231	82,631
7	105,847	13,035	155,128	38,301	70,431	83,461
10	105,863	12,686	159,723	47,996	73,023	84,145
12	105,855	12,359	167,241	24,921	74,225	84,929
15	105,937	12,641	153,605	53,422	75,235	84,775

correlated credit risk that is modeled through the correlated returns on equity indices and interest rate changes.

The downside risk on portfolios of securities diversified across industries is considerably less than that for portfolios concentrated in a particular industry. With fifteen securities in a diversified portfolio, the portfolio minimum value is approximately twice that for portfolios concentrated in a particular industry. Also the 99 percent confidence level is approximately 50 percent higher. This implies a considerably lower correlation in defaults among the securities in the portfolio and demonstrates the importance of industry diversification. Clearly, financial institution capital adequacy standards should reflect the level of industry concentration in their loan portfolio.

CORRELATED INTEREST RATE AND CREDIT RISK SIMULATION WITH INDUSTRY DIVERSIFICATION AND AVERAGE EQUITY VOLATILITY

To assess the influence of the equity volatility parameters on study results, a portfolio of fifteen initially B-rated bonds was simulated over a one-year time step using the average volatility case assumptions. The results are found in Exhibit 22–6. It is also assumed that all of the bonds are from firms that operate in different industries (i.e., their simulated return on equity is systematically related to different equity indices).

The mean value of the portfolio in Exhibit 22–6 with correlated interest rate and credit risk is essentially the same as that reported in the exhibit for the bond without credit risk and is approximately $2,000 higher than the mean values reported for the high volatility case. This reflects the fact that with the lower equity volatility assumptions there is a very low default rate. The standard deviation of the average volatility portfolio is $9,269 or about $1,500 greater than that for the bond facing only interest rate risk. This reflects both the fact that the bonds in the portfolio move out of the B-rating category 14 percent of the time and that bond upgrades (downgrades) are more likely in declining (increasing) interest rate environments.

COMPARISON OF DIFFERENT RISK ASSESSMENT METHODOLOGIES AND THE SIGNIFICANCE OF EQUITY VOLATILITY ASSUMPTIONS

For comparison, a summary of the results of the different methodologies and volatilities is found in Exhibit 22–7. A number of conclusions can be drawn. An interest rate risk analysis, as compared to an integrated risk analysis, dramatically underestimates risk as measured by standard

EXHIBIT 22–6

Simulated Portfolio Values with Correlated Interest Rate and Credit Risk, Average Equity Volatility, and Industry Diversification (per $100,000 of initial value)

Number of Bonds in Portfolio	Mean	Standard Deviation	Maximum	Minimum	99% Confidence Level	95% Confidence Level
15	$107,954	$9,269	$144,418	$73,134	$87,137	$93,568

EXHIBIT 22–7

Comparison of Results Utilizing Different Risk Measures and Assumptions (per $100,000 of initial value)

Risk Analysis	Mean	Standard Deviation	Maximum	Minimum	99% Confidence Level	95% Confidence Level
Interest Rate Risk Analysis	$107,772	$7,865	$139,448	$84,611	$91,150	$95,547
Integrated Risk Analysis						
One Industry, 15 Bonds, and High Volatility	106,135	15,750	166,284	24,588	52,024	88,480
15 Industries and Average Volatility	107,954	9,269	144,418	73,134	87,137	93,568
15 Industries and High Volatility	105,937	12,641	153,605	53,422	75,235	84,775

deviation or confidence level. For a high yield bond portfolio to be well diversified, it must hold bonds from a cross section of industries as well as having at least ten bonds. Finally, the results highlight the significant impact of equity return volatility on the risk profile of a high yield bond portfolio.

SUMMARY

Methodologies are needed to assess correlated interest rate and credit risk in various types of portfolios. Such risk analysis is important for portfolio management, for setting capital adequacy standards at financial institutions, and for other purposes. This chapter reports the results of Monte Carlo simulations of high yield portfolios under conditions of correlated interest rate and credit risk. It has been found that ten to fifteen bonds are adequate to minimize portfolio risk levels. It has also been found that diversifying across industries is very effective in reducing portfolio risk. The equity volatility assumptions including the volatility of the return on market indices, as well as the beta coefficient of the firm, and the firm-specific equity volatility are shown to significantly affect the distribution of simulated bond rating changes and defaults. As the dispersion of possible bond rating changes increases, the importance of capturing correlated interest rate and credit risk also increases.

REFERENCES

Altman, E. and A. Kishore (1996). "Almost Everything You Wanted to Know about Recoveries on Defaulted Bonds." *Financial Analysts Journal* 52, no. 6, pp. 57–64.

Barnhill, T. (1998). "Portfolio Risk Analysis Utilizing Correlated Interest Rate and Credit Risk Simulations." Working paper, The George Washington University.

Duffie, D. and J. Pan (1995). "An Overview of Value at Risk," *Journal of Derivatives* 4, no. 3, pp. 7–49.

Gupton, G.; C. Finger; and M. Bhatia (1997). *CreditMetrics™—Technical Document.* 1st Edition. New York: J. P. Morgan & Co.

Hull, J. and A. White (1994). "Numerical Procedures for Implementing Term Structure Models I: Single-Factor Models." *Journal of Derivatives.* Fall, pp. 7–16.

Longerstaey, J. and P. Zangari (1996). *RiskMetrics™—Technical Document.* New York: Morgan Guaranty Trust Co.

PART SIX

Investing In Distressed Securities

CHAPTER 23

Do Seniority Provisions Protect Bondholders' Investments?

Lenders need not fear expropriation.

Edward I. Altman

Allan C. Eberhart

INTRODUCTION

A number of recent studies document that violations of the absolute priority rule (APR) are commonplace and can be of large magnitude. The APR states that senior creditors should be fully compensated before junior creditors receive a payoff, and that junior creditors should be paid in full before shareholders receive any portion of the bankrupt firm's value.

Studies finding that the rule is violated about 75 percent of the time include Betker (1992b), Eberhart, Moore, and Roenfeldt (1990), Eberhart and Sweeney (1992), Fabozzi et al. (1993), Franks and Torous (1989), Hotchkiss (1993), LoPucki and Whitford (1990), Weiss (1990), and White (1989). All these studies note that the lowest-priority claimants—that is, the shareholders—benefit from APR violations.[1]

Edward I. Altman is the Max L. Heine professor of finance at the Stern School of Business of New York University in New York (NY 10012).

Allan C. Eberhart is a visiting assistant professor of finance at the Stern School, and assistant professor of finance at the School of Business at Georgetown University in Washington (DC 20057).

1. The term *benefit* perhaps should be placed in quotation marks because it implies a wealth transfer. As we discuss in this article, however, the capital markets appear to anticipate APR violations as well as other influences on the bankruptcy emergence payoffs to securityholders. Eberhart and Senbet (1993) show that anticipated APR violations can be beneficial in reducing the risk incentive for financially distressed firms.

415

Estimates of the percentage of firm value that shareholders receive in violation of the rule range from 2.4 percent (Betker 1992b) to 7.6 percent (Eberhart, Moore, and Roenfeldt 1990). Junior creditors, though, can be helped or harmed by APR violations.[2]

Departures from the APR have a potentially pernicious effect on the ability of firms to borrow money. If seniority provisions in bond contracts are routinely violated by the bankruptcy court, their value my be negligible. Jensen (1991) forcefully argues that APR violations are harmful. He posits that senior creditors may respond to deviations from the APR by refusing to lend to risky firms for fear of expropriation.

One response to Jensen's argument is that as long as lenders anticipate the possibility (and the size) of a departure from the APR, they should not be averse to lending to high-risk firms because they will be compensated with a lower price/higher yield. In other words, in an efficient market investors are protected against expropriation.

Overall, the empirical evidence supports the efficient market hypothesis at the time firms default or file for Chapter 11. This implies that investors who purchase a firm's bond at this time pay an appropriate (i.e., efficient) price. It does not imply (although it is by no means inconsistent) that at the time the bonds are issued, the market prices these bonds efficiently.

The market for distressed securities is dominated by sophisticated institutional investors called "vultures" who specialize in these securities; Altman (1991) estimates that there are at least sixty institutional investors and many broker/dealers who specialize in distressed and defaulted securities. The proportion of informed investors who purchase bonds at issuance is likely to be smaller.

To the extent this is true, there is a greater chance that, for example, senior bond prices at issuance do not reflect the potential dilution of seniority provisions in states of default. That is, investors may be overpaying for seniority provisions that they believe will offer more protection against the severity of default (i.e., the magnitude of the loss in states of default) than an informed investor would expect.[3]

---

2. For example, Eberhart and Sweeney (1993) show that the Wickes' 9 percent convertible subordinated debenture holders received over $449.93 less per $1,000 face value bond than they would have received if the APR had been followed. On the other hand, they also note that the Baldwin United 10 percent subordinated debenture holders collected over $576 more per $1,000 face value bond than they were entitled to under the APR.

3. For some more recent evidence on the probability and/or severity of default, see Altman (1989, 1992), Altman and Kao (1991), Fons, Carty, and Girault (1993), and Lucas and Lonski (1991, 1992).

This study investigates the efficiency of the market for bonds of firms that default and subsequently file for Chapter 11. To the best of our knowledge, our sample of 91 firms with 232 bonds that filed for and emerged from Chapter 11 between 1980 and 1992 is larger and more recent than for any other sample in this area.

We conduct two types of tests with this sample. First, we test the efficiency of these bonds as of the default date. Unlike previous researchers, we test for efficiency within each priority category. For the statistically most reliable sample, the results are generally supportive of efficiency.

Our second, and more important, test focuses on the efficiency of bond prices at issuance. Because we have, ex post, chosen those bonds that went into bankruptcy, we cannot conduct traditional efficiency tests. Rather we attempt to answer the question: Do seniority provisions protect bondholders' investments? In other words, do investors receive compensation for the seniority provisions they pay a premium for at issuance? If not, this suggests that, for example, senior bonds are overpriced at issuance.

We answer this question by documenting the losses that bankrupt firms' bondholders experience over the entire life of the bond. We find that, on average, higher seniority is associated with higher payoffs at emergence, providing evidence (albeit indirect) that the bonds are efficiently priced at issuance.

LITERATURE REVIEW

Studies of the market for distressed securities by Warner (1977), Betker (1992a), and Eberhart and Sweeney (1992) report results that, overall, are supportive of efficiency. Other studies that find support for efficiency in this market include Eberhart, Moore, and Roenfeldt (1990) and Gilson, John, and Lang (1990). Branch and Ray (1992) provide a complete discussion of investing in bankrupt firm securities.

Warner (1977) finds that the average cumulative abnormal return (ACAR) for a sample of bankrupt railroad bonds is generally insignificantly different from zero (during the bankruptcy period). He concludes therefore that the market is efficient.

Betker (1992a) also reports that the ACAR for his sample of bankrupt firms' stocks, and bonds is generally insignificantly different from zero. His study covers returns through 1990 for post-1978 Bankruptcy Code filings (so do Eberhart and Sweeney 1992). He segregates bonds into secured versus unsecured categories, but does not analyze different priority bondholders within the unsecured class (e.g., senior versus junior, etc.).

Eberhart and Sweeney (1992) test the efficient market hypothesis for a sample of bankrupt firm bonds using the ACAR and price-unbiasedness tests. This latter test asks if the actual return for each bond during the bankruptcy period, cross-sectionally regressed or the bond's expected rate of return, falls along a forty-five-degree line. The authors demonstrate that this can be a more powerful test of efficiency than the ACAR test. Overall, their results support efficiency. In a more recent study, Eberhart and Sweeney (1993) note that although APR violations may not bias distressed security prices, they can introduce additional noise (i.e., uncertainty about a security's intrinsic value).

A working paper by Datta and Iskander (1992) analyzes daily price changes for bankrupt firm stocks and bonds. Although some of these results are consistent with our results, this study has a very small sample size (under thirty issues). Hradsky and Long (1989) provide an analysis of the post-default monthly performance of bonds for up to twenty-four months after default. For a comparison of the new versus the old Bankruptcy Code, see Bradley and Rosenzweig (1992) and Altman (1993a).

Our study provides further insight into the degree of efficiency in the market for distressed securities by testing for abnormal performance during the default period for each category of bond. As mentioned earlier, we also include more recent defaults than previous studies.

DATA AND METHODOLOGY
Data

The sample is composed of 91 firms (with 232 bonds) that defaulted, filed for Chapter 11, and completed a bankruptcy/reorganization between January 1980 and July 1992. We collected information on the coupon and seniority of each bond as well as the issue price, the price just after default, and the price/payoff of the debt securities upon emergence from Chapter 11.[4]

Our pricing sources include: Standard & Poor's *Bond Guide; Capital Changes Reporter;* OTC dealers' quotes (bid); *The Wall Street Journal; The Bankruptcy Datasource;* Standard & Poor's *Daily Stock Price Record;* annual reports, 10-Ks, 8-Ks, and investor files. For a small number of issues (eight), we use data from T. Rowe Price Associates, which did an internal

---

4. Although the confirmation date can precede the emergence date, they are often the same date. Thus, we use the terms interchangeably. More generally, these dates represent the completion of the bankruptcy process, as some of these firms were liquidated or acquired.

study of defaulted bond investor performance. Broker dealers' quotes are from B.D.S. Securities, Merrill Lynch & Co., and Salomon Brothers. Our sample represents the vast majority of defaulting issues in the sample period that have gone through the entire bankruptcy/reorganization process, and probably well over 90 percent of relevant defaulting dollars.[5]

The subordinated category is the largest portion of the sample (38 percent; 89 issues), with senior-unsecured next (33 percent; 76 issues). The vast majority of issues are straight (non-convertible) (189; 81.5 percent). Only five issues are original-issue, discounted, non-cash-pay bonds.

The average time spent in Chapter 11 is 1.97 years, which is slightly longer than what Altman (1993a) reports. Note that the time from default to emergence is slightly longer than from bankruptcy to emergence because some firms default on debt issues prior to the actual Chapter 11 filing. (Because the default date and Chapter 11 filing date are often the same, we use the phrases default period, Chapter 11 period, and reorganization period interchangeably.)

Post-Default Performance of Bonds

We measure the performance of 202 defaulting issues from the end of the default month to the completion of the Chapter 11 period.[6] Specifically, we calculate the ACARs by adjusting the raw return of each defaulting issue for the comparable-period performance on an index of high-yield "junk" bonds. The latter is represented by the returns on the "Blume-Keim Low Rated Bond Index" (Blume and Keim 1987 and Blume, Keim, and Patel 1991).[7]

The ACAR test is a test of whether the average actual return ($\bar{R}$) equals the average expected rate of return ($\overline{ER}$):

---

5. Over the period January 1980–July 1992, approximately 610 corporate debt issues defaulted from about 350 different firms. As of July 1992, at least 280 issues from over 140 firms were still being reorganized and had not emerged from Chapter 11 (see Merrill Lynch (1993a, 1993b) for a discussion of issues trading while under Chapter 11). In addition, at least 45 of the defaulting issues from 30 firms were restructured outside the confines of the bankruptcy court or for some other reason did not file for Chapter 11 protection. Therefore, our 232-issue and 91-firm sample represents at least 80 percent of the defaulting issues, and our 91 firms represent over 50 percent of the eligible defaulting companies that emerged from Chapter 11 in the sample period.
6. This sample is slightly smaller than the 232 issues because of missing price data at default on 30 issues.
7. The correlation coefficient between monthly returns on the Merrill Lynch Master Index of High Yield Debt Securities and the Altman-Merrill Lynch Index of Defaulted Debt Securities is 0.595 for the period 1987–1992 (Altman 1993b). But the two indexes are totally independent with respect to their bond issue sample.

$$ACAR = \bar{R} - \overline{ER}$$

$$= (1/N) \sum_{i=1}^{N} R_{i,Ti} - (1/N) \sum_{i=1}^{N} R_{i,Ti}$$

$$= (1/N) \sum_{i=1}^{N} CAR_{i,Ti} \qquad (23\text{--}1)$$

where

$R_{i,Ti}$ = actual rate of return for bond i over T_i months (expressed in monthly returns);

$ER_{i,Ti}$ = expected rate of return for bond i over T_i months (expressed in monthly returns);

$CAR_{i,Ti}$ = cumulative abnormal return for bond i (expressed in monthly returns);

N = sample size;

T_i = number of months from default to emergence from Chapter 11 for bond i.

We express each CAR in terms of monthly returns because there are large cross-sectional differences in the amount of time each firm spends in default.[8] To test the statistical significance of the ACAR, we use a simple t-statistic based on the cross-sectional variation in the CARs.

Loss Measures

We calculate three loss measures to measure the degree of protection that seniority provisions offer:

$$L_1 = \frac{P_c - P_o}{P_o} \qquad (23\text{--}2)$$

$$L_2 = \frac{P_c - (P_o + FI)}{P_o} \qquad (23\text{--}3)$$

$$L_3 = \frac{P_c - (P_o + FI + IFI)}{P_o} \qquad (23\text{--}4)$$

---

8. Specifically, $R_{i,Ti} = (P_{Ti}/P_d)^{1/Ti} - 1$, and $ER_{i,T}$ is the average monthly rate of return on the market (i.e., the Blume-Keim Junk Bond Index).

where

$L_1, L_2,$ and L_3 = the three loss calculations;
     P_o = original issue price;
     P_c = price/payoff at confirmation;
     FI = forgone interest during the reorganization period including one-half lost coupon at default, not including reinvestment of the interest;
    IFI = interest on FI.

L_1 is the most straightforward measure of the lost principal from original issuance purchase until the end of the reorganization period. L_2 considers the opportunity cost of holding a debt security during an investment period when no interest is being paid. For our calculations, we use the coupon amount on the specific issue as the forgone interest. Finally, L_3 also encompasses lost return on reinvestment of the interest that would have been received if the bond had not defaulted.[9] Of course, $L_1 > L_2 > L_3$; the L_1 loss (gain) is "less severe" than L_2, which is "less severe" than L_3.

Sample Selection Bias Issues

Our sample of defaulted bonds is limited to those of issuers that eventually filed for Chapter 11. Curing default outside Chapter 11 has been shown to be a less costly way to resolve financial distress (Gilson, John, and Lang 1990). Consistent with this finding is the observation by Betker (1992a) that bonds experience negative reactions to Chapter 11 announcements.

Hence, the sample of defaulted bonds that did not go through Chapter 11 likely experienced higher returns; this suggests that our measure of average returns during the default period may be biased downward. This insight is important to keep in mind when interpreting the efficiency results. (This bias is likely greater than the possible opposite bias in our default-period sample, which analyzes thirty fewer issues than the sample covering returns/losses from issuance to emergence.)

---

9. We calculate interest on interest at 8 percent. Ideally, we would use a rate that changes with market conditions (and thus reflects the true opportunity cost of the interest), but the magnitude of these amounts involves such a small portion of the loss measure that we consider our approximation reasonable.

EMPIRICAL RESULTS

Prices at Issuance and Emergence

Exhibit 23–1 shows the average issuance price and the average payoff at emergence for the overall sample and each priority class. Note that the average initial price (P_o) is (with the exception of discounted bonds) close to, but not equal to, 100; that is, 100 percent of the bond's face value. These average values range from a high of 99.67 for secured bonds to 95 for senior-subordinated bonds. The overall sample average is 96.33. It should be noted that 84 of the 232-bond sample (38 percent) have initial prices less than face value, including the five discounted bonds; five issues have initial prices greater than face value.

The overall average emergence payoff is 50.46; approximately 50 cents on the dollar. For the sample of bonds with prices at default (202 issues), the average price just after default is 38.44 (shown in Exhibit 23–2).

The average emergence payoff sorted by seniority shows the highest average value recorded for secured bonds (100.91) followed by 76.94 for senior bonds and just 4.78 for noncash-pay subordinated debt.[10] The one exception to this hierarchy is the senior-subordinated average of just 23.30 versus 28.41 for subordinated issues. This is explained by the fact that the firms represented for each of these two categories are not identical.

E X H I B I T   23–1

Average Bond Price at Issuance
and Average Emergence Payoff

Debt Issue Type	Sample Size	Issuance Price (P_o)	Emergence Payoff (P_c)
Overall Sample	232	$96.33	$50.46
Non-Convertible	189	95.83	56.91
Convertible	43	98.52	22.12
Overall Sample by Seniority			
Secured	24	99.67	100.91
Senior	76	98.85	76.94
Senior-Subordinated	38	95.00	23.30
Subordinated (cash-pay)	89	96.19	28.41
Subordinated (noncash-pay)	5	54.88	4.78

---

10. The average emergence/confirmation price for straight, non-convertible senior bonds is 81.05, about 4 more than the sample of senior bonds that includes convertibles (five issues).

E X H I B I T   23–2

Average Bond Price at Default and Average Emergence Payoff

Debt Issue Type	Sample Size	Default Price (P_d)	Emergence Payoff (P_c)
Overall Sample	202	$38.44	$52.57
Non-Convertible	171	41.16	57.16
Convertible	31	23.41	27.25
Overall Sample by Seniority			
Secured	23	69.36	102.24
Senior	68	46.02	77.78
Senior-Subordinated	32	25.69	21.32
Subordinated (cash-pay)	74	29.80	30.71
Subordinated (noncash-pay)	5	2.48	4.78

Hence, we also calculate the average prices for those firms that have *both* senior-subordinated and subordinated debt outstanding, and we then find the expected ordering (for the twenty senior-subordinated bonds the average P_c is 22.62; for the twenty-eight subordinated bonds the average P_c is 10.75).[11] Although the loss measures discussed below make a stronger case for the value of seniority, these results are consistent with the notion that investors pay an appropriate price for higher priority.

Efficiency Tests at Default

Exhibit 23–2 lists the average prices at default (P_d) and at emergence (P_c) for the subsample of 202 bonds with prices available at default. Note that for many, but not all, priorities and types of issues, as well as the entire sample of 202 defaulted issues, the average price at the end of the reorganization period is greater than the average price at default; this is what we would expect in an efficient market.

---

11. When we update our results through September 1993, the sample size increases to 321 bonds (152 firms). The senior-secured and senior-unsecured average payoffs at confirmation/ emergence drop substantially to 88.79 and 58.2, respectively (the senior-subordinated and junior-subordinated remain virtually unchanged). These changes are driven by the Continental Airlines bonds. When these bonds are removed, the results are qualitatively similar. These results are available from the authors.

We find one exception, however; the average emergence payoff to the senior-subordinated bonds (21.32) is lower than the average default price (25.69). This suggests the bonds are overpriced at default.

On the other hand, the secured and senior bond samples appear to have done exceptionally well, at least with respect to absolute price differences. Of course, these comparisons provide only informal evidence on the efficiency of defaulted bond prices.

Exhibit 23–3 presents the excess return (i.e., ACAR) results. The overall sample average excess returns are significantly negative (-1.29 percent, t $= -2.49$). The average excess returns to the secured, subordinated (cash-pay), and convertible bonds are also significantly negative; this suggests these bonds are systematically overpriced at default. The median returns, however, are generally much lower in magnitude. Because extreme outliers are not unusual in this sample, the median return results are a better indicator of "typical performance."

The results include multiple debt issues for a number of companies. For example, the twenty-three secured observations were issued by just eight companies; the sixty-four straight senior bonds by thirty-one companies; the thirty straight senior-subordinated bonds by twenty-six companies; and the forty-nine straight subordinated issues by thirty-seven companies. The positive correlation among bonds from the same firm causes the t-statistics to be biased toward larger magnitudes.

To circumvent this problem, we calculate the equal-weighted average return among bonds from the same firm (see Warga and Welch, 1993). These independent excess return results are shown in Exhibit 23–4 and, overall, are supportive of efficiency.

The subordinated-straight bonds are the only exception, as they display negative and significant returns of -4.16 percent (t $= -4.03$). Although this suggests these bonds are overpriced at default, the inefficiency is probably not exploitable because we have not accounted for the transaction costs, which are likely to be high. Moreover, the implied arbitrage strategy is to short-sell these bonds; given the negative average reaction to default announcements (Betker, 1992a), implementing this strategy may be impossible.

Loss Measures

Exhibit 23–5 summarizes the average and median results for the three loss measures. In the majority of cases (164 issues; 70.7 percent), we use actual market values for the payoff upon emergence. For the cases where market values are not available, we use the stated book values of the package of securities exchanged for the old debt.

E X H I B I T   23-3

Efficiency Tests for Sample of All Bonds

Debt Issue Type	Sample Size	Monthly Excess Returns (%) (ACARs)			
		Mean	Median	Standard Deviation	T-Test
Overall Sample	202	(1.29)	0.14	7.35	(2.49)
Non-Convertible	171	(0.67)	0.38	6.56	(1.34)
Convertible	31	(4.73)	(2.22)	10.03	(2.63)
Overall Sample by Seniority					
Secured	23	1.23	(1.14)	1.99	2.96
Senior	68	0.60	1.07	5.43	0.91
Senior-Subordinated	32	(1.88)	(2.41)	7.76	(1.37)
Subordinated (cash-pay)	74	(3.95)	(1.40)	8.65	(3.93)
Subordinated (noncash-pay)	5	4.34	1.85	7.32	1.33

E X H I B I T   23-4

Efficiency Tests for Independent Sample

Debt Issue Type	Sample Size	Monthly Returns (%)		
		Absolute	Excess	T-Test
Secured	8	2.07	1.46	1.49
Senior	33	0.81	0.01	0.01
Senior-Subordinated	27	(1.45)	(2.12)	(1.37)
Subordinated (cash-pay)	54	(4.16)	(4.67)	(4.03)
Subordinated (noncash-pay)	4	6.16	4.99	1.24

The results using the 164-issue sample where only market values are available are qualitatively similar to the results with our larger sample. Some average results showed lower losses with the reduced sample, however. For example, L_1 for senior bonds is −7.30 percent versus −22.1 percent for the larger sample.

For all defaulted bond investors, the average L_1 is −48.38 percent (median = −65.6 percent). In fact, many issues suffer virtually a 100% loss, and fifty-three issues suffer L_1 losses of over 90 percent. Also, the range of values is high; for example, the range for L_1 is +74.1 percent to −100 percent.

E X H I B I T   23-5

Three Loss Measures

Debt Issue Type	Sample Size	L_1 Mean	(%) Median	L_2 Mean	(%) Median	L_3 Mean	(%) Median
Overall Sample	232	(48.38)	(65.60)	(79.81)	(91.57)	(83.37)	(92.64)
Non-Convertible	189	(41.70)	(49.00)	(74.42)	(83.53)	(78.07)	(85.10)
Convertible	43	(77.75)	(90.00)	(103.51)	(112.71)	(106.66)	(113.12)
Overall Sample by Seniority							
Secured	24	1.68	(0.75)	(32.15)	(29.73)	(36.29)	(33.49)
Senior	76	(22.05)	(12.59)	(52.57)	(39.10)	(56.51)	(41.46)
Senior-Subordinated	38	(75.13)	(86.04)	(109.51)	(113.97)	(113.09)	(116.38)
Subordinated (cash-pay)	89	(70.58)	(79.57)	(99.54)	(106.62)	(102.59)	(108.36)
Subordinated (noncash-pay)	5	(90.38)	(91.38)	(145.74)	(133.91)	(149.44)	(137.23)

The average L_2 and L_3 for the entire sample are considerably lower (greater losses) than the L_1 figure, with $L_2 = -79.8$ percent and $L_3 = -83.4$ percent. Median losses are also again lower than the mean ($L_2 = -91.6$ percent and $L_3 = -92.6$ percent). Therefore, average losses to investors almost double when one includes the lost opportunities for an issue that trades "flat" (i.e., without interest).

The importance of lost interest in a bankruptcy/reorganization is clearly demonstrated for a firm where there are some issues that accrue interest and others that do not during the reorganization. For example, in the LTV Corp. bankruptcy, all the LTV issues were unsecured and were trading flat, while several of the firm's Youngstown Sheet & Tube subsidiary bonds were secured and had interest accruing during the seven years of reorganization. When LTV emerged from Chapter 11 in July 1993, the unsecured parent company bonds were selling for about 26 cents on the dollar, while the two Youngstown bonds were over $160 per $100 face value. Of course, the price of the latter bonds would be less than par value if not for the accrued interest.

These results underscore one of the many potential benefits of a shortened bankruptcy process (i.e., the possibility of lower losses). See Altman (1993a) and LoPucki (1993) for a discussion of the average time in bankruptcy.

Loss by Seniority

The L_1, L_2, and L_3 losses by seniority are also shown in Exhibit 23–5. Secured bonds (twenty-four issues) show an average L_1 of 1.68 percent, although the median is slightly negative (-0.75 percent). When we adjust for lost interest and also lost interest on interest, though, the secured bonds incur average returns of -32.2 percent (L_2) and -36.3 percent (L_3). Some of the secured bonds are sold "flat," although in a few cases their prices reflect post-petition accrued interest, (e.g., Public Service Corporation of New Hampshire). L_1 values are a modest -22.1 percent for senior bonds, although the L_2 and L_3 rates are significantly greater at -52.6 percent and -56.5 percent, respectively.

Lower-priority senior-subordinated and subordinated bond issues do quite poorly, with L_1 losses of 75.1 percent and 70.6 percent, respectively. When we include forgone interest, the senior-subordinated bonds incur losses of 109.5 percent (L_2) and 113.1 percent (L_3). The comparable loss rates for subordinated bonds are slightly less.[12] Again, if you stratify these two samples with firms that have both senior-subordinated and subordinated debt outstanding, the anomaly disappears, (i.e., the senior-subordinated bond L_1 is -76.4 percent versus -87.4 percent for subordinated bonds).

Exhibit 23–5 also lists our results for convertible bonds versus straight debt. The convertible bonds, which have more equity-like features, do somewhat worse than their straight-debt counterparts. Losses due to the equity-like features are neutralized, however, by the lower average coupon rate for convertibles. This is because L_2 and L_3 are affected by the lower coupon, but our measures ignore the fact that convertibles have the lower coupon in the first place due to the conversion features of the bonds. Hence, by accounting for the lost coupon payments only from the default date, we are underestimating the loss to convertibles vis-à-vis non-convertible issues.

As noted above, the L_1 experience of senior-secured debt is slightly positive and modestly negative for the senior-unsecured class. The L_1 loss percentage for all subordinated bonds, however, is about 50 percentage points worse than the loss for senior-unsecured bonds (-70.6 percent versus -22.1 percent). These results clearly show that despite the existence of widespread—and potentially large—APR violations, higher seniority,

---

12. This anomaly is possible because the senior-subordinated bonds were issued during periods of high interest rates; thus, their higher average coupon rate increases the magnitude of L_2 and L_3.

ceteris paribus, leads to greater protection of a bondholder's investment (i.e., lower losses/higher payoffs at emergence from Chapter 11). This is consistent with the efficient pricing of bonds at issuance, because bondholders pay a premium for the higher seniority.

SUMMARY AND CONCLUSIONS

The dramatic rise in debt ratios for many firms during the 1980s has been followed by an equally dramatic rise in the number of firms filing for bankruptcy in the late 1980s and early 1990s (Altman 1991). Some resulting research shows that absolute priority rule (APR) violations occur in approximately 75 percent of Chapter 11 bankruptcy cases, and that these violations can be considerable.

The regularity and frequency of APR violations has led some observers to argue that they may make lenders hesitant to lend to anything less than stellar credit rating firms for fear of expropriation. If the market is efficient, however, lenders need not fear expropriation, because they are compensated for any possible dilution of their priority in case of a bankruptcy with a lower purchase price/higher yield.

This study conducts two tests of efficiency of the market for bonds of firms that default and subsequently file for Chapter 11. Our sample is composed of 91 firms (232 bonds) that defaulted, filed for Chapter 11, and emerged from Chapter 11 between January 1980 and July 1992. Our first test focuses on the efficiency of these bonds as of the default date. Some of the results within priority categories suggest that bonds are overpriced at the time of default. The results with the statistically most reliable sample, however, generally support efficiency.

Our second, and more important, test focuses on the efficiency of bond prices at issuance. Because we have, ex post, chosen bonds that went into bankruptcy, we cannot conduct traditional efficiency tests. Rather we provide some indirect evidence on efficiency by calculating the extent to which seniority provisions protect bondholders' investments. Specifically, we document the losses bankrupt firm bondholders experience over the entire life of the bond. We find that bonds with seniority provisions receive significantly higher payoffs (lower losses) at emergence than subordinated bonds, providing indirect evidence that the bonds are efficiently priced at issuance.

ENDNOTES

The authors wish to express their appreciation to the Standard & Poor's Corporation for its financial and technical support of this project. T. Rowe Price Associates also supplied some valuable data. Ben Branch, Ned Elton, and Lisa Fairchild provided helpful comments. The project was assisted by the staff at the New York University Salomon Center, especially Suzanne Crymes, Sally Eddy, and Kenneth Zekavat. Eberhart received support from a Georgetown University Junior Faculty Fellowship and a Summer Research Grant.

REFERENCES

Altman, E. (1989). "Default Risk, Mortality Rates and the Performance of Corporate Bonds." *Journal of Finance* September, pp. 909–22.

———. *Distressed Securities.* Chicago: Probus Publishing Co., 1991.

——— (1993a). "Evaluating the Chapter 11 Bankruptcy-Reorganization Process." *Columbia Business Law Review* No. 1, pp. 1–25.

——— (1993b). "The Performance of Defaulted Debt Securities: 1987–1991." *Financial Analysts Journa,* May/June.

——— (1992). "Revisiting the High Yield Debt Market." *Financial Management* Summer, pp. 78–92.

Altman, E., and D.L. Kao (1991). "Corporate Bond Rating Drift: An Examination of Rating Agency Credit Quality Changes over Time." Charlottesville, VA: Research Foundation of the Chartered Financial Analysts Federation.

Betker, B. (1992a). "An Analysis of the Returns to Stockholders and Bondholders in a Chapter 11 Reorganization." Working Paper, The Ohio State University.

——— (1992b). "Equity's Bargaining Power and Deviations from Absolute Priority in Chapter 11 Bankruptcies." Working Paper, The Ohio State University.

Blume, M., and D. Keim (1987). "Lower Grade Bonds: Their Risks and Returns." *Financial Analysts Journal* July/August, pp. 26–33.

Blume, M.; D. Keim; and S. Patel. "Returns and Volatility of Low Grade Bonds." *Journal of Finance.* March, pp. 49–74.

Bradley, M., and M. Rosenzweig (1992). "The Untenable Case for Chapter 11." *Yale Law Journal* March, pp. 1043–95.

Branch, B., and H. Ray (1992). *Bankruptcy Investing.* Chicago, IL: Dearborn Press.

Datta, S., and M. Iskander (1992). "The Valuable Effects of Chapter 11 Bankruptcy Filing on Different Classes of Security Holders: An Empirical Investigation." Working Paper, Northern Illinois University, July.

Eberhart, A.; W. Moore; and R. Roenfeldt (1990). "Security Pricing and Deviations from the Absolute Priority Rule in Bankruptcy Proceedings." *Journal of Finance.* December, pp. 1457–69.

Eberhart, A., and L. Senbet (1993). "Absolute Priority Rule Violations and Risk Incentives for Financially Distressed Firms." *Financial Management,* 22 (Autumn), pp. 101–116.

Eberhart, A., and R. Sweeney (1992). "Does the Bond Market Predict Bankruptcy Settlements?" *Journal of Finance.* July, pp. 943–80.

———— (1993). "Noise: The Case of the Market for Bankrupt Firms' Securities." Working Paper, New York University and Georgetown University.

Fabozzi, F.; J. Howe; T. Makabe; and T. Sudo (1993). "Recent Evidence on the Distribution Patterns in Chapter 11 Reorganizations." *Journal of Fixed Income* March.

Fons, J. (1987). "The Default Premium and Corporate Bond Experience." *Journal of Finance* March, pp. 81–97.

Fons, J.; L. Carty; and D. Girault (1993). "Corporate Bond Defaults and Default Rates, 1970–1991." *Moody's Special Report,* January.

Franks, J., and W. Torous (1989). "An Empirical Investigation of U.S. Firms in Reorganization." *Journal of Finance.* July, pp. 769–97.

Gilson, Stuart C.; Kose John; and Larry H.P. Lang (1990). "Troubled Debt Restructurings: An Empirical Study of Private Reorganization of Firms in Default." *Journal of Financial Economics.* October, pp. 315–54.

Hotchkiss, Edith S. (1993). "The Post-Bankruptcy Performance of Firms Emerging from Chapter 11." Unpublished Dissertation, New York University.

Hradsky, Gregory T., and Robert D. Long (1989). "High-Yield Default Losses and the Return Performance of Bankrupt Debt." *Financial Analysts Journal.* pp. 38–49.

Jensen, Michael C. (1991). "Corporate Control and the Politics of Finance." *Journal of Applied Corporate Finance.* Spring, pp. 13–33.

LoPucki, L. (1993). "The Trouble with Chapter 11." *University of Wisconsin Law Review,* June.

LoPucki, L., and W. Whitford (1990). "Bargaining Over Equity's Share in Reorganization of Large Publicly Held Companies." *University of Pennsylvania Law Review.* November, pp. 125–96.

Lucas, D., and J. Lonski (1992). "Changes in Corporate Credit Quality." *Journal of Fixed Income,* March, pp. 7–14.

———— (1991). "Corporate Bond Default Rates." In S. Levine, ed., *Investing in Bankruptcies and Turnarounds.* New York: Harper Business.

Merrill Lynch (1993a). "Defaulted Bonds: Supply, Demand and Investment Performance." High Yield Securities Research.

————. (1993b). "Defaults and Returns on High Yield Bonds: Analysis through 1992." High Yield Securities Research.

Warga, A., and I. Welch (1993). "Bondholder Losses in Leveraged Buyouts." *Review of Financial Studies.*

Warner, Jerold B. (1977). "Bankruptcy, Absolute Priority, and the Pricing of Risky Debt Claims." *Journal of Financial Economics* 4, pp. 239–76.

Weiss, L. (1990). "Bankruptcy Costs and Violations of Claims Priority." *Journal of Financial Economics* 27, October, pp. 285–314.

White, Michelle (1989). "The Corporate Bankruptcy Decision." *Journal of Economic Perspectives* 3, Spring, pp. 129–51.

CHAPTER 24

Investing in Distressed Situations: A Market Survey

Stuart C. Gilson

Preface

My original purpose in writing this article was to provide a useful "instructional manual" on the business of buying and trading distressed claims, for use in a course that I teach at the Harvard Business School on corporate restructuring. I have since been pleased to discover that a need for this kind of research also exists in the real world. Because much of what is known and practiced in this business is not based on any formal theory, but rather on experience and "doing," a survey article always runs the risk of losing currency if the world changes too quickly. Fortunately, in the year since this article was published, events and trends in the market for distressed investments have made the conclusions of the article seem even more relevant.

For any market to work well, there must be both supply and demand. On the supply side, the past year has seen a number of encouraging developments: a resurgence of highly leveraged deals (coupled with the return of zero coupon and pay-in-kind subordinated debt financings), a number of prominent public bond defaults (such as Discovery Zone and Fokker), and predictions that total U.S. bankruptcy filings in 1996 will top one million for the first time *ever.* And of course we are entering the third year of the junk bond market's historical three-year 'boom and bust" cycle, following a record $73 billion of new high yield issues in 1993. So if the junk bond prognosticators are correct, the next few years should see a significant increase in corporate defaults.

On the demand side, things look equally robust. T. Rowe Price Associates, Rothschild Inc., Prudential Mutual Fund Management, and Oak Hill Partners have recently assembled big pools of investment capital for the purpose of buying distressed securities. And many deep-pocketed investment banks have been actively making markets in distressed claims.

In my article, I argued that the biggest returns to buying and trading distressed securities have historically gone to investors who have a comparative advantage in valuing corporate assets. The value of corporate assets—the left-hand side of the balance sheet, or the "pie" that is sliced into the firm's various claims and securities—ultimately determines how much money one makes from investing in the firm's securities. For a number of reasons, I predict that superior skill at valuing these assets, through painstaking fundamental analysis, will become increasingly important over the next few years.

First, increasing competition on the demand side—more money chasing each opportunity—will reduce the investor's margin for error; mistakes in valuing a company will carry an increasingly heavy penalty, in the form of either lost opportunities or overpayments.

Second, during the last "bankruptcy boom," some investors, who in a previous life had made their living underwriting junk bonds for the original corporate issuers, were able to profit handsomely because they knew—better than anyone else—who *owned* the bonds when they crashed. Such knowledge is of course immensely valuable in a workout or bankruptcy. This source of comparative advantage has largely disappeared, however, as competition among junk bond underwriters, and liquidity in the secondary market for junk bonds, have both grown.

Finally, by most reckoning, many of the defaults that we will see over the next few years will be concentrated in certain industries—technology, telecommunications, healthcare, gambling—that are going through massive structural changes, where the "rules of the game" are being completely rewritten. With this sort of instability, valuing corporate assets will become even more challenging, and having specialized knowledge about the fundamental business factors that drive value in a particular industry—depth over breadth—will become increasingly important.

INTRODUCTION

One of the most important and enduring legacies of this period has been the development of an active secondary market for trading in the financial claims of these distressed companies. The participants in this market include many mainstream institutional investors, money managers, and hedge funds, as well as certain individuals—known as ("vultures")—who specialize in trading distressed claims.

The strategies these investors use are as diverse as the claims they trade and the companies they target. Some investors prefer to acquire the debt claims of a company while it tries to reorganize under Chapter 11 so they can either influence the terms of the reorganization or wait until the company's debt is converted into a major equity stake that can be used to influence company policy. Some investors prefer to purchase senior claims, others prefer junior claims, and still others spread their purchases throughout the entire capital structure. Some investors choose to take a passive role, seeking out undervalued claims, "hitching their wagons" to that of a more active vulture investor or holding distressed securities as part of a broadly diversified portfolio.

The business of trading in distressed debt is not new. In the chaos that immediately followed the American Revolution, Treasury Secretary Alexander Hamilton proposed to restore confidence in the financial system by redeeming, at face value, the bonds the American states had issued to finance the war. On the heels of this proposal, speculators acquired large quantities of the bonds, which had fallen greatly in value under the weight of high inflation and the massive war debt, in the hope that Hamilton's program would be completed.[1]

What is unique about today's distressed debt market is its size and scope. There is a market for virtually every kind of distressed claim: bank loans, debentures, trade payables, private placements, real estate mortgages—even claims for legal damages and rejected lease contracts. It is only a slight exaggeration to suggest that anything that is not nailed down will be traded when a firm becomes financially distressed. Two and a half years into the Chapter 11 bankruptcy of R.H. Macy, 728 of the firm's claims had traded for a total dollar value of $510 million. In the bankruptcy of Hills Department Stores, more than 2,000 claims exchanged hands.

The level of financial distress in the economy, hence the supply of distressed debt, is of course highly cyclical. As Exhibit 24–1 shows, the past few years have seen fewer opportunities to invest in distressed situations, as measured by the number or size of publicly held firms that filed for Chapter 11 (although this group represents only part of the market). In part, this trend reflects the final weeding out of poorly structured deals from the 1980s. In part, the downtrend is the result of recent improvements in the economy. The supply of distressed debt, however—both within the

---

1. See John Steele Gordon (1988). *The Scarlett Woman of Wall Street,* New York: Weidenfeld & Nicolson.

E X H I B I T   2 4 – 1

Frequency and Size of Chapter 11 Filings and
Other Corporate Restructuring Transactions
by Publicly Traded Firms, 1981–1996

	Number of Transactions				Value of Transactions ($ billions)*			
	Chapter 11 Filings	Hostile Tender Offers	Leveraged Buyouts	Spinoffs	Chapter 11 Filings	Hostile Tender Offers	Leveraged Buyouts	Spinoffs
1981	74	10	14	2	6.4	9.1	2.9	1.4
1982	84	8	15	3	11.9	3.5	2.2	0.3
1983	89	9	47	17	16.3	2.6	3.3	3.8
1984	121	9	113	13	8.3	3.5	19.8	1.4
1985	149	12	156	19	7.3	21.4	20.0	1.6
1986	149	17	238	26	16.7	21.8	59.8	4.6
1987	112	16	214	20	52.3	6.4	54.5	3.7
1988	122	28	300	34	52.8	52.9	70.5	13.6
1989	135	15	305	25	82.4	52.8	87.6	8.4
1990	116	5	201	27	90.6	9.5	19.7	5.7
1991	125	3	193	18	90.7	2.9	7.7	5.0
1992	91	1	223	19	58.3	0.5	8.6	6.1
1993	86	1	176	26	18.0	0.0†	10.7	15.2
1994	70	7	159	28	8.7	13.0	8.7	24.6
1995	84	11	165	44	24.2	11.0	6.1	55.9
1996	84	8	149	38	14.0	5.4	23.6	92.1
Total	1,691	160	2,668	359	559.0	216.5	405.5	243.4

*All dollar values are converted into constant 1996 dollars using the producer price index. For a Chapter 11 filing, "Total Value of
    Transaction" equals the book value of total assets of the filing firm. For a hostile tender offer and for a leveraged buyout,
    "Total Value of Transaction" equals the total value of consideration paid by the acquirer (including assumption of debt),
    excluding fees and expenses. For a spinoff, "Total Value of Transaction" equals the market value of the common stock of the
    spun-off entity evaluated at the first non-when-issued stock price available after the spinoff.

†Less than $0.1 billion.

Sources: The *1995 Bankruptcy Yearbook and Almanac* and Securities Data Corporation.

United States and abroad—is certain to rise again. Exhibit 24–1 also shows
that the market for distressed debt has historically provided more investment opportunities than other corporate restructuring transactions that
have traditionally attracted the interest of investors, including hostile tender offers, LBOs, and spinoffs.

This article surveys the theory and practice of investing in distressed
situations. Trading practices in the market for distressed claims have
become more sophisticated and institutionalized as the volume of activity
has grown. To investors who are unfamiliar with this market, these methods

may seem arcane and complex. One goal of this survey is to show that the core strategies for realizing value in distressed situations are relatively straightforward. Another goal is to describe and analyze the various risks—most of them highly firm-specific and idiosyncratic—that one faces when purchasing distressed claims. Understanding how to manage these risks is key to earning superior returns in this market. I conclude by discussing future opportunities in distressed situation investing.

BASIC RESTRUCTURING OPTIONS

Investing in distressed situations involves purchasing the financial claims of firms that have filed for legal bankruptcy protection or else are trying to avoid bankruptcy by negotiating an out-of-court restructuring with their creditors. In the United States, corporate bankruptcy reorganizations take place under Chapter 11 of the U.S. Bankruptcy Code. Firms that liquidate file under Chapter 7. In practice, most firms—more than nine in ten—first try to restructure their debt out of court and only when this fails do they file for bankruptcy. A recent academic study found that approximately 50 percent of all U.S. public firms that experienced financial distress in the 1980s successfully dealt with their problems by restructuring their debt out of court.[2]

An out-of-court restructuring can almost always be accomplished at much lower cost than a court-supervised reorganization. Part of this difference reflects savings in legal and other administrative costs. More importantly, Chapter 11 generally imposes a much heavier burden on the business because of the greater demands placed on management's time and costly delays engendered by litigation. Consistent with this cost differential, Gilson et al. found that firms that successfully restructure their debt out of court experience significant increases in their common stock price (approximately 30 percent, on average, after adjusting for risk and market movements) from the time they first experience financial distress to when they complete their restructuring. Over a corresponding interval, firms that try to restructure out of court but fail, experience significant average stock price declines (also on the order of 30 percent).

---

2. See Stuart Gilson, Kose John, and Larry Lang (1990). "Troubled Debt Restructurings: An Empirical Study of Private Reorganization of Firms in Default," *Journal of Financial Economics,* vol. 27, no. 2, October, pp. 315–53; and Stuart Gilson (1991). "Managing Default: Some Evidence on How Firms Choose between Workouts and Chapter 11," *Journal of Applied Corporate Finance,* vol. 4, no. 2, Summer, pp. 62–70.

Chapter 11, however, also provides certain benefits to a distressed firm. While in Chapter 11, the firm does not have to pay or accrue interest on its unsecured debt (and it only accrues interest on its secured debt to the extent the debt is overcollateralized). Chapter 11 also allows the firm to reject unfavorable lease contracts and to borrow new money on favorable terms by granting lenders superpriority over existing lenders ("debtor-in-possession" financing). Moreover, a reorganization plan in Chapter 11 can be passed with the approval of fewer creditors than a restructuring plan negotiated out of court (which generally requires creditors' unanimous consent).

From an investor's perspective, Chapter 11 can also be attractive because the firm is required to file more financial information with the court (e.g., monthly cash flow statements) than is generally available in an out-of-court restructuring.

Lately, in an attempt to realize the benefits of both out-of-court and court-supervised reorganization, an increasing number of distressed firms have made "prepackaged" Chapter 11 filings. Since 1989, about one in four bankruptcy filings by public firms has been of this kind. In a "prepack," the firm simultaneously files for bankruptcy and presents its claimholders with a formal reorganization proposal for a vote (having already solicited creditors' approval for the plan). As a result, the bankruptcy usually takes much less time. TWA completed a prepack in only three months. Prepacks work best for firms whose problems are more financial than operational in nature and that have relatively less trade and other nonpublicly traded debt outstanding.

STRATEGIES FOR CREATING VALUE

The Bankruptcy Code does not explicitly regulate trading in distressed claims. As a general legal principle, an investor who purchases a distressed claim enjoys the same "rights and disabilities" as the original claimholder. Thus, with some exceptions, the investor can assert the claim's full face value in a bankruptcy or restructuring, regardless of how much he or she paid to acquire it.

A plan of reorganization—whether negotiated in or out of court—is essentially a proposal to exchange the firm's existing financial claims for a new basket of claims (possibly including cash). The firm's immediate objective is to reduce the total amount of debt in the capital structure. In Chapter 11, the management of the firm (the "debtor") has the exclusive right to propose the first reorganization plan for 120 days following the bankruptcy filing. This period is routinely extended in many bankruptcy jurisdictions.

In deciding whether to vote for a plan, claimholders need to consider the total value, as well as the type, of new claims they are to receive under the plan. The treatment that a particular claim receives in either Chapter 11 or an out-of-court restructuring is not prescribed by formula. Under the "rule of absolute priority," no claimholder is entitled to receive any payment unless all more senior claims have been made whole. This rule must be followed in a Chapter 7 liquidation. In Chapter 11, certain claims are given a higher priority to receive payment than others (see Exhibit 24–2), but absolute priority does not have to be followed exactly. Small deviations from absolute priority are in fact routine in Chapter 11 cases, as senior claimholders willingly leave some consideration on the table for more junior claimholders to ensure passage ("confirmation") of the reorganization plan. (The precise legal rules that must be followed for a reorganization plan to be confirmed are described in the appendix.) Deviations from absolute priority are also common in out-of-court restructurings—which makes sense because the main alternative to restructuring is to file for Chapter 11.[3]

A simple but useful model to use in analyzing the returns to vulture investing is to view the firm as a pie. The size of the pie represents the present value of the firm's assets. The pie is cut into slices, with each slice representing a financial claim on the firm's cash flows (e.g., common stock, bonds, bank debt, trade claims). A vulture investor purchases one or more slices of the pie and profits if the slice grows larger. Viewed this way, a vulture investor can follow three strategies to earn a positive return on this investment. He or she can

- Make the entire pie larger by taking an active management role in the firm and deploying its assets more efficiently.
- Make someone else's slice smaller, thereby increasing the size of the investor's slice (even if the total pie does not become any larger).
- Do nothing (buy undervalued, inefficiently priced claims and wait for them to appreciate).

The first two strategies are proactive: The investor has to be able to influence the outcome of the reorganization proceedings and exercise some degree of control over the firm. The third strategy is passive: If the investor has correctly identified an undervalued claim, all he or she has to

---

3. See Julian Franks and Walter Torous (1994). "A Comparison of Financial Recontracting in Distressed Exchanges and Chapter 11 Reorganizations," *Journal of Financial Economics,* vol. 35, no. 3, June, pp. 349–70.

EXHIBIT 24–2

Hierarchy of Claims in Chapter 11
from Most Senior to Most Junior

---

1. Secured claims
2. Superpriority claims (e.g., debtor-in-possession financing)
3. Priority claims
   a. Administrative expenses (including legal and professional fees incurred in the case)
   b. Wages, salaries, or commissions
   c. Employee benefit claims
   d. Claims against facilities that store grain or fish produce
   e. Consumer deposits
   f. Alimony and child support
   g. Tax claims
   h. Unsecured claims based on commitment to a federal depository institutions regulatory agency
4. General unsecured claims
5. Preferred stock
6. Common stock

---

do after purchasing the claim is wait (until the market discovers its "error"). Of course, some combination of all three strategies is also possible.

PROACTIVE INVESTMENT STRATEGIES

An appealing analogy can be drawn between the market for distressed debt and the market for corporate control. In both markets, proactive investors seek to profit either by redirecting the flow of corporate resources to more highly valued uses or by bargaining for a larger share of those resources. The mechanisms for acquiring and exercising influence in these two markets differ in fundamental ways, however.

Taking Control of the Business

In Chapter 11, there are several ways that an investor can influence how the firm's assets are deployed. He or she can;

Submit a reorganization plan to be considered and voted upon by the firm's claimholders. The reorganization plan specifies what financial consideration will be delivered to each of the firm's outstanding claims and proposes a business plan for the firm once it leaves Chapter 11. In addition to current management, any person who holds any of the firm's claims is entitled to submit a reorganization plan. The judge in the case can permit more than one plan to be voted upon at the same time. In the Chapter 11 bankruptcy of Revco D.S., a total of five plans were filed during the case, including two by the debtor, one by a coalition of creditors and preferred stockholders, and one each by two competitors (Jack Eckerd and Rite-Aid). Although every claimholder in a Chapter 11 case is entitled to submit a reorganization plan, the judge must approve the plan before it can be put to a formal vote. Toward this end, an investor's credibility with the judge (and creditors) will be enhanced if he or she owns many of the outstanding claims in a class.

Purchase currently outstanding debt claims with the expectation that these eventually will be converted into voting common stock under the firm's reorganization plan. Owning a large block of common stock will enable the investor to exercise control over the firm's assets after it reorganizes. This strategy has been used successfully by vulture investors Sam Zell and David Schulte through their investment vehicle, the Zell/Chilmark Fund. During the Chapter 11 bankruptcy of Carter Hawley Hale Stores, for example, Zell/Chilmark made a tender offer for the company's bonds and trade claims explicitly for the purpose of becoming the company's majority stockholder once these claims were converted into common stock under the reorganization plan. In the end, Zell/Chilmark controlled 73 percent of the retailer's equity.[4]

Purchase new voting stock (and other securities) that are to be issued under the firm's reorganization plan. This approach is known as "funding the plan." The recent Chapter 11 reorganization of Continental Airlines was premised on an infusion of $450 million from a group of outside investors, which included Air Canada, in return for a majority of Continental's common stock and a package of notes, warrants, and preferred stock.

In each of these cases, the investor's goal is to assume a management or control position in the company and directly influence its investment and operating policies. The investor earns a return by causing the company to be run more profitably, thus increasing the value of its assets (and the value of the financial claims held against those assets).

Outside of Chapter 11, control over the firm's assets can be acquired by purchasing a large block of the firm's equity and waging a proxy contest or forcing management to hold a special stockholders' meeting. In principle, special stockholders' meetings are also possible inside Chapter 11, subject to the judge's approval. One goal of having such a meeting

---

4. As Zell remarked at the time, "I clearly have no intention of being a bondholder . . . . If I'm going to make an investment, I'm going to be an owner of equity." See Francine Schwadel, "Zell 'Vulture Fund' Offers Investment in Carter Hawley," *The Wall Street Journal,* July 25, 1991.

might be to force management to propose a more "stockholder friendly" reorganization plan. Such meetings have been permitted in several high-profile Chapter 11 cases, including Lionel, Allegheny International, and Johns–Manville.

In practice, however, purchasing equity is generally an ineffective way to acquire or exercise control in a financially troubled company. Most bankruptcy judges are reluctant to approve special stockholders' meetings. The Bankruptcy Code already includes a procedure for replacing management (with a "trustee") when management is shown to be guilty of "fraud, dishonesty, incompetence, or gross mismanagement."[5] In addition, under state and federal law, the managers and directors of a Chapter 11 debtor are generally considered fiduciaries of both stockholders and creditors; thus, management may be legally unable to pursue a course of action that favors stockholders over creditors. (In an out-of-court restructuring, these constraints do not apply, but management always has the option of filing for bankruptcy if a proxy fight threatens.)

Finally, prebankruptcy stockholders' interests are often severely diluted by the issuance of new common shares to creditors under the firm's bankruptcy or restructuring plan. Any control one has over a financially distressed firm by virtue of being a large stockholder is therefore usually short-lived. Stockholders of Wheeling–Pittsburgh Steel, which spent more than five years in Chapter 11, received less than 10 percent of the reorganized firm's stock. This percentage is fairly typical.

As a rule, more-senior claims in the capital structure receive more-senior claims (debt or cash) in a reorganization or restructuring; more-junior claims typically receive more of the common stock. The trick—if the goal is to emerge from the reorganization as a major equity holder—is to concentrate on buying relatively junior claims, but not so junior that one ends up receiving nothing (i.e., because the firm's assets are worth too little to support distributions that far down the capital structure). Investors who are better able to value the firm's assets have a clear advantage in trying to achieve this goal.

"Bondmail"

An investor can also increase his or her return by acquiring a sufficiently large percentage of an outstanding debt issue to block the firm's reorganization plan. As described in the appendix, in every Chapter 11 case, the firm's financial claims are grouped into distinct "classes." Each class votes

---

5. Section 1104(a) of the U.S. Bankruptcy Code.

separately on whether to approve the reorganization plan(s) under consideration. A class is deemed to have accepted a plan if at least two-thirds in value held and one-half in number of the claimholders in that class who vote, vote affirmatively (the latter criterion is referred to as the "numerosity" requirement). Claimholders who do not vote are not counted. A "consensual" plan of reorganization cannot be approved unless every impaired class votes for the plan (see the appendix).

Thus, an investor needs only slightly more than one-third of the claims in a particular class to block a reorganization plan. In this case, the investor can threaten to hold up the firm's reorganization unless he or she is given a higher recovery—a practice that has come to be known as "bondmail." (To return to the pie analogy, the investor can try to enlarge his or her slice at the expense of other sliceholders.)

Note, however, that an investor who holds a blocking position in a class cannot demand more favorable treatment under a plan than other members of the class. Section 1123(a)(4) of the Bankruptcy Code requires that all holders within any given class be treated identically under a reorganization plan (except for holders who agree to be treated differently). Thus, the practice of "greenmail"—seen in many 1980s-style corporate takeovers—is not allowed in Chapter 11.

In determining whether the numerosity requirement has been satisfied, the courts treat a holder of multiple claims within a class as a single holder if the claims are effectively identical, such as publicly traded debentures or notes. In the case of nonidentical claims—for example, different bank loans grouped within the same class—several recent court decisions suggest that the holder is entitled to one vote for each claim he or she holds in this class.

The distinction is an important one in terms of how much voting control a given-sized block of claims confers on the holder. If an investor holds, say, 35 percent of the outstanding principal amount of a debenture issue representing a single class, he or she can block the class from approving a reorganization plan but cannot force the class to approve a plan: As long as one other holder is represented in the class, the investor cannot account for more than half of all holders. Only by controlling 100 percent of the claims can he or she have complete control over how the class votes. Even if the investor forms a voting coalition with other class members, most judges will treat the coalition as a single "holder" when tallying votes. In contrast, an investor may be able to satisfy the numerosity requirement with less than 100 percent ownership of the claims in a class when the claims are nonidentical (e.g., bank loans, trade claims).

A blocking strategy is riskier if the investor purchases his or her claims before the firm files for Chapter 11. The reason is that claimholder classes are defined within the reorganization plan. The Bankruptcy Code requires only that a class contains "substantially similar" claims; it does not require that substantially similar claims be put in the same class. Thus, the plan proposer has considerable opportunity to gerrymander claims and reduce the voting power of particular claimholders. One way the investor can preempt this possibility is to propose his or her own plan.

An investor's ability to coerce a higher payment from the firm is also limited by the threat of a bankruptcy "cram-down." As discussed in the appendix, a reorganization plan can be confirmed over the objections of a claimholder class (i.e., "crammed down" on that class) if the present value of the consideration class members are to receive under the plan equals the allowed value of their claims or if no more-junior class receives any consideration. In practical terms, an investor who holds a blocking position in a class can still be forced to accept a low recovery if the firm's assets are worth too little to support any additional payments to that class. Even if the cram-down is never used, the threat of a cram-down can be enough to reduce an investor's recovery drastically. Thus, investors in distressed debt (especially junior debt) need to assess carefully whether the claims they are thinking of buying are "in the money."

One invariable byproduct of the strategy is intense conflict among different creditor classes. While Revco D.S. was in Chapter 11, vulture investor Talton Embry of Magten Investments purchased blocking positions in the company's subordinated bonds in an attempt to reduce the recoveries realized by holders of Revco's senior bank debt. Conflicts between junior and senior creditors were also much in evidence in the bankruptcy of Gillette Holdings, in which Apollo Advisors held a blocking position in the company's senior claims and Carl Icahn held a blocking position in its junior bonds.

PASSIVE INVESTMENT STRATEGIES

The explosive growth in the demand side of the distressed debt market has greatly reduced the number of opportunities for buying underpriced claims. Most participants now consider this market to be relatively efficient, and several recent academic studies confirm this view.

These studies consider various buy-and-hold strategies that investors might pursue to exploit possible overreaction in the market for distressed bonds or common stock (data limitations preclude looking at the market for most nonpublic claims). After publicly traded bonds go into default, they typically trade at about 30 percent of their face value; the average discount

EXHIBIT 24–3

Weighted Average Price of Defaulted Bonds at End of Default Month as a Percent of Face Value, January 1, 1977–March 31, 1991

Bond Class	Price/ Face Value
Senior Secured	54.6%
Senior Unsecured	40.6
Senior Subordinated	31.3
Subordinated	30.1
Junior Subordinated	23.0
All Bonds	34.2

Source: Salomon Brothers study (April 18, 1991).

for more-junior bonds is even larger (see Exhibit 24–3). Market overreaction therefore seems at least plausible. These studies, however, fail to find evidence of abnormal returns (adjusting for risk and transaction costs) to buying portfolios of distressed bonds at the end of the default month, the end of the bankruptcy-filing month, or on other key dates.[6] Systematic abnormal returns also do not appear to be avaliable from buying bankrupt firms' common stock.[7]

Although no comparable empirical studies have been done for trading in bank or trade claims, increasing liquidity in this market makes the existence of profitable trading rules seem unlikely here, too. In the mid-1980s, news of a bank loan default typically might have resulted in the bank's workout department being approached by one or two interested potential buyers. In the current market, a bank's digital trading desk might receive up to a hundred inquiries in the case of a large credit.

Although a passive strategy may be unlikely to yield positive abnormal returns, a number of institutional investors hold large amounts of distressed debt as part of a broader portfolio diversification strategy. Included

---

6. See Alan C. Eberhart and Richard J. Sweeney (1992). "Does the Bond Market Predict Bankruptcy Settlements?" *The Journal of Finance,* Vol. 47, no. 3, July, pp. 943–80; and Chapter 23.

7. See Dale Morse and Wayne Shaw (1988). "Investing in Bankrupt Firms," *The Journal of Finance,* Vol. 43, no. 5, December, pp. 1193–1206. In spite of this evidence, a number of investment funds have specialized in buying common stock in companies that have recently emerged from Chapter 11. The rationale for this strategy is that such stocks are undervalued because (1) Few analysts follow them (hence the alternate label "orphan stocks") and (2) These stocks are in oversupply because creditors tend to unload the shares they receive in a bankruptcy reorganization quickly. See Matthew Schifrin, "Reborn and Deleveraged," *Forbes* (August 15, 1994).

in this group are Trust Company of the West, Foothill, T. Rowe Price, and Cargill, among others. These investors, of course, retain the option to become actively involved in a bankruptcy or restructuring.

Careful fundamental analysis of an individual firm's situation may still yield opportunities to purchase claims for less than their intrinsic value. Careful scrutiny of the covenants of a bond issue may, for example, turn up a weakness in a subordination agreement. Junior bondholders in the Zale and R.H. Macy bankruptcies realized higher-than-expected recoveries—at the expense of senior creditors—because the bonds were released from the subordination agreement under a special exemption. Often, these kinds of provisions are buried in the indenture document; inspecting only the bond prospectus may be insufficient.[8]

RISKS OF INVESTING IN A DISTRESSED SITUATION

The risks in investing in distressed claims are highly firm-specific. Many are legal and institutional in nature, and most can be controlled through careful planning and by conducting adequate due diligence. Having a sound working knowledge of bankruptcy law is important; many successful investors in this market are either former practicing bankruptcy attorneys or have access to legal counsel experienced in bankruptcy matters.

The following list of relevant risk factors is undeniably long, but the large number of risks alone has not prevented investors from earning huge returns in this market, on a par with those earned in many corporate takeover contests of the 1980s. Experience has shown that investors who understand and are adept at managing these risks consistently earn the highest returns from trading in distressed debt.

The "J" Factor

To encourage consensual bargaining among bankrupt firms' claimholders, the U.S. Bankruptcy Code is designed to be flexible. As a result, the outcome of any case may significantly depend on prior case law or on how a

---

8. In contrast to these buy-and-hold strategies, some investors alternatively specialize in short selling the common stock of companies that are in or near Chapter 11. Such activity, however, is much more limited in scale than the buy-and-hold approach, and the participants in this market are highly sophisticated. In addition, shares in a firm are generally thought to be more difficult to locate after the firm files for bankruptcy. Short sellers are known to have made large (multimillion dollar) returns in such bankruptcies as Circle K, ZZZZ Best, and LTV.

particular judge rules. The judge's track record should therefore be carefully factored into an investor's purchase decision.

Judges can significantly influence investment returns through their control of the administration of a bankruptcy case. Of particular importance to proactive investors is the judge's prerogative to decide whether a particular claim is allowed to vote on a reorganization plan or is entitled to any recovery, whether a proposer's reorganization plan can be put up for a vote, and whether an allowed plan is confirmable. At a critical point in the bankruptcy of Integrated Resources, the judge would not permit creditors *check* to see vulture investor Steinhardt Partners' competing reorganization plan until after they had voted on management's plan—even though management's exclusive right to file a plan had expired.

Judges can also influence investor returns because their approval is required before the debtor can undertake major actions that lie outside the "ordinary course" of its business (such as selling off an operating division or making a major investment in new equipment). Interventionist judges have been known to permit a firm to take actions that are potentially harmful to creditors' interests. In the Eastern Airlines bankruptcy, the judge allowed management to spend almost $200 million of cash that had been placed in escrow for Eastern's unsecured creditors, on the grounds that the "public interest" would be better served if Eastern were to continue flying. (The Bankruptcy Code does not give judges this particular charge, however.)

In some jurisdictions, especially the Southern District of New York, judges are thought to systematically favor the interests of management and stockholders over creditors. One alleged consequence of this bias is that the debtor's "exclusivity period"—during which only the debtor can propose a reorganization plan—is more often extended in this district. This policy allows debtor management to remain in control of the firm longer to the possible detriment of the firm's creditors. To seek a more favorable outcome, some firms go "forum shopping," filing in districts that are believed to be debtor friendly.[9] Eastern Airlines filed for Chapter 11 in the Southern District of New York, even though it was incorporated in Delaware and headquartered in Miami. Eastern accomplished this feat by attaching its bankruptcy filing to that of a small subsidiary headquartered in New York, which had filed for Chapter 11 only six minutes before. The subsidiary was less than 1 percent of Eastern's size by total assets and operated a string of airport travel lounges.[10]

---

9. See Lynn M. LoPucki and William C. Whitford (1991). "Venue Choice and Forum Shopping in the Bankruptcy Reorganization of Large, Publicly Held Companies," *Wisconsin Law Review,* Vol. 1991, no. 1, pp. 13–63.

10. For an analysis of the Eastern Airlines Bankruptcy, see Lawrence Weiss, "Restructuring Complications in Bankruptcy: The Eastern Airlines Bankruptcy Case," Manuscript (1994).

Title Risk and the Mechanics
of Transferring Claims

When an investor purchases a claim against a financially distressed firm, a number of steps need to be taken to ensure that the investor is legally recognized as the new owner. In practice, one may encounter various hidden hazards during this process.

Transfers of claims in Chapter 11 are regulated by Federal Bankruptcy Rule 3001(e). To understand the application of this rule, it is necessary first to describe the procedure the court follows in identifying the firm's claimholders. Within ten days of filing for Chapter 11, the debtor is required to file a schedule of assets and liabilities with the court clerk, including the name and address of each creditor. The debtor then sets a "bar date." Creditors with disputed or contingent claims must file a "proof of claim" by this date or forfeit their rights to participate in the reorganization plan; all other claimholders are automatically assumed to have filed a proof of claim.[11] (Exhibit 24–4 provides a time line of key dates in a typical Chapter 11 reorganization.)

Under Rule 3001(e), an investor who purchases a claim against a firm after a proof of claim has been filed by the selling creditor is required to provide the court with evidence of the transaction. If, after approximately 20 days, the seller does not object to the transaction, the judge automatically approves the transfer of ownership. If the transaction takes place before proof has been filed, no formal notification of the court is required and filing a proof of claim becomes the investor's responsibility. In neither case does the investor have to reveal the number of claims purchased or the price paid. Also, Rule 3001(e) does not apply to the purchase and sale of publicly traded securities; here, as in other matters, the Bankruptcy Code defers to relevant securities law.

Prior to August 1991, when the current version of Rule 3001(e) was adopted, more rigorous disclosure requirements had to be satisfied. In general, an investor had to disclose the terms of the transaction to the court— including the number of claims purchased and, in some circumstances, the transaction price. The transfer of claims also had to be approved by a court order. In a number of widely cited cases, judges refused to approve claims

---

11. Generally, it is a good idea for even these creditors to physically file a proof of claim, however, to help resolve any future disputes over title and ownership.

E X H I B I T   24–4

Time Line of Key Events and Dates in a Chapter 11 Reorganization

Filing of Chapter 11 petition.
Filing of schedule of assets and liabilities.
Bar date.
Filing of plan of reorganization and disclosure statement.
Hearing on disclosure statement.
Balloting on plan.
Plan confirmation hearing.
Effective date of plan/distribution of new claims under plan.

transfers on the grounds that the sellers were not adequately informed about the value of the claims they were selling.[12] Removing the judge from this process (under revised Rule 3001(e)) has arguably had the effect of increasing liquidity in the secondary market for distressed claims.

Notwithstanding this revision, an investor may still encounter a number of problems in trying to establish title to a claim. For example, the seller may have sold a given claim more than once, creating multiple holders of the claim. Such redundant sales may be purely fraudulent or the result of oversight on the part of larger lenders who inadvertently assigned responsibility for selling the loan to more than one person. Small trade creditors are thought to be especially guilty of this practice, and one prominent vulture investment fund now avoids purchasing trade claims altogether.

---

12. For example, in the Chapter 11 reorganization of Revere Copper and Brass, the judge refused to approve vulture fund Phoenix Capital's purchase of unsecured trade debt at 28 cents on the dollar, on the grounds that trade creditors may have mistakenly believed the company was being liquidated, causing them to sell out at too low a price. Evidently, one factor in her decision was a *Wall Street Journal* story published shortly after most of these purchases had been made, which reported that the company's reorgainzation plan would likely propose creditor recoveries between 65 and 100 cents on the dollar. The judge argued that Phoenix did not provide trade creditors with information that would enable them to make an "informed" decision. She specifically cited Section 1125 of the Bankruptcy Code, which prohibits solicitation of claimholders in regard to a plan of reorganization before they have received a copy of the disclosure statement (which describes the plan terms and related pertinent information). Eventually, as a condition of approving the transfer of claims, the judge required Revere to offer selling creditors a full refund.

An investor can take several measures to reduce the risk of buying a redundant claim.[13] If the seller has already filed a proof of claim or granted the buyer a power of attorney to file a proof of claim in the seller's name, virtually no risk exists, because the court assigns the claim a number. By referring to this number when buying the claim, the buyer can establish himself or herself as the true owner. Short of this arrangement, the buyer can insist that the seller provide him or her with a title guarantee; however, legal costs make this option relatively unattractive for smaller claims. The buyer can also file a proof of claim or notice of transfer of claim with the court, even if he or she is not required to do so. Filing either of these forms creates a physical record of the transaction. Unfortunately, the mere existence of this record does not necessarily preclude another investor from buying the same claim; the original record must first be identified. The court eventually compiles a "master list" of all such records that have been filed in the case, but this process can take several months, which leaves the investor to search physically through the many hundreds or thousands of forms that may have been filed in the case to date.[14]

Finally, title issues are important in "multiple debtor" cases in which related parent and subsidiary corporations have all individually filed for Chapter 11. These cases are often "administratively consolidated," meaning the cases are collectively assigned a single case number and name for administrative convenience even though each individual case also receives its own name and number. Creditors who have debt outstanding at the parent company level that is guaranteed by one or more subsidiaries are generally advised to file proofs of claim for each individual parent or subsidiary case, as well as for the consolidated case.[15] One consequence of this procedure is that the total debt outstanding in a case is often significantly overstated because of temporary double-counting. Total claims in Wheeling–Pittsburgh Steel's bankruptcy started out at $14 billion, even though only $1 billion in actual claims were outstanding.

---

13. The remainder of this section is based on the excellent discussion of the claims trading and title transfer issues in Thomas Moers Mayer, "Claims Trading: Problems and Failures," Manuscript (1994).
14. Title problems can also arise as a result of how the court records proofs of claim. In most jurisdictions, the court mails creditors the official notice of the bar date along with a computer-coded proof-of-claim form (based on the debtor's schedule of liabilities). Sometimes, however, creditors choose to substitute their own forms. As a result, the same claim will be recognized twice, once as an entry in the debtor's schedule of liabilities and once as a "new" claim listed on the creditor's personalized proof-of-claim form. Such duplication may not be corrected for several months. In the meantime, the investor may be hindered in asserting his or her claim because the debtor chooses to recognize only the "parallel" claim noted on its schedule of liabilities. See Mayer, "Claims Trading."
15. See Mayer, "Claims Trading."

Risk of Buying "Defective Merchandise"

An investor who purchases distressed debt may inherit certain legal "baggage" or liabilities from the original lenders that the investor had no role in creating. These liabilities can be significant and present a major risk to participants in this market.

Fraudulent Conveyance   An investor who buys debt in a troubled LBO may become liable for damages under an outstanding fraudulent conveyance suit. Roughly speaking, a fraudulent conveyance occurs when (1) Property is transferred from a firm in exchange for less than "reasonably equivalent" value, and (2) As a result, the firm is left insolvent (or it was insolvent when the transfer took place). The first criterion is almost always satisfied by an LBO.[16]

In filing a fraudulent conveyance suit, the debtor attempts to recover the property that was fraudulently transferred. In theory, this course of action may mean trying to recover the payments that were made to the selling shareholders; in practice, such efforts are mainly directed at large, deep-pocketed claimholders, who make attractive targets for litigation. An investor who buys up and consolidates a large number of smaller claims may be especially at risk. If a fraudulent conveyance action is successful, lenders' claims can be subordinated or stripped of their security interest if the debt is secured. Under Section 548 of the Bankruptcy Code, a fraudulent conveyance action can be brought within one year of an LBO.[17]

Avoidable Preferences   Chapter 11 allows a debtor to recover certain payments, known as "avoidable preferences," that it made to creditors within 90 days prior to filing for bankruptcy.[18] The point of this provision

---

16. In an LBO, the firm borrows a large sum of money and uses the proceeds to buy out the public stockholders. Under the law, this payout of cash is considered a transfer of assets. Neither the cash received by stockholders nor any appreciation in the value of the firm's assets due to the LBO, however, is included in the calculation of reasonably equivalent value.

17. Fraudulent conveyance actions can also be brought under various state laws patterned after either the Uniform Fraudulent Conveyance Act or the Uniform Fraudulent Transfers Act. Applicable state laws generally have a longer statute of limitations (up to six years). In practice, fraudulent conveyance suits are almost always settled before going to final judgment, typically for less than ten cents on the dollar. (See Jack Friedman (1993). "LBO Lawsuits Don't Pick Deep Pockets," *The Wall Street Journal,* January.) Such suits, however, are often brought as a negotiating ploy during a Chapter 11 case to induce larger concessions from the LBO lenders (or current holders of LBO debt). These concessions are an additional cost to the investor from a fraudulent conveyance attack.

18. This period increases to one year if the creditors had an insider relationship with the debtor. Such a relationship might be deemed to exist, for example, if a lending bank is represented on the debtor's board of directors at the time the debtor files for Chapter 11.

is to discourage insolvent firms from cutting side deals with key creditors.[19] Payments to creditors made in the normal course of business and on normal business terms are not recoverable. Payments on LBO debt, however, may be recoverable, given the unusual nature of the transaction. Grants of additional security to a lender are also generally recoverable.

The Bankruptcy Code's treatment of preferences creates several risks for an investor in distressed debt. If the investor purchases debt in a firm that subsequently files for bankruptcy, he or she may have to return payments that were received on the debt within the 90-day profiling period. If the debt is purchased after the firm files for bankruptcy, the investor is not directly on the hook. The court, however, could still choose not to recognize the investor's claims until all such preferences are recovered (from the previous owners of the debt).

Equitable Subordination and Lender Liability   In Chapter 11, an investor in distressed debt risks having the debt "equitably subordinated"—made less senior—if the selling creditor is found to have engaged in "inequitable conduct" that resulted in harm to other creditors or gave the selling creditor's claim an unfair advantage in the case. (Of course, the same penalty applies if the investor is found guilty of such conduct.) Equitable subordination invariably reduces the investor's rate of return because more-junior claims almost always receive lower percentage recoveries in bankruptcy.

In determining whether inequitable conduct has occurred, basically the same standards apply as those used to assess lender liability outside of Chapter 11. A bank creditor may be considered guilty of inequitable conduct if it exercises excessive control over a firm's operations as a condition of lending the firm more money or refuses to advance funds under an existing credit line, thus impairing the firm's ability to pay its other creditors. In the bankruptcy of convenience store operator Circle K, unsecured creditors holding claims worth approximately $700 million petitioned the court to equitably subordinate $380 million of senior bank debt on the grounds that the banks had contributed to the bankruptcy by financing an ill-advised acquisition.

Environmental Liabilities   Under The Comprehensive Environmental Response Compensation and Liability Act (CERCLA), lenders can be held liable for the costs of cleaning up hazardous substances found on the borrower's property. This liability is assessed based on who currently

---

19. If preferential payments could not be recovered, creditors might, at the first hint of financial
        trouble, collectively rush to grab whatever of the firm's assets they could to protect their
        individual interests, making the firm's problems even worse.

owns or operates the property rather than on who was responsible for creating the pollution. A lender who has a security interest in certain contaminated property may be considered an "owner" or an "operator" of the property—hence potentially liable under CERCLA—if it forecloses on its security interest or assumes an active role in managing the property.

An investor in distressed debt should investigate whether the seller has engaged in past behavior that might qualify it as an owner or an operator of contaminated property. CERCLA provides secured lenders with an exemption to its definition of property "owner," but the courts have differed on how widely this exemption applies; also, this exemption does not shield a lender from liability under various state environmental laws. As a general rule, lenders do not expose themselves to liability under CERCLA simply by exercising their ordinary rights as creditors (e.g., by enforcing covenants, restructuring a loan, foreclosing on a security interest and promptly disposing of the acquired property).

Protecting against These Risks   Investors in distressed debt can reduce their exposure to these liabilities by obtaining appropriate representations, warranties, and indemnities from the seller. These protections are especially important in the case of bank, trade, and other nonpublic debt, on which less information is generally available from public sources. Representations and warranties, which effectively operate like put options, give the investor some assurance as to what "nonstandard" liabilities, if any, he or she may inherit as a result of buying the debt (especially those that arise from improper conduct by the seller).[20] As added protection, investors also often ask sellers to indemnify them against potential damages.

Obtaining representations, warranties, or indemnities can be difficult, however, because creditors who sell their claims most often wish to rid themselves of all ties to the firm. Many contemplated bank loan sales have fallen through because banks have been unwilling to grant these protections to otherwise willing buyers.[21] This attitude has grown increasingly common among banks as the number of potential buyers of distressed

---

20. Most bank loan sale agreements transfer responsibility to the buyer for the "standard" risks and liabilities that can arise in a distressed (or nondistressed) situation, including the risk that the court will disallow part or all of the claim; the risk that the buyer will realize a lower recovery on the claim than he or she initially expected; and the risk that the buyer may have to lend funds to the borrower under the unfunded portion of any letter of credit.

21. This happened, for example, in the out-of-court restructuring of Western Union and in the bankruptcies of Coleco Industries and Apex Oil. See Chaim Fortgang and Thomas Moers Mayer (1990). "Trading Clams and Taking Control of Corporations in Chapter 11," *Cardozo Law Review,* Vol. 12, no. 1, pp. 1–115.

claims has rapidly increased in recent years. Also, trading in the current market for distressed debt is characterized by a higher fraction of retrades (in which the seller is not the original lender) and hence a much shorter average holding period than was true even five years ago. In this environment, representations, warranties, and indemnities generally make less sense for both buyers and sellers.

As a result of these considerations, investors who are more familiar with the borrower's operations and management (e.g., as a result of past business dealings or superior research) have an increasing comparative advantage in assessing these risks and in accurately valuing distressed claims.

Disputed and Contingent Claims

In almost every Chapter 11 case, the status, seniority, or size of some claims is not resolved until well into the case. An investor's recovery in the case and percentage return can be greatly affected by how these disputed claims are resolved, especially if they rank senior or equal to the investor's claim in the firm's capital structure.

Claims can be disputed or contingent for many reasons. For example, creditors sometimes file multiple proofs of claim for the same underlying instrument. Another important source of dispute revolves around the issue of when a particular claim comes into existence. When the Environmental Protection Agency (EPA) has a claim outstanding against a bankrupt firm under CERCLA, for example, the debtor will typically try to argue that the claim arose before it filed its bankruptcy petition (e.g., because the actions that gave rise to the contamination occurred before the filing). The EPA, in contrast, will typically argue that the claim arose after the firm filed for bankruptcy (e.g., because the costs of cleaning up the contaminated site have yet to be actually incurred).

The date on which a claim comes into existence is important because under the Bankruptcy Code all prepetition claims are discharged when the firm leaves bankruptcy (to use an analogy, the debtor's record is wiped clean of all offenses committed before it filed for Chapter 11). If the EPA loses its case, then its claim will most likely be added to the pool of general unsecured claims, although it may still try to have its claim treated as a higher priority administrative expense. Exactly the same issues come up when the Pension Benefit Guaranty Corporation brings a claim against a Chapter 11 debtor for unfunded pension liabilities.

Finally, Chapter 11 allows a firm to reject unfavorable leases and other "executory contracts" (including collective bargaining agreements). Any economic loss the owner of the leased property suffers as a result of such rejection becomes a general unsecured claim against the estate. The owner, however, may dispute the debtor's right to reject the lease or its estimate of losses from the rejection.

Counting Votes

Investors should be aware of certain problems that can arise in connection with how, and whether, they vote their claims in Chapter 11.[22] Acquiring, say, 35 percent of the claims in a class does not always mean the investor commands 35 percent of the votes. The source of this discrepancy differs depending on whether the claims are publicly traded.

For the buyer of a bank, trade, or other nonpublic claim to be considered a "holder of record"—and thus be eligible to vote on the reorganization plan—a "statement of transfer of claim" must be received by the claims-processing agent no later than the official voting record date. The court clerk mails this statement to the claims-processing agent, who is usually located in a different state. With various delays possible, this process can take well over a week. An investor who purchases a claim too close to the record date therefore risks being disenfranchised. This problem was an issue in the Hills Department Stores bankruptcy. To guard against this possibility, the purchase agreement could include a provision that requires the seller to transmit his or her ballot to the buyer, although the seller may fail to perform its obligation in a timely enough manner. Even better, the buyer could try to obtain from the seller a power of attorney that would give the buyer the right to vote the claim on behalf of the seller.

Voting rights issues are more complicated—and interesting—in the case of publicly traded bonds or debentures than for nonpublic claims. The indenture trustee for a bond issue maintains a registry of ownership, but it rarely lists the real beneficial owners of the bonds. In practice, most bonds are held in "Street name" at various brokerage firms, which act as custodians for the real owners. When voting on a plan of reorganization commences, the balloting agent sends both a "master ballot" and a set of individual ballots to the brokerage firms registered as holders of record. Each brokerage firm is supposed to distribute the individual ballots to the actual owners. The owners return their marked ballots to the brokerage firm, which then summarizes the votes on the master ballot. Only the master ballot is returned to the balloting agent—without disclosing the identities or votes of the real owners.

---

22. This summary of voting issues is based on Mayer, "Claims Trading."

A number of things can go wrong in the process. The broker may miss the deadline for returning the master ballot to the balloting agent. In the recent bankruptcy of Spectradyne, a vulture investor who held a blocking position in a preferred stock class was unable to prevent the class from accepting the plan because his votes were not recorded in time.

Also, because no record is kept of how individual bondholders voted, confusion may ensue if bondholders are allowed to choose between two or more alternative settlements (e.g., an all-cash offer versus an all-stock offer). In particular, there is no way to establish which of the alternative settlements applies to bonds that are purchased after the end of balloting (because the bonds do not physically note which settlement option the holder of record chose). This problem was significant in the recent bankruptcies of E-II Holdings and Zale Credit Corporation.

Another risk facing investors is the potential for abuse of the voting process. A bondholder who holds his or her bonds at more than one brokerage firm (or holds the bonds in more than one account at the same firm) gets to cast a vote for each separate account (recall that the master ballot does not list the names of the voting bondholders). This means the holder can block a plan by ensuring that more than one-half of the voting "bondholders" vote against the plan—even if he or she in fact represents fewer than one-half of all voting bondholders. Such behavior is difficult to prove, although it has been rumored in several prominent cases.

Another potential abuse involves "churning" of bonds. The final tabulation of votes in a Chapter 11 case typically does not occur until about 60 days after the voting record date. During this time, a person could purchase some amount of bonds, keep the ballots (by agreement with the sellers), and immediately resell the bonds sans ballots. By repeating this sequence of transactions, the buyer could accumulate a large number of votes without having to hold as many bonds. Such behavior, although possible in theory, is discouraged by various penalties and sanctions (some criminal). Still, investors should be aware of the risk that their ownership of a class can be significantly diluted by such "vote inflation."

Disqualification of Votes

To profit from a proactive investment strategy, an investor must have some control over the outcome of the bankrupt firm's financial reorganization. In Chapter 11, however, investors who are more aggressive in asserting their interests risk having the judge disqualify their votes.

Events surrounding the bankruptcy of Allegheny International greatly helped define the limits of permissible behavior in this context.[23] Allegheny filed for Chapter 11 in early 1988. In late 1989, the company rebuffed the friendly overtures of New York-based Japonica Partners L.P. In response, Japonica purchased $10,000 of Allegheny's public debentures and filed its own plan of reorganization—even while disclosure hearings were being held on Allegheny's plan. Under its competing plan, Japonica proposed to acquire control of Allegheny, settling creditors' claims with mostly cash.

After balloting had commenced on Allegheny's plan, Japonica started to acquire senior bank debt in the company. It eventually acquired just over 33 percent of the class before the close of balloting, at progressively higher prices ranging from 80 percent to 97 percent of the claims' face value. Japonica was thereby able to block the debtor's plan. Soon after, it purchased an additional claim in this class for only 82 percent of face value.

The judge in the case subsequently granted a motion by the debtor to disqualify Japonica's votes under Section 1126(e) of the Bankruptcy Code, which allows the court to disqualify the votes of "any entity whose acceptance or rejection [of a plan] . . . was not in good faith, or was not solicited or procured in good faith." The judge reasoned that Japonica acted in bad faith because it had an "ulterior purpose": to acquire control of the debtor. According to the ruling, Japonica sought to defeat the debtor's reorganization plan to advance interests that it had other than as a creditor. As evidence of this self-interest, the judge noted that Japonica purchased most of its bank claims after balloting had already begun on the debtor's plan and paid a lower price for them after it had attained a blocking position in the class.

Japonica also purchased senior unsecured claims from some of Allegheny's insurance company lenders for 95 cents on the dollar—after they had already voted against Japonica's plan and for higher consideration than they had been offered under the plan. The judge rejected the insurance companies' request to change their ballots, finding again that Japonica had acted in bad faith in what he described as a "naked attempt to purchase votes."

After balloting had commenced on its own plan of reorganization, Japonica made a separate tender offer for the public subordinated bonds of

---

23. See Joy Conti, Raymond Kozlowski, Jr., and Leonard Ferleger (1992). "Claims Trafficking in Chapter 11—Has the Pendulum Swung Too Far?" *Bankruptcy Developments Journal,* Vol. 9, no. 2, pp. 281–355; and Richard Lieb (1993). "Vultures Beware: Risks of Purchasing Claims against a Chapter 11 Debtor," *The Business Lawyer,* Vol. 48, no. 3, May, pp. 915–41.

Allegheny and its Chemetron subsidiary—without the approval of the court and at a lower price than it was simultaneously offering to bondholders under its plan. Here, the judge found that Japonica's tender offer was a violation of Section 1123(a)(4) of the Bankruptcy Code, which requires a reorganization plan to treat all holders within a given class identically.

Although the judge's ruling has received mixed reviews from legal scholars, several key lessons emerge from the Allegheny case. An investor is more likely to be "shut down" by a judge if he or she openly proposes to acquire control of the debtor and, to achieve this goal, proposes an alternative reorganization plan to the debtor's and/or acquires a blocking position in one or more classes for the sole purpose of defeating the debtor's plan. One cannot appear to be too aggressive in the eyes of the judge. The risk of vote disqualification will also be greater if an investor does not respect the "sanctity" of a formal plan of reorganization (e.g., by simultaneously trying to buy claims both within and outside a plan).

Although the objectives of a proactive investor in Chapter 11 may be the same as those of a hostile acquirer in a conventional takeover contest, the path one must take to acquire control in Chapter 11 is almost always more circuitous given the involvement of the judge at every step.[24]

Holding Period Risk

The annual rate of return that one realizes buying distressed claims depends on two unknowns: the dollar recovery eventually realized by the claims (as specified in the firm's restructuring or reorganization plan), and the amount of time it takes to be paid this recovery. In the case of distressed debt, the potential dollar return is always "capped," in the sense that the most an investor can receive for the claim is the debt's face value (plus such interest that may accrue on secured debt during a Chapter 11 case).[25] Thus, the investor's annual percentage return is highly dependent on how long it takes the firm to restructure or reorganize. It is not uncommon for investors in distressed claims to seek annualized returns in the range of 25 to 35 percent.

---

24. In the end, Japonica's plan was defeated, and under the debtor's largely all-equity plan, it received stock in exchange for the debt claims it had purchased. Japonica was also forced to offer to purchase all the remaining common stock of Allegheny under a control provision that management had adopted earlier. Japonica was more than happy to oblige, because it believed—correctly, as things turned out—that the stock was grossly undervalued under current management.

25. In Chapter 11, interest accrues on secured debt if the debt is overcollateralized, but only up to the value of the excess collateral. As discussed earlier, no interest accrues on unsecured debt while a firm is in Chapter 11.

However, even modest extensions of the investor's holding period can result in substantial erosion of annualized returns, especially in the early years of a reorganization.

Aside from how it impacts the holding period, delay also hurts the investor's return because legal and other administrative costs of bankruptcy generally increase over time. (Professionals' fees in a large Chapter 11 case can easily exceed a million dollars a month.) These costs must be paid before any other claims are settled in Chapter 11, and therefore, they directly reduce the recoveries available for the firm's claimholders (especially holders of more-junior claims, who are last in line to be paid). Delay also destroys value because management continues to be distracted from running the business and key customers and suppliers are more likely to defect.

Chapter 11 cases typically run for two to three years, but adverse business developments or breakdowns in the negotiations can cause the proceedings to drag on for much longer. LTV spent more than six years in bankruptcy court. Cases also tend to take longer in certain jurisdictions (such as the Southern District of New York) where judges are inclined to extend the debtor's exclusivity period.[26] Negotiations will generally be completed in less time when the firm has a less complicated capital structure and/or fewer creditors, because creditors have fewer opportunities to disagree over what the firm is worth or what division of the firm's assets is "fair." Negotiations also typically take much less time and are less costly when firms restructure their debt out of court.[27] Finally, firms that require less extensive restructuring of their basic businesses are generally able to restructure their capital structures more quickly.

Because of the time factor, some institutions that invest in troubled situations specialize in companies whose problems are primarily financial rather than operational in nature (e.g., leveraged buyouts that go bust shortly after inception and/or firms that have solid managements in place). Most, when contemplating an investment in a Chapter 11 situation, also consider the reputation of the bankruptcy judge for expediting cases.

---

26. For a sample of 43 firms that filed for Chapter 11, LoPucki and Whitford, in "Bargaining over Equity's Share," found that cases held in New York take an average of 2.8 years to complete, compared with 2.1 years for other jurisdictions represented in their sample.

27. Gilson et al., in "Troubled Debt Restructurings," found that out-of-court restructurings are typically completed in about a year, in contrast to about two years for a typical Chapter 11 case. The authors suggested a number of reasons for this difference: Firms that restructure out of court do not have to work through a judge or observe the strict procedural rules of Chapter 11. They can selectively restructure only a subset of their claims if they choose to, and they tend to be financially more solvent than firms in Chapter 11.

The holding period can also drag on unexpectedly because of delays in distributing cash and new securities to creditors under a confirmed plan of reorganization. Often, several months elapse between the plan confirmation date and the distribution date. Some amount of time is needed to print and physically distribute the new securities. In the case of bonds, the SEC's approval of the bond indenture is also necessary. Delays are considered more likely when the new securities are distributed through non-U.S. agents, who have less experience processing Chapter 11 distributions than their U.S. counterparts. In the bankruptcy of Wang Laboratories, the use of non-U.S. agents was a concern of the company's Eurobond holders.[28]

The Strategic Role of Valuation

In every distressed situation, an investor's return depends on two key values: the true value of the firm's assets (*true value*) and the value of the firm's assets used in determining payouts to claimholders under the firm's reorganization or restructuring plan (*plan value*). These two values are almost always different, and an investor's returns can be significantly affected by changes in either value.

An investor should be aware that various parties in the case may have a significant financial interest in promoting plan values that differ dramatically from the firm's true value. Junior claimholders (e.g., common stockholders) benefit from a higher plan value because they are last in line to be paid. Conversely, senior claimholders (e.g., secured lenders) prefer a lower plan value because they then receive a larger fraction of the total consideration distributed under the plan (in effect, "squeezing out" more junior interests). These conflicting incentives exist even though both junior and senior claimholders may privately assign the same true value to the firm.

As a simple illustration, suppose that senior creditors are owed 200 and junior creditors are owed 100 (for total debt of 300). Suppose further that the true value of the firm's assets is 260. If this amount is also the plan value, then senior creditors are made whole in the restructuring, leaving only 60 for junior creditors and nothing for stockholders. (To simplify the example, I assume that payouts under the plan follow the absolute priority rule.) Stockholders would clearly prefer the plan value to exceed 300. Senior creditors, on the other hand, benefit when the plan value is less than the true value. For example, consider an alternative restructuring plan premised on a plan value of 180. In this case, senior creditors receive

28. See Mayer, "Claims Trading."

consideration nominally worth 180 (in the form of new debt and equity securities and possibly some cash), and junior creditors and stockholders both receive nothing. Because the firm is really worth 260, however, the new claims must eventually appreciate in value by 80 (i.e., 260 − 180)—a pure windfall to senior creditors.

Disagreement over the plan value can be a major obstacle to reaching a consensus and can result in unexpected extensions of the investor's holding period. In the bankruptcy of R.H. Macy, various parties in the case proposed plan values ranging from $3.35 billion to $4 billion. Adding to the usual tension in this case was the fact that a company director held a significant amount of Macy's junior debt and would therefore benefit from a higher valuation.

Any claimholder, of course, is free to vote against a reorganization plan that incorporates an unfavorable plan value. To promote a particular plan value more effectively, an investor may consider proposing his or her own reorganization plan in order to determine the general location of bargaining. At a minimum, the investor should understand which particular claimholder class "controls" the reorganization plan proposal process. In the bankruptcy of National Gypsum, junior classes alleged that management presented overly pessimistic revenue forecasts to enhance senior creditor recoveries—an allegation that to some is supported by the approximate quadrupling of National Gypsum's stock price that occurred during the following year.[29]

The above analysis also implies that an investor can earn superior returns by being able to estimate more precisely the firm's actual value. At Fidelity's Capital & Income Fund, for example, fund managers have historically pursued a strategy of buying senior claims in bankrupt firms whose assets they believe are fundamentally sound but currently undervalued in the market. By targeting senior claims, the fund hopes to receive more of the firm's equity—and future upside—under the reorganization plan. Key to this strategy is that the firm leaves Chapter 11 and distributes its new securities before the anticipated business turnaround takes place and the undervaluation is corrected.

---

29. Under National Gypsum's reorganization plan (confirmed on March 9, 1993), the firm's common stock was estimated by management to be worth approximately $12 a share; one year later, it was trading at about $40 a share. (Of course, an alternative interpretation is that the firm's business improved after it left Chapter 11 and that this improvement was not anticipated by management.) Accusations of management lowballing have become increasingly common in Chapter 11 cases. See Alison Leigh Cowan (1994). "Beware Management Talking Poor," *The New York Times* February.

Lack of Information about Purchases and Purchasers

Investors in distressed claims generally get to operate in relative secrecy. They do not have to disclose the terms of their purchases—either the number of claims acquired or the price paid—when they transact in Chapter 11, and no such disclosure has to be made in an out-of-court restructuring. This information does have to be reported if an investor files a Schedule 13D or 14D-1 with the SEC. In most situations, however, neither filing will be required (at least until after the firm's restructuring or reorganization plan is completed).[30]

For investors in distressed debt, this lack of disclosure can be a double-edged sword. Because no central record is kept of who holds a firm's debt, an investor may—as a bargaining ploy—be able to claim ownership of a blocking position in a class, when his or her actual holdings are more modest. One prominent vulture investor attempted this strategy in acquiring the bonds of bankrupt MGF Oil; management was able to discover through polling other bondholders that the vulture actually owned only 7 percent of the issue.[31] The same lack of information also makes it more difficult for an investor to know how many claims in a given class he or she should acquire, and at what price, when other investors are simultaneously seeking control.

Knowing who owns a firm's claims clearly provides a huge advantage in this market. Apollo Advisors is thought to be especially well informed about junk bond ownership because most of the principals at Apollo are former employees of Drexel Burnham Lambert and thus were directly involved in either designing or underwriting the bonds. This superior knowledge has been credited with giving Apollo a significant competitive advan-

---

30. A 13D filing must be made by any person who acquires more than 5 percent of an outstanding voting equity security, within ten days of crossing the 5 percent threshold. A 13D filing is not required when an investor purchases debt securities but may be required later if and when these securities are converted into equity under the firm's restructuring or reorganization plan. A 14D-1 filing must be made within five days of the announcement of an intention to solicit tenders for an equity security or any security that is convertible into an equity security. An investor who makes a tender offer for debt securities may therefore have to file a Schedule 14D-1 if these securities are convertible into equity under a contemplated restructuring or reorganization plan. A 14D-1 will not be required if the tender offer is for debt claims that are not "securities" or is formally part of a Chapter 11 reorganization plan. (The SEC has ruled that a debtor's disclosure statement includes enough information to make a 14D-1 filing unnecessary.)

31. Matthew Schifrin (1991). "Sellers Beware," *Forbes* January. To preempt this strategy, firms sometimes engage proxy solicitation firms to gather information on bond ownership.

tage when it bid to acquire the junk bond portfolio of failed insurer First Executive in 1991. Apollo eventually acquired more than $6 billion (face value) of First Executive's junk bonds—most of them Drexel issues—for $2 billion less than their true value, according to one recent estimate.[32]

Liquidation Risk

In a Chapter 7 liquidation, the firm's assets are sold for cash by a trustee and the proceeds are paid to the firm's claimholders according to the absolute priority rule. If the firm is worth more as a going concern than as a source of salable assets, then claimholders can collectively do better by keeping the firm alive and trying to reorganize (either in Chapter 11 or out of court).

An investor in distressed claims needs to be able to assess the risk that a firm will fail to reorganize and be forced to liquidate. As described in the appendix, the judge in a Chapter 11 case must convert the case to a Chapter 7 liquidation if agreement on a plan of reorganization is impossible.[33] Liquidation is more likely if the firm has "hard" and/or nonspecialized assets that retain most of their value when sold off. Liquidation is also a much more frequent outcome for small firms than for large ones. There are several reasons for the frequency of liquidation among small firms. Legal and other out-of-pocket costs of Chapter 11 exhibit significant economies of scale; the relative burden of Chapter 11 is therefore much greater for small firms. Also, small firms typically derive more of their value from intangible and/or specialized assets (e.g., a patent for a new drug). Finally, most small firms simply do not have the resources or depth of management to cope with a lengthy and complex Chapter 11 reorganization. An investor's losses in a liquidation will in general be smaller if he or she has purchased senior or secured claims or if the firm has relatively more unencumbered assets (i.e., assets that have not been pledged as collateral against some other loan).

---

32. Apollo's purchase of First Executive's junk bond portfolio is analyzed in Harry DeAngelo; Linda DeAngelo; and Stuart Gilson (1994). "The Collapse of First Executive Corporation: Junk Bonds, Adverse Publicity, and the 'Run on the Bank' Phenomenon," *The Journal of Financial Economics,* Vol. 36. no. 3, December, pp. 287–336. Apollo also had access to more financing than competing bidders (it is partnered with Altus Finance, a subsidiary of Credit Lyonnais); hence, unlike most other bidders, it was also able to satisfy the insurance regulators' preference that the portfolio be sold as a whole.
33. A firm can also liquidate as part of a Chapter 11 reorganization plan, but that is a much less common vehicle for liquidation than Chapter 7.

Insider Trading Issues

Investors who trade in a distressed firm's claims may be subject to bankruptcy court or other sanctions if they also have an inside or fiduciary relationship with the firm. The concept of insider trading is not explicitly addressed in the Bankruptcy Code (and is not well defined even in non-bankruptcy law). With respect to the publicly traded securities of a bankrupt firm, investors who trade on the basis of inside information face possible sanctions under Section 10(b) of the Securities Exchange Act—the same as investors in nondistressed securities. An investor who had advance knowledge of the debtor's reorganization plan, for example, would be unable legally to buy or sell the firm's publicly traded bonds. It is less clear whether this investor would also be barred from trading in the debtor's nonpublicly traded claims, which do not meet the legal definition of a "security."

Bankruptcy court judges generally take a dim view of trading by fiduciaries and can impose a variety of sanctions. An investor will be considered a fiduciary if he or she is also a professional advisor to some party in the case. Investment banks with large trading operations may find themselves in this dual role. An investor will also be considered a fiduciary if he or she sits on the Unsecured Creditors Committee (UCC). A UCC is appointed by the judge in every Chapter 11 case. It normally consists of the seven largest unsecured creditors who are willing to serve. The UCC is empowered to investigate all aspects of the firm's business, which gives it access to proprietary company information not normally available to investors.[34]

One way for such investors to avoid court sanctions is to erect a *Chinese Wall* to separate their trading activities from their fiduciary activities (for example, by prohibiting the same employees from serving in both capacities). In Federated Department Stores' bankruptcy, Fidelity Investments obtained the judge's special permission to erect such a wall and trade in Federated debt while simultaneously sitting on the Official Bondholders' Committee. The Chinese Wall, however, can be, and has been, challenged in bankruptcy

---

34. In addition, the UCC consults with the debtor on administrative matters related to the case and on formulating a plan of reorganization. The operating expenses of the UCC, including all reasonable legal and advisory fees, are paid by the firm. Committees can also be formed to represent other classes of claims if the judge decides these classes would otherwise be disadvantaged in the case. In out-of-court restructurings, the standard practice is to establish a "steering committee" of creditors that functions like the UCC in Chapter 11. Companies also usually reimburse these committees for reasonable operating expenses incurred. The role of UCCs in Chapter 11 is examined in Lynn M. LoPucki and William C. Whitford (1990). "Bargaining over Equity's Share in the Bankruptcy Reorganization of Large, Publicly Held Companies," *University of Pennsylvania Law Review,* Vol. 139, no. 1, pp. 125–96.

court.[35] As a result, many institutional investors refuse to sit on the UCC, even though they could make valuable contributions in that capacity.

Tax Issues

The particular strategy an investor follows to acquire control in a distressed firm can have a huge impact on the firm's tax liability, and hence the investor's after-tax return. In general, this tax penalty increases with the percentage of equity that an investor either purchases directly or acquires indirectly through the exchange of stock for debt.

Preservation of Net Operating Losses   If an investor purchases a block of claims in a distressed firm for the purpose of acquiring control, the firm may lose significant tax benefits arising from its net operating loss carryforwards (NOLs). This tax "hit" can severely reduce the investor's return. NOLs are often a distressed firm's largest single asset.[36] Before it emerged from Chapter 11, R.H. Macy had NOLs in excess of $1 billion.

Under Section 382 of the Internal Revenue Code, a firm's ability to use its NOLs can be severely restricted when it experiences an "ownership change." An ownership change takes place when any group of stockholders collectively increases its total percentage ownership of the firm's common stock by more than 50 percentage points during any three-year period.[37] Purchasing a large block of equity or debt prior to the firm's reorganization or restructuring can greatly increase the risk of an ownership change, especially if the debt is exchanged for common stock.

---

35. During the bankruptcy of Papercraft Corporation, a failed LBO, a court-appointed examiner recommended that the trading profits made by two investors in the case—Magten Asset Management and Citicorp Venture Capital Ltd.—be refunded to the debtor and that neither investor be allowed to fully vote its claims. The examiner's recommendation was based on the fact that both investors sat on the UCC and were therefore fiduciaries. Citibank Venture Capital was also an original investor in the LBO and had the right to elect a director to Papercraft's board. Significantly, it made no difference to the examiner that one investor had disclosed its "insider" relationship to the sellers of the claims or that the other's intention in buying claims was to facilitate the reorganization (as well as to make a profit).
36. One recent academic study finds that, for public companies in Chapter 11, NOLs typically exceed the total book value of assets by more than 200 percent. See Stuart Gilson (1997). "Transaction Costs and Capital Structure Choice: Evidence from Financially Distressed Firms," *Journal of Finance,* Vol. 52, pp. 161–96.
37. In calculating the percentage ownership change, percentage reductions in ownership by individual stockholders who individually own less than 5 percent of the stock are collectively treated as a single holder. In addition, convertible securities and warrants are treated as actual common shares. The increase in ownership attributed to each stockholder is determined relative to the lowest percentage of the firm's stock owned by that holder during the three-year test period.

If an ownership change does take place, the restrictions on NOL use are generally less severe if the firm is in Chapter 11. In this case, the least severe restriction applies if more than 50 percent of the firm's stock continues to be held by its prepetition shareholders and creditors (who must have been creditors for at least 18 months before the bankruptcy filing).[38] This condition can easily be violated, however, if an outside investor has acquired control of the firm's equity by purchasing claims. The most severe restriction would then apply: Annual NOL use would be limited to the value of shareholders' equity after the reorganization multiplied by a statutory federal interest rate. In practice, this calculation produces a relatively small number, making it unlikely that the firm will be unable to use up its NOLs before they expire.[39] If an ownership change occurs while the firm is restructuring its debt out of court, it can lose its NOLs altogether.[40]

Investors can manage such risks by limiting how much they invest in high–NOL firms or by targeting more solvent firms that are apt to issue less new equity in a reorganization or restructuring.

Cancellation of Indebtedness Income   If an investor purchases a financially distressed firm's debt at less than face value and later—within two years—becomes "related" to the firm by acquiring more than 50 percent of its equity, the discount may be taxable to the firm as *cancellation of indebtedness* (COD) income. Normally, such income is created whenever a firm repurchases its debt for less than full face value. The risk of creating COD income is greatest for investors who seek to control the firm's operations after it reorganizes.

Exit Strategies and Liquidity Risk

Although the market for distressed claims has become much more liquid and efficient in recent years, it is still less liquid than most organized securities markets. Investors should therefore decide on an exit strategy before

---

38. NOLs are reduced by approximately one-half the amount of any debt forgiven in the reorganization (net of any new consideration distributed) plus any interest.
39. In the United States, NOLs can be carried back 3 years and then carried forward for 15. Even if the firm manages to preserve some of its NOLs while in Chapter 11, however, it will forfeit even these if it experiences a subsequent ownership change within two years.
40. Specifically, if the firm continues in its historic line of business, annual use of NOLs is limited to the value of shareholders' equity before the restructuring is implemented multiplied by the same statutory federal interest rate used in calculating the restriction for firms in Chapter 11. If the firm changes its line of business, however, all of its NOLs are lost.

they invest in a distressed situation. Exit normally occurs in one of three ways. First, and most common, investors can simply trade out of their positions. Second, they can sell their claims in an initial public offering. This strategy is appropriate when investors acquire a large equity stake in the borrower and the borrower's stock is not publicly traded (e.g., because it went private in an LBO). Third, investors can swap their claims for cash and/or other consideration in a merger. This form of exit was available in the recent bankruptcy of R.H. Macy, which was acquired out of Chapter 11 by Federated Department Stores.

Unforeseen declines in market liquidity can substantially reduce an investor's returns by lengthening the holding period and/or reducing the exit price. In a distressed situation, such *liquidity risk* can arise in several ways. First, too many new types of claims may be created under the firm's reorganization or restructuring plan, resulting in an overly complex and fragmented capital structure. This fragmentation will undermine liquidity if the total dollar amount outstanding of a given claim is too small to support an active market in the issue. In practice, a junk bond issue must be worth at least $100 million (face value) to generate strong interest among institutional investors and analysts.

An investor's ability to trade out of his or her position may also be impaired if he or she signed a confidentiality agreement when the claims were purchased. Such agreements are fairly standard in purchases of non-public claims, such as bank debt, in which the original lenders have proprietary knowledge about the borrower's operations. (These agreements also typically prohibit the buyer from contacting the borrower.) If the investor tries to sell these claims without disclosing such material inside information, he or she could run afoul of applicable securities law if the claims are considered "securities." An investor can reduce this risk in Chapter 11 by postponing trades until after the firm files its disclosure statement (which discloses at least as much information as a typical securities offering registration statement).

The liquidity of the firm's common stock will also be impaired if the firm places trading restrictions on its stock in order to preserve its NOLs. Such restrictions reduce the likelihood of an "ownership change," which can cause the firm to lose some or all of its NOLs. After significant amounts of new common stock have been issued in a bankruptcy or restructuring, even modest trading in the stock may trigger an ownership change. To guard against this risk, Allis–Chalmers, which emerged from Chapter 11 with nearly half a billion dollars in NOLs, preempted all trading in its common stock by placing its shares in a special trust—effectively taking itself private. In some other cases, bankruptcy judges have enjoined trading in claims—going against the intent of revised Rule 3001(e)—because of concern over the potential loss of NOLs.

Finally, analysts and investors may lose interest in a firm once it becomes financially distressed (e.g., because trading in the firm's securities is suspended by the listing exchange or the SEC or because the firm ends up significantly smaller). In this case, the investor may have to take a proactive role in restoring liquidity to the market. This happened in the case of Hills Stores, which emerged from Chapter 11 in October 1993. In the summer of 1995, Dickstein Partners L.P.—which had become a major stockholder in Hills under its reorganization plan—waged a proxy fight against management with the goal of forcing an auction for the firm and increasing its share price. In spite of having shown positive operating performance since the bankruptcy, Hills was followed by relatively few analysts—its debt and equity securities had been closely held since the reorganization— and its stock price had remained flat. Dickstein's initiative has been credited with increasing Hills' stock price by more than 20 percent.[41]

DO VULTURES ADD OR SUBTRACT VALUE IN A REORGANIZATION?

The role of vulture investors in the corporate reorganization process is controversial. The very term *vulture* is pejorative, much like the tag *raider,* once used to describe proactive investors in the 1980s' takeover market. Many bankruptcy judges are philosophically opposed to the idea that people can insert themselves into a distressed situation for profit—all while the firm's original lenders and stockholders are being asked to make material financial sacrifices. The news media are often no more sympathetic,[42] and the SEC keeps revisiting the idea of bringing the market for distressed claims under the scope of the insider trading laws.

Such hostility to the activities of vulture investors overlooks the critical role they play in creating value in a restructuring situation. A key point is that trading in distressed claims is voluntary: Sellers only participate in a given transaction when they expect to benefit from doing so. When a firm becomes financially distressed, there are various reasons why the original lenders can benefit from selling their claims, even for less than full face value.

---

41. See Stephanie Strom (1994). "Giving the Pros a Taste of Their Own Medicine," *The New York Times* August, and Letter to Hills Stockholders from Dickstein Partners L.P. (dated June 12, 1995), on file with the author.
42. See, for example, Laura Jereski and Jason Zweig (1991). "Step Right Up Folks," *Forbes* March.

Bank lenders may be able to book a profit on a distressed loan sale if, as a result of prior writedowns, the sales price exceeds the current book value of the loan. By disposing of their distressed loans and improving the quality of their loan portfolios, these lenders may also be able to reduce the amount of capital that must be set aside to satisfy statutory risk-based capital guidelines. Finally, some banks prefer to sell off their loans as soon as they become troubled, rather than actively manage them through a workout department.

Trade creditors can also benefit from selling their claims against a distressed firm. Smaller vendors often cannot afford to wait until the end of a bankruptcy or restructuring for their claims to be settled and would rather receive cash up front. Other vendors may wish to continue doing business with the firm after it solves its financial difficulties and therefore sell their claims rather than risk antagonizing the firm in an adversarial Chapter 11 or restructuring proceeding.

By buying up and consolidating distressed claims, vultures can also facilitate a reorganization by reducing the so-called "holdout problem." Outside of Chapter 11, distressed firms often attempt to restructure their publicly held debt by offering bondholders the opportunity to exchange their bonds for new claims (typically consisting of either equity securities or new debt securities having a lower face value or interest rate than the original bonds). Bondholders who hold only a small fraction of a given issue have little incentive to tender their bonds, because their decision will not have a material impact on the likelihood of a successful restructuring. Moreover, if they retain their bonds and the restructuring goes through anyway, they get to receive the more generous payouts offered by the original bonds without having made any financial sacrifice. If enough bondholders behave this way, however, the restructuring must fail and everyone is worse off.[43] By buying up small holdings and consolidating them into large blocks, vulture investors help reduce the holdout problem and make it easier for firms to restructure their debt.

Vulture investors, as discount buyers, are also less wedded to receiving the full face value of their claims in a restructuring or bankruptcy; even a small (e.g., 30 percent) recovery of face value can produce large investment returns if the claims were acquired for a sufficiently low price. Banks and insurance companies, in contrast, often fiercely resist giving up loan

---

43. The holdout problem is less severe in Chapter 11 because bondholders within a class who hold out can be forced to participate in a reorganization plan as long as a sufficient number of other bondholders (representing at least two-thirds in value and one-half in number of all bondholders represented in the class) vote for the plan.

principal or taking equity in the borrower.[44] Lender resistance to principal write-downs can result in firms being saddled with excessive leverage after they come out of a bankruptcy or restructuring, forcing them to restructure again in the future. (In practice, approximately one in three firms that reorganizes in Chapter 11 makes a return trip to bankruptcy court as a "Chapter 22" or "Chapter 33.") The presence of vulture investors therefore facilitates restructuring by giving the firm greater flexibility to choose an optimal capital structure.[45]

CONCLUSION

Although the strategies for investing in distressed debt are many and varied, investors who are consistently successful in this market tend to exhibit certain key qualities. First is a superior ability to value a firm's assets. This trait not only means being better at processing information; it also means being better at locating and collecting information. When a firm becomes financially distressed, information about the firm from conventional public sources often dries up or is not sufficiently timely. In its bid to control bankrupt Allegheny International (now Sunbeam–Oster Company), Japonica Partners engaged almost a hundred outside people to help it value the company's assets; it extensively interviewed the company's distributors, customers, and line managers in order to understand its products and markets better; and it relentlessly pressured senior management to provide it with detailed and timely operating and financial data. This approach was fundamental analysis with a vengeance.

The second defining quality of a successful vulture investor is superior negotiating and bargaining skill. In large measure, this skill is a function of how accurately one values the firm's assets and of how well the

---

44. See Stuart Gilson, "Transaction Costs and Capital Structure Choice: Evidence from Financially Distressed Firms."

45. Empirical evidence on the impact of vultures is limited. One recent study finds that common stock prices of distressed firms increase, on average, when vultures acquire the firms' junior claims and decline, on average, when they acquire more-senior claims. See Edith Hotchkiss and Robert Mooradian (1997). "Vulture Investors and the Market for Control of Distressed Firms," *Journal of Financial Economics,* Vol. 43, pp. 401–32. The authors provide two possible interpretations of their evidence: (1) The vulture's decision to purchase junior (senior) claims in the capital structure signals that he or she believes the firm has a high (low) value; or (2) Vultures purchase senior claims to block the firm's reorganization plan and extract higher payments (at the expense of junior claims).

investor understands the firm's capital structure, including the legal rights and financial interests of all other claimholders.

Finally, successful vultures understand the risks of investing in distressed situations. These risks cannot be eliminated, but they can be controlled. Again, careful fundamental analysis of the firm's business and financial condition is critical.

The future will bring new opportunities from abroad, especially in Europe and Mexico. In the United Kingdom, in particular, annual trading in distressed bank loans now runs, by some estimates, into the billions of dollars. One reason for this growth is the U.K. banks' increasing willingness to break from traditional relationship banking and sell off their loans when they become nonperforming. As lenders in general become more comfortable with the idea of transacting in secondary markets for distressed debt, there is every reason to expect these trends to continue.[46]

46. I am grateful to the Harvard Business School's Division of Research for supporting this project. This article is based in part on a presentation I made at the Spring 1994 Berkeley Program in Finance.

Rules for Confirming a Chapter 11 Plan of Reorganization

Every proposed plan of reorganization assigns the firm's claimholders to different classes. The Bankruptcy Code requires that each class consist only of claims that are "substantially similar." Confirmation of a plan of reorganization can be either consensual or nonconsensual.

Consensual Plans

Under a consensual plan of reorganization, every impaired class of claims must vote for the plan. Acceptance of the plan by a particular class requires the approval of at least two-thirds of the face value of outstanding claims in that class, representing at least one-half of the claimholders in that class who vote (claimholders who do not vote or fail to show up are not counted). The plan must also satisfy the best-interests-of-creditors test: Each dissenting member of every impaired class must receive consideration worth at least what he or she would receive in a liquidation. To ensure that this requirement is satisfied, the plan sponsor normally includes an estimate of the firm's liquidation value in the official disclosure statement given to creditors prior to the vote. In practice, these reported liquidation values are usually low-ball estimates, set sufficiently low so that the best-interests-of-creditors test is almost sure to be satisfied.

Nonconsensual Plans

Under a nonconsensual plan of reorganization, one or more impaired classes vote against the plan. For such a plan to be confirmed, two additional tests must be satisfied: The plan must not discriminate unfairly, and it must be fair and equitable. If the plan meets these two conditions, then it can be "crammed down" on the dissenting classes. A plan is fair and equitable with respect to a dissenting class if the present value of the cash and securities to be distributed to the class equals the allowed value of the class members' claims or if no more-junior class receives any consideration. Stated differently, a plan is fair and equitable if the absolute priority rule holds for the dissenting class and for all more junior classes. (More-senior classes are excluded from this determination, and their recoveries need not conform to the absolute priority rule.) The rule is more complicated in the case of secured debt.

Consider the hypothetical example in Exhibit 24A–1. In this example, suppose the secured and senior unsecured classes vote for the plan, and the subordinated class votes against the plan (the common stock, which is to receive nothing, is automatically assumed to vote against the plan). The plan can be crammed down on both the subordinated and common stock classes (assuming the earlier best-interests-of-creditors test is also satisfied, as it must be under either type of plan). Note that the proposed distributions to the secured and senior unsecured classes do not conform to the absolute priority rule. Because both of these classes vote for the plan, there is no need to cram the plan down on them.

In practice, cram-downs are uncommon because they require the court to hold a valuation hearing to determine the present value of the cash and securities to be distributed to dissenting classes. These hearings tend to be extremely costly and time consuming, so it is generally in everyone's best interest to avoid them. As a consequence, senior classes often leave something on the table for junior classes, even though the junior classes would be entitled to nothing if the absolute priority rule were strictly followed. Thus, the threat of a cram-down can have as significant an influence on the outcome as an actual cram-down.

With either type of plan (consensual or nonconsensual), confirmation requires that at least one impaired claimholder class vote for the plan. If this vote is impossible to attain, the judge will convert the case to a Chapter 7 liquidation, under which the firm's assets will be sold off and the proceeds distributed to creditors according to the rule of absolute priority.

The Feasibility Test

Every plan (consensual and nonconsensual) must also be deemed feasible by the judge in order to be confirmed, which means the company will be able to generate sufficient cash flow in the future to avoid a return trip to bankruptcy court. In practice, plan feasibility is assessed by comparing projected annual debt service costs with projected earnings or cash flows (generally over a four- to six-year horizon).

E X H I B I T   24A-1

Hypothetical Chapter 11 Reorganization Plan

Claim	Allowed Value	Present Value of Consideration	Percent Recovery
Secured Debt	100	95	95%
Senior Secured Debt	240	203	85
Subordinated Debt	150	90	60
Common Stock	—	0	0

CHAPTER 25

Analyzing the Credit Risk of Distressed Securities*

Mark R. Shenkman

INTRODUCTION

For many investors, the term *distressed securities* connotes high risk and suggests avoidance; others recognize that distressed securities offer attractive risk-return opportunities. Since the shakeouts in the high yield market in 1989 and 1990, many high yield portfolio managers, hedge funds, arbitrageurs, and private partnerships have gravitated to the lucrative segment of the high yield market known as distressed investments. Although distressed investing is still considered the backwater of all investment sectors, it is gaining more acceptance each year.

A distressed investment sector has existed since the Great Depression, when a small group of sophisticated investors purchased defaulted railroad and utility bonds, but the market for distressed investments greatly expanded in the 1980s. Distressed investing came into vogue when many of the leveraged buyouts (LBOs) of the late 1980s faltered and the Resolution Trust Corporation was formed to clean up the savings and loan debacle. As in many evolving markets, the early entrants in distressed investing earned handsome profits and showed spectacular results.

This chapter will provide an overview of the process for analyzing distressed credits. In particular, this chapter highlights some of the complexities and nuances that should be considered when investing in distressed

*Reprinted, with permission, from *Credit Analysis of Nontraditional Debt Securities,* Seminar
  proceedings. Copyright 1995, Association for Investment Management and Research,
  Charlottesville, VA. All rights reserved.

companies. However, investment professionals should retain the services of experienced bankruptcy lawyers to guide them through the maze of the U.S. Federal Bankruptcy Code.

TERMINOLOGY

Distressed investing has certain terms unique to this asset class, and in many cases, terms are used interchangeably.

- *Bankrupt securities.* Any company that has actually filed a formal petition under Chapter 7 (liquidation) or Chapter 11 (rehabilitation) of the U.S. Bankruptcy Code is a bankrupt security.
- *Distressed securities.* These companies are suffering from serious financial deterioration and may be in technical or actual default with respect to their debt obligations. A company whose securities are selling at a deep discount because of market conditions or because of a low coupon is not necessarily a distressed security.
- *Fallen angels.* These companies were investment grade, but their financial conditions have deteriorated so that they are now rated below BBB. The rating agencies consider them speculative credits.
- *Prebankruptcy.* In some situations, companies are considered to be in the prebankruptcy stage. Some companies are able to avoid a formal bankruptcy filing by working out a debt restructuring with their creditors during this stage.
- *Restructuring (or recapitalization).* This process results from a company having insufficient cash flow to service its debt on a timely basis. Restructuring or recapitalization requires the company to negotiate with its creditors to recapitalize the company. The process may be accomplished without a formal bankruptcy filing.
- *Vulture investing.* This term is a pejorative used to define investments in distressed and/or bankrupt situations. It implies that in sorting through the assets of an ailing company, investors are picking over a "corporate corpse."

THE LIFE CYCLE OF A BANKRUPTCY

A system of stages can be used to identify where a company is in the cycle of the bankruptcy process.

Prebankruptcy   A company in this stage acknowledges that it is under financial distress. In many cases, informal bondholder committees are formed and start working with the company and its advisors to try to restructure the company. A prepackaged bankruptcy plan may be attempted in which creditors agree in advance on a recapitalization. The company will then file for Chapter 11 as a formal way to clear up financial problems and to implement "fresh start" accounting. The prebankruptcy stage is when investors should begin their research to determine the investment merits of a particular company.

Early Bankruptcy   This stage begins on the date of an actual bankruptcy filing and can last from six months to more than a year. Lawyers have a field day in the beginning phase; they typically have a vested interest in slowing down the process as creditor groups jockey for power. Virtually no fundamental issues are addressed in this early phase of the cycle, but many administrative, legal, and power issues play out.

This stage, given its maximum of uncertainty and confusion, may be a good time to purchase a large position and invest at a low dollar price. Some investors may prefer to wait, however, because of the time value of money. An investor in the early bankruptcy stage may end up with a large investment, but the confirmation of the reorganization plan could take several years.

Middle Bankruptcy   In the middle stage, which typically lasts from six months to two years after filing, the legal and financial advisors begin to perform their in-depth due diligence analysis with creditors' committees. During this stage, a company's operations begin to stabilize. Usually, the company has terminated contracts and leases and begins to build up cash because it is not paying interest to creditors.

During this stage, some issues cause big battles. For example, in the Macy's bankruptcy, the company had the exclusive right to present the first reorganization plan and used this middle period to receive repeated, contested extensions.

Late Bankruptcy   The late stage can last anywhere from one year to—as in the case of Manville and LTV—several years. During this stage, issues among the creditors are resolved, the enterprise value is established, and the creditors decide how the new securities and cash will be distributed.

From the standpoint of the time value of money, investing during the late stage may offer the best returns because the risk of legal paralysis is reduced. Investors can gain better insight into the valuation ranges than they can in earlier stages and have a greater ability to assess the problems and delays in the bankruptcy.

INVESTMENT ANALYSIS

In analyzing a possible investment in a distressed situation, investors need to consider the causes of the distress, the industry and company operating results, the various types of restructuring, the most advantageous position in the capital structure in which to invest, when investing is actually buying the company, the number and composition of creditor committee(s), the bankruptcy judge, and (perhaps most importantly) timing.

CAUSES OF FAILURE

Without knowing why a specific company failed, an investor cannot know how long correcting the problems will take, and the analysis of potential returns will be flawed from the very beginning. Therefore, investors must identify the reason for the enterprise's failure. Was it excessive leverage, as was the case with Macy's, Marvel Entertainment, and Levitz Furniture? Was it structural industry problems, as in the case of wireless cable operators, such as HearHand Wireless and CAI Wireless? Was it a poor acquisition strategy, as with Federated Department Stores? Was it inept management? Was it an LBO that was predicated on asset sales to deleverage? Or was it legal problems, as in the cases of Texaco, Manville, and Dow Corning?

THE INDUSTRY AND COMPANY OPERATING RESULTS

Industry structure, trends, and competitive forces can have a significant impact on a firm. Bruno'a and Grand Union, both of which went bankrupt, would be examples of companies whose financial stability was adversely affected by industry problems. Industries undergo structural changes, so investors need to determine whether a particular company has problems because of structural change in the industry or because of problems unique to the company—too much leverage, poor management, or ill-timed acquisitions.

In addition, one must carefully analyze a company's competitive position. In very competitive, or commodity-oriented, industries, a highly leveraged company should be a low-cost producer. Otherwise, stronger companies will capitalize on the company's unfavorable financial position.

Investors should also examine the distressed company's operating results from various perspectives. One should look at not only the consolidated financial statements but also the contingent liabilities and unconsolidated subsidiaries. Some companies have numerous subsidiaries, and some of their "jewels" may not have entered bankruptcy. The holding company may file for bankruptcy, but the operating company may not. Creditors may try to draw the healthy operations of the company into the bankruptcy in order to expand the asset base to be distributed to creditors.

Investors should review the company's historical revenue growth. Many companies fall on difficult times because revenues have not grown for several years. Analysis of revenue growth may reveal whether prices or failures of unit growth are responsible for poor revenue growth. Is the business cyclical and/or seasonal? Many companies have seasonal differences in cash flows. For example, Macy's was able to manage its cash flow so that reorganization occurred after the Christmas season when its cash position was at its highest level. One should also examine the company's gross margin to determine any trends.

Capital expenditures should be assessed. Many companies postpone or stop capital spending as they slide into default. These companies may need to modernize their plants and equipment in order to be competitive in postbankruptcy.

In addition to trends in cash flow, analysts should also assess the company's ability to retain experienced people. Many members of middle and senior management can be lured away during the bankruptcy process.

TYPES OF BANKRUPTCY OR RESTRUCTURING

The type of bankruptcy and the complexity of the restructuring dictate how much time and cost are involved before the investment can begin to pay off. The length of time required to resolve a bankruptcy can increase due to many factors, including intense creditor infighting, a backlog of bankruptcy cases, and a complex legal landscape. In the mid-1980s, a typical bankruptcy lasted 18–22 months; the time then progressed to 24–30 months; and today, on average, a bankruptcy takes more than 30 months to resolve.

In a *prepackaged bankruptcy,* all the details have been worked out with the creditors before filing. An *out-of-court restructuring* is typically a private exchange offer. Some companies are able to recapitalize and restructure without the protection of bankruptcy. In a *voluntary Chapter 11,* the company, senior management, and the board of directors determine on their own to put the company into bankruptcy. Placing a company into *involuntary bankruptcy* takes only three creditors that in the aggregate have a claim for $10,000. A *Chapter 7 bankruptcy* is a total liquidation of the corporation.

POSITIONING IN THE CAPITAL STRUCTURE

A major decision that an investor must make is what position in the capital structure is the most advantageous for the investment. Some investors take the lowest-dollar-cost approach, in which the debt is purchased at the cheapest price. For example, Grand Union, which in the prebankruptcy stage, was a holding company that had senior zero-coupon debt trading at 70 cents, junior zero-coupon debt trading at 75 cents, and preferred stock trading at zero. In light of the enterprise value of the operating company, the holding company would not have been a good place to invest. At the operating company level, Grand Union had 11.25 percent and 11.375 percent senior secured debentures trading flat at $86 and subordinated 12.25 percent debentures trading at $39. Is an investor better off with only 39 points of risk or at the higher dollar price of $86 with better position at the senior level of the capital structure?

In the analytical process, the investor must examine the best way to play a given situation. Investors must decide if they want to seek control or a blocking position in a given tranche. The size of different tranches is relevant; a blocking position typically requires an investment of at least 35 percent of a given tranche because most confirmation plans need two-thirds approval by each class.

BUYING THE COMPANY VERSUS INVESTING

At times in a bankruptcy situation, particularly in the case of distressed subordinated high yield debt, investors are "buying the company" because, ultimately, they will end up receiving equity in payment of their claims. Subordinated holders of distressed high yield bonds usually end up with equity in the reorganized company.

In nondistressed high yield bond analysis, one should calculate the typical financial ratios, such as total interest coverage, the ratio of total debt to earnings before interest, taxes, depreciation, and amortization (EBITDA). Then one should review the amortization schedule, the consistency and predictability of cash flows, and the industry fundamentals.

In a distressed company analysis, however, the most important factor is total enterprise value (TEV) and the value of the company to be distributed to each class of creditors. Analysis of these elements often requires developing pro forma capital structures, which estimate what the company's balance sheet may look like when it emerges from bankruptcy. The purpose is to estimate whether the company will be able to service its debt in the future. The salability of the company's assets is also critical because many reorganization plans are contingent upon asset sales. If one is going to be an equityholder in a company, one must consider whether the postbankrupt company can generate sufficient cash flow to rebuild its value.

Equityholders, in short, need to think in terms of what the future of the business is likely to be. Has or can the company correct its problems? How capable is its management? The senior management who put the company into a precarious financial position may not be able to provide the leadership necessary to take the company out of bankruptcy. If the existing management's strategies failed in the past, they may be unable to sell assets quickly or to change the complexion of the postbankrupt company.

CREDITORS' COMMITTEES

Creditors' committees are negotiating bodies that represent creditor classes. One of the fiercest battles that takes place in all high-profile cases is over the question of having separate committees for different tranches of debt. Each constituency wants to have its own committee; the banks, subordinated-debt holders, stockholders, those claiming damages, and preferred stockholders. The more committees that exist, the slower the process and the more infighting that occurs.

If a judge forces all creditors into one committee, then the composition of the committee is critical. If 7 out of 12 creditors represent banks, then the banks control the committee. Sometimes trade representatives are on the committee. Trade creditors take a different perspective from the banks' perspective because they want the company to survive in order to ship merchandise.

RECORD OF THE JUDGE

Investors should never underestimate the importance of the judge in a particular case. One should review the key rulings of the judges in large cases, particularly in the New York Southern District. Some judges favor creditors, some are pro-debtors, and some are impartial. Examination of judges' past decisions will indicate their opinions on such important issues as substantive consolidation, exclusivity, and summary judgments.

Each judge has his or her own style with respect to handling the proceedings. Some judges want to keep very tight control of the process, and others keep the process loose and let the parties seek a consensus.

Judges tend to pay careful attention in high-profile cases because their peers are watching them. These judges are also handling personal bankruptcies and small business bankruptcies. So, a judge may be handling thousands of cases at a time. If one case is a highly public, billion-dollar case, the judge is likely to focus on it. The bigger the bankruptcy, the more controlling the judge tends to be.

TIMING

The critical issue that drives the analysis of distressed investment opportunities is the amount of time the company must remain in bankruptcy. The progress of the bankruptcy process is important. Intercreditor disputes and the judge's control over conflicts could extend the time a company must contend with the bankruptcy court.

The most important factor in whether the company will be a long or short time in bankruptcy is the company's operating results during Chapter 11. Are results improving or deteriorating? If the company's cash flow deteriorates, it is not going to come out of bankruptcy any time soon. No company is going to emerge from the protection of bankruptcy if its business is inherently weak and management has failed to stop the cash flow drain.

When a company is able to curtail paying interest and to terminate leases, it should build up sufficient working capital for day-to-day operations. Many debtors, however, are forced to turn to financial institutions to obtain debtor-in-possession (DIP) financing for working capital. This DIP financing has a super-priority ranking.

VALUATION

Valuation in the distressed-company situation addresses the individual assets, enterprise value, the plan, and the tranche.

ASSETS

The discrete parts of a distressed company should be valued by using public stock market valuations and recent information on asset sales of related businesses. Investors should look at all divisions and determine the performance of each during the past several years. These results should be compared with those of the divisions' competitors.

One should analyze the company on an ongoing basis because the company may not be able to obtain the values it expects to receive from its assets. Therefore, the evaluation should include a sensitivity analysis with and without asset sales.

Finally, an investor trying to make a sound investment decision needs the opinions of outside experts. The experts might be investment bankers or specialists in distressed appraisals. In most cases, creditors' committees will obtain the proper professional assistance to obtain a fair market appraisal.

THE ENTERPRISE VALUE (TEV)

Calculating the TEV of the distressed company is probably the most important exercise to perform in analyzing a distressed investment candidate. The TEV will determine the value that creditors will divide upon confirmation of the reorganization plan. Two methods are widely used: discounted cash flow analysis and industry comparables.

Discounted Cash Flow Analysis   In this approach, the company's present TEV is the present value (PV) of its cash flows (its discounted cash flow) plus the present value of its terminal value. The appropriate discount rate to use is the company's weighted-average cost of capital (assuming a normal capital structure). Formally, the calculation is

$$TEV = PV \text{ cash flow} + PV \text{ terminal value.}$$

Analysis of Industry Comparables   This method of valuation entails calculating a market value for the enterprise based on various multiples for similar companies. The multiples can include ratios of price to sales, price-to-EBITDA, or price-to-earnings before interest and taxes (EBIT). For example, suppose one has reviewed the valuations of several companies that are direct competitors of the company being analyzed and found the following multiples (with price defined as the market value of investment capital): price-to-sales, 0.8 times; price-to-EBITDA, 5 times; and price-to-EBIT, 8.5 times. Suppose these multiples are used for a company with the forecasts shown in Exhibit 25–1. Each comparison produces a slightly different TEV, with a simple unweighted average of about $385. Depending on the importance of sales, EBITDA, or EBIT, any of the calculated TEVs, or the average could be used for estimating this company's TEV.

E X H I B I T   2 5–1

Industry Comparable Method of
Determining Enterprise Value

Measure	Multiple	Forecasted Level	TEV
Price-to-Sales	0.8x	$500	$400.0
Price-to-EBITDA	5.0	75	375.0
Price-to-EBIT	8.5	45	382.0
Average			$385.7

Source: Mark R. Shenkman.

The company's securities are then valued based on the rankings of the specific claims. First, taxes and Social Security liabilities must be subtracted. The Internal Revenue Service, hoping that it will get a piece of available cash, usually files massive claims against bankrupt companies. The IRS might put in a $2 billion claim and settle for $26 million. Any DIP financing is next in line. The remaining liabilities are then ranked on a priority basis from secured debt to trade claims, unsecured subordinated debt, any contingent claims, such as damage or health claims, preferred stock, and finally, the common equity.

All of the creditors file claims, and in most cases, the claims far exceed the amount the company accepts as its liability. The bankruptcy judge weights all of the claims; the claims may amount to billions of dollars but, in the end, the judge may find the allowable claims are only a fraction of the original claim.

Suppose a company has a TEV of $350 million and claims against it of $600 million. Legally, secured creditors are entitled to receive 100 percent of their claims before other creditors receive anything. If the banks claim $200 million, they may take it in cash or, if they are sensitive to the time value of money, they may take 80 percent in cash and 20 percent in new senior debt or equity to expedite the process.

THE PLAN

Almost every plan has a package of securities; there is no such thing as a plan under which creditors receive only cash. If a plan of reorganization is consensual, the various creditor groups have an opportunity to vote on the plan. If the creditors' committees are unable to develop a plan or reorganization, the judge can force the process along.

Plans usually include some cash, some bonds, and some equities and may include some reinstatement of old debt. The value of the bonds depends partly on their types, the size of the total issue, and whether the issue will be public or private. Small or private issues are usually priced at a discount. The investor should compare the yield of the bonds with the bonds of other companies in the same industry. Then, using various valuation methods, the investor should evaluate the likely market price of the equity. One should calculate a range of prices likely under the pro forma capital structure with contingent liabilities and cost of the bankruptcy factored in. The marketability of the equity is also a key consideration.

One of the most contentious issues is the question of prepetition interest (interest earned up to the date of a bankruptcy filing) and postpetition interest on the monies. Usually, a claimant will get prepetition interest, although postpetition interest may not be paid. The likelihood of receiving postpetition interest increases if a secured creditor is overcollaterized.

THE TRANCHE

Typically, the more junior the tranche, the more likely those creditors are to receive equity in the distribution plan. Investors should be willing to accept more equity in the following circumstances: The company has good growth prospects; it is a cyclical company at the trough of the cycle; the shareholders are proactive; the public equity markets would give these shares a premium valuation. In general, bonds are desirable if the company's operations are stabilized and deleveraging is foreseeable.

Many highly successful investors in high-profile distressed companies become involved in certain situations because they want to emerge as substantial equityholders at a very low price. However, there have been situations where the creditors received large blocks of stock, and arbitrage activities have taken place. Upon the distribution of the stock these arbitrageurs dumped their equity into the market during a very short period, causing a supply imbalance. In such cases, the stock price may plunge after the company emerges from bankruptcy.

MATRIX VALUATION APPROACH

A return matrix is useful in analyzing rates of return and relative value. Exhibit 25–2 contains an example—a Plan A distribution plan for a hypothetical bankrupt company. At the top is a description of the claims against the company before the bankruptcy. This company has three classes of claims, and for each, the description indicates the face amounts and the

EXHIBIT 25-2

Sample Valuation Matrix

Distributions per Plan A

		New 10% Debt		Common Equity		
Claim	Old Debt	Amount	Per $100 of Old Debt	Shares (millions)	Percent of Total	Per $100 of Old Debt
Trade Claims	$ 40.0	$12.9	$32.3	2.1	10.3%	5.2
11.375% Senior Notes	292.8	85.1	29.1	13.5	67.7	4.6
14.5% Senior Subordinated Notes	176.2	2.0	1.1	4.0	20.0	2.3

Market Value of New Debt at 11 Percent Yield

Note	Price per Bond	Total Value	Value per $100 of Bonds
11.375% Senior Notes	$94.0	$80.0	$27.3
14.500% Senior Subordinated Notes	94.0	1.9	1.1

Valuation of Securities Received Assuming Various TEVs (per $100 of old notes)

TEV	11.375% Senior Notes	14.5% Subordinated Notes	Trade Claims	TEV	11.375% Senior Notes	14.5% Subordinated Notes	Trade Claims
$275	$67.8	$20.9	$77.3	$325	$79.3	$26.6	$90.2
280	68.9	21.5	78.6	330	80.5	27.2	91.5
285	70.1	22.1	79.9	335	81.7	27.7	92.8
290	71.3	22.6	81.2	340	82.8	28.3	94.1
295	72.4	23.2	82.5	345	84.0	28.9	95.3
300	73.6	23.8	83.8	350	85.1	29.4	96.6
305	74.7	24.3	85.0	355	86.3	30.0	97.9
310	75.9	24.9	86.3	360	87.4	30.6	99.2
315	77.0	25.5	87.6	365	88.6	31.1	100.5
320	78.2	26.0	88.9	370	89.8	31.7	101.8
325	79.3	26.6	90.2	375	90.9	32.3	103.1

One-Year IRR for 11.375% Senior Notes

TEV = Price	$300	$310	$320	$330	$340 IRR	$350	$360	$370	$375
$65	13.2%	16.7%	20.3%	23.9%	27.4%	31.0%	34.5%	38.1%	39.9%
66	11.5	15.0	18.5	22.0	25.5	29.0	32.5	36.0	37.7
67	9.8	13.3	16.7	20.2	23.6	27.1	30.5	34.0	35.7
68	8.2	11.6	15.0	18.4	21.8	25.2	28.6	32.0	33.7
69	6.6	10.0	13.3	16.7	20.0	23.4	26.7	30.1	31.8
70	5.1	8.4	11.7	15.0	18.3	21.6	24.9	28.2	29.9
71	3.6	6.9	10.1	13.4	16.6	19.9	23.2	26.4	28.0
72	2.2	5.4	8.6	11.8	15.0	18.2	21.4	24.7	26.3

One-Year IRR for 14.5% Notes

	$300	$310	$320	$330	$340	$350	$360	$370	$375
$20	18.8%	24.5%	30.2%	35.9%	41.5%	47.2%	52.9%	58.6%	61.4%
21	13.2	18.6	24.0	29.4	34.8	40.2	45.6	51.0	53.7
22	8.0	13.2	18.4	23.5	28.7	33.8	39.0	44.2	46.7
23	3.3	8.3	13.2	18.1	23.1	28.0	33.0	37.9	40.4
24	-1.0	3.8	8.5	13.2	18.0	22.7	27.4	32.1	34.5
25	-4.9	-0.4	4.2	8.7	13.2	17.8	22.3	26.9	29.1
26	-8.6	-4.2	0.1	4.5	8.9	13.2	17.6	22.0	24.2
27	-12.0	-7.8	-3.6	0.6	4.8	9.1	13.3	17.5	19.6

Source: Shenkman Capital Management, Inc.

distributions under the reorganization plan, which must be confirmed by each creditor group (tranche). For example, pursuant to Plan A, the holders of the 11.375 percent senior notes would receive $85.1 million of new 10 percent notes plus 13.5 million shares of common stock, or about 68 percent of the outstanding stock.

The next panel deals with the problem of determining the value of the new debt. In this example, the assumption is made that the new 10 percent notes will trade at a discount to par, to yield 11 percent.

The next panel of Exhibit 25–2 shows the valuation of the securities received under various TEV assumptions. For instance, if one assumes that the company has a total valuation (total value of debt plus equity) of $300 million, then the package of securities to be received by the 11.375 percent noteholders under the plan should be worth $73.6 per each $100 of old notes.

The bottom panels are the matrixes providing internal rates of return (IRRs) for the notes at various TEVs and various note prices. For example, if the investor can purchase the 11.375 percent notes in the open market today at $65 and the TEV for the company is $300 million, then the one-year IRR is 13.2 percent.

In essence, this matrix analysis allows an investor to calculate various returns by making assumptions regarding TEVs, holding periods, and back-end security valuations. This type of analysis is most appropriate in the late stage of the bankruptcy process, when intercreditor disputes have largely been resolved. Hence, the financial health of the company can be determined, and a range of enterprise valuations can be established.

CAVEATS

The most important concept in distressed-securities investing is the time value of money. The longer the investment is held, the lower the rate of return. Therefore, investors must always keep in mind that most bankruptcy proceedings and restructurings take longer than expected—in some cases, twice as long as originally anticipated.

Investing in a bankrupt company can be fraught with delays. The process can become bogged down in both administrative and legal arguments. Working under the "squeaky wheel" theory, junior holders often make the loudest protests even though they may be entitled to only a small recovery. If the senior creditors are trying to expedite the case, the junior creditors' protests may provide them with greater value than they are entitled to.

Finally, too much money may be chasing too few good distressed plays. Huge pools of money have been raised by investment firms for the specific purpose of investing in distressed securities. These firms are competing against one another—investing in the same defaulted issues and often in the same tranches of debt. More research, more newsletters, and more court services monitoring distressed situations are now available than in the mid-1980s. Hence, the market is becoming more efficient and the high returns of previous years may not be achievable.

CONCLUSION

Distressed bonds are more volatile than regular bonds and as a general rule have no correlation with trends in interest rates or the stock market. The price of a distressed bond is driven by several factors, including the ultimate enterprise value, the amount and value of securities distributed after the reorganization plan, and the division of assets among creditors. Accordingly, investors should perform detailed analyses before making an investment in a distressed situation, take a proactive position in bankruptcy in order to maximize value, and retain experienced professionals (e.g., accountants, lawyers, and investment bankers) to help monitor and structure a realistic plan of reorganization.

In addition, investors need to be patient: They should not react to the ups and downs of each court proceeding. For example, when a judge rules against bondholders in a hearing, sometimes it has a material impact on the outcome of the case but at other times it is merely one small procedural issue.

PART SEVEN

Corporate Finance

CHAPTER 26

Strategic Financing Choices for Emerging Firms: Debt versus Equity

Mitchell Weiman

Ned Armstrong

Theodore M. Barnhill, Jr.

INTRODUCTION

Capital structure and capital budgeting decisions are among the most important that management makes. By this we mean how best to raise and deploy capital to create and enhance shareholder value through plant expansion, product development, distribution enhancement, acquisition and geographic expansion, and so on. This chapter focuses on the strategic financing choices open to emerging firms with an emphasis on the choice between debt and equity financing.

CONCEPTUAL FRAMEWORK

The objective of financial management is to maximize the value of the firm. In the context of capital structure policy this can be accomplished by financing the firm with the proportion of debt and equity that minimizes the firm's weighted average cost of capital. A number of factors affect this optimal capital structure target as well as short-term debt versus equity decisions. In some cases firms may choose to adopt capital structures that do not necessarily minimize their cost of capital. Factors that significantly affect a firm's debt versus equity financing decision include:

- Business risk.
- Tax advantages of debt financing.
- Relative cost of debt versus equity financing.

- External financing requirements.
- Industry capital structure norms.
- Competitive position in industry.
- Management's risk preferences.
- Management's opinion on whether the firm's stock is fairly, over-, or undervalued.
- Management's concerns regarding control of the firm.

One of the fundamentals of corporate finance is the balancing of business risk with financial risk. Business risk is a function of the fundamental nature of business and reflects the risk of the firm if its capital structure were all equity. Business risk is a function of a number of different factors including: the cost structure of the firm (fixed versus variable), the sensitivity of cash flows to macroeconomic changes, the competitive position of the firm within the industry, the level of control over prices (commodity goods versus differentiated goods), the amount of diversification across product lines, the dependence upon a small group of suppliers or clients, and so on. The level of a firm's business risk is assessed by examining the relative historical volatility of revenue, cost, and cash flow over different economic cycles. Financial risk on the other hand is related to the level of risk associated with the amount of debt in the capital structure. As the level of debt increases so does the firm's financial risk. It is very important that firms balance these risks. Firms with low levels of business risk can afford to take on more financial risk (debt) in their capital structure. Firms with high levels of business risk have a more limited capacity to take on financial risk. The clear demonstration of this concept is a comparison of utilities with very little business risk and a correspondingly high level of debt financing as compared to high technology firms with a great deal of business risk and a correspondingly low level of debt in their capital structure.

A major advantage of debt financing is of course the tax deductibility of interest expense. As long as the firm can earn a return on capital that exceeds the after-tax cost of debt financing its return on equity can be levered up by using debt financing. Other things being equal, this encourages firms to adopt highly levered capital structures. Of course the use of debt financing creates the risk of financial distress which in the extreme can destroy the value of owner's equity. Thus, in the selection of a target capital structure one must weigh the potential advantages and disadvantages of debt financing.

The firm's capital requirements and external financing requirements, industry capital structure norms, and competitive position are also very important considerations in establishing a target capital structure. In general, firms with large and nondeferrable capital requirements are more dependent on external financing than less capital-intensive firms. Such firms will tend to favor a lower debt ratio to give them assured access to external financing under all market conditions. Similarly, firms that are dependent on external financing must pay close attention to industry capital structure norms and their own competitive position within the industry.

Management attitudes and expectations also play an important role in establishing target capital structures and affecting the short-term decision regarding whether to finance with debt or equity at a particular time. Concerns regarding maintaining managerial control may lead some firms to use debt as opposed to equity financing. Management's risk preferences will also play an important role in establishing a target debt ratio, with more risk-tolerant managements perhaps choosing a more highly levered capital structure, and vice versa. Finally, management's view on the relative cost of debt versus equity financing and their expectations regarding future earnings relative to the current price of the firm's common stock are very important. In situations where management expects a rapid growth in earnings that are not fully reflected in the price of the firm's common stock a strong bias exists in favor of debt financing. Alternatively, if management believes that the price of the stock fully reflects future growth prospects, an equity issue may be favored even if it temporarily pushes the firm's debt to value ratio below the long-term target.

FINANCING ALTERNATIVES

There are a number of funding alternatives open for emerging firms. Each has certain advantages and disadvantages. The key sources for capital are shown in Exhibit 26–1. They are:

Capital Markets

These are public markets where debt and equity instruments are priced and traded. The capital is obtained when a company floats an offering to investors through an investment bank. These offerings can be made worldwide but are most often done in the United States. For emerging firms both high yield bond markets and public equity offerings are major sources of capital. However the cost and availability of such financing is greatly affected by market conditions.

EXHIBIT 26-1

Sources of Capital

	Capital Markets	Bank Loans	Joint Venture or Partnership	Private Capital Infusions	Internally Generated Funds
Pro	Size Availability	Size Cost Availability	Outside Outside expertise Size	Timeliness Amount	No issuance costs Simpler timing issues
Con	Fees Reporting requirements Communications Timing	Noncash costs Covenants Commitment Callability Fees	Cumbersome terms Cost	Cumbersome terms Difficulty in locating suitable investor Cost	Amount can be limited

Bank Loans

A bank loan is a commitment to borrow funds from a commercial lending institution for a specified time and to repay them with a predetermined, but usually floating rate of interest. The funds are obtained by working through a loan officer who arranges terms and funding. The actual lending institution is typically located near the business, but sometimes is part of a nationwide entity. Like the capital markets, this source is only available when the banks are conducive to lending.

Joint Venture or Partnership Arrangement

Joint ventures are undertaken with another knowledgeable party to pursue a business opportunity. They are characterized by predetermined sharing of profits and capital infusions. The entity providing the money is typically a financial investor, although this investor can also provide project specific expertise as well. The funds can be obtained anywhere, domestic or overseas, depending on the provider. Typically these arrangements are pursued when opportunity exists. Often, negotiations can be extensive.

Private Capital Infusions

These are cash infusions by private individuals or an entity, outside the bounds of the markets. Terms are negotiated between the parties involved. The transaction can be governed by contract or federal laws (Rule 144a or Regulation D) depending upon how the transaction is structured.

Internally Generated Funds

These are the funds the company generates through its normal course of business. Ongoing corporate treasury decisions determine the use of funds. They are available based on corporate performance and can be disbursed at the corporate or operating level depending on how they will be deployed.

PROS AND CONS OF USING THESE SOURCES

Each source of capital has various pros and cons as well as a cost for using it. The capital markets are typically the best way to raise large (over $50 million) amounts of capital, and access to these markets is relatively easy for firms of sufficient size. Major disadvantages include fees, reporting requirements and costs, and timing (because perceptions in capital markets can change as rapidly as the underlying fundamentals and technicals).

With regard to initial public offerings (IPOs), the advantages include new capital to finance expansion, liquidity for existing stockholders, and a new way to finance acquisitions through stock swaps. Disadvantages of an IPO include high flotation and recurring costs, financial disclosure requirements, and potential loss of control.

Bank loans are also a source for larger amounts of funds, though not always to the degree of the capital markets. In addition to interest rate and term risks (most carry floating rates and are shorter terms), bank loans come with costs and disadvantages that include restrictive covenants, commitment fees, compensating balances, and strict call provisions.

With joint ventures and/or partnerships, a company can go to outside capital, sometimes in substantial amounts. The most important advantage however, is the industry knowledge and expertise that the outside party provides. Key disadvantages are cumbersome terms and the returns demanded by the capital provider, which are often in excess of those returns required by the capital markets.

Private capital infusions can provide timely and sometimes large amounts of capital without the cumbersome filing and regulatory reporting requirements of the capital markets. However, finding the sources of private capital can be more difficult, and the terms of the transaction and the returns demanded by the capital provider could be onerous.

Internally generated funds can be more readily acquired than those from other sources and are free of issuance and due diligence costs. Naturally, the decision to tap outside sources must be made when the amount of capital required exceeds what can be generated internally.

When considering factors such as the amount of capital needed, non-cash costs such as covenants and profit sharing, term structure and overall cost, many managers choose to utilize the capital markets to obtain the funds they need. Accordingly, the decision then comes down to raising debt or equity.

If for instance, our hypothetical steel company, MW Steel (see Exhibit 26–2) needed to raise $50 million to build a new plant, these sources of capital would represent its alternatives. Internally generated funds would be insufficient, as the company does not have the earnings power to generate the required amount of capital in the short term. Like-wise, private capital infusions or a joint venture would probably be unrealistic due to competitive dynamics. Accordingly, the company must utilize the capital markets or a bank loan. For illustrative purposes we will assume that the bank loan required the company to pledge assets, something the company was unwilling to do. As a result, MW Steel must tap the capital markets for either debt or equity.

DEBT VERSUS EQUITY

In evaluating whether to utilize debt or equity, a manager must evaluate several factors. First, they must determine if a debt or equity financing is appropriate to move the firm toward its target capital structure. Second, they must look at the cost of issuing the security. This is essentially the price, direct or indirect, that shareholders bear for the issuance. Third, the amount of leverage the company can bear is important in that it will affect the company's valuation in the marketplace, as well as basic operating and credit decisions. Within this context, management must evaluate the magnitude and timing of the company's cash flows in order to determine the practicality of issuing debt as well as the terms. For instance, if positive cash flow were not expected for several years, debt—if issued at all—would need to be structured as a discount note with a zero coupon or deferred interest structure. Though each of these factors must be considered, we believe relative cost to be one of the most important factors in determining a firm's tactical debt versus equity decision.

Cost of Equity

It is convenient to distinguish between a firm's required and expected return on equity. In a capital asset pricing model framework the equilibrium required return is equal to the current risk-free interest rate, plus the firm's beta coefficient, times the required equity market risk premium.

E X H I B I T   26–2

MW Steel Co.

	1993	1994	1995	1996	1997	1998E
Sales	$300,000	$232,000	$330,000	$320,000	$350,000	$400,000
GP Margin	20%	16%	21%	21%	20%	21%
EBITDA Margin	10%	5%	10%	11%	10%	11%
EBITDA	$ 30,000	$ 11,600	$ 33,000	$ 35,200	$ 35,000	$ 44,000
Dep. & Amor.	7,000	7,000	7,200	7,300	7,500	7,800
Interest Exp.	11,050	11,050	11,050	11,050	11,050	11,050
Pretax	$ 11,950	$ (6,450)	$ 14,750	$ 16,850	$ 16,450	$ 25,150
Tax Rate	40%	40%	40%	40%	40%	40%
Net Income	$ 7,170	$ (3,870)	$ 8,850	$ 10,110	$ 9,870	$ 15,090
EPS	$ 0.72	$ (0.39)	$ 0.89	$ 1.01	$ 0.99	$ 1.51
Current Assets	$130,000	$130,000	$135,000	$140,000	$140,000	$150,000
Total Assets	$250,000	$246,130	$254,980	$265,090	$274,960	$290,050
Current Liab	$ 40,000	$ 40,000	$ 40,000	$ 40,000	$ 40,000	$ 40,000
L-T Debt	$130,000	$130,000	$130,000	$130,000	$130,000	$130,000
Equity	$ 50,000	$ 57,170	$ 53,300	$ 62,150	$ 72,260	$ 82,130
Shares Outstanding	10,000	10,000	10,000	10,000	10,000	10,000
Avg. Stock Price	6	4	8	8.5	9	
Capital Expenditures = 3% of Sales	$ 9,000	$ 6,960	$ 9,900	$ 9,600	$ 10,500	$ 12,000

Alternatively, the expected return on equity is the discount rate that equates the present value of a firm's expected future dividends and common stock price to the net proceeds of a new equity issue. Both the required return and expected return on equity fluctuate depending on the level of risk-free interest rates, perceptions regarding a firm's future profitability and risk characteristics, and overall equity market conditions.

In attempting to determine his required return on equity, an investor looks at whether he is being fairly compensated for the risk he is taking relative to the return he will receive over a risk free investment. Accordingly, the key elements of the cost of equity can be viewed as the risk-free rate of return, and the risk premium which in turn is dependent on the firm's earning power, and growth prospects, as well as larger factors involving the economy, the financial markets, and industry characteristics.

The risk-free rate can be viewed as the rate of return that the investor can achieve with no risk to his investment. Typically, the Treasury rate is used as a benchmark. The risk premium, on the other hand, is far more complex and difficult to determine. It helps to look at it within the following framework. The risk premium can be viewed as being determined by three elements: market characteristics, industry characteristics, and firm-specific characteristics.

The condition of the financial markets can affect the required rate of return because it represents a benchmark for risky returns. In other words, an investor will look at the return he demands from equity in relation to what he can get from other equities or in the market as a whole.

Various industry characteristics will determine the risk a company faces going forward. Among the factors that must be evaluated include: the threat of entry by other well-capitalized or well-staffed firms, the experience curve (how much the management still needs to learn about the business), the amount and type of competition between existing firms, extent of available substitute products, and the relative bargaining power of buyers and suppliers.

Another important variable to pricing equity is the comparison of a company's market valuation relative to its peers. The two main ratios we look at to do this are the price-to-earnings ratio (P/E ratio) and the price-to-book ratio. The price-to-earning ratio is:

Stock price per share / Earnings per share

The P/E for MW Steel in 1997 is:

$$9 / .99 = 9.1$$

In comparing companies' P/Es you need to consider the growth of a company's earnings. The higher the earnings growth of a company the higher the P/E, because people will be willing to pay more for the earnings growth. The other important valuation ratio is price to book. The price-to-book ratio is:

Stock price per share / (Equity/Shares outstanding)

The price-to-book for MW Steel in 1997 is:

$$9 / (72,260/10,000) = 1.25x$$

As with the P/E ratio, the higher the price-to-book ratio the greater the growth potential of the company and obviously the greater the risk to the investor. Book value is what investors use to determine the downside of an investment.

Firm-specific factors that must be evaluated to assess the risk premium involve the quantitative and qualitative assessment of financial data as well as management and competitive issues. One key financial variable is the liquidity—the ability of the company to meet current obligations. The ratio we use to determine a firm's liquidity is the current ratio.

Current ratio = Current assets / Current liabilities

The Current ratio for MW Steel in 1997 is:

140,000 / 40,000 = 3.5

The higher the current ratio the more liquid and conservative the company is.

One must also review the existing leverage under which the firm operates. Once the firm exceeds an acceptable level of levergage (in turn, determined by industry and firm-specific factors) the risk increases dramatically. Earnings variability is another factor that helps determine risk. This factor is driven by events within the firm as well as the economy and the industry in which the firm operates.

Another consideration is the size of the firm. Often, but not always, smaller firms are viewed as riskier.

Growth is another key element in the determination of the risk premium. Generally, strong growth characteristics can reduce the risk premium that investors demand. These characteristics are both based on the industry and firm-specific factors.

For initial public offerings (IPOs) some special considerations are necessary to determine the cost of equity. First and foremost are the growth prospects for the firm. Normally, an IPO is undertaken at a point when growth prospects are excellent. This consideration can offset other risks including the lack of public company experience and size limitations. Factors that can increase the cost of equity in an IPO include the sale of insider stock, and/or the presence of large benefits to venture capital and seed capital interests. Once all these factors have been considered there is the ubiquitous IPO discount investors demand. This further increases the cost of equity.

A final institutional factor that can influence the cost of equity is the investment banking firms involved in the issuance of the equity. For instance the large well-known (Bulge Bracket) firms may be able to reduce the price demanded by investors who are comfortable and confident with the firms' distribution breadth and capabilities. Also, certain niche firms that have excellent relationships with specific investors can enhance the pricing for a stock.

For low growth firms a "quick and dirty" way to estimate the expected return on equity is the inverse of the P/E ratio. In the case of MW Steel (see Exhibit 26–2), we can use the inverse of the P/E ratio or earnings yield as a proxy for the cost of equity.

Cost of equity = Earnings per share/Price per share

MW Steel Cost of equity for 1997 is .75/9 = 8.3%

Management and their financial advisors are likely to have the best information available to assess a firm's dividend levels, stock price, expected return on equity, and expected future profitability. In circumstances where the expected and required returns are approximately equal, the firm would be considered to be fairly valued and the debt versus equity decision would be based on other considerations. In circumstances where the expected return is high relative to the equilibrium return, management may conclude that the stock is undervalued and that it is not in the current stockholders' best interests to issue new equity at that time. This will often occur when the firm's price-earnings ratio is unusually low. For example, if the managers of MW Steel are raising $50 million to build a new plant and they feel that this plant will grow their earnings dramatically, they might try to issue debt instead of equity because they feel that they would be selling equity too cheaply based on their future growth and earnings expectations. A good strategy in a situation like this would be to issue debt initially and wait to raise more equity until the earnings have increased and the stock can be sold at a higher valuation.

Alternatively, if the expected return is low relative to the equilibrium-required return, management may conclude that the stock is fully valued and that it is a particularly attractive time to issue equity. This will often occur when the firm's price earnings ratio is unusually high. These decisions regarding the issuance of equity capital determine the amount of ownership management will give to new shareholders at the expense of existing shareholders.

Cost of Debt

A potential debt issuer will be viewed as being investment grade or noninvestment grade based on a quantitative and qualitative assessment of the firm's creditworthiness. This difference will determine the cost of the debt, with noninvestment-grade being the more costly. Key fundamental issues that investors will examine to determine the proper interest rate for a debt offering are the leverage ratio, interest coverage ratio, quality of cash flow, and cyclicality of the issuer's earnings.

The most important consideration in determining whether a company will use debt financing is obviously the after-tax interest rate that the company will pay on the debt.

$$\text{After-tax cost of debt} = \text{Interest rate} \times (1 - \text{Tax rate})$$

Also, to the extent feasible, firms and their financial advisors attempt to assess whether current interest rates are high or low relative to likely future rate levels. During periods of relatively low interest rates, firms may be inclined to finance at fixed rates for longer terms. However, during recessionary times, the noninvestment-grade market and more specifically, the market for newly issued B-rated bonds, can become very thin. Hence, firms may wish to issue high yield bonds but find themselves in a time period when the market for new issues has essentially disappeared.

Finally, firms will also evaluate the relative cost of equity versus debt financing. While equity financing will almost always have a higher required return than debt, the relative cost fluctuates. A bias exists towards using the type of financing that is found to be relatively cheaper. Of course, major capital structure decisions are far more complex than a comparison of the short-term relative costs of different financing methods and these decisions require consideration of the full range of issues previously given. These factors must in turn be considered within the context of the capital markets and its technicals, the U.S. economy, and the world economy.

FUNDAMENTAL ISSUES

The amount of leverage that a company has on its balance sheet is determined by dividing the total amount of long-term debt a company has by its equity. This is a very important ratio in determining debt pricing because it will quickly show how levered a company is compared to its peers. When looking at a leverage ratio, one must compare companies in the same industry because different industries can operate safely with different amounts of leverage. For example, banks and thrifts operate with much higher leverage ratios than companies in cyclical industries such as steel or heavy machinery. This is due to the fact that banks and thrifts derive their earnings from interest rate spreads. They borrow at rates lower than those at which they lend and match their maturities as closely as possible. For example if they can borrow for 5 years at 6 percent and lend for 5 years at 8 percent, they will lock in a 2 percent interest margin for 5 years. In industries that are cyclical such as steel, there is no way to accurately predict a company's return on capital year-after-year because of the cyclicality of the business. Therefore a company in a cyclical industry must maintain a lower leverage ratio in order to operate prudently.

The leverage ratio of MW Steel for 1997 is 2.07x.

$$\text{LT debt / Equity} = \text{Leverage ratio}$$
$$130{,}000/62{,}780 = 2.07x$$

If the company raises \$50 million in debt the leverage ratio will go to 3.19x.

$$(130{,}000 + 50{,}000)/62{,}780 = 2.86x$$

Another ratio that measures leverage is Debt/EBITDA. This is simply another measure of a company's leverage. MW Steel's Debt/EBITDA is:

$$130{,}000/35{,}000 = 3.71$$

If the company raises \$50 million in debt, the Debt/EBITDA ratio goes to:

$$(130{,}000 + 50{,}000)/35{,}000 = 5.14$$

The other major ratio that debt investors look at is the interest coverage ratio. This ratio is the amount of earnings before interest, taxes, and depreciation (EBITDA) less capital expenditures, divided by interest expense. In industries with large capital expenditures a higher interest coverage ratio is beneficial, as the company will theoretically have more room for cash flow disappointments.

The interest coverage ratio for MW Steel in 1997 is 3.26x.

$$(\text{EBITDA} - \text{Capital EX}) / \text{Interest expense} = \text{Interest coverage ratio}$$
$$(35{,}000 - 10{,}500)/7{,}500 = 3.26x$$

This means that MW Steel's EBITDA less capital expenditures can fall by 71 percent before it will be unable to meet interest payments.

If MW Steel raises \$50 million of debt at 10 percent, the interest coverage ratio will go to 1.96x

$$(35{,}000 - 10{,}500)/(7{,}500 + 5{,}000) = 1.96x$$

In examining this ratio an investor must also look at the quality of a company's EBITDA. For instance, a company might have a large portion of its revenues in one year from one project that may not recur. In the MW Steel example, there was a large drop off in revenues for 1994. This could be because in 1993 the company had a large contract that it lost in 1994. A very important aspect of revenue quality is that there be no large concentration of revenues from one source.

Operating and profit margins are key components in assessing the quality of a company's EBITDA. To determine the quality of a company's margins, one must compare companies in the same industry. If a company's margins are higher than those of its peer group, one must take a closer look to determine why. In most cases a company will not be able to consistently surpass its peers' margins. For example, a company might have a technological advantage that will enable it to produce a product more cheaply, but eventually its competitors will get the same advantage and drive the firm's margins back down. These are things one must look at when examining the quality of a company's EBITDA. *One must determine if a company's EBITDA level is sustainable.*

STRUCTURE OF DEBT

The structure of the debt will also determine its pricing. Major debt structuring issues are: secured versus unsecured debt, senior debt versus subordinated debt, covenants, length of maturity, cash pay versus zero coupon, call features, and private versus public debt.

Secured Debt versus Unsecured Debt

Secured bonds are collateralized by some type of asset (e.g., real estate, machinery, or the stock of subsidiary companies). The more liquid the underlying asset, the higher its quality to the investor. If a secured bond issuer defaults on a secured bond, the bondholder has the right to foreclose on the collateral and either liquidate it or transfer it to the bondholder's name. Unsecured debt is debt that is not backed by a pledge of specific collateral. Unsecured debt is basically a general debt obligation backed only by the integrity of the borrower. Because there is no collateral associated with unsecured debt, it is risky for the bondholder and therefore more expensive for the issuer. Most high yield bonds are unsecured.

Senior Debt versus Subordinated Debt

Senior debt has a claim prior to junior or subordinated debt and equity on a corporation's assets in the event of liquidation. Senior debt typically takes the form of bank loans, insurance company notes and bonds, or debentures not expressly defined as junior or subordinated. Subordinated debt is junior in claim to other debt on assets. That is, it is repayable only after other debt with a higher claim has been satisfied. Some subordinated debt may have an even lower claim on assets than other subordinated debt. For example, a junior subordinated debenture ranks below a subordinated debenture. Senior debt is cheaper for a company to issue than subordinated debt because it bears less risk. In the event of liquidation, an investor in senior debt technically will be paid in full before the owner of a subordinated debt gets back any money. There is a definite cost spread for senior debt versus subordinated debt in the high yield debt market. The spread in today's market is from 30–130 basis points, depending on the quality of the credit and the industry. The weaker the credit, the larger the spread between senior and subordinated debt.

Covenants

These are another important issue in pricing debt. In a trust indenture a covenant is a promise that certain acts will be performed and others refrained from. Designed to protect the lender, covenants cover such matters as working capital, debt-to-equity ratios, and dividend payments. Covenants give the lender rights if one of the covenants is broken. A typical covenant might be a debt-to-equity limitation of, for example, five times. Should the company exceed this, an event of default is declared. An event of default typically has a cure period of several months, and if the default is not cured, bond repayment can be demanded immediately. For example, in Exhibit 26–2 MW Steel's long-term debt would have to exceed $360 million before it would be in violation of a 5x debt-to-equity covenant.

Maturity Term

The maturity term of the bond can also affect pricing. Typically, the longer a bond's maturity, the higher the interest rate. The exception to this rule is in an inverted yield curve environment. The risk in issuing shorter-term debt is that interest rates may be higher when the bonds mature and are in need of refinancing. For example, suppose MW Steel decides to issue 5-year bonds at +400/5-year U.S. Treasury notes, or 9.5 percent. In 5 years the company must refinance the bonds. Suppose the 5-year U.S. Treasury note rates will have gone from 5.5 percent to 7.5 percent. Assuming the company can issue debt at the same spread to Treasuries, the company must now pay 11.5 percent. In this case the company would have been better off issuing 10-year bonds at the outset. This example can also work in favor of the issuer if the treasury rates were to decline.

Cash-Pay Bonds versus Zero Coupon Bonds

Cash-pay bonds are simple bonds, which pay their interest in cash. A zero coupon bond makes no periodic interest payments but instead is sold at a deep discount from its face value. The buyer of such a bond receives the effective coupon rate of return by the annual accretion of the discount to par by a specified maturity date. Typically, companies who issue zero coupon bonds are higher-risk growth companies. Quite often companies that issue zero coupon bonds are unable to pay cash interest because they have huge outlays for capital expenditures, and their revenues won't support interest payments. The telecommunications industry today is a perfect example. Many companies in this business are being created that have no revenues or assets. These companies can raise money through zero coupon bonds and use the funds to build out telephone networks. These companies, as well as the investors in the bonds, are predicting that the networks being built will produce enough cash flow to pay off the bonds at maturity. The company can commit the capital to the buildout of its business rather than the interest service on the bonds each year until maturity. (Most zero coupon bonds in the high yield market are actually zeroing coupons for the first 3–5 years, and then become cash-paying coupon bonds from that point to their maturity.) There is a definite premium an issuer must pay in the high yield market to issue a zero because of the risk. In today's market that premium is roughly 150 basis points.

Another type of bond structure that is becoming more popular today is an interest reserve covenant. This type of structure makes the company hold a specified number of interest payments in a reserve account that may only be used if the company cannot pay interest from its operations. Interest reserve bonds are typically priced slightly higher then zero coupon bonds. The same type of company that issues zero coupon bonds will also consider interest reserve bonds as an alternative.

Call Feature

A call feature of a bond gives the bond issuer the right to redeem a bond before maturity on a specified date, at a specified price. Most bonds issued are callable, however, in rare circumstances noncallable bonds are issued. The longer the call protection for the investor, the lower the interest rate on the bond. An investor wants the bond outstanding as long as possible and thus would prefer a bond with 5-year call protection versus 3-year call protection. Today the call feature of a high yield bond has become fairly standardized. A typical call feature for a 10-year high yield bond is 5 years at par, plus one-half the coupon. This means that the call price of a bond issued at 10 percent is 105, five years after it is issued.

Private versus Public Debt

The decision of whether to issue debt publicly or privately will affect its pricing. Private bonds are more expensive to the issuer then public bonds because they are not SEC registered, and the secondary trading market is less liquid. Over the past several years because of rule 144a, differences between the public and private markets have begun to blur. Most traders in the high yield market today will tell you that there is very little penalty for issuing private bonds under rule 144a, and due to the fact that SEC review and registration are not necessary, the speed with which they can be brought to the market is advantageous. Between January and May 1998, there was $83 billion of high yield debt issued, of which 77 percent was privately placed under Rule 144a.

FREQUENCY OF ISSUANCE AND REPUTATION OF ISSUER

A first-time issuer in the high yield market will pay a premium over a company with similar credit characteristics who has accessed the market before and has a good reputation with investors. This is because in the high yield market credibility with investors is extremely important and can take quite some time to earn. There are actually instances where one company is a better fundamental credit risk than its competitor but gets priced more expensively in the market because it has not yet earned investor confidence. Investors are interested in management's ability to improve the credit quality of the company. Their objective is to select bonds that outperform the market and tighten to the treasury curve.

IMPORTANCE OF THE RATING AGENCY ON BOND PRICING

The rating agencies provide an extremely important and objective review of bond issues. They objectively rate issues based on companies' fundamentals and place a rating on any bond upon request for a fee. Moody's and Standard & Poor's are the main rating agencies for high yield bonds. High yield bonds are rated Ba1/BB+ or lower. Investors use these ratings to help them determine the yield at which a bond should trade. There is a positive correlation between ratings and the pricing of bond issues. However, bonds with the same rating in different industries often trade at different yields. This is due to the investor's perception of risk in different industries. For example a B-rated homebuilder may trade tighter than a B-rated long distance telephone company because investors feel that the long distance telephone industry currently carries more risk than the homebuilding industry. Therefore, when trying to price a bond according to its rating, it is important to compare companies within the same industry.

SUMMARY AND CONCLUSIONS

Capital allocation is one of the most important choices management makes. A key part of the decision is how, where, and at what cost to raise the capital. While several alternatives exist, the most effective and efficient choice is normally the capital markets. Within the framework, management must choose between debt and equity. There are many factors that influence this choice; however, the most important is cost.

To determine the cost of equity, management must consider several factors. The first of these is the risk-free rate, or the return investors can get with no risk. Second, management must consider the risk premium required to compensate investors for the risk of owning the company's equity. This premium is influenced by a number of factors, including macroeconomic events, industry factors, and firm-specific factors such as liquidity, leverage, and earnings volatility. The resultant required rate of return is the cost of equity. For low-growth firms, the earnings yield is a shorthand method used to quantify this cost.

The cost of debt is quantified by the after-tax cost of interest on the debt. Several factors influence the interest rate. These factors include, first and foremost, the financial fundamentals of the issuer. These financial fundamentals include their cash earning volatility, amount of leverage, and interest coverage. Other factors are also important. Among these are terms (secured and unsecured), seniority, call features, covenants, method of interest payments, rating, and whether the debt is public or private. All of these factors interact to determine the interest cost on the debt.

Once management has raised the funds and spent them, the financial markets will continually review their choices and their success or failure resulting in a dynamic cost of capital process that must be constantly reviewed.

CHAPTER 27

The Advantages and Disadvantages of Public versus Private Issuances of High Yield Debt Securities

Norman B. Antin

Jeffrey D. Haas

I. INTRODUCTION

During the last 20 years, the high yield "junk" bond market has grown from an insignificant portion of the corporate fixed income market to one of the fastest growing and innovative segments of corporate finance. Aggregate new issues of public and private high yield debt have increased from a relatively small $1.6 billion during 1970 to $232.1 billion during 1997.[1]

As the market for high yield debt has expanded, the ability of corporate issuers to access the high yield bond market has increased significantly. Initially, the high yield market lacked liquidity and stability, which resulted in many potential issuers relying primarily on bank financing. An issuer of high yield debt could look only to the public markets in order to complete a debt offering. However, as the high yield bond market became more diversified and liquid, companies have recognized that the time and expense saved in a private transaction may, under the right circumstances, more than offset the modest premium in pricing (when compared to a public offering) that is often required by investors. The private placement segment of this market has thus emerged as a viable alternative within the high yield bond market. As a result, companies that only a few years ago might not have been able to access the fixed income markets at all, now can not only complete an issuance of high yield debt, but can also consider whether it is in their best interests to do so publicly or privately.

The dramatic expansion of the high yield bond market has accentuated the choice available to issuers about whether to issue debt through the medium of the public or the private capital markets. As in all corporate financing decisions, there are advantages and disadvantages associated with each course of conduct. As an initial proposition, a company should seek to raise capital through the easiest method available at the least possible cost. Whether to raise money publicly or privately depends upon a great many factors, any of which may change from time to time. Some of these factors are highlighted below and discussed in greater detail in this article.

• *Pricing considerations.* A public debt offering generally offers more competitive pricing than a private debt financing. Because of, among other things, the possible lack of secondary market liquidity, the generally smaller size of the offering, and the potential lack of public ratings, a private debt offering will generally offer a higher yield to investors compared to a public debt offering.

• *Marketing the issue to investors.* The U.S. public debt market is the largest and most liquid market for U.S. dollar-denominated securities. For this reason, a public offering offers the largest potential for market penetration, with active participation at both the retail and institutional levels. A private offering is primarily limited to institutional investors, and issuers must be careful to ensure that those participating in the placement comply with applicable requirements.

• *The size of the issue.* The recent expansion of the private placement market has made the issue of size not as relevant as it once was; nevertheless, larger transactions (i.e., $100 million to $1 billion or more) are generally sold publicly, while smaller transactions are usually issued privately. Thus, the larger size of public transactions contributes to enhanced secondary market liquidity and a higher public profile.

• *Secondary market liquidity and trading.* A public offering provides a potential issuer of debt securities with stronger secondary market liquidity and a greater public profile when compared to a private offering. In addition, there are no resale restrictions with respect to publicly issued debt as there are with privately offered debt.

• *Registration of the issue and related matters.* An issuer who contemplates a public debt offering must file a registration statement with the

Securities and Exchange Commission (SEC) pursuant to the Securities Act of 1933, as amended (the Securities Act). A public debt offering requires SEC-mandated disclosures that are not required in a private placement. To the extent not exempted, the issuer must also register the debt securities under the securities laws of the various states in which the offer and sale are to be made. In addition, a public offering of debt securities will often require compliance with the Trust Indenture Act of 1939, as amended (the TIA). Companies that issue securities publicly also become subject to the ongoing periodic reporting requirements of the Securities Exchange Act of 1934, as amended (the Exchange Act). In contrast, a private debt offering generally will not require federal or state registration and is generally exempt from the provisions of the TIA.

• *Expenses.*   As a result of the registration and disclosure obligations associated with a public offering, a public debt offering has higher upfront expenses (i.e., SEC registration, state securities filing fees, printing costs, accounting and legal fees, and other out-of-pocket expenses) and higher ongoing expenses (i.e., costs associated with continuous periodic public reporting responsibilities and compliance with the TIA). A private debt offering generally has lower upfront and ongoing expenses.

• *Timing.*   Timing is one of the more important factors in distinguishing between public and private debt offerings. Due primarily to the amount of time necessary to comply with applicable federal and state securities laws, a public offering will take approximately 8 to 12 weeks to be completed (up to 24 weeks for a first-time issuer), while a private placement can generally be completed within 2 to 8 weeks.

• *Underwriting.*   Both public offerings and certain types of private transactions are generally conducted on a firm commitment underwritten basis, which enhances the prospects for completion of the transaction. In some instances, a public transaction can only be done on a "best efforts" basis; in this case the underwriter does not commit to purchasing the issue for resale. Traditional private placements are generally sold through an agent on a best efforts basis, and may sometimes be sold by the issuer directly.

• *Public ratings.*   As the market for high yield debt has expanded, the necessity of obtaining public ratings has declined. Nevertheless, public ratings are generally obtained in public debt offerings but not in traditional private debt offerings.

• *Indenture terms and covenants.*   An indenture is a legal document that defines the rights and obligations of the borrower and lender with respect to a bond issue. In public offerings, the documentation is generally more standardized and not negotiated with individual investors, whereas most terms in traditional private transactions are subject to extensive negotiations. The nature of the covenants will be highly dependent upon the financial condition and operations of the issuer. A more seasoned company with a stronger balance sheet and established track record will require less restrictive covenants. As for other terms that may be imposed, a public debt offering will often require less onerous call provisions and call premiums compared to a private debt offering.

The purpose of this article is to examine the advantages and disadvantages of public versus private high yield debt issuances. For purposes of this discussion, a public offering of high yield debt securities is one which is registered with the SEC pursuant to the Securities Act. A private offering of high yield debt securities is one that is exempt from registration with the SEC under the Securities Act. Although there are a multitude of possible exemptions from registration pursuant to which companies can issue high yield debt securities, this article focuses on the two basic types of private offerings: (1) the traditional private placement (most often conducted pursuant to Regulation D under the Securities Act) and (2) the Rule 144a private placement.

II. THE PUBLIC SALE OF HIGH YIELD DEBT SECURITIES

A. Overview of Applicable Federal and State Securities Laws

The public sale of debt securities is primarily a matter of federal law and is governed principally by the Securities Act. The Exchange Act, the TIA, and various state securities (or *blue sky*) laws also apply to the public sale of debt securities. In general, the Securities Act applies to the offer and sale of securities, while the Exchange Act applies to trading in securities once they have been sold. The philosophy of both acts is one of full disclosure, and neither seeks to regulate the substance or fairness of securities. The premise underpinning both statutes is that investors should be free to make their own investment decisions with the benefit of all necessary information.

Prior to the offer or sale of debt securities, issuers are required to file a detailed and requirement specific registration statement with the SEC, unless one of many enumerated exemptions from registration is available.[2] While *offers* to sell securities may be made prior to such registration statement's effectiveness, *sales* may not be made until that time, and until prospective investors have been furnished with a prospectus based on the information included in the registration statement.

In addition to the registration and prospectus provisions, other sections of the Securities Act make certain conduct in connection with an offering of securities unlawful or actionable. The Securities Act includes several antifraud provisions, violations of which give rise to civil liability. The Securities Act also makes it a crime to willfully violate any provision of the Securities Act or to include a misstatement or half-truth in a registration statement.[3]

In contrast to the Securities Act, which does not mandate or regulate the terms of securities, the TIA has various substantive requirements. The TIA requires that every debt instrument subject to its terms (practically every debt security registered under the Securities Act) must be issued subject to certain standardized terms. These requirements are set forth in a document referred to as an *indenture,* entered into by the issuer of the debt instrument and at least one independent trustee.

In addition to federal requirements, each of the states of the United States requires some form of registration, absent an appropriate exemption, prior to the offer and sale of securities within the state. Consequently, a company proposing to issue public or private high yield debt securities has numerous federal and state legal requirements to consider in planning for a transaction.

B. The Federal Registration Process

1. General

Section 5 of the Securities Act requires that all securities offered by mail or other channels of interstate commerce be registered with the SEC. Federal registration is a process designed to ensure that adequate and accurate information relating to the issuing company will be filed with the SEC and distributed to prospective investors in a narrative format, which is referred to as a *prospectus.*

The SEC has no authority to approve or disapprove of particular securities or companies. Rather, its authority is limited to determining the adequacy and accuracy of the proscribed information that is required to be included in the registration statement and the prospectus to be distributed to prospective investors. The basic requirement of the Securities Act is that unless an exemption from the registration requirements is available, no security may be publicly offered unless a registration statement has been filed with the SEC, and no security can be sold unless the registration statement has become effective.

2. Conduct during the Registration Process

When considering the requirements and rules of conduct involved in the process of publicly issuing debt securities, it is common to divide the registration process into (1) the prefiling period, (2) the waiting period, and (3) the posteffective period.[4]

a. The Prefiling Period   The prefiling period represents the period of time until the filing of a registration statement with the SEC. Except for negotiations between the issuer and prospective underwriters and among members of the proposed underwriting group, all activities to condition the market for the proposed offering prior to the filing of a registration statement are prohibited. During this prefiling period, which is often referred to as the *quiet period,* no offering of debt securities for sale, whether orally or in writing, is permitted.[5]

During the prefiling period, the issuing company will focus on selecting an investment banker and preparing the applicable registration statement. The company contemplating a public offering of debt securities will usually seek an investment banking firm to act as underwriter. In most instances, securities offered publicly will be offered by an underwriting group consisting of several broker-dealer firms. The formation of an underwriting group helps to spread the risk and facilitates the sale of the issue. Typically, one or two investment banking firms will take the lead in organizing the underwriting group, and it is the lead or managing underwriter that will conduct the negotiations with the company with respect to an underwriting agreement.[6]

The applicable registration statement is also prepared during the prefiling period. Preparation of the registration statement and the prospectus (which is an integral part of the registration statement), is a significant undertaking that requires the coordinated efforts of counsel for the company (who prepares the registration statement and most of the ancillary documents), the company's independent public accountants (who prepare the financial statements), various personnel of the company, and the managing underwriter. A full-blown registration statement is a lengthy and extensive document that contains virtually everything an investor would want to know about the issuer, its business and finances, and the terms of the debt securities to be offered. Abbreviated registration forms are available for use by companies whose securities are actively traded and about which the same sort of information that would be required in a registration statement is publicly available.[7] Abbreviated registration forms are also available for particular types of transactions[8] as well as for "small business issuers."[9] For the company seeking to sell its securities to the public for the first time, however, the registration process can be arduous and expensive.[10]

b. The Waiting Period   The second stage of the registration process is the waiting period, which represents the period of time between the filing of a registration statement and the declaration of effectiveness of the registration statement by the SEC. Once the registration statement is completed, it is filed pursuant to the Securities Act with the SEC's principal office in Washington, D.C. The SEC requires that all public debt offering registration statements (as well as certain other registration statements, proxy statements and reports under the Exchange Act) be filed with the SEC in the appropriate electronic form.[11] The registration statement will be processed by one of the SEC's examining groups within the Division of Corporate Finance. Based upon the staff's review, the company will normally receive one or more comment letters which will become the basis for filing one or more amendments to the registration statement.

The waiting period is intended to provide a period of time during which those who will ultimately be involved in the distribution process, as well as the investing public, will have an opportunity to become informed about the security being offered without having to make an immediate decision under sales pressure.

During the waiting period, the underwriter will market the securities within the confines of the Securities Act.[12] After the registration statement has been filed, although sales cannot be effected, the underwriter can take steps to organize a selling group and to condition the market for the offering. These steps must be undertaken, however, in compliance with the applicable requirements of the Securities Act, which permit unrestricted oral communications and limited and prescribed written communications during this period. The principal method of disseminating information concerning the proposed offering during this period is the preliminary prospectus, which is essentially an incomplete version of what will ultimately be distributed as the definitive prospectus. The preliminary prospectus omits certain information such as the offering price or rate, the underwriters' and dealers' discounts and commissions, the amount of proceeds, conversion rates, call prices or other matters dependent on the offering price or rate. Offers to buy—which can be accepted only after the registration statement becomes effective and which can be revoked at any time prior to acceptance—as well as indications of interest, can be solicited subsequent to the filing of the registration statement and prior to its effective date.

Upon filing of the registration statement, the issuing company will often take steps to secure a credit rating for the debt issue and to list the securities on an exchange or automated quotation service. Investors often rely on such public ratings in order to assess the credit risk or default risk of an issue. Credit risk or default risk refers to the risk that the issuer of a fixed income security may default (i.e., the issuer will be unable to make timely principal and interest payments on the security). Credit risk is gauged by quality ratings assigned by commercial rating companies such as Standard & Poor's Corporation (S&P), Moody's Investors Service (Moody's), Fitch Investors Service (Fitch), and Duff & Phelps Investment Research Co. (Duff & Phelps).[13]

In the case of a public offering of debt securities, the issuing company needs to determine whether it wants to list the debt security on an exchange or rely on the over-the-counter market. Most public debt offerings are traded in the over-the-counter market, where a large number of securities firms are available to publish quotations. The over-the-counter debt market is generally believed to be as deep and as liquid as the auction market of the principal exchanges. Nevertheless, many issuers will opt for a stock exchange listing simply because they believe it provides a certain status that will help them in their businesses.[14]

c. The Posteffective Period   The third and final phase of the registration process, the posteffective period, begins when the registration statement is declared effective by the SEC. The sequence of events following the declaration of effectiveness depends on whether pricing of the debt issue has occurred before the registration statement has become effective or thereafter. If pricing of the debt issue occurs before the registration statement is declared effective, generally the evening before, the underwriter will notify members of the underwriting group of the relevant pricing information and the distribution will take place promptly by the underwriting syndicate or group. The lead underwriter, acting on behalf of members of the underwriting group, will have available substantial offers to buy or indications of interest from broker-dealers which are turned into contracts of sale by phone. The broker-dealers, in turn, through their salesmen, will have been in contact with prospective investors. The members of the selling group employ similar means to contact interested investors among their clientele. During the same or following day, written confirmations accompanied by the final prospectus will be sent by the selling dealers and confirmations will be exchanged between the lead underwriter and members of the selling group.

If pricing has not occurred before the registration statement has been declared effective, marketing of the debt securities continues for a brief period of time after the effective date. Until pricing, the preliminary prospectus can be used in the same manner as before the effective date. The manner in which indications of interest and offers are solicited is subject to substantially the same restrictions that apply during the waiting period. Once there has been an agreement with respect to pricing, a final prospectus including the pricing information is filed pursuant to Rule 424(b)(1) under the Securities Act. The sequence of events after pricing does not differ significantly from that which would be followed if pricing were determined prior to the effective date.

C. The Trust Indenture Act

The TIA was passed by Congress in 1939 in reaction to perceived abuses associated with the public issuance of various debt instruments. Specifically, the TIA was enacted in order to provide full and fair disclosure, not only at the time of issuance of bonds, notes, debentures, and other similar securities, but throughout the life of such securities, and to provide for independent trustees pursuant to indentures, with the emphasis being to protect and enforce the rights of holders of debt securities issued thereunder.[15] The mechanics of the TIA are closely integrated with the registration procedure that is set forth in the Securities Act. Thus, every debt instrument that is offered to the public by use of the mails or otherwise by interstate commerce must be issued under an indenture that has been qualified by the SEC.[16] No indenture may be qualified under the TIA unless certain standardized requirements with respect to the indenture have been met and the trustee satisfies the TIA's specific requirements of independence.

The procedure for qualification of indentures is straightforward and may be coordinated with the filing of a registration statement under the Securities Act. The issuer must include various information and documents prescribed by the SEC in order to permit a determination as to whether the trustee is eligible to act under the TIA's trustee qualification standards, discussed below, as well as an analysis of certain provisions of the indenture. In order to assess a trustee's qualifications, the SEC has prescribed particular forms for institutional and individual trustees.[17] In addition, the information with respect to the debt security that is specified in the registration forms filed by an issuer under the Securities Act is used by the SEC to analyze the indenture provisions. The indenture is qualified when the registration statement becomes effective under the Securities Act.

Under Section 310 of the TIA, at least one trustee (an *institutional trustee*) must be a United States corporation that is authorized to exercise corporate trust powers, is subject to governmental supervision or examination, and has at all times a combined capital and surplus of $150,000 or more. While an indenture may provide for additional cotrustees, the institutional trustee must be able to exercise all of the rights and duties of any of the trustees, either alone or jointly with others, unless such trustee is precluded from performing a particular act by the law of a particular jurisdiction. Under Section 310, a trustee will be disqualified if subject to any one of certain specifically enumerated "conflicting interests," and a trustee must eliminate the conflicting interest or resign within 90 days after becoming aware of any such conflict.[18] In the event the trustee resigns for any reason, the issuer will be required by the terms of the indenture to take prompt steps to have a successor trustee appointed.

In addition to indenture provisions on eligibility and disqualification of the trustee, the TIA details the provisions that must be included in all qualified indentures. These provisions, which are set forth in Sections 311 through 318 of the TIA, have become largely "boilerplate."[19]

The TIA contains several important exemptions. The TIA exempts any security other than (1) a note, bond, debenture or evidence of indebtedness; (2) a certificate of interest or participation in any such debt; or (3) a temporary certificate for, or a guarantee of, any such debt. The TIA also exempts many issuances of debt securities that are exempt from the provisions of the Securities Act. For example, private placements of debt securities are exempt, as are certain small issuances, when (1) not more than $5 million of such debt securities are issued within any period of 12 consecutive months or (2) not more than $10 million of such debt securities are issued during any period of 36 consecutive months.[20]

D. State Securities Laws

In addition to federal regulatory requirements, an issuer of either public or private high yield debt securities needs to be concerned with the state regulation of such securities. State regulation of securities in the United States dates back to 1911, when Kansas adopted what is considered to be the first comprehensive system of securities regulation. These laws are popularly referred to today as "blue sky" laws, because early sponsors viewed them as being designed to reach "speculative schemes which have no more basis than so many feet of blue sky."[21] Today, a Uniform Securities Act is law in most jurisdictions and securities laws in some form are in effect in all 50 states, plus the District of Columbia, Guam, and Puerto Rico.[22] In general, the Uniform Securities Act as well as the blue sky laws of the other jurisdictions are generally focused on the registration of securities, the registration of broker-dealers, agents (or sales representatives) and investment advisors, and fraudulent and other prohibited practices.

Like the Securities Act, the state securities laws generally require the registration of any security before it is offered or sold in the state, unless the security or the transaction is exempted. Registration is generally accomplished through the process of *coordination, qualification,* or *notification.* The coordination procedure is significant in that it represents an attempt by state regulators to help minimize the duplication inherent in a system of dual regulation (i.e., regulation at both the federal and state level). In essence, if a prospectus included in a registration statement filed with the SEC (together with any additional information filed with the SEC that is desired by the state administrator) is filed timely with the state administrator, the registration statement will automatically become effective at the state level when it becomes effective at the SEC, unless the administrator has otherwise instituted a stop order proceeding under the state law. The dual structure permits the state to continue its traditional regulation without sacrificing the disclosure philosophy of the federal statute.[23]

A streamlined procedure called "registration by notification" is available in approximately 60 percent of the states for companies that have been in continuous operation for five years, satisfy a net earnings test, and have not had a default for the prior three years in the payment of principal, interest, or dividends with respect to any securities having fixed maturity interest or dividend provisions. The notification procedure requires the filing of limited data[24] and such registration automatically becomes effective at a specific time unless the administrator institutes a stop order proceeding to deny effectiveness.

The qualification procedure, in which the state administrator exercises plenary authority to decide what information is required as well as when a registration statement will become effective, must be used when the other procedures are not available.[25]

All state securities laws provide exemptions from the applicable registration requirements. The Uniform Securities Act, like the Securities Act, provides exemptions for both particular securities and particular transactions.[26]

Of significance to issuers of private high yield debt securities are exemptions recurrent in most state laws providing for (1) an exemption for offerings to financial institutions and institutional investors,[27] and (2) the Uniform Limited Offering Exemption (ULOE), which exempts any offer or sale of securities sold in compliance with Regulation D of the Securities Act.[28]

The National Securities Markets Improvement Act of 1996 amended Section 18 of the Securities Act to preempt state securities registration and merit review requirements for certain securities, including securities listed on the NYSE, the AMEX, or the Nasdaq National Market System; securities sold to "qualified purchasers" (which is to be determined through SEC rulemaking); and securities sold in private placement transactions under Rule 506 of Regulation D, discussed below. The various states retain the right to require parties filing documents with the SEC to file copies thereof with such states for notice purposes along with a consent to service of process and the required fee. State administrators retain the authority to investigate and bring enforcement actions with respect to fraud or deceit or unlawful conduct by a broker or dealer.

E. The Exchange Act

The Exchange Act requires registration by every issuer of a nonexempt security that is listed on a national securities exchange[29] or is held of record by at least 500 persons, if the issuer has total assets exceeding $10 million[30] (and if the issuer is engaged in interstate commerce or in a business affecting interstate commerce, or any of its securities are traded by use of the mails or any means of interstate commerce). Unlike the Securities Act, whose disclosure scheme is transaction oriented, registration under the Exchange Act is designed to afford more or less continuous disclosure. The Exchange Act accomplishes this in four ways:

1. Periodic reports must be filed under Section 13 (and in some cases under Section 15(d)) of the Exchange Act. The principal periodic reports required to be filed with the SEC by reporting companies consist of: (1) the annual report on Form 10-K (or Form 10-KSB for small business issuers), which is required to be filed within 90 days after the end of the company's fiscal year; (2) the quarterly report on Form 10-Q (or Form 10-QSB for small business issuers), which is required to be filed within 45 days after the end of the company's fiscal quarter-end other than the year-end quarter; and (3) the current report on Form 8-K, which is required to be filed within 15 days or 5 days of the earliest event to occur, depending on the event that requires the filing of the Form 8-K report.[31]

2. Under Section 14(a) of the Exchange Act, the solicitation of proxies must comply with applicable SEC rules.[32]

3. Sections 13(d)–(e) of the Exchange Act require the filing of certain beneficial ownership reports and Sections 14(d)–(f) of the Exchange Act regulate tender offers.[33]

4. Section 16 of the Exchange Act imposes certain requirements with respect to insider trading practices.[34]

F. Federal Antifraud Provisions

Both the Securities Act and the Exchange Act contain provisions that regulate fraud under a number of different scenarios. Many of those provisions apply to both public and private transactions. The general antifraud provisions under the federal securities laws include:

1. Section 17(a) of the Securities Act, which makes it unlawful to (a) make an untrue statement of a material fact; (b) make a statement which is misleading because of the omission of a material fact; (c) employ any device, scheme, or artifice to defraud; or (d) engage in any practice which operates as a fraud or deceit. This is the general pattern for defining fraud under the federal securities laws, but it is limited in Section 17(a) to the sale or offer for sale of securities.

2. Section 10(b) of the Exchange Act makes it unlawful "in connection with the purchase or sale" of any security to use "any manipulative or deceptive device or contrivance" as defined by regulations of the SEC. The SEC has adopted Rule 10b-5 pursuant to this section, which defines fraud essentially in the same terms as Section 17(a) of the Securities Act, except that it is applicable to purchases as well as to sales of securities. While broader than Section 17(a) in the sense that it is applicable to purchases as well as sales, it is narrower in that it is not applicable to offers.

3. Section 14(a) of the Exchange Act delegates to the SEC authority to regulate by rule the solicitation of proxies. Pursuant to this authority, the SEC has adopted Rule 14a-9 under the Exchange Act that makes it unlawful in connection with the solicitation of proxies to (a) make a false statement, (b) make a statement which is misleading because of the omission of a material fact, or (c) fail to correct an earlier statement which has become false or misleading.

4. Section 14(e) of the Exchange Act defines fraud in connection with tender offers and the solicitation in favor or opposition to a tender offer as (a) an untrue statement, (b) a statement that is misleading because of the omission of a material fact, or (c) "to engage in any fraudulent, deceptive or manipulative acts or practices." The SEC has rule-making authority under Section 14(e) to further define fraudulent, deceptive, or manipulative acts or practices.

5. Sections 15(c)(1) and (2) of the Exchange Act authorize the SEC to proscribe, to broker-dealers effectuating or attempting to effectuate the purchase or sale of a security, by devices, contrivances, acts, and practices which are "manipulative, deceptive, or otherwise fraudulent." The SEC, pursuant to this authority, has adopted a number of rules, including Rule 15c1-2 which defines such practices to include (a) an untrue statement of a material fact, (b) a statement which is misleading because of the omission of a material fact, or (c) a practice which operates or would operate as a fraud or deceit upon any person.

6. Section 9 of the Exchange Act pertaining to the manipulation of listed securities.

All of the foregoing provisions are enforceable in a variety of actions brought by the SEC. However, none of the above, except Section 9 of the Exchange Act, expressly provides for a private action for damages. Nevertheless, the courts have construed several of the general antifraud provisions of the federal securities laws (particularly Rules 10b-5, 14a-9, and Section 14(e)) as allowing private parties an implied cause of action based on a violation of these provisions.[35]

III. THE PRIVATE SALE OF HIGH YIELD DEBT SECURITIES

A. Overview

Private placements play an important role in capital formation within the United States. In general, private offerings are utilized to provide financing for established companies through a placement made primarily, if not exclusively, to institutional investors, such as insurance companies and pension funds. As in the case of a public offering, such placements are often handled by investment banking firms which receive a commission for their efforts in placing the securities. However, a private placement may also be the means by which a start-up company raises its initial capital, either because it is not seasoned enough to pursue a public offering or because it wants to defray the costs of undertaking a public offering. Private placements may also be utilized for venture capital investments, to issue securities by a company in connection with acquisitions of closely held corporations where all or part of the consideration consists of securities of the acquiring corporation as well as in isolated asset acquisitions.

Private placements have been increasingly utilized within the high yield bond market, particularly under circumstances where timing is a primary concern. Within the United States today, there are two basic methods of conducting a private placement of high yield debt securities: (1) a traditional private placement conducted pursuant to Regulation D, which is negotiated in a confidential manner with a limited number of investors, and (2) a Rule 144a private offering, which is generally conducted more like a public offering, with nonnegotiable terms and distribution to a broader investor universe. Each of these private offering distribution methods are discussed below.

B. Regulation D Private Placement Market

1. History

While Section 5 of the Securities Act requires that all securities offered by the use of the mails or other channels of interstate commerce be registered with the SEC, Congress provided a number of exemptions in the Securities Act from such registration requirements where there was no practical need for registration or where the public benefits were too remote. Section 3 of the Securities Act contains exemptions primarily for many types of particular securities.[36] In some cases, the exemptions under Section 3 do not relate to the type of security at all but rather to the way it is sold. For example, Section 3(a)(11) provides an exemption from the registration requirements for any offer or sale of securities to residents of a single state by an issuer who resides in or is incorporated in the same state and does business in that state. In contrast, Section 4 of the Securities Act exempts certain specific transactions in securities, including "transactions by any person other than an issuer, underwriter, or dealer" and transactions by an issuer not involving any public offering, which is more fully discussed below. Significantly, none of the exemptions in either Section 3 or Section 4 exempts an issuer from the antifraud or civil liability provisions of the federal securities laws.[37]

Among the exemptions, Section 4(2) of the Securities Act exempts from the registration and prospectus delivery requirements of Section 5 "transactions by an issuer not involving any public offering." This is the so-called *private offering* or *private placement* exemption, which is the most utilized exemption under the Securities Act. The private placement exemption has had a long history. Because the language of the statute is imprecise, interpreting what in fact constitutes a "transaction not involving a public offering" has been left to the courts. In the early years following the adoption of the Securities Act, the SEC's emphasis was on the number of offerees. However, a 1954 decision of the U.S. Supreme Court shifted the emphasis from the number of offerees and established the basic principle that the private offering exemption is available only for an offering made exclusively to persons able "to fend for themselves."[38] The ability to fend for oneself in this context depends on access to the same kind of information as that which would be included in a registration statement and the sophistication of the offerees.

In addition to the statutory exemptions referenced above, Section 3(b) of the Securities Act provides the SEC with authority to exempt offerings not exceeding $5 million and Section 4(6) of the Securities Act exempts transactions not exceeding $5 million made solely to one or more "accredited investors."[39] Over the years, the SEC has adopted a series of rules, compliance as to which constitutes a safe harbor for issuers relying on particular exemptions.[40] In order to simplify and clarify judicial interpretation of Section 4(2) of the Securities Act and certain of the SEC rules promulgated thereunder, as well as expand the availability of such rules and achieve some form of uniformity, in 1982 the SEC promulgated Regulation D.

2. Requirements for Compliance with Regulation D

a. General   Regulation D provides a safe harbor so that transactions complying with its requirements will not be considered public offerings. The SEC adopted Regulation D to provide certain issuers with limited offering exemptions from the registration and prospectus delivery requirements of the Securities Act. While Regulation D is an exemption for the issuer from the registration requirements of Section 5 of the Securities Act, it does not exempt an issuer from the antifraud or civil liability provisions of the federal securities laws.[41]

Regulation D exempts offerings which comply with one of three Rules: Rule 504 is available for offerings up to $1 million; Rule 505 is available for offerings up to $5 million; and offerings exceeding $5 million must comply with Rule 506. Rules 501 through 503 set forth definitions and common elements shared by more than one of the specific exemptions. Specifically, Rule 501 sets forth the definitions of various terms used in Regulation D; Rule 502 sets forth the information required to be provided to investors under each of the exemptions;[42] and Rule 503 describes the notice requirement which applies to each of the exemptions.[43]

b. Rule 504   Rule 504 is available to any issuer (domestic or foreign) that is not subject to the reporting requirements of the Exchange Act and is not an investment company. The exemption is available irrespective of the issuer's legal structure (i.e., it may be a corporation, partnership, venture, trust, or other entity) or line of business and irrespective of the total number of offerees or purchasers. An eligible issuer can offer securities pursuant to Rule 504 provided the aggregate offering price of the securities offered pursuant to Rule 504 or any other Section 3(b) exemption does not exceed $1 million during any 12-month period.[44]

The securities received in a Rule 504 offering, unlike under other Regulation D exemptions, are not restricted securities and the issuer is not precluded from advertising or engaging in a general solicitation. No disclosure document need be used, but the offering is subject to the antifraud provisions of the Securities Act. Such offerings must also comply with applicable blue sky laws. In this regard, while most states generally do not have a specific exemption for Rule 504 offerings, many of them have adopted Form U-7 for registration of Rule 504 offerings.[45] An offering conducted pursuant to Rule 504 can be viewed as an exempt public offering rather than a truly private offering.

c. Rule 505   Rule 505 is available to any issuer (domestic or foreign), whether or not it is a reporting company, which offers and sells up to $5 million of securities during any twelve-month period.[46] Rule 505 may not be used by an issuer that is an investment company or by certain other disqualified parties. A Rule 505 offering can be made to an unlimited number of offerees provided that there is no general solicitation or advertising. Sales of the securities can be completed with an unlimited number of accredited investors,[47] as well as up to 35 nonaccredited purchasers, who do not have to meet any sophistication or suitability requirements and do not have to be able to bear the risk of the investment. As long as the offerings are not combined under certain integration rules, an issuer may utilize this exemption on multiple occasions (as long as the aggregate purchase limitation is not exceeded during the 12-month period), each with up to 35 nonaccredited investors.[48]

d. Rule 506   Rule 506 provides an exemption to any issuer (including investment companies), whether or not the issuer is a reporting company, that offers and sells an unlimited amount of securities without general advertising or solicitation to an unlimited number of accredited investors and to not more than thirty-five nonaccredited investors. With respect to nonaccredited investors, the issuer must reasonably believe, immediately prior to making the sale, that the nonaccredited persons understand the merits and risks of the offering. Unlike a Rule 505 transaction, the nonaccredited purchasers in a Rule 506 offering either alone or with the assistance of a purchaser representative must have sufficient knowledge and experience in financial and business matters to be capable of evaluating the merits and risk of the prospective investment.[49] Because of the sophistication requirement, issuers will generally prefer to utilize Rule 505 unless the size of the offering exceeds the Rule 505 threshold.

C. Rule 144a Private Placement Market

1. General
The SEC adopted Rule 144a in April 1990. Rule 144a was proposed to simplify the existing private placement rules, which was expected to facilitate a significant expansion of the private placement market.[50] Rule 144a has been quite successful, and has directly contributed to a significant increase in private placement transactions during the 1990s. Rule 144a provides a limited safe harbor exemption from the registration requirements of the Securities Act and provides for the resale of unregistered securities to "qualified institutional buyers" (QIBs), discussed below. Rule 144a is not intended to provide an exemption from registration for issuers or dealers, who must find their own exemptions in connection with the initial sale of securities. Rather, Rule 144a was promulgated to provide an efficient, liquid market among institutional investors with large securities portfolios (i.e., in excess of $100 million) for securities issued in exempt offerings or in reliance on Regulation S under the Securities Act.[51] Consequently, Rule 144a is best considered an exemption with respect to secondary trading. Because of the manner in which the process is conducted, as described below, a Rule 144a offering is in many respects similar to a public offering. Indeed, it has been observed that "most 144a deals are considered private placements by the [SEC,] but public securities by the market."[52]

2. Requirements for Compliance with Rule 144a
Several requirements need to be observed in order to comply with Rule 144a. First, the seller must take reasonable steps to assure that the buyer is aware that the seller may rely on Rule 144a. Second, the rule excludes "fungible securities," which are securities that, when issued, are part of the same class as securities listed on a U.S. securities exchange or traded in an automated U.S. interdealer quotation system (which includes the Nasdaq). Thus, securities not traded in any organized securities market or only traded in the "pink sheets" or other nonautomated interdealer trading system, as well as securities traded in an offshore securities market, are not fungible securities and are therefore eligible for the Rule's safe harbor provisions. Third, offers and sales may be made only to QIBs. There are three

broad categories of QIBs under the rule. The first is a long list of institutional investors[53] which, to be qualified, must own and invest on a discretionary basis at least $100 million in securities of issuers that are not affiliated with the entity. Second, banks and savings and loan associations, in addition to the $100 million portfolio requirement, must meet a $25 million net asset requirement and be subject to federal or state regulation. Third, securities dealers registered under the Exchange Act need only meet a $10 million securities portfolio requirement.[54]

If an issuer of securities sold in a Rule 144a transaction is a reporting company under the Exchange Act and complies with each of the foregoing conditions, no further conditions are imposed. However, if the issuer is a nonreporting company, the issuer must commit to make available to the holder and a prospective buyer limited information about the issuer's business and the products or services it offers, and its most recent balance sheet, and profit and loss and retained earnings statements for the preceding two years, which should be audited to the extent reasonably available.

In connection with the SEC's promulgation of Rule 144a, the SEC approved an NASD proposal to create a PORTAL Market, which is a computerized, screen-based quotation, trading, settlement and clearing system for securities sold in reliance on Rule 144a. The PORTAL market is limited to QIBs for both initial private placements and subsequent trading in Rule 144a eligible securities. The concept was for PORTAL to act as a closed market on which designated PORTAL securities would be placed with and traded among Rule 144a QIBs, with PORTAL approved dealers acting as market intermediaries.

3. Application of the Rule

We have previously observed that a Rule 144a offering operates in many respects like a public offering. While not required, the issuer and its counsel will typically work with the initial purchasers (usually, investment banking firms; hereinafter Initial Purchasers) and their counsel, to prepare an offering memorandum that is subject to completion and is analogous to a preliminary prospectus. Certain information, such as the applicable price and/or rate of the securities, discounts and commissions, proceeds to the issuer, interest payment dates, and redemption dates ordinarily are omitted from the preliminary offering memorandum. The offering memorandum will generally contain the information that would be included in Part I of a registration statement for the offering on a form the issuer would be entitled to use.[55] The offering memorandum is circulated prior to pricing, during a period which is similar to the waiting period in a registered transaction. During this time, the Initial Purchasers *presell* the securities.

Counsel to the Initial Purchasers will generally prepare a purchase agreement, which is analogous to a firm commitment underwriting agreement, that sets out the terms of the purchase of the securities by the Initial Purchasers from the issuer. The terms of the purchase agreement are negotiated by the issuer and the Initial Purchasers, unlike a more traditional private placement where the issuer negotiates directly with the ultimate purchasers of the securities.

At an agreed-upon time, the securities are priced, the price and price-related information are added to the purchase agreement and the offering memorandum, and the offering memorandum is completed, printed and delivered promptly to the Initial Purchasers. At the same time that the issuer and Initial Purchasers enter into the purchase agreement, the Initial Purchasers enter into an agreement among themselves with respect to distribution. The purchase agreement may provide that the securities will be issued in book-entry and/or nonbook-entry form. The Initial Purchasers will finalize orders from the ultimate purchasers and distribute the final offering memorandum. Prior to the closing with the issuer, arrangements will be made for the securities to clear through the Depository Trust Company (DTC) and to be eligible to trade in PORTAL. At the closing, among other things, the issuer and the trustee execute the indenture; the issuer delivers the securities, either in book-entry form, by causing DTC to credit the securities to the account of the Initial Purchasers, or in certificated form, by delivering the actual certificates to the trustee; and the Initial Purchasers make payment for the securities.

D. Registration Rights Generally

In connection with the private placement of debt securities, the purchasers will often demand and receive registration rights. Under the typical registration rights agreement, the holders of a specified amount of the securities may demand registration at the issuing company's expense. There may be a cutoff period when the registration rights expire. In some cases, registration rights may be exercised only once, and in other cases, the holders will be entitled to demand registration on more than one occasion. The purchasers of the debt securities also may be granted incidental registration rights, so that if the issuer files a registration statement covering other securities or securities of the same class, the holders will be entitled to include their debt securities in the registration statement. The agreement may require such holders to sell the offering through the same underwriters that the issuer is using in order to assure an orderly distribution. Such holders also may be required to refrain from making any sales until a specified period of time after the completion of the distribution.

Another type of registration right that is often utilized in high yield debt offerings does not require the purchasers of the debt securities to demand registration. Instead, the issuing company undertakes to file either a shelf registration statement or a registration statement in connection with an exchange offer (whereby fully registered securities are exchanged for the restricted debt securities issued in the private placement). In either case, the intention is the registration of the securities by the holders as soon as practicable after the initial sale. This type of registration right is intended to place the securities in a position where they are freely tradable with the delivery of a prospectus at the earliest feasible date. Rather than giving the buyers the right to demand registration to cover specific sales that they may make at some future time, all of the securities are registered regardless of the buyers' intentions to hold or to sell. To induce the issuer to register the securities promptly, the indenture under which they are issued frequently provides either that the interest rate will be reduced as soon as a registration statement becomes effective or that the interest rate will be increased if a registration statement is not filed by a specified date or is not declared effective by the SEC by a specified date. Prior to effectiveness, the initial purchasers can make resales to other institutional investors, as in the case of any other secondary sale of a privately placed security. An exchange offer registration statement or a shelf registration statement covering resales, however, increases the marketability of the securities. The terms of any registration rights agreement will vary from transaction to transaction.

IV. THE ADVANTAGES AND DISADVANTAGES OF PUBLIC VERSUS PRIVATE HIGH YIELD DEBT ISSUANCES

A. Pricing Considerations

A public offering has the advantage over either a traditional private placement or a Rule 144a offering in being able to provide the issuer of debt securities with the most competitive pricing terms. Public issues are generally priced more attractively because of a combination of a number of factors described below, such as the size and secondary market trading and liquidity of the issue. A debt security issued under Rule 144a will generally require a modest premium when compared to a public issue (i.e., 5–10 basis points, depending on factors such as the credit quality of the issuer),[56] but will generally require a lower premium when compared to a traditional private placement. When the lower overall transaction costs of a Rule 144a offering are considered, however, the costs of a Rule 144a offering and a public offering (without giving effect to an issuer's ongoing reporting requirements under the Exchange Act) could be quite similar. A traditional private placement is generally the most costly financing alternative from a pricing standpoint when compared with either a Rule 144a transaction or a public offering (i.e., it will require a premium of 10–25 basis points when compared to a public offering),[57] due to the relative lack of liquidity of a privately placed security.

B. Potential Investor Participation

The U.S. public debt market is the largest and most liquid market for U.S. dollar-denominated securities. For this reason, a public issuance offers a potential issuer of debt securities additional marketing flexibility that is not available with either of the private financing alternatives. Specifically, a public offering offers an issuer the largest potential for market penetration, with active participation at both the retail and institutional levels. In contrast, Rule 144a offerings may only be conducted with QIBs, primarily large institutional investors; and traditional private placements are limited to accredited investors and a limited number of nonaccredited investors. Issuers conducting a private placement must be careful to ensure that those participating in the placement qualify under applicable requirements, which would not apply in a public offering.

C. Size of the Offering

The size of a contemplated debt offering is likely to play a factor in the type of financing considered. In general, the public markets still probably offer the most flexibility to an issuer, because both smaller issuances as well as very large transactions can be undertaken. The Rule 144a market can also accommodate both large and smaller debt issues. However, with respect to smaller transactions, there is a preference for issues of at least $100 million, in order to provide liquidity in the form of secondary market trading. In today's market, however, transactions of $50 million or less can and have been completed. In contrast, traditional private placements generally involve smaller sized transactions, partly due to the fact that traditional private placements are more individually negotiated, as discussed below. Here too, however, the present market environment is tending to ignore the foregoing distinctions, and larger transactions are being completed.

D. Secondary Market Liquidity and Trading

A public offering offers a potential issuer of debt securities with stronger secondary market liquidity and a greater public profile as compared to a private offering. In addition, there are no resale restrictions with respect to publicly issued debt as there are with respect to privately offered debt, and the public market is the only market that has an active and liquid long-term sector (of up to 30 years). Although there is less secondary market liquidity than in a public offering, a Rule 144a transaction offers much greater liquidity than is available with respect to investments in traditional private placement transactions, due primarily to Rule 144a's relaxation of the resale restrictions. While the establishment of the PORTAL system by the NASD was intended to facilitate trading by QIBs in securities issued in Rule 144a transactions, the system has not significantly enhanced trading in Rule 144a transactions to date. The traditional private placement market has generally provided investors with little or no secondary market liquidity. However, to the extent an issuer agrees to provide registration rights at some later date, the liquidity of the debt issue will be enhanced.

E. Registration

A public offering of debt securities requires the filing of some form of registration statement with the SEC and, to the extent not exempted, to the state, under the securities laws of the various states in which the offer and sale are to be made. In addition, such a transaction requires filings under and compliance with the TIA. However, companies can now register with the SEC for a Rule 415 shelf registration, which allows the company to issue bonds continuously over a two-year period up to a maximum predetermined amount.

In both Rule 144a transactions and traditional private placements, an issuer of debt securities is not required to register with the SEC or to have an indenture qualified under the TIA. Both Rule 144a transactions and traditional private placements are also generally exempt from state blue sky laws. Registration fees can be expensive, and private financings accordingly represent a cost savings when compared to financings in the public markets. However, in Rule 144a transactions, QIBs may be provided with registration rights that require the issuing company to register the securities at some point with the SEC and, if required, with the various states, and at such time qualify the indenture and comply with the TIA. Registration rights may also be provided in traditional private placements. Registration rights serve to defer the costs of registration and the obligations of continuous public reporting under the Exchange Act until such time as the rights are exercised and the debt securities are registered.

F. Disclosure

An issuer of public debt securities must provide the investing public with full SEC mandated disclosure. Holders and prospective purchasers of Rule 144a securities also have the right to obtain current business and financial information about the issuer unless periodic or certain other reports are filed under the Exchange Act by domestic and non-U.S. issuers, respectively. Issuers in Rule 144a transactions generally prepare an offering memorandum, which closely resembles a public offering prospectus. The offering memorandum will include a description of the terms of the securities offered, the anticipated use of proceeds, a description of the issuer's business, and copies of the issuer's financial statements. In contrast, limited public disclosure is utilized in a traditional private placement, and confidentiality is maintained to a much greater extent.

G. Expenses

A company contemplating an issuance of public debt securities will generally incur higher upfront and ongoing costs as a result of the registration and disclosure obligations associated with conducting a public offering, the continuous public reporting responsibilities under the Exchange Act thereafter, and expenses associated with compliance with the TIA. A Rule 144a transaction will generally be less expensive to conduct than a public offering (there are no registration fees, for example) and will not produce the same ongoing costs as are associated with a public offering. Rule 144a transactions do involve more costs than traditional private placements (the least expensive form of financing) because the offering memorandums that are utilized in such transactions tend to follow the disclosure requirements that apply to registered transactions, with information prepared by the issuer's attorneys and accountants. In addition to the costs that are involved in conducting a private financing, to the extent that registration rights are provided to investors (under either private financing alternative), the issuer will incur the additional costs associated with registering the debt securities, ongoing public reporting, and compliance with the TIA when the registration process begins.

H. Timing

As a result of the time involved in complying with applicable federal and state securities laws, a public offering will usually take more time to complete than either private placement alternative. A public offering can generally take between 8 to 12 weeks to complete in the case of an issuer that is a reporting company and sometimes up to twice as long (i.e., 24 weeks) for a first-time issuer. However, to the extent that an issuer has filed a shelf registration pursuant to Rule 415, an issuer can achieve almost immediate access to the marketplace. Both a Rule 144a transaction and a traditional private placement can be accomplished in a relatively short period, ranging from 2 to 8 weeks for a 144a transaction and 2 to 9 weeks for a traditional private placement, with transactions averaging around 6 weeks. The shorter time frames permit issuers in private placement transactions to take advantage of market conditions more quickly.

I. Underwriting

Both public offerings and Rule 144a transactions are generally conducted on a firm commitment underwritten basis, which enhances the prospects for completion of the transaction. Firm commitment transactions are undertaken pursuant to an underwriting or purchase agreement that is negotiated by the underwriter, or representative thereof, and the issuer, and contain fairly standardized representations and warranties as well as covenants and undertakings. In some instances, a public transaction will only be done on a best efforts basis, in which case the underwriter does not commit to purchase the issue for resale. Traditional private placements are generally sold through an agent on a best efforts basis, and may sometimes be sold by the issuer directly. The undertakings and terms associated with a traditional private placement are typically subject to more individual negotiations between the issuer and the investor.

J. Public Ratings

As the market for high yield debt has expanded, the necessity of obtaining public ratings has declined. Nevertheless, public ratings are generally obtained in public debt offerings and are not generally obtained in traditional private debt offerings. The sophisticated investors who generally invest in private placements will typically have their own investment staffs perform credit analysis with respect to the issuer. To the extent that it is not clear whether the issuer is above or below investment-grade quality, the issuer or its placement agent may seek to obtain a rating to determine the issuer's credit standing.

K. Covenants and Other Terms

An indenture utilized in a public debt offering will generally contain standard public market covenants as compared to an indenture utilized in a private offering of debt, which will generally contain more restrictive covenants.[58] In both public offerings and Rule 144a transactions, the documentation is more standardized and is not negotiated with individual investors, whereas most terms in traditional private transactions are subject to extensive negotiation. With respect to covenants generally, their nature will be highly dependent upon the financial condition and operations of the issuer. A more seasoned company with a stronger balance sheet and an established track record will generally require less restrictive covenants. As for other terms which may be imposed, a public debt offering will often require less onerous call provisions and call premiums as compared with private financing transactions. In private transactions, investors are more likely to be matching assets to liabilities, with the result that longer call protection and higher call premiums will be necessary. Traditional private placements lend themselves to more flexibility with respect to certain types of transactions, as they are more readily able to accommodate various complicated corporate credit and noncredit structured transactions when compared to Rule 144a and public transactions. This is because a traditional private placement is typically subject to more individual negotiation between the issuer and the investor.

V. CONCLUSION

While the high yield junk bond market has existed in some form since the late 1800s, this market has experienced phenomenal growth over the last 20 years, reaching record levels during both 1996 and 1997. Aggregate issuances of public and private high yield debt amounted to $232.1 billion during 1997, which reflected an increase of $109.3 billion or 88.9 percent from the $122.9 billion of high yield debt issued in 1996. As the market for high yield debt has expanded and become more developed and liquid, the private placement segment of this market has emerged not only as a viable alternative to public distribution but, since 1995, has been the medium of choice for issuers of high yield bonds. In 1997, private issuances of high yield debt amounted to $200 billion, which constituted 86.1 percent of the total high yield new issues market.

This article has described some of the fundamental requirements with which an issuer of high yield debt securities must comply when conducting a public offering or a private placement under either Rule 144a or Regulation D. The dramatic expansion of the high yield private placement market in recent years reflects the general recognition by issuers that the time and expense saved in a private offering may, under the right circumstances, compensate the issuing company for the modest premium in pricing (when compared to a public offering) that is often required by investors with respect to such securities.

A company that is contemplating the issuance of high yield debt has to evaluate a number of factors in determining whether to proceed with a public or private transaction. As we have indicated, there are advantages and disadvantages to each of the financing alternatives that are available. For example, under circumstances where pricing, potential investor participation, size, and liquidity are of prime importance, an issuing company will generally prefer issuing its securities publicly. Alternatively, under circumstances where timing and expense are the primary considerations or where the issuing company has concerns with respect to complying with applicable federal and state securities laws and/or with the types of disclosures that are generally required pursuant to such securities laws, a company will generally prefer to issue its securities privately. In any event, with the growth and acceptance of the high yield private placement market generally, the Rule 144a offering, which has many characteristics similar to a public offering but can generally be accomplished more quickly and less expensively, has emerged as an alternative means of issuing high yield debt that combines many of the advantages of the public markets, while addressing many of the disadvantages of the private markets. Consequently, each potential issuer of high yield debt will need to weigh the various factors discussed herein to determine what mix best suits the circumstances that give rise to the financing in question.

ENDNOTES

1. Securities Data Corporation.

2. See Section III of this chapter.

3. See Section II F of this chapter.

4. See Harold S. Bloomenthal and Holme Roberts & Owen, *Securities Law Handbook—Comprehensive Overview of the Law of Securities Regulation, Plus Recent Developments* (West Publishing Group, 1998).

5. The term "offer to sell" in Section 2(3) of the Securities Act is broadly defined to include "every attempt or offer to dispose of, or solicitation of an offer to buy, a security or interest in a security, for value."

6. Underwritings are generally conducted either on a *firm commitment* basis or on a *best efforts* basis. In a firm commitment underwriting, the underwriters become contractually obligated to purchase the debt securities to be offered from the issuer for resale to investors. Thus, the underwriting firm or group assumes the risk for any unsold securities. Because of such risk, the underwriters will not commit to purchase the debt securities and sell the issue until immediately before the registration statement becomes effective under the Securities Act. To expedite the rapid distribution of debt securities in a public offering (as well as to spread the risk), the tendency has been to involve several underwriters who each have strong distribution networks or, alternatively, to form a selling group of additional broker-dealers.

   When a company is not well established, it is less likely to find an underwriter that will give a firm commitment and assume the risk of distribution. Under such circumstances, the underwriting firm will undertake to use its "best efforts" to sell the debt securities. Instead of buying the issue from the issuer and reselling it as principal, the underwriter sells it for the issuer as an agent. If no debt securities are sold, there is no liability to the underwriter and no proceeds to the company. In some instances, generally when other alternatives are not available, the company may attempt to market the debt securities without an underwriter in a so-called *self underwriting*.

   The agreement to purchase or distribute the issuer's debt securities and other related terms are set forth in an underwriting, purchase, or agency agreement. For a discussion on the role and obligations of underwriters and underwriting agreements, see Coopers & Lybrand, *A Guide to Going Public,* 2d ed. (1997) pp. 10–46.

7. Forms S-1, S-2, and S-3 provide the basic framework for the registration of securities under the Securities Act. The same information is required to be part of each of these registration statements. The differences among the forms primarily reflect the SEC's determination as to (1) when this required information must be presented in full in the prospectus delivered to investors, (2) when certain of the required information may be presented in an abbreviated

form and supplemented by documents incorporated by reference but delivered to investors, and (3) when certain information may be incorporated by reference from documents filed pursuant to the Exchange Act without delivery to investors. Generally, it is the portion of the information relating to the issuer, as opposed to the transaction-specific information, which sometimes may be satisfied otherwise than through full prospectus presentation.

The information that is required to be included in a registration statement (as well as reports and proxy statements under the Exchange Act) is set forth in Regulation S-K (other than required financial information, which is the subject of Regulation S-X, the SEC's general accounting regulation). In preparing a registration statement, counsel for the issuer will first select the proper registration form, which will, in turn, direct him or her to the appropriate sections of Regulation S-K for that form's specific disclosure requirements. The required data for a Form S-1 registration statement includes information with respect to: (1) the issuer and its subsidiaries; (2) directors and officers of the issuer; (3) aggregate remuneration of such directors and officers; (4) stockholders owning 10 percent or more of the outstanding shares of any class of equity of the issuer; (5) promoters; (6) selling holders of the securities other than the issuer; (7) capitalization; (8) securities offered, price and underwriting data; and (9) use of proceeds.

8. For example, a Form S-3 may be used for certain (1) secondary offerings, (2) rights offerings, dividend or interest reinvestment plans and conversions, (3) offerings of investment-grade asset-backed securities, and (4) majority-owned subsidiaries. A Form S-4 is available for companies issuing securities in connection with a merger, consolidation, transfer of assets or reorganization; and a Form S-8 is available for companies issuing securities pursuant to specific types of employee benefit plans.

9. In 1992, the SEC adopted a new integrated registration, reporting and disclosure system applicable to *small business issuers.* A small business issuer is defined as a U.S. or Canadian entity that is not an investment company and which has annual revenues of less than $25 million and voting stock with a public float of less than $25 million. See Rule 405 under the Securities Act. Regulation S-B sets forth the required disclosures of small business issuers, and is basically a simplified version of Regulation S-K. Forms SB-1 and SB-2 are the Securities Act registration forms that can be utilized by small business issuers. Each form attempts to simplify the registration process and reduce the burdens and costs of registration for small businesses.

10. The SEC is constantly striving to simplify the registration process. For example, Rule 415 under the Securities Act permits issuers of certain kinds of securities to prepare and file a registration statement well in advance of when such issuer intends to market its securities (so called *shelf registrations*). Rule 415 has significantly liberalized the registration process (particularly with respect

to issuers of debt securities) and has made it possible for qualified issuers to obtain access to the capital markets more readily than in the past. Pursuant to Rule 415, an issuer can file a registration statement with the SEC with respect to an offering of debt securities that is expected to occur over a period not to exceed two years. Consequently, such an issuer would be in a position to act quickly to take advantage of favorable *market windows* as they occur from time to time. Sales *off the shelf* can be made almost instantaneously by filing either a post-effective amendment or a supplement with the SEC.

11. In 1996, the SEC adopted final rules (set forth in Regulation S-T) designed to implement its Electronic Data Gathering, Analysis and Retrieval System (EDGAR). Pursuant to Regulation S-T, most filings under the Securities Act, the Exchange Act and the TIA must be made in electronic format. Generally, anything that is to be incorporated by reference in a filing must also be filed electronically. In order to gain access to EDGAR, a filer must apply for an access code. Filings may be transmitted until 10:00 PM on business days (although filings that begin after 5:30 PM are treated as if filed on the next business day). Filing fees must be forwarded (by hand, by mail, or by wire transfer) to the SEC's lock box at the Mellon Bank in Pittsburgh, Pennsylvania; filings will not be deemed accepted until the appropriate fee is paid. Filings under EDGAR are available to the public on the same day that they are filed.

12. The underwriter also is required to have the reasonableness of its proposed compensation reviewed by the National Association of Securities Dealers, Inc. (NASD). The basis for such regulation is Article III, Section 1 of the NASD's Rules of Fair Practice, which obligates members to observe high standards of commercial honor and just and equitable principles of trade. See NASD Man. (CCH) ¶2710(c).

13. S&P and Moody's are the most widely recognized and utilized of the rating agencies, although Fitch and Duff & Phelps are becoming more frequently used. If a company desires a rating on an issue, it must apply to the rating agency. The agency, in turn, charges a one-time fee, for which it reviews the issue periodically while it is outstanding; at least one formal review is made annually.

All of the rating agencies designate debt quality by assigning a letter rating to an issue. S&P ratings range from AAA to D, with AAA obligations having the highest quality investment characteristics and D obligations being in default. In a similar fashion, Moody's ratings extend from Aaa to C, Fitch's from AAA to D, and Duff & Phelps' from AAA to CCC.

14. In order to have a security traded on a national securities exchange, it must meet the listing requirements for the exchange and be admitted to listing by the exchange. Listed markets purport to be continuous auction markets in which a buyer or seller can execute transactions through members of the exchange on

the exchange floor at any time during exchange business hours. There are eight registered national securities exchanges, including the New York Stock Exchange (NYSE) and the American Stock Exchange (AMEX).

Securities not listed on an exchange as well as some listed securities trade in the over-the-counter market. The primary prerequisite for a debt security to trade in the over-the-counter market is the decision of a dealer to act as a marketmaker with respect to that particular security (i.e., be willing to purchase or sell the security in a normal trading lot to other dealers at a quoted ask or bid price). Securities that do not attract marketmakers, in effect, have no organized market in which they can readily be purchased or sold.

The NASD has developed a computerized system to facilitate trading in the over-the-counter market. This system is called the Nasdaq stock market (Nasdaq). Nasdaq permits marketmakers to electronically submit their quotations with respect to specific securities and lets subscribing broker-dealers receive current quotations for a substantial number of over-the-counter securities. Except under certain limited circumstances, only securities that are registered under the Exchange Act are eligible for quotation on Nasdaq. The company whose securities are to be quoted must apply for listing on Nasdaq and pay a prescribed annual fee. In addition, at least two NASD members (three in the case of securities listed on the Nasdaq's National Market System) must register as marketmakers with respect to the security.

For a discussion of securities markets, see Coopers & Lybrand, *A Guide to Going Public,* p. 29.

15. See Section 302 of the TIA. See Louis Loss and Joel Seligman, *Securities Regulation,* 3d ed. (1989), pp. 1591–1690.

16. An indenture is a legal document entered into by the issuer and a corporate trustee that defines the rights and obligations of the borrower and the lender with respect to a bond issue. The corporate trustee acts in a fiduciary capacity as a representative of the interests of bondholders, as discussed in the text below. Among the trustee's functions are authenticating the bonds issued, keeping track of all the bonds sold, making sure that the bonds do not exceed the principal amount authorized by the indenture, and seeing that the issuer complies with all of the covenants set forth in the indenture.

An indenture will generally set forth the terms of a bond issue, including any required covenants and related provisions. Covenants provide the mechanism by which the trustee can accelerate the maturity date of the bonds in the event of adverse developments with respect to the business of the issuer or with respect to its financial condition. There are generally two types of covenants, affirmative covenants and negative covenants. Affirmative covenants are intended to maintain or insure the ongoing integrity of the issuer's corporate existence and business operations and generally include, among other items, agreements: (1) to continue to conduct the activities of the issuer along the same lines of business as presently conducted; (2) to maintain the corporate existence of the issuer and its material subsidiaries, maintain insurance, pay taxes, and maintain properties necessary for the conduct of the issuer's business; (3) to comply with applicable laws and regulations; and (4) to deliver to investors certain financial and other information relating to the issuer and its subsidiaries. Negative covenants are intended to insure that the issuer will conduct its business in a manner that will preserve its financial integrity throughout the term of the financing and protect the issuer's assets and cash flow from the claims of investors and other creditors. Typical negative covenants include, among others, required ratios with respect to liquidity, net worth and capitalization and various restrictions with respect to: (1) the incurrence of long-term or short-term debt; (2) the incurrence of rental obligations under operating leases; (3) mergers and consolidations, unless after giving effect thereto, the surviving corporation is able, among other things, to issue $1.00 of additional long-term debt and no event of default would exist; (4) the sale of all or a substantial portion of the assets of the issuer other than in the ordinary course of its business; (5) the sale of stock of the issuer's subsidiaries; (6) the incurrence of liens, claims and other encumbrances (other than liens incurred in the ordinary course of the issuer's business); (7) the amount of cash dividends, stock redemptions and, in certain cases, payments with respect to subordinated indebtedness of the issuer; (8) investments by the issuer (other than investments made in the ordinary course of the issuer's business); and (9) transactions with affiliates.

An indenture also addresses other terms of the debt issue including whether the instrument is callable (i.e., can be prepaid). Many indentures prohibit the ability of an issuer to call the underlying bonds during the early years of the issue (generally referred to as call protection). Similarly, many indentures will permit the issuer to call the bonds (in whole or in part) upon the payment of a specified make-whole premium. Typically, the make-whole premium will be set at an amount equal to the present value of the difference between the coupon rate of the bonds being prepaid and a Treasury bond of similar duration plus an applicable credit spread.

17. The Trust Indenture Reform Act of 1990 amended the TIA to facilitate Rule 415 shelf offerings. See footnote 10. The SEC subsequently adopted rules together with amendments to Forms T-1 (used for institutional trustees) and T-2 (used for individual trustees) in order to permit an issuer to delay the naming of a trustee under an indenture when securities are to be sold on a shelf registration basis.

18. A trustee is deemed to have a conflicting interest if the indenture securities are in default and (1) It acts as a trustee under more than one indenture of the same issuer, subject to several exceptions; (2) It or any of its directors or executive

officers is an underwriter for an issuer of the indenture securities; (3) It directly or indirectly controls or is directly or indirectly controlled by or is under direct or indirect common control with an underwriter for an issuer; (4) Both the trustee and the issuer (or an underwriter) have more than one director or executive officer in common, or the trustee or any of its directors or executive officers is a "partner, employee, appointee or representative" of the issuer (or of any such underwriter), subject to certain exceptions; (5) More than specified percentages of the trustee's voting securities are beneficially owned by the issuer, the underwriter, or their respective directors, partners or executive officers; (6) The trustee owns beneficially, or in any representative capacity, more than specified percentages of the securities of an issuer, an underwriter, or a person who stands in a control relationship with an issuer or who owns substantial percentages of its voting securities; or (7) Except under certain circumstances, the trustee shall be or become a creditor of the issuer.

19. Section 311 is designed to prevent a trustee that is also a creditor of the issuer from improving its own creditor position at the expense of the bondholders under specified circumstances. Section 312 addresses bondholders' lists and provides that the indenture shall require the issuer to furnish the trustee (at six-month intervals or, on request, more often) all information in its possession or control as to the names and addresses of the bondholders, and specifies how such lists may be accessed by bondholders. Section 313 addresses reports by the trustee while Section 314 addresses reports by the issuer. Section 315 addresses the duties and responsibilities of the trustee before and after default. Section 316 permits the indenture to contain provisions authorizing the holders of not less than specified percentages of the principal amount of the indenture securities outstanding to take actions with respect to (1) remedies available to the trustee, (2) waivers of past defaults, or (3) the postponement of any interest payment for a specified period, but requires the indenture to provide that the right of any indenture securityholder to receive his principal and interest when due and to bring suit therefor may not be impaired without his consent. Section 317 requires the indenture to confer upon the trustee the power to recover judgment, in its own name as trustee, against the issuer in the event of a principal default or an interest default that has continued for whatever period the indenture provides and the power to file proofs of claim on behalf of all holders in the event of judicial proceedings affecting the issuer or its property. Section 318 requires the indenture to provide that provisions required by the statute shall control in the event of conflict with other provisions.

20. See Section 304 of the TIA.

21. Hall v. Gerger-Jones Co., 242 U.S. 539 (1917). For a history of the state regulation of state securities laws, see Louis Loss and E. Cowett, *Blue Sky Law* (1958). For general information on blue sky regulation, see Loss and Seligman, *Securities Regulation*.

22. The text of each jurisdiction's blue sky statutes appears in *Blue Sky Law Reporter,* a multivolume compilation of statutes and regulations (CCH). A Uniform Securities Act was promulgated by the National Conference of Commissioners on uniform state laws in 1956. All or substantially all of this act is currently in force in 41 jurisdictions. Revisions to the 1956 Uniform Securities Act were proposed in 1985; portions of the revised act or provisions similar to such revisions have been adopted in six jurisdictions. As a result of the passage of the National Securities Markets Improvement Act of 1996 (NSMIA), the North American Securities Association is proposing amendments to the Uniform Securities Act to address NSMIA's provisions preempting state authority with respect to registration and/or filing requirements for covered securities, which includes securities issued in many private placements. See Peter M. Fass and Derek A. Wittner, *Blue Sky Practice for Public and Private Limited Offerings* §1.01 (1997).

23. See Unif. Sec. Act §303. Currently over 40 jurisdictions have either a registration by coordination procedure or an exemption for securities registered pursuant to a shelf registration with the SEC under Rule 415. See footnote 10. In many jurisdictions, the issuer is also required to file a Form U-1, Uniform Application to Register Securities, with the jurisdiction's securities administrator, when a security is filed pursuant to a shelf registration with the SEC. For a discussion of registration procedures, see Fass and Wittner, *Blue Sky Practice for Public and Private Limited Offerings,* §2.02.

24. See Unif. Sec. Act §302. The data required to be filed includes: a description of the security offered; the offering price, underwriters' discounts, or commissions and finders' fees; other selling expenses; a copy of the underwriting or selling group agreement, or a description of the plan of distribution if the securities are to be offered by a different arrangement; a description of any stock options outstanding or to be created in the offering; and a copy of any prospectus, circular, form letter, advertisement, or other sales literature to be used in connection with the offering.

25. See Unif. Sec. Act §304. The data required to be included in a registration statement subject to qualification is modeled on Schedule A of the Securities Act and the SEC's Form S-1 generally.

26. See Unif. Sec. Act §§401 and 402 and Section III A in this chapter.

27. See Unif. Sec. Act §402(b)(8). Sales to such investors are excluded on the basis that these investors can protect their own interests without any need for state intervention. The Section 402(b)(8) exemption, while resembling many aspects of the "accredited investor" definition of Regulation D (see Section III B and footnote 47 in this chapter), is different in that individuals are not included, regardless of their financial wherewithal or investor acumen. In addition, the foregoing exemption has been determined to apply in approximately 49 jurisdictions to offerings to qualified institutional buyers, as that term is defined in Rule 144a (see Section IIIC).

28. See Section III B of this chapter. The ULOE provides that an offering is exempt from state registration if it complies with Rules 501, 502, 503, 505, and/or 506 under Regulation D, provided that certain additional requirements are complied with. There is no exemption in the ULOE for securities that may be exempt under Rule 504 (i.e., offers and sales not exceeding $1.0 million). However, a simplified registration procedure called the Small Corporate Offering Registration (SCOR), with a new registration Form U-7, has been created for small offerings exempt from federal registration under Regulation D's Rule 504. In addition, securities that are exempt at the federal level under Rule 504 may still be exempt under various other limited offering exemptions available under state laws.

In addition to the ULOE, another widely used exemption is the limited offering exemption found in Section 402(b)(9) of the Uniform Securities Act. In order to take advantage of the exemption, most states preclude offers during any consecutive 12-month period to more than 10 offerees and limit the number of total securityholders within and without the particular jurisdiction. While this section has been adopted in some form by all but two jurisdictions, variations between the different state codes are widespread.

29. See footnote 14.

30. Section 12(g)(1) of the Exchange Act requires registration if total assets exceed $1 million; however, the SEC, by rule, has increased the total asset criterion to $10 million. See Rule 12g-1 under the Exchange Act.

31. Form 8-K needs to be filed in the event of a change in control; the acquisition or disposition of a significant amount of assets other than in the ordinary course of business; the appointment of a receiver and certain material orders issued in a bankruptcy or reorganization proceeding; the resignation or dismissal of the certifying accountant (with information relating to any disagreement over accounting principles and a confirming letter from the accountant to the SEC); the resignation of a director if the director has furnished the registrant with a letter describing a disagreement on any matter relating to the registrant's operations and the director requests that such matter be disclosed; and any other matter which the registrant regards as of material importance to securityholders and elects to report on in the Form 8-K.

32. Regulation 14A consists of twelve fairly detailed rules, together with Schedule 14A, which specifies in twenty-two items the information required to be set forth in a proxy statement, and Schedule 14B, which specifies the information to be included in a statement required to be filed for each participant in a contested election. The first six items of Schedule 14A apply to proxy statements generally, regardless of the type of action proposed to be taken. They call for information with respect to (1) the date, time, and place of the meeting, (2) the revocability of the proxy, (3) dissenters' appraisal rights, (4) the identity of the persons on whose behalf the solicitation is being made and who are bearing its cost, (5) any substantial interest of the solicitors and other specified persons in the matters to be acted upon, and (6) the issuer's voting securities and their principal holders. Item 7 specifies in considerable detail the information required in connection with an election of directors. Item 8 requires certain information with respect to management remuneration. Items 9 through 22 relate to proposals of various other types such as the selection of auditors; bonus, profit sharing and other remuneration plans; pension and retirement plans; options, warrants or rights; the authorization or issuance of securities otherwise than for exchange; the modification or exchange of securities; mergers, consolidations, acquisitions of another issuer's securities and similar matters; the acquisition or disposition of property; the restatement of accounts; reports of the management or of committees, as well as minutes of stockholders' meetings; matters submitted to a vote of securityholders without any requirement that they be so submitted; and charter and by-law amendments.

33. Sections 13(d)–(e) and 14(d)–(f) of the Exchange Act are collectively known as the Williams Act. Sections 13(d) and (e) require a person or group of persons in the process of acquiring a substantial block of equity securities of a company (i.e., 5 percent or more of the outstanding shares) to notify the SEC and the company that they have made such an acquisition (through the filing of a Schedule 13D or a Schedule 13G with the SEC and the company within 10 days of the triggering purchase), and to disclose, among other things, their intentions with respect to the control of the company. Sections 14(d)–(f) of the Exchange Act regulate tender offers. A tender offer is a means of buying a substantial portion of the outstanding stock of a company by making an offer to purchase all shares, up to a specified number, tendered by shareholders within a specified period at a fixed price, usually at a premium above the market price. The Williams Act requires a person making a tender offer to file certain information with the SEC and regulates the tender offer process.

34. Section 16 of the Exchange Act regulates insider trading in the following manner: (1) Section 16(a) requires the reporting by certain insiders of their stock holdings and transactions in an issuer's securities; (2) Section 16(b) imposes liability on insiders of the issuer with respect to profits derived by them from short-swing trading (a purchase and sale or sale and purchase occurring within any six-month period); and (3) Section 16(c) makes it unlawful for insiders to engage in short sales of the issuer's equity securities.

35. See Loss and Seligman, *Securities Regulation,* Chapter 9.

36. See Sections 3(a)(2) through 3(a)(8) of the Securities Act.

37. See Section II F of this chapter.

38. See SEC v. Ralston Purina Co., 346 U.S. 119, 121 (1953).

39. The Section 4(6) exemption is available for offers and sales made by any issuer exclusively to accredited investors, as defined in Regulation D (see footnote 47), where the offering does not involve public solicitation or advertising. The

availability of the exemption does not depend on the use of a disclosure document, but the offering must be reported on Form D, as in the case of Regulation D offerings. See footnote 43.

40. For example, pursuant to its authority under Section 3(b), the SEC has adopted Regulation A, which exempts public offerings not exceeding $5 million in any 12-month period. Regulation A is intended to make it easier for small start-up companies to go public. Public offers and sales of securities are exempt from the registration requirements of the Securities Act by issuers who meet the eligibility requirements set forth in Rule 251. Such eligibility requirements include the filing of an offering statement (a simplified version of a registration statement) and the distribution of an offering circular to investors in connection with the sale of securities. An offering statement has to be *qualified* by the SEC before a security offered in reliance on Regulation A can be sold.

The National Securities Markets Improvement Act of 1996 extends the SEC's authority to adopt rules or regulations exempting offerings from the registration or other provisions of the Securities Act that it deems necessary or appropriate in accordance with the public interest or protection of investors. This is a significant expansion in the SEC's ability to adopt exemptions and could, for example, result in the SEC increasing the $5 million ceiling on the Rule 505 exemption under Regulation D, discussed below, and/or the Regulation A exemption, both of which are predicated on Section 3(b). To date, the SEC has not taken any action to increase such ceiling.

41. See Section II F of this chapter.

42. If an issuer sells securities pursuant to Rule 504 or generally to accredited investors (as discussed herein), no specific disclosure is required. If securities are sold pursuant to Rules 505 or 506 to nonaccredited investors, the type of information to be furnished depends on the size of the offering and whether the issuer is subject to the reporting requirements of the Exchange Act. With respect to nonfinancial information, nonreporting issuers are required to provide the same kind of information as is required by the registration form the issuer would be entitled to use in a public offering. A reporting company will generally furnish current information required to be reported under the Exchange Act.

43. The availability of all Regulation D exemptions is dependent upon the filing of a Form D with the SEC no later than 15 days after the first sale of securities pursuant to one of the exemptions. No periodic or final Form D has to be filed thereafter. Supplemental filings are not required except, if the offering continues for a substantial period of time, or it otherwise becomes apparent that the information in the Form D is inaccurate, there may be a need to file an amendment to correct the information in the Form D.

44. In determining the aggregate amount of securities that may be sold under Rules 504 and 505, an issuer must include the aggregate offering price of securities sold during the prior 12 months as well as during the offering with reliance on all Section 3(b) exemptions (i.e., Rules 504, 505, and 506, Regulation A and Regulation B). Further, if made within six months after completion of the offering, such other offerings may be deemed integrated, in which event the amount would have to be included for Rules 504 and 505 purposes. See footnote 48.

45. See footnote 28.

46. See footnote 44.

47. An accredited investor is defined to include: (1) any bank as defined in Section 3(a)(2) of the Securities Act or any savings and loan association or other institution whether acting in its individual or fiduciary capacity; (2) any broker-dealer registered pursuant to Section 15 of the Securities Act; (3) any insurance company; (4) any investment company registered under the Investment Company Act of 1940; (5) any business dealers purchasing for their own accounts; (6) any Small Business Investment Company licensed under Section 301(c) or (d) of the Small Business Investment Act of 1958; (7) any plan established and maintained by a state or its agencies for the benefit of its employees if such plans' total assets exceed $5,000,000; (8) under certain circumstances, any employee stock ownership plan within the meaning of the Employee Retirement Income Security Act of 1974; (9) any private business development company as defined in Section 202(a)(22) of the Investment Advisers Act of 1940; (10) any organization described in Section 501(c)(3) of the Internal Revenue Code, corporation of Massachusetts or similar business trust or partnership not formed for this specific purpose of acquiring the securities offered, with total assets over $5,000,000; (11) any director, executive officer, or general partner of the issuer, or any director, executive officer, or general partner of a general partner of that issuer; (12) any natural person with a net worth (or spousal joint net worth) over $1,000,000; (13) any natural person with an individual income over $200,000 in each of the two most recent years or joint income with that person's spouse in excess of $300,000 in each of those years who has a reasonable expectation of reaching the same income level in the current year; (14) any trust with total assets in excess of $5,000,000 not formed for the specific purpose of acquiring the securities offered, whose purchase is directed by a sophisticated person as described in Rule 506; and (15) any entity in which all of the equity owners are accredited investors.

48. Integration is an important concept for determining a number of matters under Regulation D, including (1) the 35 nonaccredited investors permitted in a Rule 505 or Rule 506 offering; (2) the aggregate sales limit under Rule 504; (3) whether securities of the same single issue are offered and sold exclusively to

accredited investors; (4) the extent to which a series of Rule 506 offerings can be made; and (5) whether offerings under Rules 505 and 506 can be separated. Under Rule 502(a), sales made more than six months before the Regulation D offering and those made more than six months after the completion of the Regulation D offering are not deemed integrated with such Regulation D offering, provided that no sales of securities of the same or similar class were made (other than to certain employee benefits plans). Rule 502 also generally requires a hiatus of six months between the completion of a Rule 505 or 506 offering and the commencement of a registered offering. The SEC will not allow the withdrawal of a public offering and the commencement of a private placement without a cooling-off period, which will also generally be for six months.

49. The sophistication rule applies only to purchasers and not to offerees.

50. See "SEC Study Ready to Ease Private Placement Rules," *The Wall Street Journal*, C1, April 13, 1990.

51. Regulation S provides that offers and sales "that occur outside the United States" are not deemed an offer and sale for purposes of the registration provisions of the Securities Act. Adopted in 1990, Regulation S facilitates offshore distributions by U.S. issuers. See generally Bloomenthal and Holme Roberts and Owen, *Securities Law Handbook*, pp. 1697-1794 (1998).

52. See Kershaw, "Scouring the Globe for the Traditional Private Market," *Investment Dealers' Digest*, March 7, 1994.

53. Included in this list are the following entities: insurance companies, registered investment companies or business development companies, licensed small business investment companies, employee benefit plans, certain business development companies, charitable organizations, and registered investment advisors.

54. Dealers may take into account not only securities they own (trading accounts and investment accounts), but also securities they invest, pursuant to discretionary authority, for customers.

55. See footnote 7 in this chapter.

56. See Scott J. Gelbard, "Institutional Private Placements and Other Financing Alternatives," *PLI Course Handbook, Private Placements*, 1997.

57. Ibid.

58. See footnote 16.

CHAPTER 28

Managing Default: Some Evidence on How Firms Choose between Workouts and Chapter 11*

Stuart C. Gilson

INTRODUCTION

With the large number of high-profile corporate defaults and bankruptcies that have occurred since the start of this decade, financial economists have become increasingly interested in understanding how companies deal with financial distress. In particular, academic concern has focused on whether the costs of resolving default are excessive, and whether the process by which firms recontract with their creditors can be made more efficient.

Companies have good reason to be concerned with these issues as well. Since 1990 there have been almost half a million business bankruptcy filings in the United States, including more than 50 filings by public companies with over $1 billion of assets.[1] The costs of restructuring the balance sheets of troubled companies can be daunting. LTV Corporation, for example, spent almost $200 million on legal and other professional fees during its seven-year bankruptcy. And this figure ignores other, potentially greater, costs of financial distress such as any loss of business occasioned by the bankruptcy.

There are two basic methods for reorganizing troubled companies: private workouts and formal bankruptcy. In either case, new financial claims are exchanged for the firm's outstanding debt contracts on terms the firm

*This article is reprinted with permission from *Journal of Applied Corporation Finance,* Vol. 4, No. 2, Summer 1991.

The author is grateful for the helpful comments of Max Holmes, the valuable research assistance of Joe Basset, and the research support provided by the Division of Research of the Harvard Business School.

1. Source: *Bankruptcy Yearbook & Almanac.*

finds more affordable. The net effect of the exchange is either to reduce the level of interest and principal payments, to extend the payment dates, or to substitute equity for debt. The main difference between the two approaches is that, in bankruptcy, this exchange is supervised by the court.

Viewed in this light, the workout–bankruptcy choice has an obvious parallel with the decision faced by plaintiffs and defendants over whether to settle out of court or go to trial. If settling privately is appreciably less expensive, then both sides have an incentive to avoid going to court. But if the affected parties are unable to agree on how to split the cost savings, then a trial may still be necessary even though the combined wealth of both parties is ultimately lower.

Professor Michael Jensen has argued that today's highly leveraged companies that get into trouble have far stronger incentives to reorganize privately than their low-leveraged counterparts of the early 1980s. When a highly leveraged company misses an interest payment, management is forced to take corrective action much sooner than otherwise, thus leaving more of the company's operating value intact. In the absence of such an "early warning system," operating performance could be allowed to deteriorate much longer—in the extreme, making liquidation the only sensible alternative. To the extent private workouts are less costly than the formal Chapter 11 process, the "privatization of bankruptcy" envisioned by Jensen should ensure that more of the firm's value survives the recontracting process, thus benefiting creditors as well as shareholders.[2]

In a recently published study, Kose John, Larry Lang, and I examined a sample of 169 New York and American Stock Exchange–listed companies that defaulted on their debt during the 1980s.[3] Eighty, or almost half, of these companies successfully restructured their debt in workouts while the rest filed for Chapter 11. And for 62 of the 89 companies (or almost 70 percent) that ended up in bankruptcy, we found reports in *The Wall Street Journal* of

---

2. See Michael Jensen (1989). "Active Investors, LBOs, and the Privatization of Bankruptcy," *Journal of Applied Corporate Finance* Spring.

3. Stuart Gilson, Kose John, and Larry Lang (1990). "Troubled Debt Restructurings: An Empirical Study of Private Reorganization of Firms in Default," *Journal of Financial Economics* 26. We constructed our sample by first ranking all New York and American Stock Exchange–listed companies by their common stock returns (measured over 3 consecutive years), and then identifying all firms in the bottom 5 percent of these returns that were either in default on their debt, bankrupt, or restructuring their debt to avoid bankruptcy, based on coverage of these firms in *The Wall Street Journal*. This selection process was repeated for various years, resulting in a sample of firms that first experienced financial difficulty throughout the period 1978–1987.

attempts to restructure privately. (Because a good number of other attempts at restructuring almost certainly were unreported, this 70 percent figure should be construed as a "lower bound.")

Thus, during the 1980s, private restructuring was generally the preferred method for dealing with default. The fact that attempts at private restructuring have been so frequent would seem to confirm that workouts are indeed less costly on average than Chapter 11s.

To the alarm of many, however, a series of court rulings and tax law changes since 1990 have made such private restructurings more difficult. To understand the import of these developments, it is necessary to know more about the relative costs of a workout versus Chapter 11. In the pages that follow, I begin by reviewing recent academic research on the costs of financial restructuring. I then go on to present the findings of my own studies that attempt to determine what factors distressed companies consider in choosing between private workouts and bankruptcy.

COSTS OF WORKOUTS VERSUS CHAPTER 11

Legal and Professional Fees

For several reasons, payments for legal and other professional services are likely to be higher if a company restructures its debt in bankruptcy court. Lawyer and investment banker fees effectively accrue on an hourly basis, and therefore increase with the length of time spent in creditor negotiations. In the Gilson–John–Lang study cited earlier, the average length of time spent by 89 companies in Chapter 11 was over 20 months; the average length of the 80 workouts was about 15 months.

This difference was significantly greater in the 30 cases in our sample that involved the private restructuring of publicly traded debt. Such debt was always restructured through exchange offers in which bondholders were free to tender, or not tender, their bonds in exchange for a package of new securities. (In 87 percent of these exchanges, moreover, this package included new common stock or securities that could be converted into common stock.) The average length of exchange offers in our sample was just under seven months.

Workouts may be less time-consuming in part because firms need deal only with creditors whose claims are in default. Of the workouts we examined, 30 percent of the firms with publicly traded debt, as well as 10 percent of the firms with debt owed to banks and insurance companies, avoided having to restructure such debt. By contrast, cross-default provisions included in most debt contracts virtually guarantee that when a company files for Chapter 11, it will have to negotiate with all its creditors.

In addition, total legal fees in Chapter 11 are based on the number of billable hours.[4] Because legal and other professional fees have priority over all the firm's other claims in Chapter 11, the professional advisors involved in the case have no obvious financial incentive to minimize the amount of time the firm spends in Chapter 11. Although bankruptcy judges will often scale back requested fees or partially withhold payment of fees until the end of the case (witholding rates of 25 percent are common), lawyers can easily anticipate the adjustments and charge accordingly.

A potential solution to this problem would be to pay lawyers and investment bankers using the same securities distributed to shareholders and creditors as currency, thus giving them an interest in preserving the value of the *surviving* firm and an incentive to get out of Chapter 11 quickly.[5] An interesting alternative approach was recently taken by Ames Department Stores, which filed for Chapter 11 in April 1990. Ames had established a special bonus plan for its CEO, Stephen Pistner, which would pay him $3.5 million if Ames was successfully reorganized within 18 months of its Chapter 11 filing, and successively smaller amounts if the reorganization took longer; no bonus would be paid if Ames was still in Chapter 11 after 39 months. Such innovative compensation schemes, however, are all too rare.[6]

A direct comparison of legal and professional fees for Chapter 11 and private restructuring is difficult because firms are not required to report these costs outside of Chapter 11. Nevertheless, firms that privately restructure their bonds through exchange offers are required to disclose an estimate of all offer-related costs in the exchange offer circular distributed to bondholders. As a result, I was able to obtain reliable cost data for a sample of 18 exchange offers undertaken by New York and American Stock Exchange–listed companies.[7]

As summarized in Exhibit 28–1, these costs amounted on average to only 0.65 percent of the book value of assets (measured just prior to the

---

4. A darkly humorous account of how the Bankruptcy Code sometimes creates perverse incentives for lawyers to prolong the firm's stay in Chapter 11 (for example, by filing excessive motions with the court) can be found in Sol Stein (1989. *A Feast for Lawyers* (M. Evans and Company, Inc.).

5. See proposals by Michael Price and Wilbur Ross in their Roundtable discussion.

6. For evidence on how distressed firms pay their senior managers, see Stuart Gilson and Michael Vetsuypens (1991). "CEO Compensation in Financially Distressed Firms," *Journal of Finance*.

7. This table is taken from Gilson, John, and Lang, cited in footnote 3. Exchange offer costs include cash compensation paid to the exchange and information agent; legal, accounting, brokerage and investment banking fees; and the value of any common stock warrants issued to the firm's investment bank (as estimated in the offer circular).

E X H I B I T   28-1

Direct Costs of Exchange Offers for Troubled Junk Bonds*

	Mean	Median	Range
Exchange Offer Costs ($1,000s)	$799	$424	$200–2,500
Offer Costs as a Percentage of the Book Value of Assets	0.65%	0.32%	0.01–3.40%
Offer Costs as a Percentage of the Face Value of Bonds Restructured under Offer	2.16%	2.29%	0.27–6.84%

*Sample consists of eighteen exchange offers undertaken during 1981–1988 for which data were available. Costs consist of cash compensation paid to the exchange and information agent; legal, accounting, brokerage, and investment banking fees; and the value of any common stock warrants issued to the firm's investment bank advisor (as estimated in the exchange offer prospectus).

exchange offer); the corresponding median percentage was only 0.32 percent. By contrast, academic studies have found that average legal and professional fees reported by Chapter 11 companies range from 2.8 percent to 7.5 percent of total assets (generally measured within one year of the filing).[8] Although comparisons across studies are made difficult by differences in the samples and the definitions of costs, these results clearly suggest that private restructuring through exchange offers is much less costly than formal reorganization in Chapter 11, perhaps by as much as a factor of ten.

Management by Bankruptcy Judges

Greater waste of corporate assets is also possible in Chapter 11 because the Bankruptcy Code effectively requires judges to set corporate operating policies. Of course, judges also have the potential to add value by arbitrating disputes among the firm's claimholders, thus reducing the length of time required to restructure the debt.

In their traditional role, judges are supposed to interpret and administer the law. In Chapter 11, however, because they must approve all major

---

8. See Jerold Warner (1977). "Bankruptcy Costs: Some Evidence," *Journal of Finance* 32; James Ang, Jess Chua, and John McConnell (1982). "The Administrative Costs of Corporate Bankruptcy: A Note," *Journal of Finance* 37; and Lawrence A. Weiss (1990). "Bankruptcy Resolution: Direct Costs and Violation of Priority of Claims," *Journal of Financial Economics* 26. These studies calculate average costs using different definitions of the firm's assets, including the assets' market value (Warner, Weiss), liquidation value (Ang et al.) and book value (Weiss).

business decisions, bankruptcy judges have broad powers to influence how the firm's assets are managed. A company's future profitability may depend critically on how the bankruptcy judge rules on proposed corporate actions such as major asset divestitures and capital expenditures.

Moreover, the Bankruptcy Code does not require judges to base their decisions on whether corporate assets will be put to uses that produce the highest rate of return to all investors. For a company's plan of reorganization to be "confirmed" in bankruptcy court (the last legal hurdle to be crossed before exiting from Chapter 11), the judge is required by law to ensure only that two conditions are met: (1) Each claimholder must receive at least what he or she would have been paid if the firm were liquidated;[9] and (2) The company must not appear to be in danger of going bankrupt again in the near future. However honorable their intentions, judges have no financial interest in the outcome of reorganizations, and generally lack relevant management experience. Thus, corporate assets may systematically end up being worth less when judges set corporate policies.

Lost Investment Opportunities

To the extent dealing with creditors (and, in bankruptcy, the judge) diverts management's attention from operating the business, the firm may forgo profitable investment opportunities. Value lost by not capitalizing on such opportunities is no less real a cost of financial distress than lawyers' fees, and should also be considered in the context of the workout–bankruptcy decision. Although these costs cannot be directly measured, it is reasonable to assume that the extent of any damage will be greater the longer it takes to renegotiate the firm's debts. Hence the "opportunity costs" of financial trouble are likely to be greater in Chapter 11 than in private workouts.

Chapter 11 creates additional delays and distractions due to various procedural demands placed on managers. Before making any decision not in the ordinary course of the firm's business (such as hiring an investment bank to provide advice on asset sales), management must file an application

---

9. This is referred to as the "best interests of creditors" test in Section 1129(a)(7) of the Bankruptcy Code. Strictly speaking, this standard only applies if all impaired classes of claimholders assent to the proposed plan (which generally happens). If one or more classes votes against the plan, then the relevant standard is the "fair and equitable" test {Section 1129(b)(2)}, which basically requires that each impaired class receives the present value of its allowed claims under the plan (or whatever is available after all senior classes have been paid in full, provided more junior classes receive nothing). If a plan is fair and equitable, then dissenting classes can be forced to accept its terms under a court-imposed "cramdown."

with the court. They may file such an application, moreover, only after first notifying creditors in writing and allowing them sufficient time to file objections. Because the firm can act only after the judge approves the application, otherwise routine decisions can take months to complete. After Public Service Company of New Hampshire filed for bankruptcy in 1988, D.P.G. Cameron, the firm's vice president and general counsel, commented that "the proceedings . . . left us breathless."[10]

One proxy, admittedly crude, for the extent of a company's investment opportunities is the difference between its value as an ongoing concern and its liquidation value–what I refer to as "excess going concern value."[11] To the extent investment opportunities are more likely to be lost in Chapter 11 than in private workouts, troubled companies have incentives to avoid bankruptcy and restructure their debt privately. In the extreme, if Chapter 11 leads to liquidation, creditors and shareholders effectively forfeit all of the firm's excess going concern value by not settling privately.[12]

The importance of preserving going concern value in these situations is well demonstrated by the case of Tiger International, a cargo shipper and lessor of transportation equipment. In early 1983, the company initiated what turned out to be a successful workout. As reported at the time in *The Wall Street Journal* (February 16, 1983):

> Wayne M. Hoffman, Tiger chairman, said the company was getting "excellent cooperation" in the early meetings with lenders. He said that he expects sessions to continue "for some weeks," but that he was confident a rescheduling of debt would be the result. "It's in the lender's interests to do this. All of them agree that the going concern is the important thing."

Consistent with the outcome of this case, the Gilson–John–Lang study found that troubled companies are more likely to reorganize privately when they have greater excess going concern value. For companies that successfully restructured their debt out of court, the average ratio of excess going concern value to liquidation value prior to restructuring was 0.83; for firms that filed for Chapter 11 that average ratio was only 0.61.

---

10. See Stein, cited in footnote 4.
11. Of course, excess going concern value will also reflect other sources of value such as monopoly power and goodwill.
12. Of the Chapter 11 companies I examined (all of them New York and American Stock Exchange companies), only 5 percent were completely liquidated through a conversion to Chapter 7. For smaller, private companies, the rate is generally higher.

HOW DO SHAREHOLDERS FARE?

To the extent private workouts are less costly than Chapter 11, both share-holders and creditors should be better off when attempts to restructure debt privately succeed.[13] My own research suggests shareholders have generally done better in workouts than in Chapter 11.[14] The Gilson–John–Lang study found that shareholders of companies that successfully restructured their debt out of court realized an average 41 percent increase in the value of their common stockholdings over the period of restructuring (beginning with announcement of the default and net of general market movements). By contrast, for companies that tried to restructure privately but failed, average cumulative returns to shareholders were *negative* 40 percent over the period of restructuring that ended with a Chapter 11 filing. At least part of the 80 percent difference in these returns can be viewed as the market's estimate of the shareholder portion of the total cost savings from avoiding Chapter 11 and restructuring privately. (Some part of this 80 percent, of course, may also reflect the possibility that firms ultimately filing Chapter 11 were systematically less profitable after negotiations with creditors began–or that operating problems were far worse than investors initially suspected at the time of default–than firms that did not end up filing.)

Shareholders are also typically allowed to retain a significantly higher percentage of the equity in workouts than in bankruptcy. As I found in a recent study, creditors on average receive 20 percent of the common stock in workouts, as compared to 67 percent of the outstanding stock in Chapter 11s.[15] Shareholders will be harmed by dilution of their equity to the extent creditors effectively purchase the new shares at a below-market

---

13. If only a subset of the firm's debt is restructured, a private restructuring plan could in principle harm nonparticipating creditors (for example, participating creditors' claims could be given more security or made more senior). However, such harm will be limited by the right of nonparticipating creditors to sue the firm (and other creditors), by covenants that restrict the issuance of more senior debt, and by cross-default covenants that restrict the firm's ability to exclude certain creditors from participating in the restructuring.

14. Assessing the relative returns to creditors is more difficult because their claims trade much less frequently and market price data are either unreliable or nonexistent. There is nonetheless some evidence that creditors take bigger writedowns of their claims in Chapter 11 than in workouts. See Julian Franks and Walter Torous (1994). "A Comparison of Financial Recontracting in Distressed Exchanges and Chapter 11 Reorganizations," *Journal of Financial Economics*.

15. See Stuart Gilson (1990). "Bankruptcy, Boards, Banks, and Blockholders," *Journal of Financial Economics*. Such percentages assume that none of the warrants or convertible debt and preferred stock received by creditors are eventually converted. Assuming such securities are fully converted, the average creditor holdings increase to approximately 40 percent and 80 percent, respectively.

price, or if the value of control conferred by large blocks is dissipated by the issuance of new shares. In some Chapter 11s, of course, shareholders are completely wiped out. In workouts, obviously, shareholders never voluntarily consent to such a plan.

ADVANTAGES OF CHAPTER 11

Although evidence from the 1980s suggests that Chapter 11 is more costly than private restructuring *in the average case,* bankruptcy also provides certain benefits that offset at least part of this cost difference and cause some companies to file for Chapter 11 directly. There are four principal advantages to filing for bankruptcy.

First, the Bankruptcy Code allows firms to issue new debt that ranks senior to all debt incurred prior to filing ("prepetition debt"). Such "debtor-in-possession" (DIP) financing is valuable because the firm can borrow on cheaper terms and thus conserve on scarce cash.[16] Over the last few years, increasing sophistication of DIP lenders and growth of the market for tradable bank debt have resulted in more firms entering Chapter 11 with a DIP facility already in place.

Second, interest on prepetition unsecured debt stops accruing while the firm is in bankruptcy, again freeing up cash.[17]

Third, the Bankruptcy Code's automatic stay provision protects the firm from creditor harassment while it reorganizes, thus allowing the business to function with fewer disruptions.

Fourth, firms in bankruptcy can reject, subject to certain limitations, unfavorable leases and other "executory contracts" (while compensating the lessor for some portion of his/her loss). The threat of lease rejection alone can encourage lessors to grant the bankrupt firm more favorable terms.

Finally, it is easier to get a reorganization plan accepted in Chapter 11 because the voting rules are less restrictive. Acceptance of the plan requires an affirmative vote by only a majority (one-half in number, but representing two-thirds in value) of the claimholders in each class whose claims are impaired. By contrast, a workout cannot pass without the consent of all who participate, thus increasing the incidence of creditor holdouts.

---

16. For an excellent description of current DIP lending practices see Mark Rohman and Michael Policiano (1990), "Financing Chapter 11 Companies in the 1990s," *Journal of Applied Corporate Finance,* Summer.

17. Interest on secured debt continues to accrue up to the excess, if any, of the security's assessed value over the debt's face value.

THE HOLDOUT PROBLEM

Whether the cost savings from private restructuring are realized will depend on whether creditors unanimously agree to the terms of the restructuring. Any factors that increase the likelihood of creditor holdouts thus make attempts at private workouts less likely to succeed. Of course, many of these factors are either difficult or impossible to quantify, such as creditors' relative bargaining strength or the amount of antipathy that creditors feel towards shareholders and management. Nonetheless, some academic work has succeeded in identifying factors that can be used to predict the likelihood of holdouts.

The extent of the holdout problem depends partly on what type of debt is restructured. As noted previously, publicly traded bonds have traditionally been restructured through voluntary exchange offers. The holdout problem in these offers can be quite severe. Provided enough bonds are tendered so that the firm stays out of bankruptcy, the bondholders who do not tender (and thus, typically, do not agree to a reduction in the value of their claims) benefit at the expense of those who do. The alternative to an exchange offer—namely, modifying the interest rate, principal amount, or maturity of the outstanding bonds by a vote of bondholders—is made virtually impossible by the Trust Indenture Act of 1939, which requires *every* bondholder to agree to such changes. (Modification of all other, "noncore" covenants of the bond indenture usually requires only a simple or two-thirds majority.)

To address this problem, exchange offers are structured to penalize holdouts. New bonds offered in these exchanges, in addition to having a lower coupon rate or principal amount, are also typically more senior, and of shorter maturity, than the outstanding bonds they will replace.[18] Holders are also sometimes asked jointly to tender their bonds and vote for the elimination of non-core protective covenants in the old bonds (called an exit consent solicitation). By so doing, bondholders who tendered will be in a better position than those who did not if the firm later files for bankruptcy.

This situation changed dramatically, however, in January 1990 when Judge Burton Lifland ruled in LTV's bankruptcy that bondholders who tendered in a previous exchange offer were entitled to a claim in bankruptcy equal only to the *market* value of the bonds accepted under the offer; bondholders who held onto their original bonds were allowed a claim equal to

---

18. As pointed out to me by an investment banker acquaintance, the effect of the exchange is similar to offering passengers on the Titanic the chance to move up from steerage to first class.

the bonds' full face value. Since bonds of distressed companies usually sell at big discounts, the effect of this ruling was to reward LTV's holdouts. The LTV decision was reversed on appeal in April 1992, but in the interim period there was a dramatic fall-off in attempted exchange offers.[19]

With regard to private debt, my research suggests that holdouts are less common, and private restructurings thus more likely to succeed, when more of the firm's debt is owed to commercial banks–and, to a lesser extent, to insurance companies. The Gilson–John–Lang study found that, on average, bank debt amounted to 40 percent of total liabilities in firms that successfully restructured, but only 25 percent in firms that filed for Chapter 11 (median debt ratios were 36 percent and 20 percent, respectively).

As one would expect, bank lenders tend to be more sophisticated and fewer in number than other kinds of creditors, and are more likely to recognize the potential benefits of private restructuring. Trade creditors, by contrast, are generally less predisposed to settle. Bankruptcy professionals frequently characterize trade creditors as "unsophisticated" and "acrimonious." Consistent with this characterization, so-called vulture investors often buy out a firm's trade debt at the very start of their involvement with the company.

Our results also indicate that private restructuring succeeds more often when there are fewer distinct classes of long-term debt outstanding.[20] The simplest way to interpret this evidence is to note that having more creditors increases the likelihood that any one creditor will hold out, and thus makes disputes among creditors more likely. The number of debt classes also serves as a measure of the complexity of a firm's capital structure. Complex capital structures will be more difficult to restructure privately, especially if the claims are more difficult to value and there is greater disagreement among creditors over whether they are being treated fairly relative to other creditors or shareholders.

---

19. An additional consequence of the ruling was that companies gave up more easily (and filed for Chapter 11) when an exchange offer generated a low initial tender rate. During the 1980s, by contrast, it was not uncommon for companies to revise the terms of exchange offers up to half a dozen times until some desired tender rate was attained.

20. As identified in the notes to the firm's balance sheet in its annual 10-K report. More precisely, we deflate this variable by the book value of long-term debt, to provide a measure of the number of creditors per dollar of debt owed. The rationale for this adjustment is that smaller creditors have less of their wealth at risk if a private restructuring attempt fails, and therefore are more likely to hold out, everything else unchanged.

INCENTIVES OF MANAGERS AND DIRECTORS

Although the workout–bankruptcy decision has a significant impact on a company's stock price, surprisingly few workout proposals are formally put to a shareholder vote. In only one out of every five workouts that I studied did firms first solicit shareholders' approval, either to increase the number of authorized shares or to sell off assets. This raises the interesting question whether managers can personally gain by settling with creditors on overly generous terms, and thus at shareholders' expense. One obvious reason why managers might strike a deal with creditors is to protect their jobs.

To investigate this possibility, I analyzed turnover among the senior managers (the CEO, chairman, and president) of 126 New York and American Stock Exchange–listed firms that defaulted on their debt during the 1980s.[21] As shown in Exhibit 28–2, management turnover was substantial regardless of which restructuring method was chosen. At the end of a four-year period starting two years prior to the start of a workout or Chapter 11 filing, only 40 percent of the original senior managers remained in firms that privately restructured, and only 30 percent were left in firms that filed for Chapter 11. Turnover among directors of these firms was also high; approximately half the board was replaced during a typical workout or bankruptcy.[22]

Executives' professional reputations also appear to suffer when they are replaced. Although the average age of departing managers in my study was only 52 years, not one of these managers later found work with another exchange-listed firm for at least three years. Similarly, departing directors subsequently sat on one-third fewer boards of other companies three years after leaving, suggesting that their services as directors were valued less highly by other firms. (Of course, these individuals may also have been generally less inclined to serve with large public corporations as managers or directors after their experience with financial distress.)

In short, my own research suggests that managers and other corporate insiders do not gain from systematically choosing a particular restructuring method. Moreover, it lends no support to the popular view, so often aired in the financial press, that Chapter 11 offers a "safe harbor" for the

---

21. See Stuart Gilson (1989). "Management Turnover and Financial Distress," *Journal of Financial Economics*.
22. See Gilson, cited in footnote 15.

EXHIBIT 28–2

Percentage of Original Senior Managers (CEO, Chairman, and President) Who Remain with Their Firms throughout Period of Financial Distress

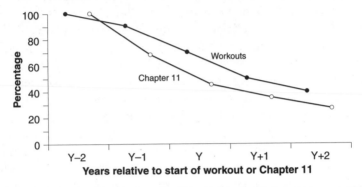

Years relative to start of workout or Chapter 11

*Sample consists of 196 managers initially employed by 126 New York and American Stock Exchange–listed companies (69 firms in Chapter 11 and 57 in private workouts) that first defaulted on their debt during 1979–1984.

firm's managers.[23] To be sure, Chapter 11 does give the filing firm the exclusive right to file the first reorganization plan for at least 120 days; and it is also true that bankruptcy judges usually grant extensions—sometimes for several years. But such extensions, however potentially costly for investors, represent at most a temporary reprieve for senior managers.

In addition to my finding that managers are routinely displaced when their firms file, I also found that one of every five top-level management changes was initiated at the behest of creditors—in particular, bank lenders. Creditors are thus far from powerless in these situations. In short, Chapter 11's automatic stay protects the *firm* from creditor harassment, but not its managers. Analysis of public company bankruptcies since 1990 suggests these trends have not changed.

POLICY IMPLICATIONS

Distressed firms can in general preserve more of their value by restructuring their debt privately, when possible, and thus avoiding Chapter 11. My

23. For example, see Roger Lowenstein and George Anders (1991). "Firms That Default Find Their Troubles May Have Just Begun," *The Wall Street Journal,* April 17, p.A1.

own research suggests that the professional fees incurred in exchange offers are about one-tenth those incurred in a typical Chapter 11 case.

Despite the cost advantage of private restructuring, however, a number of developments over the past few years have threatened to turn more troubled companies toward the bankruptcy courts. First, for nearly two years, the LTV decision undermined bondholders' incentives to tender in exchange offers for publicly traded junk debt. The second development has been a shift in the tax law toward less favorable treatment of firms that restructure their debt outside of Chapter 11.

Following the Tax Reform Act of 1986, distressed firms have found it more difficult to preserve their net operating loss carryforwards, and to avoid paying taxes on forgiveness-of-debt income when they operate outside of bankruptcy. Since 1990, firms have been subject to a new tax on private exchange offers. Under the Revenue Reconciliation Act of 1990, whenever new bonds issued in an exchange offer sell at a discount below their stated face value (as is most often the case), the firm must book the difference as taxable income. Prior to the Act, such original issue discounts were tax exempt.[24] And since the beginning of 1995, distressed firms have no longer been able to avoid taxation of forgiveness-of-debt income under the "stock for debt exception," which was repealed by the 1993 Tax Act.

Some casual evidence suggests that in the wake of these developments, troubled firms have more often chosen to deal with default in Chapter 11. I examined press reports for all firms that were identified in *The Wall Street Journal* as having filed for Chapter 11 between January 1990 and December 1996.[25] Almost two-thirds of these companies apparently made no attempt to restructure their debt privately before filing. During the 1980s, by contrast, only 30 percent of financially distressed firms sought Chapter 11 protection as a first resort. Also, for those companies that did attempt to restructure privately during this period, fewer than three months elapsed, on average, before a Chapter 11 filing. In the 1980s, companies spent an average of eight months attempting to find a private solution before filing Chapter 11.

Society loses when firms are forced to use the more expensive method for dealing with financial distress. Public policy should be directed toward breaking down barriers to private contracting (or recontracting). For

---

24. Acadia owns Reliable Drugs whose CEO, Roger Grass, formerly an executive of Rite Aid, has years of industry experience. Observers speculate that he would run Revco.

25. Alfaro, Charles (1989). "Revco receives $925 million bid from Bass Groups," *Chain Drug Review,* November 11, and Fredericls, James (1989). "Revco Draws Takeover interest," *Drug Store Review,* November 20, 1989.

example, a strong case can be made for repealing the Trust Indenture Act to facilitate private restructuring of publicly held debt.[26] Although entering Chapter 11 to preserve tax benefits helps the firm's security holders, these gains are essentially financed by other taxpayers; as such, they represent wealth transferred rather than wealth created. Corporate default could also be made less costly by relaxing the current regulatory constraints on commercial banks' ability to hold equity in distressed firms; banks are currently required to divest any stock received under a bankruptcy or restructuring in approximately two years. Allowing creditors to hold equity and debt jointly, which is the norm in Japan and Germany would also streamline the reorganization process by reducing costly, time-consuming conflicts between creditors and shareholders.

One development that offers hope is the increasing use of *prepackaged* Chapter 11, in which a firm jointly files its bankruptcy petition and reorganization plan (after having first secured creditors' informal consent to the plan). Prepackaged bankruptcy is a hybrid of private restructuring and Chapter 11—one that potentially incorporates the best features of both methods. Provided the firm has adequately disclosed details of its financial condition to creditors before filing, it is possible for the plan to be confirmed almost immediately. In late 1997, for example, Flagstar Companies completed a prepackaged bankruptcy after only five months. Such innovations in financial contracting deserve the full support of lawmakers and economists alike.

---

26. See Mark Roe, "The Voting Prohibition in Bond Workouts," *Yale Law Journal* (1987); and Robert Gertner and David Scharfstein, "A Theory of Workouts and the Effects of Reorganization Law," *Journal of Finance* (1991).